lonely planet

Berlin

Andrea Schulte-Peevers

LONELY PLANET PUBLICATIONS
Melbourne • Oakland • London • Paris

Berlin
3rd edition – March 2002
First published – August 1998

Published by
Lonely Planet Publications Pty Ltd ABN 36 005 607 983
90 Maribyrnong St, Footscray, Victoria 3011, Australia

Lonely Planet offices
Australia Locked Bag 1, Footscray, Victoria 3011
USA 150 Linden St, Oakland, CA 94607
UK 10a Spring Place, London NW5 3BH
France 1 rue du Dahomey, 75011 Paris

Photographs
Many of the images in this guide are available for licensing from
Lonely Planet Images.
w www.lonelyplanetimages.com

Front cover photograph
Reflection of Berliner Dom in the glass facade of the ill-fated Palace of
the Republic (Marvin E. Newman, Getty Images)

ISBN 1 74059 073 2

text & maps © Lonely Planet Publications Pty Ltd 2002
photos © photographers as indicated 2002

Printed by The Bookmaker International Ltd
Printed in China

Contents – Text

2 Contents – Text

Contents – Maps

The Author

Andrea Schulte-Peevers

Andrea is a Los Angeles-based writer, editor and translator who caught the travel bug early in life, hitting all continents but Antarctica by the time she turned 18. After finishing high school in Germany, Andrea decided the world was too big for her to stay in one place and moved first to London, then to Los Angeles. Armed with a degree from UCLA, she turned her wanderlust into a career as a travel writer, joining the LP team in 1995. Besides Berlin, Andrea has also coordinated, authored or updated several other Lonely Planet titles, including *Germany*, *Los Angeles*, *Baja California*, *San Diego & Tijuana*, *California & Nevada* and *Spain*.

FROM THE AUTHOR

Among the books in my Lonely Planet repertoire, *Berlin* is one of my all-time favorites. It's a city full of quirks and fascinations, imbued with an energy unrivalled in Germany and filled with surprises at all hours. Therefore, the first round of heartfelt thanks belongs to the LP folks who have made it possible for me to work on this book: to Mary Neighbour and Chris Wyness for giving me the assignment; to my editor, William Gourlay, for shepherding the project through its various stages with great competence and good humour; and to cartographer/designer Ray Thomson for producing such beautiful maps.

In Berlin, I couldn't have done without Kerstin Göllrich, who provided friendship, shelter and good company. Natasha Kompatzki of Berlin Tourismus Marketing once again helped me keep up with the city's lightning-fast changes, opened all the right doors and expertly fielded last-minute questions. She's truly a star in her job.

Heaps of thanks also go to those people who helped with the logistics of travel to and within Germany, including Johannes Fuchs, Beth Purdue, Nanci Sullivan and Barbara Hearn. Your assistance was truly invaluable and much appreciated.

Another round of applause goes to my colleague Andy Bender, whose research in Brandenburg, Saxony and Saxony-Anhalt formed the basis of this book's Excursion chapter.

Last but not least, on the home front, a great big kiss to David, my wonderful husband, for sticking with me through all of life's trials and tribulations - large and small, real and imagined - including Lonely Planet deadlines. Thanks heaps.

This Book

Andrea Schulte-Peevers and David Peevers researched and wrote the 1st edition of *Berlin*. Andrea updated the 2nd edition and, this, the 3rd edition.

FROM THE PUBLISHER

The editing of this edition of *Berlin* was coordinated in the Lonely Planet head office in Melbourne by Will Gourlay. He was ably assisted by editors Nina Rousseau, Susannah Farfor and Elizabeth Swan. Ray Thomson single-handedly took on the mapping and design as well as providing some last-minute illustrations. Mark Germanchis offered Quark support, Quentin Frayne and Emma Koch produced the Language chapter, Margie Jung designed the cover and Birgit Jordan supplied the climate charts. Photographs were provided by Lonely Planet Images, with thanks to Barbara Barbara Dombrowski and Brett Pascoe. Thanks also to Mick Weldon (MW), Kelli Hamblet (KH) and Martin Harris (MH) for providing illustrations. Darren O'Connell and Yvonne Byron also offered technical assistance. Thanks also to Kieran Grogan, Chris Wyness and Mark Griffiths for their assistance.

ACKNOWLEDGMENTS

Thanks to George Peter from Wasser- und Schifffahrtsamt Eberswalde and Klaus from the Berliner Verkehrsbetriebe (BVG) for permission to use their material.

THANKS

Many thanks to the following travellers who used the last edition and wrote to us with helpful hints, useful advice and interesting anecdotes:

Carolyn Agardy, Thomas Allen, Frank Antonsen, Charles Aschmann, John Barbano, Montse Baste-Kraan, Mark Bauer, Spencer Beggs, Fletcher Benton, Joachim Bergmann, Jan Boggess, Ben Brehmer, Christopher Carrier, Thomas Chang, Clair Chatel, Kendall Crowe, Katie Elder, Richard Elphick, Charlotte Evans, Deborah Fink, Aileen Fisher, Francessco Giovantetti, Martin & Margaret Goodwin, Frederik Grufman, Karen Grunow, Richard J Hazen, Anne Hofstede, Marie Javins, Monica Johansson, David John, Oliver Johnston, Christoph Kessel, Kurt Kunz, Francesca Lanaro, Emily MacWilliams, Peter Marshman, David McGowan, Anja Medau, Dr Michael Mittler, TJ Moore, Megan Packer, Ilaria Minio Paluello, Mari Paul, James Payne, Jan M Pennington, Steve Penny, Melanie Phipps, Krys Pogoda, Christopher Pope, Marc Purnal, Scott Reid, Chris Round, Amber Senneck, Chloe Spearritt, Julie Stenberg, Melissa Sutton, Vera Ten-Hacken, Sinead Thornton, Dave Upton, Alan Warnke, Stephan Werner, Roy Wiesner, Fiona Wilson.

Foreword

ABOUT LONELY PLANET GUIDEBOOKS

The story begins with a classic travel adventure: Tony and Maureen Wheeler's 1972 journey across Europe and Asia to Australia. There was no useful information about the overland trail then, so Tony and Maureen published the first Lonely Planet guidebook to meet a growing need.

From a kitchen table, Lonely Planet has grown to become the largest independent travel publisher in the world, with offices in Melbourne (Australia), Oakland (USA), London (UK) and Paris (France).

Today Lonely Planet guidebooks cover the globe. There is an ever-growing list of books and information in a variety of media. Some things haven't changed. The main aim is still to make it possible for adventurous travellers to get out there – to explore and better understand the world.

At Lonely Planet we believe travellers can make a positive contribution to the countries they visit – if they respect their host communities and spend their money wisely. Since 1986 a percentage of the income from each book has been donated to aid projects and human rights campaigns, and, more recently, to wildlife conservation.

Although inclusion in a guidebook usually implies a recommendation we cannot list every good place. Exclusion does not necessarily imply criticism. In fact there are a number of reasons why we might exclude a place – sometimes it is simply inappropriate to encourage an influx of travellers.

UPDATES & READER FEEDBACK

Things change – prices go up, schedules change, good places go bad and bad places go bankrupt. Nothing stays the same. So, if you find things better or worse, recently opened or long-since closed, please tell us and help make the next edition even more accurate and useful.

Lonely Planet thoroughly updates each guidebook as often as possible – usually every two years, although for some destinations the gap can be longer. Between editions, up-to-date information is available in our free, quarterly *Planet Talk* newsletter and monthly email bulletin *Comet*. The *Upgrades* section of our website (w www.lonelyplanet.com) is also regularly updated by Lonely Planet authors, and the site's *Scoop* section covers news and current affairs relevant to travellers. Lastly, the *Thorn Tree* bulletin board and *Postcards* section carry unverified, but fascinating, reports from travellers.

Tell us about it! We genuinely value your feedback. A well-travelled team at Lonely Planet reads and acknowledges every email and letter we receive and ensures that every morsel of information finds its way to the relevant authors, editors and cartographers.

Everyone who writes to us will find their name listed in the next edition of the appropriate guidebook, and will receive the latest issue of *Comet* or *Planet Talk*. The very best contributions will be rewarded with a free guidebook.

We may edit, reproduce and incorporate your comments in Lonely Planet products such as guidebooks, websites and digital products, so let us know if you don't want your comments reproduced or your name acknowledged.

How to contact Lonely Planet:
Online: e talk2us@lonelyplanet.com.au, w www.lonelyplanet.com
Australia: Locked Bag 1, Footscray, Victoria 3011
UK: 10a Spring Place, London NW5 3BH
USA: 150 Linden St, Oakland, CA 94607

Introduction

So you're planning a little trip to Berlin? Good choice. Your timing could hardly be better. Berlin is hip, cool and happening. It's also sophisticated, cosmopolitan and cutting-edge. A city in search of an identity since the Wall collapsed in 1989, the German capital is finally coming into its own. To be sure, change is still constant here, but that's just what makes the place so endlessly fascinating. Here's a quick look at what's new since the last edition of this book.

The 'corps de ballet' of cranes above Potsdamer Platz – Europe's largest building site throughout the 1990s – has given way to an increasingly vibrant new district that's a place to both work and play. North of the Brandenburg Gate, Germany's brand-new Federal Chancellery anchors the New Government District along with the historic Reichstag, where the Bundestag (German Parliament) once again convenes. The Old National Gallery on Museum Island (a Unesco World Heritage Site since 1999) has reopened after a beautiful overhaul. The new permanent exhibit of the Jewish Museum, in an eye-popping structure by Daniel Libeskind, is also poised to become one of Berlin's top attractions. Even the CityWest around Zoo station is getting a face-lift, as the drab 1950s streetscape is being enlivened by some dramatic architecture by international luminaries of the field.

And this is just some of the 'big, new' stuff that makes the headline news. Let's not forget the wealth and quality of Berlin's cultural life where opera, dance and theatre, music of all stripes and a spirited gallery scene thrive with renewed vigour. Elegant palaces, monuments and historic buildings add a sense of permanence and history to this city that's always been young at heart. And the vast green fringe of forests, parks and lakes makes escape from the urban bustle a simple matter of an S-Bahn ride.

But to truly understand what makes Berlin tick, you must venture into its neighbourhoods. Watch Schöneberg yuppies stock up on flowers and fresh vegies on Saturday's

Berlin as it appeared during the reign of Friedrich Wilhelm IV (1840–61). This original engraving comes from the 1851 edition of *The Iconographic Encyclopaedia of Science, Literature and Art.*

Winterfeldtplatz market. Listen to Turkish workers debate the latest soccer scores at a Kreuzberg cafe. Spread out a picnic beneath giant rhododendrons in Tiergarten. Join students and counter-culturalists pondering their navels in bohemian Friedrichshain. Sidle up to impeccably clad artsy types at a posh bar in Charlottenburg. Test your stamina while clubbing with scenesters in trendy Mitte. Heck, go just about anywhere – with open eyes and heart – and you're pretty much guaranteed a fun time.

Berlin's many charms certainly have not been lost on travellers. With around eight million overnight stays per year, it ranks as Germany's most popular city. At least part of Berlin's magnetism comes from its unique position in history. From 1933–45, Hitler and his henchmen orchestrated the Nazi dictatorship from here. After WWII, Berlin became the epicentre of the Cold War, especially after the construction of the Berlin Wall in 1961 brutally sliced the city in half, separating former neighbours physically and ideologically for nearly 40 years. These days, though, the German capital is positioning itself as the link between Eastern and Western Europe.

While Berlin's physical scars are definitely healing, its people have not easily rejoined. The 'Wall' that lingers in their minds and hearts has proved harder to tear down than the one they once looked across with such longing. But Berlin demands that its people get on with their lives, and they will undoubtedly rise to the challenge. Divisions among them may persist, but they're united in their resilience.

Another facet of the Berlin character is an attitude of tolerance. Some people may not like what you do or how you look, but most follow the motto coined by King Frederick the Great: 'Jeder nach seiner Façon', which loosely translates as 'live and let live'. It's no coincidence that one in every 7.5 Berlin residents is an immigrant or that Europe's liveliest gay and lesbian scene flourishes here.

All these factors make Berlin a most 'un-German' city, largely free of the rigid social structure so entrenched in much of the country. A trendsetter by nature and necessity, Berlin feeds on fledgling moods, trends, appetites and processes them into the new *Zeitgeist*, which is then exported to the rest of the country and beyond.

The world has always looked to Berlin – sometimes in fascination, sometimes in horror and sometimes even in deep sympathy. At once repellent and seductive, light-hearted and brooding, Berlin continues to be a city of exhilarating extremes.

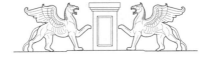

Facts about Berlin

HISTORY
Early Settlements

The area currently occupied by Berlin has been settled since the Stone Age, as numerous archaeological findings show. About 3000 BC, early forms of agriculture and animal husbandry took place, and the oldest pottery also dates from this period. Weapons, tools and jewellery from the early Bronze Age were found at digs in Spandau and Lichtenrade. From the later Bronze Age are the urn cemeteries and remains of settlements attributed to the Lausitz society.

In the first centuries AD, several tribes settled along the Havel and Spree rivers, including the Burgundians and the Germanic Semnones. After the 6th century AD, they competed for territory with the Slavic tribes called Heveller and Sprewanen. The Heveller tribe built fortresses in both Spandau and Köpenick.

After the German king Heinrich I conquered Brandenburg in 928 his son, Otto the Great, tried in vain to Christianise the Slavs. In 1134, Albrecht der Bär (Albrecht the Bear) of the House of the Askanians became margrave of the Nordmark (Northern March), a territory which included Brandenburg. Albrecht managed to increasingly suppress and squeeze out the Slavs, resettling the land with immigrants from west of the Elbe River.

Medieval Berlin

Berlin's 'modern' history began in the 13th century with the founding of the trading posts of Cölln and Berlin by itinerant merchants in the area of today's Nikolaiviertel in the Mitte district. Thanks to their strategic location at the crossroads of medieval trading routes, the two settlements soon developed into *Handelsstädte* (trade centres). In 1307, they merged into the double city of Berlin-Cölln, thus formalising the loose cooperation that had existed since their establishment.

A self-confident merchant class managed to keep the city – which was a member of the Hanseatic League in the 14th and 15th centuries – largely independent. But even they could not prevent it from eventually being absorbed into the sphere of power of the Hohenzollern dynasty. After lengthy squabbling between rival factions, this family managed to establish itself as the rulers of the Mark (March) of Brandenburg, a role it would hold until 1918.

In the 1440s, under Elector Friedrich II (ruled 1440–70), Berlin and Cölln gradually lost their independence. Their administrative council was dissolved and the foundation for a city palace, the future Berliner Schloss was laid. By the time Friedrich II's nephew Johann inherited the realm in 1486, Berlin-Cölln had become a residential city and the capital of the March of Brandenburg.

Under the electors, Berlin grew into a powerful and civilised city. It took the Thirty Years' War (1618–48) to, at least temporarily, put an end to this expansion. An outgrowth of the Reformation, the war had begun as a religious conflict between Protestant and Catholic leagues and soon degenerated into one of Europe's bloodiest dynastic wars. Over the period of hostilities the entire Holy Roman Empire, including Berlin, was ravaged.

The Phoenix Rises

As a result of the war, Berlin's pre-war population of 12,000 had been decimated to a mere 6000 people and more than one third of the city's houses lay in ruins. Replenishing the population was foremost in the mind of Elector Friedrich Wilhelm (called the Great Elector, ruled 1640–88), which he shrewdly accomplished by inviting foreigners to settle in Berlin. In 1671, for instance, he asked 50 wealthy Jewish families, who had been expelled from Vienna, to come to the city with the proviso that they bring their enormous fortunes with them.

The bulk of new settlers, though, were Huguenot refugees from France. Some 6000 arrived after King Louis XIV, in 1685, revoked the Edict of Nantes, which had granted the Protestants religious freedom. Berlin's population swelled by 25%, and the French language superseded German in some districts. By 1700, one in five inhabitants was of French descent. Some French words – or corruptions thereof – can still be heard in Berlinisch: *Feez* for *fête*; *Budiker* for *boutiquier*; *Milljöh* for *milieu*; and of course *Boulette*, a Berlin version of the meatball. The French Cathedral on Gendarmenmarkt serves as a tangible reminder of the Huguenots' influence to this day.

Berlin continued to grow in leaps and bounds throughout the 18th century, in no small part because it was known for its religious tolerance and thus remained a haven for Protestants from around Europe. The population catapulted from a mere 29,000 in 1700 to 172,000 one hundred years later, making Berlin the second-largest city in the Holy Roman Empire after Vienna.

The Age of Prussia

The Great Elector's son, Elector Friedrich III, was a man with great ambition and a penchant for the arts and sciences. Joined by his beloved wife, Sophie Charlotte, he presided over a lively and intellectual court, founding the Academy of Arts in 1696 and the Academy of Sciences in 1700. One year later, Friedrich advanced his career by promoting himself to King Friedrich I (ruling 1688–1701 as elector, 1701–13 as king) of Prussia, making Berlin a royal residence and the capital of the new state of Brandenburg-Prussia.

His son, Friedrich Wilhelm I (ruled 1713–40), was quite a different leader. Frugal and militaristic, his obsession was to build an army of 80,000, for which he was called *Soldatenkönig* (Soldier King). In the early years of his reign, some 17,000 males – including about 7000 craftsmen – left Berlin to avoid being drafted. Friedrich Wilhelm responded by enclosing the city with a wall in 1734, officially for customs-collection purposes but actually to prevent further desertions. (And, in a bizarre twist of historic irony, a different government would use this same idea to keep its own people from leaving some 230 years later.)

Everyone breathed a sigh of relief when his son Friedrich II (ruled 1740–86) – better known to English speakers as Frederick the Great and to his subjects as 'der alte Fritz' (Old Freddy) – came to the throne. He sought greatness through developing the city architecturally and was known for his political and military savvy. Berlin flourished as a great cultural centre and became known as *Spree-Athen* ('Athens on the Spree').

Friedrich's cultural side, though, was counterbalanced by a thirst for military exploits and, in particular, a desire for the territory of Silesia in today's Poland. After a series of battles stretching over a period of about two decades, victory was his. With the signing of the Peace of Hubertusburg in 1763, Austria and Saxony agreed to put Silesia officially into the Prussian camp.

The Enlightenment & Napoleonic Occupation

During Friedrich II's reign, the Enlightenment arrived in Berlin with some authority. The playwright Gotthold Ephraim Lessing, the thinker and publisher Christophe Friedrich Nicolai and the philosopher Moses Mendelssohn (grandfather of composer Felix Mendelssohn-Bartholdy) all helped make Berlin a truly international city. After 1780, intellectual salons, organised by women such as Henriette Herz and Rahel Levin, provided an open forum of discussion for anybody regardless of social standing or religious background.

After 1800, another wave of scientists, philosophers and literary greats descended on the capital. The group included Heinrich von Kleist, Clemens von Brentano, Achim von Arnim, Novalis, Johann Gottlieb Fichte and the brothers Alexander and Wilhelm von Humboldt. Many of them taught at the new university the latter founded in 1810.

Politically, Prussia went into a downward spiral after the death of Friedrich II, culminating in the defeat of the Prussian army by Napoleon's forces at Jena, some 400km south-west of Berlin, in 1806. On 27 October of the same year, Napoleon marched through the Brandenburg Gate, beginning an occupation of Berlin that lasted seven years. The French troops finally left in exchange for a handy sum in reparation payments, leaving behind a humiliated city mired in debt so deep that it would take 53 years to climb out of it. In the end, though, Napoleon didn't fare so well either: his empire was shattered by the combined forces of Austria, Russia and Prussia at the Battle of Leipzig in 1813.

Reforms & Nationalism

The first half of the 19th century was a crucial period in the development of both Germany and Europe, when a self-made class of public servants, academics, theologians and merchants – stressing individual achievement – questioned the right of the nobility to rule. Brandenburg-Prussia was caught up in the maelstrom of reforms brought on by this movement. Restrictive guild regulations were lifted, allowing anyone to take up any profession. Agricultural reforms abolished bonded labour, providing the basis for industrialisation. Jews won civic equality in 1812.

The decay of feudal structures, the redistribution of wealth and the rise of industry changed the socio-economic ground rules, eventually leading to nationalist calls for a centralised state. At the Academy of Sciences in Berlin, philosopher Johann Gottlieb Fichte gave a series of speeches, the so-called *Reden an die deutsche Nation* (Speeches to the German Nation) in which he called for a new national consciousness.

All this ferment brought relatively little change from the top, however, and so in March 1848 Berlin joined with other German cities in a bourgeois revolution demanding freedom of the press, formation of a parliament, withdrawal of the military from the political sphere and other basic democratic rights. Government troops quickly suppressed the riots, in the process sounding the death knell for 250 people and for political development spurred by the Enlightenment. Stagnation set in for the next eight years after the reactionary Friedrich Wilhelm IV (ruled 1840–61) ascended the throne.

The Industrial Age

With the manufacturing trades already well established by the 18th century, Berlin developed into a centre of technology and industry right from the dawn of the Industrial Age. The building of the German railway system (the first track from Berlin to Potsdam opened in 1838) led to the foundation of more than 1000 factories, including electrical giants AEG and Siemens and other companies in the machine, chemical, textile and food production sectors.

The abundance of factory jobs created a new class in Berlin – the proletariat – as workers flocked to the city from throughout Germany. From 1850 to 1870, the population more than tripled to about 870,000. Putting a roof over the heads of the masses became a problem that was later solved by building countless *Mietskasernen* (literally 'rental barracks'). These were labyrinthine tenements built around successive courtyards. Here, entire families subsisted in poorly ventilated, tiny flats without indoor plumbing.

New political parties formed to give a voice to the proletariat, including the *Sozialdemokratische Partei Deutschland* (SPD, Social Democratic Party). Founded in 1875 as the Socialist Workers' Party, it took its present name in 1890 and grew steadily in influence. At the height of its popularity in 1912, the SPD garnered 75% of the vote in Berlin.

Road to the German Empire

After Friedrich Wilhelm IV suffered a stroke in 1857, his brother Wilhelm became regent and, in 1861, King Wilhelm I. Unlike his brother, Wilhelm was a man who recognised more clearly the signs of the times and was not averse to progress. Besides appointing a number of liberal ministers, he made Otto von Bismarck Prussian prime minister in 1862.

Bismarck's grand ambition was to create a Prussian-led unified Germany. His techniques would be old-fashioned and effective: manipulation and war. Bismarck began by winning Schleswig-Holstein province in a war with Denmark in 1864 (with Austria as his ally), then fought and beat Austria itself in 1866 and formed the North German Confederation the following year.

With northern Germany under his control, Bismarck turned his attention to the south. Through skilful diplomacy, he isolated France and manoeuvred it into declaring war on Prussia in 1870. He then surprised Napoleon III by winning the backing of most southern German states. The war with France ended with Prussia's annexation of Alsace-Lorraine. More importantly, with the southern German princes no longer opposed to him, Bismarck's grand plan finally came to fruition: Germany was unified with Berlin as its capital. On 18 January 1871, King Wilhelm I was crowned Kaiser Wilhelm I at Versailles (the ultimate humiliation for the French), with Bismarck as his 'Iron Chancellor'. The German Empire was born.

Gründerzeit

Gründerzeit (Foundation Era) refers to the early years of the German Empire following the defeat of France in 1871. Reparations from that country and the increased magnetism of Berlin as the centre of the new empire engendered another wave of company foundings.

Otto Von Bismark; used manipulation and war to create a unified Germany

Germany was now a wealthy, unified country thanks largely to the force and vision of Bismarck. He had painted himself in liberal colours to buy inches and stop socialist demands for miles, providing health and accident benefits and retirement pensions. But the reform issue was to be his downfall. When Wilhelm II became Kaiser in 1888 (Friedrich, the son of Wilhelm I, was sick and ruled for only 99 days), divisions arose between the emperor, who wanted to extend the system of social-security, and Bismarck, who enacted stricter anti-socialist laws. In 1890 the Kaiser finally excised Bismarck from the political scene.

The period leading up to the outbreak of war in 1914 – called the 'New Direction' – was in fact an aimless one under the personal rule of Wilhelm II, who brought his weak chancellors to heel. Industrially advanced, however, (especially in the chemical and electrical industries) and having produced some of the best social-revolutionary minds, Germany paddled into the new century with incompetent leaders at its helm.

WWI & Revolution

On 28 June 1914, the heir to the Austrian throne, Archduke Franz-Ferdinand and his wife were assassinated in Sarajevo. This triggered a war between Austria-Hungary and Serbia. Russia mobilised as part of its alliance with Serbia. Germany, allied with Austria-Hungary since 1879, declared war on Russia, followed two days later by a declaration of war on France (which had taken the Russian side). The Reichstag (German parliament) immediately granted the necessary war credits. Among the general population, initial euphoria and belief in a quick victory soon gave way to disillusionment, exacerbated by the increasing hardship of food shortages in Berlin and elsewhere.

When peace came with Germany's defeat in 1918, it meant an end to fighting but it did not create stability at home. Germany paid dearly for the war. The Treaty of Versailles forced it to relinquish its colonies in Africa, to cede Alsace-Lorraine and territory in western Poland, and to pay cripplingly high reparations. Furthermore, the treaty made Germany responsible for all losses incurred by its enemies. The humiliation was huge.

The loss of the war also caused the collapse of the monarchy. Kaiser Wilhelm II abdicated on 9 November 1918, ending more than 500 years of Hohenzollern rule and paving the way for a power struggle between socialist and democratic parties. In the early afternoon of the same day, from a window of the Reichstag, Philipp Scheidemann of the SPD proclaimed the birth of the German Republic with party leader Friedrich Ebert as its head. Hours later Karl Liebknecht, founder of the German Communist Party (then known as the Spartacus League) proclaimed the Free Socialist Republic of Germany from a balcony of the Berliner Schloss.

Founded by Rosa Luxemburg and Karl Liebknecht, the Spartacus League sought to establish a republic based on Karl Marx's theories of proletarian revolution. Opposed by moderate socialists, it merged with other groups to form the Kommunistische Partei Deutschland (KPD, or German Communist Party) in the final days of 1918. Rivalry between the SPD and the Spartacus League led to a period of instability which culminated in the so-called Spartacus Revolt in Berlin

Rosa Luxemburg; co-founder with Carl Liebknecht of the German Communist Party

from 6 to 15 January 1919. Following the bloody quashing of this uprising, Luxemburg and Liebknecht were arrested and murdered by right-wing *Freikorps* soldiers. Their bodies were unceremoniously dumped in Berlin's Landwehrkanal.

The Weimar Republic

The federalist constitution of the fledgling republic, Germany's first serious experiment with democracy, was adopted in July 1919 in the town of Weimar, where the constituent assembly had sought refuge from the chaos of Berlin. It gave women the vote and established basic human rights, but it was also unwieldy and gave too much power to the president, who could rule by decree in times of emergency. This was a clause that would later be abused by Paul von Hindenburg, Germany's second president.

A broad coalition government of left and centre parties formed, led by president Friedrich Ebert of the SPD which, until 1932, remained Germany's largest party. Too many forces in Germany rejected the republic, however, and the government satisfied neither communists nor monarchists.

More trouble erupted in 1920 when the right-wing military circle staged the so-called Kapp Putsch, occupying the government quarter. Called on by the government to act (it had fled to Dresden), workers and unions went on strike, and the military putsch collapsed.

The year 1920 also saw the amalgamation of seven cities and countless communities into Gross-Berlin (Greater Berlin), making it one of the largest cities in the world with an area of 87,000 hectares and a population of nearly 4 million. It was divided into 20 *Bezirke* (administrative districts) to which the three districts of Hohenschönhausen, Marzahn and Hellersdorf were added in the 1980s. This set-up existed until reforms put into force in 2000 reduced the number of districts to 12.

The 'Golden' Twenties The 1920s began as anything but golden, marked as they were by the humiliation of a lost war, social and political instability, hyperinflation, hunger and disease. Some 235,000 Berliners were unemployed and strikes, demonstrations and riots had become nearly everyday occurrences. The introduction of a new currency, the *Rentenmark*, brought some relief but things really started to turn around only after cash, in the form of loans under the Dawes Plan, flowed into Germany after 1924. Berlin was on the rise once again.

For the next few years, the city launched into a cultural heyday that exceeded anything that had come before. It gained a reputation as a centre for both tolerance and indulgence, and outsiders flocked to a city of cabaret, Dada and jazz. Theatres, opera houses and concert halls did a brisk trade, and the film company UFA was established. Almost 150 daily newspapers competed with each other.

In 1923, Germany's first radio broadcast hit the airwaves over Berlin and, in 1931, TV had its world premiere here. In the field of science, Berliners Albert Einstein, Carl Bosch and Werner Heisenberg were awarded Nobel Prizes. A Who's Who of architecture (including Bruno Taut, Martin Wagner, Hans Scharoun and Walter Gropius), the fine arts (George Grosz, Max Beckmann, Lovis Corinth) and literature (Bertolt Brecht, Kurt Tucholsky, WH Auden, Christopher Isherwood) contributed to Berlin's reputation as the artistic centre of the world.

Karl Marx had long since met his maker when the stock market crashed on his birthday, 25 October 1929. The so-called Black Friday cast an instant pall over the Golden Twenties. Within weeks, about half a million Berliners were jobless, and riots and demonstrations once again ruled the streets. The ensuing Depression undermined an already fragile German democracy and bred support for extremist parties.

In response to the chaos, Field Marshal Paul von Hindenburg, who had succeeded Ebert as president in 1925, used Article 48 of the constitution – the emergency powers – to circumvent parliament and appoint the Catholic Centre Party's Heinrich Brüning as chancellor. Brüning immediately deflated the economy, forced down wages and destroyed whatever savings – and faith – the

middle classes had built up since the last economic debacle. It earned him the epitaph 'the hunger chancellor'.

The volatile, increasingly polarised political climate led to frequent confrontations between communists and members of a party that had only just begun to gain momentum – the Nationalsozialistische Deutsche Arbeiterpartei (National Socialist German Workers' Party, or NSDAP).

Hitler's Rise to Power

In 1930 Hitler's NSDAP made astounding gains, winning 18% of the vote. Hitler set his sights on the presidency in 1932, running against Hindenburg; he received 37% of the second-round vote. In the ensuing national elections, the Nazis became the largest party in the Reichstag with 230 seats. Berliners, though, remained comparatively sceptical; only one in four had voted for Hitler.

Shortly thereafter, Brüning was replaced as chancellor by Franz von Papen, a hardcore monarchist associated with a right-wing club for industrialists and gentry in Berlin. Papen called two Reichstag elections, hoping to build a parliamentary base, but Hindenburg soon replaced him with Kurt von Schleicher, a military old boy.

Schleicher's attempt to pump-prime the economy with public money – a policy begun by Papen – alienated industrialists and landowners. Finally on 30 January 1933, won over by the right and following Papen's advice, Hindenburg dismissed Schleicher and appointed Hitler as chancellor, with a coalition cabinet consisting of National Socialists (Nazis) and Papen's Nationalists. The Nazis were now by far the largest single party but were still short of an absolute majority.

In March 1933, without a clear majority, Hitler called Germany's last 'officially' free pre-war election. With the help of his intimidating party militia, the *Sturmabteilung* or SA, and the staged Reichstag fire, which gave him an excuse to use emergency laws to arrest communist and liberal opponents, he won 43% of the vote (31% in Berlin) – still not an absolute majority. The turning point was reached with the Enabling Law, which gave Hitler the power to decree laws and change the constitution without consulting parliament. Through the Nazi's abuse of this law, the SPD had been banned and other parties disbanded by June 1933. Hitler's NSDAP governed alone.

The Road to WWII

The totalitarian Nazi regime brought immediate far-reaching consequences for the entire population. Unions were swiftly banned. Propaganda minister Joseph Goebbels' crack-down on intellectuals and artists sent many of them into exile. On 10 May 1933, students burned 'un-German' books on Bebelplatz. Freedom of the press was nonexistent as the NSDAP took over publishing houses. Membership in the *Hitlerjugend* (Hitler Youth) became compulsory for boys aged 10 to 18; girls had to join the Bund Deutscher Mädchen (BDM, League of German Girls). The 1936 Berlin Olympics only served to legitimise the Nazi government and to distract the world from the everyday terror perpetrated in Germany – apparently with success.

The Röhm Putsch Originally formed to guard public meetings, by 1934 the SA had become a powerful force of 4.5 million men, capable of challenging and undermining Hitler's authority. With rumours of revolt circulating, on 30 June 1934 the elite SS troops (Hitler's personal guard) rounded up and executed high-ranking SA officers, including leader Ernst Röhm, in what came to be known as the 'Night of the Long Knives'. More than 1000 people lost their lives that night.

In Berlin, Hermann Göring led the death squads, with executions taking place in the SS barracks in the district of Lichtenberg. Göring and his lieutenants also exploited the occasion to settle old (sometimes homophobic) scores with a number of Hitler's opponents.

In the same year, the death of Hindenburg allowed Hitler to merge the positions of president and chancellor.

Plight of the Jews As has been thoroughly documented, Jews became the main target in Nazi Germany. In April 1933, Goebbels organised the boycott of Jewish businesses and medical and legal practices. Jews were expelled from public service and prohibited from engaging in many professions, trades and industries. The Nuremberg Laws of 1935 deprived all non-Aryans (ie, Jews, Gypsies, blacks etc) of German citizenship and prohibited their marriage with Aryans. On the night of 9 November 1938 the terror escalated with the Reichspogromnacht (also known as Kristallnacht or 'Night of Broken Glass'). On this single night the windows of thousands of Jewish businesses and shops throughout Berlin and all of Germany were shattered, the premises looted and set alight. Jews had started to emigrate after 1933, but this terror set off a new wave. Very few of those who remained in Berlin – about 60,000 – were still alive in 1945.

WWII

On 1 September 1939, Hitler attacked Poland, a move not greeted with pleasure in Berlin, whose people still remembered the hunger years of WWI and the early 1920s. Again, war brought food shortages and even greater political oppression.

Belgium and the Netherlands subsequently fell quickly, as did France. In June 1941 Hitler attacked the USSR, opening up a new front. Delays in staging what was called 'Operation Barbarossa' – caused by problems in the Mediterranean – would contribute to Germany's downfall as lines of supply were overextended. Hitler's troops, bogged down and ill-prepared for the bitter Russian winter of 1941–42, were forced into retreat. With the defeat of the German 6th Army at Stalingrad (then called Volgograd) the following winter, morale flagged both at home and on the fronts.

In 1941, the USA signed the Lend-Lease Agreement with Britain to provide and finance badly needed military equipment. In December of the same year, the unprovoked Japanese attack on the American fleet at Pearl Harbor prompted the USA to formally enter the war.

The 'Final Solution' The fate of Jews deteriorated after the outbreak of war. Heinrich Himmler's SS troops systematically terrorised and executed local populations in occupied areas, and war with the USSR was portrayed as a fight against 'subhuman' Jews and Bolsheviks.

At Hitler's behest, Göring commissioned his functionaries to find an *Endlösung* (Final Solution) to the 'Jewish question'. A conference, held in January 1942 on the shores of Berlin's Wannsee lake, laid the basis for the Holocaust: the efficient, systematic and bureaucratic murder of millions.

Concentration camps, though not a Nazi invention, now reached a new level of efficiency. Besides Jews, the main target groups were Gypsies, political opponents, priests (especially Jesuits), homosexuals and resistance fighters. In the end there were 22 camps, mostly in Eastern Europe, and another 165 work camps. Altogether, about 7 million people were sent to concentration camps. Only 500,000 survived to be freed by Soviet and Allied soldiers.

Resistance Resistance to the Nazis from socialist, social-democratic and workers' groups had been effectively quashed during the 1930s, with opponents either sent to camps or forced underground or abroad. The most famous case of resistance was that involving Claus Graf Schenk von Stauffenberg and other high-ranking army officers who set out to assassinate Hitler and seize power from the SS on 20 July 1944. The attempt failed and over 200 women and men from the underground were immediately arrested and about half of them executed. All in all, directly or indirectly as a result of the plot, over 7000 people were arrested, with hundreds of them executed.

The Battle of Berlin With the Normandy invasion of June 1944, Allied troops arrived in formidable force on the European mainland, supported by systematic air raids on Berlin and most other German cities. In the last days of the war Hitler, broken and paranoid, ordered the destruction of all remaining German industry and infrastructure, a decree that was largely ignored.

The final Battle of Berlin began on 16 April 1945. More than 1.5 million Soviet soldiers approached the capital from the east, reaching Berlin on 21 April and fully encircling it on 25 April. Two days later, they were in the city centre. On 30 April, the fighting reached the government quarter where Hitler was ensconced in his bunker behind the chancellery, along with his long-time mistress Eva Braun whom he'd married just a day earlier. In the afternoon, they committed suicide. Goebbels and his wife, who were in the bunker too, poisoned their six children, then killed themselves as well.

The capital fell two days later, and on 7 May 1945 Germany capitulated. The signing of the armistice took place at the US military headquarters in Reims (France) and at the Soviet military headquarters in Berlin-Karlshorst.

The Aftermath The war took an enormous toll on Berlin and its people. The civilian population had borne the brunt of the bombings. Entire neighbourhoods lay reduced to rubble, with more than half of all buildings and one-third of industry destroyed or damaged. With some one million women and children evacuated, only 2.4 million people were left in the city in May 1945 (compared to 4.3 million in 1939), two-thirds of them women. About 125,000 Berliners had lost their lives.

In Soviet-occupied Berlin, it was the women who did much of the initial clean-up, earning them the name *Trümmerfrauen* (literally 'rubble women'). Over the following months, enormous amounts of debris were piled up into so-called *Trümmerberge*, artificial hills such as the Teufelsberg in the Grunewald.

Small recoveries came quickly after the armistice, however. The first U-Bahn train ran on 14 May, the first newspaper was published on 15 May, and on 26 May the Berliner Philharmonie gave its first post-war concert. The first crosstown phone connection succeeded on 5 June.

The Politics of Provocation

In line with agreements reached at the Yalta Conference (February 1945), Germany was divided into four zones of occupation. Berlin was carved up into 12 administrative areas under British, French and US control and another eight under Soviet control. At the Potsdam Conference in July and August 1945, regions east of the Oder and Neisse rivers were transferred to Poland as compensation for earlier territorial losses to the Soviet Union.

Soviet demands for high reparations, a bone of contention that soon led to a breakdown in cooperation with the Allies, were ultimately met by brutalising their own zone of occupation. In practice this meant that factory production was requisitioned and able-bodied men and POWs were marched away and put to work in forced-labour camps in the Soviet Union. Due to foot-dragging by the Soviets, American and British troops didn't actually occupy their respective Berlin sectors until 4 July; the French arrived on 12 August. The Soviets also forcibly fused the communist KPD party and the SPD into the Sozialistische Einheitspartei Deutschland (Socialist Unity Party of Germany, or SED) on 22 April 1946 with Walter Ulbricht as general secretary.

The coalition of the western Allies and the USSR eventually collapsed in June 1948 with the Berlin Blockade. Proposed currency reform in the Allied zones prompted the USSR not only to issue its own currency but to also use it as a pretext for beginning an economic blockade of West Berlin (of course, with the intent of bringing the entire city under its complete control). The Allies responded with the Berlin Airlift which would last almost a year and see 278,000 flights supply the city.

The relationship between the Allies and the Germans changed as a result of the Airlift. No longer did Berliners regard them as

The Berlin Airlift

The ruined city of Berlin was still digging itself out from the rubble of WWII when the Soviet hammer fell on its people on 24 June 1948. The military leadership ordered a complete blockade of all rail and road traffic into the city. Berlin would be completely cut off; it was assumed that it would only be a matter of days before the city submitted to the Soviets.

Faced with such provocation, many in the Allied camp urged responses that would have been the opening barrages of WWIII. In the end, wiser heads prevailed. A mere day after the blockade began, the US Air Force launched 'Operation Vittles'. The British followed suit on the 28th with 'Operation Planefair'. (France did not participate in the Airlift because its planes were tied up in Indochina.)

Until May 12 of the following year only an act of astonishing determination and technical expertise kept Berlin alive. For about 11 months, the entire city was supplied exclusively from the air by Allied planes bringing in coal, food and machinery. Every day, around the clock, determined pilots made the treacherous landings at Berlin's airports – sometimes as frequently as one per minute. On one day alone – the 'Easter Parade' of 16 April 1949 – they flew 1400 sorties delivering 13,000 tons. By the end of the Airlift they had flown a combined 125 million miles in 278,000 flights and delivered 2.5 million tons of supplies. The operation cost the lives of 79 people, who are commemorated by the Airlift Memorial at Tempelhof airport.

Given the ever-escalating Allied effort – and the universal scorn of the world – the Soviets backed down and Berlin's western sectors were free once again. The heroic resolve of the pilots, the Allies and Berlin's people had caused the Kremlin to stumble.

Had Berlin fallen into the Soviet realm, we would most likely be looking at a vastly different Europe today, perhaps a vastly different world. The Berlin Airlift thus marks a historical event of incalculable significance. In a very real sense, the Berlin Wall never stood a chance of standing forever, built as it was in a city whose people and protectors had defiantly said 'We will never submit'.

occupational forces but as *Schutzmächte* (protective powers). For more details see the boxed text 'The Berlin Airlift'.

Two German States

In the dawn of the Cold War between East and West, the Allies went ahead with their establishment of government institutions and, in 1949, the Federal Republic of Germany (FRG, or BRD by its German initials) was founded. Konrad Adenauer, a 73-year-old former mayor of Cologne during the Weimar years, became West Germany's first chancellor. Bonn was chosen as the provisional capital.

Berlin remained an isolated island in the sea of the Soviet sector and was dependent on help from the west. In 1950, 300,000 Berliners were unemployed. Thanks to assistance from the FRG and the USA, that number had shrunk to practically zero a mere 10 years later.

Meanwhile, the Soviet zone evolved in 1949 into the German Democratic Republic (GDR, or DDR by its German initials), with Berlin its capital. Nominally a parliamentary democracy, the dominance of the SED meant that party boss Walter Ulbricht called the shots. The early years saw a party takeover of economic, judicial and security functions, including the establishment of the Ministry for State Security – or Stasi – which began neutralising opposition to the SED.

In 1952, the GDR began to cut off relations with the West. West Berliners were no longer allowed to travel to East Germany. Real estate and property owned by West Berliners was expropriated. At the same time, political and moral pressure was exerted on East Berliners to participate in the *Nationale Aufbauwerk* (National Reconstruction Project) which meant rebuilding the country in their spare time – for no pay. On 27 May 1952, all phone connections between East and West Berlin and between the GDR and West Germany were cut.

Uprising in East Berlin

By 1953 the first signs of discontent appeared in the GDR. Production bottlenecks stifled industrial output, heavy industry was given priority over consumer goods and increased demands on industrial workers bred bitterness. Furthermore, the death of Stalin had raised hopes of reform but brought little in the way of real change. Under pressure from Moscow, the government backed down on a decision to raise prices, but it refused to budge on tougher production goals.

Strikes and calls for reform turned to unrest in the urban and industrial centres, culminating in demonstrations and riots on 17 June 1953. Triggered by construction workers on Berlin's Karl-Marx-Allee, the unrest soon involved about 10% of the country's workers. When the GDR government proved incapable of containing the situation, Soviet troops stationed on East German soil quashed the uprising, with scores of deaths and the arrest of about 4000 people.

The Building of the Wall

As the GDR government continued to restrict the freedom of its citizens, the flow of refugees to the west increased. In 1953 alone about 330,000 East Germans fled to the west, most of them well-educated and young, thus amplifying the strain on an already brittle economy. The exodus reached such a level that on the night of 12 August 1961, with the approval of Warsaw Pact countries, fences and ditches were erected between East and West Berlin. On the 15th, construction of the Wall began, thus creating the Cold War's most potent symbol.

Formal protests from the western Allies as well as demonstrations by more than half a million people in West Berlin went unheeded. Tension rose further on 25 October 1961 as US and Soviet tanks faced off at Checkpoint Charlie. The incident was sparked by the GDR's refusal to grant free passage to some members of the US forces. Soon, the entire FRG/GDR border was fenced off and mined, the guards given the order to shoot to kill anybody trying to escape. By the time the Wall collapsed on 9 November 1989, over 80 people had died in such attempts in Berlin alone. (For more information on the Wall, see the boxed text 'The Berlin Wall' in the Things to See and Do chapter.)

Rapprochement

Restrictions that had prevented anybody from entering East Berlin and the GDR eased temporarily in 1963 with the *Passagier-scheinabkommen* (Pass Agreement). It permitted Westerners to visit relatives in East Berlin between 19 December 1963 and 5 January 1964. About 1.2 million visits were recorded in this period. From 1964 to 1966, the GDR opened up its borders three more times for such short periods.

In 1971, after Erich Honecker replaced Walter Ulbricht as SED party head, the *Vier-Mächte-Abkommen* (Four Powers Agreement) between the four victorious Allies set up permanent regulations for visits from west to east, including a transit route to Berlin from West Germany through GDR territory. Except for senior citizens, however, no-one was allowed to leave the GDR. Visitors to East Berlin were saddled with a compulsory exchange from Deutschmarks to the weak Ostmarks (based on a 1:1 exchange rate).

In December 1972 the two Germanies signed the Basic Treaty. This guaranteed sovereignty in international and domestic affairs, normalised East Germany-West Germany relations and paved the way for both countries to join the United Nations.

Economic Developments

During a period of economic stabilisation in the 1960s, the standard of living in the GDR rose to the highest in the Eastern bloc and the country became its second-largest industrial power (behind the USSR).

Meanwhile, West Germany strengthened its ties to the US and Western Europe and embarked on a policy of welfare-state capitalism. An economic boom known as the *Wirtschaftswunder* (economic miracle) lasted throughout the 1950s and most of the 1960s. Its architect, Ludwig Erhard, oversaw policies that encouraged investment and capital formation, aided by the Marshall Plan and a trend towards European economic integration. *Gastarbeiter* (guest workers) were called in from southern Europe (mainly Turkey, Yugoslavia and Italy) to solve a labour shortage. In 1958, West Germany was one of the original five countries to sign the Treaty of Rome which created the European Economic Community, now the expanded European Union.

Student Unrest & Terrorism in the West

In West Germany, CDU (Christliche Demokratische Union or Christian Democratic Union) and SPD, the two major parties, formed a broad coalition in 1966. The absence of parliamentary opposition fuelled an increasingly radical student movement with Berlin at its centre. At sit-ins and protests, students demanded an end to the Vietnam War and reform of Germany's dated university system and teaching programs.

By 1970 the student movement had fizzled, but not without having shaken up the country and brought about some changes, including women's emancipation, university reforms, and a politicisation of the student body.

A few radicals, though, didn't think that enough had been achieved and went underground. Berlin thus became the germ cell of the terrorist Red Army Faction (RAF), led by Ulrike Meinhof, Andreas Baader and Gudrun Ensslin. Throughout the 1970s, the RAF abducted and assassinated prominent business and political figures. By 1976, however, Meinhof and Baader had committed suicide (both in prison). Remaining members found themselves in prison, went into hiding or sought refuge in the GDR. Eventually, though, that country's demise would expose them to West German attempts to bring them to justice.

Collapse of the GDR

Erich Honecker's rise to the position of state secretary in 1971 rang in an era of changes to the East German constitution. Hopeful reunification clauses were struck out in 1974 and replaced by one declaring East Germany's irrevocable alliance with the USSR. Honecker fell comfortably in line with Soviet policies, rode out a world recession and an oil crisis in the early 1970s, and oversaw a period of housing construction, pension increases and help for working mothers.

In the mid-1980s, however, prices for consumer goods rose sharply and, with East Germany struggling to keep pace with technological innovations elsewhere in the world, stagnation set in. Reforms in Poland and Hungary, and especially Mikhail Gorbachev's new course in the USSR, put pressure on an increasingly recalcitrant SED leadership to introduce reforms.

The *Wende* (turning point) began in May 1989, when Hungary announced it would suspend its Travel Agreement, which had once prevented East Germans from entering the west via Hungary. The SED responded by tightening travel restrictions. Meanwhile, more and more East Germans filled West German consulates and embassies in East Berlin, Warsaw, Prague and Budapest, seeking to emigrate. The breakthrough came on 10 September 1989 when Hungary's foreign minister, Gyula Horn, officially opened the Hungarian border to Austria, allowing refugees to cross legally to the west.

Supported by church leaders, a wave of opposition groups, the Neues Forum (New Forum), emerged and led calls for human rights and an end to the SED political monopoly. This sparked a leadership crisis in the SED, which resulted in the replacement of Honecker by Egon Krenz. On 4 November 1989, about 500,000 demonstrators gathered on Berlin's Alexanderplatz. By this time, East Germany was losing citizens at a rate of about 10,000 per day.

The day of reckoning came on November 9, 1989, when the GDR *Politbüro* tried to turn events around by approving direct travel to the west. The announcement of direct travel was made in a televised press conference by leading *Politbüro* member Günter Schabowsky. Asked by one reporter *when* this would come into effect, Schabowsky searched his notes uncomfortably and, at a loss, mistakenly said, 'right away'. Tens of thousands rushed through border points in Berlin, watched by perplexed guards, who, though they knew nothing about this new regulation, did not intervene. West Berliners went into the streets to greet the visitors; tears and champagne flowed. Amid scenes of wild partying, the Wall had fallen.

Reunification

Opposition groups and government representatives soon met in so-called 'round table talks' to hammer out a course of action. In March 1990, the first free elections in East Germany since 1949 took place and an alliance, headed by Lothar de Maizière of the CDU, won convincingly. The SPD, which took an equivocal view of reunification, was punished by voters accordingly. The old SED administrative regions were abolished and the Länder (states) revived. Currency and economic union became a reality in July 1990.

In September 1990 the two Germanies, the USSR and the Allied powers signed the Two-Plus-Four Treaty, ending post-war occupation zones. One month later the East German state was dissolved and Germany's first unified post-WWII elections were held. Berlin once again became the German capital, when in 1991, a small majority (338 to 320) of members in the Bundestag (German Parliament) voted in favour of moving the government to Berlin. On 8 September 1994, the last Allied military troops stationed in Berlin left the city after a festive ceremony.

The Berlin Republic

In 1999 the German parliament moved from Bonn to Berlin, convening its first session in the restored Reichstag building on 19 April. The ministries have since followed, as have diplomats, government agencies, industrial associations, lobbyists and others – an estimated total of 15,000 people. A new government district around the Reichstag has sprung up, with new offices for parliamentarians, sleek embassies and, most notably, the striking New Federal Chancellery which opened in 2001.

Elsewhere too, the face of Berlin has been greatly changed since reunification. The dramatic Friedrichstadtpassagen have breathed new life into once languishing Friedrichstrasse; the New Synagogue on Oranienburger Strasse is a fervent symbol of the rebirth of Jewish culture in Berlin; Pariser Platz is once again becoming Berlin's 'reception room' flanked by embassies, banks, the Hotel Adlon and the Academy of Art; around Zoo station, the architectural sins of the 1950s are even being replaced with dramatic new structures. The most prominent development, though, has emerged around Potsdamer Platz, whose ballet of cranes was a symbol of the 1990s. Here, a new urban district anchored by DaimlerCity and the Sony Center was completed in 1998 and 2000, respectively.

Berlin's regained status as the German capital is gradually imbuing it with a new sophistication and an even greater internationalism than ever before. Signs of creative energy, construction and modernisation abound wherever you look. In part because of its geopolitical location, Berlin is also increasingly positioning itself as a conduit between east and west in all arenas, including politics, culture, business and finance, communication and science. Berlin has eight Russian banks, three Russian newspapers and a Russian-language TV station. Eastern European participation in Berlin's trade shows has tripled since reunification. This trend is likely to continue with the European Union's expansion into Poland and the Czech Republic.

In 2001, Berlin, which had teetered on bankruptcy for many years, plunged into a deep financial crisis. The heavily overextended coffers cost Eberhard Diepgen of the CDU, governing mayor for 15 years, his job. Accused of mismanagement, excessive spending and corruption, he was forced to resign from office. Klaus Wowereit (SPD) took over as interim mayor and was later confirmed as governing mayor in elections held in October 2001.

GEOGRAPHY
Berlin is Germany's largest city, both in terms of population (around 3.4 million) and area. Its north-south extent measures 38km, while from east to west it stretches for 45km. The city covers a total of 889 sq km. Berlin lies in the heart of the vast north German plains and, apart from rivers and lakes, lacks distinctive geographical features. Some of its rare hills, like the Teufelsberg in the Grunewald forest, are actually Trümmerberge made from rubble piles gathered during the post-WWII clean-up.

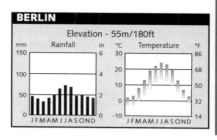

Berlin is crisscrossed by two rivers that are important for inland navigation. These are the 343km-long Havel, which has its headwaters in the Mecklenburg Lake District about 110km north-west of Berlin, and its tributary the Spree, which joins it in Spandau. On its course, the Havel travels through several canals and lakes, including the Wannsee.

CLIMATE
Berlin has a moderately cool and humid climate determined by a mixing of air masses from the Atlantic Ocean and the continental climate of Eastern Europe. Predictably, December to February are the coldest months. When the winds blow from Russia it can get mighty chilly, with temperatures dropping to below freezing. Generally, though, winters are relatively mild. More than half of the city's annual inversion days (when stagnant cold air traps warmer air below, bringing about smog) occur in these months.

July and August are warmest, though usually not chokingly hot. The nicest months are September and October which deliver the added bonus of autumn foliage. May and June, when the trees are in bloom and the outdoor cafe season kicks off, are popular months too, though rain is more likely at this time.

ECOLOGY & ENVIRONMENT
Berlin has some of the highest air pollution levels in Germany – higher than any other big city in the former West Germany, though still lower than in some eastern cities like Dresden, Halle or Chemnitz. In 1991, Berlin joined the International Climate Convention, pledging to halve CO_2 emissions by 2010.

Berlin has a vast number of trees lining its streets. Pollution and acid rain, however, are increasingly doing damage to Berlin's surrounding forests. In 2000, less than one in five trees remained healthy, with 55% displaying minor damage and 24% being either heavily damaged or dead. Oak trees are especially affected, with only 7% showing no signs of damage.

Berlin's drinking water is fine, though its lakes and rivers are not. The Havel lakes, including the Wannsee, are prone to excessive algae growth; the Spree River and the Landwehr Canal that flow right through the city are badly polluted. Only the lakes in the Grunewald forest are slightly cleaner.

Despite such problems Berlin is, in many ways, a very ecologically minded city. In order to stave off further destruction of plant and animal life, the state government has devised the ambitious Program for the Protection of Land and Endangered Species which seeks to balance the objectives of nature and conservation with urban development.

Awareness also happens on a smaller scale. Bicycle lanes abound, there are solar-powered parking voucher dispensers and even U-Bahn and S-Bahn stations have recycling bins. The city has a comprehensive and efficient public transport system; by the same token, it tries to discourage drivers through restricted parking and expensive parking meters and garages.

Greenpeace is very active in Germany. Its Berlin branch (Map 3; ☎ 28 39 15 50, fax 28 39 15 51, Ⓦ www.greenpeace.de) is at Chausseestrasse 131 in Mitte. Another important and similarly radical environmental group is the Grüne Liga (Green League, ☎ 443 39 10, fax 44 33 91 33, Ⓦ www.berlin@ grueneliga.de), whose Berlin head office is at Prenzlauer Allee 230.

FLORA & FAUNA

Berlin is a relatively green city. Parks, forests, lakes and rivers take up about one-third of its space. Nearly every neighbourhood has its own park, and a ring of forests encircles the urban sprawl.

Berlin considers itself Europe's tree capital, a result of a successful tree-planting campaign during the last two decades. Of the city's 411,000 urban trees most are linden (lime) trees (36%) and maple trees (18%); others are oak (8%), plane (6%) and chestnut (4%). The eastern district of Hohenschönhausen has the most trees per kilometre of road (134) compared to the city average of 78 per kilometre.

Animal life overall has declined dramatically since WWII. Construction and a growing population have about halved the number of existing species. Low groundwater levels have dried up biotopes, threatening the survival of reptiles, amphibians and fish. Only about 33 fish species still inhabit the city's rivers and lakes, the most common being perch, pike, roach and bream. Sparrows and pigeons are the most prevalent bird species.

At the same time, a different development has taken place in the leafy forest belt surrounding Berlin, where the population of wild rabbits, foxes, martens and even boar has increased enormously (see the boxed text 'Porcine Troubles').

GOVERNMENT & POLITICS

Along with Hamburg and Bremen, Berlin is a German city-state. Its government consists of the *Abgeordnetenhaus* (parliament, or legislative body) with 141 members and the *Senat* (Senate, or executive body). Members of parliament are voted for directly by the electorate for a five-year term. Their primary function is to pass legislation and to elect and supervise the Senate. The parliament also selects the *Regierender Bürgermeister* (governing mayor) and, at his or her suggestion, the members of the Senate.

The Senate consists of the governing mayor and eight senators. The governing mayor sets policy with the agreement of senators and represents Berlin internationally and nationally. Senators have similar roles as cabinet members, with each in charge of a particular department.

The seat of government of both the governing mayor and the Senate is the *Rotes Rathaus* (Red Town Hall). Parliament meets in the Abgeordnetenhaus on Niederkirchnerstrasse, opposite the Martin-Gropius-Bau.

Porcine Troubles

First came the politicians from Bonn, then came the wild boars from the woods…Greater Berlin's wild pig problems have reached new and undesirable heights as residents in Berlin's leafy outer suburbs wake to find their gardens ploughed up by their porcine friends. One resident reported seeing 30 wild pigs trotting along the road in front of his house, and another woke one morning to find a dead pig in his swimming pool.

The population explosion of wild pigs is said to have been caused by mild winters and an abundance of acorns and other foods. In recent years, though, the swine have expanded their food search to human habitats. Many have developed a taste for lawns, flower beds and scraps scavenged from compost heaps and garbage cans. They've learned that humans don't constitute their enemies and have lost their shyness. According to a report in the *Berliner Morgenpost* newspaper, wild pigs even wait regularly on the steps of one school to beg for food from school children in the break.

Suburbs most affected are Grunewald, Zehlendorf, Wilmersdorf, Reinickendorf and Spandau. In 2000, around 1050 wild pigs were bagged in Berlin's forests by licensed hunters.

Since 1984, the dominant party in Berlin had been the centre-right CDU led by governing mayor Eberhard Diepgen. In elections held in October 2001, however, a large number of voters turned away from the CDU as apparent payback for plunging the city into its most severe post-war financial crisis. The party, which had garnered as much as 40.8% of the vote in the 1999 elections, dropped to just 23.8% in 2001. The SPD vote now stands at 29.7%. The centrist FDP, which had not been represented at all in recent years, made a stunning comeback by more than tripling its 1999 showing to 7.7%.

Another major winner was the PDS, the successor party of the GDR's communist SED, which got 22.6% of the overall vote (17.7% in 1999). For the first time since reunification, the PDS was able to expand its appeal beyond the eastern districts, where it has traditionally received nearly every second vote. In 2001, though, it got about 15% in Kreuzberg and even garnered 6.6% in solidly bourgeois Charlottenburg-Wilmersdorf.

Some gains for the PDS seem to have come at the expense of the Green Party, which won only 9.1% of the vote, compared to 14.6% in 1995. One reason for Green voters' disenchantment may have been the

support for the war in Afghanistan that this once thoroughly pacifist party has shown on the national level.

Since no single party obtained an absolute majority, a coalition government was being formed as we went to press. It will either bring together the SPD with the PDS, or end up a so-called 'Ampelkoalition' (traffic light coalition) involving the SPD (red), the FDP (yellow) and the Greens (you figure it out).

The election results also confirmed the SPD's Klaus Wowereit as Berlin's governing mayor. Wowereit had already been interim mayor since Diepgen's resignation in spring 2001. With Wowereit, Berlin becomes the second European capital after Paris to be led by an openly gay man.

In 1920, Berlin was divided into *Bezirke* (administrative districts), each with its own local administration; the newly created districts of Hohenschönhausen, Hellersdorf and Marzahn were added in the 1980s. In January 2001, Berlin's 23 Bezirke were reduced to 12 in an effort to curb bureaucracy. This was largely a behind-the-scenes move with no impact on visitors as the old district names continue to be used. Most of the 'new' districts were created by merging existing ones so that each now has a population of roughly 300,000. The districts are: Mitte, Friedrichshain-Kreuzberg, Pankow (which includes Prenzlauer Berg), Charlottenburg-Wilmersdorf, Spandau, Steglitz-Zehlendorf, Tempelhof-Schöneberg, Neukölln, Treptow-Köpenick, Marzahn-Hellersdorf, Lichtenberg and Reinickendorf.

ECONOMY

Germany is the world's third largest economic power (behind the USA and Japan), a committed member of the EU, and has been a member of the expanded G8 group of industrial nations since 1974. In recent years, however, the German economy has weakened, in part due to pressure from foreign competition, antiquated machinery, technophobia, and high wages and social-security overheads. Berlin has been hit along with the rest of the country.

The fall of the Wall provided both an opportunity and a challenge to Berlin's economy. East Berlin was one of the GDR's manufacturing capitals, but after the Wende most of its outdated and unprofitable factories were closed. West Berlin, on the other hand, had not been an important location for industry and manufacturing after WWII because of its island status. An additional blow was the loss of most of the federal subsidies the city-state had received during the years of division.

Reunification initially generated a growth spurt, but it took only a couple of years to fizzle. While Berlin's gross domestic product leapt from DM121 billion (€61.7 billion) to DM152 billion (€77.5 billion) from 1991 to 1995, it has more or less stagnated since. In 1999, it stood at DM151 billion (€77 billion).

Unemployment figures are at record highs, especially among young people, foreigners and older workers. In July 2001, some 273,700 Berliners (or 16%) were registered as unemployed, an increase of 72,000 in just seven years (concurrent with a population drop of about 90,000). Figures would probably be even worse if entrepreneurship – especially in the service sector and among young people – hadn't picked up some of the slack. Around 158,000 people are now self-employed, with company foundings having

increased by 30% since reunification, especially in the fields of finance, corporate services, construction, commerce and tourism.

For the time being, Berlin is still in the process of painful economic restructuring, moving away from manufacturing and towards service industries.

More than half of Berlin's workforce of 1.487 million are in the service sector, including state and federal government agencies. In fact, Berlin has more than twice as many civil servants as any other big city in Germany. One in 10 people holds a government job in eastern Berlin; in the western districts it's 6.8%.

Tourism is one of the sectors that has clocked tangible growth. In 1999, about 4.2 million visitors came to Berlin, an increase of over 1 million since 1992. Another driving force is information and communication technology with around 100,000 employees. Other growth areas are software development, marketing, advertising, law and financial services.

POPULATION & PEOPLE

In November 2000, Berlin had 3.385 million inhabitants, making it the country's largest city. About 2.11 million people live in former West Berlin and 1.275 million in the eastern districts. Oddly, a post-unification population boom has been offset by a slowing birth rate and the exodus of young families from the capital to the surrounding countryside. This has resulted in a net decline of about 90,000 inhabitants since 1993. During the same period, the number of immigrants in Berlin increased by about 45,000 to roughly 450,000.

There's no doubt that Berlin is Germany's most multicultural city, with an amazing patchwork of people from 185 nations. The vast majority (83%) of immigrants live in the western districts with Kreuzberg having the highest concentration (33.6%), followed by Wedding (28.8%) and Tiergarten (26.4%). In 1999, 30% of immigrants were of Turkish descent and people from the former states of Yugoslavia accounted for 15%. Other large groups are Poles (6.5%) and immigrants from the former Soviet republics (5.6%).

About 13,000 Italians and 10,800 Greeks also reside in Berlin.

Berlin is also an extremely 'young' city. More than half of its people are under 35 and 17.5% are under 18; by contrast, only 14% are over 65 years in age. The actual number of children residing in the city is declining. While in April 1991, some 412,000 families had children under 18, that number had dropped to 366,400 by 1999, a net loss of around 11%.

EDUCATION

Berlin's public school system is built along the lines of other German federal states. Education is compulsory for 12 years and financed by the state. An overwhelming majority of students attend free public schools which, overall, are excellent.

Following an optional two or three years at kindergarten, children start attending the Grundschule (primary school), usually at six years of age. After six years, they transfer to one of three traditional secondary high school types: Hauptschule (vocational emphasis, three years), Realschule (commercial emphasis, four years), and Gymnasium (academic emphasis, seven years). The Gymnasium culminates with the Abitur, an extremely rigorous multi-day examination which must be passed in order to obtain university admission. Graduates of the Hauptschule and Realschule usually take up a two- or three-year apprenticeship taught in a system called 'dual education' where students divide their time between on-the-job training and the Berufsschule (vocational school).

Berlin also has a number of specialist schools, many of them catering for students from other countries. The John F Kennedy School in Zehlendorf has an equal proportion of German and American students, and teaches in German and English. There's also a French Grammar School, a Swedish School, a Japanese School, and others. Private schools, including private boarding schools, round out the educational offerings.

Berlin is Germany's largest university town with about 133,000 students studying at three universities, four arts colleges and nine technical colleges. The largest are the Freie Universität (41,000 students), the Technische Universität (29,000 students) and the Humboldt Universität (33,000 students). Berlin also has some 250 research institutes, including the famous Max Planck Institute.

SCIENCE & PHILOSOPHY

Germany, with its rigorous education system based on the ideas of the Berlin-born philologist and statesman Wilhelm von Humboldt (1767–1835), has made enormous contributions to the disciplines of philosophy and the natural sciences. The importance of Germans in the social sciences and physics in particular is inestimable. Up to 1939, 10 out of 45 Nobel Prizes in physics had gone to Germans.

In philosophy, it was Immanuel Kant (1724–1804) who, as a founder of German idealism, paved the way for Georg Wilhelm Friedrich Hegel (1770–1831). In *The Phenomenology of the Spirit* (1807), Hegel developed a theory of dialectics, or opposites, that culminated idealistically in pure consciousness. From 1818, he taught at the Humboldt University and actively participated in the literary salons in vogue at the time. His influence extended to Arthur Schopenhauer (1788–1860), an idealist with pessimistic predilections, who was associated with Goethe and Schiller in Weimar.

If Schopenhauer drove German idealism to its subjective limits, the Trier-born Karl Marx (1818–83) injected it with a historical basis and re-interpreted Hegel's pure consciousness as proletarian revolution. As an economist and the author of *Das Kapital*, Marx occupies a place alongside his British predecessor, David Ricardo (1772–1823). As a social theorist, his brilliance was in describing the change from feudalism to modern capitalism. As a revolutionary, he laid the groundwork for 20th-century political developments.

Friedrich Nietzsche (1844–1900) shared Schopenhauer's idealism but saw subjectivity as a positive condition. Much of his work focuses on power and the human will. His ideas on an Übermensch (superman), however, were distorted by Hitler and used to justify racial abuses.

Germany's achievements in the natural sciences are no less impressive. Geographer and naturalist Alexander von Humboldt (1769–1859), the younger brother of Wilhelm, stands out as an important figure for his study of flora and species distribution, physical geography and meteorology.

Physics, however, is the field in which Germany has particularly excelled. Born in Kiel, Max Planck (1858–1947) came to Berlin in 1889 where he concentrated his work and research on theoretical thermo-dynamics. He is considered the founder of quantum physics, a theory for which he was awarded the Nobel Prize in 1918. Planck served as president of the Kaiser-Wilhelm-Society from 1930 to 1937. First dissolved by the Allies after the war, it was refounded in 1947 and renamed the Max Planck Institute.

A close ally of Planck, Albert Einstein (1879–1955) was born in Ulm and moved to Berlin in 1913 where he became director of the Kaiser-Wilhelm-Institut for Physics and a member of the Prussian Academy of Sciences. His theories on the atomic structure of matter were followed by the publication of his theory of relativity in 1914–15. In 1921, he too received the Nobel Prize for his contributions to the field of quantum physics. A Jew and Zionist, he left Germany in 1933 for the USA, eventually becoming an American citizen in 1940.

The German tradition of excellence in the social and natural sciences continues to this day. Berlin has invested about €1.8 billion in science and R&D. The Max Planck Institute is one of the leading research facilities in the world. An important new development is a huge science and technology park in Treptow called Wissenschafts-und Wirtschaftsstandort Adlershof (WISTA, Centre for Science & Economy Adlershof).

ARTS
Painting & Sculpture
Beginnings When merchants founded Berlin in the 13th century, the fine arts were not a priority. Time, wars and the icono-clastic zeal of church reformers in the 16th century destroyed much of the small amount of medieval art there was in the first place. Among the few surviving objects are a Romanesque goblet, late-Gothic altar paintings and the faded 15th-century *Totentanz* (Dance of Death) fresco, all on view in the Marienkirche in Mitte.

The arts scene continued to slumber until the reign of Elector Joachim II (ruled 1535–71) who enlarged the city palace in the German Renaissance style and invited the era's leading artists – including Saxon painters Lucas Cranach the Elder (1472–1553) and his son, Lucas Cranach the Younger (1515–86) – to his court.

Whatever artistic spirit had developed under Joachim was quashed by the mayhem of the Thirty Years' War (1618–48). When it was over, the Great Elector Friedrich Wilhelm looked to Holland for inspiration for his two new palaces at Oranienburg and Köpenick. The painters Willem van Honthorst and Hendrik de Fromantious briefly worked on site, aided by German artists like Michael Willmann and Michael Conrad Hirt.

Baroque & Rococo In the late 17th and early 18th century the arts finally began to flourish in Berlin, partly because self-crowned King Friedrich I felt the need to surround himself with more grandeur. At the instigation of the sculptor Andreas Schlüter (1660–1714), he founded the Academy of the Arts in 1696.

Meanwhile, Schlüter enhanced Berlin's artistic landscape with several outstanding sculptures, including the *Great Elector on Horseback* (1699), now in front of Schloss Charlottenburg. The haunting *Masks of Dying Warriors* in the courtyard of the Zeughaus on Unter den Linden, construction of which Schlüter supervised, are his as well.

During this period, the allegorical fresco re-emerged as an established art form and came to adorn the ceilings of various palaces. This endeavour kept busy German painters like Johann Friedrich Wentzel and Friedrich Wilhelm Weidemann, but especially the skilled Antoine Pesne (1683–1757) who satisfied Friedrich I's taste for the French rococo style.

The arts languished under his successor, Soldier King Friedrich Wilhelm I, then took a turn towards greatness when his son, Friedrich II, ascended the throne in 1740. Friedrich drew heavily on the artistic, architectural and decorative expertise of Georg Wenzeslaus von Knobelsdorff (1699–1753), a student of Pesne. Knobelsdorff gave the world Schloss Rheinsberg (see the Excursions chapter), though he's most famous for designing the Staatsoper Unter den Linden and Schloss Sanssouci.

19th Century The 19th century saw a proliferation of styles which in some ways reflected the socio-political undercurrents rumbling through Europe at this time. New political and economic ideas coming to Germany from England and France especially resonated with the educated middle classes. This new self-confidence found expression in neoclassicism, a style which brought a formal shift to both line and body and an emphasis on Roman and Greek mythology.

A major artist of the period was Johann Gottfried Schadow (1764–1850), whose most famous work is the *Quadriga*, the horse-drawn chariot which crowns the landmark Brandenburger Tor. While basing his work on classic Greek sculpture, Schadow also imbued it with great naturalness and sensuousness.

Another important neoclassical sculptor was Christian Daniel Rauch (1777–1857), a Schadow student. Rauch had a talent for representing idealised, classical beauty in a realistic fashion. He created the sarcophagi of Friedrich Wilhelm III and Queen Luise – both on view at the Mausoleum in the gardens of Schloss Charlottenburg. His most famous work, though, is the monument of Friedrich II on horseback (1851), which stands outside the Humboldt Universität on Unter den Linden.

A student of Rauch, the sculptor Reinhold Begas (1831–1911) developed a neobaroque, theatrical style that was so ostentatiously counter-neoclassical that he met with a fair amount of controversy, even in his lifetime. The Neptune fountain (1891) outside the

Marienkirche is a Begas work, as is the Schiller monument on Gendarmenmarkt.

In painting, Romanticism began to overtake neoclassicism in popularity. A reason for this was the awakening of a nationalist spirit in Germany – spurred by the Napoleonic Wars – during the reign of Friedrich Wilhelm III (1797–1840). Romanticism was the perfect form of expression for the idealism, emotion and dreams that characterised the period.

Top billing among Romantic painters goes to Caspar David Friedrich whose works are on display at the Alte Nationalgalerie on Museumsinsel. Also here are paintings by Karl Friedrich Schinkel, Berlin's dominant neoclassical architect (see the Architecture special section) who, early in his career, created a series of romantic, moody landscapes and fantastic depictions of Gothic architecture. He also decorated the vestibule of the Altes Museum, which he designed, with frescoes.

A parallel development during the period of 1815–48 was the so-called Berliner Biedermeier. The most successful and famous artist of this period was Franz Krüger (1797–1857) whose best-known works are meticulous depictions of public parades such as *Parade auf dem Opernplatz* (Parade on the Opera Square, 1829).

There was also an interest in paintings that chronicled Berlin's constantly evolving cityscape. Important artists of the genre include Eduard Gaertner and Wilhelm Brücke. These paintings sold especially well among the middle classes, as did still lifes. Other Romantic painters, like Wilhelm Schadow and Karl Wilhelm Wach, represented a group of intensely religious artists called the *Nazarener* (Nazareths).

The Berliner Secession In 1892, an exhibit of paintings by Norwegian artist Edvard Munch shook up Berlin's art establishment. When conservative groups opposed to such nontraditional 'modern' art forced the closure of the show, a group of young artists banded together in protest. Initially calling themselves the Gruppe der XI (Group of 11), they became better known under the name Berliner Secession, adopted in 1898.

Led by Max Liebermann (1847–1935) and Walter Leistikow (1865–1908), member artists were not linked by a common artistic style, but by a rejection of reactionary attitudes towards the arts which stifled new forms of expression. They preferred scenes from daily life to historical and religious themes. They shunned the studio in favour of painting in natural outdoor light. The artists of the Berliner Secession were hugely successful and influential in inspiring new styles.

Liebermann himself evolved from a painter of gloomy naturalist scenes to one of the most important representatives of 'Berlin impressionism'. In the early 1900s, Lovis Corinth (1858–1925) and Max Slevogt (1868–1932) joined the group, as did Käthe Kollwitz (1867–1945). Kollwitz was a veritable 'Renaissance woman', active in virtually all fields of visual art. An excellent place to see her works is the Käthe Kollwitz Museum in Charlottenburg.

The 1920s If Berlin before WWI had emerged as a dynamic place where modern art could develop freely, it evolved into *the* centre of contemporary German and international art in the 1920s. Movements proliferated as a veritable Who's Who of artists flocked to Berlin. Dadaism, co-founded by George Grosz (1893–1959), emerged as a prevalent form. Dadaists rejected traditional art and considered chance and spontaneity as determining artistic elements. Collages and photo montages were art forms that grew out of dada. The works were outrageous, provocative and *everybody* was talking about them.

Parallel movements had expressionist artists like Max Beckmann (1884–1950) and Otto Dix (1891–1969) examining in their works the threats posed to humanity by urbanisation. Constructivists like El Lissitzky and László Moholy-Nagy explored the relationship between art and technology. Wassily Kandinsky, Paul Klee, Lyonel Feininger and Alexej Jawlensky formed the 'Group of the Blue Four' in 1924 and went on to work and teach at the Bauhaus art school, which moved to Berlin from Dessau

in 1932, only to be closed down by the Nazis in 1933.

The impact on the Berlin arts scene after the Nazis takeover was devastating. Many artists left the country; others ended up in prison or concentration camps, their works classified as 'degenerate' and often confiscated and destroyed. Only a few artists – Käthe Kollwitz, Gerhard Marcks and Otto Nagel – remained in Berlin, largely managing to avoid the artistic evisceration enforced by the Nazis.

Post-1945 After WWII, Berlin's art scene was as fragmented as the city itself. In the east, artists were forced to toe the 'socialist -realist' line, which Otto Nagel and Max Lingner frequently managed to leap over. In the late '60s, East Berlin established itself as an arts centre in the GDR with the formation of the Berliner Schule (Berlin School). Main members like Manfred Böttcher and Harald Metzkes succeeded at freeing themselves from the confines of officially sanctioned socialist art in order to embrace a more multifaceted realism. In the '70s, when conflicts of the individual in society became a prominent theme, underground galleries flourished in Prenzlauer Berg and art creation became a collective endeavour.

In postwar West Berlin, artists eagerly absorbed abstract influences from France and the USA. Pioneering groups included Zone 5 (a play on the four zones into which Berlin was now divided) which revolved around Hans Thiemann, and surrealists Heinz Trökes and Mac Zimmermann. At the same time, returning veteran expressionists Max Pechstein and Karl Schmidt-Rottluff provided a more 'traditional' counterweight.

In the 1960s, art went political. A new style called 'critical realism' emerged, propagated primarily by artists like Ulrich Baehr, Hans-Jürgen Diehl and Wolfgang Petrick. The 1973 movement called Schule der Neuen Prächtigkeit (School of New Magnificence) had a similar approach and involved artists like Manfred Bluth, Matthias Koeppel and Johannes Grützke.

In the 1980s, expressionism found its way back onto the canvasses of painters like Salomé, Helmut Middendorf and Rainer Fetting who were members of a group called Junge Wilde (Young Wild Ones).

Post-Wende After the Wende, Berlin's arts scene developed into one of the most exciting and dynamic in Europe. The sense of change and new beginning – coupled with the uncertainty that accompanied it – generated a fertile ground of creativity. The city, nowadays, is considered an international centre of contemporary art.

Much of it is on view in the gallery quarter around the Hackesche Höfe and Auguststrasse in Mitte, which formed soon after reunification. Pioneering galleries include Wohnmachine, Eigen + Art and Schipper & Krome. The Kunsthaus Tacheles, on Oranienburger Strasse, is home to numerous artists' studios, as is the nearby Kunst-Werke, founded in 1991, and housed in a former margarine factory. Kunst-Werke was also behind the creation of the Berlin Biennale, an exhibition of contemporary art, the second of which took place in 2001. It presents new art in unusual sites around town, including a former postal facility on Tucholskystrasse and the S-Bahn arches at Jannowitzbrücke. Also important is art forum, an annual trade show showcasing contemporary art, which began in 1996.

A new gallery frontier has emerged, of late, around Zimmerstrasse near the former Checkpoint Charlie. Galleries like Arndt & Partner and Mehdi Chouakri provide the impetus here. And, finally, there is still the established scene in Charlottenburg along Ku'damm, Uhlandstrasse, Fasanenstrasse and other streets, where Galerie Brusberg, Galerie Pels-Leuden and other doyens hold forth.

Film

In 1895, the first commercial film projection took place in Berlin. The city soon became synonymous with film making in Germany, at least until the outbreak of WWII. With filming having recently resumed in Babelsberg, Berlin has become the second-most important film centre in Germany (behind Munich). In 2000 alone, the industry received subsidies of around DM35 million (€17.85 million). Berlin hosts the single most important event in Germany's annual film calendar, the International Film Festival. Better known as Berlinale, it was founded in 1951 on the initiative of the western Allies. Held every February, it features screenings of around 750 films, with some of them competing for the Golden and Silver Bear trophies. These are awarded by an international panel of judges. In 2000, the Berlinale moved to news digs at Potsdamer Platz, also home of the Filmmuseum Berlin. Since 1971, the International Forum of New Cinema, which showcases more radical and alternative films, has taken place alongside the more traditional competition.

Berlin now has more cinemas than ever (around 265), including numerous multiplexes as well as smaller houses showing movies in their original language (see the Entertainment chapter for details).

The Early Days Berlin's pioneering role in movie history is undeniable. America had Edison, France the Lumiére brothers, and Berlin had Max Skladanowsky. A former fairground showman, his 1895 invention – the bioscope, a prototype film projector – paved the way for others to develop and improve on his technological achievement and to ring in the era of film making in Germany.

Those picking up the baton included Berlin mechanic Oskar Messter who made, patented and sold some 17 projector types between 1896 and 1913. By 1910, Berlin had 139 *Kinematographentheater* (hence the German word for cinema, Kino) showing mostly slapstick, melodramas and short documentaries.

After WWI movies finally blossomed as an artistic genre. Egged on by General Field Marshal Ludendorff, the Universum Film AG (UFA) was founded in 1917 to produce such pro-war propaganda movies as *Die Schuldigen des Weltkrieges* (The Culprits of the World War), which depicted the Allies as responsible for starting WWI. After the war, UFA began making a name for itself with Ernst Lubitsch's hugely successful but hopelessly silly monster movies. By 1922, Germany had produced 474 movies, making it the second-largest film producer after the USA. Almost all those films came out of Berlin.

The Silent Era Silent films were heavily influenced by expressionism, often adopting morbid, pathological themes and using disjointed images and clever cutting to create the warped psychology of their characters. The influence of Sigmund Freud is clear in Stellan Rye's 1913 classic *Der Student von Prag* (The Student of Prague), which tells the story of a student who sells his mirror image to a stranger and ends up fleeing his own self. *Das Kabinett des Dr Caligari* (The Cabinet of Dr Caligari, 1919) by Robert Wiene, about a hypnotist who causes his patients to commit murder, also shows expressionist influences and deals with tyranny. The world it created through bizarre visual effects was almost unthinkable, given the primitive nature of film making at the time. This style would later resonate powerfully in the works of Alfred Hitchcock.

Another *Gruselfilm* (horror, or Gothic, film) is FW Murnau's *Nosferatu* (1922), a seminal interpretation of Bram Stoker's *Dracula*. Starring Max Schreck, it inspired countless retellings of the story, including the 2001 *Shadow of the Vampire*, a fictional but spooky account of Murnau's filming of *Nosferatu* starring John Malkovich as Murnau.

Fritz Lang's *Metropolis* (1926), about the dangers of totalitarianism, stands out as an ambitious cinema classic. It depicts the revolt of a proletarian class that lives underground. Also by Lang is *M* (1931) with Peter Lorre as a child killer chased by police, and other criminals with their own ideas about justice.

The next phase of Berlin's cinema history belonged to film makers of the Neue Sachlichkeit (New Objectivity). Representatives included Georg Wilhelm Papst who had worked in New York theatre before

WWI. He came to dominate Berlin's film scene throughout the 1920s and 1930s, using montage to elucidate character and create stirring visual sequences. In *Die freudlose Gasse* (The Joyless Alley; 1925) he portrays two women – one a society lady, the other a prostitute – in order to illustrate a perceived loss of values. The most important documentary of the era was Walter Ruttmann's *Berlin – Die Sinfonie einer Grossstadt* (Berlin – Symphony of a Big City; 1927), which portrays the diversity of Berlin over the course of a 24-hour spring day.

Sound Films of the 1930s Talkie production didn't make inroads in Berlin until 1930, despite the fact that sound had been invented in Berlin. Supported by UFA, three engineers – Hans Vogt, Joseph Massolle and Jo Engel – set up a sound studio called Tri-Ergon. They developed and produced the first talkie in 1925 called *Das Mädchen mit den Schwefelhölzern* (The Girl with the Matchsticks) which premiered – and subsequently bombed – at the Metropol Theatre on Nollendorfplatz.

In 1927 UFA passed into the hands of the Hugenberg group, which was sympathetic to the burgeoning right-wing movement. The new film era resulted in the Marlene Dietrich classic *Der blaue Engel* (The Blue Angel; 1930), directed by Joseph von Sternberg and loosely based on Heinrich Mann's novella *Professor Unrat*. It tells the story of a pedantic professor who is hopelessly infatuated with a sexy cabaret singer, played by Dietrich. For Marlene, it created the vamp image that she enjoyed all her life.

Pabst's *Dreigroschenoper* (Threepenny Opera, 1931), based on the play by Bertolt Brecht (music by Kurt Weill), was set in the gangster milieu around Mackie Messer (Mack the Knife). *Das Testament des Dr Mabuse* (The Testament of Dr Mabuse; 1932) was Fritz Lang's first talkie. It is about a psychiatric patient who devises plans to take over the world. The Nazis, tellingly, prevented the German premiere, forcing Lang to shift it to Austria.

Marlene Dietrich

Marlene Dietrich, whose real name was Marie Magdalena von Losch, was born in Berlin at Sedanstrasse 53 (now Leberstrasse 65) in Schöneberg into a middle-class family on 27 December 1901. After WWI, she took acting lessons at the Max Reinhardt School and started to get small parts at the Deutsches Theater starting in 1923, the same year she married Rudolf Sieber at the Gedächtniskirche. Throughout the 1920s she also worked in the fledgling German silent-film industry, stereotyped as a hard living, libertine flapper. In the 1927 film *Wenn ein Weib den Weg verliert* (When a Girl Loses Her Way) she played a well-mannered young woman who falls into the clutches of a gigolo. Dietrich soon carved a niche in the film fantasies of lower middle-class men as the dangerously seductive *femme fatale*, best typified by her 1930 talkie *Der blaue Engel* (The Blue Angel).

MW

Dietrich, incidentally, only landed the role of Lola Lola through the insistence of the film's director, Josef von Sternberg, who convinced Heinrich Mann, on whose novel, *Professor Unrat*, the movie was based to hire her (Mann originally wanted to give the part to his lover, Trude Hesterberg, a cabaret artist). Meanwhile, the film's scriptwriter was doing his best to get his own lover into the role. Dietrich won the part and Mann lost his lover.

Filmed at the UFA studios in Babelberg, the movie also made Dietrich a Hollywood star. On the day of the premiere, 1 April 1930, she boarded a train at Anhalter Bahnhof and went to the US. Working closely with Sternberg, Dietrich built on her image of erotic opulence – dominant, severe, always with a touch of self-irony. When she put on men's suits for *Marocco* in 1930, she lent her 'sexuality is power' attitude bisexual tones, winning a new audience overnight.

Marlene stayed in Hollywood after the Nazis rose to power, though Hitler, no less immune to her charms, reportedly promised perks and the red-carpet treatment if she moved back to Germany. She responded with an empty offer to return if she could bring Sternberg, who was a Jew and no Nazi favourite.

When Allied GIs rolled into Paris in 1944, Marlene was there too. Asked once whether there was any truth to the rumour that she had slept with General Eisenhower, she reportedly replied, 'How could I have? He was never at the front'.

After the war, Dietrich continued to appear in movies, including such Billy Wilder movies as *A Foreign Affair* (1948), *Witness for the Prosecution* (1957) and *Judgment at Nuremberg* (1961). Discreet, uncompromising and, contrary to her big-screen image, always the well-bred woman from Berlin, Dietrich retreated from the public eye as age and illness gradually caught up with her in her later years.

She died in 1992, aged 90. Although Dietrich had become an American citizen in 1939 and spent her final years in Paris, she wanted to be buried in Berlin, the city of her birth. She's buried next to her mother in the Friedhof Friedenau. A large portion of her personal effects (from hair brush to glamour gowns to suitcases) are now on view at the new FilmMuseum in the Sony Center. The main plaza in the adjacent DaimlerCity also bears her name.

Nazi Period Hitler's power grab ripped through German cultural life, and the world of film was not spared. Financial trouble at UFA between 1933 and 1937 allowed the Nazis to anonymously buy out Hugenberg and step up control over the industry.

Films now required approval from Goebbels' Reichskulturkammer (Chamber of Culture). Censorship laws and bans drove over 500 actors and directors into exile. Many went to Hollywood and ended up playing parts as stereotypical Nazis. Some directors and actors were successful, but the majority struck a language barrier and sank into oblivion.

Most films produced in Berlin under the Nazis are either histories glorifying famous Germans, such as Wolfgang Liebeneiner's *Bismarck* (1940), or outright propaganda flicks like the anti-Semitic *Jud Süss* (Jew Süss; 1940) by Veit Harlan.

A tempestuous woman was to place her stamp – creatively, infamously and forever – on the capability of film to tell a story and to sway opinion and events. Leni Riefenstahl made brilliant documentaries about the Olympic Games of 1936 as well as her famous propaganda film *Triumph of the Will*, which gave an emotional boost to Hitler's psychotic Third Reich programs. Escapist comedies like Willi Forst's *Allotria* (1936) rounded out the cinematic fare.

Post-1945 Films shot directly after the war are known as *Trümmerfilme* (literally 'rubble films') and usually deal with Nazism or war. DEFA (Deutsche Film AG), a new East German film corporation, was established in the Soviet zone (the USSR was its chief shareholder), producing Germany's first post-war film, *Die Mörder sind unter uns* (The Murderers Are Among Us; 1946) by Wolfgang Staudte. Set at Christmas 1945, it tells of a guilt-ridden army doctor who encounters a commanding officer responsible for the execution of women and children in Russia. He threatens the officer with a pistol as the latter is celebrating with his wife and children.

The founding of the GDR in 1949 interrupted the artistic development of film making in the Soviet sector as the SED party prevented the production of movies not in line with party doctrine. DEFA became East Germany's film and TV production centre. Important movies of this early period include Falk Harnacks' *Das Beil von Wandsbek* (The Axe of Wandsbeck; 1951).

In West Germany, movie making comprised mostly escapist and inane entertainment. Exceptions were Robert Siodmaks *Die Ratten* (The Rats; 1955) with Maria Schell, and Billy Wilder's *Eins, Zwei, Drei* (One, Two, Three), filmed days before the Wall went up in 1961. Wilder's film was a commercial flop because its ironic portrayal of the east-west conflict was largely lost in the maelstrom of actual events. A boost to the film industry came with the first Berlinale in 1950.

1960 to 1990 When television emerged as a major competition to movies, the industry in West Berlin was particularly hard hit. Many artists and directors had already left the city because the infrastructure lagged far behind international standards. In addition, the city's 'island' status confined outdoor shoots to an urban environment, thereby limiting creative expression. The Junge Deutsche Film (Young German Film), a movement centred around directors like Volker Schlöndorf, Wim Wenders, Werner Herzog and Rainer Werner Fassbinder, took roots in Munich and only had an indirect effect on the development of the Berlin film scene. Off-beat directors like Rosa von Praunheim, who remained in Berlin, focused largely on movies portraying the city's alternative and underground culture.

In East Berlin, the government censorship loosened a little in 1971 after Erich Honecker became head of state. The most important director was Frank Beyer who made the tragicomedy *Jakob der Lügner* (Jacob the Liar; 1974), based on the book by Jurek Becker and set in a ghetto in Poland. A 1999 Hollywood remake starred Robin Williams.

Sunlight bounces off the Sony Center.

The Airlift Memorial near Tempelhof Airport.

Berlin's mascots, bears at play...

The Neues Kanzleramt anchors the New Government District in Mitte.

A perfect lazy Sunday morning – friends, coffee and plenty of chatter.

Doof-Doof…Ravers-a-go-go!

'Have you got this one in pink?'

A new day dawns for Germany's most dynamic city.

Enticed by heavy subsidies, important directors like Volker Schlöndorff, Margarethe von Trotta and Rainer Werner Fassbinder returned to Berlin in the late 1970s. Terrorism increasingly became a theme, as in Schlöndorff's *Die verlorene Ehre der Katharina Blum* (The Lost Honour of Katharina Blum; 1975), an adaptation of a Heinrich Böll short novel. Trotta, who collaborated with Schlöndorff on the film, later dealt with the theme again in *Das zweite Erwachen der Christa Klages* (The Second Awakening of Christa Klages; 1978) and in *Die Bleierne Zeit* (Leaden Time; 1981).

Huge international box-office successes were Schlöndorff's *Die Blechtrommel* (The Tin Drum, 1979), based on the Günter Grass novel, and Fassbinder's *Querelle* (1982). Perhaps the last great movie to emerge out of pre-Wende Berlin was Wim Wenders' *Der Himmel über Berlin* (Wings of Desire; 1987), starring Americans Peter Falk and Peter Coyote, which features two angels who move through divided Berlin. A 1999 Hollywood remake called *City of Angels* starred Nicholas Cage and Meg Ryan.

Post-Wende In recent years, Berlin has experienced a small renaissance with directors like Wenders and Jutta Brückner joining Volker Schlöndorff at Filmstadt Babelsberg (see the boxed text 'Hollywood on the Havel' in the Potsdam section of the Excursions chapter). One of Schlöndorff's recent productions was *Der Unhold* (The Monster) with John Malkovich. Other international successes include Dani Levy's *Stille Nacht* (Silent Night, 1995), the underground smash hit *Lola Rennt* (Run Lola Run; 1997–98) by Tom Tykwer, *Die Comedian Harmonists* (The Harmonists; 1998) about a famed group of a cappella singers whose career was cut short when their Jewish members had to flee the Nazis and *Sonnenallee* (1999) by Leander Haussmann, based on the novel by the same name by Thomas Brussig and set in East Berlin before unification. Meanwhile, Wim Wenders has won awards with *Buena Vista Social Club* (1999) and *The Million Dollar Hotel* (2000).

Theatre

Berlin's theatre scene had rather modest beginnings. The first quality productions weren't staged until the arrival of such stellar dramatists as Gotthold Ephraim Lessing and Johann Wolfgang von Goethe in the middle of the 18th century. One of the first impresarios was August Wilhelm Iffland (1759–1814) who, in 1796, took over the helm of the Royal National Theatre. Iffland was noted for his natural yet sophisticated productions (especially those of Schiller plays) and for cultivating a talented ensemble.

Iffland's act proved hard to follow and when he died in 1814, Berlin theatre languished for 80 years until Otto Brahm became director of the Deutsches Theater in 1894. Dedicated to the naturalistic style, Brahm is considered a pioneer of modern dramatic theatre. He coaxed psychological dimensions out of the characters and sought to make their language and situations mirror real life. The critical works of Gerhart Hauptmann and Henrik Ibsen were staples on his stage throughout the 1890s.

In 1894, Brahm hired a young actor named Max Reinhardt (1873–1943), who became perhaps the most famous and influential director ever in the German theatre (see the boxed text 'Max Reinhardt – Impresario Extraordinaire' in the Things to See and Do chapter). Reinhardt's path later crossed that of another seminal theatre figure, Bertolt Brecht (1898–1956), who moved to Berlin in 1924. The two worked together briefly at the Deutsches Theater until Brecht developed his own unique style, the so-called 'epic theatre' (see the boxed text 'Bertolt Brecht').

After WWII, artistic stagnation spread across German theatre for more than two decades. In West Berlin, a new period of greatness would not begin until 1970 with the opening of the Schaubühne am Halleschen Ufer under Peter Stein. The theatre, which later moved to the Ku'damm and was renamed Schaubühne am Lehniner Platz, became one of Germany's leading stages.

In East Berlin, the Volksbühne became one of the most innovative venues, along with the Deutsches Theater. Taking advantage of the relative political and artistic freedom granted to these stages by the government, they provided platforms for political exchange and renewal and contributed to the peaceful revolution of 1989. One of the driving forces was the prolific and outspoken dramatist Heiner Müller.

After the Wende, major artistic, structural and personnel changes swept Berlin's theatre landscape – both east and west. Several government-subsidised stages closed, most notably the Schiller Theater in West Berlin. Now integrated into the western system, the eastern stages underwent a significant re-orientation in form and content. At the Berliner Ensemble, Heiner Müller helped shake the dust off this venerable troupe, while *enfant terrible* Frank Castorf ignited a creative firestorm at the Volksbühne.

Meanwhile, various changes in directorships at leading stages is currently sparking inspiration in Berlin's Thespian scene. After 13 years at the famous Burg Theater in Vienna, Claus Peymann is restoring greatness to the Berliner Ensemble. Bernard Willms, who made the Maxim Gorki Theater into one of the most respected theatres in town, has moved on to the Deutsches Theater, while the young Volker Hesse has taken over at the Gorki. Also part of a new generation is Thomas Ostermeier who, along with noted dancer and choreographer Sasha Waltz, is co-directing the Schaubühne am Lehniner Platz. Generational change at the helm also seems to have translated into greater interest among younger audiences, not just in the established stages but also in the growing number of fringe theatres.

Bertolt Brecht

Bertolt Brecht (1898–1956), the controversial poet and playwright who spent the last seven years of his life in East Berlin, wrote his first play, *Baal*, while studying medicine in Munich in 1918. His first play to reach the stage, *Trommeln in der Nacht* (Drums in the Night; 1922), won the coveted Kleist Prize, and two years later he began working at the Deutsches Theater in Berlin alongside Austrian director Max Reinhardt.

MW

Over the next decade, in plays like *Die Dreigroschenoper* (The Threepenny Opera, 1928), he developed his theory of 'epic theatre' which, unlike 'dramatic theatre', forces its audience to detach themselves emotionally from the play and its characters and to reason intellectually.

A staunch Marxist, Brecht went into exile during the Nazi years, surfaced in Hollywood as a scriptwriter, then left the USA after being called in to explain himself during the communist witch hunts of the McCarthy era. He wrote most of his best plays during his years in exile: *Mutter Courage und ihre Kinder* (Mother Courage and Her Children; 1941), *Leben des Galilei* (The Life of Galileo; 1943), *Der gute Mensch von Sezuan* (The Good Woman of Sezuan; 1943) and *Der kaukasische Kreidekreis* (The Caucasian Chalk Circle; 1948).

Brecht returned to East Berlin in 1949 where he founded the Berliner Ensemble with his wife, Helene Weigel, who directed it until her death in 1971. His *Mother Courage and her Children* premiered in 1949 at the Deutsches Theater. In 1954, the troupe moved into the Theater am Schiffbauerdamm.

During his lifetime Brecht was both suspected in the east for his unorthodox aesthetic theories and scorned (and often boycotted) in much of the west for his communist principles. A staple of left-wing directors throughout the 1960s and 1970s, Brecht's plays are now under reassessment, though his influence in freeing the theatre from the constraints of a 'well-made play in three acts' is undeniable. The superiority of Brecht's poetry, so little known in English, remains undisputed.

Dance

Dance is alive and kicking up its heels in Berlin, which has three state-sponsored ballet troupes (attached to the three opera houses) as well as a thriving independent scene. New and innovative groups attract a growing audience to performances often staged in unconventional venues. Leading venues are the TanzWerkstatt Berlin and the Hebbel Theater, which organise the annual Tanz im August dance festival that draws international attention. Also of importance is the Tanzfabrik Berlin, founded in 1978, as a centre for modern, contemporary, improvisational and experimental dance. The biggest name to emerge on the scene in recent years is that of choreographer and dancer Sasha Waltz whose abstract dance spectacles are mostly staged at the Schaubühne am Lehniner Platz.

Historically, Berlin has made several contributions to the evolution of free and expressive (ie, modern) dance. The eccentric American dancer Isadora Duncan opened her own school (the Duncanschule) in Berlin in 1904. Duncan banished the ballet shoe – which she considered 'an instrument of torture' – and flitted across the stage barefoot and in her trademark flowing white gowns.

In the artistically fecund 1920s, Berlin gave birth to a new dance form, the so-called grotesque dance. Influenced by dadaism, it was characterised by excessive, and often comical, expressiveness. One of its prime practitioners was Valeska Gert. Even more influential in the long run was the vision of Mary Wigman who regarded body and movement as tools to express the universal experience of life in all its complexity. Her style inspired some of today's leading German choreographers (including Pina Bausch and Reinhild Hoffmann).

Berlin's first encounter with ballet came under the reign of Friedrich II who brought Italian star Barberina to the city in 1744. The first royal ballet company formed in 1811 but, in the absence of home-grown talent, it had to rely on imported dancers and choreographers. Ballet went commercial in the 1920s with the emergence of the glitzy revues featuring rows of leggy high-kicking showgirls, a tradition that's lately been revived at the Friedrichstadtpalast which maintains its own 80-member dance troupe.

After WWII, ballet experienced a renaissance under the Russian immigrant Tatjana Gsovsky. Initially working without a permanent stage, she choreographed a number of memorable productions, including *Hamlet* (1953) and *The Idiot* (1954) at the Theater des Westens. Gsovsky later became ballet director at the Deutsche Oper and also founded the Berliner Tanzakademie.

Gsovsky was succeeded by her solo dancer, Gert Reinholm, who produced few highlights during his 28-year tenure. One rather scandalous work was *Suzi Creamcheese* (1970), which was based on a song of the same name and featured the music of Frank Zappa. Today's ballet troupes concentrate on audience-pleasing, classical repertoires including such classic pieces as *Swan Lake* and *The Nutcracker*.

Music

For centuries, Berlin was largely eclipsed by Vienna, Leipzig and other European cities when it came to music. The few musical styles generated here were the *Lieder* (songs), hymns and ballads produced during the reign of the culture-loving Friedrich II by a trio of composers: Friedrich Wilhelm Marpurg, Johann Abraham Peter Schulz and Carl Friedrich Zelter (1758–1832). Carl Zelter served as director of the Berlin Singing Academy from 1800 to 1832, whose student body included later composers Felix Mendelssohn-Bartholdy (1809–1847) and Giacomo Meyerbeer (1791–1864).

In 1882, the Berliner Philharmonisches Orchester was established, gaining international stature under Hans von Bülow and Arthur Nikisch. In 1923, Wilhelm Furtwängler became artistic director, a post he would hold with interruptions, until 1954. His successor, Herbert von Karajan, was an autocratic figure who took the orchestra to a position of real dominance on the world stage and remained its director until 1989. He was followed by Claudio Abbado who will be succeeded by Sir Simon Rattle in 2002.

The pulsating 1920s drew numerous musicians to Berlin, including Arnold Schönberg and Paul Hindemith who taught at the Academie der Künste and the Berliner Hochschule (Berlin College) respectively. Schönberg's atonal compositions found a following here, as did his experimentation with noise and sound effects. Hindemith explored the new medium of radio broadcast and taught a seminar on film music.

The era also generated the Berlin *Schlager*, silly but entertaining songs with titles like *Mein Papagei frisst keine harten Eier* (My Parrot Doesn't Eat Hard-boiled Eggs) and *Veronika, der Lenz ist da* (Veronica, Spring is Here). Singing groups like the Comedian Harmonists built their success on this music.

New expressionistic approaches to musical theatre came from classically trained composers including Hanns Eisler and Kurt Weill, who collaborated with Brecht on *The Threepenny Opera* and *The Rise and Fall of the City of Mahogany*. Mischa Spoliansky was among the leading lights of the cabaret stages.

Contemporary Music Berlin continues to be a fertile breeding ground for new musical trends and it is estimated that in the early 21st century the scene consisted of nearly 2000 bands. But even before the Wende, numerous homegrown performers managed to leap onto the national and even international stage.

In the late '60s, Tangerine Dream hit the airwaves with its electronically charged, psychedelic sound. A decade later, East Berlin-born Nina Hagen followed her adopted father, writer Wolf Biermann, to West Germany and soon became the diva of German punk. Her laconic Berlin style blended well enough with English-American punk for the *New Musical Express* to describe her as an epileptic Edith Piaf and a cross between Johnny Rotten, Maria Callas and Bette Midler. Hagen also laid the groundwork for the major musical movement of the '80s, the Neue Deutsche Welle (New German Wave) which gave the stage to Berlin bands like Ideal, the Neonbabies and UKW.

Back in the GDR, bands like Die Puhdys and Rockhaus kept alive a vibrant underground scene; both continue to perform today.

The National Anthem

Germans have had an ambiguous relationship with their national anthem. Although a lot of young West Germans were familiar with the words, those who sang it before reunification were generally dismissed as either fools or hard-core nationalists. These days Germans feel less inhibited about singing along.

Based on an obscure Croatian folk song, the music for the German national anthem was composed by Joseph Haydn in 1797 and set to words penned by Hoffmann von Fallersleben in 1841 (including the original words 'God preserve Franz the Kaiser' – an Austrian, in fact). It didn't become the formal anthem until 1922. During the Nazi period it was usually sung in conjunction with *Die Fahne Hoch* (Raise the Flag), an uninspiring ditty composed in 1927.

The national anthem was retained after 1945 – largely due to the efforts of Konrad Adenauer – minus the first two verses, which either listed a set of borders that now lie in neighbouring countries or sounded like a drinking song. A 1990 court decision ruled that only the third verse was protected as a national symbol.

The East German national anthem, *Auferstanden aus Ruinen* (Resurrected from Ruins) joined the long list of unsung communist golden oldies once the socialist fatherland was abolished. Proclaimed in 1949, its pro-unification lyrics fell out of favour among party honchos after the construction of the Berlin Wall in 1961, when only the tune was permissible. In November 1989, it was sung in protest by demonstrators. This received the blessing of the Ministry of Culture a couple of weeks later, and the anthem was played accordingly on radio and television before being finally abolished in 1990.

West Berlin also attracted a slew of international talent. David Bowie and Iggy Pop both spent stints here, living at Hauptstrasse 152. Nick Cave owned a club, and U2's Zooropa album was inspired by Zoo station.

Coinciding with the Wende, another essentially homespun music form – techno – took over Berlin. Techno may have its roots in Detroit-based house music and the synthetic sounds of bands like Kraftwerk, but it was from Berlin that it conquered the world. Reflecting the apolitical and almost nihilist *Zeitgeist*, these aggressive, urban sounds have influenced the fashion and tastes of an entire generation. Pioneering clubs included Ufo, Planet and the extant Tresor (whose survival is threatened). The scene took a more commercial turn in the mid-1990s with the opening of the now-defunct E-werk, a converted power station with space for thousands of ravers.

Berlin also spawned the annual Love Parade which snakes through city streets every July. What began as a three-car procession with 150 ravers has turned into a weekend-long phenomenon that for years set new attendance records, culminating in 1.5 million ravers in 1999; in 2001, though, figures dropped to a mere half million (see the boxed text 'Techno Town' in the Entertainment chapter)

Despite techno's dominance, other sounds continue to be produced in Berlin. From 1993 to 1998, the two-day Metrobeat Festival at the Kulturbrauerei was a launch pad for local talent as diverse as the retro-band Rosenstolz and the female Turkish hiphop singer Aziza-A.

Literature

Since its beginnings, Berlin's literary scene has reflected a peculiar blend of provincialism and worldliness. As with the other arts, Berlin didn't emerge as a centre of literature until relatively late, reaching its zenith during the dynamic 1920s. Overall, the city was not so much a place that generated influential writers – or where they came to write – as it was one where they came to meet each other, exchange ideas and be intellectually stimulated.

Berlin's literary history begins during the Enlightenment in the late 18th century, an epoch dominated by humanistic ideals. A major author was Gotthold Ephraim Lessing (1729–81) who is noted for his critical works, fables and tragedies. In Berlin he wrote the play *Minna von Barnhelm*, though his best-known dramatic works are *Miss Sara Samson*, *Emilia Galotti* and especially *Nathan der Weise* (Nathan the Wise).

The Romantic period, which grew out of the Enlightenment, was marked by a proliferation of literary salons, usually sponsored by women, such as Rahel Levin (later Rahel Varnhagen). Men and women from all walks of life came together to discuss philosophy, politics, art and other subjects. Literary greats working in Berlin in this era included Friedrich and August Wilhelm von Schlegel (the latter translated Shakespeare into German) and the Romantic poets Achim von Arnim, Clemens Brentano and Heinrich von Kleist.

During the realist movement in the middle of the 19th century, novels and novellas gained in popularity, thanks to increased interest from the newly established middle class. Historical novels and works critical of society also caught on, such as those by Wilhelm Raabe (1831–1910) who, in his *Chronik der Sperlingsgasse* (Chronicle of Sperling Lane; 1857), examines various aspects of urban life in Berlin. The Berlin society novel was raised to an art form under the pen of Theodor Fontane (1819–98). Most of his works are set around the March of Brandenburg and in Berlin and show both the nobility and the middle class mired in their societal confinements.

Naturalism, a spin-off of realism, took things a step further after 1880. It aimed at painstakingly re-creating the milieu of entire social classes, down to the local dialect. In Berlin, Gerhart Hauptmann (1862–1946) was a main practitioner of the genre. Many of his plays and novels focus on social injustice and the harsh life of workers – subjects so provocative that several of his premieres ended in riots and scandals. In fact, an 1892 Deutsche Theater production of *Die Weber* (The Weavers), which depicted the misery of Silesian weavers, prompted the Kaiser to cancel his subscription. The play, however, was a smashing success. In 1912, Hauptmann won the Nobel Prize for Literature.

In the 1920s, renowned as a period of experimentation and innovation, Berlin became a magnet for writers from around the world. A masterpiece from that time was Alfred Döblin's (1878–1957) *Berlin Alexanderplatz*, which provides a dose of big-city lights and the underworld during the Weimar Republic. Other notables from the era were the political satirists Kurt Tucholsky (1890–1935) and Erich Kästner (1899–1974), as well as Egon Erwin Kisch, a newspaper journalist and author of critical essays. Also a dominant force, primarily in drama, was Bertolt Brecht, who was among the artists who left Germany after the Nazis came to power (see the boxed text 'Bertolt Brecht' earlier in this chapter). Many of those who stayed went into inner emigration, which essentially meant keeping their mouths shut and working underground, if at all.

After the war, different developments took hold in the two Berlins. In East Berlin, government censorship stifled author creativity and freedom of expression. The SED party organised regular cultural conferences and author congresses to hammer in the official line. Safe themes were post-war reconstruction and the historical evolution of the socialist state.

In the mid-1970s, a segment of the literary scene began to detach itself slowly from the party grip. Authors like Christa Wolf (1929–) and Heiner Müller (1929–95) belonged to loose literary circles that regularly met in private houses. Wolf is one of the best and most controversial East German writers. *Der geteilte Himmel* (Divided Heaven) has an industrial backdrop and tells the story of a woman's love for a man who fled to the west.

Müller had the distinction of being unpalatable in both Germanies. It is said that he worked for the Stasi, but that his messages were so ambiguous as to be worthless. His works, which are dense and difficult, include *Der Lohndrücker* (The Man Who Kept Down Wages) and the *Germania* trilogy of plays.

In West Berlin, the postwar literary scene didn't revive until the arrival of Günter Grass in the late 1950s. His famous *Die Blechtrommel* (The Tin Drum) humorously traces recent German history through the eyes of Oskar, a child who refuses to grow up. The book made Grass a household name, and he has followed up with an impressive body of novels, plays and poetry. In Berlin he lived and worked as part of a writers' colony which also included Hans-Magnus Enzensberger, Ingeborg Bachmann and the Swiss writer Max Frisch. Together they paved the way for the political and critical literature that has been dominant since the 1960s. In 1999, Grass became the ninth German to win the Nobel Prize for Literature.

Literary achievement stagnated at first after the Wende as writers from the east and west began a process of self-examination. Rather than working together on coming to terms with their separate pasts, the creative chasm resulting from the years of division was emphasised. Only Heiner Müller and Botho Strauss stood out amid the creative void. In the late 1990s Berlin's literary scene finally picked up steam. New books dealing with the past are characterised not by analytical introspection but by emotionally distanced, nearly grotesque, imagery. Examples here include Thomas Brussig's *Helden wie wir* (Heroes like us, 1995) and Ingo Schulze's *Simple Stories* (1998). On the more populist end of the spectrum is a revitalisation of the genre of the 'Berlin detective story' which features Pieke Biermann and Horst Bosetzky as prime practitioners.

Berlin has several literary organisation and author forums, including the Literaturforum im Brechthaus (☎ 282 20 03), Chausseestrasse 125, which hosts the Brecht-Tage (Brecht Days), among other things; the Literarisches Colloquium Berlin (☎ 816 99 60), Am Sandwerder 5; and literatur-WERKstatt (☎ 485 24 50), which in 2000 organised the Literaturfestival attended by 100,000 people.

SOCIETY & CONDUCT

Berlin is a very casual city. Except for formal gourmet restaurants, there's no need to dress up for dinner or a theatre or opera performance (though you're certainly free to do so). Some nightclubs may have dress codes, though originality and creativity are usually what matters here.

Overall, Berliners are accommodating and fairly helpful towards visitors. Many will volunteer help if you look lost and may even accompany you to make sure you get to your destination.

If you're invited to someone's home, ask if there's anything you could bring. Even if the answer is no, it's still nice to arrive clutching some flowers or a bottle of wine. After a dinner party, call the next day or send a little thank-you note.

Berliners tend to be quite opinionated and the conversation may touch on many subjects, from politics to the weather in Spain. It *is* OK to mention 'the War', if done with tact and relevance. After all, a lot of people you will meet have grown up demanding explanations. What causes offence, however, is a 'victor' mentality, which is perceived as righteous and gloating, or the idea that fascist ideas are intrinsically German.

Shaking hands is common among both men and women, as is a hug or a kiss on the cheek, especially among young people. When making a phone call, give your name at the start. Germans consider it impolite or simply get annoyed when no name is given. If you don't want to give your real name (when dealing with bureaucracy, for instance), make one up.

Like elsewhere in Germany, great importance is placed on the formal 'Sie' form of address, especially in business situations. Among younger people and in social settings, though, people are much more relaxed about 'Sie' and 'du'.

Academic titles (Herr or Frau Doktor) are important. If someone introduces herself as Dr Schmidt, that's what she wants to be called. If you have a title yourself, you may of course insist on it as well; this can be useful in situations where you want the extra respect.

RELIGION

Berlin's astonishing religious diversity is largely a result of the constant influx of newcomers from all parts of the world over the course of its history. Since the Reformation in the 16th century, Berlin has been predominantly Protestant. After 1685 it became a haven for Huguenots who fled France in droves after King Louis XIV revoked the Edict of Nantes which had granted them religious freedom. About 6000 of them settled in Berlin at the invitation of the Great Elector, Friedrich Wilhelm, accounting for about 20% of the population by 1700.

The Berlin of today is a very secular city; not even half of its population is a member of a religious institution. Among those who are, about one in three is an adherent of a Christian faith. Protestants greatly outnumber Roman Catholics: according to the latest figures, about 26% of Berliners are Lutherans, while only 9.3% are Roman Catholics.

Berlin has one of Germany's largest Jewish communities, its number (about 12,000) bolstered in recent years by the immigration of Russian Jews. The community maintains a hospital, schools, six synagogues, and the Centrum Judaicum museum and community centre on Oranienburger Strasse. In 1986, a chapter of Adass Jisroel, a conservative Jewish congregation, formed as well. It currently has about 1000 members.

With 200,000 followers (6% of the population), Islam has a significant place in Berlin's religious landscape, its number largely coming from the city's vast Turkish population. Nearly 40 other religious affiliations are represented – some, like the Unitarian Church, with fewer than 100 members.

Residents belonging to a recognised denomination have to pay a church tax amounting to 10% of their income tax.

LANGUAGE

German belongs to the Indo-European language group and is spoken by over 100 million people throughout the world, including Austria and part of Switzerland. There are also ethnic German communities in neighbouring Eastern European countries such as Poland and the Czech Republic, although expulsion after 1945 reduced their numbers dramatically.

High German is the official and proper form of the language, though most people also speak a local or regional dialect. The same is true of Berlin, though only a small number of Berliners speak pure Berlinisch.

Alphabet Soup

The Germans are not that precious about their language. It is full of English words (das Meeting) and it also has reams of French (*leger* – casual) , Greek (*Fotografie* – photography) and Latin (*Capitalismus* – capitalism) words. Things can have a 'Happy End' (happy ending) in German, and that's also the name of a favoured brand of toilet paper. For many, though, the most recent German spelling reforms did not have a 'Happy End'.

In 1902, Germans first standardised their orthography. Until then, it contained remnants of a Medieval muddle. They overhauled it again almost a century later in 1998. But for some German spelling boffins, this most recent reform went too far. The Deutsche Akademie für Sprache und Dichtung (the PEN organisation of writers) was pointedly unhappy. So was the *Frankfurter Allgemeine Zeitung* (FAZ), the conservative newspaper, which bit the bullet of reform for a couple of years but, in 2000, amid much self-righteous breast beating, reverted to old spelling. Along with other sensible or not-so-sensible changes, the FAZ threw the third 'f' in Schiff(f)ahrt (sea voyage) overboard, took the 'h' out of Känguru(h) (kangaroo), and whited out the 'f's in F(Ph)otograf(ph)ie. The cumbersome 'ß' which had been dropped in many (but not all) words, again became de rigeur over morning coffee and *das Müsli* (muesli).

Orthographic counter-revolution? Well, the FAZ is also notorious for using archaic Gothic script for some of its headlines. But bucking the reform did reflect the mood of many Germans, who had organised citizens' petitions against the changes. For teachers and school kids, things were uncertain for a while. In the end though, the reform prevailed, and both old and new ways of spelling are correct until 2005, when new orthography becomes standard usage.

See the Language chapter at the back of this book for pronunciation details and useful phrases. The glossary, also at the back, contains some common German words.

Berlin, as observers noted even in the 1920s, is 'essentially a creation of modern times'. Indeed, the fact that it's more than 750 years old is certainly not reflected in its appearance. Very little survives from the Middle Ages, with the Marienkirche and the reconstructed Nikolaikirche in Mitte being the most noteworthy examples. The Renaissance period is even more poorly represented with the ornately gabled Ribbeckhaus (1624), nearby at Breite Strasse 35–36, the only remaining residential building from that era.

Berlin's first architectural heyday came in the late baroque period, propelled by self-crowned King Friedrich I's need to immortalise himself. The arrival of master architect Karl Friedrich Schinkel marked the beginning of a veritable building boom during the reign of Friedrich Wilhelm III (ruled 1797–1840) when neoclassicism ruled the day.

The founding of the German Empire in 1871, with Berlin nominated as its capital, saw a population explosion within Berlin's city limits. It also became apparent that there was great need for mass housing. Industrial architecture emerged as a new field led by Peter Behrens, who was a trailblazer for Modernism. This later flourished in the 1920s as the International Style (under people like Walter Gropius and Ludwig Mies van der Rohe) only to be eradicated by the Nazis who favoured architecture that was essentially a parody of neoclassicism.

After WWII, the wrecking ball destroyed much of what the bombs had left standing. A 'de-construction' boom preceded reconstruction and resulted in different architectural visions on either side of the divided city.

Mirroring their Soviet colleagues, East Berlin architects followed the 'bigger is better' maxim. This is best exemplified in the Karl-Marx-Allee lined by monumental structures of Stalinist 'charm' built in a style called *Zuckerbäckerstil* (wedding cake style), a deceptively pleasant term. The GDR's own architectural vision created soulless high-rise blocks – the so-called *Plattenbauten* made from prefab building elements – which provided much needed housing.

In West Berlin, putting a roof over people's heads was also a postwar priority and it took a long time before an architectural style was consolidated. In the end, this mostly took the form of continuing and perfecting the International Style with much the same cast of practitioners as before the war.

After the Wende, Berlin experienced a veritable building boom that brought the world's best architects to the city. Construction of Potsdamer Platz, Pariser Platz, Friedrichstrasse, the New Government District and other areas has gradually turned the city into a world-class state-of-the-art metropolis. For the time being, Berlin remains a work in progress, its constantly evolving cityscape offering ever-new angles of discovery and aesthetics.

Previous Page & Inset:
The Sony Center's tented central plaza in Berlin's Potsdamer Platz (photograph by Andrea Schulte-Peevers).

ARCHITECTS

Some of the world's greatest architects have left their imprints in Berlin through the ages. Their work can be seen in various parts of the city.

Georg Wenzeslaus von Knobelsdorff (1699–1753)

Georg von Knobelsdorff was the leading light of what became known as the 'Frederician Rococo', a particular fusion of that late baroque style with neoclassical elements, which flourished under King Friedrich II. His greatest claims to fame are Schloss Sanssouci in Potsdam (1747), the Neuer Flügel in Schloss Charlottenburg (1747) and the Staatsoper Unter den Linden (1742).

Carl Gotthard Langhans (1732–1808)

A baroque architect by training, Langhans made his mark as a pioneer of pure neoclassicism. His landmark Brandenburger Tor (1791), based on a classical Greek design, was the first major structure in this style on German soil. He also designed the Belvedere in the park of Schloss Charlottenburg and an early version of the Schauspielhaus/Konzerthaus on Gendarmenmarkt.

Peter Behrens (1868–1940)

Often called the 'father of modern architecture', Behrens is best known for his industrial 'cathedrals', in particular the AEG Turbine Hall (1909) in Wedding, an airy and light-flooded factory with high ceilings and exposed structural beams. Behrens also paved the way for the up-coming generation of avant-gardists like Bruno Taut, Le Corbusier, Walter Gropius and Ludwig Mies van der Rohe.

Bruno Taut (1880–1938) & Contemporaries

Berlin's late-19th-century population explosion generated an urgent need for cheap housing, which resulted in the mushrooming of *Mietskasernen* – warren-like, claustrophobic tenements built around successive court-yards. In the 1920s, several architects started 'humanising' housing colonies by restricting their height to four storeys and integrating open green spaces. Examples include the Hufeisensiedlung (Horseshoe Colony, 1924–26) in Britz by Bruno Taut (see Neukölln in the Things to See & Do chapter); the Waldsiedlung Onkel-Toms-Hütte (Forest Colony Uncle Tom's Cabin, 1926) in Zehlendorf by Otto Rudolf Salvisberg and Hugo Häring; and Siemensstadt (1931) between Charlottenburg and Spandau by Hans Scharoun, Walter Gropius and others.

Prussia's Building Master: Karl Friedrich Schinkel

No single architect has determined the face of Berlin more than Karl Friedrich Schinkel. The most prominent and mature architect of German neoclassicism, Schinkel was born in Neuruppin in Prussia in 1781 and studied architecture under Friedrich Gilly and his father David at the Building Academy in Berlin. He followed up his studies with a two-year trip to Italy (1803–05) to study the classics close-up, but returned to a Prussia hamstrung by Napoleonic occupation. Unable to practise his art, he scraped by as a romantic painter, furniture and set designer.

Schinkel's career took off as soon as the French left Berlin. He steadily rose through the ranks of the Prussian civil service, starting as surveyor to the Prussian Building Commission and ending as chief building director for the entire state. He travelled tirelessly through the land, designing buildings, supervising construction and even developing principles for the protection of historical monuments.

His travels in Italy notwithstanding, Schinkel actually drew greater inspiration from classic Greek architecture. From 1810 to 1840, his vision very much defined Prussian architecture; Berlin was even called 'Athens on the Spree'. In his buildings, he strived for the perfect balance between functionality and beauty, achieved through clear lines, symmetry and an impeccable sense for aesthetics. Driven to the end, Schinkel fell into a coma in 1840 and died one year later in Berlin.

Aside from the major landmarks detailed in Tour I later in this chapter, Schinkel also created the Mausoleum (1810) for Queen Luise and the Schinkel Pavilion (1824) – both in the park of Schloss Charlottenburg – the neogothic war memorial in Viktoriapark atop the Kreuzberg (1821), Schloss Charlottenhof (1827), and the Nikolaikirche (1837) in Potsdam. For details on any of these, see the Things to See & Do chapter and the Excursions chapter, respectively.

Hans Scharoun (1893–1972)

Hans Scharoun was already designing apartment buildings in Charlottenburg and supervising the construction of the Siemensstadt colony (1929–31) when Hitler rose to power. After the war, he helped re-establish the Berlin Arts Academy and became a prime practitioner of a Modernist subgenre called 'organic architecture'. It was characterised by asymmetry, dynamic, round and flowing shapes and a general attempt to integrate architecture with the sensory needs of humans. One of his basic tenets was to adapt the shape of the building to its stated purpose and function, rather than the other way around. Scharoun was critically acclaimed in architectural circles and frequently honoured in competitions, but few of his designs ever made it off the drawing board. Of those that did, as for example with the Philharmonie (see Tour II later in this chapter), the results are quite dramatic.

Renzo Piano (*1937)

Born in Genoa, Italy, Renzo Piano is best known for the Centre Pompidou in Paris, a high-tech parody built in collaboration with Richard Rogers. As the main brain behind Berlin's Potsdamer Platz development, Piano has tempered his love for technology without sacrificing his characteristic mixing of materials and bold, open-plan designs imbued with a sense of lightness.

Helmut Jahn (*1940)

Although considered an American architect, Jahn was actually born in Nuremberg and trained in Munich before continuing his studies at the Institute of Technology in Chicago. His early work borrows heavily from Bauhaus-inspired geometry and minimalism, but he has since developed a style that's been called 'creative rationalism', in short: more varied and imaginative forms. He has made two major contributions to Berlin's post-Wende cityscape: the Neues Kranzler Eck in Charlottenburg and the Sony Center in Tiergarten.

STYLES

The following are some of the main styles of architecture that have flourished in Berlin throughout the centuries. You'll find examples of each scattered throughout the city.

Baroque/Rococo

The baroque, en vogue from the early 17th century to the mid-18th century, merges structures, sculpture, ornamentation and painting into a single *Gesamtkunstwerk* (complete work of art). The style was never as exuberant in Berlin as in southern Germany but retained a formal and precise bent. Rococo is a derivation of late baroque and coincided with the Enlightenment. The period's most famous practitioners in Berlin were Knobelsdorff (see Architects earlier this section), but also Johann Arnold Nering (1659–95), best known for his contributions to Schloss Charlottenburg.

Neoclassicism

Neoclassicism, which emerged in the late 18th century, has had the most lasting effect on Berlin's cityscape. A reaction against baroque flamboyance, the style brought a return to classical design elements like columns, pediments, domes and restrained ornamentation as had been typical of the Graeco-Roman period.

Neoclassicism peaked under Friedrich Wilhelm III who envisioned a link between Prussian prowess and the greatness of ancient Greece. The most prolific architects of the age were Langhans and Schinkel (see Architects and Tour I later in this chapter).

Historism

Industrialisation in the second half of the 19th century fundamentally altered the basic structure of society, and scientific discoveries undermined people's belief systems. This time of progress – but also of insecurity – gave birth to Historism (sometimes also called Revivalism), which reproduces earlier styles, even blending several together into an aesthetic hotchpotch. Good examples of this type of architecture are the Theater des Westens (1896) in Charlottenburg, the Rotes Rathaus (1869) in Mitte and, of course, the Reichstag (1894) and Berliner Dom (1905), both in the neo-Renaissance style.

International Style

The industrialisation, mechanisation and rationalisation of the outgoing 19th century fed into a new aesthetic that was a wholesale rejection of all that preceded it: the International Style, more descriptively known as 'Functionalism' or 'New Objectivity'. Its main characteristics are boxlike shapes, flat roofs, plain and unadorned facades and interior walls, and the abundant use of glass. Pioneers included Peter Behrens, Bauhaus School founder Walter Gropius, Mies van der Rohe and Le Corbusier. Suppressed in the Third Reich, the International Style re-emerged in a more mature form after WWII. Echoes of it are still with us today, both in its residential and 'corporate' forms. Tour II describes several examples of this style.

Monumentalism

Nazi architecture, like Nazism itself, revelled in pomposity. In 1937, Hitler appointed Albert Speer as his main architect and charged him with redesigning Berlin into Germania, the capital of Nazi Germany. Unfortunately for Speer, classicism already had one 'neo' prefix by the time he

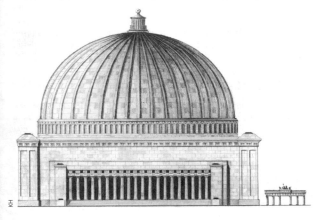

Left: The Great Hall, an example of Nazi Monumentalism. The building never got beyond planning stage. Had it been built, it would have dwarfed the Brandenburg Tor (1791), one of Berlin's major landmarks.

got his hands on it, which perhaps explains why Nazi monumentalism often seems absurd. The never-realised Great Hall, for example, boasted a 250m-diameter dome and was planned to accommodate 150,000 people. Nazi-era projects that did make it off the drawing board (and survived the war) include the Olympic Stadium in Charlottenburg, Tempelhof Airport in Tempelhof and the Reichsluftfahrtsministerium in Mitte.

Critical Reconstruction

After the Wende, city planners were faced with the challenge and opportunity to rebuild the New Berlin to reflect the Zeitgeist at the dawn of the third millennium. Rejecting anything too bold, avant-garde or monumental, the powers that be turned instead to 'critical reconstruction', an approach that sought to forge a link with history without creating replicas of earlier landmarks. Tight building regulations – extending to cornice height and construction materials used – limited architects' creativity from the onset of this formidable project. This approach can best be seen in the buildings in the new Potsdamer Platz area in Tiergarten, described in Tour III (see later in this chapter).

TOUR I – NEOCLASSICAL VISIONS: 'ATHENS ON THE SPREE' IN MITTE

Historic Mitte is a showcase of neoclassical architecture, most notably by Schinkel. This tour can be combined with the Historic Mitte Walking Tour in the Things to See & Do chapter.

Brandenburger Tor (1791)

Pariser Platz; Architect: Carl Gotthard Langhans
One of the most photographed landmarks in town, the Brandenburger Tor (Brandenburg Gate) was inspired by the entrance to the Acropolis in Athens. Around 26m high and 65m wide, it is supported by Doric columns and crowned by the Quadriga, a two-wheeled chariot drawn by four horses and driven by the winged goddess of victory (Johann Gottfried Schadow, 1793).

Schauspielhaus/Konzerthaus (1821)

Gendarmenmarkt; Architect: Karl Friedrich Schinkel
The Schauspielhaus is the unifying element of Gendarmenmarkt, which is anchored by the French and German cathedrals on its northern and southern end, respectively.

When Langhans' original 1801 design went up in flames in 1817, Schinkel rebuilt it. He retained the remaining outside walls and columns but added the massive open staircase leading to the raised Ionic portico.

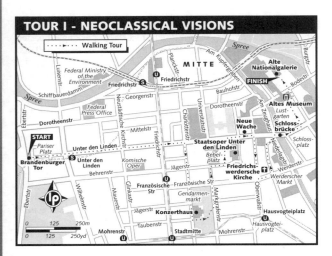

This entrance is lorded over by a much taller central structure crowned by a phalanx of statues. Badly mauled during WWII, the building was reconstructed according to Schinkel's plans. In 1994, it was renamed Konzerthaus.

Staatsoper Unter den Linden (1743)

Unter den Linden 7; Architect: Georg Wenzeslaus von Knobelsdorff
Today's Staatsoper (National Opera) on the eastern side of Bebelplatz is one of Berlin's earliest neoclassical structures, commissioned by Friedrich II as his court opera. A gabled portico is supported by six Corinthian columns and bears the inscription 'Fridericus Rex Apolloni et Musis', a reference to the king's intention to build a temple honouring Apollo and the Muses. Following a devastating fire, it was rebuilt by Carl Ferdinand Langhans in 1843–44, then enlarged in 1926 and rebuilt again after WWII.

Neue Wache (1818)

Unter den Linden 4; Architect: Karl Friedrich Schinkel
The Neue Wache (New Guardhouse) was Schinkel's first major architectural project. Looking a bit like a miniature-military-fortress-meets-Greek-temple, the dignified structure is fronted by a double row of Doric columns supporting a tympanum embellished with allegorical war scenes. Originally, it had an open inner courtyard, but this was covered up in 1931 except for a circular skylight. The sombre atmosphere inside this hall, now Germany's central memorial, is enhanced by walls clad in muschelkalk plates and a basalt floor.

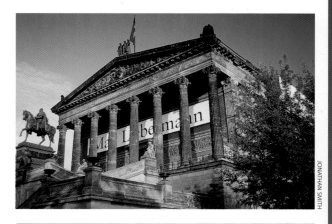

JONATHAN SMITH

JONATHAN SMITH

ANDREA SCHULTE-PEEVERS

Top: Home to works by Adolph Menzel, Monet, Degas and Renoir, the Alte Nationalgalerie has recently undergone a major facelift.

Middle: The majestic dome of Berlin Cathedral, restored to its pre-WWII splendour.

Bottom: Weinhaus Huth, the only remaining eyewitness to the first heyday of Potsdamer Platz.

Top: Berliner Volksbank features parallel rectangular office blocks connected on the seventh floor.

Middle: The atrium of the DaimlerChrysler Services Building, in Potsdamer Platz, boasts cathedral-like acoustics and dimensions.

Bottom: Ku'damm Eck in Charlottenberg – sleek lines and shimmering facades are characteristic of the modern architecture of the new Berlin.

Friedrichswerdersche Kirche (1830)

Werderscher Mark; Architect: Karl Friedrich Schinkel
Here, Schinkel unites neoclassical strict symmetry with neogothic elements, such as the use of red bricks, the building blocks of choice in medieval northern Germany. The church is easily recognised by its characteristic roofline punctuated by a row of slender, square turrets. The same turrets crown the pair of square towers. Inside, the single nave construction is supported by a series of pillars buttressing a gallery which contains a Schinkel exhibit.

Altes Museum (1830)

Lustgarten; Architect: Karl Friedrich Schinkel
A phalanx of 18 Ionic columns holds up the 87m-long portico of the Altes Museum (Old Museum) on the northern edge of the Lustgarten. Considered Schinkel's most mature work, it is reached via an open staircase flanked by sculptures of an amazon and a lion tamer. Inside the rectangular structure are two inner courtyards and the famed central rotunda, modelled after Rome's Pantheon, with its Roman statues of Greek gods.

Schinkel also designed the lovely **Schlossbrücke** (Palace Bridge) which links Museum Island with Unter den Linden. The bridge is lined with eight clusters of white marble statues portraying the training and development of a Greek warrior.

Alte Nationalgalerie (1876)

Bodestrasse 1–3; Architect: Friedrich August Stüler
In December 2001, the Alte Nationalgalerie (Old National Gallery) re-opened after a thorough three-year restoration. The building, which resembles a Greek temple, is accessed by a sweeping double staircase. Stüler, a disciple of Schinkel, also designed the Neues Museum, which is currently being resurrected from its wartime ruins and is expected to re-open in 2005.

TOUR II – EXPERIMENTAL VISIONS: MID-CENTURY MODERNISM IN TIERGARTEN

After WWII, the district of Tiergarten became the experimental stage for new city planning, flanked by the Hansaviertel on the park's northern edge and the Kulturforum on its southern. Both developments allow for a survey of the architectural acumen of that day's internationally known modernists. Since the places covered are a fair distance apart from each other, this tour is best done by bicycle.

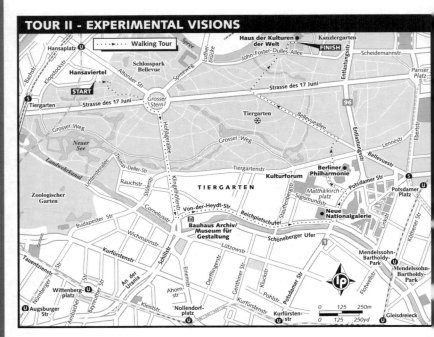

Hansaviertel (1953–57)

The Hansaviertel (Hansa Quarter) on the north-western perimeter of the Tiergarten is a loosely-structured residential community for 3500 people. A mix of high-rises and single-family homes – plus a commercial centre with shops, two churches, a school and library – it escapes sterility thanks to a reasonable amount of open areas and green spaces.

The Hansaviertel was the result of an architectural competition in 1953 and represents the cutting edge of architectural vision in the 1950s. More than 50 renowned architects from 13 countries, including Walter Gropius, Luciano Baldessari, Alvar Aalto and Werner Düttmann, participated in the building of the Hansaviertel.

Bauhaus Archiv/Museum für Gestaltung (1976–79)

Klingelhöferstrasse 14; Architect: Walter Gropius

Founded in Darmstadt in 1960, the Bauhaus Archiv/ Museum für Gestaltung (Bauhaus Archive/Museum of Design) moved to Berlin in 1971 and into its current home, built by Alexander Cvijanovic after Gropius' death, in 1979. Sharply structured, the complex consists of two parallel two-storey wings, connected by an undulating ramp and lower central edifice. The most distinctive – and attractive – element is the angled shed roofs which give the museum its unmistakable silhouette.

Neue Nationalgalerie (1968)

Potsdamer Strasse 50; Architect: Ludwig Mies van der Rohe
Completed shortly before its architect's death in 1969, the Neue Nationalgalerie (New National Gallery) clearly epitomises the 'less is more' approach typical of Mies van der Rohe, one of the 20th century's leading architects. His structures are simple shapes in solitary settings that make no attempt at blending with their surroundings. This temple-like art museum is a 50m by 50m glass-and-steel cube perching on a raised granite podium reached via two large open staircases. The coffered rib-steel roof defies gravity with the help of eight steel pillars and a floor-to-ceiling glass front. The interior has a continuous, open floor plan.

Berliner Philharmonie (1963)

Herbert-Von-Karajan-Strasse 1; Architect: Hans Scharoun
Scharoun's design principle 'form follows function' is given perfect expression in this glorious concert hall. The architect ditched the traditional stage in favour of a complicated layout of three pentagonal sections twisted and angled around a central orchestra pit. The audience is seated in terraced blocks with every seat offering perfect views and acoustics. It's all covered by a tent-like roof that gives the building its unique shape. The gold-coloured aluminium facade was added in 1981.

Haus der Kulturen der Welt (1957)

John-Foster-Dulles-Allee 10; Architect: Hugh A Stubbins
Nicknamed 'pregnant oyster', the design of the Haus der Kulturen der Welt (House of World Cultures) certainly ranks among the most eccentric of Berlin's mid-century buildings. Stubbins designed a dynamic, playful structure that was the American contribution to the International Building Exposition. Its most stunning element – the free-flowing roof – was a pioneering vision at the time. The building was fraught with disaster right from the start and nearly burned down during construction. It partly collapsed in 1980 but was faithfully rebuilt by 1987.

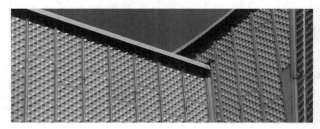

Right: Detail of the gold aluminium facade of the Philharmonie by Hans Scharoun (photograph by Andrea Schulte-Peevers)

TOUR III – CUTTING-EDGE VISIONS: THE NEW BERLIN AT POTSDAMER PLATZ

Images of the ballet of cranes hovering over Potsdamer Platz and the lipstick-red Infobox went around the world in the 1990s, a symbol of the rebirth of united Berlin. From an ugly wasteland has sprung a dynamic new urban district swarming with shoppers, tourists, musical fans, restaurant patrons and, of course, office workers.

There are essentially two parts to the new Potsdamer Platz: DaimlerCity, completed in 1998, and the Sony Center, inaugurated in 2000. Roughly pie-shaped, the former Daimler City consists of 19 buildings of varying heights arranged in an irregular grid of 10 streets some new, some revived like the Alte Potsdamer Strasse. Three high-rises mark the edges of the development. About 50% of the space is taken up by offices, 20% by flats and 30% by mixed-use facilities (hotels, theatres etc).

The Sony Center, north of Neue Potsdamer Strasse, is a complex of eight buildings enclosing a central plaza and comprising Sony's European headquarters, the FilmMuseum, apartments and office buildings.

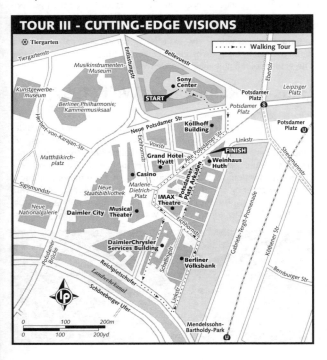

TOUR III - CUTTING-EDGE VISIONS

An international team of the finest and brightest minds in contemporary architecture was tapped to design the various structures based on a masterplan by Renzo Piano and Christoph Kohlbecker. Design criteria included wide footpaths, ground-floor arcading and facades made from natural materials like terracotta, sandstone or clinker. Renzo Piano himself designed six of the 19 structures, including the entertainment ensemble of Musical Theater, IMAX and Casino, all orbiting a central plaza called Marlene-Dietrich-Platz.

Some of the complex's main buildings include the following:

Sony Center (2000)

Neue Potsdamer Strasse/Bellevuestrasse; Architect: Helmut Jahn
Helmut Jahn has used the 26,500 sq metres of the Sony Center lot to create a playful, visually interesting environment. The central focus is the so-called Forum, an oblong plaza spatially divided by a semicircular hedge and a circular fountain. It is canopied by a dramatic tentlike glass roof supported by steel beams emanating like the spokes of a bicycle wheel. The plaza is flanked by five buildings, all but one with rounded facades to match the outline of the Forum. They include the FilmMuseum and the Esplanade Residence which integrates the Kaisersaal (Emperor's Room) salvaged from the historic Hotel Esplanade. The structures are clad in mirrored glass which generates an interesting interplay between shapes, colours and the light refracted through the tent roof. Standing a bit apart, facing Potsdamer Platz, is the 100m-high Sony Tower with its svelte, semicircular glass facade.

Kollhoff Building

Potsdamer Platz 1; Architect: Hans Kollhoff
This office building with retail establishments on the ground floor occupies a vast triangular space emanating south-west from Potsdamer Platz. The structure is highest (22 storeys) where it borders the square and, together with Helmut Jahn's Sony Tower, forms a gateway to the new Potsdamer Platz district. Away from the square, the building height moves down in two steps. The entire structure is clad in a mantle of reddish-brown bricks (clinker), with a grey-green granite base, giving it the rather old-fashioned, traditional appearance typical of Kollhoff's designs.

Hotel Grand Hyatt (1998)

Marlene-Dietrich-Platz 2; Architect: Rafael Moneo
The famed Spanish architect didn't strain his imagination on the exterior of this luxury hotel: its monotonous facade, with its rows of square windows, is more functional than aesthetic, despite the use of shiny, sleek, red sandstone. However, the interior projects sophistication with Zen-like minimalism, while the rooftop fitness centre provides fitting environs for a thorough indulgence of the senses.

DaimlerChrysler Services Building (1997)

Reichspietschufer/Eichhornstrasse; Architect: Renzo Piano
The most arresting feature of the DaimlerChrysler Services Building is its dramatic atrium with dimensions of a postmodern basilica that force an upward gaze. It's anchored by Jean Tinguely's bizarre *Méta-Maxi* sculpture. DaimlerChrysler Services is a subsidiary of the DaimlerChrysler corporation. Its logo – an all-green 'Rubik's cube' – tops the 83m-tall tower on the structure's southern end near Reichspietschufer. Incidentally, the tower doubles as a chimney for the exhaust from the underground tunnel snaking beneath the structure.

Berliner Volksbank (1997)

Complex framed by Eichhornstrasse, Linkstrasse and Reichpietschufer; Architect: Arata Isozaki
The Japanese postmodern master architect has created one of the most interesting and appealing structures in DaimlerCity. Two rectangular parallel office blocks are connected on the 7th floor via several glass-covered bridges, while the waffle-patterned mocha-coloured facade boasts subtle wavelike curves. The tunnel-like space between the two buildings is taken up by an urban garden.

Potsdamer Platz Arkaden (1997–98)

Off Linkstrasse; Architect: Richard Rogers
Rogers has designed three office-residential-commercial blocks linked by a stylish three-storey interior mall. Sheltered by a glass canopy, it's enlivened by marble and leafy plants, and thoughtfully placed benches allow you to take it all in at leisure.

Weinhaus Huth (1912)

Alte Potsdamer Strasse 5; Architects: Conrad Heidenreich & Paul Michel
This majestic structure, dwarfed by its postmodern neighbours, is the only eyewitness to the first heyday of Potsdamer Platz. It survived both WWII and the Wall, thanks in large part to its steel skeleton, an innovation at the time. The building has a shell-limestone facade; inside, marble staircases lead to a gourmet restaurant and to the flats on the upper storeys.

Left: Waffle-patterned, mocha-coloured facade of the Berliner Volksbank building by Arata Isozaki (photograph by Andrea Schulte-Peevers)

TOUR IV – FUTURISTIC VISIONS: GLASS & STEEL IN THE CITYWEST

While all the attention is focused on the new construction in Berlin's historic centre, the CityWest too is gradually enhancing its drab image. To be sure, the 1950s look cannot be eradicated overnight, but the following buildings are clearly setting accents of renewal in Charlottenburg.

Ludwig-Erhard-Haus (1997)

Fasanenstrasse 83–84; Architect: Nicholas Grimshaw
Structure, Space, Skin – these are the building blocks of the philosophy of British architect Nicholas Grimshaw. His Ludwig-Erhard-Haus, a prime example of 'organic' architecture, perfectly reflects these principles. The underlying high tech design was inspired by the armadillo: the supporting structure consists of a series of up to 38m-high arching steel girders that vaguely resemble a rib cage. The entire building is wrapped in a glass skin. The main elements on the inside are a 'street-like' walkway paralleling the length of the building, and an atrium that provides access to the offices. The building houses the Berlin Stock Exchange as well as the Chamber of Commerce and Industry.

Kantdreieck (1995)

Fasanenstrasse 81; Architect: Josef Paul Kleihues
This award-winning office building sets an extravagant visual accent in the CityWest. Its vaguely nautical theme is generated by a strict modular pattern based on square, triangle and circle. The building consists of two

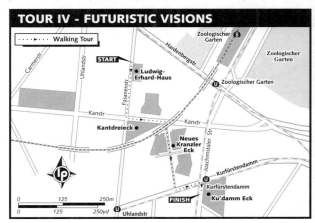

main components: a five-storey triangular glass-and-slate base and an 11-storey square tower which is topped by a giant triangular 'sail', which shifts in the wind like a weather vane.

Neues Kranzler Eck (2000)

Joachimstaler Strasse/Kurfürstendamm; Architect: Helmut Jahn
Helmut Jahn, designer of the Sony Center (see Tour III), also dreamed up this minimalist and edgy office-and-retail complex; it is bisected by a pedestrian walkway connecting Ku'damm and Kantstrasse. The up to 60m-high glass palace has cool, angular geometry with a concrete core and a neon-lit atrium. The starkness is softened by two large birdcages with 110 exotic birds in its courtyard. Also incorporated into the complex is the rotunda of the Café Kranzler, which is all that remains of this once popular – if touristy – coffeehouse.

Ku'damm Eck (2001)

Kurfürstendamm/Joachimstaler Strasse; Architects: Gerkan, Marg & Partner
Out with the old, in with the new – that's the motto at this urban street corner. Its previous incarnation torn down in 1998, the new Ku'damm Eck does its part in catapulting the district into the 21st century. Ten storeys-high (44m), its most distinctive element is the graduated rounded facade of the main building, which is buttressed by lower base floors with a slightly undulating facade. Housing a hotel and the C&A clothing store, its exterior also features an electronic billboard and sculptures by Markus Lüppertz.

Facts for the Visitor

WHEN TO GO

Berlin is a fascinating city year-round, although most visitors arrive between May and September when the weather is the most reliable. Naturally, this is also when museums and tourist attractions get the biggest crowds and cheap rooms are harder to find. But summer in Berlin is lovely mostly because much of life moves outdoors. Beer gardens and cafes bustle at all hours; outdoor events and festivals enliven the city's streets, squares and parks; and swimming in the lakes is a refreshing delight – at least as long as the weather plays along. Remember that rain is a possibility in any month.

From November to early March, skies tend to be gloomy and the mercury often drops below freezing. On the plus side, there are fewer visitors and shorter queues. Just pack the right clothes and keep in mind that there are only six to eight hours of daylight. In December, the sun (if there is any) sets around 3.30pm.

Avoid major holidays like Easter, Christmas and New Year and special events like the Love Parade when the city bursts at the seams (unless, of course, that's what brings you here in the first place).

ORIENTATION

Berlin sits in the middle of the region known from medieval times as the Mark (March) of Brandenburg, now the *Bundesland* (federal state) of Brandenburg. The state of Berlin measures some 892 sq km while the municipal boundaries encompass 234 sq km.

Roughly one-third of the state of Berlin is made up of parks, forests, lakes and rivers. There are more trees here than in Paris and more bridges than in Venice. Much of the natural beauty of rolling hills, quiet shorelines and bucolic riverbanks is in the south-east and south-west of the city.

The Spree River wends its way across the city for over 30km, from Grosser Müggelsee, the city's largest lake, in the east to Spandau in the west. North and south of Spandau, the Havel River widens into a series of lakes, from Tegel to below Potsdam. A network of canals links the waterways to each other and to the Oder River on the Polish border, and there are beautiful walks along some of these canals.

In 2001, Berlin's previous 23 administrative districts *(Bezirke)* were reduced to 12 in an effort to curb bureaucracy. In most cases this has meant merging existing districts, a behind-the-scenes administrative move with no impact on visitors as the old district names continue to be used. The eight 'core' ones are: (clockwise from the west) Charlottenburg, Tiergarten, Mitte, Prenzlauer Berg, Friedrichshain, Kreuzberg, Schöneberg and Wilmersdorf. Kreuzberg, quite different in its eastern and western sections, is split in this book into Kreuzberg 36 and Kreuzberg 61 for clarity, according to its old postal codes.

Berlin continues to have two centres that reflect its 40-year division. The CityWest near Zoo station and Kurfürstendamm in Charlottenburg (Map 6); and Mitte in the east along Unter den Linden and around Alexanderplatz (Map 7).

Unter den Linden, the fashionable avenue of aristocratic old Berlin, and its continuation, Karl-Liebknecht-Strasse, extend east from the Brandenburger Tor to Alexanderplatz, once the heart of socialist East Germany. Some of Berlin's finest museums are on Museumsinsel in the Spree. One of several epicentres of nightlife has sprung up in the Spandauer Vorstadt around the Hackesche Höfe and along Oranienburger Strasse, although the area is getting serious competition from Prenzlauer Berg, north-east of here.

South of the Brandenburger Tor, in areas once occupied by the Wall, Berlin's newest quarter has emerged around Potsdamer Platz. East of here, office buildings have sprung up around the former Checkpoint Charlie, the infamous border crossing. The Wall itself, Berlin's grim erstwhile landmark, hasn't

DISTRICTS OF BERLIN

Existing Districts — Treptow

New Districts within existing boundaries — XII

Pankow
IV
Reinickendorf
XII
Hohenschönhausen
Weissensee
Wedding
Spandau
V
Prenzlauer Berg
XI
Tiergarten
I
Marzahn
X
Hellersdorf
Charlottenburg
II
Mitte
Friedrichshain
Kreuzberg
III
Lichtenberg
Wilmersdorf
Schöneberg
VII
Zehlendorf
VI
Steglitz
Tempelhof
Neukölln
VIII
Treptow
IX
Köpenick

0   5   10km
0   3   6mi

been vanquished altogether; sections remain for public viewing around the city (see the boxed text 'The Berlin Wall' in the Things to See & Do chapter).

Back in the CityWest, the ruin of the Kaiser-Wilhelm-Gedächtniskirche, on Breit-scheidplatz near Zoo station, is the most visible landmark. The main tourist office and dozens of shops are in the Europa-Center on the eastern side of the square. The Kurfürstendamm (known as the 'Ku'damm'), the main thoroughfare here, runs 3.5km west from Breitscheidplatz to Halensee.

To the north-east, between Breitscheidplatz and the Brandenburger Tor, is Tiergarten, a district named after the city park that was once a royal hunting domain. The area north of the park, along the bend in the Spree (the Spreebogen) and between Lehrter Stadtbahnhof and Bellevue S-Bahn stations, is being transformed into the New Government District. The Lehrter Stadtbahnhof now operates as an S-Bahn station, but eventually

will become the capital's main station for long-distance and suburban train travel.

While in central Berlin, keep in mind that the street numbers usually run sequentially up one side of the street and down the other (important exceptions are Unter den Linden and, in Schöneberg, Martin-Luther-Strasse and Lietzenburger Strasse). Number guides usually appear on most corner street signs. Be aware, too, that a continuous street may change names several times along its length, and that on some streets (eg Kurfürstendamm, Kantstrasse, Knesebeckstrasse etc) numbering sequences continue after interruptions caused by squares.

MAPS

The maps in this book should suffice in most cases. However, if you plan to travel extensively in the outer suburbs, or want to look up specific streets, you may need a more detailed map. Lonely Planet's laminated Berlin city map has three scales (Berlin & Vicinity

1:60,000; Central Berlin 1:34,500; and Zoo, Tiergarten, Mitte 1:20,000) and an index of all streets and sights. It includes an S-Bahn and U-Bahn network map, essential information, an English-German glossary and a walking tour (AUS $7.95, UK £3.99, US$5.95).

Available locally from newsagents and bookstores are maps by Falkplan, which come either as the standard sheet map or the Falk Megaplan with a patented folding system, ADAC and the RV Verlag Euro City. All are good choices and cost from €4.50 to €7.50.

If you plan to stay in Berlin for several months, a street atlas, such as the one published by RV Verlag (€12.90), might come in handy. It has more than 150 detailed maps (1:20,000) of the city, suburbs and Potsdam, a street name index, public transport routes, plus descriptive information and listings (in German).

TOURIST OFFICES
Local Tourist Offices
The main office of Berlin Tourismus Marketing (BTM; Map 6) is on the ground floor of the Europa-Center at Budapester Strasse 45 near Zoo station. It is open from 8.30am to 8.30pm Monday to Saturday and 10am to 6.30pm Sunday. A second branch (Map 7) is in the southern wing of the Brandenburg Gate and is open from 9.30am to 6pm daily. Staff at both offices can make room reservations for free, but only at BTM partner hotels.

Smaller tourist office branches with limited services, called Info Points, are in the main hall of Tegel airport at the left-luggage office opposite Gate O (open from 5am to 10.30pm daily); and in the Reisecenter on the ground floor of the KaDeWe department store (Map 6) at Tauentzienstrasse 21 (open 9.30am to 8pm weekdays, 9am to 4pm Saturday).

The newest BTM branch is the Info-Cafe in the lobby of the TV Tower (Map 7), where you can pick up information and also grab a snack or relax over coffee.

For information on the telephone, call the BTM Call Centre on ☎ 0190-01 63 16. This number is valid from within Germany only and calls are charged at higher than regular phone rates ranging from €0.41 to €1.20 per minute. From outside Germany call ☎ (49) 1805 75 40 40. Room and select events reservations can be made at ☎ 030-25 00 25 at regular phone rates. The Call Centre is staffed from 8am to 7pm Monday to Friday and from 9am to 6pm on weekends. All services are also available on the BTM's Web site at 🆆 www.berlin-tourism.de.

All tourist offices sell maps, books and the heavily touted Berlin WelcomeCard (€16). It entitles one adult and up to three children (under 14 years of age) to 72 hours of public transport within the Berlin-Potsdam area and to minor discounts on admissions to museums, shows, attractions, sightseeing tours and boat cruises. The WelcomeCard is also available at hotels and public-transport ticket offices.

Tourist Offices Abroad
Germany's national tourist office (Deutsche Zentrale für Tourismus, DZT) has its headquarters at Beethovenstrasse 69, 60325 Frankfurt/Main (☎ 069-97 46 40, fax 75 19 03, 🄴 info@d-z-t.com, 🆆 www.germany -tourism.de). Staff can answer questions over the phone or send promotional brochures of Berlin and many other destinations within Germany. Branch offices around the world include the following:

Australia (☎ 02-9267 8148, fax 9267 9035, 🄴 gnto@germany.org.au)
 PO Box A980, Sydney South, NSW 1235
Austria (☎ 01-513 27 92, fax 513 27 92 22, 🄴 Deutschland.reisen@d-z-t.com)
 Schubertring 12, 1010 Vienna
Canada (☎ 416-968-0372, fax 968 1986, 🄴 gnto@aol.com)
 PO Box 65162, Toronto, Ontario M4K 3Z2
France (☎ 01-40 20 07 46, fax 40 20 17 00, 🄴 gntopar@d-z-t.com)
 47 Avenue de l'Opéra 75002 Paris
Japan (☎ 03-3586 0380, fax 3586 5079, 🄴 gntokyo@d-z-t.com)
 7-5-56 Akasaka, Minato-ku, Tokyo 107-0052
Netherlands (☎ 020-697 8066, fax 691 2972, 🄴 gntoams@d-z-t.com)
 Hoogoorddreef 76, 1101 BG Amsterdam ZO
Russia (☎ 095-7376 408, fax 7376 409, 🄴 dztmow@glasnet.ru) c/o
 Lufthansa German Airlines, Hotel Renaissance, Olimpiski prospekt 18/1, 129 110 Moscow

South Africa (☎ 011-643 1615, fax 484 2750)
c/o Lufthansa German Airlines, 22 Girton Rd,
Parktown, PO Box 10883, Johannesburg 2000
Switzerland (☎ 01-213 22 00, fax 212 01 75,
🖻 gntozrh@d-z-t.com)
Talstrasse 62, 8001 Zürich
UK (☎ 020-7317 0908, fax 7495 6129,
🖻 gntolon@d-z-t.com)
PO Box 2695, London W1A 3TN
USA *New York:* (☎ 212-661 7200, fax 661 7174,
🖻 gntonyc@d-z-t.com)
Chanin Bldg, 122 East 42nd St, 52nd Floor,
NY 10168-0072
Los Angeles: (☎ 323-655 6085, fax 655 6086,
🖻 gntolax@aol.com)
8484 Wilshire Blvd. Suite 440, Beverly Hills,
CA 90211

Additional offices are in Brussels, Budapest,
Copenhagen, Helsinki, Hong Kong, Madrid,
Mexico City, Milan, Oslo, Prague, São Paulo,
Seoul, Stockholm, Tel Aviv and Warsaw.

TRAVEL AGENCIES

Many travel agencies offering cheap flights
advertise in the *Reisen* classified section
(Kleinanzeigen) of the popular city magazines *Zitty* and *Tip* (see the Listings section in
the Entertainment chapter for details). A good
discount operator specialising in unpub-
lished, discounted fares to anywhere is Alternativ Tours at Wilmersdorfer Strasse 94 in
Wilmersdorf (Map 6; ☎ 881 20 89; U-Bahn:
U7 to Adenauerplatz). Another outfit specialising in flights and package tours is Travel
Overland at Goltzstrasse 14 in Schöneberg
(Map 4; ☎ 217 38 90). Frauen Unterwegs,
specialising in travel for women only, is at
Potsdamer Strasse 139, also in Schöneberg
(Map 4; ☎ 215 10 22).

Rainbow Tours operates incredibly
cheap multi-day bus trips to Prague, London, Munich and Paris. It's at Kantstrasse
116 (Map 6; ☎ 318 63 00) For further information visit the Website (German only)
🖳 www.rainbowberlin.de.

STA Travel is the main agency catering
for young people and student travellers, although anybody can buy tickets there. It
also issues GO25 and ISIC cards (see Student & Youth Cards later in this chapter)
and has branches all over Berlin, including
in Charlottenburg at Hardenbergstrasse 9

(Map 6; ☎ 310 00 40) and at Goethestrasse 73
(Map 6; ☎ 311 09 50); in Mitte at Dorotheen-
strasse 30 (Map 7; ☎ 20 16 50 63) and in
Prenzlauer Berg at Gleimstrasse 28 (Map 3;
☎ 281 51 33).

Among general full-service travel agencies, Atlas Reisewelt has a good reputation.
There are branches at Alexanderplatz 5 (Map
7; ☎ 242 73 70) and Münzstrasse 14 (Map 7;
☎ 247 76 48) in Mitte, as well as at Schönefeld airport (☎ 60 91 56 50). These are good
places for train, bus or ferry tickets as well
as for booking package tours.

Several agencies specialise in travel to
Eastern Europe. For travel to Poland, try
Polnisches Reisebüro Darpol in Charlot-
tenburg at Kaiser-Friedrich-Strasse 19 (Map
4; ☎ 342 00 74; U-Bahn: U7 to Richard-
Wagner-Platz). If Russia is in your travel
plans, check with Sputnik Travel in Mitte at
Friedrichstrasse 176 (Map 7; ☎ 20 30 22 46).
Help with travel to the Czech Republic is
available from Cedok Travel at Leipziger
Strasse 60 (Map 7; ☎ 204 46 44). Ungarn
Tours sells bus and air tours to Budapest and
beyond; it's at Karl-Liebknecht-Strasse 9
(Map 7; ☎ 247 82 96).

DOCUMENTS
Visas

European Union (EU) nationals and those
from certain other European countries, including Switzerland and Poland, require only
a passport or their national identity card to
enter and stay in Germany. Citizens of Australia, Canada, Israel, Japan, New Zealand,
Singapore and the USA need only a valid
passport (no visa) if entering as tourists for
up to three months.

Nationals from most other countries need
a so-called Schengen Visa, named after the
Schengen Agreement that abolished passport
controls between Austria, Denmark, the
Netherlands, Belgium, Luxembourg, Germany, France, Spain, Portugal, Italy, Greece,
Finland, Iceland, Norway and Sweden. Residency status in any of the Schengen countries
negates the need for a visa, regardless of your
nationality.

Three-month tourist visas are issued by
German embassies or consulates. A fast-track

visa system has been introduced so that visas can be issued while you wait, but this still might not be the case everywhere. Inquire early about how long it takes, or leave enough time before departure to apply. You'll need a valid passport and sufficient funds to finance your stay. Fees vary depending on which country you apply in.

Travel Insurance

Make sure you have a travel insurance policy to cover medical problems, theft and loss in Germany. A policy with a higher medical-expense option is best suited. A wide variety of policies is available, so check the small print and know what to do in case you need to file a claim. Some policies specifically exclude 'dangerous activities', which can include scuba diving, motorcycling, even trekking. A locally acquired motorcycle licence is not valid under some policies.

You may prefer a policy that pays doctors or hospitals directly rather than you having to pay on the spot and file a claim later. If you have to claim later, make sure you keep all documentation. Some policies ask you to call back (reverse charges) to a centre in your home country where an immediate assessment of your problem is made. Check that the policy covers ambulances or an emergency flight home.

Also check your medical policy at home, since some policies already provide coverage worldwide, in which case you only need to protect yourself against other problems (see Health later in this chapter).

Paying for your airline ticket with a credit card often provides you with limited travel-accident insurance, and you may be able to reclaim the payment if the operator doesn't deliver. Ask your credit card company what it's prepared to cover.

Driving Licence & Permits

If you plan to drive in Germany, you need to carry a valid driving licence. Although you are not required by law to have an International Driving Permit (IDP), having one helps Germans make sense of your unfamiliar local licence (but make sure you take that with you too) and simplifies the car and motorcycle rental process. IDPs are valid for one year and may be obtained for a small fee from your local automobile association – bring a passport photo and your regular licence.

Hostel Cards

You must be a member of a Hostelling International-affiliated organisation in order to stay at hostels run by the Deutsches Jugend-herbergswerk (DJH). Non-Germans who don't have an HI card may obtain a so-called International Guest Card (IGC) at any hostel. It costs seniors/juniors €18/10 and is valid for one year. If you don't have it, €3.10 per night will be added to your regular hostel rate; you'll be given a pass that is stamped once for each night and after six nights you automatically get the IGC. German citizens or residents can also buy the DJH/HI cards for seniors/juniors €18/10 at the hostel when checking in.

Independent hostels don't require a card.

Student & Youth Cards

The International Student Identity Card (ISIC), a plastic ID-style card with your photograph, provides discounts on many forms of transport (including airlines and local public transport) and on admission to museums and sights, as well as cheaper meals in university cafeterias.

If you're under 26 but not a student, you can apply for an IYTC (International Youth Travel Card) issued by the ISTC (International Student Travel Confederation), or the Euro<26 card, which goes under different names in various countries. Both give much the same discounts and benefits as an ISIC.

All these cards are issued by student unions, hostelling organisations and youth-oriented travel agencies.

Copies

All important documents (passport data page and visa page, credit cards, travel insurance policy, air/bus/train tickets, driving licence etc) should be photocopied before you leave home. Leave one copy with someone at home and keep another with you, separate from the originals.

EMBASSIES & CONSULATES
German Embassies Abroad

German embassies around the world include the following:

Australia (☎ 02-6270 1911, fax 62 70 19 51)
119 Empire Circuit, Yarralumla, ACT 2600
Austria (☎ 0222-711 54, fax 713 83 66)
Metternichgasse 3, Vienna 3
Canada (☎ 613-232 1101, fax 594 93 30)
1 Waverley St, Ottawa, Ont K2P 0T8
France (☎ 01 53 83 45 00, fax 01 43 59 74 18)
13–15 Ave Franklin Roosevelt, 75008 Paris
Ireland (☎ 01-269 3011, fax 269 39 46)
31 Trimleston Ave, Booterstown, Dublin 4
Japan (☎ 03-5791 7700, fax 34 73 42 43)
4-5–10 Minami-Azabu, Minato-ku, Tokyo 106
Netherlands (☎ 070-342 0600, fax 365 19 57)
Groot Hertoginnelaan 18–20, 2517 EG The Hague
New Zealand (☎ 04-473 6063, fax 473 60 69)
90–92 Hobson St, Wellington
Russia (☎ 095-937 95 00, fax 938 23 54)
Ulitsa Mosfilmovskaya 56, 119285 Moscow
South Africa (☎ 012-427 8900, fax 343 94 01)
180 Blackwood St, Arcadia, Pretoria 0083
Switzerland (☎ 031-359 4111, fax 359 44 44)
Willadingweg 83, 3006 Bern
UK (☎ 020-7824 1300, fax 78 24 14 35)
23 Belgrave Square, London SW1X 8PZ
USA (☎ 202-298 4000, fax 298 4249)
4645 Reservoir Rd NW, Washington, DC 20007-1998

Embassies in Berlin

Almost all embassies are now located in Berlin. Most operate consular sections at the same address which you will need to contact for visa and other applications (consulates located at a different location are mentioned below).

Australia (Map 7; ☎ 880 08 80, fax 880 08 83 10) Friedrichstrasse 200, Mitte
Austria (Map 7; ☎ 20 28 70, fax 229 05 65) Friedrichstrasse 60, Mitte
Belgium (Map 7; ☎ 20 35 20, fax 20 25 22 00) Friedrichstrasse 95, Mitte
Canada (Map 7; ☎ 20 31 20, 20 31 25 90) Friedrichstrasse 95, Mitte
Czech Republic (Map 8; ☎ 22 63 80, fax 22 94 033) Wilhelmstrasse 44, Mitte
Denmark (Map 4; ☎ 25 00 10, ☎ 50 50 20 00, fax 50 50 20 50) Rauchstrasse 1, Tiergarten

France (Map 7; ☎ 206 390 00, fax 206 390 10) Kochstrasse 6–7, Mitte;
consular section: (Map 6; ☎ 88 59 02 43, fax 882 52 95) Kurfürstendamm 211, Charlottenburg
Hungary (Map 7; ☎ 20 31 00, fax 229 13 14), Unter den Linden 76, Mitte;
consular section: (Map 7; ☎ 20 31 01 08/09, fax 394 13 85), Wilhelmstrasse 61 – same building, different entrances
Ireland (Map 7; ☎ 22 07 20, fax 22 07 22 99) Friedrichstrasse 200, Mitte
Israel (Map 4; ☎ 89 04 55 00, fax 89 04 52 22) Schinkelstrasse 10, Wilmersdorf;
consular division (☎ 89 04 55 07)
Japan (Map 4; ☎ 030-21 09 40, fax 21 09 42 22) Hiroshimastrasse 6, Tiergarten
Netherlands (Map 7; ☎ 030-20 95 60, fax 20 95 64 41) Friedrichstrasse 95, Mitte
New Zealand (Map 7; ☎ 20 62 10) Friedrichstrasse 60, Mitte
Poland (Map 1; ☎ 22 31 30, fax 22 31 31 55) Lassenstrasse 19–21, Grunewald;
consular division: (Map 1; ☎ 22 31 30, 22 31 32 12) Richard-Strauss-Strasse 11, Grunewald
Russia (Map 7; ☎ 226 63 20, 229 11 10, fax 229 93 97) Unter den Linden 63–65, Mitte;
consular division: (☎ 229 12 07) Behrenstrasse 66, Mitte
Slovakia (Map 7; ☎ 2012030, ☎ 47 30 23 24) Leipziger Strasse 36, Mitte
South Africa (Map 7; ☎ 22 07 30, fax 22 07 31 90) Friedrichstrasse 60, Mitte
UK (Map 7; ☎ 20 45 70) Wilhelmstrasse 70–71, Mitte

The bear has been the symbol of Berlin for centuries. Some say the city's name comes from the German word Bärlein, meaning 'Little Bear'.

USA (Map 7; ☎ 830 50) Neustädtische Kirchstrasse 4–5;
consular division: no tel, Clayallee 170, Zehlendorf, open 8.30am-noon Mon-Fri; American Citizen Services: (☎ 832 92 33, fax 83 05 12 15); Visa Information Service – in English or German – (☎ 0190-85 00 58 00 automated, 24/7); (☎ 0190-85 00 58 live operator) 7am-8pm Mon-Fri – services are charged at €1.80 per minute

Your Own Embassy

As a tourist, it's important to realise what your own embassy – the embassy of the country of which you are a citizen – can and can't do to help you if you get into trouble while in Germany. Generally speaking, your embassy won't be much help in emergencies if the trouble you're in is remotely your own fault. Remember that you are bound by German laws and not your own country's. Your embassy will not be sympathetic if you end up in jail after committing a crime locally, even if such actions are legal in your own country.

In genuine emergencies you might get some assistance, but only if other channels have been exhausted. If all your money and documents are stolen, for instance, your embassy will help you get a new passport. Having a photocopy of the important pages of your passport will make replacement that much easier. But forget about a free ticket if you need to get home urgently – after all, that's what travel insurance is for.

CUSTOMS

Articles that you take to Germany for your personal use may be imported free of duty and tax with some conditions. The following allowances apply to *duty-free goods* purchased at the airport or ferries: 200 cigarettes or 100 cigarillos or 50 cigars or 250g of loose tobacco; 1L of strong liquor or 2L of less than 22% alcohol by volume *and* 2L of wine; 500g of coffee or 200g of extracts *and* 100g of tea or 40g tea extracts; 50g of perfume or scent *and* 0.25L of eau de toilette; and additional goods up to a value of €179.

You must be 17 years or over to bring in tobacco products and alcohol; the importation of duty-free coffee is, oddly, barred to those under 15. There are no currency import restrictions.

Do not confuse duty free with *duty-paid* items (including alcohol and tobacco) bought at normal shops and supermarkets in another EU country and brought into Germany, where certain goods might be more expensive. Then the allowances are more generous: 800 cigarettes or 200 cigars or 1kg of loose tobacco; 10L of spirits (more than 22% alcohol by volume), 20L of fortified wine or aperitif, 90L of wine or 110L of beer.

Note that duty-free shopping within the EU was abolished in mid-1999. This means that you can still take duty-free goods into an EU country, like Germany, from a non-EU country like the USA or Australia. You can't, however, buy duty-free goods in an EU-country unless you're headed for a non-EU country.

MONEY
Currency

In January 2002, Germany introduced euro notes and coins. There are seven euro notes (five, 10, 20, 50, 100, 200 and 500 euros) and eight coins (one and two euro coins, and one, two, five, 10, 20 and 50 cent coins). Germans, like everyone else, will be relatively unfamiliar with euros for some time, so it's a good idea to take extra care when you pay.

Exchange Rates

country	unit		euro
Australia	A$1	=	0.58
Canada	C$1	=	0.71
Denmark	Dkr1	=	0.13
Japan	¥100	=	0.92
New Zealand	NZ$1	=	0.47
South Africa	R1	=	0.12
Switzerland	Sfr1	=	0.68
UK	UK£1	=	1.62
USA	US$1	=	1.13

Exchanging Money

The easiest places to change money are banks or foreign-exchange counters at airports and train stations. Post offices often have money-changing facilities as well, and their rates for cash – though not for travellers cheques – are sometimes better than at banks.

Bye Bye Deutschmark, Hello Euro

As you're reading this, the venerable Deutschmark is history. In January 2002, Germany – along with 11 other member nations of the European Union – introduced euro notes and coins. The euro is now the common currency of Austria, Belgium, Finland, France, Germany, Greece, Ireland, Italy, Luxembourg, the Netherlands, Portugal and Spain. The value of the euro against the dollar and all other currencies – including those of the four EU members remaining outside the euro zone – will fluctuate according to market conditions.

Each of the euro bills represents a different epoch in European cultural history (Gothic, Renaissance, baroque, etc). They feature a generic 'European' bridge on one side and a vaguely familiar but unidentifiable arch on the reverse. Each country will be permitted to design coins with one side bearing a national emblem (the other side will be standard for all euro coins).

If you happen to have Deutschmarks left over from an earlier trip, you can still exchange them at the Landeszentralbank Berlin (Map 7; ☎ 347 50), Kurstrasse 40 in Mitte, from 8.30am to 1pm weekdays.

Research for this edition took place just before the euro big bang. Whenever possible, we obtained the euro price. Sometimes, however, euro prices were not yet available and we had to convert the DM price. Readers therefore might find slight differences in the price we give and the actual price in euros.

At banks and exchange offices, the charge usually comes to between €3 and €5 per transaction. Occasionally you'll see currency exchange machines but they rarely give good rates. Established exchange offices in Berlin include:

AGW Exchange (Map 6; ☎ 882 10 86), Joachimstaler Strasse 1–3, open 9am to 7pm Monday to Friday, 10am to 3pm Saturday.

American Express (Map 7; ☎ 20 45 57 21) Friedrichstrasse 172 in Mitte; and (Map 6; ☎ 21 47 62 92) at Bayreuther Strasse 37 near the KaDeWe department store, open 9am to 7pm Monday to Friday, 10am to 2pm Saturday. There is no commission charged when cashing American Express travellers cheques.

Euro-Change (Map 6; ☎ 261 14 84), on the street level of the Europa-Center facing Breitscheidplatz, open 9am-6pm Monday to Friday, to 4pm Sat. There are branches at Friedrichstrasse 80 and on Alexanderplatz, both in Mitte (Map 7) and at Tempelhof airport (Map 5).

Reisebank (Map 6; ☎ 881 71 17), Hardenbergplatz 1 outside Zoo station, open from 7.30am to 10pm daily. Other branches are at Ostbahnhof (Map 5; ☎ 296 43 93) and at Bahnhof Friedrichstrasse (Map 7; ☎ 20 45 50 96) with shorter hours.

Thomas Cook (Map 7; ☎ 20 16 59 16), Friedrichstrasse 56, open 9.30am to 6pm weekdays, from 10am to 2pm Saturday. No commission is charged for exchanging Thomas Cook travellers cheques.

Cash Nothing beats cold, hard cash for convenience…or risk. If you lose it, it's gone forever and few travel insurers will come to your rescue. Those who will, limit the amount to about US$300. But since Germany is still a cash-based society, you can't avoid having at least some cash, say €100 or so, in your pocket at all times. Plan to pay in cash almost everywhere (see Credit Cards later in this section for likely exceptions). Remember that banks only exchange foreign paper money, not coins.

Travellers Cheques The main idea of carrying travellers cheques rather than cash is the protection they offer from theft, though their popularity is waning as more travellers – including those on tight budgets – deposit their money in their bank at home and withdraw it as they need it through ATMs.

In Germany, travellers cheques are *not* commonly used to pay for store-bought goods, at restaurants or hotels. Cheques issued in any other currency must be exchanged into local currency at a bank or exchange office (bring your passport). The Reisebank charges €3 for amounts under €50, and 1% or a minimum of €6 for higher transactions. The most commonly recognised are American Express and Thomas Cook cheques, and neither company charges commission for exchanges at their own offices. Both also have efficient replacement policies.

ATMs Automatic teller machines are common in central Berlin, though occasionally you may have to swipe your card through a slot to gain entry to a secure area. All of them only accept four-digit PIN codes. Most machines take Visa and MasterCard, and if your bank at home is part of the Cirrus, Plus, Star or Maestro network systems, you'll be able to use your ATM card to withdraw money directly from your home account. Check the fees and availability of services with your bank before you leave. Always keep handy the telephone number for reporting lost or stolen cards.

Credit Cards All the major international cards – eg MasterCard, Visa and American Express – are recognised and becoming more widely accepted, especially at major hotels, petrol stations, travel agencies and large shops and department stores. It is, however, best not to assume that you'll be able to pay for your meal, room, ticket or purchase with a card – inquire first.

Some stores may require a minimum purchase, others may refuse to accept a credit card even if that credit-card company's logo is displayed in the window. Nevertheless, it can't hurt to take your card along, if only for emergencies or for renting a car.

Check with your credit card issuer about fees and interest rates for cash withdrawals through ATMs. Make a note of where to call in case your card is lost or stolen.

International Transfers Depending on the country of origin, money sent by wire transfer from your bank to a bank in Berlin should reach you within a week. Note that some banks charge an exorbitant amount just for receiving the money (fees of €25 and up are typical), unless you have an account with them. Opening an account, however, may well be impractical or even impossible to do.

As an alternative, Western Union or MoneyGram offer ready and fast international cash transfers through agent banks such as Postbank (branches at many post offices) or Reisebank (see Exchanging Money earlier in this chapter). Cash sent becomes available as soon as the order has been entered into the computer system, ie, instantly.

Commissions are paid by the person making the transfer; the amount varies from country to country. Since commissions can be costly, you should use this service in emergencies only.

Security
Be cautious – but not paranoid – about carrying money. Use the safe at your hotel or hostel for your valuables and excess cash. Don't display large amounts of cash in public. A moneybelt worn under your clothes is a good place to carry excess currency when you're on the move or otherwise unable to stash it in a safe. Avoid carrying your wallet in a back pocket of your pants. This is a prime target for pickpockets, as are handbags and the outside pockets of moneybelts worn outside the clothing.

Costs
As you might expect, spending lots of money in Berlin is not hard, but it's a bit harder to spend little. The secret to staying within budget is to cut costs where you can, such as with accommodation and food. If you're very economical, you can expect to survive on €45 per day. If you can afford to spend twice that, you'll start living quite comfortably.

Rooms at simple pensions often cost around €25 per person or less per night. Staying in a room with a shared bathroom will save at least 30% off fully equipped bathrooms. Hostels are cheaper still and there's now a great number of quality places in central locales.

Buying passes keeps public transport costs way down (see the Getting Around chapter). Students with valid ID (see Student & Youth Cards earlier in this chapter), seniors and children are usually eligible for discounted prices.

Preparing your own meal or getting food from an *Imbiss* (snack bar) can save you a bundle, and many cafes and restaurants have

Making an Art of Discounts

There are many ways to cut costs while exploring Berlin.

Savings are particularly large if you happen to be a student, senior or child. At museums, sights and attractions, you can expect to save as much as 50% off the regular admission price. Reduced rates are also available for some forms of public transport, and admission to public pools, ice rinks and other such facilities. Students also qualify for unsold or returned tickets available at box offices immediately before curtain, usually at half price.

Anyone can save on theatre and musical tickets by buying them from Hekticket, a last-minute booking agency (see the Entertainment chapter). During the off-season, you can negotiate discounted room rates at some hotels or ask for a reduction for stays of more than three nights. The concept of Happy Hour – usually an hour or two early or late in the evening when you can get cheaper or half-price drinks – has become a big hit as well.

Opera, ballet and classical music fans under 27 can get incredibly cheap tickets by buying the new Classic Card. A cooperation between the Konzerthaus Berlin, the Berliner Philharmonie and the Deutsche Oper, this card costs €25 and allows you to attend as many performances as you wish within one year at these venues on a best-seat-available basis. Concert tickets cost €5-8, opera and ballet €10. The card is available at each venue's box office and the Dussmann Kulturkaufhaus (see the Shopping chapter).

small, inexpensive dishes or lunchtime specials that are tasty and filling. At restaurants, cut down on drinks since even non-alcoholic beverages are quite expensive.

Tipping & Bargaining

At restaurants, the service charge *(Bedienung)* is always included in bills and tipping is not compulsory. If you're satisfied with the service, add about 5% to 10%. Rather than leaving the money on the table, tip as you're handing over the money by announcing the amount you intend to pay. For example say '30, bitte', if your bill comes to €28 and you want to give a €2 tip. If you have the exact amount, just say 'Stimmt so' (roughly 'that's fine'). Taxi drivers, too, expect a small tip, usually about 10%.

Bargaining rarely occurs in Germany, certainly not in shops or restaurants. At hotels, you can sometimes ask for a lower rate which you may get if business is slow. Haggling is commonplace at flea markets, however, and you should be able to get at least 10% to 25% off the asking price. Prices at produce markets are usually not negotiable, though vendors may throw in an extra tomato or two towards the end of the day.

Taxes & Refunds

Most German goods and services include a value-added tax (VAT) called *Mehrwertsteuer* (or MwSt) of 16%. Non-EU residents leaving the EU can have this tax (minus processing fee) refunded for goods (not services) bought, which is definitely worth it for large purchases.

Check that the shop where you're buying has the necessary Tax-Free Shopping Cheque forms. The shop will issue you a cheque for the amount of VAT to be refunded, which you can cash in at VAT Cash Refund offices when leaving the country. Before you can get your money, the Tax-Free Shopping Cheque, together with the invoices or receipts, must be stamped by German customs as you leave the country. You're not allowed to use the items purchased until you have left Germany.

If you're flying out of Germany, have the paperwork stamped at the airport *before* you check in for your flight (with the exception of Frankfurt airport, where you check in first and then proceed to customs with your luggage). Note that you will have to show the goods. Refunds are made directly at VAT Cash Refund desks at the airports. There are customs offices at all three Berlin airports.

If you're travelling via another EU country, you must go through this procedure at the EU airport from which you depart for your non-EU destination.

If you want to avoid the queues at the VAT Cash Refund office, you can mail the customs-stamped forms and receipts to them after you return home and ask that the refund be issued to your credit card or mailed as a cheque.

Those unable to obtain the necessary seal or stamp before leaving Germany may obtain it at a German embassy or consulate back home. The items purchased must be shown to a mission official and sales slips, tax forms and passport must be presented.

Some 17,000 shops, including Germany's biggest department stores, are affiliated with the Tax-Free Shopping Cheque service; they can be identified by a special label on their window reading 'Tax-Free for Tourists'. Printed information is available at affiliated shops, some tourist offices, major hotels, airports and harbours.

POST & COMMUNICATIONS

There are dozens of post offices throughout Berlin, most with restricted opening hours (usually from 8am to 6pm weekdays, until noon on Saturday). An exception is the main post office (Map 6; ☎ 01802-33 33) in the Neues Kranzler Eck at Joachimstaler Strasse 7, near Zoo station, which is open from 8am to midnight Monday to Saturday, and from 10am on Sunday and holidays. Most post offices exchange currency and travellers cheques and are good places to fall back on when the banks are closed.

Postal Rates Within Germany and the EU, sending a normal-sized postcard costs €0.51, a 20g letter is €0.56 and a 50g letter is €1.12. Postcards to non-EU destinations cost €1.02, a 20g airmail letter is €1.53 and a 50g airmail letter is €2.05. If the postcard or letter is oversized, there is a significant surcharge, sometimes up to triple the base rate. German postal workers can be very finicky about this and are bound to measure any letter that looks even remotely non-standard. A parcel up to 2kg within Germany costs €3.68. Surface-mail parcels up to 2kg within Europe are €7.67 and to destinations elsewhere €9.71. Airmail fees are €14 for a 2kg parcel sent somewhere within Europe, and €27 for the same parcel going anywhere else in the world.

Sending & Receiving Mail Stamps are sold at post offices, and some branches have stamp machines outside the main entrance. Occasionally souvenir and postcard shops also carry stamps.

Letters sent within Germany usually take only one day for delivery; those addressed to destinations within Europe or to North America take four to six days and to Australasia five to seven days.

Mail can be sent poste restante to any post office. Select one, then inquire about the address, which usually consists of the postal code only (that of the main post office at Joachimstaler Strasse 7 is 10623 Berlin). Ask those sending you mail to mark the letter or package *Postlagernd* and to write your name clearly, followed by the postal code. German post offices will hold mail for two weeks. Bring your passport or other photo ID when picking up mail. This is a free service.

American Express (see Exchanging Money earlier in this chapter for branches) offers a free client-mail service to those with an American Express card or travellers cheques (€1 per item otherwise). The sender should include the words 'Client Mail' somewhere on the envelope. Branches will hold mail for 30 days but won't accept registered post or parcels.

Telephone

Making phone calls in Germany is simple, and with a little forethought it is not necessarily expensive. To ring abroad, dial 00 followed by the country code, local area codes and number. If you're calling Germany from abroad, the country code is 49. The area code for Berlin is 030.

A German operator can be reached on ☎ 0180-200 10 33. Reverse charge calls through this number can only be made to some countries, but it's cheaper to use a home direct service, whereby you reach an operator in your home country for a reverse charge call from Germany. To reach a US operator dial ☎ 0800-888 0013 (Sprint), ☎ 0800-225 52 88 (AT&T) or ☎ 0800-888 8000 (MCI). To Canada dial ☎ 0800-080 1014, to the UK ☎ 0800-0800 044 and to Australia ☎ 0800-0800 061 (Telstra).

For directory assistance within Germany, dial ☎ 11833 (☎ 11837 for information in English). It costs €1 for the first minute and €0.49 after that. For numbers abroad, call ☎ 11834, which will cost you €1.48 for the first minute and €0.97 for each additional minute.

Telephone Rates Rates for calls made from a private phone are split into local and national calls. A local call, which usually extends 20km beyond the city or town limits, costs about €0.06 per 90 seconds during the peak period from 9am to 6pm. National calls cost about €0.12 per minute.

If you are calling internationally from a private phone, you can reduce your cost significantly by using a private call-by-call service which requires you to dial an access code first; ☎ 01050, ☎ 01066 and ☎ 01051 are popular. Dial the access code, then 00 plus the country and area codes.

Most pay phones in Berlin will only accept phonecards. Those sold by Deutsche Telekom (DT) are available for €6.14 and €25.56 at post offices and occasionally at tourist offices, news kiosks and public transport offices. Local calls cost around €0.10 per minute and a call to anywhere else in Germany is about €0.20 per minute. Unlike calls from private phones, calls from public telephone boxes cost the same no matter what time of day you ring.

If you're making an international call from a pay phone, don't use DT cards unless you've got money to burn. Instead, use a prepaid card offered by private companies. These are sold at large newspaper stands, kiosks and discount telephone call shops. ACC is one that is widely available, but there are lots of others, and sometimes the vendor will have leaflets comparing the various cards, countries and costs. Calls to most places cost less than €0.40 per minute, much less to the USA and Canada. Some cards may charge you a connecting fee of €0.50 or so; buy one that doesn't.

If you can, refrain from calling from your hotel room, since you'll often be charged €0.30 or even €0.40 per call unit. If you have a direct-dial phone, you can save considerably if the person you're contacting is willing to call you back. Just place a short call to relay your hotel and room number and tell whoever is calling you back to dial their international access code plus 4930 (Germany code plus Berlin area code) and that number. You can sometimes do the same thing from pay phones that also receive calls by passing on the number next to the notation '*Standort*' (location) somewhere in the box/booth.

Mobile/Cell Phones The mobile/cellular phone craze has spread through Germany as everywhere else. Note that calls made *to* mobile/cellular phones cost a lot more than those to a stationary number, though how much more depends on the service used by the cellular-phone owner. Most mobile/cellular phone numbers begin with 017 or 016. Numbers starting with 0800 are toll-free, while 01805 numbers cost around €0.12 per minute and 0190 numbers are €0.62 per minute.

Germany uses GSM 900/1800, which is compatible with the rest of Europe and Australia but not with the North American GSM 1900 or the totally different system in Japan (though some North Americans have GSM 1900/900 phones that do work here). If you have a GSM phone, check with your service provider about using it in Germany, and beware of calls being routed internationally (very expensive for a 'local' call).

eKno Communication Service Lonely Planet's eKno global communication service provides low-cost international calls – for local calls you're usually better off with a local phonecard. eKno also offers free messaging services, email, travel information and an online travel vault, where you can securely store all your important documents. You can join online at W www.ekno.lonelyplanet.com, where you will find the local-access numbers for the 24-hour customer-service centre. Once you have joined, always check the eKno Web site for the latest access numbers for each country and updates on new features.

Fax

If you're staying at upmarket hotels, fax transmissions are generally not a problem. There's usually no fee for receiving faxes, though sending them can cost a bundle, so it pays to check in advance. Most copy shops will also let you send faxes (see Doing Business later in this chapter for addresses), as will most Internet cafes (see boxed text 'Where to Log On' later in this section).

If you carry a laptop with a fax modem, you only pay for the cost of the telephone call (keep in mind that hotel phone rates are exorbitant). Cheaper, in most cases, is the use of public fax-phones at some post offices and train stations. These operate with a Deutsche Telecom phonecard from which the regular cost of the call, plus a €1.02 service charge, is deducted if the connection succeeds.

Email & Internet Access

Travelling with a portable computer is a great way to stay in touch with life back home, but unless you know what you're doing it's fraught with potential problems. Remember that the power supply voltage in Germany is 220, so make sure that your AC adaptor is compatible; you may also need a plug adaptor for German outlets.

Your PC-card modem may or may not work in Germany – and you won't know for sure until you try. The safest option is to buy a reputable 'global' modem before you leave home, or buy a local PC-card modem if you're spending an extended time in any one country.

The most common modem plug used in Germany is the TAE-N. It has larger notches in some places than phone plugs, so it's useful to carry an adaptor with three inputs (one for the modem plug) that can be plugged into most telephone sockets. You can buy them anywhere in Germany for a couple of euros.

International adapters for German telephone plugs usually accept US RJ-11 plugs, but these are not stocked by all electronics stores, so it's advisable to shop around at home first or seek out a specialist store. Some mid-range and upmarket hotels have telephone sockets that accept RJ-11.

Hardwired telephones (ie, wired to the wall) or complex telephone systems requiring you to adjust your modem string will sometimes be a problem. For more information on travelling with a portable computer, see **W** www.teleadapt.com or **W** www.warrior.com.

Major Internet service providers such as AOL (**W** www.aol.com) and CompuServe (**W** www.compuserve.com) have dial-in nodes in Germany.

If you access your Internet email account at home through a smaller ISP or your office or school network, your best option is either to open an account with a global ISP, like those mentioned above, or to rely on cyber-cafes and other public access points to collect your mail.

DIGITAL RESOURCES

The World Wide Web is a rich resource for travellers. You can research your trip, hunt down bargain air fares, book hotels, find out about weather conditions or chat with locals and other travellers about the best places to visit (or avoid!).

One place to start your Web explorations is the Lonely Planet Web site (**W** www.lonelyplanet.com). Here you'll find succinct summaries on travelling to most places on earth, postcards from other travellers and the Thorn Tree bulletin board, where you can ask questions before you go or dispense advice when you get back. You can also find travel news and updates to many of our most popular guidebooks, and the subWWWay section links you to the most useful travel resources elsewhere on the Web.

There are dozens of Internet Web sites dedicated to Berlin, its culture, institutions, events etc. AOL has a useful page with lots of good links (keyword: Berlin). Most of the sites listed here also provide useful links.

W www.berlin.de Official Web site of the Berlin Senate. Excellent, with thorough information on all aspects of the city, including culture, transport, the economy, politics etc. In English and German.

W www.berlin-tourism.de Web site maintained by the BTM tourist office with information, hotel reservation system, links and historical information. In German and English. Searchable.

Where To Log On?

Most hostels and some hotels now provide Internet access, but Berlin also has plenty of cybercafes to get you online. You'll need three pieces of information to access your email account: your incoming (POP or IMAP) mail server name, your account name and your password. Your ISP or network supervisor will be able to give you these. Armed with this information, you should be able to access your Internet mail account from any net-connected machine in the world, provided it runs some kind of email software (remember that Netscape and Internet Explorer both have mail modules). It pays to become familiar with the process for doing this before you leave home.

In Charlottenburg, Cyberb@r (Map 6; ☎ 88 02 41 98), Joachimstaler Strasse 5–6, is on the top floor of Karstadt Sporthaus, a large sporting goods store. It's open 9am to 8pm Monday to Friday, to 4pm Saturday and has 12 terminals. Computer usage fee is €1/3 for 15/60 minutes of surfing.

Threatening to squash all competition is easyEverything (Map 6; ☎ 88 70 79 70), Kurfürstendamm 224, also in Charlottenburg. This Internet 'factory' has around 350 terminals and is open 24 hours. Surfing costs €1.50 per hour.

In Mitte, one option is Webtimes (Map 3; ☎ 28 04 98 90) at Chausseestrasse 8. Enter through the alleyway to get to this cafe where surfing costs €2.50/4.50 for 30/60 minutes. It's open 2pm till midnight, but closed on Sunday.

The Alpha Internet Café (Map 3; ☎ 447 90 67; S-Bahn: S8 or S10 to Prenzlauer Allee), Dunckerstrasse 72 in Prenzlauer Berg, is a well-kitted out, relaxed place. Boasting 10 computers, printers, scanners and other equipment, it is open from 2pm to midnight daily and charges €1/3/5 for 10/30/60 minutes of online time.

Schöneberg has Internet Café Hai Täck (Map 4; ☎ 85 96 14 13; U/S-Bahn: U9 or S4/45/46 to Bundesplatz) at Brünnhildestrasse 8. This cafe has AOL and compuserve, a fax service and good food.

W www.berlinfo.com This is a useful and, for the most part, well-researched English-language Web site written by a network of locals. Much of the information is geared towards expats, but there's plenty of useful stuff for visitors too.

W www.people-in-berlin.de Low-tech Web site in German, English and French specifically targeted to young, international budget travellers. Lots of links.

W www.berlin-hidden-places.de This wonderful Web site offers a virtual tour of less well-known architectural, cultural and commercial places throughout Berlin. In German and English.

W www.dhm.de Web site of the Museum of German History, but best for its links to other museums in Berlin and Brandenburg. In English and German.

W www.chemie.fu-berlin.de This Web site maintained by the Chemistry Institute of the Free University has the best link collection to Berlin-related sites. (To get to the right page, switch to the English version at the bottom of the home page, then click on the User Pages link, then on About Berlin under Miscellaneous.) In German and English (though not all links).

BOOKS

Most books are published in different editions by different publishers in different countries. As a result, a book might be a hardcover rarity in one country while it's readily available in paperback in another. Fortunately, bookshops and libraries search by title or author, so your local bookshop or library should be able to advise you on the availability of any of the books recommended in this guide.

Lonely Planet

Lonely Planet's *Germany* is an excellent source for those planning to travel around the country extensively. It contains up-to-date information on all popular mainstream travel spots, as well as eye-opening destinations that are off the beaten track. Lonely Planet's *Central Europe*, *Western Europe* and *Europe* all include a big Germany chapter for those on a grand 'shoestring' tour, in which case the *Central Europe Phrasebook* might also come in handy. Lonely Planet also publishes a *German Phrasebook* so you can chat with the locals. If you plan to spend some time in other German cities, look into the *Munich* city guide and the *Frankfurt Condensed* guide. All books are available at good book-stores or may be ordered from the Lonely Planet Web site at **W** www.lonelyplanet.com.

Guidebooks

Berlin for Young People, which is published by Herden Studienreisen Berlin, gives a quick overview of clubs, museums, hang-outs, tours, restaurants and other information. Published in English and German, it sells for around €5 at the tourist office and major bookstores.

History

Berlin, Then and Now by Tony Le Tissier is a fascinating record of the modern history of Berlin told largely in black and white photo-graphs. The accompanying text is heavy sledding, perhaps because the author was the warden of Spandau prison, a time he has chronicled in *Farewell to Spandau*. It was actually on his watch that Prisoner No 7 committed suicide; a man by the name of Rudolf Hess.

The Biography of a City by Anthony Read and David Fisher is an excellent social his-tory tracing the life of the city from its be-ginnings to post-Wall times. The *very* expensive *Berlin and its Culture* by Ronald Taylor is lavishly illustrated and traces the cultural history of Berlin from medieval be-ginnings through to the 1990s.

A wide body of work deals with the years between WWI and WWII and the artistic brilliance and moral decadence that marked the city in the 1920s. The list includes *Before the Deluge* by Otto Friedrich, but a more en-gaging read is *A Dance Between Flames* by Anton Gill.

There's a plethora of English-language books about Nazi Germany and Berlin's role during those 12 years. *The Rise and Fall of the Third Reich* by William Shirer, a one-time Berlin correspondent, remains one of the most powerful works of reportage ever written. His portrait of the Berlin of those times – a city which he loved, grew to fear and eventually fled – is considered a giant of the genre.

Inside the Third Reich by Albert Speer is one of the best books about the day-to-day operations of Hitler's inner clique. It was written by the brilliant architect who stood at the Führer's elbow and built much of the Berlin that would be bombed into rubble. For another take on the same troubling sub-ject there's *Albert Speer: His Battle With Truth* by Gitta Sereny. In over 700 pages, you'll learn of the life and times of one of the more controversial – and somehow oddly tragic – Nazi figures.

The Fall of Berlin, another co-production by Anthony Read and David Fisher, is con-sidered one of the standards on the subject of the apocalyptic last days of the war and the Wagnerian death of Adolf Hitler. Still the defining work on the subject is *The Last Days of Hitler* by Hugh Trevor-Roper, in which much idle speculation about Hitler's ultimate fate is firmly laid to rest. The writ-ing style is atrocious but the content makes it forgivable: it was written by a young in-telligence officer in 1947. *The Road to Berlin* by John Erickson is an exhaustive military chronicle of the Soviet Union's war against the Nazis.

Jews in Germany: After the Holocaust by Lynn Rapaport is based on interviews with nearly 100 Jews who continue to live in Ger-many and deals with how the memory of the Holocaust has affected their lives. There are many touching passages about the love/hate aspects of the German/Jewish relationship and much insight into how difficult it is to develop real friendships between Jews and Germans.

Books dealing with life and society dur-ing the GDR era include *Man Without a Face: The Memoirs of a Spymaster* by Markus Wolf and Anne McElvoy. It is the autobiography of Wolf himself. He was the enormously successful chief of East Ger-many's intelligence services – the hated Stasi – and, like Albert Speer, he is regarded by some as an admirable monster. For a more withering portrait of Wolf, seek out *Spymaster: The Real Life Karla* by Leslie Colitt, who concludes that there's ab-solutely nothing admirable about the man who ruined lives with such perverse joy and then prospered from the agony and destruc-tion he engineered.

Berlin and The Wall by Ann Tusa is a saga of the events, trials and triumphs of the Cold War, the building of the Wall and its effects on the people and the city of Berlin. For a chilling read about the days after the fall of the Wall there's *The File* by Timothy Garton Ash, an author who discovered his own Stasi files while doing research in Berlin. The book is full of personal accounts of the confrontations between the author and those who stalked him.

General

Christopher Isherwood will always be synonymous with Berlin because of the classic film *Cabaret*, which was based on his semi-autobiographical work *Goodbye to Berlin*. It remains a must-read because of its often hilarious descriptions of a young man lost in the Berlin of the 1920s, an anarchic and lurid age. It should be read for its wonderful descriptions of the people and events of the time.

Aimée & Jaguar by Erica Fischer is the true story of two women in Berlin who fell in love during the warped and dangerous days of 1942. It's all the more remarkable a tale in that one of the women was a mother of four and married to a German soldier while the other was Jewish. The photographs are poignant, to say the least. It was made into a movie in 1999.

Billing herself as 'Berlin's most distinguished transvestite', Charlotte von Mahlsdorf has written a rollicking account of her outlaw life as celebrated crackpot, museum owner and GDR cultural fixture in the ironically titled *I Am My Own Woman*.

Architecture students and professionals will love *Bauwelt Berlin Annual: Chronology of Building Events 1996–2001*, a series of annual volumes chronicling the new face of Berlin as it emerges. *Berlin/Brandenburg*, published by Ernst & Sohn, is a good general primer on the subject, in English and German, with copious photographs.

FILMS

For a discussion of films set in Berlin and/or made locally, see the Arts section in the Facts about Berlin chapter.

NEWSPAPERS & MAGAZINES
German

The newspaper with the largest circulation in Berlin is the *BZ*, which is borderline sensationalist and practically devoid of meaningful content. It is, believe it or not, a step up from *Bild*, which woos readers with headlines like 'Sex Waves From Space' and photographs of scantily clad young women. *BZ* is not to be confused with the respected *Berliner Zeitung*, a left-leaning daily newspaper that is most widely read in the eastern districts.

The *Berliner Morgenpost* is especially noted for its vast classified section; its Sunday edition is where to look first for cars, flats, second-hand appliances etc. *Der Tagesspiegel* has a centre-right political orientation, a solid news and foreign section and decent cultural coverage. At the left end of the spectrum is the alternative *taz* which appeals to an intellectual crowd with its news analysis and thorough reporting.

Early editions of some dailies are available after 9pm from newspaper vendors passing through pubs and restaurants or positioned outside theatres and U-Bahn stations.

Die Zeit is a highbrow national weekly newspaper with in-depth reporting on everything from politics to fashion. Germany's most widely read weekly news magazines are *Der Spiegel* and the much lighter *Focus*. Both offer hard-hitting investigative journalism and a certain degree of government criticism between covers often featuring scantily-clad models. *Stern* bites harder on the popular nerve.

Zitty and *tip* are Berlin's best bi-weekly what's-on magazines. See Listings in the Entertainment chapter for details.

English

English-language newspapers and magazines – most from the UK and the USA – are readily available. Look for them in larger bookstores and at international newsagents, especially those at larger train stations.

The *International Herald Tribune*, edited in Paris with wire stories from the *New York Times* and *Washington Post*, is the most commonly available English-language daily paper; it sells for €2.05.

The biggies from the UK include *The Guardian* (€2.05), the *Financial Times* (€2.20) and *The London Times* (€2.50). From the USA, *USA Today* (€2.05) has made huge inroads, and the *Wall Street Journal* (€2.15) is also available.

As for magazines, *The Economist* (€4.10) is on sale widely, as are the international editions of *Time* and *Newsweek* (both €4.10). In addition, practically the whole gamut of women's, car, lifestyle and speciality magazines are available as well. *Spotlight* (€4.90) is a monthly English-language magazine for Germans who want to learn English, with good feature articles and travel pieces.

RADIO & TV

Berlin has a bewildering choice of radio stations, many increasingly modelled on US-style contemporary music shows interspersed with inane talk and advertisement. If you like that kind of thing, check out the youth-oriented Fritz at 102.6, the techno-driven Kiss at 98.8 or Radio Energy at 103.4. The BBC broadcasts at 90.2. Among the more sophisticated stations is Radio Eins (95.8) which has lots of high-quality programming with topical information and political and social themes. SFB4, aka Radio Multikulti (106.8), is an excellent multicultural station with music and event information about various ethnic groups. It occasionally broadcasts in the respective languages. Jazz fiends should check out Jazzradio at 101.9, while classical music rules Klassik-Radio at 101.3. InfoRadio at 93.1 has an all-news format, including live interviews.

Most mid-range and all top-end hotel rooms have a television set and most will be hooked up to a cable connection or a satellite dish, providing access to at least 15 channels. English-language channels broadcast within Germany include CNN, BBC World, CNBC and MSNBC. The quality of the reception, though, depends on the location, on whether the TV is hooked up to cable or to a satellite dish and on the quality of the television set.

Germany has two national public channels, the ARD (Allgemeiner Rundfunk Deutschlands, commonly known as Erstes Deutsches Fernsehen) and the ZDF (Zweites Deutsches Fernsehen). The Berlin channels B1 and ORB (Ostdeutscher Rundfunk Brandenburg) are regional public stations. Generally, programming is relatively highbrow featuring political coverage, discussion forums and foreign films. Advertising is limited to the two hours between 6pm and 8pm.

Private cable TV offers the familiar array of sitcoms and soap operas (including many dubbed US shows), chat and game shows and, of course, feature films of all stripes. DSF and EuroSport are dedicated sports channels, and MTV and its German equivalent VIVA can also be received. Commercial breaks are frequent on these stations.

The content of private TV is often salacious – a copulating couple advertising margarine, a 13-year-old kid advising her parents on successful orgasm techniques, and that sort of thing. Some of it is within a hair of being X-rated. Several Turkish-language channels cater for Germany's large population with roots in Turkey.

VIDEO SYSTEMS

German video and television operates on the PAL (Phase Alternative Line) system that predominates in most of Europe and Australia. It is not compatible with the American and Japanese NTSC or French SECAM standards; pre-recorded video tapes bought in countries using those standards won't play in Germany and vice versa.

PHOTOGRAPHY & VIDEO
Film & Equipment

German photographic equipment is among the best in the world. All makes and types are readily available, as are those manufactured in other countries, though bargains are rare. Print film is sold at supermarkets and chemists, but for B&W and slide film you'll have to go to a photographic store. The latter two are hard to find (or sold at inflated prices) outside the city, so stock up if you're taking a day trip from Berlin.

For general-purpose shooting – either prints or slides – 100 ASA film is the most useful and versatile as it gives you good colour and enough speed to capture most situations on film. For shooting in dark areas or in brightly lit night scenes without a tripod, switch to 400 ASA.

The best and most widely available films are made by Fuji, Kodak and Agfa. Fuji Velvia and Kodak Elite are easy to process and provide good slide images. Stay away from Kodachrome: it's difficult to process quickly and creates major headaches if not handled properly. For print film you can't beat Kodak Gold, though Fuji and Agfa have just about perfected their films for print as well.

Film of any type is inexpensive in Germany, so there's no need to stock up at home. For a roll of 36-exposure standard print film, expect to pay around €3. The cost for good slide film should be around €5 to €7. The cost per roll goes down significantly if you buy in packages of five or 10 rolls, so shop around. Occasionally, processing is included with the purchase of the film, which is a great deal if you have the time to wait. Slide film comes back unframed, unless you specify that you want the images framed (gerahmt) in which case an extra charge applies.

Chemists and supermarkets are cheap places to get your film processed, provided you don't need professional quality developing. Standard developing for print film is about €2, plus €0.20 for each 10cm by 15cm print (allow about four days), and about €0.30 per print for overnight service. Processing slide film costs about €1.75 in these shops; if you want it mounted, your total comes to about €3.50. All prices quoted are for rolls of 36.

Full-service professional developers include PPS (Map 7; ☎ 726 10 90) at Alexanderplatz 6 in Mitte, open 8am to 8pm Monday to Friday and noon to 5pm Saturday. In Tiergarten at Potsdamer Strasse 98 is Jacobs & Schulz (Map 4; ☎ 261 80 20) which has even better hours: 8am to 10pm weekdays and (almost unheard of in Germany!) from noon to 6pm both Saturday and Sunday. Many of the staff at both places speak English.

Video recorders bought in North America or Japan can record with German-bought tapes and then play back with no problems. The size of the tapes is the same, only the method of recording and playback differs between PAL and NTSC standards. A standard VHS tape costs between €3 to €5.

Airport Security

In the wake of the terrorist attacks in the USA on 11 September, 2001, basic security checks at all airports around the world have been upgraded.

Immediate measures include the increased use of high-intensity x-ray scanners to inspect (checked) luggage, which will damage all unprocessed film.

Be sure to carry film and loaded cameras in your carry-on luggage. Currently, the standard conveyor belts for x-ray scanning of carry-on baggage should not cause damage to unprocessed film. However, to make absolutely sure that your film is not damaged, ask security staff to inspect it manually. Pack all your film into a clear plastic or mesh bag that you can quickly whip out of your luggage. Manual inspection may not be available at all airports, however.

TIME

Throughout Germany clocks are set to Central European Time (GMT/UTC plus one hour), the same time zone as Madrid and Warsaw. Daylight-saving time comes into effect on the last Sunday in March, when clocks are turned forward one hour. On the last Sunday in October they are turned back an hour. Without taking daylight-saving times into account, when it's noon in Berlin, it's 11am in London, 6am in New York, 3am in San Francisco, 8pm in Tokyo, 9pm in Sydney and 11pm in Auckland. Official times (eg, shop hours, train schedules, film screenings etc) are usually indicated by the 24-hour clock, eg, 6.30pm is 18.30.

ELECTRICITY

Electricity is 220V, 50 Hz AC. Plugs are the European type with two round pins. Your 220V appliances may be plugged into a German outlet with an adaptor, though their

110V cousins (eg, from North America) require a transformer. Some electric devices – shavers and most laptops – work on both 110V and 220V.

WEIGHTS & MEASURES

Germany uses the metric system – there's a conversion table on the inside back cover of this book. Like other Continental Europeans, Germans indicate decimals with commas and thousands with points (ie 10,000.00 is 10.000,00). Cheese, vegetables and other food items are often sold by the *Pfund* (pound), which means 500 grams.

Clothing sizes – especially for women's clothing – are quite different from those in North America (NA) and Great Britain. Women's size 8 in NA (size 10 in the UK) equals size 36 in Germany. Sizes then increase in increments of two, making German size 38 an NA 10 (UK 12) and so on.

Shoes are another matter altogether. NA size 5 (UK 3) is size 36 in Germany. It continues in increments of one, so that NA 6 (UK 4) equals size 37. Just to make things more complicated, men's sizes are a bit different. A men's 41 equates to an NA 8 (UK 7). A men's 42 would be an NA 9 (UK 8) etc.

LAUNDRY

Coin-operated laundrettes *(Münzwäscherei)* are normally open from 6am to 9pm or 10pm. A load of washing costs €3 to €3.50, including soap powder; the dryer is €0.50 per 10 minutes. In most laundrettes you select your machine and deposit the coin(s) in a central machine with numbers corresponding to the washers and dryers. The panel also distributes soap powder, so have at the ready one of the plastic cups you'll find strewn around the laundrette.

The Schnell + Sauber chain has many laundrettes across Berlin, including at Torstrasse 115 in Mitte (Map 3), Uhlandstrasse 53 and Leibnizstrasse 72 in Charlottenburg (Map 6), Bergmannstrasse 109 in Kreuzberg 61 (Map 5), Karl-Marx-Strasse 19 in Kreuzberg 36 (Map 5), and Raumerstrasse 7 in Prenzlauer Berg (Map 3). Mitte also has Eco-Express at Rosenthaler Strasse 71 (Map 3).

TOILETS

Public toilets are not ubiquitous in Berlin and you may have to pay €0.10 to €1 for the privilege of using one. Sneaking into a bar or restaurant is an easy alternative, though it's best to pick a busy place to avoid withering stares from the staff. The public facilities in department stores are usually a better choice. If there's an attendant, it's nice to tip €0.25 or so if the toilet was clean. All train stations have toilets; Zoo station even has a spic-and-span establishment called McWash where you can take a shower for €6, soap and towel included. Overall, the standard of hygiene is high, although toilets in some pubs and nightclubs can be outright disgusting.

Occasionally you'll also see self-cleaning toilet pods (€0.25), some of which are gay hang-outs, such as the public toilet below Alexanderplatz near the World Time Clock.

LEFT-LUGGAGE

There are storage facilities at the airports and all major train stations. The cost is around €2 per piece per day. Also see the Getting There & Away and Getting Around chapters.

HEALTH
Medical Services

Berlin has about 6000 doctors and 2600 dentists, so you're quite likely to find one nearby by checking under *Ärzte* in the phonebook. Alternatively, or in emergencies, call the 24-hour referral service at ☎ 31 00 31. Hotel staff can usually make recommendations as well.

To find out where to turn for after-hours emergency dental care, call ☎ 89 00 43 33. The Zahnklinik Medeco has some English-speaking doctors. There are several branches throughout Berlin of which the most central is at Stresemannstrasse 121, just south of Potsdamer Platz (Map 7; ☎ 23 09 59 60). It's open from 7am to midnight daily (appointments till 9pm, emergencies till midnight).

Make sure you have adequate health insurance (see Travel Insurance in the Documents section earlier in this chapter). The standard of health care is excellent in Germany, but is expensive unless you're an EU citizen, in which case first aid and emergency health care are free with an E111 form.

No vaccinations are required to visit Germany, except if you're coming from an infected area – a jab against yellow fever is the most likely requirement. If you're going to Berlin with stopovers in Asia, Africa or Latin America, check with your travel agent or with the German embassy or consulate nearest you.

If you're travelling on to a country where vaccinations are required, you can get them at the Tropen- und Reisemedizinisches Institut (☎ 395 64 34) at Wiclefstrasse 2 in Tiergarten (U9 to Birkenstrasse).

Berlin's tap water is safe to drink.

Hospitals There are hospitals all over Berlin but the following are university affiliated and have large, 24-hour emergency rooms. If you need an ambulance, call ☎ 112.

Uniklinikum Benjamin Franklin (☎ 844 50, emergencies ☎ 84 45 30 15/25), Hindenburgdamm 30 in Steglitz.

Uniklinikum Charité (Map 3; ☎ 282 00, emergencies ☎ 28 02 47 66), Schumannstrasse 20–21, just off Luisenstrasse in Mitte (U-Bahn: U6 to Oranienburger Tor). This is the most central major hospital.

Uniklinikum Rudolf Virchow (Map 2; ☎ 450 50, emergencies ☎ 45 05 20 00), Augustenburger Platz 1 in Wedding.

Pharmacies German drugstores (*Drogerie*) do not sell any kind of medication, not even aspirin. Even for over-the-counter *(rezeptfrei)* medications for minor health concerns, like flu or a stomach upset, you need to go to a pharmacy *(Apotheke)*. For more serious conditions, you will need to bring a prescription *(Rezept)* from a licensed physician. If you need medication after hours, call ☎ 31 00 31. The names and addresses of pharmacies open after hours (these rotate) are posted in any pharmacy window. Alternatively call ☎ 011 41.

Infectious Diseases

HIV & AIDS Infection with the human immunodeficiency virus (HIV) may lead to acquired immune deficiency syndrome (AIDS), which is a fatal disease. Any exposure to blood, blood products or body fluids may put the individual at risk. The disease is often transmitted through unprotected sex or dirty needles, including those used for vaccinations, acupuncture, tattooing and body piercing. Fear of HIV infection should never preclude treatment for serious medical conditions.

There are a couple of major organisations in Berlin in case you need support. The Berliner AIDS-Hilfe (Berlin AIDS Help; Map 6; ☎ 885 64 00), at Meinekestrasse 12, is dedicated to prevention, counselling and support for those infected with HIV. Counselling by phone is from 10am to midnight daily. The Deutsche AIDS-Hilfe (German AIDS Help; Map 5; ☎ 690 08 70), at Dieffenbachstrasse 33 in Kreuzberg is mostly a political interest group fighting for the rights of the HIV-positive.

Sexually Transmitted Diseases HIV/AIDS and hepatitis B can be transmitted through sexual contact, as can gonorrhoea, herpes and syphilis; sores, blisters or rashes around the genitals and discharges or pain when urinating are common symptoms. In some STDs, such as chlamydia or wart virus, symptoms may be less marked or not observed at all, especially in women. Chlamydia infection can cause infertility in men and women before any symptoms

---

Everyday Health

Normal body temperature is up to 37°C (98.6°F); more than 2°C (4°F) higher indicates a high fever. The normal adult pulse rate is 60 to 100 per minute (children 80 to 100, babies 100 to 140). As a general rule the pulse increases about 20 beats per minute for each 1°C (2°F) rise in fever.

Respiration (breathing) rate is also an indicator of illness. Count the number of breaths per minute: Between 12 and 20 is normal for adults and older children (up to 30 for younger children, 40 for babies). People with a high fever or serious respiratory illness breathe more quickly than normal. More than 40 shallow breaths a minute may indicate pneumonia.

have been noticed. Syphilis symptoms eventually disappear completely but the disease continues and can cause severe problems in later years. While abstinence from sexual contact is the only 100% effective prevention, using condoms is also effective. The treatment of gonorrhoea and syphilis is with antibiotics. The different sexually transmitted diseases each require specific antibiotics.

WOMEN TRAVELLERS

Women shouldn't encounter too many difficulties or harassment in Berlin, though naturally it pays to use common sense. Getting hassled in the streets is rare and most common when walking past a bunch of construction guys on their break. Cat-whistles and hollering are best ignored as any immediate response to them will be interpreted as encouragement.

Younger German women are quite emancipated and just as likely to initiate contact with the opposite sex as men are. Such confidence, however, hasn't yet translated into equality in the workplace where sexual harassment is more commonplace and tolerated than in other countries like the USA, UK and Australia.

Many women juggle jobs and children, but there's an extensive network of public, church-run and private kindergartens and daycare centres to fall back on.

The women's movement is very active in Germany and women's centres abound. These include EWA (Map 3; ☎ 442 55 42 or ☎ 442 72 57), at Prenzlauer Allee 6 in Prenzlauer Berg, open 2pm to 8pm Monday to Thursday; Frieda (Map 3; ☎ 422 42 76), Proskauer Strasse 7 in Friedrichshain; and Paula Panke (☎ 485 47 02), Schulstrasse 6 in Pankow.

Organisations

The following organisations may prove useful in times of crisis:

Frauenkrisentelefon (Women's Crisis Hotline; ☎ 615 42 43 and ☎ 615 75 96) is a listening and referral service for anyone wanting to talk about any kind of problem. It's staffed from 10am to noon Monday and Thursday, from 7pm to 9pm Tuesday, Wednesday and Friday, and from 5pm to 7pm weekends.

LARA (☎ 216 88 88) is a rape crisis and advisory centre for women. The staff provide free and anonymous support and referrals to therapy, medical and legal help from 9am to midnight Monday to Thursday and 24 hours Friday to Sunday.

Medical Kit Check List

Following is a list of items you should consider including in your medical kit – consult your pharmacist for brands available in your country.

- ☐ **Aspirin or paracetamol (acetaminophen in the USA)** – for pain or fever
- ☐ **Antihistamine** – for allergies, eg, hay fever; to ease the itch from insect bites or stings; and to prevent motion sickness
- ☐ **Cold and flu tablets, throat lozenges and nasal decongestant**
- ☐ **Multivitamins** – consider for long trips, when dietary vitamin intake may be inadequate
- ☐ **Antibiotics** – consider including these if you're travelling well off the beaten track; see your doctor, as they must be prescribed, and carry the prescription with you
- ☐ **Loperamide or diphenoxylate** –'blockers' for diarrhoea
- ☐ **Prochlorperazine or metaclopramide** – for nausea and vomiting
- ☐ **Rehydration mixture** – to prevent dehydration, which may occur, for example, during bouts of diarrhoea; particularly important when travelling with children
- ☐ **Insect repellent, sunscreen, lip balm and eye drops**
- ☐ **Calamine lotion, sting relief spray or aloe vera** – to ease irritation from sunburn and insect bites or stings
- ☐ **Antifungal cream or powder** – for fungal skin infections and thrush
- ☐ **Antiseptic (such as povidone-iodine)** – for cuts and grazes
- ☐ **Bandages, Band-Aids (plasters) and other wound dressings**
- ☐ **Water purification tablets or iodine**
- ☐ **Scissors, tweezers and a thermometer** – note that mercury thermometers are prohibited by airlines

GAY & LESBIAN TRAVELLERS

Germans are generally fairly tolerant of homosexuality and Berlin is certainly the country's most progressive city. It's estimated that up to 500,000 gays and lesbians call Berlin their home. The sight of homosexual couples holding hands is not uncommon and kissing in public is becoming more practised and accepted. Gays are known as *Schwule* (formerly a pejorative term equivalent to 'queer' but now a moniker worn with pride and dignity), lesbians are *Lesben*.

Information

The best and most up-to-date publication is the free monthly *Siegessäule*. Visit the associated (German only) Web site at **w** www .siegessaeule.de. This and *Sergej* can be found at bars, clubs and information centres. Another option is the slick monthly *Männer Aktuell* (€7.50), available at newsagents.

Another source (in German only) is *Homopolis* (€14.50) by Micha Schulze and published by the people from *Siegessäule* magazine. A thorough guide (in English and German) to Berlin's gay scene is the piquantly named *Berlin von Hinten* (Berlin from Behind, €11.50) by Bruno Gmünder, available at mainstream and gay bookshops (see the Shopping chapter). Lesbians who read German should check out Traude Bührmann's *Lesbisches Berlin* (€12.25), an exhaustive overview of the scene, its history and cool places.

Organisations

Berlin has numerous organisations you can turn to for information or support. Lesbians might also want to check out the women's centres listed in the previous Women Travellers section.

International Lesbian & Gay Association (☎ 392 53 11), at Ebersfelder Strasse 23, is ILGA's Berlin chapter; Hartmut Schönknecht is the contact person.

Lesbenberatung (Map 4; Lesbian Advisory Service, ☎ 215 20 00) is at Kulmer Strasse 20a in Schöneberg and open 4pm to 7pm Monday, Tuesday and Thursday, Wednesday 10am to 1pm and 2pm to 5pm Friday.

Mann-O-Meter (Map 4; ☎ 216 80 08 or 0700-MANNOMETER, **e** info@mann-o-meter.de, **w** www.mann-o-meter.de), Bülowstrasse 106 in Schöneberg, is Berlin's best-established and oldest information and support centre. Geared primarily towards gay men, it is open from 5pm to 10pm Monday to Saturday, from 4pm Sunday. Come here for free publications, flyers and pamphlets, to pick the volunteer staff's brains about the local scene or to find a place to stay (see 'Gay & Lesbian Hotels' in the Places to Stay chapter). Mann-O-Meter also operates the Gay Attack Hotline (☎ 216 33 36) which documents violent attacks against gays and lesbians and provides support to the victims (staffed 6pm to 9pm daily).

Miles (Map 5; ☎ 44 00 82 40, helpline 0174-604 61 06), at Katzbachstrasse 5 in Kreuzberg, offers legal, coming-out and other counselling to non-Germans, also in English. It's staffed 10am to 5pm Monday to Thursday, to 2pm Friday.

Schwulenberatung (Map 6; Gay Advisory Service, ☎ 19446 or 32 70 30 40) is just what it says and is located at Mommsenstrasse 45, on the corner of Wilmersdorfer Strasse, in Wilmersdorf. Staff are usually around from 11am to 7pm Monday to Friday.

DISABLED TRAVELLERS

Overall, Germany does reasonably well in catering for the needs of disabled people *(Behinderte)*, especially the wheelchair-bound. You'll find access ramps and/or lifts in many public buildings, including toilets, train stations, museums, theatres and cinemas. Other disabilities, like blindness or deafness, are less catered for, and the German organisations for disabled people continue to lobby for improvements.

Getting around Berlin on public transport in a wheelchair is possible but requires some planning. Buses with a blue wheelchair symbol have special ramps which can be pulled out. This works fine as long as the driver knows how to do it or the equipment isn't broken. Getting onto U-Bahn and S-Bahn trains isn't as much of a problem as getting onto the platform itself. Many stations have lifts (marked on route maps with the blue symbol), but these don't always work. To find out which are working, you can call Berlin public transport (BVG) at ☎ 194 49. BVG also publishes a brochure with helpful hints on using their system with a wheelchair. The easiest way to get around, of course, is by calling a taxi company and asking for a *Behindertentaxi*.

Disabled people can turn for information and support to the Berliner-Behinderten-Verband (☎ 927 03 60), Bizetstrasse 51–53 or Movado (☎ 471 51 45, **W** www.movado.de) at Langhansstrasse 64, both in Weissensee. Movado's Web site is in German and English. The Verband Geburts-und anderer Behinderter (Disabled Persons' Association; ☎ 341 17 97) operates a free wheelchair-hire service.

SENIOR TRAVELLERS

Museums and other sights, public swimming pools, spas and some forms of transport such as Deutsche Bahn (DB) trains usually offer discounts to retired people, old-age pensioners and those over 60. Even if discounts are not posted, it's worth asking *'Gibt es Ermässigungen für Senioren?'* If you're on a tight budget, keep in mind that there's no age limit for stays at most of Berlin's independent and DJH hostels, and that student cafeterias at universities, which offer cheap meals, are open to anyone.

BERLIN FOR CHILDREN

Successful travel with young children requires planning and effort. Don't try to overdo things; even for adults, packing too much into a day can cause fatigue and frustration. And make sure the activities include the kids as well – balance that day on Museum Island with a visit to the zoo or a park. Include the kids in the planning; if they've helped to work out where you are going, they will be much more interested when they get there. Lonely Planet's *Travel with Children* by Cathy Lanigan is a good source of information on this subject.

Most car-rental firms in Germany have children's safety seats for hire at a nominal cost, but it is essential to book them in advance. The same goes for highchairs and cots (cribs); they're common in restaurants and hotels, but numbers are limited. The choice of baby food, infant formulas, soy and cow's milk, disposable nappies (diapers) etc is great in Berlin supermarkets, but keep in mind store-trading hours – run out of nappies

on Saturday afternoon and you're facing a very long and messy weekend. Nappy-changing stations can be found in many public toilets at train stations and department stores as well as family-oriented restaurants.

It's perfectly acceptable to bring your kids, even toddlers, along to casual restaurants (though you would raise eyebrows at upmarket ones, especially at dinner time), cafes and daytime events. They're even allowed in bars and pubs, although the cigarette smoke may be uncomfortable for them.

Baby-sitting service is offered by most of the larger hotels and others may be able to help you make arrangements. Alternatively, there are a number of agencies you could contact. The Heinzelmännchen (☎ 831 60 71) can arrange for students from the Free University to come at short notice. Prices are €35/40 for three/four hours, or €7.50 per hour for five hours or more. TUSMA (☎ 315 93 40) has similar rates. Another one is Aufgepasst (☎ 851 37 23), which has 200 registered and background-checked baby-sitters and charges €6 to €7.50 per hour, plus a fee to the agency (negotiable).

Museums

Most of Berlin's museums are not particularly kid-friendly. In fact, the security staff's penetrating stares are unpleasant to most adults, let alone to little ones. Sucking on a bottle or eating a banana are out of the question in most places and don't even think about letting your tots run around – their movement may set off the sensitive alarms. Following is a list of museums where kids – and you – don't have to feel like social outcasts. Most are mentioned in greater detail in the Things to See & Do chapter.

Domäne Dahlem in Zehlendorf, this farming estate from 1560, illustrates the daily workings of a large Berlin farm at that time (see Western Districts – Zehlendorf section in the Things to See & Do chapter).

Juniormuseum, part of the Museum of Ethnology in Dahlem, has changing kid-oriented exhibits and events intended to awaken tolerance of and teach understanding for other cultures (see Western Districts – Zehlendorf section in the Things to See & Do chapter).

Museum für Naturkunde (Museum of Natural History; Map 3) is a sure winner with dinosaur fans (see Mitte section in the Things to See & Do chapter).

Museum Kindheit & Jugend (Museum of Childhood & Youth; Map 7; ☎ 275 03 83, Wallstrasse 32, Mitte; adult/concession €2/1; open 9am-5pm Tues-Fri) Also known as the School Museum, this place traces the history of education from the late 19th century to the 1950s. You can see textbooks and notebooks, ink pots, grade reports and chalkboards, plus pick up fascinating tidbits like the purpose of the *Eselskappe* (donkey hat) which had to be worn by undisciplined kids.

Museumsdorf Düppel (Düppel Museum Village), a re-created medieval village with Sunday demonstrations of old-time crafts (see Western Districts – Zehlendorf).

Puppentheater-Museum Berlin (Map 5; ☎ 687 81 32, Karl-Marx-Strasse 135, rear building, Neukölln; adult/child €2.50/2; open 9am-4pm Mon-Fri, 11am-5pm Sun; U-Bahn: U7 to Karl-Marx-Strasse) Changing exhibits tell the history of puppet theatre while displaying a wealth of hand puppets, marionettes, stick figures and other dolls from around the world. Puppet theatre performances (€4.50 per person) take place each Saturday.

Spectrum at Deutsches Technikmuseum (German Technical Museum; Map 5) has around 300 experiment stations where kids can discover why the sky is blue or how a battery works (see Kreuzberg section in Things To See & Do).

Theatre

For children's and youth-oriented theatre, see the Entertainment chapter.

LIBRARIES

Berlin has a comprehensive network of about 350 public libraries with a total of 5 million tomes. Most libraries also have international periodicals, videos, CD-ROMs, photocopiers and games. Internet access is becoming more common. As a visitor you may go to any library and browse for as long as you want for free, but only Berlin residents may obtain a library card needed to borrow materials.

Amerika-Gedenkbibliothek (AGB; Map 5; America Memorial Library; ☎ 69 08 40, Blücherplatz 1, Kreuzberg) U-Bahn: U7 to Mehringdamm. Open 3pm-7pm Mon, from 11am Tues-Sat. Commemorating the Berlin Airlift, this is the largest circulating library in Germany.

Staatsbibliothek (National Library; branches: Map 7, ☎ 266 12 30, Unter den Linden 8, Mitte; & Map 2, ☎ 26 61, Potsdamer Strasse 33, Tiergarten) Open 9am-9pm Mon-Fri, to 7pm Sat. The Mitte branch, the so-called Old National Library – has books published until 1955, while the New National Library stocks post-1955 works. The Staatsbibliothek is not part of the public library system. You need ID to enter, so bring your passport or other ID. To understand how to read or borrow books, pick up the leaflet 'Notes for First-Time Users' by the entrance.

Zentrum für Berlin-Studien (Centre for Berlin Studies; Map 7; ☎ 20 28 61 49, Breite Strasse 35–36, Mitte). Open 10am-7pm Mon-Fri, 1pm-6pm Sat. This studious place is packed with anything you ever wanted to know about Berlin (350,000 items).

Berliner Stadtbibliothek (Berlin City Library; Map 7; ☎ 90 22 60, Breite Strasse 32–34, Mitte). Open 10am-7pm Mon-Fri, to 6pm Sat. Recently renovated, this public library next door, specialises in the fields of mathematics, computer and natural sciences and law.

UNIVERSITIES

Berlin has the largest student body in Germany with a total of 133,000 students, of which 17% are foreigners. The three largest universities are the Humboldt Universität (Map 7; ☎ 209 30) at Unter den Linden 6 in Mitte, the Freie Universität Berlin (☎ 83 81) at Kaiserwertherstrasse 16–18 in Zehlendorf and the Technische Universität (☎ 31 40) at Hardenbergstrasse and Strasse des 17 Juni in Charlottenburg. Berlin also has 10 polytechnics, four arts academies and around 80 state-subsidised research facilities. (Also see Education in the Facts about Berlin chapter and individual entries in the Things to See & Do chapter.)

INTERNATIONAL CENTRES

Cosmopolitan Berlin has a number of international cultural institutes. Most have active events schedules as well as libraries with books, videos and periodicals from the country they represent. Other offerings include message boards, information about exchange programs, language courses and exhibitions. Some even have cafes and cinemas.

Amerika Haus, Hardenbergstrasse 22–24 in Charlottenburg (Map 6; ☎ 31 10 73)

British Council, Hackescher Markt 1, Mitte (Map 7; ☎ 311 09 90)

The Wall Victim's Memorial is dedicated to the 191 people who died attempting to cross the Wall.

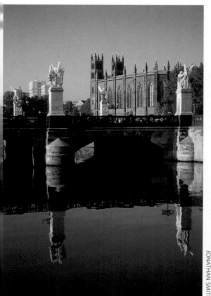

Schlossbrücke and Friedrichwerdersche Kirche.

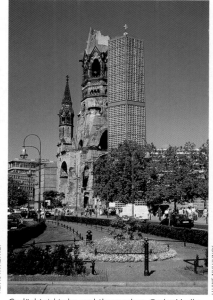

Gedächtniskirche and the modern Gedenkhalle.

Intertwined metal beams – the 'Berlin' sculpture.

An 'industrial cathedral' on the Spree.

Gateway, tourist attraction and Berlin landmark, the Brandenburger Tor.

Finnland-Institut (Finland Institute), Alt Moabit 98, Tiergarten (Map 2; ☎ 399 41 41)

Haus Ungarn (Hungary House), Karl-Liebknecht-Strasse 9, Mitte (Map 7; ☎ 240 91 46)

Institut Français, Kurfürstendamm 211 in Charlottenburg (Map 6; ☎ 885 90 20)

Italienisches Kulturinstitut (Italian Cultural Institute), Askanischer Platz 4, Tiergarten (Map 7; ☎ 269 94 10)

Polnisches Kultur-Institut (Polish Cultural Institute), Karl-Liebknecht-Strasse 7, Mitte (Map 7; ☎ 242 30 60)

Tschechisches Zentrum (Czech Centre), Leipziger Strasse 60, Mitte (Map 7; ☎ 208 25 92)

DANGERS & ANNOYANCES

By all accounts, Berlin is among the safest and most tolerant of European cities. Walking alone at night is not usually dangerous, although of course there's always safety in numbers in any urban environment.

Despite some bad press, racial attacks are quite infrequent in Germany and in Berlin. Having said that, while people of any skin colour are usually safe in the central districts, prejudice towards foreigners and gays is more likely to rear its ugly head in the outlying eastern districts, where unemployment and a general dissatisfaction with post-Wende society are rampant. In order to report a racially motivated attack, telephone the SOS-Rassismus hotline at ☎ 200 25 40 or ☎ 251 2277. No matter what skin colour you are, if you see any 'white skins' (skinheads wearing jackboots with white boot laces) run the other way – and fast.

Berlin has an estimated 5000 prostitutes who are harmless but annoying with their solicitations. On Friday and Saturday nights the Ku'damm is crawling with day-tripping Polish whores. Other night-time stomping grounds include Oranienburger Strasse, Kurfürstenstrasse, Lietzenburger Strasse, Strasse des 17 Juni and Stuttgarter Platz.

Drugs should be generally avoided for obvious reasons but also because a lot of the stuff going around is distributed by mafia-like organisations and is often dangerously impure.

Most U/S-Bahn stations are equipped with electronic information and emergency devices labelled 'SOS/Notruf/Information' and illustrated with a large red bell. If you require emergency assistance simply push the 'SOS' button. The Information button allows you to speak directly with one of the station masters. Fierce-looking private guards accompanied by even fiercer-looking muzzled dogs occasionally ride along in U-Bahn trains and are a convincing deterrent.

Very annoying but not usually dangerous are the many panhandlers, often positioned at U-Bahn exits. The days when beggars sat passively on the pavement with a hat before them are a thing of the past. The new millennium bum can be quite aggressive and tends to unleash a tirade of dissatisfaction with life, wife and government on anyone who fails to hand over some cash. At night in restaurants you'll be swarmed by vendors of roses or kitschy plastic toys. They're a pain but harmless and will move away as soon as you indicate lack of interest.

Also irritating *in extremis* are the security staff at most Berlin museums, who follow you from room to room and watch your every move lest you breathe too close to a Picasso or touch the pharaoh's death mask (God forbid).

LEGAL MATTERS

Berlin police are well trained, fairly 'enlightened' and usually treat tourists with respect. Most members of the police force can speak some English. By German law, you must carry some form of picture ID like your passport, a national identity card or a driving licence.

Reporting theft to the police is a simple, if occasionally time-consuming, matter. The first thing you will have to do, however, is show ID.

Drivers should carry a driving licence and obey road rules carefully. Occasionally, you may find yourself caught in a 'mousetrap' – a temporary spot-check station set up randomly by police. Pull over immediately if signalled to do so. You will be asked to show your driver's licence and registration papers and may be subjected to an alcohol test.

Penalties for drinking and driving are stiff. The highest permissible blood-alcohol level is 0.05% nationwide. If you are caught with

Emergency 101

If there's an emergency that requires police attention call ☎ 110. Otherwise, there are police stations all over the city, including the City-Wache (Map 6) at Joachimstaler Strasse 14–19 just south of Zoo station, and the station at Jägerstrasse 48 in Mitte (Map 7). For mishaps on trains your first recourse should be the *Bahnpolizei* (train police) with offices at all major stations.

The general emergency number for the fire brigade (*Feuerwehr*) throughout Berlin is ☎ 112. Police headquarters (Map 5; ☎ 69 90) and the municipal lost & found office (Map 5; ☎ 69 93 64 44/46) are at Platz der Luftbrücke 6 beside Tempelhof airport. The latter is on the right-hand side as you walk towards the airport entrance and keeps erratic hours; call for details.

If you've lost something on public transport, contact the BVG (Map 4; ☎ 25 62 30 40), Potsdamer Strasse 180–182 (U-Bahn: U7 Kleistpark), between 9am and 6pm Monday to Thursday (to 2pm Friday). The Deutsche Bahn has a central lost and found number at ☎ 01805-99 05 99.

The German auto club ADAC (☎ 868 60) has an office at Bundesallee 29 in Wilmersdorf. Their emergency helpline is ☎ 0180-222 22 22; assistance is free to members of ADAC or any of its foreign affiliates.

Another service is the 24-hour American Hotline (mobile ☎ 0177-814 15 10) which provides free referrals for people in need of psychological, medical, social or legal help. You don't have to be American to use it.

---

higher alcohol blood levels, you will receive an immediate driving ban. If you are involved in a car accident and you have blood-alcohol levels exceeding 0.03%, your license will usually be confiscated, even if the accident was not caused by you. A court then decides within three days whether you get it back. If your licence is confiscated, you should lodge a formal objection (*Widerspruch einlegen*) at the police station. The police will then examine the confiscation to ensure that everything was done by the book.

Drug possession is illegal in Germany, but in liberal Berlin laws are not always strictly enforced. Carrying small amounts (less than 10 grams) of hash or grass for personal consumption is treated as a minor offence and will not usually be prosecuted. The same cannot be said for harder drugs like heroin, cocaine or crack cocaine, possession of which results not only in considerable fines but may let you make the acquaintance of a Berlin jail as well.

Political demonstrations in Berlin do on occasion take on a violent character, especially when the *Autonomen*, a left-wing anarchist group, clash with right-wing neo-Nazi demonstrators. Most take place on the 1 May holiday and are usually centred in Kreuzberg and Prenzlauer Berg. Police will often seal off side streets and entire blocks and ask passers-by to prove their identity. It's a good idea to avoid such demonstrations.

If you are arrested, you have the right to make a phone call. However, in some circumstances (ie, a call might compromise the case against you) this can be denied.

For a referral to a lawyer, contact your embassy.

BUSINESS HOURS

Official shop trading hours in Germany are from 7am to 8pm on weekdays, and to 4pm on Saturday. Some bakeries are also open on Sunday but with reduced hours. In the outer, more residential, districts, though, retail stores may close earlier, like 6pm on weekdays and 2pm on Saturday. Exceptions are supermarkets and department stores. In suburban areas and smaller towns in Brandenburg, you'll also find that many stores close for two or three hours at lunchtime.

Laws for after-hour shopping have recently been relaxed, but so far few places take advantage of this development. Places to stock up on some items after 8pm include the larger train stations, including Zoo Station, Friedrichstrasse and Ostbahnhof; petrol stations; and small Turkish grocers (more prevalent in Kreuzberg and Neukölln). At all places, prices are generally higher than at regular markets. On Sundays, the Lidl budget supermarket chain opens its branches at the U-Bahn station Innsbrucker Platz in Schöneberg and at the Ostbahnhof (Map 5).

Banking hours are generally from 8.30am to 1pm and from 2.30pm to 4pm Monday to Friday (with some branches extending hours to 6pm on one day, usually Thursday), though many banks in Berlin's centre stay open throughout the day. Travel agencies and other offices are usually open from 9am to 6pm weekdays and til noon or 1pm on Saturday. Government offices, though, close for the weekend as early as 1pm on Friday. Opening hours for museums vary greatly, although some are open late one evening per week; most are closed on Monday.

All shops and banks are closed on public holidays.

PUBLIC HOLIDAYS & SPECIAL EVENTS

National public holidays observed in Berlin include: New Year's Day, Good Friday, Easter Sunday, Easter Monday, Labour Day (1 May), Ascension Day (40 days after Easter), Whit/Pentecost Sunday and Monday (in May or June), Day of German Unity (3 October), and Christmas and Boxing/St Stephen's Day (25 & 26 December).

Banks, shops and offices are closed on these days but entertainment venues are usually not. Museums, sights and other attractions are most likely closed on 24, 25, 26 and 31 of December as well as on 1 January. Restaurants are open except on December 24 and 25.

Berlin's calendar is filled with an interesting collection of cultural events, festivals and fairs. For gay and lesbian events, see the Entertainment chapter.

January
Internationale Grüne Woche (International Green Week) Officially a week-long consumer fair for food, agriculture and gardening, it's actually more like an excuse for hopping from booth to booth gorging on exotic morsels from around the world. It's held at the ICC trade fair centre. Information on ☎ 303 80.

February
Internationale Filmfestspiele Berlin (International Film Festival Berlin) Also known as Berlinale, this is Germany's answer to the Cannes and Venice film festivals and attracts its own stable of stars (few) and starlets (plenty), directors and critics from around the world. About 750 films are shown in a two-week span at various theatres around town. Check listings in newspapers or the entertainment magazines *Zitty* and *tip* for details. Many performances are quickly sold out, so check the schedule as soon as you can, then call the cinema for ticket availability. Tickets can be bought at the theatres and at ticket offices. Information on ☎ 25 92 00. Check the Web site at **w** www.berlinale.de

March
Internationale Tourismus Börse or ITB (International Tourism Fair) The world's largest travel show with exhibitors from everywhere takes over the trade show grounds. It's open to the public on the weekend. Information on ☎ 303 80 or **w** www.itb-berlin-online.de

April
Festtage (Festival Days) An annual 10-day festival of gala concerts and operas which brings renowned conductors, soloists and orchestras to Berlin. Concerts are held at the Philharmonie, operas at the Staatsoper Unter den Linden. Information on ☎ 20 35 45 55 or **w** www.staatsoper -berlin.org/fsttg/ftgprgr.htm

May
Karneval der Kulturen (Carnival of Cultures) Berlin's answer to London's Notting Hill Carnival, this is a lively street festival with a parade of whacky costumed people dancing and playing music on floats. Information is available on ☎ 622 20 24 or at **w** www.karneval-berlin.de

Theatertreffen Berlin (Theatre Meeting Berlin) Three weeks of new productions by emerging and established German-language ensembles from Germany, Austria and Switzerland. Held around town. Information on ☎ 25 48 90 or **w** www .berlinerfestspiele.de/theatertreffen

June
Mozart Festival This festival is sponsored by the Berliner Philharmonie and is held over Whitsun/ Pentecost. Information on ☎ 25 48 80.

Bach Tage Berlin This is an annual one-week festival featuring music by Bach and his contemporaries. Information on ☎ 301 55 18.

July
Classic Open Air Gendarmenmarkt A series of classical concerts held al fresco on the Gendarmenmarkt in early July. Information on ☎ 843 73 50 or **w** www.classic-openair.ch/

Love Parade Berlin's top annual techno parade, held in mid-July, with up to a million ravers, is followed by nonstop partying in clubs and bars. Information on ☎ 28 46 20. Visit the Web site at ⓦ www.loveparade.de

August
Internationale Funkausstellung (International Consumer Electronics Fair) This huge fair is open to the public and takes place at the trade show grounds. Information on ☎ 303 38.

September
Berliner Festwochen (Berlin Festival Weeks) A month-long celebration featuring concerts, exhibits, plays and other cultural events with a particular focus (eg, Gustav Mahler in 1999, Arthur Schönberg in 2001). Information is available on ☎ 25 48 90 or ⓦ www.berlinerfestspiele .de/berlinerfestwochen/

October
aaa – Die Hauptstadt Auto-Show (Car Show) This international car exhibition is held from late Oct to early Nov. Information on ☎ 303 80.

art forum Berlin An international contemporary art fair hosted by Berlin's leading galleries. Information on ☎ 303 80 or check the Web site ⓦ www.art-forum-berlin.com/

November
JazzFest Berlin Top-rated jazz festival with performances held at venues throughout the city. Information on ☎ 25 48 91 00 or ⓦ www.berliner festspiele.de/jazzfest/

December
Weihnachtsmärkte (Christmas markets) Christmas markets are held from late November to around 21 December at several locations around Berlin, including Breitscheidplatz (Map 6; 10am to 9pm or 10pm daily); Alexanderplatz (Map 7; 1 to 10pm daily); and the Marktplatz in Spandau (9am to 7pm daily). The outlying district of Köpenick sets up stalls from mid-December around the town hall (from noon to 8pm weekdays, from 10am to 8pm weekends).

DOING BUSINESS
With the world's third largest economy, Germany has long been Europe's most important address for doing business. Enormous funds have been pouring into Berlin to make it a corporate showcase on a level with London and New York. Of all German cities, Berlin has the highest concentration of English speakers, which makes getting around – and

getting down to business – a great deal easier. Before you arrive, contact the trade or commercial office of the German embassy in your country, which can provide you with valuable assistance. Your own embassy in Berlin may be able to help as well. Useful local organisations include the Berliner Industrie- und Handelskammer (Berlin Chamber of Commerce & Industry, ☎ 31 51 06 66), Fasanenstrasse 85, and the Wirtschaftsförderung Berlin (Berlin Economic Development Corporation, ☎ 39 98 00), Hallerstrasse 6, both in Charlottenburg.

Business Services
Regus Business Centers provide the full range of turnkey business operations (such as office rental, secretarial services, convention organisation and telecom needs, including video conferencing). There are five Berlin branches, including one in the Kollhoff Building at Potsdamer Platz 1 in Tiergarten (☎ 25 94 40); check the Yellow Pages for other branches.

Full-service copy shops are found everywhere, but for some reason there's a cluster of them near U-Bahn station Eisenacher Strasse in Schöneberg. Copyhaus has two branches on Grunewaldstrasse at No 18 and 78 (Map 4; ☎ 235 53 80). They are open from 8am to midnight Monday to Saturday and from 1pm to 9pm on Sunday. The staff tend to be on the snobbish side. Cheaper and friendlier for basic copy and print needs is Kopier Blitz nearby at Akazienstrasse 15 (Map 4; ☎/fax 782 49 11). Pro Business (Map 4; ☎ 216 70 67) at Maassenstrasse 7 is a full-service digital printing and copy store.

Most larger hotels offer fax and Internet connections, though usually at inflated prices. To rent audio-visual equipment such as projectors and sound systems you might try General Audio & Television Equipment (GATE; ☎ 393 20 21) at Reuchlinstrasse 10 in Tiergarten-Moabit.

Translators abound in cosmopolitan Berlin. Places to try include Language Consultancy (☎ 89 09 23 40), Joachim-Friedrich-Strasse 27 in Charlottenburg, and English Express (☎ 68 05 85 40) at Ringbahnstrasse 23 in Neukölln.

All major international courier services operate in Berlin, but none have actual offices. To schedule a pick-up, call ☎ 0800-123 08 00 for FedEx, ☎ 0800-882 66 30 for UPS or ☎ 01803-25 82 58 for DHL.

Exhibitions & Conferences

If you're planning a larger event in Berlin, your first contact should be Berlin Tourismus Marketing (BTM; ☎ 264 74 80, fax 26 47 48 99) at Am Karlsbad 11 in Tiergarten. Their regularly updated publication *Meeting and Incentive in Berlin* (in English and German) provides a detailed overview of available facilities and services. The ICC Berlin (Internationales Congress Centrum Berlin) at Messedamm 22 in Charlottenburg is the city's major conference space (Map 4; ☎ 30 38 30 00, fax 30 38 30 30).

WORK

Finding work in Germany is not all that easy, especially in eastern Germany where the official unemployment rate is almost 20% and the unofficial rate probably twice that. An additional difficulty for foreigners is the great importance Germans place on formal qualifications – especially German qualifications.

However, like most other European countries, Germany lacks qualified workers in the computer and software industries. It has therefore introduced a so-called temporary 'Green Card' for foreign specialists. Information on the scheme is available in English on the Web at Ⓦ ww.arbeitsamt.de/hst/international/egcindex.html, or ask at any German embassy.

All non-EU citizens wishing to work in Germany must apply for a work permit at the *Arbeitsamt* (Employment Office) and for a residency permit at the *Ausländerbehörde* (Foreigners' Office), a tedious process to say the least. Special conditions exist for citizens of so-called 'recognised third countries', including the USA, Canada, Australia, New Zealand, Japan, Israel and Switzerland. Citizens of these countries who have a firm

job offer are usually granted the necessary permits, providing the job cannot be filled by a German or EU citizen.

You can begin your job search either before leaving home or on arrival in Germany. You must be well qualified and be able to back up your skills with an impressive array of certificates. Once you receive a firm offer, the Arbeitsamt checks that the position cannot otherwise be filled, then issues a work permit specific to that position.

EU citizens don't need a work permit, and basically enjoy the same rights as Germans. However, they do need an EU residency permit *(EU-Aufenthaltserlaubnis)* from the local authority.

The Arbeitsamt also operates an electronic database of vacant positions and can help with finding part-time work. Temp agencies are another option, with ADIA (☎ 884 10 00), at Ku'damm 220, being one of the largest. The Saturday edition of the *Berliner Zeitung*, the *taz* and the Sunday edition of the *Berliner Morgenpost* are also good places to start looking.

You may be able to find work teaching English at language schools or privately, but you will still need work and residency permits, as well as valid health insurance at all times. Teaching English is certainly no way to get rich, but it might help to keep your head above water or prolong a trip. The hourly rate varies dramatically – from a low of €10 per hour rising to about €40 for qualified professionals in large cities. Local papers are the best way to advertise, but other good places to start are notice boards at universities, photocopy shops or even local supermarkets.

Work as an au pair is relatively easy to find and there are numerous approved au pair agencies you can approach. *The Au Pair and Nanny's Guide to Working Abroad* by Susan Griffith & Sharon Legg will help. *Work Your Way Around the World*, also by Susan Griffith, is another suggestion.

In Germany, busking is often associated with begging.

Getting There & Away

If you live outside Europe, chances are you'll be flying into Berlin. Even if you're already in Europe, a flight may still be the fastest and cheapest option, especially from faraway places like Greece, Spain or southern Italy. The train is the next best option, though cross-country buses are a viable – and cheaper – alternative. Bear in mind that, no matter which method of transport you choose, seats fill up quickly and prices often increase considerably during summer school holidays.

AIR

Direct flights to Berlin from overseas are scarce and, depending on the airline you use, you're likely to fly first into another European city like Frankfurt, Amsterdam, Paris or London, then catch a connecting flight. Taking the train is another option. From Frankfurt, for instance, super-fast ICE trains leave every other hour and make the trip to Berlin

in about four hours (€104). From Düsseldorf, ICE trains also need four hours to arrive at Zoo station (€90).

Buying Tickets

If you're flying to Berlin from outside Europe, your plane ticket is likely to be the biggest expense in your budget. With a bit of research – ringing around travel agents, checking Internet sites, perusing the travel ads in newspapers – you can often get yourself a good travel deal. Start early as some of the cheapest tickets need to be bought well in advance and popular flights can sell out.

Full-time students and people under 26 years (under 30 in some countries) have access to better deals than other travellers. You have to show a document proving your date of birth or a valid International Student Identity Card (ISIC) when you are buying your ticket and sometimes again when checking in at the airport.

For long-term travel there are plenty of discount tickets that are valid for 12 months, allowing multiple stopovers with open dates. For short-term travel within Europe, cheaper fares are available by travelling mid-week, staying away at least one Saturday night or taking advantage of short-lived promotional offers.

When you're looking for bargain air fares to Berlin, there is rarely any advantage in buying a ticket direct from the airline. Discounted tickets are released to selected travel agents and specialist discount agencies, and these are usually the cheapest deals going.

One exception to this rule is the expanding number of 'no-frills' carriers, which mostly sell directly to travellers. Unlike the 'full service' airlines, no-frills carriers often make one-way tickets available at half the return fare, making it easy to put together a return ticket when you fly to one place but leave from another.

The other exception is booking on the Internet. Some online airlines sell seats by auction or simply cut their prices to reflect the

Warning

The information in this chapter is particularly vulnerable to change: Prices for international travel are volatile, routes are introduced and cancelled, schedules change, special deals come and go, and rules and visa requirements are amended. Airlines and governments seem to take a perverse pleasure in making price structures and regulations as complicated as possible. You should check directly with the airline or a travel agent to make sure you understand how a fare (and ticket you may buy) works. In addition, the travel industry is highly competitive and there are many lurks and perks.

The upshot of this is that you should get opinions, quotes and advice from as many airlines and travel agents as possible before you part with your hard-earned cash. The details given in this chapter should be regarded as pointers and are not a substitute for your own careful, up-to-date research.

Air Travel Glossary

Alliances Many of the world's leading airlines are now intimately involved with each other, sharing everything from reservations systems and check-in to aircraft and frequent-flyer schemes. Opponents say that alliances restrict competition. Whatever the arguments, there is no doubt that big alliances are the way of the future.

Courier Fares Businesses often need to send urgent documents or freight securely and quickly. Courier companies hire people to accompany the package through customs and, in return, offer a discount ticket which is sometimes a bargain. However, you may have to surrender all your baggage allowance and take only carry-on luggage.

Fares Airlines traditionally offer 1st class (coded F), business class (coded J) and economy class (coded Y) tickets. These days there are so many promotional and discounted fares available that few passengers pay full fare.

Lost Tickets If you lose your airline ticket, an airline will usually treat it like a travellers cheque and, after inquiries, issue you with another one. Legally, however, an airline is entitled to treat it like cash and if you lose it then it's gone forever. Take very good care of your tickets.

Onward Tickets An entry requirement for many countries is that you have a ticket out of the country. If you're unsure of your next move, the easiest solution is to buy the cheapest onward ticket to a neighbouring country or a ticket from a reliable airline which can later be refunded if you do not use it.

Open-Jaw Tickets These are return tickets where you fly out to one place but return from another. If available, this can save you backtracking to your arrival point.

Overbooking Since every flight has some passengers who fail to show up, airlines often book more passengers than they have seats. Usually excess passengers make up for the no-shows, but occasionally somebody gets 'bumped' onto the next available flight. Guess who it is most likely to be? The passengers who check in late. If you do get 'bumped', you are normally offered some form of compensation.

Reconfirmation Some airlines require you to reconfirm your flight at least 72 hours prior to departure. Check your travel documents to see if this is the case

Restrictions Discounted tickets often have various restrictions on them – such as needing to be paid for in advance and incurring a penalty to be altered or cancelled. Others are restrictions on the minimum and maximum period you must be away.

Round-the-World Tickets RTW tickets give you a limited period (usually a year) in which to circumnavigate the globe. You can go anywhere the carrying airlines go, as long as you don't backtrack. The number of stopovers or total number of separate flights is decided before you set off and they usually cost a bit more than a basic return flight.

Ticketless Travel Airlines are gradually waking up to the realisation that paper tickets are unnecessary encumbrances. On simple one-way or return trips, reservations details can be held on computer and the passenger merely shows ID to claim their seat.

Transferred Tickets Airline tickets cannot be transferred from one person to another. Travellers sometimes try to sell the return half of their ticket, but officials can ask you to prove that you are the person named on the ticket. On an international flight, tickets are compared with passports.

reduced cost of electronic selling. Airlines such as buzz or Ryanair offer very competitive fares to Web surfers.

The days when some travel agents routinely fleeced travellers by running off with their money are, happily, almost over. Paying by credit card generally offers protection, as most card issuers provide refunds if you can prove you didn't get what you paid for. You may decide to pay slightly more than the rock-bottom fare by opting for the safety of an established travel agent.

Firms such as STA Travel and Council Travel with offices worldwide, Travel CUTS in Canada, and Flight Centre in Australia are not going to disappear overnight, and they do offer good prices to most destinations, especially to students and to those aged under 26.

Always make a photocopy of your ticket and keep it somewhere separate. This will simplify getting a replacement in case of loss or theft.

Travellers with Special Needs

Most international airlines can cater for travellers with special needs – those with disabilities, people with young children and even children travelling alone.

Travellers with special dietary preferences (vegetarian, kosher etc) can request appropriate meals with advance notice. If you are travelling in a wheelchair, most international airports can provide an escort from check-in desk to plane where needed, and ramps, lifts, toilets and phones are generally available.

Guide dogs for the blind will often have to travel in a specially pressurised baggage compartment with other animals, away from their owner, though smaller guide dogs may be admitted to the cabin.

Deaf travellers can ask for airport and in-flight announcements to be written down for them.

Airlines usually allow babies up to two years of age to fly for 10% of the adult fare, although a few may allow them to fly free of charge. Reputable international airlines usually provide nappies (diapers), tissues, talcum and all the other paraphernalia needed to keep babies clean, dry and half-happy. For children between the ages of two and 12, the fare on international flights is usually 50% of the regular fare or 67% of a discounted fare.

Departure Tax

A departure tax of around €4 to €5 per person and airport security fees are included in the price of an airline ticket purchased in Germany. You shouldn't have to pay any more fees at the airport, although in view of the cost of heightened security measures as a result of the terrorist attacks on 11 September 2001, additional fees are a possibility.

Other Parts of Germany

Scheduled domestic flights connect Berlin to all major German airports and vice versa, usually via Tempelhof and Tegel airports. Lufthansa has by far the largest network of flight routes serving basically all German airports. Flights are also offered by Eurowings, Deutsche BA, and LTU. For contact details see Airlines Offices later in this section.

The USA

Flights to Germany from major cities in the USA abound, though only Lufthansa has nonstop flights into Berlin (six times weekly from Washington DC). Lufthansa also connects Frankfurt with Atlanta, Boston, Chicago, Detroit, Los Angeles, New York and Philadelphia. American carriers serving Frankfurt include American Airlines, Delta and United Airlines.

There are also direct flights to other German cities, including LTU's flights to Düsseldorf from Los Angeles, Orlando and Miami. Since LTU caters mainly for holiday travellers, some of these flights may not be offered year-round. Generally, flights to Frankfurt are the cheapest.

Air fares rise and fall in a cyclical pattern. The lowest fares are available from early November to mid-December and then again from mid-January to Easter, gradually rising in the following months. Peak months are July and August, after which prices start dropping again.

The *New York Times*, the *Los Angeles Times*, the *San Francisco Examiner*, the *Chicago Tribune* and many other major Sunday newspapers produce weekly travel sections in which you'll find lots of travel agents' advertisements. Scour the Web for cheap fares; try W www.orbitz.com, W www.expedia.com, W www.travelocity.com or W www.ticketplanet.com.

Council Travel (☎ 800-226 8624, W www.counciltravel.com) and STA Travel (☎ 800-777 0112, W www.sta-travel.com) are reliable budget travel agencies with offices throughout the USA. Call or check their Web sites for the branch nearest you.

Stand-by Fares Flying stand-by can be a cheap way to reach Europe from the US if you are flexible. 4standby, part of Whole Earth Travel, offers stand-by fares from the East Coast of the USA from $169 one way and from the West Coast for $249.

Providing stand-bys from New York to Frankfurt, also from $169, is Airtech (☎ 212-219 7000, W www.airtech.com), Suite 204, 588 Broadway, New York, NY 10012. Flights offered may not get you exactly where you want to go, but the savings are so huge that you might opt for an onward train or bus. Another outfit offering much the same is Airhitch (W www.airhitch.org) with offices in New York (☎ 800-326 2009 or ☎ 212-864 2000), Los Angeles (☎ 800-397 1098 or ☎ 310-726 5000) and San Francisco (☎ 800-834 9192 or ☎ 415-834 9192).

Courier Flights Travelling as a courier means that you accompany freight to its destination. You don't have to handle any shipment personally, either at departure or arrival, and most likely will not even get to see it. All you need to do is carry an envelope containing the freight papers with you on board and hand it to someone at your destination. The freight takes the place of your check-in luggage, so you will be restricted to what you are allowed to carry on the plane.

There are other restrictions as well. Courier tickets are sold for a fixed date and schedule changes can be difficult to make. If you buy a return ticket, your schedule will be even more rigid. You need to clarify before you fly what restrictions apply to your ticket, and don't expect a refund once you've paid.

You may have to be a US resident and present yourself in person before the company will take you on. Also keep in mind that only a relatively small number of these tickets is available, so it's best to call two or three months in advance and be somewhat flexible with departure dates.

For more information, contact the International Association of Air Travel Couriers (IAATC; ☎ 352-475-1584, W www.courier.org).

Canada

Lufthansa flies to Frankfurt from all major Canadian airports. LTU flies from Toronto to Düsseldorf. Travel CUTS (☎ 800-667-2887, W www.travelcuts.com) is Canada's national student travel agency and has offices in all major cities. Also check the travel sections of the *Globe & Mail*, the *Montreal Gazette*, the *Toronto Star* and the *Vancouver Sun* for travel agents' ads.

Australia

From Australia, Lufthansa and other major international airlines offer a range of flights and fares to Frankfurt, with onward travel to Berlin. Some travel agents, particularly smaller ones, advertise cheap air fares in the travel sections of weekend newspapers. Also consider getting a Round-the-World (RTW) ticket, which can be excellent value and allows you to see a whole lot more of the world. Expect to pay around A$2300 to A$2800 for a RTW ticket.

Two well-known agents for cheap fares are STA Travel and Flight Centre. STA Travel (☎ 03-9349 2411, ☎ 131 776 Australia-wide, W www.statravel.com.au) has its main office at 224 Faraday St, Carlton, in Melbourne, with offices in all major cities and on many university campuses. Flight Centre (☎ 131 600 Australia-wide, W www.flightcentre.com.au) has a central office at 82 Elizabeth St, Sydney, and there are dozens of offices throughout Australia.

New Zealand

Cathay Pacific, Korean Air and Garuda all have good fare deals from Auckland to Berlin, usually via Frankfurt. RTW travel to or from New Zealand can often be the best value – sometimes RTW will be cheaper than a return ticket in the high season. RTW tickets from New Zealand start from around NZ$2929.

The *New Zealand Herald* has a travel section in which travel agents advertise fares. Flight Centre (☎ 09-309 6171) has a large central office in Auckland at National Bank Towers (corner of Queen and Darby streets) and many more branches throughout the country.

STA Travel (☎ 09-309 0458, W www.sta travel.com.au) has its main office at 10 High St, Auckland, and has offices elsewhere in Auckland as well as in Hamilton, Palmerston North, Wellington, Christchurch and Dunedin.

The UK

Discount air travel is big business in London. The main airlines connecting Berlin and London are Lufthansa and British Airways, with several flights daily. For the latest fares, check out the travel page ads of the Sunday newspapers, *Time Out* and the freebie *TNT*.

Some of the cheapest flights are offered by Buzz, a low-cost, no-frills airline which flies from London's Stansted airport to Berlin-Schönefeld several times daily from £35 each way. The cheapest way to purchase tickets for this airline is to go through its Web Site (W www.buzzaway.com).

For students or travellers under 26, a popular travel agency in the UK is STA Travel (☎ 020-7361 6144, W www.sta travel.co.uk), which has an office at 86 Old Brompton Rd, London SW7 3LQ, and other offices in both London and Manchester. This agencies sells tickets to all travellers but caters especially to the travel needs of both young people and students.

Other recommended travel agencies in London include the following suggestions: Trailfinders (☎ 020-7938 3939), 194 Kensington High St, London W8 7RG; Bridge the World (☎ 020-7734 7447), 4 Regent Place, London W1R 5FB; and also Flightbookers (☎ 020-7757 2000), 177–178 Tottenham Court Rd, London W1P 9LF.

Continental Europe

Discount flights to Berlin are available from many major cities in Continental Europe. From southern Europe, it's often cheaper than land transport. Lufthansa connects all major cities directly with Berlin-Tegel. Eurowings flies to Berlin-Tegel and Berlin-Tempelhof from Amsterdam. Air Berlin, Aero Lloyd and LTU are holiday airlines flying to/from many southern European countries, including Spain, Italy and Greece. Air France flies to Tegel from Paris and Nice.

France has a network of student travel agencies that sells discount tickets to travellers of all ages. OTU Voyages (☎ 01 44 41 38 50, W www.otu.fr) has a central Paris office at 39 ave Georges Bernanos (5e) and 42 offices around the country. Acceuil des Jeunes en France (☎ 01 42 77 87 80), 119 rue Saint Martin (4e), is another popular discount travel agency. Other service- and bargain-oriented Paris agencies are Nouvelles Frontières (☎ 08 03 33 33 33, W www.nouvelles -frontieres.com), 5 Ave de l'Opéra (1er); and Voyageurs du Monde (☎ 01 42 86 16 00), 55 rue Sainte Anne (2e).

In Belgium, Acotra Student Travel Agency (☎ 02-512 86 07), at rue de la Madeline, Brussels, and WATS Reizen (☎ 03-226 16 26), at de Keyserlei 44, Antwerp, are both well-known agencies. In Switzerland, SSR Voyages (☎ 01-297 11 11, W www.ssr.ch), which specialises in student, youth and budget fares, has branches in major Swiss cities, including in Zurich at Leonhardstrasse 10. In the Netherlands, NBBS Reizen is the official student travel agency with offices around the country; the Amsterdam office (☎ 020-624 09 89) is at Rokin 66.

Airline Offices

Lufthansa City Center (Map 6; ☎ 88 75 38 00) has fancy new digs in the Neues Kranzler Eck at Kurfürstendamm 21. The 24-hour central reservation number is ☎ 0180-380 38 03. Contact numbers for other airlines serving Berlin and the airports at which they are based include:

Aeroflot ☎ 60 91 53 70 (Schönefeld)
Aero Lloyd ☎ 41 01 27 55 (Tegel)

Air Berlin ☎ 0180-173 78 00 (Tegel)
Air France ☎ 01805-36 03 70 or ☎ 41 01 27 15 (Tegel)
Alitalia ☎ 41 01 26 50 (Tegel)
British Airways ☎ 0180-526 65 22 (Tegel)
Buzz Airlines ☎ 069- 50 07 01 33 (Schönefeld)
Deutsche BA ☎ 0180-535 93 22 (Tegel)
Eurowings ☎ 69 51 28 53 (Tempelhof)
El Al ☎ 201 77 90 (Schönefeld)
KLM ☎ 01805-21 42 01 or ☎ 41 01 38 44 (Tegel)
LOT Polish Airlines ☎ 0180-300 03 45 (Tegel)
LTU ☎ 41 01 37 07 (Tegel)
Malév Hungarian Airlines ☎ 41 01 28 45 (Tegel)

TRAIN

With the completion of the Lehrter Bahnhof pushed back well into this decade, most trains will continue to go through Bahnhof Zoo in the western city centre and Ostbahnhof in the eastern centre. Many long-distance trains stop at both. Depending on your final destination, you may find services arriving at one station link with services leaving from another. To connect, take the U/S-Bahn (€2.10), but allow ample time for transfer. If you have a train ticket to or from Berlin – or a rail pass – you may use it to travel on any S-Bahn (but not the U-Bahn) for free.

For ticket and timetable information (available in English) by telephone you can ring ☎ 01805-99 66 33 from anywhere in Germany for €0.12 per minute. The same information is available on the Internet at **W** www.bahn.de (look for the link to 'International Guests' for information in English).

Bahnhof Zoologischer Garten

Bahnhof Zoo (Zoo station; Map 6) is where many visitors first arrive. It features shops and Imbiss stands with extended hours, car rental offices, newsstands and bookstores; coin lockers are €1 or €2 per 24 hours; the left-luggage office (open from 5am to 11pm) charges €2 per item per day.

The large Deutsche Bahn Reisezentrum (ticket reservation and information office) is open from 5.15am to 11pm daily. In the back of the main hall, in the basement, is an establishment called McWash which has spic-and-span toilets (€0.75) and showers (€6). Next to McWash is EurAide, a quasi tourist office and excellent one-stop service station

geared towards English-speaking travellers. Staff can help with buying the right train ticket, making a seat reservation or finding a place to stay. EurAide is open from 8am to noon and 1pm to 4.30pm daily; hours may be extended to 6pm from April to October.

Outside the entrance on Hardenbergplatz is the BVG transport information kiosk, where you can get maps, information and tickets.

Other Parts of Germany

The German train system is justifiably known as the most efficient in Europe. There are more than 41,000km of track serving over 7000 German cities and towns. All trains have 1st- and 2nd-class compartments; long distance trains have a restaurant car.

Bahnhof Zoo is the main station for long-distance trains to cities west of Berlin, including Hanover, Frankfurt and Cologne. There are also frequent services to Hamburg and Munich and a direct train to Leipzig. Ostbahnhof handles regional services around Brandenburg, Saxony and, less so, Mecklenburg-Western Pomerania.

Another large station is Bahnhof Lichtenberg on Weitlingstrasse in the eastern district of Lichtenberg. This is the hub for trains to Stralsund, Rostock and other cities in Mecklenburg-Western Pomerania, as well as services to Cottbus, Dresden, Erfurt, Halle and Magdeburg.

Train Types

The Deutsche Bahn (DB) operates several types of trains:

InterCity Express (ICE) – long-distance space-age bullet train, stops at major cities only, special tariffs apply
InterCity (IC) & EuroCity (EC) – long-distance trains almost as fast as the ICE, stops at major cities only, surcharge applies
InterRegio (IR) – long-distance trains with more frequent stops than ICs
RegionalBahn (RB) – local trains in rural areas with frequent stops
Regional Express (RE) – regional trains serving primarily rural areas
StadtExpress (SE) – regional trains primarily connecting cities
Stadtbahn (S-Bahn) – local trains operating within a city and its urban area

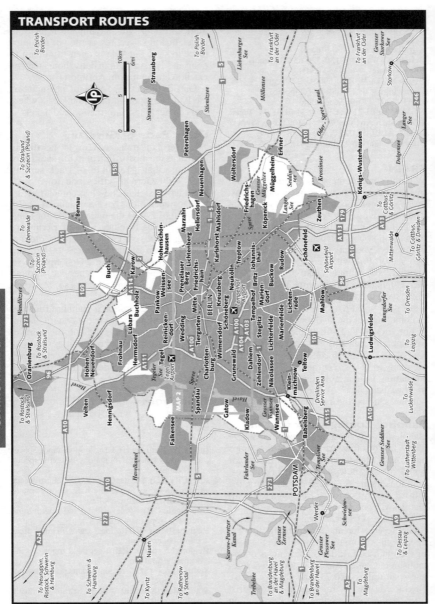

TRANSPORT ROUTES

Buying Tickets

The best places to buy your tickets are at train stations or at authorised travel agencies (look for the DB logo). Conductors also sell tickets at a surcharge of €2.50 (€5 in ICE trains). Most regional and local trains now operate without a conductor, requiring passengers to buy a ticket *before* boarding or else risk paying a fine. We definitely recommend that you make reservations for long-distance travel, especially if you're taking an ICE and IC train or are travelling on a Friday or Sunday afternoon, during holiday periods or in summer. Reservations cost €2.50 and can be made as late as a few minutes before your train departs.

Costs

The average price of 2nd-class train travel throughout Germany is currently €0.14 per km; for 1st class it's €0.21 per km. Travelling on IC or EC trains requires a supplement ticket of €3.50 (€4.50 if bought from the conductor), regardless of the distance travelled.

Though train travel in Germany is efficient, it's not necessarily cheap. Children, students and seniors qualify for reduced prices but if you're neither, and don't have a rail pass, you can cut costs by taking advantage of several special tickets and offers. If you have some flexibility, the following two offer mind-boggling savings:

Guten-Abend-Ticket This ticket is valid for unlimited train travel from 7pm until 3am (from 2pm Saturday) and costs €30 in 2nd class (€36 on an ICE train); a surcharge of €8 applies from Friday to Sunday.

Schönes-Wochenende-Ticket This ticket allows you and up to four other people to travel anywhere in Germany on *one day* from midnight Saturday or Sunday until 3am the next day for just €21 (yes, that's five people for €21!) The catch is that you may only use local trains and *not* ICE, IC, EC or IR trains. That's not so bad, though. It might take a while longer, but it is still possible to get clear across the country on the slower trains. DB is likely to alter the stitch of this deal in late 2002 in favour of families – ask at the counter or look on the Web site at **W** www.bahn.de for the latest information.

German Rail Passes A Deutsche Bahn rail pass is available to non-EU residents only and available through your travel agent or at major train stations in Germany (bring your passport). Passes are available for unlimited travel on four to 10 days within a one-month period. For example, regular 2nd-class rates for travelling on four, seven or 10 days are US$174/240/306, respectively. If you're aged between 12 and 25, you will qualify for the German Rail Youth Pass which costs US$138/174/239. Two adults travelling together should check out the German Rail Twin Pass for US$261/360/459.

If Prague is on your itinerary, consider buying the Prague Excursion Pass. It covers round-trip travel (and all supplements) to Prague from the Czech border and back within seven days. The 2nd class pass costs €31 (€23 if you're under 26) and is available from Deutsche Bahn offices or EurAide.

Europe

Berlin is well connected through direct rail links to several other European countries. Trains to Paris, Amsterdam and Brussels depart from Zoo station, while those headed to destinations east – like Moscow, Prague, Budapest and Vienna – leave from Bahnhof Lichtenberg.

It's not worth spending the extra money on a 1st-class ticket, since travelling 2nd class on German trains is perfectly comfortable. If you are *in* Germany and want to travel internationally, the Deutsche Bahn has lots of deals (mostly on return trips) to cut costs. Tell the person at the counter where you want to go, the length of stay, and ask for the cheapest deal. The Web site **W** www.bahn.de is a good place to start looking.

Long-distance trains between major German cities and other countries are called EC (EuroCity) trains. Travelling overnight to Germany from within Europe is the most comfortable option. Supplements vary a bit. If it's calculated as a supplement to the standard ticket price, expect to pay per person from €14 to €20 for a bunk in a six-person couchette, €21 to €27 in a four-person couchette, and €42 to €62 in two-person compartments.

If you have a sleeper or sleeping berth on international train trips, the train conductor will usually collect your ticket before you go to sleep and hand it back to you in the morning. If you're in a regular seat, however, expect to be woken up by conductors coming aboard in each country to check your ticket.

Eurail Passes Eurail Passes are convenient and excellent value if you're covering lots of territory in a very limited time. Available to non-residents of Europe only, they should be bought before arriving in Europe. A limited number of outlets also sells them within Europe, but your passport must show that you've been there for less than six months.

Eurail Passes are valid for unlimited travel on national railways (and some private lines) in 17 European countries. They also cover many international ferries, eg, from Sweden to Germany, as well as steamer services in various countries. A variety of passes is available.

If you're under 26, a Eurail Pass Youth gives unlimited 2nd-class travel for periods of 15 or 21 consecutive days (US$388/499) or one/two/three months (US$623/882/1089). The Youth Flexipass, also for 2nd class, is valid for travel on freely chosen days within a two-month period: 10 days of travel cost US$458, 15 days are US$599.

For those aged over 26, the equivalent passes cost more but provide 1st-class travel. The standard Eurail Pass for unlimited travel on 15 or 21 consecutive days costs US$554/718 and for one/two/three months US$890/1260/1558. The Eurail Flexipass gives you unlimited travel on 10 or 15 days of your choice within a two-month period for US$654/862. Children aged four to 11 get 50% off on any of these passes.

For non-EU residents, an excellent place to buy passes, including the German Rail Pass (see above), is Rail Europe (US ☎ 888-382-7245, Canada ☎ 800-361-7246, W www.raileurope.com). This company specialises in the full palette of Eurail Passes described here and also sells point-to-point rail tickets throughout Europe.

BUS

Berlin's central bus station is the Omnibusbahnhof am Funkturm (Map 4), in the north-western corner of Masurenallee and Messedamm in Charlottenburg. You can reach the bus staion by U/S-bahn. Take U2 to Kaiserdamm or S45 to Witzleben. Tickets may be bought at the travel agency within the station (☎ 301 80 28 for information, ☎ 302 52 94 for reservations). It's open 9am to 6pm weekdays and to noon Saturday. They're also available from other travel agencies and some ride-share agencies (*Mitfahrzentralen*). (See Hitching & Ride Services later in this chapter.) The left-luggage office is open from 5.30am to 9.30pm daily.

Other Parts of Germany

Berlin-based BerlinLinienBus (☎ 861 93 31, e info@berlinlinienbus.de, German-only W www.berlinlinienbus.de) is a co-operative of several bus companies providing services to around 350 destinations within Germany and beyond. Buses are comfortable, air-conditioned and have on-board toilet and cabin lights; smoking is not permitted. Seat reservations are required on most trips. A variety of fares is available; round-trip fares are cheaper than one-way fares. Discounted fares, called SuperSpar, are available to anyone aged under 28 and over 60. Most trips from Berlin are operated by Bayern Express & P Kühn (☎ 86 30 60 or 0180-154 64 36).

Destinations within Germany, their frequencies (in the peak summer months), trip durations and full fares and SuperSpar fares include:

destination	frequency	duration (hours)	full fares/ SuperSpar
Bremen	daily	6½	€44/28.50
Düsseldorf	3 weekly	9	€61.50/37
Frankfurt/ Main	daily	9½	€57/40
Hamburg (express)	8 daily	3¼	€22 (full fare only)
Hanover	daily	3¾	€31/18
Munich	daily	8½	€66/39

Europe

The main bus companies serving destinations throughout Europe from Berlin are BerlinLinienBus (see above) and Gullivers Reisen (☎ 31 10 21 10, fax 311 02 10, e citycenter@gullivers.de, German-only w www.gullivers.de). The latter has an office at Hardenbergplatz 14, outside of Zoo station, which is open daily from 8am to 8pm. If you are outside Germany, call toll-free ☎ 00800-48 55 48 37. Their discounted fares apply to students and anyone under aged 26 or over 60. Bikes may be taken on one way/return for €25/40. On overnight routes, super-comfortable sleeper seats (practically full beds) are available for around an additional €10. The following table shows sample destinations with one-way/return fares. Buses leave once daily from Zoo station.

BerlinLinienBus also serves these and other destinations at more or less the same rates. Check their Web site for details.

destination	duration (hours)	full fare	discount fare
Amsterdam	9	€ 50/90	€40/75
Brussels	12	€50/90	€40/75
Copenhagen	7.5	€35/60	€30/55
London	17.5	€80/140	€65/120
Paris	14	€70/125	€55/100

Busabout (UK ☎ 020-7950 1661, fax 7950 1662, e info@busabout.com, w www.busabout.com) is a UK-based budget alternative, which runs coaches along interlocking European circuits. Though aimed at younger travellers, it has no upper age limit. The Busabout Pass costs £169 (£149 for youth and student card holders) for 14 days of consecutive travel on any of the circuits. Also available are Flexi Passes good for travel on a limited number of days within a specified period. Passes for 10 days of travel within two months, for example, cost £259, 15 days of travel are £369.

From Berlin, there are direct routes to/from Amsterdam (10 hours) and Prague (eight hours). Buses pick up and drop off at the Hotel Transit in Kreuzberg (see the Places to Stay chapter). Tickets are available online or from STA Travel, Council Travel, Flight Centre, and other youth-oriented travel agencies.

CAR & MOTORCYCLE

The A10 ring road links Berlin with other German and foreign cities in every direction, including the A11 to Szczecin (Stettin) in Poland; the A12 to Frankfurt/Oder; the A13 to Dresden; the A9 to Leipzig, Nuremberg and Munich; the A2 to Hanover and the Ruhrgebiet cities; and the A24 to Hamburg.

BICYCLE

Bicycles can travel by air. You *can* take them to pieces and put them in a bike bag or box, but it's much easier simply to wheel your bike to the check-in desk, where it should be treated as a piece of baggage. You may have to remove the pedals and turn the handlebars sideways so that it takes up less space in the aircraft's hold; check all this with the airline well in advance, preferably before you pay for your ticket.

On trains, you will need to purchase a separate ticket for your bike. These cost €3 for travel on local and regional trains and €8 on IC, EC and IR trains. If you are travelling long distance you are also required to make a reservation for your bike (free). Most trains (excluding ICEs) have a 2nd-class carriage at one end with a bicycle compartment. DB's bike hotline is ☎ 01805-15 14 15 (€0.12 per minute).

HITCHING & RIDE SERVICES

Hitching *(Trampen)* is never entirely safe in any country, and we don't recommend it. Travellers who decide to hitch should understand that they are taking a small but potentially serious risk. People who do choose to hitch will be safer if they travel in pairs and let someone know where they are planning to go. It's illegal to hitchhike on autobahns or their entry/exit ramps, but service stations can be very good places to pick up a ride. Prepare a sign clearly showing your intended destination in German.

Aside from hitching, the cheapest way to travel to and within Germany is as a paying passenger in a private car. Such rides are arranged by *Mitfahrzentralen*, ride-share agencies that can be found in all major cities and many smaller ones as well. You pay a fixed amount to the driver plus commission, ranging from €5 for short distances to €10 for longer trips. Generally, a ride from Berlin to Hamburg (or vice versa) costs €17, Cologne €34, Munich €35 and Amsterdam €38 (including commission).

Berlin has several *Mitfahrzentrale* agencies, the two big ones being ADM and Citynetz. ADM has branches at Zoo station on the Vinetastrasse platform of the U2 (Map 6; ☎ 194 40); at Yorckstrasse 52 in Schöneberg (Map 4; ☎ 194 20); in U-Bahn station Alexanderplatz, as you cross from U2 to U8 (Map 7; ☎ 241 58 20); and at Odersbergerstrasse 45 in Prenzlauer Berg (Map 3; ☎ 440 93 92).

CityNetz has a big office at Joachimstaler Strasse 17 in Charlottenburg (Map 6; ☎ 194 44) and another at Bergmannstrasse 57 in Kreuzberg 61 (Map 5; ☎ 693 60 95).

The people answering the phone in these offices usually speak English well. If you arrange a ride a few days in advance, it's a good idea to call the driver the night before and again on departure morning to make sure they're definitely going.

ORGANISED TOURS

There are many options for organised travel to Berlin. The German National Tourist Office in your country may be able to provide a list of tour operators (see Tourist Offices in the Facts for the Visitor chapter). It is always worth shopping around, but such tours rarely come cheap. While they can save you hassles, they also rob you of independence.

Especially within Europe, major airlines often offer short city-break packages, which include air fares, accommodation, transfers and sometimes a guided city tour with additional time for independent explorations. Look for these deals in the travel sections of national newspapers or check with your travel agent.

Getting Around

Driving in Berlin is easier than in most big cities, but it's no walk in the park either. There's still plenty of construction going on, which often results in gridlock, mysteriously re-routed roads and sudden dead ends. A better choice is not to drive at all and to use Berlin's excellent public transport system – one billion passengers a year can't be wrong. A huge network of U-Bahn (underground) and S-Bahn (suburban-metropolitan) trains, buses, trams and ferries extends pretty much into every corner of Berlin and the surrounding areas, and tickets are quite economical.

THE AIRPORTS

Berlin has three airports; the general information number for all is ☎ 0180-500 01 86.

Tegel (TXL) is about 8km north-west of Zoo station and primarily serves destinations within Germany and Europe. In the main hall you'll find the left-luggage office (open from 5.30am to 10pm), a BTM tourist Info Point, a post office and a bank.

Schönefeld airport (SXF), about 22km south-east of Zoo station, mostly handles international flights within Europe, with a particular emphasis on Eastern Europe, as well as to and from Asia. Facilities here include a currency-exchange desk and a post office. The baggage-storage office is in front of Terminal C and opens from 5.30am to 10pm daily.

Berlin-Tempelhof (THF; Map 4) is the most central airport and functions as the main hub for domestic departures and flights to and from central Europe.

Annual flight passenger volume through Berlin is expected to double to 20 million by 2010, which is why plans have been devised to expand Schönefeld into Berlin's single mega-airport by 2007. Renamed the Berlin Brandenburg International (BBI), it will have the capacity to serve around 30 million passengers per year. As a result, Tegel is expected to be closed down and services to and from Tempelhof will be limited.

TO/FROM THE AIRPORTS
Tegel

Tegel is connected to the Mitte district by the JetExpressBus TXL, which drops off and picks up at such strategic stops as Potsdamer Platz, Friedrichstrasse and Unter den Linden. The trip takes about 30 minutes and costs €3.10. To get to the CityWest district around Zoo station, take bus No X9, which takes 20 minutes, or bus No 109, which needs five minutes more. Tickets for either are €2.10. The nearest U-Bahn station to the airport is Jakob-Kaiser-Platz (U7), which is also served by both bus No 109 and X9. You can also take bus No 128 to Kurt-Schumacher-Platz to connect to the U6. A taxi between Tegel and the CityWest costs about €18.

Schönefeld

Schönefeld airport is served by the Airport Express train (Regionalexpress or RE trains) from Zoo station about every half-hour from 4.30am to 11pm; the trip takes 30 minutes and costs €2.10. Trains also stop at Bahnhof Friedrichsstrasse, Alexanderplatz and Ostbahnhof. The airport train station is about 300m away from the terminal to which it is linked by a free shuttle bus every 10 minutes. A slower alternative (50 minutes) is the S9, which runs from Zoo station via Alexanderplatz every 20 minutes between 4am and midnight. The less frequent S45 links Schönefeld and Tempelhof airports. Bus No 171 links the terminal directly with the U-Bahn station Rudow (U7) with connections to central Berlin. For a taxi between Schönefeld and the CityWest figure on spending between €25 and €35.

Tempelhof

Tempelhof airport (Map 5) is served by the U6 (get off at Platz der Luftbrücke) and by bus No 119 from Kurfürstendamm via Kreuzberg. A taxi to/from the CityWest costs about €15.

PUBLIC TRANSPORT

Berlin's public transport system is jointly operated by the Berliner Verkehrsbetriebe (BVG; ☎ 194 49 for 24-hour information) and Deutsche Bahn (DB; ☎ 194 19 for information 6am to 11pm, ☎ 0180-599 66 33 for 24-hour hotline). The BVG operates the U-Bahn, buses, trams and ferries, while DB is in charge of the S-Bahn, Regionalbahn (RB) and Regionalexpress (RE) trains.

One type of ticket is valid on all forms of transport (with the few exceptions noted below). The system is fairly efficient but, given the continued construction around the city, delays and schedule changes may occur. For 24-hour up-to-date BVG route information call ☎ 25 62 25 62. For DB's information service, dial ☎ 29 71 29 71.

The BVG information kiosk on Hardenbergplatz, outside Zoo station (Map 6), has free route maps and general information on all means of transport. It's open daily from 6.30am to 8.30pm and also sell tickets and passes. For information on S-Bahn, RE and RB connections, visit the Reisezentrum office inside any train station.

Tickets & Passes

Berlin's metropolitan area is divided into three tariff zones – A, B and C. Tickets are valid in at least two zones – AB or BC – or in all three zones, ABC. Unless you're venturing to Potsdam or the very outer suburbs, you'll only need the AB ticket. Dogs and one piece of luggage are free. The most common types of tickets are:

Kurzstrecke (Short Trip)
 This ticket (€1.20) allows three stops on U/S-Bahn, or six stops on bus or tram; one change is allowed, but only between trains (not bus to train or bus to bus).
Zones AB or BC
 This ticket buys unlimited travel for two hours within two of the three zones (AB or BC) for €2.10.
Zones ABC
 You have unlimited travel for two hours in zones ABC (€2.40).
Tageskarte (Day Pass)
 This pass provides unlimited travel for one day (€6.10 for zones AB or BC, or €6.30 for zones ABC).

7-Tage Karte (Seven-Day Pass)
 This transferable pass allows unlimited travel for a week after validation (€22 for zones AB, €23 for zones BC and €28 for zones ABC).

Buying & Using Tickets

Bus drivers sell single and day tickets, but tickets for U/S-Bahn trains and multiple, weekly or monthly tickets must be purchased before boarding. Most are available from the orange vending machines (which feature instructions in English) in U/S-Bahn stations, as well as from the ticket window at station entrances and the BVG information kiosk.

Tickets must be stamped (validated) in a red machine (Entwerter) at the platform entrances to U/S-Bahn stations before boarding, or aboard buses upon entering. If you're using a timed ticket like the Langstrecke, validate it just as your train arrives to ensure full value. If you're caught by an inspector without a ticket (or even an unvalidated one), there's a €30 fine.

U/S-Bahn

The most efficient way to travel around Berlin is by U/S-Bahn. There are 10 U-Bahn and 13 S-Bahn lines which operate from 4am until just after midnight. Exceptions are the U1 and the U9 which operate all night on a limited service (about two trains an hour). Most S-Bahns also run hourly on Saturday and Sunday between midnight and 4am. Rail pass holders can use the S-Bahn for free.

The next station is announced on most U-Bahn (but not S-Bahn) trains and is also displayed at the end of carriages on some newer trains. It's best, though, to know the name of the station before you get to the one you need. To help you do this, large route maps are plastered on the ceilings above the doors in most U-Bahn cars. Large versions of the same maps are on station platforms.

Regional Trains

The S-Bahn network is supplemented by the Regionalbahn (RB) and the Regionalexpress (RE) trains whose routes are also marked on the BVG network map. Only BVG Ganzstrecke and DB rail tickets (including rail passes) are valid on these trains.

Bus

Berlin's buses are rather slow, but being comfortably ensconced on the upper level of a double-decker is a mighty fine – and inexpensive – way to do some relaxed sightseeing (see boxed text 'All Aboard! Berlin from Bus No 100 & 200').

Bus stops are marked with a large 'H' (for *Haltestelle*) and the name of the stop. Drivers sell tickets and can give change. The next stop is usually announced over a loudspeaker or displayed on a digital board. Push the button on the handrails to signal to the driver that you want to get off. After 8pm, you can only board through the front door and, if you already have a ticket, you must present it upon entering.

Nightbus Some 70 bus lines take over from the U/S-Bahn between 1am and 4am, running roughly at 30-minute intervals. Buses leave from the major nightlife areas like Zoo station, Hackescher Markt in Mitte and Nollendorfplatz in Schöneberg, and cover the entire Berlin area, including the outer districts. Normal fares apply.

Changeovers at major transfer stations are timed in such a way that you should only have to wait a few minutes. A free network map is available at the BVG kiosk (Map 6).

Tram

Trams used to be rickety throwbacks to the days before U/S-Bahns but most have been replaced by comfortable new models. They

---

All Aboard! Berlin From Bus No 100 & 200

For years, one of the best and cheapest ways to see Berlin has been aboard bus No 100, which shuttles between Zoo station in the CityWest to Prenzlauer Berg, passing by nearly every major historic sight. The cost? A mere €2.10 standard ticket, which even allows you to get off as often as you like within the two hours of its validity. If you plan on exploring all day, consider investing in a *Tageskarte* (Day Pass) for €6.30.

The first sight you see after the bus leaves Zoo station is the landmark Gedächtniskirche and the beginning of the Ku'damm before reaching the famous Berliner Zoo. From here, the bus turns north into the Tiergarten where you'll pass the triumphant golden figure atop the Siegessäule. Look quickly right as the bus crosses the Strasse des 17 Juni and you'll spot the Brandenburger Tor down the broad boulevard. Your next stop is Schloss Bellevue, the Berlin residence of Germany's president. The bus then follows streets paralleling the Spree river before passing the Reichstag. Soon after, it'll drive right through the Brandenburger Tor, a privilege given only to taxis and city buses.

Now you're in former East Berlin and heading down Unter den Linden, passing such sights as the Berliner Dom and Humboldt Universität. Next you'll reach Alexanderplatz with its monster TV tower, before travelling north-east through Friedrichshain all the way to the Michelangelostrasse terminus near Europe's largest Jewish cemetery.

Bus No 100 has been such a big hit that the BVG, which operates Berlin's buses, has added a second line: bus No 200. It, too, starts at Zoo station, then takes a more southerly route swinging by the Gedenkstätte Deutscher Widerstand, the Kulturforum, Potsdamer Platz, and the Martin-Gropius-Bau before heading north to the Brandenburger Tor and then east on Unter den Linden.

If you don't interrupt your trip, the entire one-way journey on either route takes about 45 minutes (more during heavy traffic). Since there's usually no commentary (unless you're lucky to have a chatty bus driver), it's a good idea to pick up a map and information leaflet from the BVG information kiosk outside Zoo station.

operate only in the eastern sections, having been abolished in the western city in 1967.

About 30 lines crisscross the entire eastern half of Berlin and a network map is available at the BVG kiosk (Map 6).

Ferry

The BVG operates several ferry services but the only one you're ever likely to need is the F10, which shuttles between Kladow and Wannsee. The trip in itself is quite scenic and, since regular BVG tickets apply, makes for an inexpensive excursion. Ferries operate hourly all year, weather permitting, usually from 9am to sunset. For information about sightseeing cruises, see Boat Tours later in this chapter.

CAR & MOTORCYCLE

Berlin is easier to drive in than many other big European cities because it was more or less rebuilt from scratch after WWII with a modern city layout. However, until roadworks and construction – especially in the eastern parts – are finished (and who knows when that will be), you may encounter some confusion. In spite of the massive building projects, traffic generally moves fairly smoothly. A real convenience is the A10 ring road which gets you easily around the urban perimeter.

Parking in garages is expensive (about €1 to €1.50 per hour), but it'll often be your only choice if you want to be near the main shopping areas or other attractions. In the CityWest(Map 6), for instance, you'll find car parks on Augsburger Strasse, in the Europa-Center and immediately west of the zoo on Budapester Strasse. The day rate is around €12.50.

Free street parking, while impossible to find in these central areas, is usually available in residential streets, especially in the eastern districts. Watch for signs indicating parking restrictions or you risk a ticket or even being towed.

Parking meters are rare but the 'pay and display' system is quite widespread. This requires you to buy a ticket for the time you intend to park from a ticket-vending machine as soon as you've parked your car (it should be kerbside just a few metres away). Then display your receipt visibly on the dashboard inside the car. Hourly rates are around €1. Check the machine or signposts for enforcement hours.

If you're staying at a hotel, keep in mind that most don't have their own garages and that you will either have to find parking on your own or have the hotel staff park it for you; this will add about €12.50 per night to your bill.

Car Rental

You'll find all the major international car-rental chains represented in Berlin. Their lowest standard rates begin at around €50 per day and between €200 and €250 per week, including VAT and unlimited kilometres. The best deals are special weekend tariffs, in effect from noon Friday to 9am Monday, from €65. Some arrangements also include collision insurance which can save up to €20 a day. You must be at least 21 to rent from most agencies.

Robben und Wientjes, a local agency with branches at Prinzenstrasse 90–91 in Kreuzberg (Map 5; ☎ 61 67 70) and at Prenzlauer Allee 96 (Map 3; ☎ 42 10 36), usually has the best deals in town with cars from €15 per day, including 100km, and trucks from €3 per hour.

International agencies cluster on and around Budapester Strasse near Zoo station. Hertz (Map 6; ☎ 261 10 53) is at Budapester Strasse 39, Avis (Map 6; ☎ 230 93 70) is next door at number 41; SixtBudget (Map 6; ☎ 219 90 90) and Europcar (Map 6; ☎ 235 06 40) are both at Kurfürstenstrasse 101; Europcar is also at Karl-Liebknecht-Strasse 19–21 (Map 7; ☎ 240 79 00) in Mitte. For other branches and agencies, check the Yellow Pages under *Autovermietung*.

A company usually offering great deals (although these are likely to fluctuate with the exchange rate) is US-based AutoEurope, which negotiates low rates and excellent conditions with all the major agencies. Reservations can be made via a 24-hour toll-free number with an English-speaking operator. Cars are available in all sizes and categories, and there's no surcharge for one-way rentals or airport drop-offs. In addition, there is no charge for cancellations or changes, and the minimum rental age is 19. They even let you travel into Poland and the Czech Republic if you tell them at the time of booking, though there is an extra charge. There is, however, a three-day minimum rental (but no penalty for turning it in early).

If you need a car and you're already in Germany, dial ☎ 0130-82 21 98. From North America call ☎ 800-223-5555; from Australia ☎ 800-12 64 09; from New Zealand ☎ 0800-44 07 22; from France ☎ 0800-901 17 70; and from Britain ☎ 0800-899 893.

A small economy car will cost you around US$90 for the three-day minimum and US$150 for the weekly rental, including unlimited kilometres, VAT and third-party insurance but not collision insurance. If this is not covered by your credit card, you have to add up to US$15 per day to your rate.

Car Purchase

Unless you're staying in Berlin or Germany for an extended time, buying a car here is more hassle than it's worth due to the costs and paperwork involved. EU nationals must register the car with the Ordnungs-und Strassenverkehrsamt (Public Order & Traffic Office). You will need proof of ownership, proof of insurance and a passport or ID. You'll also be subject to a motor vehicle tax.

Non-EU nationals quickly find themselves in a Catch 22 situation. While allowed to *buy* a car, they may not *register* it, since you have to be a German or EU resident to do so. You could ask a local friend or relative to register a car for you, but since this puts their own driving record and insurance rates at risk, it's not really a popular option.

But if you're undeterred, Berlin is among the best places in Germany to shop around for used cars. A good place to look is the weekly newspaper *Zweite Hand*, which has a separate car edition with thousands of listings. Make sure the vehicle has a valid 'TÜV' certificate of roadworthiness.

Motorcycle Rental

Numerous outfits in Berlin rent motorcycles, which are fun for excursions to the countryside. Harley fans could contact Classic Bike Harley-Davidson (Map 5; ☎ 616 79 30), Skalitzer Strasse 127–128 in Kreuzberg 36. They open from 10am to 10pm and rent a wide range of models for €50 to €130 per day (includes 300km), and on the weekend – 4pm Friday to 10am Monday – for €195 to €325 (includes 600km). The latter rate also applies to rentals from 4pm Monday to 1pm Friday (includes 900km). Prices include VAT and insurance. Helmets are €5 per day.

Another company worth trying is V2-Moto (Map 5; ☎ 61 28 04 90), nearby at Skalitzer Strasse 69, which rents models like Voxan Cafe Racer and Roadster and Laverda 750 Sport per day for €95-115. Weekend rentals (starting Fri 4pm to Mon 10am) cost €245-290. The same rates applies if you rent the bike from Mon 4pm to Fri 1pm.

TAXI

Taxi stands with 'call columns', *Rufsäule*, are beside all main train stations and throughout the city. Flag fall is €2.50, then it's €1.50 per kilometre up to 7km and €1 for each additional kilometre. A fifth passenger costs an extra €1.25 and bulky luggage is €1 per piece. To order a taxi by phone, call ☎ 194 10, ☎ 21 02 02 or ☎ 26 10 26.

If you need to travel quickly over a short distance, you can use the €3 flat rate which entitles you to ride for 2km. This only applies if you flag down a moving taxi and ask for the €3 rate before getting in.

If you have a problem with a cabbie (this is unlikely to happen), get a receipt showing the price, date, time and route, have them sign and stamp it, then complain to Innung des Berliner Taxigewerbes (☎ 23 62 71 01), Martin-Luther-Strasse 3, Schöneberg.

Velotaxi

A nonpolluting alternative for short hops is a Velotaxi, a comfortable pedicab aided by an electric engine, that seats two people. They operate along four routes: Kurfürsten-damm, Unter den Linden, Friedrichstrasse and Tiergarten. Simply flag one down or call

☎ 0172-32 88 88 88. The cost is €1 per km; travel along a set route is €2.50 per person; half-hour tours are €8 per person.

BICYCLE

Berlin is fairly user-friendly for cyclists, although you need to keep your wits about you in heavy traffic, even where there are bike lanes. Helmets are not required by law. Taking a bike in marked carriages of the U/S-Bahn costs €1.25. On U-Bahn carriages, bikes are allowed between 9am and 2pm and between 5.30pm and closing time on weekdays (any time on weekends). Taking your bike on a DB train costs €3 on local and regional trains and €8 on IC, EC and IR trains. For long-distance travel, you need to make a reservation for your bike (free). DB's bike hotline is on ☎ 01805-15 14 15 (€0.12 per minute).

Fahrradstation is the largest bike rental outfit with several branches around town and a central information and reservation hotline (☎ 0180-510 80 00). You'll find them in courtyard No VII of the Hackesche Höfe in Mitte (Map 7; ☎ 28 38 48 48); at nearby Auguststrasse 29a (Map 3; ☎ 28 59 96 61) and at Bahnhof Friedrichstrasse, Friedrichstrasse 141–142 (Map 7; ☎ 20 45 45 00). There's another one in Kreuzberg 61 at Bergmannstrasse 9 (Map 5; ☎ 215 15 66).

Fahrradstation also sells bicycles and organises guided bike tours throughout Berlin and into the surrounding countryside. Rates per day/three-day-weekend/week for city cruisers start at €10/25/35, and with mountain bikes cost €20/45/65.

An alternative is Fahrradservice (Map 7; ☎ 28 04 73 31), Reinhardtstrasse 5 in Mitte, which charges €10 to €20 for 24-hour rental.

WALKING

The historic centre of Berlin is surprisingly compact and best explored on foot. Walking lets you experience the city at ground level and generally gives you a better sense of the different flavours of the various neighbourhoods. It's safe to walk anywhere in the central city, including in the large parks like Tiergarten, though be extra careful at night time. Several great self-guided walking tours are outlined in the Things to See & Do chapter later in this book. If you don't want to walk by yourself, you can also join a guided English-language tour (see the Walking Tours section later in this chapter).

ORGANISED TOURS
Bus Tours

Most city sightseeing tours operate on the get-on, get-off as often as you wish principle and there's very little difference between operators. The main competitors take in 12 main sights – including Kurfürstendamm, Brandenburger Tor, Schloss Charlottenburg, Berliner Dom and Alexanderplatz – on loops that take about two hours without getting off. Taped commentary comes in (count 'em) eight languages. Buses leave roughly every half-hour, with the first tour usually around 10am somewhere on Kurfürstendamm near Zoo Station; buses stop running around 6pm (earlier in winter). The cost is €18.

The buses of Severin + Kühn (Map 6; ☎ 880 41 90) leave from Kurfürstendamm 216; BVB (Map 6; ☎ 88 68 37 11) from Kurfürstendamm 225 opposite the Kranzler Eck; and Berolina (Map 6; ☎ 88 56 80 30) from Kurfürstendamm 220, corner of Meinekestrasse.

These operators also have a Super Berlin Tour, a more conventional, narrated nonstop 3½-hour tour that costs €21 and is offered in the morning and in the afternoon. Children under 13 travel for half price.

Between Easter and October, there's also the BVG Top Tour (☎ 25 62 47 40), which has departures every 30 minutes from the Kranzler Eck at Kurfürstendamm 18. It makes 23 stops and costs €18 (€15 for children aged six to 14). Tickets bought after 3pm are valid until the end of the following day.

Tempelhofer (☎ 752 40 57) is slightly cheaper (€15/€12.50), makes 14 stops and has live commentary. Buses depart year round from Kurfürstendamm 231 (outside the Hertie bei Wertheim department store, Map 6) and from Unter den Linden 14, corner of Friedrichstrasse (Map 7).

Walking Tours

Berlin has three companies offering English-language tours which are excellent, informative and entertaining.

Among the best walking tours we've ever taken are the ones from The Original Berlin Walks (☎ 301 91 94, W www.berlinwalks .com). Its three- to four-hour Discover Berlin tour covers all the highlights of the city, giving interesting and unbiased historical background and architectural information. It leaves daily at 10am and 2.30pm from April to October and 10am the rest of the year, and ends at Checkpoint Charlie. Berlin Walks also offers the fascinating Infamous Third Reich Sites (March to December) and Jewish Life in Berlin (May to mid-October), which run on a more limited schedule.

Tours for those over/under 26 cost €9/7.50 (€6.75 with Welcome Card), free if under 14. A discount coupon for €1 can be printed from the Web site. Tours leave from outside the main entrance of Zoo station (Map 6) at the top of the taxi rank. You'll need a BVG *Langstrecke* ticket (€2.10; see Public Transport in the Getting Around section) or buy one from the guide. Rail-pass holders don't need one for the Discover Berlin and Jewish Life tours as the S-Bahn is used.

A very popular alternative are tours with Brewer's Best of Berlin (☎ 70 13 10 37), which has received ringing endorsements from some of our readers. Run by Terry Brewer, a former diplomat at the British Embassy in East Berlin, tours leave twice daily from May to October (once daily from February to April and from November to mid-December; no tours from late December to early January) from the New Synagogue, as well as the Circus, Clubhouse and Odyssee hostels (see the Places to Stay chapter). Entertaining and informative, they run at least five hours, cover a lot more than the basics and offer an incredible bargain at €7.50. Call or check with the hostels for specific departure times.

The Insider Tour (☎ 692 31 49) runs 3½-hour tours of all main sights in both western and eastern Berlin for €10/€7.50 (€6.50 with Welcome Card). Tours leave daily at

9.45am and 2.15pm from the Reisebank at Zoo station and at 10am and 2.30pm from outside McDonald's, also at Zoo station. From November to March only the morning tours are offered. From May to September, Insider Tour also operates four-hour bike tours for €17.50/€15, including bike rental. These leave at 10.30am from the Fahrradstation branch at Bahnhof Friedrichstrasse.

Boat Tours

In the warmer months, tourist boats cruise Berlin's waterways, calling at main historical sights in the centre as well as picturesque villages, parks and palaces. Food and drink are sold on board, but are quite expensive, so take something along with you.

Stern und Kreis Schifffahrt (☎ 536 36 00) operates boat cruises from landing docks throughout the city from April to December. Boats depart from the Schlossbrücke near Schloss Charlottenburg (Map 2); from Friedrichstrasse, the Nikolaiviertel and Jannowitzbrücke, all in Mitte (Map 7); and from Hafen Treptow in Treptow (Map 5). Popular cruises include the 3½-hour trip (€8.50 one way, €14 return) from Jannowitzbrücke (Map 7) near the Märkisches Museum, past the northern boundary of Tiergarten park to Schlossbrücke, near Charlottenburg Palace runs up to eight times daily. A one-hour spin around Museumsinsel from the Nikolaiviertel (Map 7, €7.50) operates up to 17 times daily. Night tours (€13.50, 2½ hours) start at 7.30pm and run Friday and Saturday.

Children under six travel for free, those under 14 get a 50% discount. Students and seniors get 15% off, though not on weekends or holidays. A Kombi-Tageskarte, giving you unlimited rides aboard regular Stern und Kreis cruises as well as U/S-Bahn, buses and trams in Berlin and Potsdam, costs €13.50.

Reederei Bruno Winkler (☎ 349 95 95) has sightseeing cruises on the Spree River or the Landwehr Canal from March to September. The main landing stage is at Schlossbrücke, just east of the Schloss Charlottenburg (Map 2). Three-hour tours leave twice daily at 10.20am and 2.20pm and at 7pm Friday (€12.25/€11.25). You can also hop aboard at the Friedrichstrasse landing (Map 7) at the Reichstagsufer (€10.25/€9.25). English-language audiotapes with commentary are available, but only when boarding at Schlossbrücke. Several other tours are also offered.

Berliner Wassertaxi Service (Map 7; ☎ 65 88 02 03), a water-taxi service based near the Schlossbrücke in Mitte, has one-hour spins (€6/€4.50) along the Spree between Spree Canal and Bahnhof Friedrichstrasse, leaving every half-hour between 10am and 4.30pm.

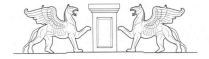

Things to See & Do

THINGS TO SEE & DO

Berlin is such a vibrant city that it's unlikely you'll run out of things to do. And it's all changing at such lightning speed that you'll be able to make your own discoveries. Just pick a quarter to wander in, soak up the atmosphere and try to imagine where it will all be a few `years hence.

Places of interest, museums, sights and other diversions are described in this chapter by district. Each of Berlin's seven core districts – Charlottenburg, Friedrichshain, Kreuzberg, Mitte, Prenzlauer Berg, Schöneberg, Tiergarten – are covered in great detail in alphabetical order. Some sections feature neighbourhood walking tours. Subsequent sections provide an overview of what there is to see and do in Berlin's outer districts. The chapter concludes with a listing of recreational activities. Berlin's wonderful public transport system is the best method of getting around the city, other than your own two feet.

Charlottenburg

To anyone travelling to Berlin before the collapse of the Wall, Charlottenburg was the place to go. This was where hotels, restaurants, shops and nightlife clustered. In the 1990s, as all attention turned to Mitte and Prenzlauer Berg, Charlottenburg gradually lost its popularity, but this is not to say that it is no longer worth a visit. As the following section shows, there's plenty to see and do in what is also now referred to as City-West. Hotels here, while older, offer good value, the shopping is still some of the best in town and there's even some exciting new architecture to spice up the bland post-war cityscape.

Charlottenburg was born out of the tragic early death of a beloved queen. When Sophie Charlotte, wife of King Friedrich I, died in 1705, the king gave town rights to the little settlement that had sprung up around the queen's summer palace and named the whole

Berlin Highlights

Berlin offers a veritable cornucopia of experiences, locations, sights and attractions – picking out the best is no easy endeavour. What follows is a highly subjective list – in no particular order – of personal favourites that we hope you will enjoy as well.

- Surveying the New Government District from the magnificent Reichstag cupola
- Greeting the sunrise after a night of bar hopping
- Exploring the city with Berlin Walks, Brewer's Best of Berlin or Insider Tours
- Walking in the footsteps of history along Unter den Linden
- Clubbing – everything from swing to electrojazz, often in unusual sites
- Shopping and fine architecture in the Friedrichstadtpassagen
- Visiting the 'must-see' museums: Pergamon Museum, Jüdisches Museum, Gemäldegalerie, Ägyptisches Museum
- Browsing KaDeWe and snacking in its opulent food hall
- Checking out the scene during breakfast in Schöneberg
- Discovering Berlin's newest district: Potsdamer Platz
- Feasting on some of the best doner kebabs this side of Istanbul
- Attending a classical concert at the Philharmonie
- Cruising Berlin's lakes, rivers or canals
- Strolling and picnicking in the fairytale setting of Pfaueninsel
- Sightseeing aboard Bus No 100 or No 200
- Enjoying the best bird's-eye views: Berliner Dom, Französischer Dom, Panorama Observation Deck

thing in her honour. Its fledgling population grew slowly. Even in 1870 the area still had a distinct rural character and a mere 17,000 inhabitants.

Not until Berlin became capital of the German Empire did the population grow in leaps and bounds. In 1890, there were 77,000 people. In 1914, there were 320,000. These years also saw the founding of the Technische Universität (1884) and the Hochschule der Künste (University of the Arts, 1902). During the Weimar years, Charlottenburg became Berlin's cultural epicentre, with theatres, cabarets, jazz clubs and literary cafes lining its main artery, the fashionable Kurfürstendamm. In fact, much of the unbridled creativity – and decadence – of the 'Golden Twenties' had its roots here. Though considerably more tame these days, Charlottenburg remains a vibrant and interesting part of the city.

CITYWEST WALKING TOUR (Map 6)

This walking tour meanders through the core of the CityWest, starting and finishing at Zoo station. It's intended to give you a flavour of the district's commercial and residential areas and will take you to historic landmarks, museums, shopping areas and the design and gallery district. The loop entails a distance of 4.5km and will take you two to three hours – longer if you linger.

Zoo station to Breitscheidplatz

Our tour begins at Zoo station, which opened in 1881 and gets its name from the **Zoologischer Garten** just east of here (for more on the zoo itself, see the Tiergarten section later in this chapter). Along with the Ostbahnhof in Friedrichshain, Zoo station is Berlin's busiest train station, especially for long-distance travel. In the '70s and '80s, the area around it was a notorious drugs haunt, a grim reality graphically portrayed in *Wir Kinder vom Bahnhof Zoo* (The Children of Bahnhof Zoo). It's the biography of the teenager Christiane F, who managed to escape the cycle of heroin addiction, prostitution and violence. The book was later made into a movie.

From here, head east on Budapester Strasse past the Zoo-Palast cinema, which until 1999 hosted the Berlin International Film Festival. On the ground floor is a branch of Hekticket where you can get half-price theatre tickets for same-day performances (see the theatre section in the Entertainment chapter for details).

A short walk away towers one of Berlin's most famous historic landmarks, the ruined **Kaiser-Wilhelm-Gedächtniskirche** (Kaiser Wilhelm Memorial Church, 1895). Allied bombing left only the husk of the neo-Romanesque church's west tower intact; it now stands quiet, poignant and dignified, engulfed in roaring commercialism. The **Gedenkhalle** *(Memorial Hall, open 10am-4pm or 5pm Mon-Sat)* contains the original ceiling mosaics, marble reliefs, liturgical objects and photos of the building before and after the bombing. In 1961, a modern octagonal **hall of worship** *(admission free; open 9am-7.30pm daily)* was built next to it. It has intensely midnight-blue stained glass windows and a larger-than-life golden Jesus figure 'floating' above the altar. On your right, as you enter, is the so-called **Stalingrad Madonna** (1942), a haunting charcoal drawing of a mother cradling her child. It was drawn on the back of a map of Russia by Kurt Reuber, a German priest and doctor, while under siege in Stalingrad; Reuber died as a Soviet POW in 1944.

On its southern side, the Gedächtniskirche flanks **Breitscheidplatz**, a lively square ruled by pedestrians that is the heart of the CityWest. Everyone from footsore tourists to seasoned street performers gathers around the quirky **Weltbrunnen** (World Fountain, 1983) by Joachim Schmettau. Made from reddish granite it shows a world split open with sculptures of humans and animals clustering in various scenes. Naturally, Berliners have found a nickname for it: Wasserklops (water dumpling).

Providing a modern counterpoint to the Gedächtniskirche is the **Europa-Center**, a soaring shopping and restaurant complex that was Berlin's first high-rise when it opened in 1965. It stands on the site of the

Romanische Café, the gathering place of choice for Weimar Republic intellectuals. Inside, the **Flow of Time Clock** by Bernard Gitton measures hours, minutes and seconds via a series of vials and spheres that fill up with radioactive-looking green liquid. The main **BTM tourist office** is on the ground floor of the centre's Budapester Strasse (north) side.

From Breitscheidplatz, you could take a detour south-east along Tauentzienstrasse to Wittenbergplatz for a browse through that wonderful temple of temptations, the KaDeWe department store (see the Shopping chapter). En route, note the iconic sculpture of intertwined metal beams called 'Berlin' by Brigitte and Martin Matschinsky-Denninghof on the centre strip.

Berlin Nicknames

Berliners are known for having a way with words. They also have a fertile imagination, evidence of which you'll find in the numerous nicknames they've given to their landmarks. Here's a sample:

Kaiser Wilhelm Gedächtniskirche	Hohler Zahn (Hollow Tooth)
Gedenkhalle	Lippenstift & Puderdose (Lipstick & Powdercase)
Haus der Kulturen der Welt	Schwangere Auster (Pregnant Oyster)
Reichstag Cupola	Eierwärmer (English Egg Cosy)
TV Tower	Telespargel (Tele-Asparagus)
Funkturm	Langer Lulatsch (Long Lulatsch)
ICC Congress Centre	Raumschiff (Space Ship)
Siegessäule	Gold Else (Golden Else)
Luftbrückendenkmal	Hungerharke (Hunger Rake)
Wilhelminian pissoirs	Café Achteck (Café Octagon)
Weltbrunnen	Wasserklops (Water Dumpling)

Kurfürstendamm

Breitscheidplatz is the eastern terminus of the broad, 3.5km-long Kurfürstendamm, known as Ku'damm for short. It is the CityWest's main shopping street with speciality, chain and department stores vying for customers.

It was Bismarck who was responsible for making Ku'damm into a Berlin version of Paris' Champs-Elysée. Of this mere riding path until 1880, leading to the hunting grounds in the Grunewald forest, Bismarck envisioned a 53m-wide paved boulevard flanked by grandiose residential buildings. The 1920s added the luxury hotels and shops, art galleries, restaurants and entertainment venues that still characterise the avenue today.

Stroll west on Ku'damm where, on the corner of Joachimstaler Strasse, now looms Helmut Jahn's edgy glass office and retail complex called the Neues Kranzler Eck (see the Architecture special section). It stands on the site of the old Cafe Kranzler, one of the western city's most traditional coffeehouses of which only the rooftop rotunda remains.

Fasanenstrasse

Continue west on Kurfürstendamm, then hook south into fashionable Fasanenstrasse with fancy galleries and expensive jewellery and haute couture boutiques. Palatial late-19th-century town houses, some of which have been converted into pensions or hotels (see the Places to Stay chapter), line this quiet, leafy avenue. Sneak a peek into some of the foyers to discover stucco ceilings, romantic murals, marble fireplaces or even a frilly Art Nouveau lift, made from wrought iron or brass, and resembling a giant bird cage.

From the same period dates the stately trio of proud villas, connected by a small sculpture garden, on the western side of the street, collectively known as the **Wintergarten-Ensemble**. At Fasanenstrasse 23 is the Literaturhaus, where you can attend readings and literary discussions, check out the gallery, browse the bookstore or enjoy a meal at the sophisticated **Café Wintergarten** (see the Places to Eat chapter). At No 24 is the **Käthe-Kollwitz-Museum**, followed by the Villa

Grisebach, which houses the Galerie Pels-Leusden and an auction house. Note the frilly iron grillwork and witch's hat slate turret on this building.

Käthe-Kollwitz-Museum

Dedicated to one of Germany's greatest woman artists is this exquisite private museum (☎ 882 52 10, Fasanenstrasse 24; adult/concession €4/2; open 11am-6pm Wed-Mon). Kollwitz was born in 1867 in Königsberg (today's Kaliningrad) and died in Moritzburg near Dresden in 1945, however for most of her life she lived in Berlin's working-class Prenzlauer Berg district. She studied at art schools in Berlin and Munich and also spent time in Florence and Paris. Through her art Kollwitz expressed deep commitment to and concern for the working class, the underdog, the suppressed and the poor in a timeless and easily assimilated fashion.

Lithographs, graphics, woodcuts, sculptures and drawings form the core of the collection. Amassed by the painter and gallery owner Hans Pels-Leusden (died 1993), it shows her work in all its versatility and complexity. Highlights include the anti-hunger lithography *Brot* (Bread; 1924) and the woodcut series *Krieg* (War; 1922–23).

Käthe Kollwitz: one of Germany's greatest woman artists

Among Kollwitz' favourite themes were motherhood and death; sometimes the two are strangely intertwined as in works that show death as a nurturing figure, cradling its victims. The collection also includes sculpture and several self-portraits (1889–1938). Also here is a copy of the Kollwitz monument by Gustav Seitz (1958), the original of which stands on Kollwitzplatz (see the Prenzlauer Berg section later in this chapter). Two or three special exhibits annually supplement the permanent collection.

It's worth noting that the eagle-eyed guards, so prevalent at most of Berlin's museums, are refreshingly absent here, creating an intimate, almost meditative atmosphere.

A taped audio tour (in English, French or German) is available for an additional €2.

From the museum, continue south to Lietzenburger Strasse, then west one block and north on Uhlandstrasse back to Ku'damm where you turn left.

Story of Berlin

Soon on your left is the Ku'damm Karree, a shopping mall that also contains an excellent, if somewhat pricey, local history museum with a 21st-century multi-media twist: the Story of Berlin (☎ 88 72 01 00, Kurfürstendamm 207-208; adults/children to 14 €9/3; open 10am-8pm daily, last admission 6pm). Outfitted with space-age headphones and commentary (in English or German) that activates automatically as you enter a room, you time-travel through the fascinating history of Berlin from its founding, in 1237, right up to today. Admission also includes a tour of the fully functional atomic bunker underneath the building. Budget at least two hours to make the most of this museum.

Afterwards, head west along Ku'damm, then head north on Bleibtreustrasse. When you've passed the elevated S-Bahn tracks, you can either turn right into Savignypassage (in which case, go straight to the 'Savignyplatz back to Zoo Station' section later), or you can take a short detour by continuing north to Kantstrasse, then one block west and north on Schlüterstrasse which will take you to…

Das Verborgene Museum

Berlin's Verborgene Museum (Hidden Museum, ☎ 313 36 56, Schlüterstrasse 70; admission €1.50/1; open 3pm-7pm Thur-Fri, noon-4pm Sat-Sun) is run by a nonprofit women's organisation. Its mission is to exhibit the work of women artists, primarily those working in 1920s and 1930s Berlin, who have been 'forgotten' – in other words, 'overshadowed' – by their male counterparts. Up to three exhibits are mounted annually representing media ranging from photography to sculpture, architecture to painting. Readings and concerts take place as well. Backtrack to Savignypassage to continue the tour.

Savignyplatz back to Zoo Station

In the 1980s, Savignypassage was the first place in Berlin where the support archways of the elevated S-Bahn tracks were converted into galleries, stores and restaurants, a concept since copied throughout the city, especially in Mitte. The pedestrian-only passageway leads to the southern end of Savignyplatz, a green expanse that has been Charlottenburg's nightlife hub since long before the Wall collapsed. The atmosphere here, though, is more mature, mainstream and intellectual than its pendants in the eastern districts. Check the Places to Eat and Entertainment chapters for suggestions of restaurants and bars around here.

The tour, however, continues east on Kantstrasse. Its intersection with Uhlandstrasse has emerged as a centre of interior design anchored by the humungous **Stilwerk**. This multi-level atrium-style mall contains branches of The Conran Shop, Bang & Olufsen, Alessi and other big names (see the Shopping chapter). The space is also used for classical concerts and special exhibits.

Farther east, at the corner with Fasanenstrasse, looms the **Kantdreieck** (see the Architecture special section). A few steps south stands the **Jüdisches Gemeindehaus** (Jewish Community House, ☎ 88 02 82 60, Fasanenstrasse 79-80) on the site of a synagogue destroyed during Kristallnacht (9 November 1938). Its lone surviving feature – the portal – is integrated into today's modern structure.

There's a memorial to victims of the Nazi regime, meeting rooms, exhibition space, a library and a kosher restaurant called **Arche Noah** (Noah's Ark, see the Places to Eat chapter). As with most Jewish sites in Berlin, this place is usually patrolled by police.

Continuing east on Kantstrasse soon gets you to the magnificent **Theater des Westens** (1896) whose architect, Bernhard Sehring, managed to squeeze a multitude of architectural styles – baroque, neoclassical, Art Nouveau – into a single building. Briefly the western city's opera house, it's primarily a musical venue today.

A few steps east, at the corner of Kantstrasse and Joachimstaler Strasse, is Berlin's **Erotik Museum** (☎ 886 06 66, Joachimstaler Strasse 4; adult/concession €5/4, over-18 only; open 9am-midnight daily). Inside is a surprisingly tasteful and artful exhibit that is the brainchild of Beate Uhse, Germany's recently deceased (at age 82) sex-toy marketing queen. Well-lit and sophisticated displays tell the story of human sexuality through the ages. On view are meerschaum-smoking devices engraved with time-honoured themes, extremely funny scrolls from 19th-century Japan, Balinese fertility demons, 'pillow books' and hilarious erotic films from the very early days of cinema. The selection of 17th-century chastity belts elicits lots of giggles, especially from women.

From here it's just one block north back to Zoo station and the end of the tour.

SCHLOSS CHARLOTTENBURG (Map 2)

Schloss Charlottenburg is an exquisite baroque palace and one of the few remaining sites in Berlin that still reflects the former splendour and grandeur of the royal Hohenzollern clan. Commissioned at the end of the 17th century by Elector Friedrich III (later King Friedrich I) as a summer residence for Queen Sophie-Charlotte (1668–1705), it is on Spandauer Damm, 3km northwest of Zoo station. Along with several important buildings in the **Schlossgarten** (Palace Garden; free), there are several fine museums in and around the palace. To get

THINGS TO SEE & DO

Short Primer on Berlin's Museum Scene

Around 170 museums contribute to Berlin's extraordinarily rich and diverse cultural tapestry. While a few collections are still closed for reorganisation, restoration, consolidation and various other 'ations', many more are once again open to the public. The year 2001, for instance, saw the inauguration of the spectacular Jewish Museum and the re-opening of the Alte Nationalgalerie.

Many of Berlin's top museums are administered by the pompously named Staatliche Museen zu Berlin – Preussischer Kulturbesitz (State Museums Berlin – Prussian Cultural Collection, denoted in this book with 'SMPK'; information hotline ☎ 20 99 55 55). Admission to an SMPK museum is either €2/1 per entry, or €4/2 for a *Tageskarte* (day pass) valid at all SMPK museums. A day pass is obligatory at such crowd-pleasers as the Pergamon Museum, Hamburger Bahnhof, Neue Nationalgalerie, Neue Gemäldegalerie, Ägyptisches Museum and the Sammlung Berggruen.

Budget-minded travellers, listen up: Admission to all SMPK museums is **free** on the first Sunday of the month.

Dedicated museum lovers should pick up the **SchauLust Museen Berlin**, a museum pass selling for €8/4 that gives access to some 50 Berlin museums, including all the state museums, over a three-day period. It's available at the tourist offices in the Europa-Center and the Brandenburger Tor.

Display captions are often in German only, although this is changing as exhibits are being modernised. Some places have English-language pamphlets available for borrowing or purchase – just ask. Increasingly popular are taped, self-guided audio-tours in several languages (free to €4).

Unless noted otherwise, museums detailed in this chapter are closed on Monday.

here, take U2 to Sophie-Charlotte-Platz and then bus No 210 for three stops (or walk north about 1km from the station along Schlossstrasse to the entrance). Each of the palace buildings charges separate admission (see following section). A special ticket, the **Kombinationskarte Charlottenburg** (€7/5), is good for admission to the Neuer Flügel (including audio-guide), Neuer Pavillon, Mausoleum, Belvedere and sections of the Altes Schloss. On some weekends and during summer holidays the demand for tickets may exceed capacity, so show up as early as possible.

Begun by Johann Arnold Nering, Schloss Charlottenburg was later expanded by Johann Friedrich Eosander. Over time, as the representational needs of the Hohenzollerns grew, other noted architects – like Schinkel, Knobelsdorff and Langhans – also took a whack at it. Nothing less than Versailles provided the inspiration for the three-wing structure which got its landmark central domed-tower in 1812. It's topped by a gilded statue of the goddess Fortuna that moves with the wind, making it a sort of glamorous weather vane.

Bombed in 1943, reconstruction became a priority, especially after the GDR leadership dynamited the only other halfway surviving Hohenzollern palace, the Berliner Stadtschloss in Mitte, in 1951. When completed in 1966, the restored **equestrian statue of the Great Elector** (1699) by Andreas Schlüter also returned to the courtyard outside the main entrance.

Altes Schloss

Also known as the Nering-Eosander Building after its two architects, this is the central – and oldest – section of the palace *(☎ 32 09 11; adult/concession €8/5; tours 9am-5pm Tues-Fri, 10am-5pm Sat-Sun, last tour at 4pm)*. It contains the former royal living quarters, which must be visited on a long-winded, 50-minute tour in German (ask for a pamphlet with detailed room-by-room descriptions in English at the ticket office).

The tour takes in 21 rooms, each of which are extravaganzas in stucco, brocade, gilt and overall opulence. Highlights include the **Hall of Mirrors** (Room 118); the lovely **Oval Hall** (Room 116) with views of the French gardens and the Belvedere; the wind gauge in **Friedrich I's bedchamber,** which also contains the first-ever **bathroom** in a baroque palace (Room 96); the fabulous **Porcelain Chamber** (Room 95), smothered in Chinese blueware and figures from floor to ceiling; and the **Eosander Chapel** (Room 94) with its trompe d'oeil arches. Finally, the **Great Oak Gallery** derives a dignified English feel from its rich wainscoting and large oil canvasses.

After the tour, you are free to explore the upper floor with more paintings and silverwork, vases, tapestries, weapons, Meissen porcelain and other items essential to a royal lifestyle. A lavish banquet table laid out with plates, cutlery, decorations etc – all made of silver – unashamedly displays the extreme luxury to which the royal family was accustomed.

Neuer Flügel

The reign of Friedrich II saw the addition, in 1746, of a new wing, the elongated Knobelsdorff-Flügel (☎ *32 09 11; adult/concession €5/2.50, with audio-guide, €4/3 without; open 10am-6pm Tues-Fri, 11am-5pm Sat-Sun).* You'll find some of the palace's most beautiful rooms, including the confection-like **White Hall**, the former dining hall with its elaborate concave ceiling; the **Golden Gallery,** a rococo fantasy of mirrors and gilding; and the **Concert Hall**. All rooms feature precious paintings by 18th-century French masters like Watteau, Chardin, Boucher and Pesne.

To the right of the staircase are the comparatively austere **Winterkammern** (Winter Chambers) of Friedrich Wilhelm II. Noteworthy here are the four Gobelin tapestries in rooms 351 and 352. On the ground floor is the Schinkel-designed bedroom of Queen Luise.

Schlossgarten

The Palace Garden was originally laid out in French style according to plans by Godeau, but this was changed when natural English gardens came into vogue at the turn of the 18th century. After WWII, a compromise was struck; the area adjacent to the palace is in the French style, the English park is behind.

Several ornate buildings are dotted around the grounds. The **Neuer Pavillon** *(adult/concession €2/1.50 with guided tour summer only, €1.50/1 without guided tour winter only; open 10am-5pm Tues-Sun),* also known as Schinkelpavillon after its builder, briefly served as the summer residence of King Friedrich Wilhelm III in 1824. It contains paintings, sculpture and crafts from the early 19th century, including works by Schinkel himself.

The 1788 rococo folly known as **Belvedere** *(adult/concession €2/1.50; open 10am-5pm Tues-Sun Apr-Oct, noon-4pm Tues-Fri & noon-5pm Sat-Sun Nov-Mar)* was designed by Langhans and served as a teahouse for Friedrich Wilhelm II. Today it contains an impressive porcelain collection by the royal manufacturer KPM, covering styles from rococo to Biedermeier.

The neoclassical **Mausoleum** *(adult/concession €2/1.50; open 10am-5pm Tues-Sun Apr-Oct)* contains the tombs of Queen Luise (1776–1810) and her husband Friedrich Wilhelm III (1770–1840), among others. It features sculpture by Christian Daniel Rauch.

Museum für Vor- und Frühgeschichte (SMPK)

Occupying the west wing (or Langhans Building) of Schloss Charlottenburg is the Museum für Vor- und Frühgeschichte *(Museum of Primeval & Early History; ☎ 20 90 55 55; adult/concession €2/1; open 10am-6pm Tues-Fri, 11am-6pm Sat-Sun).* It presents archaeological artefacts from European and Middle Eastern cultures from the Stone Age to the Middle Ages.

On the ground floor, a selection of **skulls** (some real, some partly reconstructed) from proto-humans to Homo Sapiens illustrates the evolution of human life. The 10,000-year-old **elk skeleton** is a crowd pleaser, as are the **dioramas** of prehistoric cave life and hunting scenes. There are remarkable collections of Bronze Age tools, weapons and ornaments and thorough explanations of how various human cultures became known – in archaeological circles – by the shape of the pottery they created or by their burial practices.

The most outstanding collection is that of Trojan antiquities on the 2nd floor in the **Schliemann Saal**, named after archaeologist Heinrich Schliemann (1822–90) who discovered the site of ancient Troy in Hisarlik in today's Turkey. After the fall of Berlin in 1945, many of the objects unearthed by Schliemann were looted by the Red Army and taken to museums in Moscow and Leningrad (now St Petersburg). The booty that remained in Berlin includes an impressive array of bronzes, huge clay amphorae for storing wine and oil, and other objects. Also here are replicas of jewellery from Schliemann's 'Priamos Treasure' whose originals are at the Pushkin Museum in Moscow.

Display panels are in several languages, including English.

SCHLOSS AREA MUSEUMS (Map 2)

In addition to the splendour of the royal palace and its outbuildings, there are five museums nearby, including a couple that are definitely on the must-see list.

Ägyptisches Museum (SMPK)

A journey through 3000 years of ancient history is offered at the Ägyptisches Museum *(Egyptian Museum; ☎ 20 90 55 55, Schlossstrasse 70; adult/concession €4/2; open 10am-6pm Tues-Sun)*. Its prize possession is the **bust of Queen Nefertiti**, she of the long graceful neck and stunning looks (even after all these years – about 3300, give or take a century or two). The bust, dramatically spotlit in a darkened room, was never finished (the right eye, for example, is not inlaid) as this was just a model for other portraits of the queen, who was the wife of Pharaoh Ikhnaton (ruled 1379–62 BC). His bust is in the main exhibition room.

The exhibit is divided into darkened niches, each devoted to a particular person or subject such as 'Ikhnaton's family', 'courtier and soldiers', or 'women and music'. All objects, including more busts, statues, reliefs and totemic animal figurines, hail from the Nile city of Amarna, which was excavated by German archaeologists in 1912. An exception is the **Kalabsha Gate**, a sandstone

arch given to Germany as a gift for its help in saving archaeological treasures during the construction of the Aswan Dam (1960–70).

A circular upstairs room holds the museum's second-most cherished object, the **Berliner Grüner Kopf**, a small male head sculpture (500–400 BC) carved from green stone that is almost expressionistic in style.

Sammlung Berggruen (SMPK)

Just opposite the Egyptian Museum is the Sammlung Berggruen *(Berggruen Collection; ☎ 20 90 55 55, Schlossstrasse 1; adult/concession €4/2; open 10am-6pm Tues-Fri, 11am-6pm Sat-Sun)*. Entitled 'Picasso and His Time', it's on loan until at least 2006 from private art collector and FOP (friend of Picasso) Dr Heinz Berggruen.

Around 75 paintings, drawings and sculptures provide a thorough survey of Picasso's work. The Blue and Rose periods (eg *Seated Harlequin*, 1905) are followed by early cubist paintings (eg the portrait of George Braque, 1910). These contrast greatly with the classicist *Seating Act, Drying her Feet* from 1921. Later paintings seem more familiar, such as *The Yellow Pullover* (1939) which shows a woman, Dora Maar, with lion claws for hands.

On the 2nd floor, the emphasis shifts to Paul Klee who's represented with 31 smaller pieces created between 1917 and 1940. Paintings by Cézanne and Van Gogh, as well as African sculpture – all of which inspired both Picasso and Klee – round out the collection. There are also a range of works by their contemporaries Gauguin, Braque and Giacometti.

An excellent 50-minute audio tour is available for hire though, unfortunately, it's in German only (€3.50/2.50).

Bröhan Museum

The lovely Bröhan Museum *(☎ 32 69 06 00, Schlossstrasse 1a; adult/concession €4/2; open 10am-6pm Tues-Sun)*, just south of the Berggruen Collection, focuses on decorative arts and design (including Art Nouveau, Art Deco and Functionalism) from 1889 to 1939. It was donated to the city by Karl Bröhan in 1982.

University founder, Wilhelm von Humboldt.

The legendary Captain of Köpenick.

Treasures await in Sanssouci Park, Potsdam.

Standing guard over Tiergarten, the Russian War Memorial.

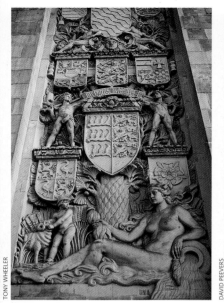

German coats of arms, Reichstag.

Schiller stands tall in Gendarmenmarkt.

Inside the new Reichstag dome, home of the German parliament.

On the ground floor are the outstanding fully furnished and decorated **Art Nouveau and Art Deco rooms** (eg, by Hector Guimard and Émile Ruhlmann). The collection of silverwork, glass, porcelain and enamelware seems endless but astonishes at every turn. There's furniture from France, porcelain from Scandinavia and Germany and paintings by members of the Berliner Secession from the late 19th to early 20th century, including Jaeckel and Baluschek.

The top floor has changing exhibitions and a remarkable **Henry van de Velde** (1863–1957) room with furniture, tableware and various other objects designed by this multi-talented Belgian.

Abgusssammlung Antiker Plastik

Lots of naked guys without noses are on view at the Abgusssammlung Antiker Plastik (*Collection of Classical Sculpture;* ☎ *342 40 54, Schlossstrasse 69b; admission free; open 2pm-5pm Thur-Sun*) with copies of Greek and Roman sculpture from 600 BC to 400 AD. It's in the same building as the **Heimatmuseum Charlottenburg** (☎ *34 30 32 01; admission free; open 10am-5pm Tues-Fri, 11am-5pm Sat-Sun*), the district's local history museum.

FUNKTURM AREA (MAP 4)

About 3km south-west of Schloss Charlottenburg, near Theodor-Heuss-Platz, is Berlin's trade fair centre (Messe) and the ICC (International Congress Centre). By far the most visible structure in this area, though, is the **Funkturm** (radio tower, Map 1) whose fili gree outline bears similarities to Paris' Eiffel Tower. It dates from the 1920s and measures 138m in height. There's a restaurant at 55m and a viewing platform at 125m.

From the top there's a good view of the **AVUS**, Germany's first car-racing track at its opening in 1921; AVUS stands for *Automo-bil-, Verkehrs- und Übungsstrecke* (auto, traffic and practice track). The Nazis made it part of the autobahn system, which it still is today. Until a few years ago, the AVUS had no speed limit but, owing to pressure from environmentalists, the maximum is now 100km/h.

OLYMPIA-STADION AREA (Map 1)

The Olympic Stadium (☎ *301 11 00; tours by appointment only, 10-person minimum; tours €5; U-Bahn: U2 to Olympia-Stadion Ost, then 15-minute walk*), commissioned by Hitler for the 1936 Olympic Games, lies about 4.5km west of Schloss Charlottenburg. African-American runner Jesse Owens won four gold medals here and put paid to Nazi theories that Aryans were all-powerful *Übermenschen* (a super race). Designed by brothers Walter and Werner March, the colosseum-like structure replaced an earlier stadium completed by their father Otto in 1913. It is one of the best examples of Nazi-era monumentalist architecture.

Today the stadium is still very much in use for soccer, track and other sporting events. Until at least 2005, however, it will be under gradual renovation intended to bring it up to scratch for the 2006 Soccer World Cup championship final. Plans call for a new translucent roof to cover the 76,000 seats. For a preview at what the revamped stadium will look like, visit a new multimedia exhibit called Olympia-Stadion - Die Ausstellung (*Olympic Stadium - The Exhibit; adult/concession €2.50/1.50; open 10am-6pm Wed & Sun*), which also chronicles the structure's often turbulent history.

The **Maifeld**, a vast field west of the stadium, was used for Nazi mass rallies (it holds more than half a million people) and later became the drilling ground for occupying British forces which, until 1994, had their headquarters nearby. Today it is used for large-scale pop concerts. On its western edge is the 77m **Glockenturm** (*Clock Tower; adult/children €2/0.75; open 9am-6pm daily Apr-Sept*), which offers good views over the stadium, the city and the Havel. Check out the Nazi-era bell: it weighs 2.5 tonnes and was rung only twice; to signal the start and the finish of the Olympic Games.

North-west of here, the **Waldbühne** sits on the corner of Glockenturmstrasse and Passenheimer Strasse. It is a lovely outdoor amphitheatre for 20,000 that is now used in summer for concerts, film screenings and other cultural events.

Friedrichshain

Friedrichshain is today what Prenzlauer Berg was in the early to mid-1990s: a gentrification frontier. Rents are low, buildings are still awaiting their face-lifts, and restaurants, bars and clubs retain a creative, unpolished edge. Traditionally a working-class quarter, it is now popular with students and other people without fat bank accounts, which is reflected in overall prices.

Friedrichshain has few sights, but you'll probably find your way to Boxhagener Platz, the epicentre of the vibrant nightlife scene that has sprung up all around here, especially on Simon-Dach-Strasse. Underground culture flourishes on Rigaer Strasse, north of the Frankfurter Allee, where squatters operate makeshift bars and clubs in their occupied buildings. To the south, Mühlenstrasse, paralleling the Spree, is also lined with intensely popular dance clubs.

It was the Spree that helped entice industry to settle in Friedrichshain in the late 19th century. The GDR kept many of the factories going, but since the Wende most have closed due to lack of profitability, thus eliminating 20,000 jobs. Friedrichshain's appearance certainly reflects its humble origins. Much of it is still crisscrossed by block after block of dilapidated Mietskasernen, with only the Volkspark softening the grey monotony.

KARL-MARX-ALLEE (Map 3)

Karl-Marx-Allee, leading south-east off Alexanderplatz, was East Germany's 'first socialist boulevard' and the backdrop for military parades. It is a unique open-air showcase of GDR architecture and a perfect metaphor for the inflated sense of importance and grandeur of the former GDR regime. First called Stalinallee after WWII, it was renamed in 1961 following Stalin's death.

Built in two segments between 1952 and 1965, the older section, which runs from Strausberger Platz to Frankfurter Tor, is a good example of the bombastic Zuckerbäckerstil (wedding cake style) in vogue in Stalinist Russia. Both sides of the 90m-wide boulevard are flanked by so-called *Volkspaläste* (people's palaces) inspired by those that line Lenin Allee in Moscow. These concrete behemoths are each between 100m and 300m long, seven to nine storeys high and honeycombed with tiny workers' flats. In an ironic twist, it was the very construction of these 'palaces' that led to the workers' uprising on 17 June 1953, which brought the GDR to the brink of collapse (see the History section in the Facts about Berlin chapter for details).

To be fair, the flats here offered a major step up in comfort, outfitted as they were with private sanitary facilities, central heating and lifts. But construction materials were poor and it didn't take long before they started to crumble. If you look closely, you'll see some partly eroded facades revealing how they were made: Placed atop the concrete shell is a steel grid upon which are glued huge rectangular tiles, now shattered and grimy with age. In 1993, a large bank bought most of these buildings and began restoring them.

Between 1959 and 1965, the second segment of Karl-Marx-Allee was constructed from Alexanderplatz to Strausberger Platz. Five- to 10-storey apartment blocks, in finest GDR prefab, line this section, which is 125m wide. But, just to show that the GDR regime wanted their people to have *some* fun as well, the boulevard also boasts two large cinemas which, after recent renovations, are once again operational. They are the **Kosmos** (1962) at No 131 and the **International** (1963) at No 33. The latter hosted many premieres of movies made by DEFA, the GDR's film studios.

Since no buses run along Karl-Marx-Allee, its monumentalism is best appreciated by bike or, alternatively, by car or on foot.

VOLKSPARK FRIEDRICHSHAIN (Map 3)

Berlin's first public park dates back to 1840 in celebration of the centenary of Friedrich II's ascension to the throne. Peter Lenné provided the original plans and in 1875 his student, Gustav Meyer, designed an expansion. During WWII, the park sported two flak towers which doubled as repositories for treasures from Berlin museums. Most of these fell victim to a devastating fire in 1945. Blown up after the war, the towers' remains were topped with rubble from bombed buildings to form the two artificial mounds called **Bunkerberge** at the park's centre and on its north-eastern edge.

One of the park's nicest features is the **Märchenbrunnen** (Fairytale Fountain; 1913) on the corner of Am Friedrichshain and Friedenstrasse, though it would benefit from some restoration. Flanked by a romantic, half-moon-shaped superstructure, it consists of multiple, tiered basins studded with sculptures representing fairytales of the Brothers Grimm (eg, Cinderella, the Frog Prince). In the warmer months, the fountain is a popular cruising spot for gay men. You can reach the park on bus No 100 or 200.

The park also has a couple of GDR-era monuments. A short walk south-east of the fountain, along Friedenstrasse, stands the **Gedenkstätte für die Deutschen Interbrigadisten**, a memorial dedicated to the German soldiers who fought against fascism as part of the International Brigades in the Spanish Civil War (1936–39). Just look for the sculpture of a sword-swinging, raised-fisted soldier. The bronze relief on the left depicts the battle of Madrid.

In the park's north-eastern corner is another monument (1972) commemorating the joint fight of Polish soldiers and the German resistance during WWII. On the southern edge is the cemetery for nearly 200 demonstrators who died during the revolutionary riots in March 1848.

Kreuzberg

Until the Wende, Kreuzberg was the ugly duckling of Berlin's western districts. Located right on the border with East Berlin, it became a catch basin for the socially disadvantaged – the poor and immigrants – and for students, squatters, punks and supporters of an alternative lifestyle. Subcultures flourished in this climate and so did some radical – and occasionally violent – spin-offs. All

were attracted by cheap rent and accepted the often sub-standard living conditions.

With reunification, Kreuzberg (which lies south of Mitte and west of Friedrichshain) was no longer a border district but was now positioned in the heart of the city. As a result, it's been slowly undergoing gentrification, especially in the western half.

Indeed, Kreuzberg is still unofficially divided into two distinct sections. The western half (referred to as Kreuzberg 61 after the old postal code) is more upmarket, with dignified 19th-century apartment houses with ornate facades. The eastern half, Kreuzberg 36, was once the hub of the alternative political scene and known for its raging nightlife. Things quieted down in the '90s, but have picked up again in the last couple of years. This neighbourhood is largely populated by Berlin's Turkish community and their culture dominates much of the street life around Kottbusser Tor and Görlitzer Bahnhof. The U1, which goes through here, has even been nicknamed the 'Istanbul Express'.

KREUZBERG WALKING TOUR (Map 5)
Though devoid of major conventional sights, this tour will introduce you to the many intriguing faces of this district. It starts at Mehringdamm U-Bahn station in Kreuzberg 61, the charming, middle-class neighbourhood around the Kreuzberg hill, and travels via Südstern into the heart of Kreuzberg 36, the epicentre of Turkish Berlin, to end at Görlitzer Bahnhof U-Bahn station. The tour covers about 6km and will take the better part of a morning or afternoon.

Mehringdamm to Viktoriapark
From the U-Bahn station, head south, cross Gneisenaustrasse and walk a few more steps to the **Schwules Museum** (*Gay Museum;* ☎ *693 11 72, Mehringdamm 61, Kreuzberg; adult/concession €3.50/2; open 2pm-6pm Wed-Sun, to 7pm Sat*). There's no permanent exhibit (yet), but a team of dedicated volunteers works hard to present a changing roster of shows dealing with all aspects of gay culture, history and daily life. These are supplemented by discussions,

readings and other events. Topics range from an exploration of the life of Oscar Wilde to the persecution of homosexuals under the Nazis. The Gay Museum also maintains a steadily growing library and archive. Ask about tours in English.

Retrace your steps back north to the intersection, then turn west into Yorckstrasse where you'll walk past the spiky twin towers of the **Bonifatiuskirche**, a neogothic concoction wedged in between a row of regular apartment buildings. Next up, look for the two giants buttressing a balcony and an ornate iron gate. These belong to the attractive **Riehmers Hofgarten**, a vast block-shaped complex wrapped around a leafy sculpture-studded courtyard. A home for the well-to-do in the early 20th century, it now contains a lovely hotel (see the Places to Stay chapter). For a close-up look, enter the courtyard through the iron gate. Exit on the other (south) side on Hagelberger Strasse, turn right, then turn left on Grossbeerenstrasse (if the gate's closed, walk to the corner of Grossbeerenstrasse and Yorckstrasse, then turn left here). A few more steps and you're at the foot of the Kreuzberg, the hill for which the district is named.

Kreuzberg & Viktoriapark

Note the rather decrepit **Café Achteck**, the nickname given to the green, octagonal late 19th-century *pissoirs* (public latrines) from the Wilhelminian era. This one is no longer functioning and is fenced off to be quietly consumed by rust (there's a better one on this tour). Also here is a suggestive **statue of Neptune** showing the god and an ocean nymphet obviously enjoying each other's company. The pond behind it acts as the catchment for an artificial **waterfall** which comes rushing down a narrow, rock-lined canal – quite a lovely sight, though enjoyed only if city coffers allow the faucets to be turned on.

Most of the Kreuzberg, which rises 66m, is covered by the rather unruly, rambling **Viktoriapark** which can be 'climbed' via some steep, short trails. It was designed by Gustav Meyer, a student of the famous garden architect Peter Lenné.

Punctuating the peak is the recently restored Schinkel-designed **Kreuzberg memorial** to the Wars of Liberation which pitted Napoleon against Prussian troops in 1813. It's a 19m-high, cathedral-like spire decorated with dramatic detail. Incidentally, it's laid out in the shape of a cross and is also topped by one. *Kreuz* is the German word for 'cross' and so this is actually what gave the hill – which was previously known as Tempelhofer Berg – its name.

The views from up here are, yes, fabulous, especially in winter when it's easy to peer over the leafless treetops. On New Year's Eve, the entire hill becomes party-central with thousands of youngsters celebrating while gawking at the fireworks. In summer, there's a rather nice beer garden called **Golgatha** on the park's western side (see the Entertainment chapter).

Descend the Kreuzberg on its eastern side to get to Methfesselstrasse, then head south. This will take you past the emerging **Viktoria Quartier**, a mixed-use district that's being developed from a former brewery. It will contain offices, loft apartment buildings and the Berlinische Galerie, a museum of modern art, photography and architecture tentatively scheduled to open in late 2003. Continue to Dudenstrasse, then turn left (east) to arrive at the Platz der Luftbrücke.

Luftbrückendenkmal & Tempelhof Flughafen

Platz der Luftbrücke is easily recognised by the **Luftbrückendenkmal** (Airlift Memorial, 1951), which locals call the *Hungerharke* (hunger rake). The trio of spikes represents the three Allied air corridors that ensured the city's survival during the Berlin Airlift of 1948–49 (see the boxed text 'The Berlin Airlift' in the Facts about Berlin chapter). But the monument itself really is a symbol of when the Allies became protectors instead of occupiers. The names of the 79 airmen and other personnel who died during this amazing effort are engraved in the plinth.

Tempelhof airport (technically in the district of Tempelhof) was one of the main landing sites for Allied planes during the airlift. Its humungous, chunky structures that appear to stretch on endlessly look like textbook Nazi architecture. In fact, Tempelhof pre-dates the Third Reich by some 10 years, though the Nazis hired Ernst Sagebiel to enlarge it into one of the most bombastic building complexes in continental Europe. A huge central courtyard leads to the 100m-long terminal and a 400m-long building with numerous gates. From both sides of this structure, a succession of hangars extends in a semicircular arrangement over a total length of 1200m.

East of Mehringdamm

Walk north on Mehringdamm, then turn right on Fidicinstrasse past the home of the English-language theatre Friends of Italian Opera (see the Entertainment chapter) and the windowless brick **Wasserturm** (1888), looking very much like Rapunzel's tower.

Turn left into Kopischstrasse, then follow it to **Chamissoplatz**, a gorgeous square anchored by a peaceful little park and framed by stately 19th-century buildings with wrought-iron balconies. One of the few Berlin neighbourhoods largely untouched by WWII, it timewarps you back to the late 19th century and has an almost unreal, movie-set quality. Indeed, directors often use these streets as backdrops for films set in 'Old Berlin'. A still-functioning Café Achteck pissoir on Chamissoplatz further adds authenticity to the scene.

One block north of the square is Bergmannstrasse, the lively main artery of Kreuzberg 61. It's a fun road teeming with funky second-hand and book shops, restaurants and cafes. Take in the atmosphere while strolling along here, eventually making your way east to Marheinekeplatz. The highlight of this large square is the **Marheineke Markthalle**, one of Berlin's three surviving historic market halls. Browse through the aisles where produce, cheeses and sausages are piled high and try to ignore the ones with junky clothing and toys. The impressive redbrick church situated at the square's northeastern corner is the **Passionskirche**, the site of occasional classical concerts.

Continue east on Bergmannstrasse past a cluster of **cemeteries**. Lots of notables lie buried here, Weimar Republic chancellor Gustav Stresemann being one of the better known. Also here are the architect Martin Gropius (died 1880), the sculptor Adolf Menzel (1905) and Schiller's girlfriend, Charlotte von Kalb (1843). Just beyond is U-Bahn station Südstern.

Südstern to Kottbusser Tor

Südstern marks the unofficial end of more upmarket Kreuzberg 61. Beyond here lies Kreuzberg 36 (sometimes still known as SO36, after its old postal code), much of which has the atmosphere of a bustling bazaar thanks to its predominantly Turkish population. The **Turkish Market**, held every Tuesday and Friday afternoon along the Maybachufer is a great place to absorb the scene (see the Shopping chapter). To get there from Südstern, walk north-east on Körtestrasse and its northern continuation, Grimmstrasse, then right on Planufer which becomes Maybachufer east of Kottbusser Damm. This is a particularly scenic section of the Landwehrkanal. Both banks are lined by handsomely renovated pre-WWI apartment buildings and, in good weather, throngs of happy folk gather on lawns and in cafes and restaurants.

Less appealing is the architecture around Kottbusser Tor U-Bahn station, a few steps north along Kottbusser Damm, where the sins of the '70s are all too apparent. Take a look at the hideous **Neue Kreuzberger Zentrum** for a perfect example of misdirected modernisation.

Kottbusser Tor is the hub of Turkish Kreuzberg. Grocers, bakeries, supermarkets, shops, department stores and cafes have a distinctive oriental flavour. Turkish women bustle about, their hair hidden beneath colourful kerchiefs and their bodies concealed beneath shapeless frocks. The younger ones often spice up the traditional garb with pink lipstick, their coats just short enough to reveal ankles in black nylons. More often than not, though, they prefer the same contemporary fashions as their German peers.

Oranienstrasse to Görlitzer Bahnhof

From the Kottbusser Tor station, head north on Adalbertstrasse where the **Kreuzberg Museum** (☎ 50 58 52 33, Adalbertstrasse 95a; admission free; open 2pm-6pm Wed-Sun) is located in a converted factory. Still a work in progress, the exhibit for now is limited to the 1st floor where Kreuzberg's industrial history – especially as it pertains to publishing and printing – is the focus. Future plans include sections that will chronicle such themes as city development, migration, protest and gentrification.

Adalbertstrasse finally intersects with **Oranienstrasse**, Kreuzberg's (in)famous nightlife drag, which is being rediscovered. Many of its cafes, bars and clubs retain the radical underground feel that helped SO36 make headlines in the wild '80s. For details about the scene, see the Entertainment chapter. If you follow Oranienstrasse east, you soon arrive at U-Bahn station Görlitzer Bahnhof, where this tour ends.

Elsewhere in Kreuzberg 36

A short walk north of Oranienstrasse is the **Künstlerhaus Bethanien** (☎ 25 88 41 51, Mariannenplatz 2; admission varies, often free; open 2pm-7pm Tues-Sun), an art centre with studios rented cheaply to young artists. The building began life in 1847 as a hospital and Theodor Fontane, before becoming a writer, spent a brief stint here as a pharmacist. The house organises frequent exhibits.

Kreuzberg is linked to Friedrichshain across the Spree by the **Oberbaumbrücke** (1896). A red-brick bridge with jaunty turrets and pinnacles, crenellated walls and arched walkways, it looks very much like a medieval drawbridge leading up to a fortified castle. Just beyond is the East Side Gallery, the longest stretch of surviving Wall (see boxed text 'The Berlin Wall' in the Mitte section of this chapter).

NORTHERN KREUZBERG (Map 5)

The area described here roughly encompasses the triangle formed by U-Bahn stations Kochstrasse to the north, Yorckstrasse to the south-west and Mehringdamm to the south. While not the prettiest part of the city, there are several good reasons to venture here anyway, most notably the amazing **Jewish Museum**, one of Berlin's new flagship attractions. **Checkpoint Charlie** (see the Mitte section later in this chapter) is nearby as well.

Jüdisches Museum

September 2001 saw the much anticipated opening of the exhibit at Berlin's Jüdisches Museum (Jewish Museum; ☎ 25 99 33 00, ticket hotline ☎ 308 78 56 81, Lindenstrasse 9-14; adult/concession €5.50/2.75; open 10am-8pm daily, last admission 7pm; guided tours €3.50, in English 5pm Sat & Sun, in German 11am & 2pm Sat & Sun; closed on Jewish high holidays and Christmas Eve). The largest such museum in Europe, it celebrates the achievements of German Jews and their contributions to culture, art, science and other fields. Arranged in a chronological fashion, the exhibit also includes one section about the Holocaust, although this is by no means the museum's entire focus. In fact, what makes Berlin's Jewish Museum different is that it looks at Jewish history beyond the very narrow context of the 12 years of Nazi rule. Jews are not exclusively presented as victims but as vital citizens who've played enormously important roles in Germany through the centuries. One part of the exhibit also deals with the resurgence of Berlin's Jewish population since reunification.

The museum building itself is a stunning work of art designed by Daniel Libeskind and an excellent example of crisp modernism in the landscape of the New Berlin. Zinc-clad walls rise skyward in a sharply angled zigzag ground plan that's an abstract interpretation of a star. The general outline is echoed in the windows: triangular, trapezoidal and irregular gashes in the building's gleaming skin.

The interior too is not merely exhibit space but a metaphor for the history of the Jewish people. The museum is entered through an underground walkway from the adjacent Berlin Museum. It leads to a small interior plaza from which three 'roads' radiate. The first road is a cul-de-sac, leading to the **Holo-caust Tower**, one of a series of 'voids' that symbolise the loss of humanity, culture and people. The second street culminates in the **ETA Hoffmann Garden**, a field of concrete columns which represents Jewish emigration and exile. The main walkway leads to a flight of stairs providing access to the exhibition floors.Tickets are available at the museum or at the Ticket Shop at Unter den Linden 36–38.

Tickets to the Jewish Museum also give admission to the **Blindenwerkstatt Otto Weidt** (*Otto Weidt Workshop for the Blind; ☎ 28 59 94 07, Rosenthaler Strasse 39, Mitte; admission to workshop only €1.75; open 1pm-4pm Tues-Fri*) **Map 7**. It contains an exhibit called 'Blind Trust – Life in Hiding at the Hackescher Markt, 1941–1943' which tells the story of Otto Weidt, a broom and brush manufacturer, who was able to protect his blind and deaf Jewish and non-Jewish workers from the Nazis until 1943.

Willy-Brandt-Haus

The flatiron building at the intersection of Stresemannstrasse and Wilhelmstrasse contains the 1996 Willy-Brandt-Haus (*☎ 25 99 37 12, Wilhelmstrasse 140; admission free; galleries open noon-6pm Tues-Sun, to 8pm Fri*). The headquarters of the SPD party, it is named after the one-time Berlin mayor and later German chancellor (1969–74). A sculpture by artist Rainer Fetting – showing Brandt in cool pose, one hand in pocket, the other outstretched – stands in the light-flooded triangular atrium. The atrium, as well as several galleries, is also used for art exhibits, discussions and concerts.

Anhalter Bahnhof

As you emerge from the Anhalter Bahnhof U-Bahn station, you'll spot some elegant arches which are all that remain of the neo-Renaissance Anhalter Bahnhof, until WWII the finest and busiest railway station in Berlin. It was from here, in 1930, that Marlene Dietrich began her journey out of Berlin that would take her to Hollywood. Badly bombed, the station languished for years and was finally demolished in the early 1960s by

the East Germans. For some reason, they kept a small piece of the facade which now stands forlornly on the giant empty lot. The tent-like structure just south of here is the new permanent home of the cultural centre, **Tempodrom** (see the Entertainment chapter).

Gruselkabinett

Just west of the Anhalter Bahnhof ruin is Berlin's Gruselkabinet (*Cabinet of Horrors; ☎ 26 55 55 46, Schöneberger Strasse 23a; adults/students/children €6/5/4.50; open 10am-7pm Sun-Tues & Thur, 10am-8pm Fri, noon-8pm Sat*). It is housed in the only publicly accessible above-ground air-raid shelter in Berlin (enter via the gap in the long red-brick building on Schöneberger Strasse). Inside is a somewhat contrived exhibit that is a combination war-museum, medieval house of horrors and country-fair spook show. In the 'historical section', you'll find a smattering of actual belongings left behind by those who holed up here to escape bombing raids.

A broken-through section of the outer wall reveals its 2.13m thickness. The ground floor is given over to the gory subject of medieval surgery techniques, graphically (and laughably) demonstrated by groaning dummies. And then there's the top level where you'll be accosted by giant gorillas leaping out of the dark. If all this sounds like it might be fun for children, well, be warned that it's pretty intense.

Deutsches Technikmuseum

The giant Deutsches Technikmuseum (*German Museum of Technology; ☎ 90 25 40, Trebbiner Strasse 9, Kreuzberg; adult/ concession €2.50/1; open 9am-5.30pm Tues-Fri, 10am-6pm Sat-Sun; U-Bahn: U15 to Möckernbrücke or Gleisdreieck*) is an engaging and stimulating museum and one of the largest of its kind in the world. Its 14 departments examine technology through the ages – from printing and transport to computers – with many interactive stations. It's easy to spend an entire day here, especially if you bring the kids.

Demonstrations of historical machines and models take place throughout the museum. Visitors can also be active themselves, printing business cards on historical machines, making paper, grinding corn or stepping behind the microphone at a faux TV studio. There's a copy of the world's first computer – the Z1 by Konrad Zuse – plus demonstrations of computer music and games.

The six-hectare **Museumspark** features working windmills and watermills, railway track systems and a historical brewery.

Massively popular with kids is the interactive **Spectrum** annexe (enter from Möckernstrasse 26, about 300m east of the main museum building), where they can participate in around 300 experiments that explain the scientific underpinnings of technology. If you ever wondered why the sky's blue or how a battery works, this is the place to get the lowdown.

A new building, completed in 2001, will house exhibits on ship navigation (set to open in late 2002) and aviation (late 2003).

Mitte

Mitte (literally: Middle) is Berlin's birthplace and packed with sights and museums, entertainment and hotel options. Whether part of the Brandenburg-Prussia kingdom, the German Empire, the Weimar Republic, the Third Reich or the GDR, Mitte has always been the nexus of politics, culture and commerce. And it didn't take long after the Wende before it became the hub of united Berlin.

Your sightseeing choices here are immense. You'll find world-class museums in profusion. Some of the greatest architects – Schinkel, Nering, Langhans among them – have left their mark with neoclassical and baroque structures dotted throughout the district. A stroll along **Unter den Linden**, Berlin's grand boulevard, will take you past a phalanx of sites that tell the city's story. The **Spandauer Vorstadt**, around the Hackesche Höfe, has evolved into Berlin most popular nightlife centre. You can sip cocktails in a cool lounge, watch the sun rise after a night in a throbbing nightclub, attend an acclaimed opera or see top-notch theatre.

Mitte covers roughly the same area taken up by all of Berlin at the beginning of the 19th century. WWII reduced nearly 80% of the historical buildings into bombed-out and smouldering husks, mere shadows of their former grandeur. Since the district was part of the Soviet sector, it fell to the GDR to do the clean-up. Indeed, some of the restoration work from the decades when East Berlin was the GDR capital, is exemplary as can be seen, for instance, on Gendarmenmarkt or along Unter den Linden. But the regime also bungled big-time when destroying – for ideological reasons – such perfectly salvageable structures as the Hohenzollern's Stadtschloss (City Palace) and replacing them with aesthetic eyesores like the Palast der Republik. Entire quarters like the Spandauer Vorstadt and Friedrichstadt were left to languish through decades of neglect.

Mitte adjoins several areas of major interest located in other districts, most notably Tiergart en with which it was administratively joined in 2000. The New Government District, anchored by the **Reichstag** and the **New Federal Chancellery** is just north of the Brandenburger Tor, while the **Potsdamer Platz** precinct is on Mitte's south-western periphery. See the Tiergarten section later in this chapter for details. **Checkpoint Charlie**, the famous Cold War symbol, is right on Mitte's border with Kreuzberg.

HISTORIC MITTE WALKING TOUR (Map 7)

This is an amble through Berlin's historic centre, starting at the landmark Brandenburger Tor and heading east along Unter den Linden, with a small detour along Friedrichstrasse to Gendarmenmarkt. The tour ends at the Schlossbrücke, the gateway to Museumsinsel, whose fabulous collection of museums is covered separately. If this is your first time in Berlin, this tour, which covers a distance of about 3km, is a good introduction to some of the best Berlin has to offer in terms of historic sights. Allow at least two hours, more if you plan a more thorough investigation of the places mentioned. This tour can be combined with Tour I of the Architecture special section.

Brandenburger Tor

One of Berlin's most photographed sites, the Brandenburger Tor (Brandenburg Gate) was once the boundary between East and West Berlin. It was against this backdrop in 1987 that then-US president Ronald Reagan uttered the famous words: 'Mr Gorbachev – Tear down this Wall.' The Wall came down in 1989 and the gate – long a symbol of division – became the very epitome of German reunification.

Berlin once had 18 city gates, of which only the Brandenburg Gate survives. It was designed by Carl Gotthard Langhans in 1791 in neoclassical style and crowned by an ornate sculpture representing the goddess Victory. And what a 'well-travelled' goddess she is: spirited to Paris in 1806 by Napoleon after his occupation of Berlin, she triumphantly returned in 1814, freed from the French by a gallant Prussian general. The gate's north wing contains the **Raum der Stille** *(Room of Silence; open 11am-6pm Apr-Oct, to 5pm Nov & Jan-Mar, to 4pm Dec)*, where the weary can sit and contemplate peace. The south wing contains a tourist office branch (see the Tourist Offices section in the Facts for the Visitor chapter). A restoration, begun in 2001, covered the gate in plastic sheeting; it should be completed by the time you're reading this.

Pariser Platz

The Brandenburg Gate opens onto Pariser Platz, which is being restored to its pre-war grandeur, when it was known as the 'emperor's reception hall'. By the time construction is finished, it will be framed on three sides by the embassies of the United States and France as well as banks, offices and the Academy of Arts. Holding court, since 1997, from the south-eastern corner is the **Hotel Adlon** *(☎ 226 10, Unter den Linden 77)*, former and once again grande dame of Berlin caravansaries. On the outside at least, the building is a fairly faithful replica of the 1907 original, which counted Charlie Chaplin, Greta Garbo and Thomas Mann among its guests. Presidents, musicians, diplomats, actors and the merely moneyed shack up here these days, welcomed by liveried doormen and a majestic lobby underneath a stunning stained-glass cupola. The hotel is operated by the Kempinski chain and officially called the Adlon Hotel Kempinski (see the Places to Stay chapter).

Holocaust Memorial

Just south of Pariser Platz, on the east side of Ebertstrasse, is the site of the Memorial to the Murdered Jews of Europe, colloquially known as the Holocaust Memorial. It was designed by New York architect Peter Eisenman who envisions around 2700 concrete pillars positioned in a grid pattern on a gently sloping ground. An underground information centre is intended to personalise the abstract experience of the memorial itself. Exhibits will tell the life stories of some of the victims, provide details about their origins and create virtual bridges to other memorials.

Unter den Linden

Berlin's most splendid boulevard extends for about 1.5km from the Brandenburger Tor to the Schlossbrücke. Before being developed into a showpiece road, Unter den Linden was merely a riding path connecting the Berliner Stadtschloss with the Tiergarten, once the royal hunting grounds. Under Elector Friedrich Wilhelm (ruled 1640–88), the eponymous linden trees were planted, but it took another century to complete the harmonious ensemble of baroque, neoclassical and rococo structures. Wartime brought especially heavy destruction to the western end of Unter den Linden; most of what you see here today reflects postwar architectural tastes. The stretch east of Friedrichstrasse, though, has been beautifully restored.

Pariser Platz to Charlottenstrasse

Strolling east on Unter den Linden, you'll see the hulking **Russian Embassy** *(☎ 226 63 20, Unter den Linden 63-65)*, a Stalinist behemoth in white marble dating from 1950. It is built in the so-called *Zuckerbäckerstil* (wedding-cake style) of architecture in

The Holocaust Memorial – Anatomy of a Debate

Capping more than a decade of debate and indecision, Berlin may be finally poised to build a memorial to the six million Jews killed during the Holocaust. The design by Peter Eisenmann was approved by the German parliament in June 1999. Construction was set to begin soon thereafter but has since been postponed several times. At the time of writing, late 2001 was given as the latest date, although that may change again. The cost, around €7.5 million, is to be shared equally by the state of Berlin, the federal government and a nonprofit organisation. The creation of this memorial has been one of the most complicated and sensitive debates in the reunified Germany.

Here's a short timeline:

1988
The story begins pre-Wende with journalist Lea Rosh's call for a monument to the murdered Jews. The West German government shows interest but the issue gets buried amid reunification euphoria. When picked up again in 1993, Chancellor Kohl supports the idea of a monument and calls for a design contest.

1995
A committee decides on a design by Jackob Marcks consisting of a gigantic slanted concrete plane engraved with the names of ALL murdered Jews. Kohl boycotts the idea and demands a new discussion. Others want a new contest. Rosh likes Marcks' design. The Berlin Senate postpones a decision.

1996
The Bundestag debates the issue without results.

1997
A new contest begins.

1998
A monumental design by Peter Eisenmann is favoured by Kohl and others. Cultural and political leaders, including Günter Grass, Elie Wiesel, Martin Walser and Berlin's mayor, want to scratch the memorial altogether. Eisenmann creates a less grandiose version, but there are voices demanding a third contest. Others propose to set up a branch of Steven Spielberg's Shoa Foundation instead. Lea Rosh insists on a memorial.

1999
More confusion ensues when a group of politicians and clerics support a design by theologian Richard Schröder in the form of a column inscribed with the 6th Commandment 'Thou Shalt Not Kill' in German, Hebrew and other languages. The idea is rejected by the Bundestag (now led by Chancellor Gerhard Schröder).

June 1999
Eisenmann's downscaled version finds enough supporters (314 vs 209) in the Bundestag. It takes the form of a huge accessible field comprised of 2700 concrete pillars of varying height which, from afar, looks like a cemetery. An information centre is planned as well.

Summer 2001
Work on the memorial, having been postponed numerous times, finally began in late October 2001.

vogue during the Stalin era. A tall wall allows only glimpses of the compound, but if you're interested in this type of monumental building, swing by Karl-Marx-Allee east of Alexanderplatz, which is lined with them (see the Friedrichshain section earlier in this chapter).

A few steps further on is the box office of the **Komische Oper** (☎ 47 99 74 00, Unter den Linden 41), one of Berlin's three opera houses. A theatre has stood in this spot since 1764, but the core of the current structure dates only to 1892. After WWII, the original interior – a plush, richly festooned baroque extravaganza – was largely restored, clashing with the decidedly functional '60s facade. (See the Entertainment chapter.)

On the north side of the next block, just before Charlottenstrasse, **Berlin Story** (☎ 20 16 61 39, Unter den Linden 40; open 10am-8pm) is an exhaustive bookstore cum bilingual history exhibit (see the Shopping chapter). The latter is organised by the Berlin Historical Society, an organisation dedicated to preserving the historical appearance of Mitte, especially along Unter den Linden. Much of its effort is geared towards reconstructing the Stadtschloss, which once stood in the place of the hideous Palast der Republik (see later in this section). On view are photos, pictures, scale models and the quaint Kaiserpanorama, a sort of primitive movie theatre.

Deutsche Guggenheim Berlin

In the south-eastern corner of Unter den Linden and Charlottenstrasse is the Deutsche Guggenheim Berlin (☎ 202 09 30, Unter den Linden 13-15; adult/concession €2.50-4/1.50-2.50, free Mon; open 11am-8pm daily, to 10pm Thur). A joint venture between Deutsche Bank and the Guggenheim Foundation, it is the fifth permanent – and smallest – exhibition space courtesy of this New York-based family, which incidentally is of German descent. The 510 sq metre gallery, with soaring ceilings and minimalist architecture, hosts three or four high-calibre shows of modern and contemporary art annually. There's also a small shop and cafe.

Alte Staatsbibliothek

Opposite the Deutsches Guggenheim Berlin is the 1914 Alte Staatsbibliothek (Old National Library; ☎ 266 12 30, Unter den Linden 8; admission free; open 9am-9pm Mon-Fri, to 7pm Sat). At 107m long and 170m wide, it is one of the largest buildings in central Berlin. Founded by the Great Elector Friedrich Wilhelm in 1661, the library's collection encompasses nine million books and periodicals, including precious manuscripts (eg, the poems of Hafiz, 1560), original musical sheets (eg, by Bach, Mozart and Beethoven) and maps (eg, Germany by Nicolas von Kues, 1491). The ivy-covered building is accessed via a tranquil inner courtyard where a nice cafe offers a respite from the bustle. Free tours run at 10.30am every first Saturday of the month. Books published after 1955 are housed at the Neue Staatsbibliothek (New National Library) near Potsdamer Platz.

Continue the tour by heading south on Charlottenstrasse, then one block west on Französische Strasse before turning south on Friedrichstrasse.

Friedrichstrasse

Friedrichstrasse was once the main artery of Friedrichstadt, a residential community built to plan by Friedrich I. Over the centuries, it evolved into one of Berlin's liveliest and most elegant boulevards, until WWII and division put an end to this nexus of urban vitality. After the Wende, Friedrichstrasse became the focus of an ambitious renewal project to breathe new life into the boulevard. Between Französische Strasse and Mohrenstrasse, an international team of architects created a trio of interconnected office and shopping complexes: the **Friedrichstadt-passagen**. Called 'Quartiers,' these structures are like jewel boxes, their sleek exteriors hiding sparkling treasures within.

Quartier 207 is home to French department store **Galeries Lafayette** where Jean Nouvel has created a central translucent glass funnel that reflects light with the intensity of a hologram. At **Quartier 206** the usual clique of international designer boutiques grace its hallowed halls. Take a look even if

Donna Karan doesn't do it for you: the Art deco decor is definitely worth it for the elegant composition in multi-hued marble, kaleidoscopically arranged in geometric patterns beneath a tent-like glass roof. **Quartier 205** has ceilings of cathedral dimensions and a light court accentuated with a towering installation by John Chamberlain.

Quartier 205 ends at Mohrenstrasse, where you turn east to reach the southern end of Gendarmenmarkt in one short block.

Gendarmenmarkt

Once a thriving marketplace, quiet, graceful Gendarmenmarkt is Berlin's most beautiful square. From 1736 to 1782, it was used by a military regiment, the 'gens d'arms' – hence the name – which had its headquarters and main stables here. The twin churches of **Deutscher Dom** (German Cathedral) and **Französischer Dom** (French Cathedral) combine with Schinkel's **Konzerthaus** to form a superbly harmonious architectural trio. Unifying elements include the columned porticoes and the domed towers of the two churches. Only the French cathedral is used as a place of worship.

A magnificent **statue of Friedrich Schiller**, one of Germany's greatest dramatists, stands in the centre of the square. Squirreled away by the Nazis, it ended up in the west, from where it returned to East Berlin in 1988 following an exchange of artworks between the two German states.

Deutscher Dom The German Cathedral, completed in 1708, consists of a pentagonal central structure surrounded by apses. Eighty years later it got its dazzling galleried dome, designed by Karl Gontard, which is supported by a ring of slender Corinthian columns. Renovated after the Wende, the Dom reopened in 1996 as a museum featuring **Fragen an die Deutsche Geschichte** (Questions on German History; ☎ 22 73 21 41; admission free; open 10am-6pm Tues-Sun). This exhibit focuses on the history of parliament and democracy in Germany and is sponsored by the Deutsche Bundestag (German Parliament). Since 1999, it has been undergoing a gradual revamping set to

be completed in 2002. Most sections remain open during this process. Spread over four floors, you can learn about Germany's brief flirtation with democracy during the 1848–49 Revolution and also find out about the inner workings of the Bundestag. Other sections chronicle the years of the Weimar Republic and the Third Reich as well as the decades of division after WWII.

Französischer Dom The mirror image of the Deutscher Dom, the French Cathedral was once the main house of worship of Berlin's large population of French Huguenots who, persecuted in their own country, settled here in the late 17th century. Built between 1701 and 1705 by Louis Cayart, the church was modelled after the main Huguenot church in Charenton, which had been destroyed in 1688. By 1785 it too had acquired its landmark Gontard-designed, domed tower, matching that of the German Cathedral.

Since 1929, the French Cathedral has housed the **Hugenottenmuseum** (Huguenot Museum, ☎ 229 17 60, Gendarmenmarkt 5; adult/concession €1.50/1, church free; open noon-5pm Tues-Sat, 11am-5pm Sun) which chronicles the fate of these French Protestants in France and in Berlin-Brandenburg from the 17th to the 20th century. On display are books, art, manuscripts and documents. Descriptions are in French and German.

For a great view, climb the tower to an outdoor **viewing gallery** (adult/concession €3/2; open 9am-7pm daily Apr-Oct, 10am-6pm Nov-Mar). Concerts on the church's **carillon** take place periodically on Saturday and Sunday.

The French Cathedral marks the northern end of Gendarmenmarkt. Continue the tour by strolling another block north on Markgrafenstrasse, then one block east on Behrenstrasse to Bebelplatz.

Bebelplatz

Originally known as Opernplatz, Bebelplatz was renamed in 1947 for August Bebel, the co-founder and leader of the Social Democratic Party (SPD). On 10 May 1933 the Nazis held their first official book burning here. They torched the works of authors they considered subversive, including Bertolt Brecht, Heinrich Mann and Jack London. It was a portentous event that signalled the death of the cultural greatness Berlin had achieved over the previous two centuries. A poignant below-ground memorial of an empty library by the Israeli artist Micha Ullmann marks the spot, but unfortunately it's hardly visible through the scratched glass window.

Bebelplatz is framed by several historical buildings. On the eastern side of the square is the renowned **Staatsoper Unter den Linden** (*National Opera; ☎ 203 55 40, Unter den Linden 7*), built in 1743, one of Berlin's earliest neoclassical structures (see the Architecture special section).

Opposite is the **Alte Königliche Bibliothek** (Old Royal Library), nicknamed *Kommode* (chest of drawers) for its bulky shape; it's now part of the Humboldt Universität school of law. On the square's south-eastern corner looms the giant copper dome of the **St-Hedwigs-Kathedrale** (*☎ 203 48 10, Behrensstrasse 39; admission free; open 10am-5pm Mon-Sat, 11pm-5pm Sun*), built in 1773 and partly modelled on the Pantheon in Rome. It was Berlin's only Catholic church until 1854 and has been the location of the Berlin bishopric since 1929. During WWII, it was a centre of Catholic resistance under Father Bernard Lichtenberg (1875–1943), who was imprisoned by the Nazis and died in a cattle car en route to Dachau concentration camp.

Humboldt Universität

Bebelplatz also borders Unter den Linden on the northern side of which looms the grandiose Humboldt University (*☎ 209 30, Unter den Linden 6*). It began life in 1753 as a palace of Prince Heinrich, brother of King Friedrich II, and became a university in 1810 on the initiative of Wilhelm von Humboldt, then minister of cultural affairs. Humboldt managed to assemble an illustrious faculty that included the philosophers Hegel and Fichte, and the university quickly rose to prominence throughout Europe. Marx and Engels both studied here,

and notable professors included the Brothers Grimm, Albert Einstein, Max Planck and the nuclear scientist Otto Hahn. Numerous Nobel Prize winners came out of Humboldt.

In November 2000, after three years of restoration, the equestrian **statue of Friedrich II** (1851) by Christian Daniel Rauch was returned to its usual place in the middle of Unter den Linden, standing in front of the university.

Neue Wache

Continue the tour by strolling east on Unter den Linden where the next structure on the north side is the Neue Wache (*New Guardhouse; Unter den Linden 4, admission free; open 10am-6pm daily*), built in 1818 by Schinkel for King Friedrich Wilhelm III. Germany's central memorial to the victims of fascism and militarism, it contains the tombs of an unknown soldier, a resistance fighter and a concentration camp victim, as well as Käthe Kollwitz's sculpture *Mother and her Dead Son*. (See the Architecture special section.)

Zeughaus & Kronzprinzenpalais

The rose-coloured building just east of the Neue Wache is the baroque Zeughaus (*Royal Arsenal; Unter den Linden 2*), built in 1706 by Andreas Schlüter. It normally contains the Museum of German History, but a renovation and extension by Chinese-American architect IM Pei will keep it closed until at least 2003. Pei's plans call for a dramatic glass roof to cover the central courtyard (Schlüterhof) of the historic edifice and the addition of a new modern wing to house special exhibits. Pei, one of the world's most eminent architects, is best known for the glass pyramid entrance to the Louvre in Paris.

Meanwhile, changing themed exhibits drawn from the museum's permanent collection are on view across the street at the colonnaded **Kronzprinzenpalais** (*Crown Princes' Palace; ☎ 20 30 40, Unter den Linden 3; admission free; open 10am-6pm Thur-Tues*). Originally built in 1664, it indeed served as a royal residence until the demise of the monarchy at the end of WWI. The National Gallery took over the space in 1919 to exhibit its contemporary art collection, including top artists like Lovis Corinth, Otto Dix, Paul Klee and Lyonel Feininger. The Nazis, who regarded modern art as 'degenerate', closed down the museum in 1933. The building was bombed to bits in WWII, but in the late 1960s the GDR government had a replica built, which it used as a guesthouse for visiting dignitaries. On 31 August 1990, the Treaty of German Unification was signed here.

The counterpart of this building is the 1811 Crown Princesses' Palace next door (west). Now known as the **Opernpalais**, it houses a stuffy restaurant-cafe (☎ 20 26 83, *Unter den Linden 5)* famous for its cake selection, as well as a pub and cocktail bar. The best time to visit is summer when the beer garden is in session.

The Historic Mitte Walking Tour ends here.

MUSEUMSINSEL (Map 7)

East of the Royal Arsenal, the lovely **Schlossbrücke** (Palace Bridge), with its Schinkel-designed marble statues, leads to the Spreeinsel (Spree island), the southern tip of which was the site of Berlin's earliest medieval settlement. Its northern half is better known as Museumsinsel (Museum Island), although a more poetic name might well be 'Treasure Island' because of the world-class calibre of the exhibits. Made a Unesco Heritage Site in 1999, the complex is undergoing a complete overhaul projected to be completed by 2010. The **Neues Museum**, severely damaged by WWII, is being completely rebuilt and will house the collection of Egyptian antiquities from 2007. Closed until at least 2005 is the neobaroque **Bodemuseum** on the island's northern tip. Late 2001 saw the reopening of the **Alte Nationalgalerie**, bringing the number of museums open for business back to three.

Museum Island is an outgrowth of a late-18th-century trend among Europe's royal houses to share their private collections with the public. The British Museum in London, the Louvre in Paris, the Prado in Madrid and the Glyptothek in Munich all date back to this time. Not to be outdone – and egged on by his advisers and supporters – Friedrich Wilhelm III commissioned Schinkel for the construction of the **Altes Museum** (1829). As a result of the royal collections' growth, in 1841, Friedrich Wilhelm IV decided to turn the entire island into a museum complex. The Neues Museum was completed in 1855, followed by the Alte Nationalgalerie (1876), the Bodemuseum (1904) and finally the **Pergamon Museum** (1930).

Alte Nationalgalerie (SMPK)

The Alte Nationalgalerie *(Old National Gallery; ☎ 20 90 55 55, Bodestrasse 1-3; adult/concession €4/2; open Tues-Sun 10am-6pm)* reopened in December 2001 after a thorough restoration. A showcase of 19th-century European art, it also incorporates the paintings previously on view at the Gallery of the Romantics at Schloss Charlottenburg. Artists like Caspar David Friedrich, Adolph Menzel, Lovis Corinth and Impressionists like Monet, Degas, Renoir and Cezanne are all well represented, as are sculptures by Rodin and others.

Altes Museum (SMPK)

Art and sculpture from ancient Rome and Greece are on view at the Altes Museum *(Old Museum; ☎ 20 90 55 55, Museumsinsel, enter from Lustgarten; adult/concession €4/2; open 10am-6pm Tues-Sun, to 10pm Thur)*. An imposing neoclassical edifice (1830) by Karl Friedrich Schinkel, this was the first building on museum island and has a famed rotunda featuring sculptures of Zeus and his entourage. (See the Architecture special section.)

Pergamon Museum (SMPK)

If you only have time for one museum while in Berlin, make it the Pergamon Museum *(☎ 20 90 55 55, Am Kupfergraben; adult/concession €4/2; open 10am-6pm Tues-Sun, to 10pm Thur)*. A feast of classical Greek, Babylonian, Roman, Islamic and Middle Eastern art and architecture, it will amaze and enlighten you – and possibly make your head spin if you're not careful.

Under the roof of a monumental edifice that took nearly 20 years to build (completed in 1930) are three world-class collections: the Antikensammlung (**Collection of Classical Antiquities**), the Vorderasiatisches Museum (**Museum of Near Eastern Antiquities**); and the Museum für Islamische Kunst (**Museum of Islamic Art**). Audio-guides with taped commentary are included in the admission price. For in-depth information on selected exhibits, look for plastic trays holding sheets in English, French and German. A small fee is charged per sheet and payment is by an honour system; just place the money in the box as you exit.

You'll need at least two hours to do this place justice. If your time is limited, stick to the highlights detailed below.

Antikensammlung The first major exhibit of the Collection of Classical Antiquities is also one of the most spectacular and the museum's namesake: the **Pergamon Altar** (165 BC) from Asia Minor, a gargantuan raised marble shrine the height of a three-storey building. It's mindboggling to think that what you see here was merely the entrance to a vast complex. Check out the scale models to help put it all in perspective.

The 120m **frieze** framing the hall's wall shows the gods doing battle with the giants. Note the anatomical precision, down to pectorals and facial expressions. Behind the altar, and reached by walking up its steps, is the **Telephos Frieze** which depicts the life story of the legendary founder of Pergamon.

The museum continues past the north (left) door with plenty of antique sculpture. If you're pressed for time, skip it or just check out the **Hellenistic architecture** of Room 8, entered through the marble foyer of a 2nd-century-BC temple, where you'll find a stunning floor mosaic.

Another highlight awaits in Room 6 (Roman architecture), behind the south (right) door: the splendidly preserved **Gate of Miletus**, built under Emperor Hadrian in the early 2nd century AD. Merchants and customers once flooded through here onto the market square of Miletus, a Roman trading town in Asia Minor that functioned as a bridge between Asia and Europe. Note the gate's symmetry and intricate decorative detail. The **Orpheus Mosaic** in the same room is from a villa in Miletus.

Vorderasiatisches Museum As you pass through the Gate of Miletus, you seamlessly enter another culture and century: Babylon during the reign of Nebuchadnezzar II (604-562 BC). This is the first room of the Museum of Near Eastern Antiquities whose *pièce de résistance* is the world famous **Ishtar Gate** fronted by a 30m-long 'Processional Way' (the original was 250m long). The walls of both the gate and way are covered in cobalt blue and ochre glazed bricks and feature reliefs of striding lions (a symbol of the goddess Ishtar), horses, dragons and unicorns. The walls of the gate itself are 15m high, which is presumed to be only half of their original height.

Room 5 is also worth a closer look for its unique **mosaic wall** from a temple in Uruk (3000 BC). The wall is put together from countless clay pegs in different colours arranged in a decorative pattern. This was not done so much for aesthetic reasons but rather to add a layer of reinforcement to the temple's brittle adobe walls.

Museum für Islamische Kunst The Museum of Islamic Art is on the upper floor and showcases art and objects from the 7th to the 19th centuries AD, including carpets, wood carvings, ceramics and books. The first highlight awaits in Rooms 9 and 10 in the form of the exterior wall of the fortress-like **Caliph's Palace in Mshatta**, probably built during the reign of Caliph al-Walid II (743–44 AD). Mshatta itself, which means 'winter camp', was located near today's Jordanian capital, Amman. The section on display here is part of a wall that once surrounded a complex measuring 144m by 144m and was guarded by 25 towers. The delicate-looking facade is smothered in decorative detail featuring vines and tendrils as well as whimsical animals and mythical figures.

Room 14 contains an impressive **Mihrab** (1226 AD), a prayer niche from Kaschan in Iran, ablaze with shiny golden, blue and turquoise tiles with Arabic inscriptions and adornments. Not to be missed either is the 17th-century **Aleppo Room** (Room 17) from the house of a Christian merchant in today's Syria. Each square centimetre of wall space is overlaid with colourful wooden panelling painted with dizzying detail. If you look closely, you can make out *The Last Supper* and *Mary and Child* amid all the ornamentation (straight ahead, on the right of the door).

Berliner Dom

Overlooking the cluster of museums is the neo-Renaissance Berliner Dom *(Berlin Cathedral;* ☎ *20 26 90, Am Lustgarten; adult/concession €5/3 for church, crypt & viewing gallery, €4/2 for church & crypt; open 9am-8pm Mon-Sat & noon-8pm Sun Apr-Sept; to 7pm Oct-Mar; viewing gallery last admission 5pm Apr-Sept, 4pm Oct-Mar).* It is the former court church of the royal Hohenzollern family, members of which are buried in its crypt. It's almost miraculous that this ostentatious symbol of monarchical power survived the GDR's fervour for erasing all traces of Berlin's imperial past, especially since it suffered grave damage during WWII. Rebuilt mostly with money pouring in from the western churches, its restoration was not completed until 1993, three years after the Wende.

The colossal structure (114m long, 73m wide, 85m high) is crowned by a central copper dome topped with a golden cross and ringed by four smaller towers. To get a sense of its vastness, climb the 270 steps to the **viewing gallery** at the base of the dome. Besides giving you nice views over the central city, it also lets you admire the intricate church design from a bird's-eye perspective.

The main church itself is richly decorated. The niches in the northern and southern apses hold the ornate sarcophagi of members of the Hohenzollern family. More of these elaborate coffins, including those designed by Schlüter for King Friedrich I (1713) and his second wife Sophie Charlotte (1705), are on view in the **crypt**.

English services are held at 6pm Thursday. A busy schedule of lectures, readings and concerts takes place throughout the year. Free organ recitals take place at 3pm Wednesday to Friday from May to September.

Lustgarten

The cathedral is fronted by the Lustgarten (Pleasure Garden) which began life in the late 16th century as a vegetable and herb garden for the adjacent palace kitchen. In 1650, Berlin's first potatoes were harvested here. The Soldier King, Friedrich Wilhelm I, had it converted into a parade ground, but in 1830 Schinkel turned it back into a small park to complement his then brand-new Altes Museum. The Nazis paved it over and now, after much debate, the garden has been restored to its Schinkel-era appearance.

SCHLOSSPLATZ & AROUND (Map 7)

Nothing of today's sterile Schlossplatz, south of the Lustgarten and called Marx-Engels-Platz under the GDR, serves as a reminder of the magnificent edifice that stood here from 1451 to 1951: the Berliner Stadtschloss (City Palace). Begun as a fortress-like structure during the reign of Elector Friedrich II, it was enlarged, then reconfigured and renovated many times, finally taking up the entire area of today's square. A rectangular building with two inner courtyards, its most captivating architectural features were a triumphal-arch portal and an octagonal chapel with a huge cupola.

WWII left its mark, but structurally the palace was not irreparable. It even served as a makeshift museum after 1945. In 1950, though, the GDR's Walter Ulbricht arbitrarily declared that it was 'a ruin not worthy of reconstruction' and, arrogantly ignoring protests from east and west, had the 500-year-old building blown up. In its stead was put the nerve centre of the GDR government, anchored by the Palast der Republik, the Staatsratsgebäude and the Marx Engels Forum. It was a decision even some East Berlin political honchos later regretted.

Palast der Republik

Until 1990, the Palace of the Republic, a clumsy pile of concrete and steel built in 1976 with a glitzy facade of rust-coloured mirror glass, was home of the GDR parliament (the Volkskammer, or People's Chamber) and site of SED party conventions. The complex was also accessible to the common people during congresses, balls and concerts held in a hall that seated up to 5000 (Harry Belafonte once sang here). There was also a gallery, restaurants and bars.

In 1990 it was discovered that the 'palace' was contaminated with asbestos, forcing its immediate closure. For years demolition looked inevitable but, while discussion about its fate has continued, it's been left to crumble, an eyesore in a blossoming Berlin. In 1993–94, one step ahead of Christo and his wrapped Reichstag, a French artist clad the structure with plastic sheets designed to look like the old Berliner Schloss. This sparked interest in rebuilding the original structure and the formation of the Berlin Historical Association. (See the section on the Berlin Story exhibit earlier in this section).

Around Schlossplatz

Only the triumphal-arch portal from which Karl Liebknecht proclaimed a Socialist German Republic in 1918 was spared during demolition of the Stadtschloss. In the early 1960s, it was incorporated into the **Staatsratsgebäude** *(State Council Building;* ☎ *40 00 21 16, Schlossplatz 1)* which, after the Wende, served as the Federal Chancellery. See if the doors are open to sneak a peek at the colourful windows in the foyer which depict the 'historical evolution' of the GDR from the ill-fated revolutionary days of 1918–19 to the founding of the communist state in 1949. The portraits in the centre show Rosa Luxemburg and Karl Liebknecht, co-founders of the German Communist Party (KPD). Incidentally, the building is the future home of the Bundesnachrichtendienst (Federal Intelligence Service).

East of the State Council Building is the **Neue Marstall** *(New Royal Stables; Breite Strasse)* once home to horses and carriages and now containing the City Archives. Note the bronze reliefs on the wall facing the Palace of the Republic which depict socialist heroes and pivotal revolutionary events.

Immediately south at Breite Strasse 35–36 is the ornately gabled **Ribbeckhaus**, Berlin's only remaining late Renaissance building (1624). Today it contains a library, the Zentrum für Berlin-Studien (Centre for Berlin Studies; see Libraries in the Facts for the Visitor chapter).

Schinkelmuseum (SMPK)

Just west of Schlossplatz is the Schinkel-designed **Friedrichswerdersche Kirche** (1830) which now contains the Schinkelmuseum *(☎ 20 90 55 55, Werderscher Markt; adult/ concession €2/1; open 10am-6pm Tues-Sun)*. No longer a place of worship, the church houses an exhibit of German neoclassical sculpture representing all major practitioners of the time, including Johann Gottfried Schadow, Christian Friedrich Tieck and Christian Daniel Rauch. Upstairs is an exhibit on the life and work of Schinkel, the multiskilled architect and sculptor. (For more on Schinkel and the building, see the Architecture special section.)

The chunky-looking structure south of the church once housed the Reichsbank, the German national bank under the Nazis. In GDR days, the central committee of the SED party had its headquarters here. In united Germany, the building with its modern extension is the home of the Bundesaussenministerium (Federal Foreign Office).

ALEXANDERPLATZ (Map 7)

East of the Schlossbrücke, Unter den Linden gives way to Karl-Liebknecht-Strasse which culminates in Alexanderplatz, once East Berlin's main commercial hub. Known as 'Alex' for short, the square was named in honour of Tsar Alexander II, who visited Berlin in 1805. Until then it had been called Ochsenplatz (oxen square). Today it's a mere shadow of the low-life district Alfred Döblin called 'the quivering heart of a cosmopolitan city' in his novel *Berlin Alexanderplatz* (1929). Redesigned several times in the late 1920s and badly bombed in WWII, its current socialist look dates from the 1960s. On 4 November 1989, some 700,000 people gathered here to rally against the GDR regime. They were vociferous but peaceful, and they were heard; five days later, the Wall came down.

The first impression of Alexanderplatz is overwhelming. Nothing seems to be built on a human – or humane – scale. A cacophonous jumble of concrete and glass high-rises combines with a treeless asphalt desert to form one of the most hideous and disorienting squares this writer has ever seen. This is a good place for a quick overview of the soulless architectural styles in vogue in the GDR. It's hard to imagine that it actually looked even more drab before the Wende – at least the giant billboards atop rooflines and the neon advertisements have added, well, splashes of colour.

Alexanderplatz has forever been a major public-transport hub. Today, trains stop both below ground and on the elevated tracks slicing right through the square.

Alexanderplatz has few sights, a minor one being the **World Time Clock** (1969) by Erich John with its enamel and aluminium panelling (don't use the subterranean men's toilet nearby unless you want to be stared down by 101 men on the prowl).

One of the other attractions is the **TV Tower** (*☎ 242 33 33, Panoramastrasse 1a; adults/concession €6/2.50; open 9am-1am Mar-Oct, 10am-midnight Nov-Feb*), a spiky 365m-tall monstrosity built in 1969. Just below the antenna is a shiny steel sphere which, when hit by sunlight, produces the reflection of a huge cross – once a source of embarrassment to the atheist GDR and of glee in the west where they dubbed this phenomenon 'the Pope's revenge'. If it's a clear day and the queue isn't too long, it's worth paying to go up. At the 207m level is the **Telecafé** (*☎ 242 33 33; open 10am-1am Mar-Oct, 10am-midnight Nov-Feb*) which makes a complete revolution every half an hour and has live music at 7pm Tuesday to Saturday. There's also a tourist office in the foyer.

Marienkirche
The Gothic Marienkirche (*☎ 242 44 76, Karl-Liebknecht-Strasse 8; admission free; open 10am-noon & 1pm-4pm Mon-Thur, noon-4pm Sat-Sun*), a Lutheran church just west of Alexanderplatz, is one of Berlin's few surviving medieval buildings (1270). Inside, note the baroque alabaster pulpit by Andreas Schlüter (1703) with its lavish canopy topped by a gaggle of cherubs set against gilded rays of sunlight. Another major attraction is the *Totentanz* (Dance of Death, 1485) fresco, which portrays a shrouded figure of Death in 14 guises leading people from all walks of life to their graves. It's been under restoration for years and may still not be back in place during your visit.

Nearby is the opulent **Neptunbrunnen** (Neptune Fountain, 1891) by Reinhold Begas which was moved here from Schlossplatz. The female figures symbolise the rivers Rhine, Elbe, Oder and Weichsel.

SOUTH OF ALEXANDERPLATZ (Map 7)
The area south of Alexanderplatz, roughly bounded by the Spree canal and Alexanderstrasse, is the oldest and most historic part of Berlin.

Rotes Rathaus
The palatial Rotes Rathaus (Red Town Hall, 1860), home of Berlin's governing mayor and the Berlin Senate, is the largest building in this area. It gets its name from the colour of the brick used in its construction (not from the political leanings of its occupants). The design successfully blends Italian Renaissance elements with northern German architecture. Note the terracotta frieze on the facade (1879) which depicts the entire city history from the 13th century onward. The representative staircase, with its four allegorical statues symbolising various trades, as well as the ceremonial halls, may be visited (*admission free; open 9am-6pm Mon-Fri*), except during official functions.

Nikolaiviertel
The Nicholas Quarter, a cute maze of narrow, car-free lanes lined by diminutive houses, lies just south-west of the Red Town Hall and is bounded by the broad Mühlendamm to the south. Some of Berlin's oldest houses stood here until levelled by bombs in 1944. What you see today is the not entirely unsuccessful attempt by socialist architects

to re-create a medieval village. Sure, purists will be shocked to learn that only a few of these buildings have actual historical origins or that most are made with the same ubiquitous prefab concrete slabs so popular in GDR-era construction (some wags have even dubbed it 'Disneyviertel' because of the artificial nature of the place). Nonetheless, some buildings stand out from the crowd. The house **Zum Nussbaum** *(☎ 242 30 95, Am Nussbaum 3)*, for instance, contains a convivial restaurant-pub, the original of which once stood on the nearby Fischerinsel (see the Places to Eat chapter). In the 1920s, it was the favourite watering hole of local legend, humorist and cartoonist Heinrich Zille. The reconstructed courthouse – the **Gerichtslaube** – also stands in Poststrasse and contains a couple of pricey restaurants.

Also part of the Nikolaiviertel are the following small and moderately interesting museums. If you wish to visit all three, you should get the *Verbundkarte* (combination ticket) for €3/1.50 available at either place; admission is free on Wednesday.

Museum Nikolaikirche Lording over the Nikolaiviertel are the spindly twin spires of the late-Gothic Nikolaikirche (1230), Berlin's oldest church. One of the few buildings that was restored rather than newly built, it is no longer a place of worship but contains the Museum Nikolaikirche *(☎ 24 00 21 82, Nikolaikirchplatz; admission €1.50, €5/3 during special exhibits, free Wed; open 10am-6pm Tues-Sun)*. The exhibit documents the various construction periods of the church and its role in local history. Perhaps more interesting is the sculpture dotted around the hall, including a tomb portal by Andreas Schlüter and several Renaissance gravestone epitaphs.

Museum Knoblauchhaus Dating from the 18th century, the Knoblauchhaus *(☎ 240 02 01 71, Poststrasse 23; adult/concession €2.50/1.25, free Wed; open 10am-6pm Tues-Sun)* is the oldest original residential building in the Nikolaiviertel. It served as the home of the Knoblauch family for nearly 170

years until 1928. One of the family members, Eduard Knoblauch, was the architect of the original synagogue in Oranienburger Strasse. On the 1st floor are four period rooms showcasing bourgeois living in the age of Biedermeier. The upper floor houses changing exhibits. In the basement is the rustic yet elegant **Historische Weinstuben** restaurant.

Ephraim-Palais The Ephraim-Palais *(☎ 24 00 21 21, Poststrasse 16; adult/concession €2.50/1.25, free Wed; open 10am-6pm Tues-Sun)* was the home of Friedrich II's treasurer, Veitel Heine Ephraim. It features a curved rococo facade with delicate gilded ironwork balconies and sculptural ornamentation and is considered one of Berlin's prettiest buildings.

Although the original, which stood some 20m from the current location, was destroyed during the construction of the Mühlendamm bridge in 1936, the precious facade was dismantled and stored for decades in West Berlin. In 1984, it was given to East Berlin to be used in the construction of the Nikolaiviertel.

These days, the Ephraim-Palais hosts changing exhibitions about various aspects of local art and cultural history.

Molkenmarkt & Around
The busy intersection of Mühlendamm, Stralauer Strasse and Spandauer Strasse, immediately south of the Nikolaiviertel, marks the centre of the Molkenmarkt area, which is full of hidden gems. The name refers to its medieval origin as a dairy market, though it requires a good imagination to recognise it as such amid the roaring traffic. On the south side of Mühlendamm stands the building complex of the GDR Ministry of Culture which incorporated the former **mint** (1935) and the baroque **Palais Schwerin**.

Looming above it all is the **Alte Stadthaus** *(Jüdenstrasse 34–42)* built by Ludwig Hoffmann from 1902–11 as an extension to the Red Town Hall and distinguished by an 80m-high colonnaded and domed tower. From 1960–90, it served the GDR as the Haus des Ministerrates (House of the Ministry Council). Since 1995, it has been in the process of being restored to its former glory – it may be completed by the end of 2002. Major exterior enhancements include the re-creation of the mansard roof, the refurbishment of the tower and the return of a gilded Fortuna sculpture which will reclaim its historic perch atop the cupola.

Head north on Jüdenstrasse, then right on Parochialstrasse which leads to the baroque **Parochialkirche**, built in 1703. Designed by Johann Arnold Nering (whose other works include the oldest section of Schloss Charlottenburg), the church still bears the wounds of WWII. It's unrestored layout reveals four conches framing a central square tower. With its bare walls, open ceiling (you can actually see the roof timbering), draughty doors and stone floors, it has at least as powerful an effect as Charlottenburg's Gedächtniskirche. The Parochialkirche is now primarily used for exhibits and concerts.

Also on Klosterstrasse is the **Palais Podewil** *(Klosterstrasse No 68–70)*, a lovely early-18th-century patrician manor turned cultural centre (see the Entertainment chapter).

A few steps farther north is another church ruin, that of the **Franziskaner Klosterkirche** (Franciscan Abbey Church). Built in the first half of the 14th century, it was converted into a grammar school in 1574. Famous pupils include Karl Friedrich Schinkel and Otto von Bismarck. Badly damaged in WWII, the ruins were preserved and now form the backdrop for a popular summer series of outdoor music and theatre events.

The building behind the church ruins is the **Justizpalast** *(Courts of Justice, Littenstrasse 13–17)*, built in the early 20th century and worthwhile checking out for its handsome Art Nouveau staircases. The historic restaurant-pub **Zur letzten Instanz** *(☎ 242 55 28, Waisenstrasse 14)* is nearby. (See the Entertainment chapter.)

Märkisches Ufer

The area around Märkisches Museum U-Bahn station yields a couple of moderately interesting sights. Head east from the station, then north on Inselstrasse to get to the spot where the Spree canal rejoins the river.

To the left loom the monotonous high-rises of the **Fischerinsel**, the name given to the southern tip of the Spree island (Museum Island occupies the northern end). As the name suggests, this used to be a fishing settlement, a crammed maze of alleyways lined by simple two-storey houses with claustrophobic courtyards, all interspersed with raucous pubs and tiny stores. Not much fishing happens these days.

Turning left into Märkisches Ufer leads to the baroque **Otto-Nagel-Haus** *(Märkisches Ufer 16-18)* which is now home of the Prussian Picture Archives. At No 12 is an exact copy of a rococo house that once stood on the opposite bank. The highlight here is the **Ermeler-Haus** *(Märkisches Ufer 10)*, one of Berlin's most handsome town villas, despite being replica. Now part of the **art'otel berlin mitte** (see the Places to Stay chapter), its lovely rococo interior is best enjoyed during a meal in the upmarket restaurant.

Backtrack to Wallstrasse, and turn left towards the Märkisches Museum within the small **Köllnischer Park**. This area once formed a part of the city fortifications built under Soldier King Friedrich Wilhelm I. A reminder is the so-called **Wusterhausensche Bär** (literally 'Bear of Wusterhausen'), a guard tower which, despite the name, has nothing to do with the three brown bears housed in a pit in the park. They are the **official city mascots** and are named Schnute (born 1981), Maxi (1986) and Tilo (1990).

Märkisches Museum The red-brick pile is the Märkisches Museum *(Museum of the March of Brandenburg, ☎ 30 86 62 15, Am Köllnischen Park 5; adult/concession €4/2, free Wed; open 10am-6pm Tues-Sun)*. The exterior is a hotchpotch of replicas of actual buildings in Brandenburg. The tower, for instance, is modelled after that of the bishop's palace in Wittstock, while St Catherine's Church in the town of Brandenburg inspired the Gothic gables. A copy of the Roland statue from the same town guards the museum entrance.

On view is a new permanent exhibition documenting cultural history in Berlin from the Middle Ages to the present. Several thematic sections chronicle such waystations as Berlin as a royal residence, Berlin as capital city, Berlin under the Nazis, Berlin's infrastructure and several more. A highlight is the nifty **automatophones**, 18th-century mechanical musical instruments, which are wound up and made to go through their noisy paces at 3pm Sunday (separate admission €2/1).

SPANDAUER VORSTADT (Maps 3 & 7)

The Spandauer Vorstadt (Spandau suburb) is one of Berlin's hippest areas and teems with nightclubs, bars and restaurants. Besides Oranienburger Strasse, the main artery, much of the action takes place in side streets like Auguststrasse and Tucholskystrasse.

The quarter, bordered by Friedrichstrasse in the west and Karl-Liebknecht-Strasse/ Prenzlauer Allee in the east, gets its name from the time when the main road to Spandau – today's Oranienburger Strasse – ran right through here. These days, it's often mistakenly called 'Scheunenviertel' (Barn Quarter), which is actually only the small section of Spandauer Vorstadt around Rosa-Luxemburg-Platz (see Scheunenviertel later in this chapter).

For centuries, the area was the centre of Berlin's **Jewish community** and since the opening of the **New Synagogue** it has become so again today.

The S1 or S2 to Oranienburger Strasse, the U6 to Oranienburger Tor or any S-Bahn to Hackescher Markt will put you right in the thick of things.

Hackesche Höfe (Map 7)

Tourists flock to the beautifully restored Hackesche Höfe (Hackesche Courtyards, 1907) like bears to the honey jar. After a three-year restoration, the warren of eight courtyards reopened to great fanfare in late 1996. A multi-use complex combining apartments with restaurants and cafes, theatres, galleries and boutiques, it's one of Berlin's greatest success stories. Although somewhat tainted by an overly commercial feel, it's definitely worth a visit.

Fronted by a beautiful facade, the main entrance off Rosenthaler Strasse immediately puts you into the prettiest courtyard, Hof I (Endellscher Hof). Its facades are smothered in kaleidoscopic, intricately patterned tiles by Art Nouveau artist August Endell. Also here is the **Chamäleon Varieté** (see the Entertainment chapter), which has adapted the ballroom of the former and fashionably famous wine-restaurant Neumann. Hof II (Theaterhof) features the Hackesches Hof-Theater, which celebrates **Yiddish culture**, and several architects' studios. The other six courtyards contain more galleries, fashion boutiques, cafes and bookstores.

Sophienstrasse (Map 3)

The Hackesche Höfe spill out onto Sophienstrasse, which was lavished with attention by the GDR regime in preparation for the city's 750th anniversary in 1987. At the time, many of the 19th-century houses along here were placed under protection and restored.

Of historical interest is the **Handwerkervereinshaus** *(Sophienstrasse 18)* with the former assembly halls of the craftsmen's association founded in 1844. This group later formed the germ cell of the workers' movement in Berlin, eventually leading to the founding of the Sozialdemokratische Partei (SPD) in 1869 by August Bebel and Wilhelm Liebknecht. Both spoke to the workers in several meeting halls here, the largest of which held 1400 people. Now renamed **Sophiensaele** *(☎ 283 52 66, Sophienstrasse 18)*, the space has evolved into a cutting-edge venue for innovative fringe theatre, concerts and dance. Quality can be high and some productions have gone on to bigger venues. Acclaimed dancer and choreographer Sasha Waltz, now co-director of the Schaubühne am Lehniner Platz, got her start here.

Just past the Handwerkervereinshaus look for the entrance to the quiet and dignified **Sophie-Gips-Höfe** whose trio of courtyards contains galleries and the popular **Barcomi's** cafe (see the Places to Eat chapter). The connecting walkways are lined with primary-coloured neon lights.

Already in view is the hulking outline of the baroque **Sophienkirche** *(☎ 282 58 77,*

Grosse Hamburger Strasse 29) surrounded by a gated churchyard. The only church in Mitte to survive WWII, it's a single-nave, galleried confection with understated decor and a delicate stucco ceiling. The tower, with its copper and gilded top, is the only baroque tower in Berlin. Unfortunately, the church is usually closed and can only be seen on tours (in German; call for details). You can usually stroll around the churchyard, though. If the gate off Sophienstrasse is locked, walk to the corner with Grosse Hamburger Strasse, turn left and the entrance will be via a gap between two apartment buildings.

Also on Grosse Hamburger Strasse, a short walk south of here, used to be Berlin's oldest Jewish cemetery (1672). Destroyed by the Nazis in 1938, it contained the graves of more than 10,000 people, including the philosopher Moses Mendelssohn. Several memorials stand in its space today.

Neue Synagoge (Map 3)

The beautifully rebuilt New Synagogue *(Oranienburger Strasse 29)* is crowned by the gold and silver Schwedler Dome, once again a Berlin landmark. Built in a Moorish-Byzantine style by Eduard Knoblauch (also see the Knoblauchhaus earlier in this section),

the synagogue opened in 1866 as the nation's largest (3200 seats) in the presence of Otto von Bismarck and several other Prussian dignitaries.

During the Kristallnacht pogrom on 9–10 November 1938, SS thugs tried to set fire to it – as they had to almost all of Berlin's other 13 synagogues – but were prevented by Wilhelm Krützfeld, a local police chief. A plaque on the synagogue facade commemorates this act of courage. The synagogue was nonetheless desecrated by the Nazis, though it was not destroyed until hit by bombs in 1943.

In the GDR era the ruins were left to linger until the mid-80s. Reconstruction began before the Wende on the 50th anniversary of Kristallnacht with a ceremony attended by Erich Honecker. The building reopened in May 1995, this time in the presence of then-Chancellor Helmut Kohl and then-President Roman Herzog.

Today it is not a house of worship but a research and community centre called **Centrum Judaicum** (☎ 88 02 84 51, *Oranienburger Strasse 28-30; adult/concession €2.50/1.50; open 10am-8pm Mon-Sun, 10am-6pm Tues-Thur, 10am-5pm Fri May-Aug; 10am-6pm Sun-Thur & 10am-2pm Fri Sep-Apr; guided tours (in German) €2/1,*

Berlin's Jewish Renaissance

Like a phoenix rising from the ashes of those killed by the Nazis, Jewish life is once again thriving all over Germany, but nowhere as vigorously as in Berlin. The capital now has the world's fastest growing Jewish community, thanks largely to a wave of immigrants from the former Soviet Union. In July 2001, the city's official Jewish population stood at 12,500 people, and figures may even be higher because statistics only count Jews affiliated with a synagogue.

The community supports seven synagogues, two mikve ritual baths, several schools and a handful of Kosher restaurants. The rebuilt New Synagogue on Oranienburger Strasse in the historic Jewish quarter has become a symbol of Jewish renewal. Their story in this city, though – as just about everywhere else in Europe – is a tortured one of persecution, murder and injustice.

The first Jewish settlers arrived as early as 1295, but throughout the Middle Ages they had to contend with being blamed for any kind of societal or economic woe. When the plague struck in 1348–49, the suspicion that the Jews had poisoned the wells led to the city's first major pogrom. In 1510, 38 Jews were publicly burnt after being accused of desecrating communion wafers and of killing Christian children. All other Jews were expelled.

The tide turned somewhat in 1671 when Great Elector Friedrich Wilhelm invited 50 wealthy Jewish families who had been banished from Vienna to settle in Berlin. Although he may have been – at least initially – motivated by financial interests, he later extended the offer to Jews in general. For the *tours 4pm Wed and 2pm and 4pm Sun).* Its permanent exhibit documents the history of the building and Jewish life and culture in Berlin and Brandenburg. On display are photographs, original furnishings, documents and liturgical objects. Hushed 'sound fragments' of the synagogue's construction and destruction, as well as murmurings of prayer and everyday life in the quarter before the Holocaust, heighten the mood. Expect a lot of security checks to get inside.

Next door is the **Jüdische Galerie Berlin** *(Jewish Gallery Berlin;* ☎ *282 86 23, Oranienburger Strasse 31; admission free; open 12.30pm-6.30pm Mon-Thur, 1am-5pm Fri, 11am-3pm Sun),* which – no surprise here! – displays the works of Jewish artists.

Kunsthaus Tacheles (Map 3)

Graffiti-covered walls, brittle staircases, dilapidated facades – the Kunsthaus Tacheles *(*☎ *282 61 85, Oranienburger Strasse 54-56)* is pretty much the antithesis of prettified Mitte. Yet it's also one of the city's major attractions, and not just for anarchic, underground artists and those who love them. This is still the place to come for mind-bending art, the warped sounds of tomorrow and an almost infectious burst of creativity.

Originally part of a shopping complex built in 1909, the Tacheles became an exhibition hall for AEG electrical products during the Weimar Republic. After WWII it pretty much languished for decades until the heady days of reunification. Shortly after 1989, about 50 artists moved into the ruinous building hoping to have it declared a protected building. The squatters accomplished this in 1992, paving the way for the vast alternative art and culture centre it still is today. There are artists' studios, galleries, a theatre and a cinema, as well as a cafe and nightclub. The chaotic backyard is a constantly evolving 'sculpture garden'. It's all run by a self-governed nonprofit organisation which is largely made up of the artists themselves.

Over the years, the Tacheles has lost little of its edge, even though it's included in tourist office advertising material and is on the route of tour buses from Denmark and Bavaria. But that edginess may soon evaporate after all.

The area surrounding the building is poised to be developed into what is termed the 'Johannisviertel' (St John's Quarter). If plans are approved, it will encompass apartment and office buildings, restaurants, shops

---

Berlin's Jewish Renaissance

first time, Jews were allowed to publicly practise their faith. Berlin's oldest Jewish cemetery, on Grosse Hamburger Strasse, dates from this time, as does the first synagogue.

In 1743, philosopher Moses Mendelssohn, who paved the way for Jewish emancipation, came to Berlin. The first Jewish family was granted full civic rights about 50 years later and in 1812 the Emancipation Edict finally made all Jews full citizens of Prussia with equal rights and duties. By the late 19th century, many of Berlin's Jews, numbering about 5% of the population, had become thoroughly German in speech and identity. The community continued to grow, partly thanks to a wave of Hasidic Jews escaping the pogroms of Eastern Europe who settled in the Scheunenviertel, then an immigrant slum. By 1933, one in three (around 170,000) German Jews lived in Berlin. The well-documented terrors of the Third Reich sent most into emigration and left 60,000 dead. About 7000 Jews survived the war years in Berlin, calling themselves 'U-Boats' for their ability to submerge in the wartorn city.

After WWII, the Jewish population remained tiny until the collapse of the Soviet Union brought a new wave of immigrants. Jewish Berlin has flourished ever since, and interest in their culture is high among Berliners. An appreciation of traditional Jewish foods is a growing trend, and cultural events of all sorts are well attended by Jews and non-Jews alike. Case in point is the Hackesches Hof-Theater (☎ 283 25 87) in the Hackesche Höfe, which performs Yiddish theatre and music. An excellent source about the community is the English-language Web site at Ⓦ www.hagalil.com/brd/berlin/berlin.htm.

and a luxury hotel. The Tacheles is supposed to be integrated into the spanking-new district while being allowed to keep a popular anarchic flair, although exactly how that is to be accomplished is hard to imagine. Stay tuned.

Scheunenviertel (Map 3)

The Scheunenviertel (Barn Quarter) is framed by Münzstrasse, Alte Schönhauser Strasse, Torstrasse and Karl-Liebknecht-Strasse. U-Bahn station Weinmeisterstrasse is in the heart of it.

This was traditionally a poor area of narrow lanes lined by dumpy houses. Prostitution, petty and not-so-petty crime and revolutionary rumblings flourished here in the 19th century until WWII. In the early 20th century, the Scheunenviertel absorbed huge numbers of new Jewish immigrants from Eastern Europe, and its streets and shops soon rang with the sound of Yiddish. Most newcomers were Hasidic Jews who, at least initially, had trouble assimilating to the existing and more liberal Jewish community living a few blocks west.

The Scheunenviertel got its name because in 1672, the Great Elector, Friedrich Wilhelm, decided to move the hay barns – a fire hazard – beyond the then-city limits to the area of today's Rosa-Luxemburg-Platz. This square is now occupied by the **Volksbühne**, a theatre founded by workers in 1913 and first helmed by Max Reinhardt. It has always had a reputation for avant-garde, radical productions, a tradition continued under its current director Frank Castorf. Nearby is the **Karl-Liebknecht-Haus** (Kleine Alexanderstrasse 28), which housed the central committee of the KPD, the communist party from 1926 to 1933. Appropriately, the PDS, the successor party of East Germany's SED, has its offices here today.

ORANIENBURGER TOR AREA (Map 3)
Brecht-Weigel Gedenkstätte

From 1953 until their respective deaths in 1956 and 1971, Bertolt Brecht and his wife, Helene Weigel, made their Berlin home in this building that now contains the Brecht-Weigel Gedenkstätte (Brecht-Weigel Memorial House; ☎ 283 05 70 44, Chausseestrasse 125; tours adult/concession €3/1.50; tours (in German) every half hour 10am-noon Tues-Fri, 5pm-7pm Thur, 9.30am-noon & 12.30pm-2pm Sat, hourly 11am-6pm Sun). Inside, Brecht's spacious but rather modest living and working quarters upstairs are functionally furnished with leather chairs from the 1930s and also some Biedermeier pieces. His large library contains everything from German classics to books on the FBI and detective stories. The tiny bedroom where he died (probably of a heart attack) remains as if he'd just left, with hat and woollen cap hanging on a door hook and Chinese artwork on the walls.

Weigel's living quarters on the ground floor are comparatively cluttered and have a surprisingly petit bourgeois character, reflected in her passion for collecting jugs, porcelain, glass etc.

Call for reservations since tours are limited to eight people. The entrance is upstairs to the right from the rear courtyard.

Museum für Naturkunde

A short walk north is the fascinating Humboldt University-affiliated Museum für Naturkunde (Natural History Museum; ☎ 20 93 85 91, Invalidenstrasse 43; adult/concession €2.50/1.25; open 9.30am-5pm Tues-Sun; U-Bahn: U6 to Zinnowitzer Strasse). The world-famous **Dinosaur Hall** takes pride of place with its star exhibit, a 23m-long and 12m-tall skeleton of a Brachiosaurus brancai, in fact the world's largest exhibited dinosaur skeleton. The other six dinosaur skeletons in the hall are smaller but no less interesting and neither is the fossilised **archaeopteryx**, the prehistoric species that forms the evolutionary link between reptiles and birds.

Evolution is the general underlying theme of the exhibits in 16 vast rooms. Another show-stopper is 'Bobby', a preserved gorilla that was the first such animal raised in captivity from baby to adulthood.

At Invalidenstrasse 44, just west of the museum, is the **Bundesministerium für Verkehr, Bau- und Wohnungswesen** (Federal Ministry of Transport, Building & Housing).

Hamburger Bahnhof (SMPK)

In a former train station, about a 10-minute walk west of the Natural History Museum, is Berlin's premier contemporary art museum, the Hamburger Bahnhof (☎ 20 90 55 55, Invalidenstrasse 50-51; adult/concession €4/ 2; open 10am-6pm Tues-Fri, to 10pm Thur, 11am-6pm Sat-Sun). It picks up where the Neue Nationalgalerie at the Kulturforum leaves off. Big names, including Joseph Beuys, Andy Warhol, Robert Rauschenberg, Anselm Kiefer and Keith Haring, form the core collection, which spans the second half of the 20th century. Traditional and modern media are represented, from painting to video, sculpture to light installations.

At least as interesting as the art (and to some, perhaps even more so) is the architecture of the building. A late neoclassical structure from 1847, the gleaming white, three-winged ex-train station exudes a palatial aura, though the clock in the right tower gives away its more mundane origin. At night, a light installation by Dan Flavin bathes the building in mystical blue and green hues. Josef Paul Kleinhues (who also designed the Kantdreieck, see the Architecture special section), created the magnificent exterior. It is centred on a vaulted central hall with the loftiness of a Gothic cathedral. Inside, whitewashed walls are supported by an exposed skeleton of steel beams, the perfect environment for megasized canvases and large scale installations. Smaller art is displayed in the 80m-long vaulted Ostgalerie and side wings.

FRIEDRICHSTRASSE (Map 7)

The area around Bahnhof Friedrichstrasse has been Berlin's premier theatre district since the late 19th century, although the station itself has an even more 'dramatic' history. Until 1990, it was the main gateway for western German visitors to East Berlin. The squat building just north of the U-Bahn station exit once housed the border checkpoint. Nicknamed **Tränenpalast** (Palace of Tears; ☎ 206 10 00, Reichstagsufer 17), here western visitors had to say goodbye to their eastern friends and family. Many tears were shed within these walls, hence the name. A slab of the Wall reminds of these times. Today it's a cultural centre hosting international events (see the Entertainment chapter).

Just across Weidendammbrücke is the **Berliner Ensemble** (☎ 28 40 81 55, Bertolt-Brecht-Platz 1), originally called Theater am Schiffbauerdamm (the name refers to the shipbuilders who used to work here on the banks of the Spree). It made headlines within days of its 1892 opening when it premiered Gerhart Hauptmann's The Weavers, a play under imperial ban for its critical social stance. The Kaiser responded by cancelling his subscription to the royal box. In 1903, Max Reinhardt got his first crack at directing here, and after WWII, his one-time protégé, Bertolt Brecht, moved in with his newly founded Berliner Ensemble. A **statue** outside the theatre shows the seated Brecht, hands folded in his lap and surrounded by three black marble pillars engraved with quotations from his works.

About 200m east of the theatre, still on Schiffbauerdamm, the **Bundesministerium für Umwelt** (Federal Ministry of the Environment) is located right across the road from the **Bundespresseamt** (Federal Press Office) on Reichstagufer.

Heading north on Albrechtstrasse will soon bring you to the **Deutsches Theater** (☎ 28 44 12 25, Schumannstrasse 13a). Classical operettas formed the standard repertoire here until Otto Brahm – a dedicated supporter of Hauptmann and other naturalists – took over in 1894. The theatre experienced its heyday under Reinhardt, who succeeded Brahm and who directed it, with interruptions, from 1905 to 1932 (See the boxed text 'Max Reinhardt – Impresario Extraordinare').

East of here, back on Friedrichstrasse, is the **Friedrichstadtpalast** (☎ 23 26 24 74, Friedrichstrasse 107) with its garish facade. The structure you see today dates from just 1985, replacing the 1869 original. First a market hall, it later housed a circus and only became a theatre in 1919 under Max Reinhardt. Lavish, commercial musical revues with showgirls and live orchestras take place here today.

For more on any of these theatres, see the Entertainment chapter.

Max Reinhardt – Impresario Extraordinaire

Max Reinhardt (1873–1943) was one of the seminal figures in the history of German theatre. Under his stewardship, Berlin became the country's leading theatre town in the first three decades of the 20th century. Born in Vienna of Jewish descent (his birth name was Max Goldmann), Reinhardt soon traded a traineeship in banking for a career in the theatre. In 1894, Otto Brahm hired him as an actor at the Deutsches Theater (DT), which launched Reinhardt's mercurial career path.

At the age of 27, while still acting at the DT, he co-founded Berlin's first literary cabaret – Schall und Rauch – on New Year's Eve 1900. In 1902 he became director of the Kleines Theater and simultaneously ran the Neues Theater from 1903 to 1906, making a name for himself with a production of Maxim Gorki's *Nachtasyl* (Night Asylum, 1903). In 1905 he inherited the mantle of the Deutsches Theater from Brahm and, on the side, also founded the Kammerspiele a year later.

Stylistically, Reinhardt completely turned his back on the Naturalism favoured by his mentor Brahm and broke new ground by using technological innovations to enhance the illusionary effects of the theatre. He integrated light effects, music, the new turning stage and other devices into his lavish productions, including his famous version of Shakespeare's *A Midsummer Night's Dream*. He demanded and extracted great performances from his actors.

During WWI, Reinhardt also directed the Neue Volksbühne, which he had helped found in 1913. In 1919, he opened the Grosse Schauspielhaus (later the Friedrichstadtpalast) and co-founded the Salzburg Festival. In 1920, he suddenly handed the directorship of his Berlin theatres to Felix Hollaender and spent the next four years shuttling between theatres in Vienna, Salzburg and Berlin. Drawn back to the Berlin of the 'Golden Twenties' in 1924, he founded the Komödie am Kurfürstendamm and returned to run the DT until 1932. Reinhardt left Germany as soon as Hitler came to power, first going to Austria until 1938, then emigrating to the USA after the *Anschluss* (annexation). He died in New York on 30 October 1943.

THIRD REICH GOVERNMENT QUARTER (Map 7)

Wilhelmstrasse, south of Pariser Platz, was Berlin's traditional government centre from the late 18th century through the Third Reich era. The chancellery, presidential palace and the foreign ministry were all located along here. During the Third Reich the area became the nexus of power and perversion in Hitler's Nazi Germany. Except for the Reich Aviation Ministry, nothing has survived from that time, so you'll have to exercise your imagination to picture what the area must have looked like. All other structures were either destroyed outright in the war or later demolished by the Soviets and East Germans.

For an immersion into the quarter's history, take the 'Infamous Third Reich Sites' walking tour offered by The Original Berlin Walks (see Walking Tours in the Getting Around chapter).

Neue Reichskanzlei

Hitler's Neue Reichkanzlei (New Chancellery, 1938) must have been an impressive sight. More than 400m long, it ran nearly the entire length of Vosstrasse, west of Wilhelmstrasse. Hitler's head architect, Albert Speer, worked some 4000 people through a mad 24-hour schedule, completing the massive structure in only 11 months, two days ahead of schedule. Built of yellow stucco and grey stone, it featured a columned entrance leading to a large inner courtyard.

One of the hallways inside measured 146m, just slightly longer than the Hall of

Mirrors in Versailles (where the humiliating WWI peace treaty was signed). Only the finest building materials were used, including various kinds of marble, bronze, glass and mosaics. The Führer allegedly asked Speer to make the floors particularly slippery, joking that diplomats should have no trouble making their way here as they were used to walking on slippery terrain.

After the war, the Russians stripped out all that marble and creatively recycled it in their memorials in Treptower Park and on Strasse des 17 Juni.

Hitler's Bunker

The legendary Führerbunker, where Hitler, Eva Braun and the Goebbels family committed suicide on 30 April 1945, was about 200m west of the New Chancellery in the garden of the old chancellery. Today, the spot is covered by a large grassy area with some fledgling trees.

Hitler had the bunker built in 1943 but only spent his last six weeks in it. It was entered through an earlier shelter from 1935, known as the Vorbunker, and was extremely deep. The ceiling plate was 1m below ground, and the roof alone consisted of 30cm-thick concrete topped by 20cm of soil. After the war, the Soviets tried to blow up the whole thing but the concrete proved impervious to explosives and so they burned and flooded it. The ceiling was reportedly blown up bit by bit until the whole thing caved in. It was filled with rubble during construction of the adjacent apartment building in 1988.

Reichsluftfahrtsministerium

One of the most prominent relics of Nazi architecture – Hermann Göring's Reichluftfahrtsministerium (Reich Aviation Ministry, 1936) – stands at Leipziger Strasse 5–7, corner of Wilhelmstrasse. Designed by Ernst Sagebiel, the massive building survived Allied bombing largely unscathed. It took a mass of workers less than a year to build this beehive-like complex honeycombed with more than 2000 offices. The concrete and steel structure, up to seven storeys tall, wraps around three inner courtyards and opens to a park at its rear. A facade of crushed shells hides the concrete and steel skeleton.

During the GDR era, the building was the seat of the Council of Ministers. After reunification, the Treuhand-Anstalt, the agency charged with selling off East German companies and property, moved into the complex, which had been renamed Detlev-Rohwedder-Haus (after the first Treuhand chief who was murdered by Red Army Faction terrorists in 1991). It is now the home of the Bundesfinanzministerium (Federal Ministry of Finance).

Gestapo Headquarters & Topographie des Terrors

On Prinz-Albrecht-Gelände just east of the Martin-Gropius-Bau once stood some of the most feared institutions of the Third Reich. The Gestapo came first, appropriating the School of Applied Arts at Prinz-Albrecht-Strasse 8 (now Niederkirchner Strasse) in 1933. The following year, the SS central command moved into the Hotel Prinz Albrecht next door, and Hitler henchman Richard Heydrich established the headquarters of the SS Sicherheitsdienst (Security Service) around the corner at Wilhelmstrasse 102. In 1939, finally, the Reich Security Office moved here as well. Countless people, including many members of the resistance movement, were brought here to be imprisoned, interrogated, tortured and killed; when the Berlin thugs were done with them, many were sent on to perish in concentration camps.

The buildings were all demolished after the war, but a haunting exhibit called 'Topography of Terror' (☎ 25 48 67 03, Stresemannstrasse 110; admission free; open 10am-6pm daily) graphically documents the crimes committed in this complex. Still housed provisionally in the former Gestapo torture cellars, a permanent facility is being planned.

The neo-Renaissance building across the street was originally the **Preussischer Landtag** (Prussian parliament; ☎ 23 25 10 64, Niederkirchner Strasse 3; admission free; open 9am-3pm Mon-Fri), then went through a brief stint under the Nazis as the notorious

People's Court (1934–35), before being turned into an air force officers' club by Göring. Since reunification it has been the **Abgeordnetenhaus**, the seat of Berlin's parliament. There's a free exhibit called '100 Years of the Prussian Parliament' on the ground floor. A stretch of the **Berlin Wall** runs along Niederkirchner Strasse from the Martin-Gropius-Bau to Wilhelmstrasse. (See the boxed text 'The Berlin Wall' later in this chapter.)

Martin-Gropius-Bau

The Martin-Gropius-Bau *(☎ 25 48 60, Niederkirchener Strasse 7; admission varies; usually open 10am-8pm Wed-Mon)* started life in 1881 as a museum of applied arts and is now used for large-scale special exhibits of international calibre. Designed by the uncle of Bauhaus architect Walter Gropius, it's a beautiful Italian Renaissance-style cube with a generous light court and facades decorated with mosaics and terracotta reliefs.

On the 2nd floor is the **Museum der Dinge** *(Museum of Things, ☎ 25 48 69 00; admission free; open 10am-8pm Wed-Mon, to 10pm Sat)*, previously known as Werkbundarchiv, which documents daily life throughout the 20th century through art, objects and bric-a-brac.

CHECKPOINT CHARLIE & AROUND (Map 7)

A potent symbol of the Cold War, Checkpoint Charlie – at the intersection of Friedrichstrasse and Zimmerstrasse – was the main gateway for non-Germans between the two Berlins from 1961 to 1990. Shortly after the Wall was built, the world held its breath as US and Soviet tanks dramatically faced off across the border post in October 1961.

For nearly four decades, an American flag flew on top of a guardhouse, a jeep was stationed in front and a sign in English, Russian, French and German warned; 'You are now leaving the American sector'. This being the third Allied checkpoint, it was named 'Charlie' – the third letter (alpha, bravo, charlie…) in military lingo. In 2001, a replica guardhouse was returned to the site

(the original is in the Allied Museum in Zehlendorf; see later in this chapter), as was a copy of the famous sign. Also here are huge photos of an American soldier looking east and a Russian soldier looking west. All around here a new office district, with buildings designed by Philip Johnson and other international architects, has sprouted.

Haus am Checkpoint Charlie

The history of the Berlin Wall is commemorated through photographs, documents and objects in the Haus am Checkpoint Charlie *(☎ 25 29 62 45, Friedrichstrasse 43-45; adult/concession €6/3; open 9am-10pm daily, including holidays)*. You'll learn about the development of the inhuman border security installations and come across fascinating nuggets about the heroic efforts of GDR citizens to escape their keepers. Interesting displays include a handcrafted one-man submarine and photographs of people fleeing in concealed compartments in cars and luggage. One family actually made its way to freedom in a homemade hot-air balloon.

Another part of the exhibit chronicles the history of the two Berlins since the end of WWII, focusing on major events such as the 1953 workers' uprising, the construction of the Wall and the Four Powers Agreement. Events involving Checkpoint Charlie in particular are also addressed, such as the stand-off between USA and Soviet tanks and the death of would-be escapee Peter Fechtner, who bled to death after being shot by GDR border guards.

Multilingual displays help make a visit of this museum an engrossing experience for everyone, even if the rooms themselves are grimy and confusingly organised. A much-needed renovation was being planned at the time of writing. The cafe serves dishes from the UK, USA, Russia and France.

Museum für Kommunikation

The famous Red and Blue Mauritius stamps, the world's first telephone and several generations of computers are among the main draws at Berlin's newly revamped Museum für Kommunikation *(Museum of*

The Berlin Wall

More than a decade has passed since the tumbling of 'die Mauer', the ugly scar and symbol of inhumanity and oppression that bisected Berlin for 28 years. The East German government erected this so-called 'Anti-Fascist Protection Barrier' in 1961 to curb the exodus of its own people to the west. Extended several times, it snaked around West Berlin for some 155km. Its ugly prefab concrete slabs – which you could reach out and touch or paint on the western side only – were flanked by a no-man's land of barbed wire, land mines, attack dogs and around 300 watch towers on the eastern side. Such measures made a mockery of the East German government's euphemistic description of the structure.

More than 5000 people tried to scale the Wall; 3200 were captured, 191 were killed. The first victim, who tried to jump into the west from the window of his house, died only a few days after the Wall went up. The full extent of the cruelty of the system became blatantly apparent on 17 August 1962 when 18-year-old Peter Fechtner was shot during his escape attempt and then left to bleed to death while the East German border guards looked on.

After the end of the Cold War, nearly all of this potent symbol was eagerly dismantled. Memento seekers chiselled away much of it and entire sections ended up in museums around the world. Most of it, though, was simply recycled for use in road construction.

Today, little more than 1.5km of the Wall is left, but throughout Berlin, segments, memorial sites, museums and signs keep alive this horrifying but important chapter in German history.

To help people identify the course of the Wall, about 8km of its length has been mapped out with a double row of flagstones in the ground.

East Side Gallery (Map 5)

This is the longest, best preserved and most interesting surviving stretch of Wall and the one to see if you're pressed for time. Paralleling Mühlenstrasse in Friedrichshain, the 1300m-long section is an open-air gallery created by international artists in 1990; some freshened up their work in 2000. A few of the murals have political messages, others show surreal imagery, yet others are purely decorative. Here you'll find the famous paintings of the Trabant bursting through the Wall, and the kissing couple of Erich Honecker and Leonid Brezhnev.

Just to avoid confusion: this is not a gallery where you have to pay admission; you can simply walk along it and enjoy the art.

Dokumentationszentrum Berliner Mauer (Map 3)

Surrounded by high steel walls, this memorial on the corner of Bernauer Strasse and Ackerstrasse is the only site in Berlin where you can see what the death strip in all its horrifying detail looked like, complete with front-line wall, coarse gravel strip, patrol path, illuminated strip and back wall. Also here is the nonprofit Documentation Centre (☎ 464 10 30, Bernauer Strasse 111; admission free; open 10am-5pm Wed-Sun; S-Bahn: Nordbahnhof). It shows photographs, films and other exhibits about the Wall.

Wall Victims Memorial (Map 7)

Just south of the Reichstag, on the eastern end of Scheidemannstrasse, is this moving memorial to the 191 people who died trying to cross the Wall – the last only nine months before it collapsed and Berliners were able to move freely across their city again.

Niederkirchner Strasse (Map 7)

This 160m section runs along Niederkirchner Strasse from Martin-Gropius-Bau to Wilhelmstrasse.

THINGS TO SEE & DO

Communication; ☎ 20 29 40, Leipziger Strasse 16; admission free; open 9am-5pm Tue-Fri, 11am-7pm Sat-Sun). The museum reopened in 2000 in an attractive late-19th-century building, just north of Checkpoint Charlie. It wraps around a central light court where visitors can communicate with robots and try various interactive exhibits in the adjacent communication gallery. Upstairs is the hands-on computer gallery, while in the basement awaits the museum's 'treasure chamber', whose exhibits include the precious stamps. There's a nice restaurant on the premises as well. At night, the building is lit from within and glows blue like a crystal.

Prenzlauer Berg

Prenzlauer Berg has, in recent years, evolved from a working-class backwater to one of the prettiest and most happening of Berlin's neighbourhoods. The facades that still bore the scars of war after the Wende have been restored at a furious pace. At the same time, a wonderfully diverse cafe and pub scene has sprouted. Eager young entrepreneurs have opened up shops, studios, galleries and offices, bringing with them energy, ideas, and optimism needed to inject new life and colour into this district.

Even during GDR days, Prenz'lberg – as Berliners refer to it – was a special district. In many ways it was the mirror image of Kreuzberg. Both were frontier districts, wedged against the Wall, neglected and brimming with old, claustrophobic living spaces. Both attracted people in search of an alternative lifestyle: avant-garde artists, writers, homosexuals and political activists. Even squatting was prevalent here.

The Prenzlauer Berg tradition of going against the majority goes a long way back. A comparatively low 23% voted for the Nazis in 1932, and during GDR elections in 1986 some 5% protested silently against the regime by refusing to participate in the voting – sham that it was, with only the SED party on the ballot. If 5% seems small, remember that the simple act of not voting meant extending an invitation to the Stasi.

Today, Prenzlauer Berg retains some of its experimental edge, although the area around Kollwitzplatz has been gentrified almost too much for its own good. For a look at a less polished neighbourhood, head north of Danziger Strasse.

WALKING TOUR (Map 3)

This walk takes in the southern section of Prenzlauer Berg between U-Bahn stations Senefelderplatz and Eberswalder Strasse. It covers a distance of about 2.5km and can be done in under two hours without lingering.

The tour starts on **Senefelder Platz** (take the southern U-Bahn exit), a triangular patch of green named for the inventor of lithography, Aloys Senefelder (1771–1834); there's a monument to the man in the square's little park. Also note one of the last remaining **octagonal pissoirs** (nicknamed Café Achteck) from the late 19th century in the north-eastern corner. From here, walk east on Metzerstrasse, then turn north on Kollwitzstrasse.

Immediately on your left, at Kollwitzer Strasse 35, you'll pass a rather unusual **adventure playground** which engages children in creative play. There's a workshop where kids actually build with hammers and nails, a bike-repair shed, a smithy, various climbing structures and much more. The playground, open to kids aged six to 14, is supervised by a social worker and is free. This progressive project was the first such playground in eastern Berlin when it opened in 1990.

Continuing north, you'll soon get to Kollwitzplatz, the heart of Prenzlauer Berg. This square, which until a few years ago was still framed by dilapidated buildings pockmarked with war wounds, has been thoroughly gentrified. Tourist buses plough through here and trendy restaurants, cafes and bars have popped up all over.

In the centre of Kollwitzplatz stands an expressive bronze **sculpture** of an aged Käthe Kollwitz by Gustav Seitz (1958). She looks tired, possibly from a lifetime of concern with the destitute around her. Children often clamber around this larger-than-life sculpture or sit in her maternal lap. Kollwitz, who produced an entire series of mother and child drawings, would probably have liked this. Between 1891 and 1943, she and her physician husband Karl lived on the corner of Kollwitzstrasse and Knaackstrasse. The house was destroyed in 1943. (See the Käthe-Kollwitz-Museum entry in the Charlottenburg section earlier this chapter.)

Turning south-east into Knaackstrasse will soon get you to the statuesque **Wasserturm** (water tower, 1875). Resting atop a slight mound, it now contains flats, but during the Third Reich its basement functioned as a torture chamber. Further east Knaackstrasse soon runs into Prenzlauer Allee where, around the corner, is the **Prenzlauer Berg Museum** (☎ 42 40 10 97, *Prenzlauer Allee 227; admission free; open 11am-5pm Tues & Wed, 1pm-7pm Thur, 2pm-5pm Sun).* It presents various facets of local history during changing exhibitions accompanied by readings, films and guided tours.

Backtrack to the water tower, then go north on Rykestrasse. On your left, at No 53, is the only Berlin **synagogue** to survive both Kristallnacht (apparently because Nazi party officials resided nearby) and Allied bombing. It's actually set back from the street and usually inaccessible, though you can see it from the pavement through a gate.

Turning left on Wörtherstrasse will take you back to Kollwitzplatz. From here, head north on **Husemannstrasse**. This entire street received a serious sprucing up from the East German government for Berlin's 750th anniversary celebrations in 1987. Yet Husemannstrasse has the same artificial patina as the Nikolaiviertel in Mitte, created at the same time. Lots of cutesy, supposedly turn-of-the-century shops opened here. Today they contain antiques and junk, along with a fairly meagre selection of furniture, books and GDR paraphernalia.

Turn left into Sredzkistrasse, where the giant complex of the former **Schultheiss brewery**, once the largest brewery in the world, will soon come into view. The mid-19th-century yellow-brick Art Nouveau complex survived time and wars relatively intact. Production ceased in 1967 and the factory lingered until 1991 when it became

the cultural centre called **Kulturbrauerei** (☎ 441 92 69, *Knaackstrasse 97*). Following a complete restoration, it has more going on than ever before although some of the edgy underground ambience has been lost (see the Entertainment chapter). The entrance is near the corner of Knaackstrasse and Danziger Strasse.

If you want, you can continue north of Danziger Strasse where you'll find lots more cool bars and restaurants along Lychener Strasse and around Helmholtzplatz.

Alternatively, turn left on Danziger Strasse, which takes you right to Eberswalder Strasse U-Bahn station. Before boarding the train, make a quick detour south to Kastanienallee 7–9 where you'll find the historic **Berliner Prater**. Originally a beer hall, it became an assembly place for the Berlin workers' movement late last century. August Bebel and Rosa Luxemburg were among those who fired up the crowds with rousing speeches here. Today, the Prater serves as a secondary stage of the Volksbühne theatre, with provocative, offbeat productions. The vast beer garden just behind it attracts an intergenerational crowd in summer. In winter, the adjacent restaurant is a traditional favourite with the grey-haired set. This is the end of the tour.

NORTHERN PRENZLAUER BERG (Map 3)

Northern Prenzlauer Berg, around U-Bahn station Schönhauser Allee, is quite different from the Kollwitzplatz area and still preserves more of a genuine GDR era ambience. It too, though, is up-and-coming as evidenced not just by the establishment of the local gay and lesbian scene on Gleimstrasse (see the Entertainment chapter), but also by the arrival of a major museum, the **Vitra Design Museum Berlin** (☎ 473 77 70, *Kopenhagener Strasse 58; adult/concession €5/3, free if under 12; open 11am-8pm Tues-Sun).* The visions of Frank Lloyd Wright, Issey Miyake, Charles and Ray Eames, Verner Panton and other design and architectural bigwigs are the focus of exhibits here. A branch of its 'mother' museum in Weil on the Rhine River near the Swiss border, the Vitra occupies a beautifully converted transformer plant built by Hans Heinrich Müller in 1926. Exhibits change several times per year and are supplemented by tours and talks.

East of Schönhauser Allee, on Stargarder Strasse, is the **Gethsemane Kirche**, one of the centres of the dissident movement that led to the collapse of the East German government. Further east, where Stargarder Strasse meets Prenzlauer Allee, looms the dome of the **Zeiss Grossplanetarium** *(☎ 42 18 45 12, Prenzlauer Allee 80; shows adult/concession €4/3; shows 9.30am Mon-Fri & Wed, Sat-Sun afternoons, 8pm Fri-Sat, 2pm Sun; S-Bahn: S4, S8 or S10 to Prenzlauer Allee)*. It has Berlin's most modern telescope, which explores the universe as part of multimedia shows with music and laser. It's popular with school kids, so pick the evening show if you want quiet.

North-east of the planetarium, between Sültstrasse and Sodtkestrasse, is an interesting housing development from 1930 called **Flamensiedlung** (Flemish Colony), so named because it was inspired by the architecture of the low countries. Architects Bruno Taut and Franz Hillinger tried to break up the monotony of the dark and dim Mietskasernen by creating green open spaces and adding balconies.

Schöneberg

South of Tiergarten, Schöneberg is a comfortable transition zone between the sedateness of its western neighbour, Wilmersdorf, and the wackiness of Kreuzberg to the east. Tastefully restored 19th-century apartment buildings line residential streets, many of them packed with pubs, cafes and global-village restaurants.

It's hard to imagine that as recently as the 1980s Schöneberg – especially the area around Winterfeldtplatz – was a squatter's stronghold. An ambitious gentrification program finally pushed them out, making room for upwardly mobile Generation Xers, including many young families. Schöneberg is trendy and chic, its people having the necessary money and education to appreciate the finer things in life.

Schöneberg has also been an active centre of the gay scene since the 1920s, a period vividly chronicled by one-time area resident Christopher Isherwood in *Goodbye to Berlin*. There are plenty of gay haunts around Nollendorfplatz and along Motzstrasse and Fuggerstrasse with all scenes catered for.

Schöneberg's most famous daughter is Marlene Dietrich who grew up on Leberstrasse and is buried in Friedhof Friedenau (see boxed text 'Cemetery Hopping' later this chapter and the boxed text 'Marlene Dietrich' in the Facts about Berlin chapter). Another famous name associated with this district is John F Kennedy. It was at Schöneberg's town hall where he told the world: 'Ich bin ein Berliner' – I am a Berliner.

NOLLENDORFPLATZ AREA (Map 4)

Nollendorfplatz marks the beginning of the gay district. Christopher Isherwood lived at Nollendorfstrasse 17, a block south of the square. The treatment of homosexuals under the Third Reich is commemorated by a triangular red granite **memorial plaque** set into the wall of the south-western exit of Nollendorfplatz U-Bahn station. Homosexuals suffered tremendously from persecution under the Nazis although their plight has been generally ignored. Those who didn't conceal their orientation had to wear pink triangles and were, at best, socially ostracised. Many were imprisoned, sent to concentration camps and murdered.

The imposing neobaroque building right on Nollendorfplatz is the former **Metropol Theater**, which currently hosts one-off gay parties (see the Entertainment chapter). Note the tastefully erotic frieze gracing its facade.

From the square, Maassenstrasse leads south to the **Winterfeldtplatz**, site of a wonderful **produce market** on Wednesday and Saturday mornings (see the Shopping chapter). The Saturday market especially is perfect for observing the trendy Schöneberg scene at play. Young families with small children gather on the square's east side for a chat and a coffee, while fashionable 'dinks' (double income, no kids) dig into lavish breakfasts at the many cafes. The church looming above the square is the **St-Matthias-Kirche**.

KLEISTPARK AREA (Map 4)

A number of interesting sites cluster around U-Bahn station Kleistpark. The park itself is a few steps north on Potsdamer Strasse and is entered via the graceful sandstone **Königskolonnaden** (Royal Colonnades), designed in 1780 by Karl von Gontard (who also created the domes atop the German and French cathedrals on Gendarmenmarkt). Sculptural ornamentation, including figures of angels and gods, decorate the arcades. The colonnades originally stood at the end of Königsstrasse (today's Rathausstrasse) in Mitte but were moved here in 1910 because of road construction. Kleistpark itself used to be a botanical garden.

Near the western end of the park stands the imposing **Kammergericht** (chamber courts of justice) which was where the notorious Nazi Volksgericht (People's Court), led by the fanatical judge Roland Freisler, held some of its show trials. About 2500 political prisoners received death sentences here, many of them going on to be executed at Plötzensee Prison (see Gedenkstätte Plötzensee in the Tiergarten section later in this chapter). From 1945 to 1990, the Allied Control Council had its seat here. These days, the Berlin Constitutional Court uses a part of the building.

North of here, on the corner of Goebenstrasse and Potsdamer Strasse, stood the **Sportpalast**, a huge hall with room for up to 9000. Besides hosting bicycle races and concerts, it was also here where, on 18 February 1943, Goebbels, standing before thousands of war-chastened but still fanatical Berliners, exclaimed: *'Wollt ihr den totalen Krieg?'* (Do you want total war?) The answer was 'yes', and the rest is history. In 1973, the Sportpalast was torn down.

Potsdamer Strasse is a fairly grotty, run-down street that has actually seen *worse* days when it was a haven for drug addicts and prostitutes. Some of that still goes on

today, but mostly this is a completely normal business street with second-hand boutiques, junk and photo stores, fruit and vegie shops etc. Only the **Wintergarten-Das Variété** adds some sparkle (see the Cabaret section in the Entertainment chapter). South of Kleistpark station, Potsdamer Strasse turns into Hauptstrasse where, at No 152, David Bowie and Iggy Pop once lived.

RATHAUS SCHÖNEBERG (Map 4)

Schöneberg's town hall on John-F-Kennedy-Platz is most famous for being the place where JFK gave his 'Ich bin ein Berliner' speech. From 1948 to 1990, the Rathaus was the seat of the West Berlin Senate and the governing mayor (now back at the Rotes Rathaus in Mitte). Its clock tower used to rise 81m but was shortened by 10m in 1950 to accommodate the **Liberty Bell**. Seven million Americans donated money towards this replica of the original Philadelphia Bell which was given to Berliners as a gesture of support. It was presented to the city by General Lucius D Clay, commander of the US army in Germany.

A permanent exhibition *(☎ 787 70 70; admission free; open 10am-6pm daily)* on the life and work of former chancellor Willy Brandt (1913–1992) is shown inside the town hall.

Tiergarten

Named for the sprawling city park, the district of Tiergarten, wedged in between Zoo station in the west and the Brandenburger Tor in the east, is home to two of the most visible and important post-Wende developments: the **New Government District** in its north-eastern corner and the **Potsdamer Platz** area in the south-eastern corner. The area south of the park is once again the diplomatic quarter. Older attractions – aside from the park itself – include interesting mid-century modernist architecture (see Tour II of the Architecture special section) and, above all, the complex of world-class museums at the Kulturforum.

Cemetery Hopping

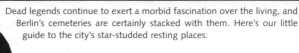

Dead legends continue to exert a morbid fascination over the living, and Berlin's cemeteries are certainly stacked with them. Here's our little guide to the city's star-studded resting places:

Dorotheenstädtischer Friedhof – Mitte (Map 3)

This one wins, hands down, the top award for greatest density of celebrity corpses. A veritable pantheon of German greats lie buried here, including the architects Schadow and Schinkel (who designed his own tombstone), composers Paul Dessau and Hanns Eisler, Heinrich Mann, Bertolt Brecht and his wife, Helene Weigel. Brecht, in fact, lived in the house bordering the cemetery, allegedly to be close to his idols, the philosophers Hegel and Fichte, who are also buried here. In 1985, German playwright and Berliner Ensemble director Heiner Müller joined their ranks; fans still leave cigars in his honour on his grave.

The cemetery (☎ 461 72 79) is located at Chausseestrasse 126, near U-Bahn station Zinnowitzer Strasse. Look for a chart of grave locations at the end of the walkway leading to the gated graveyard. It's open roughly from 8am to sunset, though it's best to check the sign by the entrance for details or else you'll be in for a fence climbing adventure if the gates are locked.

Jüdischer Friedhof – Prenzlauer Berg (Map 3)

The second of Berlin's Jewish cemeteries is on Schönhauser Allee. It opened in 1827 after the oldest one on Grosse Hamburger Strasse in Mitte ran out of space. Look for the graves of impressionist painter Max Liebermann (1935), composer Giacomo Meyerbeer (1864) and the publisher Leopold Ullstein (1899). It's closed on weekends and Friday afternoon. Men must cover their head upon entering. Take the U2 to Senefelder Platz.

NEW GOVERNMENT DISTRICT (Maps 2 & 7)

The decision by the federal government, in 1991, to relocate from Bonn to Berlin prompted an ambitious construction program to house all branches of government, elected officials and their staff, not to mention the diplomatic corps, lobbyists and the media. The heart of the new government district is the so-called Band des Bundes, a band of government buildings anchored by the Reichstag and the Neues Kanzleramt (New Federal Chancellery) along with parliament and government buildings in the eastern part of the Spreebogen (a bulge in the flow of the Spree river).

Reichstag (Map 7)

Only a few steps north of the Brandenburger Tor (see the Mitte section earlier in this chapter) stands another landmark, the Reichstag (*tours free; reservations made at Deutscher Bundestag, Besucherdienst, 11011 Berlin or* ☎ *22 73 21 52*) built by Paul Wallot in 1894. In May 1999, the Bundestag – the German parliament – moved into the building, which British architect Sir Norman Foster had turned into a state-of-the-art parliamentary facility, preserving only the historical shell to which he added a striking giant **glass dome**.

A major tourist attraction, the dome is accessible via a lift that whisks you to a rooftop **viewing terrace** *(admission free; open 8am-midnight, last entry 10pm)*; there's a fancy restaurant here, too. From here, a spiral ramp leads to the top of the glistening 'beehive' at whose centre is a mirror-clad funnel that reflects the light in myriad directions. Lifts down operate until midnight. This is an immensely popular attraction and you'll likely have to queue for the lift up; waits of 30 minutes to an hour are fairly common.

Cemetery Hopping

Friedhof Friedenau – Schöneberg (Map 4)

To pay homage to the city's most fabled daughter, Marlene Dietrich, you have to travel to this tiny cemetery. Here the 'Blue Angel' makes her final home in a not terribly glamorous plot near her mother's. Her tombstone bears her first name only, as well as the inscription: 'Here I stand on the marker of my days'. The cemetery is at Stubenrauchstrasse 43–45; look for the map inside the entrance to find her grave located near the Fehlerstrasse (north) side of the cemetery. Pianist and composer Ferruccio Busoni is also buried here. Take the U9 to Friedrich-Wilhelm-Platz, then walk about 400m north-west on Görresstrasse to Südwestkorso, the entrance is west of the street.

Matthäus-Kirchhof – Schöneberg (Map 4)

This pretty little churchyard holds the bones of the famous Brothers Grimm, who taught at the Humboldt Universität, as well as the physician and politician Rudolf Virchow. There's also a memorial tombstone to Claus Schenk Graf von Stauffenberg and his fellow conspirators executed by the Nazis after their failed attempt to assassinate Hitler in 1944. A pamphlet with additional names and grave locations is available for €0.50 from the cemetery office. Take the S1/U7 to Yorckstrasse or U7 to Kleistpark.

Jüdischer Friedhof – Weissensee (Map 3)

This is Berlin's – and Europe's – largest Jewish cemetery (1880) with more than 100,000 graves. Even before the Wende, West Berlin Jews buried their dead here. Just beyond an imposing yellow-brick gate lies a circular area with a memorial to concentration camp victims. A chart by the entrance reveals the locations of the plots of some of the better known residents, including painter Lesser Ury and publisher Samuel Fischer. The cemetery is closed on Saturday and Jewish holidays. Men must cover their heads upon entering. Take bus No 100 to the eastern terminus, cross Michelangelostrasse and walk through the housing estate to Puccinistrasse. After about 100m, turn right into Herbert-Baum-Strasse.

An imposing structure – measuring 137m by 97m – the Reichstag has been the focus of momentous events in German history. After WWI, Philipp Scheidemann proclaimed the German Republic from one of its windows. The Reichstag fire on the night of 27 February 1933 destroyed large sections, allowing Hitler to blame the communists and to cement his power. A dozen years later, bombs and the victorious Soviets nearly finished the job. The photograph of a Red Army soldier raising the red flag atop the burning building is world famous. Restoration – *sans* dome – wasn't finished until 1972.

At midnight on 2 October 1990 the reunification of Germany was enacted here. In the summer of 1995 the Reichstag again drew the world's attention when the artist Christo and his wife Jeanne-Claude wrapped it in fabric for two weeks. Sir Norman's reconstruction began shortly thereafter.

Neues Kanzleramt (Map 2)

The Neues Kanzleramt *(New Federal Chancellery; Willy-Brandt-Strasse 1)* stands obliquely opposite the Reichstag. Designed by Axel Schultes and Charlotte Frank, the building generated a storm of controversy even before its occupants had settled into their new offices. Much of the debate centred on its size. Some critics considered it too immodest, while others thought the design itself was not suitable as a government office. Even Chancellor Gerhard Schröder didn't exactly show enthusiasm, preferring instead to distance himself from what had, after all, been a pet project of his disgraced predecessor Helmut Kohl.

The Chancellery consists of three main sections. The offices of the chancellor and his staff, his residence, as well as the cabinet meeting room and a conference room, are housed in a central white cube, which rises nine storeys high and has semi-circular openings. It is flanked by two elongated office blocks, giving the complex an 'H' shape if viewed from a bird's eye perspective. On the eastern side of the building is the **Ehrenhof** (Court of Honour), fronted by a transparent glass wall through which a forest of pillars (a Schultes trademark) is clearly visible on the inside. Behind the Chancellery is the **Kanzlergarten** (Chancellor's Garden). The Chancellery is not accessible to the public but to get a good sense of its dimensions, walk across Moltkebrücke to the northern Spree bank.

MOABIT (Map 2)

North of the New Government District, the traditionally blue-collar neighbourhood of Moabit is poised to undergo dramatic changes in the near future. Suits are gradually replacing workers' overalls as it morphs into a place of work and play for members of parliament and their staff, lobbyists, service industries and whoever else has an interest in being near Germany's government. The **Bundesinnenministerium** (Federal Ministry of the Interior) has already moved into spanking new digs at the **Spree-Bogen Complex** on Alt Moabit.

East of here, the gaping holes and pivoting cranes around the Lehrter Stadtbahnhof S-Bahn station point to the development of the **Lehrter Zentralbahnhof**, Berlin's futuristic central train station. (Completion dates have been pushed back many times, so we won't even venture a guess here.) A costly extension of the U5 from Alexanderplatz to this station, another project instigated by Helmut Kohl, has been rather controversial and construction has been slowed and even halted for lack of funds. Berliners have already found a nickname for it: Kanzlerlinie (Chancellor Line). Another major undertaking is the 3.3km-long **Tiergarten Tunnel** which will reroute traffic beneath the park away from the government buildings.

Moabit was originally settled in 1718 by French Huguenots, who called their colony *Terre des Moabites* (Land of the Moabits) because that was where, according to the Old Testament, Eli Melech and his family had found refuge. In the late 19th century, the area became part of the ring of working-class neighbourhoods that encircled the city centre to the north and east.

Moabit's face is changing but for now its few charms are quickly absorbed on a stroll along Alt-Moabit from U-Bahn station Turmstrasse, the area's commercial heart. Before heading east, however, take a quick detour north to the **Arminius Markthalle** (☎ 396 09 50, *Bremer Strasse 9*), the nicest of the three surviving historical market halls (see the Shopping chapter). You reach it by walking a few steps west on Turmstrasse from the station and turning right into Jonasstrasse. The market hall is right there on the corner with Arminiusstrasse.

Back on Turmstrasse, head south one block to the road called Alt-Moabit and walk east. The Spree-Bogen Complex with the Ministry of the Interior will soon emerge on your right. Just past here is the **St Johanniskirche** (1835), an early work by Karl Friedrich Schinkel. It has an arcaded Italianate portico and an extremely steep staircase leading up to the church door, which is usually locked.

Farther east lies the vast **Justizzentrum** (Centre of Justice) which incorporates the criminal courts, the municipal courts and a fortress-like prison that has hosted such top crooks as Red Army Faction (RAF) terrorists, Erich Honecker and Erich Mielke, the final Stasi director.

Gedenkstätte Plötzensee (Map 2)

About 3km north of the centre of Moabit (and technically in Charlottenburg) is the Gedenkstätte Plötzensee (*Plötzensee Memorial;* ☎ 344 32 26, *Hüttigpfad; admission free; open 8.30am-4.30pm Jan & Nov, 8.30am-5.30pm Feb & Oct, 8.30am-6pm Mar-Sept, 8.30am-4pm Dec; U-Bahn: U9 to Hansaplatz, then bus No 123 to Gedenkstätte Plötzensee*). It commemorates the 3000 victims of the Nazi regime who were executed here, most of them political prisoners of all persuasions and nationalities. In a single night in 1943, following an air raid, 186 prisoners were hanged only so that they could not escape from the partly destroyed prison.

A year later, many of the conspirators of the failed assassination attempt on Hitler on 20 July 1944 – and their (mostly uninvolved) relatives and friends, a total of 86 people – were also hanged here; a process the Führer had captured on film.

The chillingly simple memorial is housed in a plain brick shed at Plötzensee prison. Most haunting is the execution room, its emptiness pierced by an iron bar bearing five hooks. The other room documents the arbitrary practices of the Nazi judicial system.

An excellent free English brochure is available at the desk.

TIERGARTEN PARK
(Maps 2, 4 & 6)

Berlin's green lung bristles with huge shady trees, groomed paths, woodsy groves, lakes and meadows and is a great place for a jog, picnic or stroll. At 167 hectares, it is also one of the world's largest city parks. In spring, when the rhododendron bushes are in full bloom, the area around Rousseau Island becomes an oasis for the senses. Chime concerts ring out at noon and 6pm daily from the 68-bell, black marble and bronze **Carillon** – the largest in Europe – on John-Foster-Dulles-Allee just south of the New Chancellery (Map 2).

The Great Elector, Friedrich Wilhelm (ruled 1640–88), used the land as hunting grounds, though he made the job easy on himself by having the animals confined to a fenced-off area measuring 1km by 3km. It became a park in the 18th century and was landscaped by master gardener Peter Lenné (1789–1866) in 1830. During the frigid winter of 1946–47, Berliners chopped down virtually all the trees for firewood.

Strasse des 17 Juni (Map 2)

The broad boulevard known as Strasse des 17 Juni, which bisects Tiergarten, was built by King Friedrich I to connect the Stadtschloss with Schloss Charlottenburg. Hitler's showy entrance to Berlin, it was called East-West Axis during the Nazi era. Its present name commemorates the 1953 workers' uprising in East Berlin, which brought the GDR to the brink of collapse.

On the northern side, just west of the Brandenburger Tor, is the **Sowjetisches Ehrenmal** (Soviet Memorial), flanked by the first two Russian tanks (Nos 200 and 300) to enter Berlin in 1945. The reddish marble is said to have come from Hitler's Neue Reichskanzlei on Wilhelmstrasse. (More of this recycled marble was used in building the Soviet Memorial in Treptower Park.)

Like the arms of a starfish, five large roads merge into the roundabout called Grosser Stern, farther west along Strasse des 17 Juni. At its centre is the 69m-high **Siegessäule** (Victory Column, Map 4), which rather cockily commemorates 19th-century Prussian military exploits. The mosaic frieze behind the curtain of columns on the raised ground floor depicts the founding of the German Empire in 1870–71. The Nazis moved the column here in 1938 from Königsplatz (now Platz der Republik) in front of the Reichstag. Crowned by a gilded statue of Victory (called 'Gold-Else' by Berliners), it has a spiral staircase (285 steps) leading to the top for an eyeful of the park and surrounds *(adult/ concession €1/0.50, free if under 12; open 9.30am-6.30pm Mon-Thur, to 7pm Fri-Sun).*

Schloss Bellevue (Map 2)

Just north-east of the Siegessäule is Schloss Bellevue (1785), built for Prince Ferdinand, the youngest brother of Friedrich II, and now the German president's official residence. Until 2005, Johannes Rau and his family will reside in this neoclassical, U-shaped structure whose chalk-white facade is broken up by Corinthian columns and topped by a tympanum with sculptural decoration. Kaiser Wilhelm II disliked the building and used it as a school for his children. The Nazis turned it into a museum of German ethnology and later a guesthouse.

Zoologischer Garten (Map 6)

After putting the finishing touches on Tiergarten, Peter Lenné turned his attention to the south-western corner of the park where King Friedrich Wilhelm IV had donated the grounds for a zoo *(☎ 25 40 10, Budapester Strasse 34; adult/concession/children to age 15 €7.50/6/3.75 each for zoo & aquarium,*

THINGS TO SEE & DO

€12/9.50/6 for combination ticket; open 9am-dusk, 6.30pm at the latest, aquarium to 6pm). Germany's oldest zoo was largely stocked with the king's pheasants and animals from the Pfaueninsel (see the Zehlendorf section later in this chapter) at its 1844 opening. Nowadays, around 19,000 animals representing about 1500 species roam the grounds (many in open, moated habitats), making the Berlin Zoo the most varied in the world. Enter via the impressive **Elephant Gate** (complete with chinoiserie roof).

The adjacent **Aquarium** opened in 1869 and has 10,000 animals from 650 species. Highlights include sharks and jelly fish as well as the terrarium with snakes, alligators and crocodiles.

Bauhaus Archiv/Museum für Gestaltung (Map 4)

About 1km to the east of the zoo is the Bauhaus Archive/Museum of Design *(☎ 254 00 20, Klingelhöferstrasse 14; adult/ concession €4/2; open 10am-5pm Wed-Mon)*. It is devoted to the members of the Bauhaus School who laid the basis for much of contemporary design and architecture (see boxed text 'The Bauhaus'). The collection includes works by Paul Klee, Walter Gropius, Wassily Kandinsky and Oskar Schlemmer and other leading Bauhaus practitioners. Furniture, blueprints, models and graphic prints are presented in an appealing and easily assimilated fashion. The original model of the 1925 Bauhaus building in Dessau is a prized highlight. (For more on the building itself, see the special Architecture chapter.)

POTSDAMER PLATZ

The ballet of construction cranes no longer dances above Potsdamer Platz, Berlin's newest neighbourhood, the most visible symbol of the 'New Berlin' and a major tourist attraction. The new quarter sprawls south and west of the square for which it is named, hemmed in by Potsdamer Strasse in the east and Linkstrasse in the west. The

---

The Bauhaus

The Bauhaus School was the most influential force in 20th-century architecture. Founded in Weimar in 1919 by Berlin architect Walter Gropius, it aimed to unite art with everyday functionality, from doorknobs and radiators to the layout of entire districts and apartment blocks. The movement attracted some of the era's most talented artists and architects, including Paul Klee, Wassily Kandinsky, Piet Mondrian, Lionel Feininger and Oskar Schlemmer.

Gropius' radical ideas raised too many eyebrows in Weimar and in 1925 the Bauhaus relocated to Dessau, where it enjoyed its most fruitful phase. Disciples peppered the city with Bauhaus structures and mass-marketed their successes – simple but elegant lamps, chairs and wallpaper, to name a few items.

In 1932 the Bauhaus moved to Berlin to escape oppression by the Nazis, who claimed the movement undermined traditional values. (How could a German roof be flat? they asked.) The school was dissolved by Hitler in 1933 and its leading lights fled the country. After WWII, the Bauhaus was hailed as the cutting edge of modern architecture but its chief followers remained in exile.

– Jeremy Gray

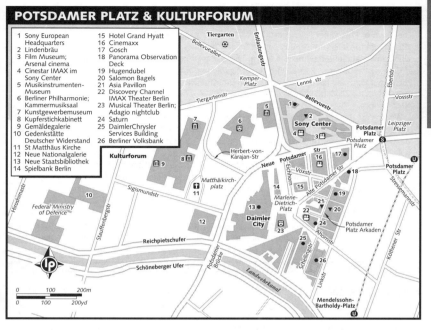

POTSDAMER PLATZ & KULTURFORUM

1 Sony European Headquarters
2 Lindenbräu
3 Film Museum; Arsenal cinema
4 Cinestar IMAX im Sony Center
5 Musikinstrumenten-Museum
6 Berliner Philharmonie; Kammermusiksaal
7 Kunstgewerbemuseum
8 Kupferstichkabinett
9 Gemäldegalerie
10 Gedenkstätte Deutscher Widerstand
11 St Matthäus Kirche
12 Neue Nationalgalerie
13 Neue Staatsbibliothek
14 Spielbank Berlin
15 Hotel Grand Hyatt
16 Cinemaxx
17 Gosch
18 Panorama Observation Deck
19 Hugendubel
20 Salomon Bagels
21 Asia Pavillon
22 Discovery Channel IMAX Theater Berlin
23 Musical Theater Berlin; Adagio nightclub
24 Saturn
25 DaimlerChrysler Services Building
26 Berliner Volksbank

European equivalent of Times Square until WWII, it was scarred by the Wall and the death strip until reunification.

The reincarnated complex consists of two sections: **DaimlerCity**, inaugurated in 1998 and home to a large shopping mall, an IMAX theatre, a musical theatre, a casino, a luxury hotel, several restaurants, cafes and office buildings; and, a block north, across Neue Potsdamer Strasse, the **Sony Center**, which opened in June 2000. The FilmMuseum, a Sony Store, a multiplex movie theatre with 3D IMAX and a Bavarian restaurant called Lindenbräu (see the Places to Eat chapter) are the main attractions here.

Both complexes are a showcase of the work of the world's best architects (although the jury is still out on whether the world's best really gave their best on Potsdamer Platz). For details, see Tour III of the Architecture special section.

For a birds-eye view of the quarter, you can take what is billed as the world's fastest elevator to the **Panorama Observation Deck** *(Potsdamer Platz 1; adult/concession €3/2; open 11am-8pm Tues-Sun)*.

Filmmuseum Berlin

A multi-media journey through German film history and a behind-the-scenes look at special effects are what awaits visitors to the Filmmuseum Berlin *(☎ 300 90 30, Potsdamer Strasse 2; adults/concession €6/4; open 10am-6pm Tues-Sun, to 8pm Thur)*. Opened in late 2000, the museum kicks off with appropriate theatricality as it sends you through a warped mirror room straight from *The Cabinet of Dr Caligari*. Themes include pioneers and early divas, Fritz Lang's silent epic *Metropolis*, Leni Riefenstahl's awe- and fear-inspiring Nazi-era *Olympia* and post-WWII movies. As she did in real life, though, it is *femme fatale* Marlene Dietrich who steals the show – highlights from her private collection form the museum's centrepiece.

Potsdamer Platz – Coming Full Circle

The dawn of Potsdamer Platz coincided with the construction of the first railway line to Potsdam in 1838. From the late 19th century to the Golden Twenties, the square evolved into the heart of metropolitan life and entertainment in Berlin. Thousands of people came through daily, stopping for tea at Café Josty, a beer at Pschörr brewery or gathering in the lobby of the elegant Hotel Esplanade. Potsdamer Platz had become such an important traffic nexus that Europe's first (hand-operated) traffic light was installed in 1924 to control the daily flow of more than 100,000 people, 20,000 cars and 30 tram lines.

World War II sucked all life out of Potsdamer Platz, which was 80% destroyed. The area soon plunged into a coma and languished in the shadow of the Wall. On the GDR side was the infamous 'death strip', while in the west sprawled an abandoned and desolate wasteland. Nearly all the remaining historical buildings were demolished at that time, except the ruined Hotel Esplanade, the erstwhile *belle* of Bellevuestrasse. Two of its lavish rooms – the Kaisersaal and the Frühstückssaal (breakfast room) – were moved 75m, with the help of some wizardly technology, when the hotel was finally torn down in 1996. Now part of the Sony Center and fully restored to their previous opulence, the rooms were in the process of being converted into an exclusive restaurant at the time of writing.

With the fall of the Wall – and communism – capitalism took over instantly. Investors and developers were quick to realise the enormous commercial potential of this huge slice of prime real estate, which was soon gobbled up by powerful corporations like Daimler-Benz (now DaimlerChrysler), Sony and A&T, a development company.

KULTURFORUM

During the 1950s, one of Germany's premier architects of the time, Hans Scharoun, was asked to create a design concept for what would become known as the Kulturforum. This cluster of top-notch museums and concert venues took shape on the south-eastern edge of Tiergarten, just west of the Potsdamer Platz quarter.

Scharoun started things off with the **Berliner Philharmonie** (1961), Herbert-von-Karajan-Strasse 1, a concert hall with otherworldly acoustics (see the Architecture special section and the Entertainment chapter). He also designed the adjacent smaller **Kammermusiksaal** (Chamber Music Hall, 1987), the Musical Instruments Museum (1985) and the Neue Staatsbibliothek (1978) across the street at Potsdamer Strasse 33. The other museums were designed by Ludwig Mies van der Rohe (Neue Nationalgalerie, 1968) and the team of Heinz Hillmer, Rolf Gutbrod and Christoph Sattler (Museum of Applied Art and Museum of Prints & Drawings).

Standing a bit lost and forlorn within the modern museum complex is the red-brick **St Matthäikirche** (☎ 261 36 76, *Matthäikirchplatz; tower admission €0.50; open noon-6pm Tues-Sun*) dating from 1846. The neo-Romanesque confection was designed by Friedrich August Stüler. A well-kept secret is the bird's-eye view of Kulturforum and Potsdamer Platz from atop the bell tower. The nearest U/S-Bahn station is Mendelssohn-Bartholdy-Park, a 10-minute walk east. Bus Nos 129, 142 and 148 stop closer to the complex.

Gemäldegalerie (SMPK)

If you only see one Kulturforum museum, make sure it is the Gemäldegalerie *(Picture Gallery; ☎ 20 90 55 55, Matthäikirchplatz; adult/concession €4/2; open 10am-6pm Tues-Sun, to 10pm Thur)*. Opened in June 1998 and housed in a gloriously designed building, it focuses on European painting from the 13th to the 18th centuries with more than 1300 paintings on view. The collection's particular strengths are the works of 15th- and 16th-century Dutch masters as well as Italian painting from the 14th to the 18th centuries. Visitors make a suitably grand entrance to the galleries from the amazing football field-sized, pillared Great Hall, lit via circular skylights.

To keep the overwhelm factor to a minimum, grab a map in the huge foyer and prepare to spend at least two hours just to gain an overview. Admission includes free audioguides (German or English) with commentary on selected paintings. If you want to concentrate on particular masters, here are some of the highlights:

Dürer (room 4)
Cranach the Elder (room 5)
Holbein the Younger (room 6)
Rubens (rooms VII and VIII)
Rembrandt (room 16)
Gainsborough and Reynolds (room 20)
Canaletto and Tiepolo (room XII)
Caravaggio (room XIV)
Titian and Tintoretto (room XVI)
Botticelli (room XVIII)

Musikinstrumenten-Museum (SMPK)

The Musical Instruments Museum (☎ 25 48 10, Tiergartenstrasse 1; adult/concession €2/1; open 9am-5pm Tues-Fri, 10am-5pm Sat-Sun) focuses on the evolution of musical instruments from the 16th to the 20th centuries. Harpsichords from the 17th century, medieval trumpets and shepherds' bagpipes may not start a stampede for tickets, but the museum displays them all in a unique and interesting way. Historical paintings and porcelain figurines portray people playing the instruments, and there are earphones sprinkled throughout the museum to hear what they sound(ed) like. Other nuggets include Steinway pianos and curiosities like a musical walking stick.

Pride of place goes to the **Gray Organ** (1820) from Bathwick, England, but our favourite is the **Mighty Wurlitzer** (1929), an organ with more buttons and keys than a troop of Beefeater guards. From a ramp above, you can peer through windows at the bizarre collection of percussion and other instruments connected to this musical behemoth, which give it control over an entire orchestra of sound effects.

Guided tours (€1.50) at 11am on Saturday culminate with a noon recital on this white and gold confection (you don't have to go on the tour to hear this). Chamber music concerts (many free) take place most weeks at 11am on Wednesday and at 3.30pm on Sunday.

Kunstgewerbemuseum (SMPK)

The never-ending marble ramps inside the Kunstgewerbemuseum (Museum of Applied Art; ☎ 20 90 55 55, Matthäikirchplatz; adult/concession €2/1; open 10am-6pm Tues-Fri, 11am-6pm Sat-Sun) have an almost Escher-like quality. It shows arts and crafts ranging from 16th-century chalices of gilded silver to Art Deco ceramics and 20th-century appliances.

Medieval treasures include the 34 pieces of silverware that once belonged to town councillors of Lüneburg, gem-encrusted reliquaries; and the famous **Welfenschatz** (Guelf treasure), which includes a domed reliquary supposed to have contained the head of St George. The Renaissance is represented with beautiful Venetian glass, decorated earthenware (majolica) and other items.

Upstairs (Renaissance to Art Deco), don't miss Carlo Bugatti's crazy suite of furniture (1885) blending elements of Islamic, Japanese and Native American design. Also here are historical board games, amazing works in (unfortunately) ivory and Meissen porcelain. The Chinese Room from the Graneri Palace in Turin, Italy, is another highlight.

The basement houses the New Collection, showcasing international 20th-century product design from top practitioners, including Charles Eames.

Kupferstichkabinett (SMPK)

One of the world's finest and largest collections of graphic art is housed at the Kupferstichkabinett (Museum of Prints & Drawings; ☎ 20 90 55 55, Matthäikirchplatz; adult/concession €2/1; open 10am-6pm Tues-Fri, 11am-6pm Sat-Sun). Fans of Albrecht Dürer, Pieter Brueghel the Elder, Rembrandt, Lucas Cranach the Elder, Picasso and Giacometti will be happy here. The illustrations to Dante's

Divine Comedy by Botticelli are highlights. Illuminated manuscripts round out the displays.

What you see is in fact only a fraction of the entire collection, as exhibits are rotated to prevent deterioration of the fragile paper. This is also the reason for the protective glass casings and muted lighting. All explanatory panels are in German only, so it's better if you already know how to appreciate this type of art.

Neue Nationalgalerie (SMPK)

The New National Gallery (☎ *20 90 55 55, Potsdamer Strasse 50; adult/concession €4/2; open 10am-6pm Tues-Fri, 11am-6pm Sat-Sun)* lies a short walk south of the main Kulturforum complex. It focuses on paintings and sculpture of the 20th century up until the 1960s and represents all major genres: cubism (Picasso, Gris Leger), surrealism (Dali Miró, Max Ernst), new objectivity (Otto Dix, George Grosz), Bauhaus (Klee, Kandinsky) and, above all, German expressionism (Kirchner, Schmitt-Rottluff, Heckel). Among many highlights are the warped works of Otto Dix (eg, *Old Couple;* 1923), Beckmann's triptychs, the wonderful 'egghead' figures of George Grosz, and Kirchner's *Potsdamer Platz*, 1914, which provides an impression of what the newly incarnated square looked like in its early-20th-century heyday.

The exhibitions echo the fearful symmetry of the building; paintings on the walls just zoom away from you like railroad tracks into the distance. You'll definitely be treated to predatory stalking by the always attentive staff, but there's a hopping cafe in the basement where you can escape them. And the sculpture garden in the back is a great place to put up your feet and catch a few rays if the sun is shining. (For more on the building's design, see the Architecture special section.)

Neue Staatsbibliothek

The rambling building on the east side of Potsdamer Strasse houses Scharoun's Neue Staatsbibliothek *(New National Library;* ☎ *26 61, Potsdamer Strasse 33; admission free; open 9am-9pm Mon-Fri, to 7pm Sat; free tours 10.30am third Sat of the month).* Open since 1978, it is an academic lending and research library with huge reading rooms. Classical concerts take place in the Otto-Braun-Saal.

Gedenkstätte Deutscher Widerstand

Housed in the former Third Reich army command centre south-west of the Kulturforum is the Gedenkstätte Deutscher Widerstand *(The German Resistance Memorial Museum;* ☎ *26 99 50 00, Stauffenbergstrasse 13-14; admission free; open 9am-6pm Mon-Fri, 9am-1pm Sat-Sun, tours 11am Sun).* It addresses an important – and often neglected – facet of the Third Reich: home-grown resistance efforts against the Nazi terror regime. Photographs, documents and explanatory panels show how such diverse groups as workers, students, Jews, soldiers, prisoners, exiles and others risked life and livelihood to thwart Hitler's mob.

Perhaps the most famous act of resistance was the conspiracy to kill Hitler in 1944 led by Claus Schenk Graf von Stauffenberg. Hitler, of course, survived, resulting in the executions of the main conspirators in the courtyard of the Bendlerblock on the night of the attempt. All in all, more than 200 people were accused of involvement in the plot; about half were hanged or beheaded in Plötzensee prison, also a war memorial today (see earlier in this section).

Northern Districts

PANKOW

Pankow, Berlin's northernmost district, was once the centre of the East German government elite. Since 2001, it has also incorporated the old districts of Prenzlauer Berg (see earlier in this chapter) and Weissensee. Pankow itself has preserved a pleasant, small-town atmosphere but is modest in terms of visitor attractions. Part of its appeal lies in the forests and parks that blanket more than one-third of the land. Its main artery, Breite Strasse, is reached after a 500m-walk north from Pankow S-Bahn station (S8 and S10) along Berliner Strasse. Where the two streets meet stands the medieval **Dorfkirche**, a diminutive Gothic red-brick church with octagonal towers (open only for Sunday service). Another 500m or so west is Pankow's imposing neobaroque **Rathaus**, site of the Soviet show trial of the commander of the Sachsenhausen concentration camp. Still farther west is the popular **Bürgerpark** (people's park); it merges into the Schönholzer Heide with a Soviet cemetery for soldiers fallen in the Battle of Berlin.

Schloss Niederschönhausen

Pankow's main sight is Schloss Niederschönhausen (1664) which, after the founding of the GDR in 1949, became that country's 'White House' for Staatspräsident (State President) Wilhelm Pieck, who lived here until 1960. His successor, Walter Ulbricht, used the palace for four more years until the completion of the Staatsratsgebäude (State Council Building) on Schlossplatz in Mitte (see that section earlier in this chapter). It then became a government guesthouse hosting, among many others, Mikhail Gorbachev and Fidel Castro. Until 1991, the entire compound was completely inaccessible to the general public. After the fall of the Wall, some of the Round Table discussions that paved the way to reunification took place here.

The rather unremarkable two-storey palace is set within a walled garden (closed from December to Easter) that is surrounded by the Peter Lenné-designed Schlosspark (always open). The little Panke, the river that gives Pankow its name, flows through here. Access to the Schloss area is via formerly guarded iron gates. Coming from Breite Strasse, walk north on Ossietzkystrasse where, after about 750m, you'll reach the southern gate. You can also take tram No 52 or 53 from S-Bahn station Pankow to the Tschaikowskystrasse stop and walk east on Tschaikowskystrasse for about 400m, which will lead you to the western gate.

The entire quarter around the palace, especially along Majakowskiring, was a closed community where the party top brass lived

side by side with prominent artists, scientists and writers, including Hanns Eisler, Christa Wolf and Arnold Zweig. Access passes were needed to get inside, thus ensuring that the general public couldn't see the lavish villas and overall luxury in which their rulers wallowed – while denying almost everyone else basic amenities like a car or telephone.

Weissensee

Thinly populated Weissensee is one of the more pleasant among the former East Berlin districts, having preserved a provincial flair and a fair amount of green space. Weissensee escaped large scale destruction during WWII and much of its 19th-century architecture survived.

Weissensee gets its name from the **Weisser See**, an almost circular lake on Berliner Allee (U2, S8 or S10 to Schönhauser Allee, then tram No 23 or 24 to Berliner Allee/Indira-Gandhi-Strasse stop). On a nice day, the place is crawling with families and young couples, and fleets of rowing and pedal boats dot the placid waters. On its eastern shore is an old-fashioned lakeside pool.

East of here, is the **Brecht-Haus** (☎ 926 80 44, Berliner Allee 185; admission varies; open 2pm-6pm Wed-Sun) where Bertolt Brecht and Helene Weigel first lived after returning from exile in 1949. The neoclassical villa, which abuts the lake, is now an art and cultural forum with frequent readings, concerts and exhibits. North of the lake, in a little park, is an open-air theatre, the Freilichtbühne, where concerts and film screenings take place in the warmer months.

Weissensee is also home to Europe's largest Jewish Cemetery (see the boxed text 'Cemetery Hopping').

Hundemuseum Clocks that bark on the hour, stuffed and porcelain pooches, medals, posters, dog-shaped candlesticks, even a 'doggie-draft notice' from 1945 – you'll find it all at the quirky Hundemuseum (Dog Museum; ☎ 474 20 31, Alt-Blankenburg 33; adult/concession €1/0.50; open 3-6pm Tues, Thur & Sat, 11am-5pm Sun; S-Bahn: S8 or S10 to Blankenburg, then 10mins walk east). This delicacy for canine lovers is the lifetime passion of Margarete and Gerhard Laske who have crammed as many as 20,000 dog-related items into their seven exhibition rooms, garnering themselves a listing in the *Guinness Book of Records*.

Eastern Districts

LICHTENBERG

Since 2001, nondescript Lichtenberg, west of Friedrichshain, has also incorporated the old district of Hohenschönhausen. In 1995, Lichtenberg was the first Berlin district to elect a mayor from the Partei Demokratischer Sozialisten (PDS) party, successor to the GDR's SED. Nostalgia for the communist era is surprising given that Lichtenberg was home to the headquarters of the feared Ministry for State Security – or 'Stasi' – as well as one of its main prisons. From its offices on Normannenstrasse, the invasive surveillance system extended less to foreign

enemies than to the GDR's own citizens (see the boxed text 'The Stasi – Fear and Loathing in the GDR'). Lichtenberg also has a **zoo**, a **Schloss** and another important memorial exhibit, the **Museum Karlshorst**.

More green space, a couple of lakes (Orankesee and Obersee) and a villa colony make **Hohenschönhausen** slightly more appealing. As far as sights, there's really just one and a pretty chilling one it is.

Schloss Friedrichsfelde & Tierpark

Schloss Friedrichsfelde (☎ *513 81 41, Am Tierpark 125; U-Bahn: U5 to Tierpark)*, is a late-baroque palace (1695). It survived WWII practically intact, but after the war, parts of it were used to house animals from the adjacent Tierpark. Only a complete restoration from 1973 to 1981 gave it back its elegant look. At the time of writing, the palace was closed to the public, while its future purpose was being decided.

The Stasi – Fear and Loathing in the GDR

The walls had ears. Modelled after the Soviet KGB, the East German Ministerium für Staatssicherheit (Ministry for State Security, 'Stasi' for short) was founded in 1950. It was secret police, central intelligence agency and bureau of criminal investigation, all rolled into one. Called the 'shield and sword' of the paranoid SED leadership – which used it as an instrument of fear and oppression to secure its power base – the Stasi grew steadily in power and size over the four decades of its existence. By the end, the ministry had about 91,000 official full-time employees. Its secret weapons, though, were the 173,000 IMs (inoffizielle Mitarbeiter: unofficial employees) recruited from among the general public to spy on their co-workers, friends, family and neighbours. Even the tiniest piece of information was documented. By the time the system collapsed, there were files on six million people.

The Stasi's all-pervasiveness is unimaginable, as is the extent of the invasion of privacy it perpetrated on its own citizens. Its methods knew no limits with wire-tapping, video-tape observation, and opening of private mail being the more conventional techniques. Perhaps the most bizarre form of Stasi terror was the conservation of a suspected 'enemy's' body odour. Samples taken during interrogations – usually by wiping the unfortunate victim's crotch with a cotton cloth – were stored in hermetic glass jars. If a person needed to be identified, specially trained groin-sniffing dogs – euphemistically known as 'smell differentiation dogs' – sprang into action.

In order to see the original office of Erich Mielke, the last Stasi director, as well as cunning surveillance devices, communist paraphernalia and blood-chilling documents about GDR internment camps, travel to the former Stasi headquarters in the eastern district of Lichtenberg. The so-called 'Stasi Museum' (☎ *553 68 54, Ruschestrasse 103 – Haus 1; admission €2.50/1.50; open 11am-6pm Mon-Fri, 2pm-6pm Sat-Sun; U-Bahn: U5 to Magdalenenstrasse)* is a memorial exhibit about this creepy organisation and life in the GDR in general. It is sponsored by the Forschungs- und Gedenkstätte Normannenstrasse (Normannenstrasse Research & Memorial Centre).

To compensate its citizens for the loss of the famous Zoologischer Garten in West Berlin, the government of East Berlin converted the former Schlosspark into a zoo. **Tierpark Friedrichsfelde** *(☎ 51 53 10; adult/student/child €7/6/3.75; open 9am-4pm Nov-Feb, 9am-6pm Mar & Oct, 9am-7pm Apr-Sep)* opened in 1954 and at last count (end of 2001) had over 8000 animals representing nearly 1000 species living in open moated habitats. Star residents include many species of rare hoofed animals, including wild horses, oryx-antelopes and Vietnamese sika stags, all of which are extinct in nature.

Museum Berlin-Karlshorst

This fascinating memorial exhibit *(☎ 50 15 08 10, Zwieseler Strasse 4, cnr Rheinsteinstrasse; admission free; open 10am-6pm Tues-Sun)* focuses on the relationship between Germany and the Soviet Union from 1917 to the Wende. Documents, objects, uniforms and photographs explore every stage in the relations, with a particular focus on WWII. Themes such as German-Soviet relations before Hitler's rise to power, the daily grind of life as a soldier, and the fate of Soviet civilians during the war are all dealt with in an informative and objective manner.

The villa which houses the exhibit has a turbulent history. It was here, on the night of 8 May 1945, that the unconditional surrender of the German army was signed, thus officially ending WWII in Europe.

During the war, the building served as an officers' mess of the Wehrmacht pioneer school; in 1945, it became the headquarters of the Soviet Military Administration in Germany (SMAD). In this building, the GDR was given statehood in 1949. The **office of Marshal Zhukov**, the Soviet supreme commander, can still be seen, as can the **Great Hall** in which the terms of surrender were signed. Outside is a battery of **Soviet military weapons**, including a Howitzer canon and the *Katjuscha* multiple rocket-launcher (called a Stalin organ).

To get here, take the S3 to Karlshorst, north on Treskowallee, then right on Rheinsteinstrasse for a 10-minute walk. Display panels are in German and Russian only, but an English-language pamphlet (free) and also a well-written booklet (€2.50) are available.

Gedenkstätte Hohenschönhausen

The Gedenkstätte Hohenschönhausen *(Hohenschönhausen Memorial Site; ☎ 9862 42 19, Genslerstrasse 66; admission & tours free; tours 1pm Tues-Thur, 11am Fri-Sat and by arrangement)* is in a feared ex-prison that went through three notorious incarnations. From May 1945 to October 1946, it served as the Soviet-run 'Speziallager Nr 3' (Special Camp No 3), a processing centre for as many as 20,000 German prisoners of war destined for the Gulag. The Soviets then turned it into a regular prison, mostly dreaded for its 'U-Boats' – windowless, subterranean cells where the imprisoned were subjected to various forms of torture. In 1951 the place was turned over to the GDR government which converted it into its central Stasi prison. Suspected enemies of the regime were detained, interrogated and tortured here until as late as 1989.

For now the memorial can only be seen on guided tours (in German). Call ahead for a reservation. Take the S7 to Marzahn, then head back south on tram No 6, 7, or 17 to Genslerstrasse.

MARZAHN-HELLERSDORF

If you're curious about what was considered 'state-of-the-art' housing in the GDR as late as the 1980s, just take the S7/75 to Springpfuhl, followed by tram Nos 8 or 18, and you'll find yourself in the heart of Marzahn. After being 'assaulted' by the hideous aesthetics, get ready for a serious mind-warp: **Alt-Marzahn**, a minuscule patch of medieval history reconstructed amid the soulless concrete canyons. It's all here: a lovely church with step-gabled tower, cobblestone lanes, a wooden windmill, even a small farm. Sort of Disneyland – GDR-style – built on the grounds of the actual settlement from the 1300s.

Also here is the **Dorfmuseum Marzahn** *(☎ 541 02 31, Alt-Marzahn 13; adult/concession €2.50/1.25, free on Wed; open 10am-6pm Tues-Sun)*, which actually contains two

'Luxury Living' GDR-Style

Marzahn, Hohenschönhausen and Hellersdorf are eastern satellite cities, created with test-tube efficiency in the late '70s and early '80s. Their most distinctive feature is row upon row of gigantic, nondescript, prefab housing developments – the so-called *Plattenbauten* – rushing skyward like concrete stalagmites. In Marzahn alone, more than 62,000 flats for 160,000 people were built between 1976 and 1979, giving it the dubious distinction of being Germany's largest new-building complex. Most of these warrens of tiny apartments rise up to 17 storeys high. Entrance doors are painted with colours, symbols or animals to make it easier – especially for kids – to find one's way home. The people of the GDR even had a nickname for their petite abodes: Arbeiterschliessfächer (Workers' Lockers).

Fact is, these flats were in hot demand in communist Germany. Unlike buildings in older districts in central Berlin, for example in Prenzlauer Berg and Friedrichshain, they came with such relative luxuries as private baths, lifts and central heating. Other amenities, like playgrounds and parking, were considered desirable bonuses as well.

In the years immediately after the Wende, it was mostly people from the lower end of the social spectrum who lived in these concrete boxes. But as of late, the neighbourhoods have seen a growing influx of the young and hip but cash-poor, many coming here from other parts of Germany. Artists, architects, journalists and other creative types especially seem drawn to these functional environments. They like this uncompromising urbanity and find appeal in its brutalised architecture. Lower rents entice too, but more than anything, this new-found appeal may be a backlash against the increasing prettification so pervasive elsewhere in town. Faceless Plattenbauten as individual lifestyle expression – what would GDR city planners say to that?

MW

---

small museums: the surprisingly interesting **Friseurmuseum** (Hairdressing Museum) and the **Handwerksmuseum** (Handicrafts Museum). The former sheds not just light on the mysteries of washing, cutting, curling and dying hair, but also provides a glimpse into the intricate world of wig-making. A highlight is furniture designed by Art Nouveau pioneer Henry van de Velde for a Berlin hair salon. The Handwerksmuseum upstairs has changing exhibits on various crafts during medieval Berlin.

Hellersdorf is a mirror image of Marzahn with Plattenbauten ghettos galore containing 40,000 flats. Whatever charm there is can be found amid the 19th-century villas in the suburb of Mahlsdorf.

Gründerzeit Museum

Hellersdorf is also the home of one the more unusual among Berlin's museums, the Gründerzeit Museum (☎ 567 83 29, Hultschiner Damm 333; admission €3.50/1.50; open Wed & Sun 10am-6pm; S-Bahn: S5 to Mahlsdorf, then tram No 62 for 2 stops). Housed in the Mahlsdorfer Gutshaus, a historic manorhouse, it is the brainchild of Charlotte von Mahlsdorf, born Lothar Bergfelde, and the GDR's most famous transvestite. One of Charlotte's passions was collecting furniture and objet d'arts from the late 19th century, which she lovingly arranged into a museum of period rooms, including living rooms, kitchen, laundry room and maids' quarter. Alas, like Britain's Quentin Crisp *(The Naked Civil Servant)*, who saw greener pastures in New York, Die Charlotte flew the coop to Sweden in 1995.

Some of the famous pack rat's collection went with her, but lots was left behind and bought by the Hellersdorf district administration. Volunteers now take visitors on tours through the house. Call before you venture out.

Southern Districts

NEUKÖLLN (Map 5)

Neukölln, Berlin's most densely populated district, is a study in contrasts. The north, bordering Kreuzberg, has traditionally been a stronghold of the proletariat and continues to be dominated by poorer segments of the population, including many immigrants. The main drag, Karl-Marx-Strasse, is a busy high street peopled by the pale and downtrodden and lined by cheap import stores and low-end chains.

The southern suburbs of Britz, Buckow and Rudow, on the other hand, have preserved a tranquil small-town character, with tree-lined avenues, single-family homes and a largely middle-class population. An exception is Gropiusstadt, a massive high-rise housing development that is a good example of the kind of architectural sins committed in the 1970s.

Volkspark Hasenheide

This wonderful rambling park links Neukölln with Kreuzberg and was originally the royal family's rabbit preserve (hence the name: literally 'rabbit heath'). Landscape architect Peter Lenné also worked his magic in the Hasenheide in 1838. After WWII it was turned into a public park, with walking paths, playgrounds, an outdoor theatre and an animal sanctuary. Today it is still a popular hangout for neighbourhood folks who meet up for a game of *boules*, a chat or a stroll. The 70m-high **Rixdorfer Höhe** is another one of Berlin's Trümmerberge (rubble mountains).

Britz

A delicacy for architecture fans awaits in the **Hufeisensiedlung** (Horseshoe Colony), an expressionist housing development from the late 1920s in the suburb of Britz. It is the brainchild of Bruno Taut and Martin Wagner, who set out to create generous and humane living spaces as appealing alternatives to the cramped and lightless tenements of the inner city.

The structure on Lowise-Reuter-Ring perfectly illustrates the principles at work.

Around an existing pond, they created a park-like area and surrounded it with a rounded three storey structure in the form of a horseshoe. What looks like a huge single building actually consists of individual sections each set at a slightly different angle to achieve the rounded effect. All the flats have balconies facing the park and each section has its own small garden. It all looks clean, neat and quite handsome.

While here, also check out the street called **Hüsung** just west of Lowise-Reuter-Ring. Here you'll find uninterrupted rows of narrow, two-storey, single-family homes that follow the diamond-shaped outline of the street. Their tiny front lawns are separated from the pavement with hedges of identical height; trees are evenly spaced, about 10m apart. The amazing symmetry and homogeneousness of this development is both a tad oppressive and visually interesting.

The 'Horseshoe' and the 'Diamond' are easily reached by taking the U7 to Parchimer Allee and walking north for about 250m.

Another attraction in Britz is **Schloss Britz** (☎ *606 60 51, Alt-Britz 73; exhibits adult/concession €3/2; tours on request; park open 9am-dusk daily; €2/1*), reached by walking about 500m west from Parchimer Allee U-Bahn station (U7). Not really a palace but a large estate, it was the home of a courtier and built in 1706 in French Renaissance style. After WWII, it first served as an orphanage, but has now been restored for exhibits, receptions, concerts and other cultural events. Most of the rooms are decked out in period furniture and can be visited on tours. The estate park, though, is a nice enough place for relaxing and a picnic.

Gropiusstadt

South-east of Britz is Gropiusstadt, West Berlin's answer to Marzahn and other barren colonies of the former East Berlin. Built from 1964 to 1975, it's a glass and concrete desert with flats for some 50,000 people. Although based on designs by Bauhaus founder Walter Gropius, the end result probably made him spin in his grave. His vision of a pedestrian-friendly community with lots of green, open spaces and up to four-storey tall buildings was turned into a forest of high-rises – some with as many as 31 floors – that stand close enough together to see the neighbours brush their teeth. There are no real attractions here for visitors, but if you just want to get a feel for the place, get off at any of the four U-Bahn stations south of, and including, Johannisthaler Chaussee (U7). There's a shopping centre at the Wutzkyallee stop.

TREPTOW

Treptow gets its character from the Spree River and the large recreational area formed by the Plänterwald forest and Treptow Park which stretch along the western river bank. **Stern und Kreis Schifffahrt** (☎ 536 36 00, *boats leave from Hafen Treptow, near S-Bahn station Treptower Park*) operates cruises from May to October, and rowing and pedal boats are available for rent as well.

Once a manufacturing stronghold, Treptow is staking its future on high-tech. The former GDR television production site in Adlershof, in the southern part of the district, is being turned into a huge technology park called Wissenschafts- und Wirtschaftsstandort Adlershor (WISTA, Centre for Science & Economy Adlershof). Part of the complex is the life sciences campus of the Humboldt Universität.

Prime attractions for visitors are the monumental **Soviet War Memorial** in Treptow Park and, primarily for kids, the Spree-Park.

Museum der Verbotenen Kunst (Map 5)

Still standing in what used to be the former 'Death Strip' is the only remaining accessible watchtower, from which GDR soldiers guarded the German-East German border. A group of young artists not only prevented its demolition but also created a unique museum inside, the Museum der Verbotenen Kunst (*Museum of Forbidden Art;* ☎ 229 16 45; *admission free; open noon-6pm Wed-Sun*). Exhibits change constantly but usually feature art works either from or dealing with the period of the country's division. Upstairs is a documentation on the oppressive nature of the border system. In summer, performances, concerts and outdoor

movie screenings take place in the area surrounding the tower. From U-Bahn station Schlesisches Tor (U1/15) walk south-east for about 10 minutes or take bus No 265. From S-Bahn station Treptower Park, it's about the same distance north-west.

Sowjetisches Ehrenmal (Map 1)

Right at the heart of Treptow Park is the city's largest Soviet memorial (1949), a gargantuan complex attesting both to the immensity of the losses of WWII and to the overblown self-importance of the Soviet state under Stalin. The monument is always open. From the S-Bahn station Treptower Park, head south for about 750m on Puschkinallee, then enter the park through the bombastic stone gate.

As you approach the complex, you'll first pass a statue of Mother Russia, grieving for her dead children. The actual entrance to the memorial is flanked by two mighty walls made from red marble retrieved from Hitler's New Chancellery and fronted by kneeling soldiers.

From here a wide plaza, lined on either side by eight sarcophagi representing the then 16 Soviet republics, opens up. Each of the blocks is covered with reliefs portraying scenes from the war and quotes from Stalin (in Russian and German). The large field in the centre is the burial site of the 5000 soldiers who fell in the Battle of Berlin. It culminates in a mound topped with a 13m-high statue of a Russian soldier clutching a child, his great sword resting on a shattered swastika. In the plinth is a socialist-realism mosaic of grateful Soviet citizens, including workers, peasants and some Central Asian minorities.

Archenhold Sternwarte (Map 1) A

short walk south of the monument is Germany's oldest public observatory (☎ 534 80 80; *adult/concession €2/1.50; open 2pm-5.30pm Mon-Thur, 2pm-7.30pm Fri-Sun*). It opened in 1909 at the initiative of astronomer Friedrich Simon Archenhold. In 1915, Albert Einstein introduced his theory of relativity here. The modernised museum contains a **giant refracting lens**

Check out the art at the East Side Gallery.

Memorial to the Wars of Liberation, Kreuzberg.

GDR-era murals still grace some buildings.

Three storeys high, the Pergamon Altar is a highlight of the Pergamon Museum.

Zoo station – transit point for commuters, inspiration for a U2 song.

Kronprinzenpalais, one of many stately buildings on Unter den Linden, Berlin's famous boulevard.

(demonstrations 3pm Sun, public viewing 8pm second Fri of the month Oct-Mar) and several exhibitions on space-related themes. It is best reached by walking north into the park from S-Bahn station Plänterwald.

Spree-Park Plänterwald (Off Map 1)

Smaller children especially enjoy the Spree-Park Plänterwald *(☎ 53 33 50, Kiehnwerderallee 1-3; adult/children ages 3-12 €15/14 including rides; usually open 9am-6pm Mon-Fri, 10am-7pm Sat-Sun Mar-early Nov)*. It has its origin in what was once the biggest amusement park in the GDR with as many as 1.5 million visitors annually. In 1991, it was sold to a private company which has updated the rides and attractions. It's still pretty low-key with some (not so) wild water-rides, a Ferris wheel, a roller coaster and the 'cowboy town' of Colorado City. A number of casual eateries and snack bars are on the grounds as well. The closest S-Bahn station is Plänterwald, from where it's a 15- to 20-minute walk north-east. Or you can take U1 or U15 to Schlesisches Tor, then bus No 265 to the Rathaus Treptow stop. The entrance is on Neue Krugallee.

Anna Seghers Gedenkstätte (Off Map 1)

Fans of the writer Anna Seghers (1900–83) might be interested in making a pilgrimage to the small memorial exhibit inside her former flat *(☎ 677 47 25, Anna-Seghers-Strasse 81; adult/concession €2/1; open 10am-4pm Tues-Wed, 10am-6pm Thur; S-Bahn: S6, S8, S9, S45 to Adlershof)*. The original cramped living room and office with her precious library are still there, as is a small exhibit documenting her life and work. A committed communist, Seghers (whose real name was Netty Radvanyi, nee Reiling) spent WWII in Mexico before choosing East Berlin as her domicile upon her return from exile. Her most famous work is *The Seventh Cross* (1941), a chilling account of the terrors of the Nazi regime. The nearest S-Bahn station is Adlershof.

KÖPENICK

Köpenick, at the far south-eastern tip of Berlin, was administratively merged with Treptow in 2001 and is by far the greenest district, with forests and lakes covering about two-thirds of the land. Berlin's largest lake (Müggelsee), largest forest (Köpenicker Stadtforst) and highest natural elevation (Müggelberge, 115m) are all here. There's lots of boating, swimming, sailing, windsurfing, rowing and hiking.

Köpenick, the area's third medieval settlement after Spandau and Berlin, was granted town rights in 1232, a full 30 years before Berlin, from which it remained independent until 1920. Culture and architecture fans have a protected **Altstadt**, **baroque palace** and the former fishing village, Kietz, to look forward to.

Despite its obvious natural assets, the GDR located lots of industry in Köpenick. At one point, there were about 100 factories with 35,000 jobs. Most have since closed, though smaller companies and 'cleaner' industries – like electronics and cosmetics companies – remain.

Easily reached on the S3 from all major central Berlin S-Bahn stations, Köpenick makes an excellent half-day or day break from the big-city bustle of Berlin. Start at the district's **tourist office** *(☎ 655 75 50, Alt-Köpenick 34; open 9am-7pm Mon-Fri, 10am-2pm Sat-Sun)*.

Gedenkstätte Köpenicker Blutwoche

In the early 20th century, Köpenick was a stronghold of the KPD (communist) and SPD (Social Democrat) parties. In March 1920, local workers did their part in staving off the attempted putsch of right-wing radical Wolfgang Kapp (see the History section in Facts about Berlin). Under the leadership of Alexander Futran, they stalled troops loyal to Kapp as they marched on Berlin. Futran was captured and executed, but Köpenick remained red. Thirteen years later, when Hitler rose to power, the communist flag was defiantly raised over Köpenick.

The Nazis naturally didn't let such provocation pass unpunished. In the week of

Der Hauptmann von Köpenick

A bronze statue of the Hauptmann von Köpenick (the Captain of Köpenick), a legendary character famous for making a laughing stock of Prussian authority, stands guard outside the Rathaus. Born Wilhelm Voigt, he was a ne'er do well who had spent much of his life in prison for petty offences. Upon his final release in 1906, the unemployed cobbler decided to turn honest and start over in another country. All he needed was a passport. There was only one problem; as an ex-con without job or money, chances of being granted one were pathetically slim.

Voigt's frustration soon reached boiling point. But then he had an ingenious idea. He dressed himself in a captains' uniform he had found at a costume shop, walked into the street and took command of the first group of soldiers who happened to pass by, ordering them to march on the Rathaus of Köpenick. There, he and his men occupied the town hall, arrested the mayor and confiscated the city treasury. No one ever bothered to ask who he was or whether he had the authority to do so. His uniform was all the identification they needed. With everyone standing stiffly at attention, Voigt disappeared with the money.

As soon as the press got wind of the ruse, the entire world scoffed at the absurdity of Prussian militarist authority and Voigt became an instant media celebrity. Voigt, however, didn't get away with his trickery. Ten days later, he was caught and sentenced to four years in prison. But even the Kaiser was so amused by the incident that he ordered the cobbler released after only two years. For the next few years, Voigt travelled to all corners of the world – Vienna to London, Budapest to New York City – giving interviews and signing film, book and music contracts.

But with the outbreak of WWI, Voigt's fame fizzled; no one was laughing at Prussian militarism any longer. Dejected, he settled in Luxembourg and died in 1922, as poor and downtrodden as he had been most of his life.

The Rathaus Köpenick has dedicated a small, free exhibit in his – ahem! – honour.

21–26 June 1933, the SA arrested and brutally tortured hundreds of Nazi opponents, killing 91. Badly mangled bodies, sewn into cloth sacks, were still being retrieved weeks later from the surrounding rivers. The atrocities, which went down in history as the *Köpenicker Blutwoche* (Köpenick's Bloody Week), took place in the courthouse prison of the **Amtsgericht Köpenick**. Today it contains a small **memorial exhibit** (☎ *657 14 67, Puchanstrasse 12; admission free; open 10am-4.30pm Tues-Wed, 10am-6pm Thur, 2pm-6pm Sat)*, including a reconstructed cell. A **monument** (1969), showing a raised clenched fist, honours the victims of the Blutwoche; it's on Platz des 23 April just south of here.

Altstadt

Much of Köpenick's Altstadt, including buildings and roads, has recently been restored. Unlike most of Spandau's old town, Köpenick's Altstadt is not pedestrianised

and many of its ancient cobblestone streets still follow their medieval layout. The oldest street is Böttcherstrasse but for a parade of historic houses go to Strasse Alt-Köpenick. The oldest is the one at No 36 (built in 1616). House No 14 dates to 1800, Nos 6 and 10 to 1830.

Easily recognised is the **Rathaus** (1904), a red-brick, neo-Gothic jumble with frilly turrets and a jutting 54m tower. Also note the step-gabled mock facade typical of northern German architecture. A statue of the legendary Hauptmann von Köpenick stands outside the main entrance.

Schloss Köpenick

The simple but graceful Köpenick Palace stands on the Schlossinsel, an island in the Dahme, and was built in Dutch baroque style between 1677 and 1682. It served as a residence for Prince Friedrich until he became Elector Friedrich III (and later King Friedrich I). Subsequently it went through periods as a prison and a teaching seminary before the GDR moved its Museum of Applied Arts here in 1963. After the Wende, the museum became the sister branch of the Museum of Applied Arts at the Kulturforum. Its collections, however, remain hidden from public view until the building's thorough restoration is completed, a process that could drag on beyond 2004.

In October 1730, cruel justice was meted out by a military court assembled in the Schloss' Wappensaal, a lavishly decorated 2nd-floor hall. The accused? Captain Friedrich and Captain Hans. Their crime? Attempted desertion. The verdict(s)? The guillotine for Hans, the throne for Friedrich, who just happened to have the good fortune of being the son of King Friedrich Wilhelm I – the future King Friedrich II.

Opposite the Schloss is the baroque **Schlosskapelle** (1885), built according to plans by Charlottenburg palace architect Johann Arnold Nering. It's all surrounded by the lovely **Schlosspark**.

Kietz

South-east of the Altstadt, the Kietz is Köpenick's medieval fishing village and is still lined by nicely restored single- and two-storey buildings where the fisherfolk lived as far back as the 18th century. The Kietz is home to the unique **Wäschereimuseum** *(Laundry Museum, ☎ 656 38 21, Luisenstrasse 23; tours adult/concession €2/1; tours 3-6pm first Fri of the month only; tram: No 62 to Müggelheimer Strasse/Wendenschlossstrasse)*. It dates back to the 19th century when Köpenick was a centre of the laundry business and includes steam-powered washing machines, gas-fuelled irons and ancient mangles among its displays.

Guided tours (in German) are delivered with lots of humour but unfortunately are run only once a month.

Grosser Müggelsee

The Müggelsee is called 'Grosser' for good reason. Measuring 4km in length and 2.5km in width, it's the largest lake in the Berlin area. The north-western shore is bordered by the suburb of **Friedrichshagen**, best reached on tram No 61 from S-Bahn station Friedrichshagen. In 1753, Friedrich II settled this area with 100 Bohemian families whose job it was to grow mulberry trees to feed the silkworms that supplied silk for weaving. At the end of the 19th century, a circle of poets and writers that included Gerhart Hauptmann gathered here as well.

Where the Spree merges with the lake are the **Stern und Kreis Schifffahrt** *(☎ 536 36 00)* cruise company's landing docks. Several boats daily make the half-hour trip to the forested southern shore (with good hiking – this is where you'll find the Müggelberge) and back between May and October. One-way costs €2 or €3.50 depending on where you get off, return is €5.50. West of the lake, the **Köpenicker Stadtforst** stretches southward for miles, eventually leading to the Müggelberge.

Also on the shore are two lakeside pools; **Seebad Friedrichshagen** just east of the north shore landing docks, and **Strandbad Müggelsee** on the eastern shore in the medieval fishing village of Rahnsdorf (take tram No 61).

Grünau

Grünau is a handsome colony founded in 1749 on the western bank of the Dahme River, south of the Köpenick Altstadt. This section of the river, called **Langer See**, was the site of the Olympic regattas in 1936. Here you'll find the **Wassersportmuseum** *(Water Sports Museum, ☎ 674 40 02, Regattastrasse 141; admission free; open 2pm-4.30pm Sat)*, with an exhibit on the history of water sports in Berlin-Brandenburg. On display are flags, medals, clothing, newspaper articles, photos, boats and boat accessories. To get there, take the S8 to Grünau, followed either by a five minute walk north or otherwise take a short ride on tram No 68 to the Wassersportallee stop. Alternatively, you could take tram No 62 to the Müggelbergallee stop and cross the Dahme on a little ferry on the same ticket.

THINGS TO SEE & DO

Western Districts

SPANDAU

Spandau, about 10km north-west of Zoo station, makes a lovely excursion and respite from the city. Having been spared from heavy bombing, it is one of the few places in Berlin that still has a historic centre – the Altstadt – complete with narrow cobblestone lanes, a market square and a medieval church. Its most striking attraction, though, is the almost entirely intact 16th-century citadel.

Spandau's other main asset is its forests (especially the **Spandauer Forst** in the north), which take up about one-quarter of the district and are great for walking. You might encounter deer, rabbits and, though rarely, wild boar.

As the locals will quickly tell you, Spandau is not Berlin. Ever since 1920, during the formation of Greater Berlin, the people of Spandau have greatly resented their loss of independence. To this day, they talk about 'going to Berlin' when travelling outside their district.

Several ex-Nazis sentenced to imprisonment at the Nuremberg Trials served their time at the former **Alliierte Kriegsverbrechergefängnis** (Allied War Criminal Prison) on Wilhelmstrasse in the western Spandau suburb of Staaken. Among them was Albert Speer, who was released in 1966, and Rudolf Hess. The prison was torn down as soon as Hess, who was the only prisoner in the end, died in 1987.

Spandau Zitadelle

The extremely well-preserved Spandau Citadel (1560–94) is an impressive Renaissance structure on a little island in the Havel River. A moat protects it on three sides, while the fourth opens up to the river. Its basic layout is that of a square with each corner protected by a bastion – essentially a stony section shaped like an arrowhead. Its

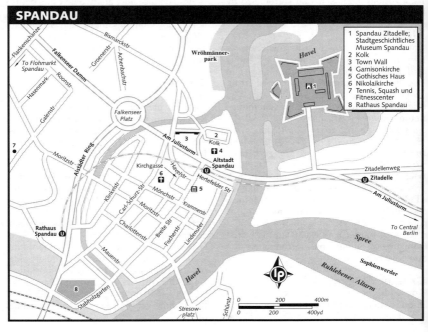

SPANDAU

1 Spandau Zitadelle;
  Stadtgeschichtliches
  Museum Spandau
2 Kolk
3 Town Wall
4 Garnisonkirche
5 Gothisches Haus
6 Nikolaikirche
7 Tennis, Squash und
  Fitnesscenter
8 Rathaus Spandau

dramatic outline is best appreciated in winter when you can see it through the leafless trees of the surrounding park.

As you enter via the bridge off Strasse Am Juliusturm, you will pass the gate featuring the restored coat of arms of the Hohenzollern dynasty with its distinctive two black eagles. Wandering around the central courtyard is free but besides a few sculptures and statues there isn't that much to look at.

More interesting is a climb up the 36m-high **Juliusturm**, the crenellated tower in the south-west corner, from where you can better appreciate the citadel's layout and also enjoy a view over the Havel and Spree rivers and to the Altstadt. From 1873 to 1919, Bismarck had the *Reichskriegsschatz* (literally 'imperial war treasure') stored here. This was an amount in gold equivalent to 120 million Reichsmark, which was a portion of the reparation payments collected from the French after the war of 1870–71.

Also of interest is the **Stadtgeschichtliches Museum Spandau** (☎ *354 94 40, adult/concession €2/1, including Juliusturm; open 9am-5pm Tues-Fri, 10am-5pm Sat-Sun)*, the local history museum in the former Zeughaus (armoury). Another exhibit detailing the history of the citadel is inside the **Kommandantenhaus** (commander's house), on your right as you enter through the gate. Also here is the ticket office where tickets, good for both museums and the tower (weather permitting) are sold. The citadel is about 200m west of the U-Bahn station Zitadelle (U7).

Altstadt

The Altstadt lies a short walk west of the citadel and consists of two sections separated by Strasse Am Juliusturm. The older part, called **Kolk**, lies immediately on your right (north) after you've crossed the Havel. Compared with the vastness of the citadel, this area seems toy-sized. Wander the quiet, narrow lanes lined by tiny houses, including a few half-timbered ones. The **Garnisonskirche** (Garrison Church), also known as Marienkirche, dates from 1848 but was destroyed in WWII and rebuilt in 1964. West

of here stands a 78m-long remnant of the medieval 6m-high **town wall**.

Most of the pedestrianised Altstadt lies south of the Strasse am Juliusturm. This is Spandau's commercial heart, and shops line both its main streets, Carl-Schurz-Strasse and Breite Strasse. The graceful church on the corner of Carl-Schurz-Strasse and Mönchstrasse is the **Nikolaikirche** (☎ *333 12 51, Carl-Schurz-Strasse; admission free; open 11am-2pm Wed, 3pm-6pm Thur, 11am-3pm Sat, 2pm-4pm Sun)*. It played a pivotal role during the Reformation, when the first public Protestant service in Brandenburg was held here in 1539. This was made possible when Elector Joachim II, whose statue stands outside the church, became the first Brandenburg ruler to convert to Protestantism in 1539. A Protestant minister delivered the sermon while a Catholic priest ministered the holy communion. Within only a few years, Protestantism became the dominant religion in the entire March of Brandenburg.

The Nikolaikirche was first mentioned in a record of 1240 but the structure you see today dates from the 15th century. The walls of the west tower, which doubled as fortress and watchtower, are up to 3m thick. The church itself is a three-nave Gothic hall design, its whitewashed walls decorated with oil paintings. Of interest is the bronze **baptismal font** (1398) and the **baroque pulpit** (1714). Pride of place, though, goes to the late-Renaissance **altar** (1582) whose centre panel depicts the Last Supper. During WWII, a wall erected around the altar protected it from the fire storm of 1944.

Another important medieval building is the **Gotisches Haus** (Gothic House; ☎ *333 93 88, Breite Strasse 32; admission free; open 10am-5pm Mon-Fri, 10am-1pm Sat)*. Possibly dating back to the 13th century, it is a very rare example of a town house made entirely from brick (instead of wood). It contains a small exhibit chronicling construction in Spandau's old town from the Middle Ages to recent times. Look for the beautiful net-vaulted ceiling from around 1500.

WILMERSDORF (Map 1)

The sprawling district of Wilmersdorf runs from Kurfürstendamm in the north to Zehlendorf in the south, with about half of its area taken up by the Grunewald forest. Like its neighbours to the north and east – Charlottenburg and Schöneberg, respectively – it's largely middle-class residential. Although short on sights and attractions, many visitors become familiar with Wilmersdorf because of its density of affordable hotels. Restaurants and bars abound as well, though the quarter is hardly considered trendy, except perhaps for the area around Ludwigkirchplatz and along Pariser Strasse.

Grunewald

The Grunewald, a sprawling forest covering a total area of 32 sq km, is bordered by the Havel River in the west, Heerstrasse in the north, Clayallee in the east and the Schlachtensee lake in the south. It is bisected by the A115 autobahn (AVUS), which separates the northern Wilmersdorf section from the Zehlendorf section. Sights in the latter are covered under Zehlendorf.

Until 1903 the forest served as the private hunting grounds for the royal family. Freezing Berliners felled about 70% of all the trees to survive harsh winters during WWII and the Berlin Blockade, so what you see today is mostly new-growth forest. The Grunewald is at the top of the list of favourite outings among Berliners and provides just as much entertainment, respite and distraction for visitors.

Teufelsberg The forest's northern section is dominated by the Teufelsberg, at 115m the highest Trümmerberg (literally 'Rubble Mountain') in Berlin, made from 25 million cubic metres of war debris. Since 1950, it has been a popular recreational spot, especially on rare snowy days when the sledding and ski slopes (!) and the small ski jump have kids howling with glee. There's also a climbing rock and trails for mountain bikes, and in autumn the sky is filled with colourful kites. The little lake at the bottom of the hill is the **Teufelssee** (not suitable for swimming). Just north of the lake is the high moor, Teufelsfenn.

Havelchaussee A lovely footpath runs along the entire right bank of the Havel River. For drivers there's the Havelchaussee which cuts through the forest from Scholzplatz/Am Postfenn (south off Heerstrasse and the only place from where the drive can be started) in the north to the Zehlendorf suburb of Nikolassee in the south. If you can, avoid driving here on sunny spring Sundays, when it's bumper to bumper for the entire 6km.

About 2.5km into the drive or the walk is the **Grunewaldturm** (*Havelchaussee 61; adult/concession €1/0.50; open 10am-dusk, in summer often to midnight; S-Bahn: S1 or S7 to Wannsee, then bus No 218 to Grunewaldturm*), built in 1899, a 56m-high tower formerly known as Kaiser-Wilhelm-Turm after Wilhelm I, whose marble statue stands in the tower hall. From the **viewing gallery**, reached after climbing 204 steps, a marvellous view extends over the river, the suburbs of Gatow and Kladow and all the way to the Pfaueninsel (see the Zehlendorf section), sometimes even to Potsdam. There's also a nice restaurant, which serves breakfast until 3pm.

ZEHLENDORF

Zehlendorf is one of Berlin's greenest districts (only Köpenick is greener), with about half of its land covered by forest, rivers and lakes. The elegant suburbs of Dahlem and Wannsee with their villas and estates contribute greatly to Zehlendorf's small-town character. To visitors and locals, the district has much to offer. The southern half of Grunewald forest and Wannsee lake are great areas for outdoor activities, while several museums provide intellectual stimulation. A couple of palaces, important historical sites, a university and lovely gardens further add to its appeal.

Dahlem Museum Complex

The leafy suburb of Dahlem is home to an extraordinary cluster of museums focused on the art and culture of peoples from around the world. In 2000, two collections – the Museum of Indian Art and the Museum of East Asian Art – reopened to the public.

Ethnologisches Museum (SMPK) The Museum of Ethnology (☎ *830 14 38, Lansstrasse 8; adult/concession €2/1; open 10am-6pm Tues-Fri, 11am-6pm Sat-Sun; U-Bahn: U1 to Dahlem-Dorf)* has one of the world's largest and most outstanding collections of pre-industrial, non-European art and objects. It's impossible to describe fully the museum's extraordinary wealth. Budget at least two hours to walk through its labyrinthine network of halls on an eye-opening journey of discovery that'll fly by in no time. Note that this museum is being given a gradual overhaul, meaning that some sections may be closed at any given time.

African and **pre-Columbian civilisations** are particularly well represented. Highlights of the latter include stone sculptures from Guatemala, and figurines, sculptures and weapons from the Mayan culture. The gold jewellery and helmets are sparkling examples of these rich civilisations. Major crowd-pleasers include the **South Seas** section where cult objects from New Guinea, Tonga, Melanesia and other islands can be seen. The island seafaring tradition is paid tribute in the Boat Hall, home to several enormous outriggers, including a double-hull boat from Tonga that can be entered.

The **Africa exhibit** goes a long way towards debunking stereotypical preconceptions of supposedly 'primitive' cultures on that continent. There are lots of masks, ornaments, vases, musical instruments and other objects of ceremonial and everyday life, mostly from West African countries such as Cameroon, Nigeria and Benin. The high level of craftsmanship is especially evident in a beaded throne that was a gift from King Njoya of Cameroon to Emperor Wilhelm II.

Admission to the Ethnology Museum also gives you access to the recently revamped **Museum für Indische Kunst** (Museum of Indian Art). On view are fine and applied art from India, South East Asia and Central Asia from the 2nd century BC to the present. The museum is especially noted for

its fine terracottas, stone sculptures and bronzes as well as wall paintings and sculptures scavenged from Buddhist cave temples along the Silk Route.

In the same complex is the **Museum für Ostasiatische Kunst** (Museum of East Asian Art), which was also recently reorganised. Ceramics, bronzes, laquerware, jade objects, graphics from China, Japan and Korea are exhibited here.

Museum Europäischer Kulturen (SMPK) The many facets of the cultural heritage of European peoples and countries is the subject matter of the Museum of European Cultures (☎ *20 90 55 55, Im Winkel 6-8; adult/concession €2/1; open 10am-6pm Tues-Fri, 11am-6pm Sat-Sun; U-Bahn: U1 to Dahlem-Dorf)*. The exhibit – entitled Cultural Contacts in Europe: the Fascination of the Image – is based on a fairly abstract and heady concept: it seeks to depict the cultural commonalities and diversity of European countries in the context of the production, distribution and use of images. Fortunately, on the exhibition floor this translates into more tangible – and often quite interesting – displays of furniture, tiles, carpets, paintings, photography, film and TV and wherever else images play a role in people's daily lives.

Domäne Dahlem Travel back in time to pre-industrial Berlin at this large farming estate turned open-air museum called Domäne Dahlem (☎ *832 50 00, Königin-Luise-Strasse 49; adult/concession €2.50/1.25, free on Wed; open 10am-6pm Wed-Mon; U-Bahn: U1 to Dahlem-Dorf)*. The complex centres on a large 1560 manor, one of the city's oldest buildings, which contains exhibits on the region's agricultural history, rural crafts and bee keeping. A highlight is a historic dry goods store lovingly furnished with great authenticity. Smaller buildings contain workshops where volunteers demonstrate such crafts as spinning, weaving, pottery-making, furniture-painting and more. Actual (organic) farming is also still practised, with the produce sold in the Hofladen. The complex also hosts popular themed markets – pottery, textile, Christmas etc. Call for details of upcoming events.

Freie Universität

The buildings of the Freie Universität *(Free University, FU; ☎ 83 81; U-Bahn: U1 to Dahlem-Dorf)* are scattered about Dahlem. It was founded in 1948 as a counterpoint to Berlin's traditional Humboldt Universität in Mitte which was falling increasingly under the influence of Marxist-Leninist doctrine. The Free University's democracy-minded students and professors risked harassment, dismissal and even arrest. Initially, lectures at the *free* university took place in empty villas but in 1955, the Henry-Ford-Bau opened as the first permanent structure, financed with a grant from the Henry Ford Foundation.

Creating an entirely new university was also an opportunity to do away with elements of Germany's antiquated university system. FU students were given a voice through a student council, while quaint organisations like (saber) duelling fraternities were prohibited. In the 1960s, students at the FU provided the spark for the nationwide student movement which, among other things, demanded further reforms in the political and university systems.

Botanischer Garten

Berlin's stunning botanical garden *(☎ 83 85 01 00, or ☎ 83 85 00 27 for recorded message, Königin-Luise-Strasse 6-8, enter from Unter den Eichen or Königin-Luise-Platz; adult/concession €4/2 for gardens & museum, half-price if arriving two hours before closing; open 9am-dusk, latest 9pm)* is a symphony of perfume and colour about a 15-minute walk east of U-Bahn station Dahlem-Dorf (U1). Little over 100 years old, it boasts more than 20,000 plant species from around the world beautifully arranged on 43 hectares. Also on the grounds is the **Botanisches Museum** *(same tel; adult/concession €1/0.50; open 10am-6pm daily)*. It complements the garden by providing scientific background information about the world of plants.

Alliierten-Museum

The Alliierten-Museum *(Allied Museum; ☎ 818 19 90, Clayallee 135; admission free; open 10am-6pm Tues-Sun; U-Bahn: U1 to Oskar-Helene-Heim)* is an engaging multimedia exhibit in the former Outpost cinema for US troops. It documents the history and challenges faced by the western Allies in Berlin during the Cold War. The original guard trailer from Checkpoint Charlie, a brightly painted piece of the Wall, a GDR guardtower, a US military plane and a French military train are vivid relics greeting you in the museum's yard.

The exhibit itself is divided into two periods. The first, from 1945 to 1950, covers the Allied victory, the relationship between the occupiers and the vanquished, and the tough times of the Berlin Airlift. It all continues next door, culminating with the fall of the Wall, reunification and the withdrawal of occupying forces in 1994.

One especially fascinating exhibit is the partial re-creation of the Berlin Spy Tunnel, built by the CIA in order to tap into the central telephone system of the Soviets. Two metres wide and 450m long, it recorded half a million calls from May 1955 to 1956 until a double agent blabbed to the Soviets.

This fascinating museum is sadly undervisited, probably because it's perceived as being in a remote location. This is not really the case: the U-Bahn ride from, say, Nollendorfplatz in Schöneberg, takes about 20 minutes, followed by a five- to 10-minute walk north on Clayallee. It's worth the effort. All explanatory panelling is in German, English and French.

Grunewaldsee & Jagdschloss Grunewald (Map 1)

The southern half of the Grunewald forest boasts a couple of fine sights and several swimming lakes (Grunewaldsee, Schlachtensee and Krumme Lanke). The largest, the Grunewaldsee, is doggie paradise and even has a dog beach. Unfortunately, the concept of 'pooper-scoopers' hasn't yet caught on here which means you have to keep an eye on the trail. It also renders the place basically unsuitable for small children.

Jagdschloss Grunewald *(☎ 969 42 02 or 813 34 42, Am Grunewaldsee 29; adult/concession €2/1.50; open 10am-5pm Tues-Sun May-Oct, 10am-4pm Sat-Sun Nov-Apr)*, south of Grunewaldsee, is the oldest existing palace in Berlin. A Renaissance palace built by Elector Joachim II in 1542, it stands on the lakeshore. Joachim called the place 'Haus am Grünen Walde' (House in the Green Woods), which is how the forest and the area got their name. Inside is a surprisingly good gallery with German and Dutch paintings from the 15th to the 19th centuries. Exquisite works include oils by Lucas Cranach the Elder, an early-15th-century altar and *Venus and Armor* by the Dutchman Jan Lievens (1630–73). Another exhibit, the **Jagdzeugmagazin** (Hunting Collection) with hunting-related items, antlers and paintings depicting hunting scenes, can easily be skipped.

Take the U1 to Dahlem-Dorf, then bus No 183 to the Clayallee stop, followed by a 15-minute walk west through the forest; alternatively take the U7 to Fehrbelliner Platz, then bus No 115 to Pücklerstrasse, then walk west.

Brücke Museum (Map 1)

Works by the expressionist artists' group Die Brücke (The Bridge; 1905–13) can be seen at this small but extremely worthwhile museum *(☎ 831 20 29, Bussardsteig 9; adult/concession €4/2; open 11am-5pm Wed-Mon; U-Bahn: U1 to Dahlem-Dorf, then bus No 115 to Pücklerstrasse, then short walk west)*. The museum is just east of the Jagdschloss Grunewald. Founders Karl Schmidt-Rottluff, Erich Heckel and Ernst Ludwig Kirchner were soon joined by other heavy-weights, including Emil Nolde, Max Pechstein and Otto Müller. Their goal was to break with the conventions of traditional art academies. Shapes and figures that teeter on the abstract – without ever quite getting there – bright, emotional colours and unusual perspective characterise their paintings. The Nazis, predictably, called this work subversive and had much of it destroyed. Fortunately, plenty survived, including 400 or so paintings and thousands of

sketches and watercolours by all major Brücke members from which this museum's changing exhibits are drawn.

Museumsdorf Düppel

Find out what a medieval village in the Berlin area might have looked like during a visit to the Museumsdorf Düppel *(Düppel Museum Village; ☎ 802 66 71, Clauertstrasse 11; adult/concession €2.50/1.25; open 3pm-7pm Thur, 10am-5pm Sun Apr-early Oct, admission til one hour before closure; S-Bahn: S1 to Mexicoplatz, then bus No 211 or 629)*. A re-creation on the grounds of an actual 12th-century settlement, it features over a dozen reed-thatched buildings surrounded by fields and woods. Museum volunteers are also engaged in protecting threatened plant species as well as breeding a special kind of local sheep called 'Skudde' and the Düppeler Weideschwein (Düppel pasture pig), both of which are endangered. Demonstrations of various old-time crafts such as blacksmithing and pottery take place on Sunday. The museum is located in Düppel, a neighbourhood in southern Zehlendorf.

Wannsee

Villa-studded Wannsee, Zehlendorf's westernmost suburb, is one of the most rewarding parts of town. The area gets its name from the Wannsee lake which consists of the Grosser Wannsee and the Kleiner Wannsee. On the shores of the latter, the Romantic poet Heinrich Kleist and his lover Henriette Vogel committed suicide in 1811. **Kleist's grave** is located on the south-eastern side of Wannsee bridge (enter at Bismarckstrasse 3).

The lake environment is a paradise for sailors, windsurfers and rowers, and the **Strandbad Wannsee**, a popular lakeside pool since 1907, provides welcome respite from the heat on summer days (see the Swimming section later in this chapter). In the northeast, the Grunewald forest hugs the lake's shore, while the **Berliner Düppel Forest** sprawls out to the west.

Cruises Various cruises leave from the docks near S-Bahn station Wannsee (S1 and S7). Children under six travel for free, those under

14 get a 50% discount. Students and seniors get 15% on weekdays.

Stern und Kreis Schifffahrt (☎ 536 36 00) cruises the Wannsee and adjacent waters between April and October.

The **Grosse Havelrundfahrt** (*Big Havel Tour, up to four times daily, €7/9 one-way/return, about 1¼hr each way*) runs from Wannsee to Kladow and Pfaueninsel to Potsdam and back.

The **7-Seen-Rundfahrt** (*Seven Lakes Tour; 2-hr tour €8, six to eight times daily*) takes you through various Havel lakes, passing by the Pfaueninsel and the Glienicke Bridge. You can get on and off as you wish.

If you just want a little spin on the water, take **Ferry No 10** which operates hourly year round (weather permitting) between Wannsee and Kladow for the price of a regular BVG ticket (€2.10).

Pfaueninsel

As if lifted from a magical fairytale, the dreamy Pfaueninsel in the Havel River is one of the most enchanting places in Berlin and great for escaping the city. The island was the romantic fantasy of King Friedrich Wilhelm III. Here, in 1797, he built a frilly little **mock-medieval palace** perfect for frolicking around with his mistress away from the curious eyes of the court. The exoticism of the exterior continues inside, which may be toured (☎ 805 30 42; adult/concession €3/2.50, includes ferry; tours 10am-5pm Tues-Sun Apr-Oct).

The prolific Peter Lenné designed the lovely gardens where the peacocks that gave the island its name still strut their stuff proudly. Since the entire place is a protected reserve, the *verboten* list is rather long and includes smoking, cycling, swimming, animals and radios. Picnicking, though, remains legal and this is a nice place to do it.

Ferries leave from the docks at the end of Nikolsloer Weg (*fare & island admission €1; boats 8am-8pm May-Aug, to 6pm Apr & Sept, 9am-5pm Mar & Oct, 10am-4pm Nov-Feb*). If you're driving, take Nikolsloer Weg (your map may show other routes but they're off limits). Bus No 216 makes the trip hourly from S-Bahn station Wannsee.

Haus der Wannsee Konferenz

In January 1942, a group of elite Nazi officials led by Reinhard Heydrich, chief of the Reich Security Main Office, met at this idyllic villa right on the lakeshore. The purpose of their gathering was to decide on the fate of the Jewish people. Debate was swift and deadly. The 'Final Solution', they agreed, would be to deport and exterminate all European Jews in a systematic and organised fashion, starting immediately.

These days, the same building is home to the **Wannsee Conference memorial exhibit** (☎ 805 00 10, Am Grossen Wannsee 56-58; admission free; open 10am-6pm Mon-Fri, 2pm-6pm Sat-Sun; S-Bahn: S1 to Wannsee, then bus No 114 right to the Haus). You can stand in the room where discussions took place and study the minutes of the conference, taken by Adolf Eichmann. Also here are the portraits and career synopses of the main perpetrators, many of whom were allowed to live to ripe old age. The rest of the exhibit chronicles, in a thorough and graphic way, the horrors leading up to and perpetrated during the Holocaust. Photographs and documents portray the ever-increasing acts of cruelty inflicted upon the Jews, from the ghettos to Auschwitz.

You must ring the bell to enter. For background information, borrow an English-language pamphlet from the desk or invest in the excellent English booklet on sale for €2.75.

Schloss Glienicke & Around

Schloss Glienicke, on Königsstrasse at the very south-western tip of Berlin, is surrounded by a romantic Lenné-landscaped park. The palace itself, a rambling cluster of buildings, got its current look from the prolific Karl Friedrich Schinkel who, in 1826, expanded the earlier structure to create a summer residence for Prince Carl of Prussia (third son of King Friedrich Wilhelm III). Inside the Schloss is an exhibit (☎ 969 42 02; adult/concession €3/2.50; open 10am-5pm Sat-Sun mid-May–mid-Oct) on the intricacies of landscape gardening and a few furnished period rooms, which are seriously skippable.

More interesting than the palace, the site of occasional concerts, is the surrounding garden. Here, Schinkel created the gazebolike **Grosse Neugierde** (Great Curiosity), inspired by the monument to Lysicrates in Athens. You'll find it in the park's southwestern corner from where it overlooks the Havel and the outskirts of Potsdam. Schinkel also converted a former billiard house into the **Kasino**, an Italian villa with a double pergola, west of the palace. The **Klosterhof** nearby consists of reassembled pieces of an Italian Carthusian monastery.

Prince Carl himself was an avid collector of antiquities and much of what you see he personally brought to Berlin (some might say, stole) from places like Pompeii and Carthage.

The palace south of Königsstrasse is the **Jagdschloss Glienicke** *(Glienicke Hunting Palace, 1682;* ☎ *80 50 10, Königstrasse 36b),* built under the Great Elector and later used as a wallpaper factory before being purchased by Prince Carl in 1859; it was he who ordered it expanded in French neobaroque style by Ferdinand von Arnim. Since the end of WWII, it has been used an international conference and education venue.

As spy novel aficionados will know, the **Glienicker Brücke** just west of the palaces was the dramatic setting of spy exchanges during the Cold War. The green steel construction spans the Havel over a length of 125m and connects Berlin with Potsdam.

To get to the park and the bridge, take the S7 to Wannsee, then via bus No 116, which runs at 20 minute intervals.

Activities

Berlin's many parks and forests are tailormade for walking and jogging. There are also dozens of pools to choose from. Soccer, volleyball, handball and other team sports are popular too, but you usually have to join a club to participate.

In the outer suburbs, you'll find large sports centres that combine, all under one roof, a pool, squash and tennis courts, fitness studio, sauna etc. One of the more central is

the Sport-und Erholungszentrum (SEZ, Map 3) in the district of Friedrichshain (see Indoor Pools later in this section), which even incorporates an ice rink.

For details about tickets to sports events (soccer, basketball, ice hockey, horse racing and more), see the Spectator Sports section in the Entertainment chapter.

CYCLING

The Berlin office of the cycling association called Allgemeiner Deutscher Fahrradclub (General German Bicycle Club, ADFC) has put out a *Radwegekarte* map that shows all bike routes in Berlin. The map costs €7.80 and is available at bookstores and at the ADFC office *(☎ 448 47 24, Brunnenstrasse 28, Mitte; open noon-8pm Mon-Fri, 10am-4pm Sat; U-Bahn: U8 to Bernauer Strasse).*

The countryside surrounding central Berlin offers many lovely cycling routes. Check at major bookshops (see the Shopping chapter) for guides with detailed route descriptions. *Mit dem Rad durch Berlin* by Peter Becker is one option, another is *Auf Tour – Ohne Auto Mobil,* published by the BVG public transport agency. See the Getting Around chapter for details on bike rentals and on taking your bike on public transport.

GYMS & FITNESS CENTRES

Berlin gyms are expensive and may not be of the same standard as you're used to back home. Many are membership-based clubs and require you to sign a contract (usually one year minimum), shell out a registration fee and pay monthly dues. The following are among the ones that sell day passes for what seems to be the going rate of €23, though some may also be willing to give you a free trial workout. It won't hurt to ask.

A women-only facility with an active fitness class schedule, weight-lifting equipment, saunas and more is **Jopp Frauen Fitness** *(☎ 21 01 11, Tauentzienstrasse 13a, Charlottenburg; open 7am-11pm Mon-Fri, 10am-8pm Sat-Sun)* **Map 6**; *(☎ 24 34 93 55, Karl-Liebknecht-Strasse 13, Mitte; open 8am-10pm Mon-Fri, 10am-5pm Sat-Sun)* **Map 7**. Check the Yellow Pages for additional branches.

What's Free

It's easy to spend a fortune in Berlin and most museums and activities will cost some money. What follows is a list of places you can go and things you can do while keeping your wallet closed. Everything is described in greater detail in this book.

Museums & Memorial Exhibits (Always Free)
- Alliierten Museum
- Abgusssammlung Antiker Plastik
- Heimatmuseum Charlottenburg
- Kreuzberg Museum
- Fragen an die Deutsche Geschichte at Deutscher Dom
- Deutsches Historisches Museum at Kronprinzenpalais
- Neue Wache
- Museum Berlin-Karlshorst
- Gedenkstätte Deutscher Widerstand
- Museum der Dinge at Martin-Gropius-Bau
- Gedenkstätte Hohenschönhausen
- Dokumentationszentrum Berliner Mauer
- Museum für Kommunikation
- Prenzlauer Berg Museum
- Haus der Wannsee Konferenz
- Willy-Brandt-Haus
- Gedenkstätte Köpenicker Blutwoche
- Museum der Verbotenen Kunst
- Wassersportmuseum in Grünau
- Gotisches Haus in Spandau
- Topographie des Terrors
- Reichstag Cupola
- Gedenkstätte Plötzensee

Museums (Occasionally Free)
- Deutsche Guggenheim Berlin – Monday
- Märkisches Museum – Wednesday
- Museum Nikolaikirche – Wednesday
- Museum Knoblauchhaus – Wednesday
- Ephraim-Palais – Wednesday
- Dorfmuseum Marzahn – Wednesday
- Domäne Dahlem – Wednesday
- All SMPK Museums – First Sunday of the month (these include the Altes Museum, Schinkelmuseum, Pergamon Museum, Hamburger Bahnhof, Gemäldegalerie, Kupferstichkabinett, Kunstgewerbemuseum, Neue Nationalgalerie, Ägyptisches Museum, Sammlung Berggruen, Alte Nationalgalerie, Museum für Vor- und Frühgeschichte, Ethnologisches Museum, Museum Europäischer Kulturen)

Entertainment
- Carillon (glockenspiel) recitals in the Tiergarten, Französischer Dom, organ recitals at the Berliner Dom
- Monday or Tuesday at the A-Trane jazz club
- Free movies at Filmriss (Entertainment chapter)
- Concerts at the Hochschule für Musik Hanns Eisler
- Tours of the Alte and Neue Staatsbibliothek

For the discerning fitness freak, there's the state-of-the-art **Healthland** (☎ *20 63 53 00, Behrenstrasse 48, Mitte; day pass €25; open 6am-11pm Mon-Fri, 10am-10pm Sat-Sun)* **Map 7**. At 2500 sq metres, it's a huge place with extensive cardio training and free weights areas. It also offers spinning classes.

In Kreuzberg 36 there is a rare German branch of the US chain, **24-Hour Fitness** (☎ *69 80 79 90, Hermannplatz 10, Kreuzberg 36)* **Map 5**. It offers all the latest equipment, free weights and fitness classes. And, as the name suggest, it's open 24/7.

Various forms of yoga classes (iyengar, asthanga, power-yoga) ensure physical and spiritual well-being at this low-key studio, **Moveo** (☎ *69 50 52 54, Am Tempelhofer Berg 7d, Kreuzberg 61)* **Map 5**. A trial class is €7.50, regular classes are €12.50. Some are even taught in English.

The granddaddy of gyms is **Gold's Gym** (☎ *442 82 94, Immanuelkirchstrasse 3-4, Prenzlauer Berg; open to 11pm Mon-Fri, to 6pm Sat-Sun)* **Map 3**. It has a weights room, aerobics classes and sauna. Take tram No 1 from U-Bahn station Rosa-Luxemburg-Platz to Knaackstrasse.

Ars Vitalis (☎ *788 35 63, Hauptstrasse 19, Schöneberg; open 8am-11.30pm daily)* **Map 4** is a modern gym with aerobics, weights and cardio training, plus sauna and pool.

ICE SKATING

Berlin has several well-maintained municipal indoor ice rinks that are usually open from mid-Oct to early March. The cost is €3/1.50 per skating session, plus €2.50 to €3.50 to rent skates. Skating periods vary with each facility but usually last three hours. Call for schedules. The rink at the SEZ (see the Indoor Pools section later in this section) is open 9am to 10pm daily between November and March (to 8pm Sun). Day admission is €3 adult/concession, plus €3 for skate rental.

Municipal rinks include the following:

Horst-Dohm-Eisstadion (☎ *823 40 60, Fritz-Wildung-Strasse 9, Wilmersdorf; U-Bahn: U1 to Heidelberger Platz)* **Map 4** Admission buys two hours of skating time.

Erika-Hess-Eisstadion (☎ 45 75 55 57, Müllerstrasse 185, Wedding; U-Bahn: U6 to Reinickendorfer Strasse) **Map 3**

Sportpark Neukölln (☎ 62 84 40 07, Oderstrasse 182, Neukölln; U-Bahn: U8 to Hermannstrasse) **Map 1**

RUNNING

Berlin is a great place for running because of its many parks. By far the most popular – because of its size and central location – is the Tiergarten, though the Volkspark Hasenheide in Neukölln, the Tegeler Forst in Tegel and the Grunewald in Wilmersdorf/Zehlendorf are also popular. The trip around the scenic Schlachtensee here is 5km. If you prefer to run in historic surroundings, try the gardens of Schloss Charlottenburg, though seasoned joggers might feel under-challenged because of its relatively small size.

SWIMMING

Berlin has plenty of outdoor and indoor pools in each district. Some may be closed on some mornings when school groups take over. Others are restricted to specific groups – women, men, nudists, seniors – at certain times of the week. Outdoor and lakeside pools are usually open 8am to 8pm daily, from May to Sept. During that time, some of the indoor pools may be closed. In general, opening hours vary by day, pool and season. For specifics, either call the pool directly or the **BBB Hotline** on ☎ 01803-10 20 20, check the German-language Web site at Ⓦ www.bbb.berlin.de, or pick up a pamphlet at any pool. Unless otherwise noted, tickets are €3.25/2.25 adult/concession.

Indoor Pools

Berlin has indoor pools, of varying standards, in just about every district.

Bad am Spreewaldplatz (☎ *69 53 52 10, Wiener Strasse 59h, Kreuzberg 36; U-Bahn: U1 or U15 to Görlitzer Bahnhof)* **Map 5** has a wave pool, water cascades and a slide in addition to a 25m lap pool. Sauna admission is adult/concession €5.50/7.50.

A modern 'fun' pool with a whole lot of attractions is **Blub Badeparadies** (☎ *60 90 60, Buschkrugallee 64, Neukölln; 4hr admission adult/concession €11/9, day pass €13/11.50;*

open 10am-11pm; U-Bahn: U7 to Grenzallee). There is a wave pool, a waterfall, a 120m slide, a saltwater pool, hot whirlpools, sauna landscape and restaurants.

Sport- und Erholungszentrum *(SEZ Sports Centre, ☎ 42 18 23 20, Landsberger Allee 77, Friedrichshain; pool admission adult/concession €5.25/2.75 for 2½ hours, €3.25/1.75 for 1½ hours, €4.25/2.25 7pm-10pm; S-Bahn: S8 or S10 to Landsberger Allee)* **Map 3** is a mega sports facility encompassing seven pools (including a wave pool) and a slide. The complex also houses an ice-skating rink and a fitness studio. Sauna admission is an extra €5/7.50 adult/concession.

Try the two pools at **Stadtbad Charlottenburg** *(Alte Halle ☎ 34 38 38 60, Neue Halle ☎ 34 38 38 65, Krumme Strasse 10; U-Bahn: U2 or U7 to Bismarckstrasse)* **Map 2**. Its Alte Halle (Old Hall) is one of the world's few pools that's also a protected monument. With its Art Nouveau ceiling and colourful tiles dating back to 1898, it definitely has museum character, a 25m pool with warmish water (28°C) and a sauna. (During nude bathing on Tuesday, Wednesday and Friday nights, the place is crawling with gay men.) The modern Neue Halle (New Hall) is more suited for serious swimmers and has a 50m lap pool. Sauna admission is €11.50.

Stadtbad Mitte is in a renovated 1928 Bauhaus structure *(☎ 30 88 09 10, Gartenstrasse 5; S-Bahn: S1 or S2 to Nordbahnhof)* **Map 3**. This place has a 50m lap pool; it feels like swimming in a glass cube. The water is kept at 28°C.

Stadtbad Neukölln was called the most beautiful pool in Europe at its opening in 1914 *(☎ 68 24 98 11, Ganghoferstrasse 3; admission to sauna area adult/concession €13/11; U-Bahn: U7 to Rathaus Neukölln)* **Map 5**. It's one of Berlin's most impressive bathing temples with mosaics and frescoes, marble and brass. There are 25m and 20m pools. The sauna area also has a dry sauna, Russian-Roman bath and steamroom (separate admission, €10/12.50 adult/concession).

Outdoor & Lakeside Pools

One of the great summer delights in landlocked Berlin is its many lakes. Swimming is

allowed but if you prefer some amenities try one of the public lakeside pools listed below. Sommerbad Kreuzberg and Sommerbad Olympia-Stadion are regular outdoor pools that are central if you just want a chance to cool off quickly.

Freibad Halensee is well situated in a forest *(☎ 891 17 03, Königsallee 5a, Wilmersdorf)* **Map 4**. This lakeside pool is popular with those who prefer to do their swimming *au naturel*. It is occasionally closed for poor water quality. To get here take bus No 115 to Herbertstrasse. Coming from Kurfürstendamm, walk down Bornstedter Strasse, then via a pedestrian bridge across the autobahn.

Sommerbad Olympia-Stadion was built for the 1936 Olympic Games *(☎ 30 06 34 40, Olympischer Platz, Osttor (eastern gate), Charlottenburg; U-Bahn: U2 to Olympia-Stadion Ost)*. You can do your laps in the same 50m pool where top athletes have swum. You'll be watched by oversized sculptures and four gigantic clocks.

The most central, multicultural and popular facility is **Sommerbad Kreuzberg** *(☎ 616 10 80, Prinzenstrasse 113-119, Kreuzberg 36)* **Map 5**. Better known as Prinzenbad (Princes' Pool), this is often crawling with hormone-crazed teenagers. There are two 50m pools, a slide and a nudist section.

Strandbad Müggelsee has a nice sandy beach and is idyllically located on the Müggelsee's eastern shore *(☎ 648 77 77, Fürstenwalder Damm 838, Köpenick; S-Bahn: S3 to Friedrichshagen, then tram No 61 to Strandbad Müggelsee)*. It's especially suitable for children because of its sandy beach and flat water with reasonable quality.

Claiming to be the largest lakeside pool in Europe, **Strandbad Wannsee** has been in business since 1907 *(☎ 803 56 12, Wannseebadweg 25, Zehlendorf; S-Bahn: S1, S3 or S7 to Nikolassee, then bus No 513 to Strandbad Wannsee)*. Often referred to as Berlin's 'Lido', its kilometre of sandy beach are about as crowded as the real thing in Italy. Besides swimming, you can rent boats, take an exercise class, eat and drink at several restaurants or relax in a giant wicker chair typically found at German coastal resorts. The water quality is decent.

Saunas

Germans are far from prudish and saunas are usually mixed and nude, so check your modesty at the reception desk. There are, however, hours set aside for women only, so call ahead to find out those times. The cheapest saunas are those at public pools (see Swimming – Indoor Pools earlier in this section).

Privately operated facilities usually have more amenities and may even be luxurious.

The *Thermen am Europa-Center* (☎ 257 57 60, *Nürnberger Strasse 7; one hour €9.20, additional hour €4.10, day admission €17.90; open 10am-midnight Mon-Sat, 10am-9pm Sun)* **Map 6** is a stylish facility next to the Gedächtniskirche. It incorporates nine saunas, indoor and outdoor pools filled with salt-rich thermal waters, fitness rooms, restaurants and a terrace for tanning.

Hamam (☎ 615 14 64, *Mariannenstrasse 6, Kreuzberg; admission €6 for 1 hour, €9 for 2½ hours; open noon-10pm Tues-Sun, 3pm-10pm Mon)* **Map 5** is a Turkish-style bathhouse downstairs from the Schoko Café open to women only. Relax in the steam room or enjoy some of the beauty services.

TENNIS & SQUASH

Most of the larger racquet-sports centres are in the suburbs and are generally inconvenient to reach by public transport.

One of the largest and more central ones is **Tennis & Squash City** (☎ 873 90 97, *Brandenburgische Strasse 53, Wilmersdorf; open 7am-1am daily; U-Bahn: U7 to Konstanzer Strasse)* **Map 6**. Prices vary according to court, time of day and day of the week but range from €12 to €30 for one hour of tennis and from €5 to €16 for 45 minutes of squash. There's also a solarium and a sauna.

Tennis, Squash und Fitnesscenter (☎ 333 40 83, *Galenstrasse 33, Spandau; U-Bahn: U7 to Rathaus Spandau)* offers indoor tennis and squash courts, plus sauna, solarium and a fitness studio.

For squash fans only, a good central option is **Fit Fun** (☎ 312 50 82, *Uhlandstrasse*

194; rates from adult/concession €10/6; open 9am-midnight)* **Map 6**. Its 13 courts are often busy with students from the nearby Technical University.

COURSES
Language

The Goethe Institut promotes German language and culture abroad. It is a nonprofit, government-subsidised cultural and language organisation that also offers German language courses in various cities, including Berlin.

The Berlin branch of the **Goethe Institut** (☎ 25 90 63, *fax 25 90 64 00, Neue Schönhauser Strasse 20, Mitte)* **Map 7** offers courses for all age groups and stages of proficiency – from absolute beginner to professional level. The program is run on three general levels of proficiency: *Grundstufe* (basic), *Mittelstufe* (intermediate) and *Oberstufe* (advanced); each is further divided into sublevels.

Intensive courses cost from around €1546 to €1602 (eight weeks), €862 to €878 (four weeks) and €694 (two weeks), excluding accommodation and meals. The institute also runs three-week **summer programs** for children and youths aged 10 to 20 years from €1750 including accommodation and meals. Courses are offered throughout the year, but it's best to contact the Goethe Institute directly to find out the specific dates. The staff in the Berlin office are knowledgeable, helpful to a fault and speak excellent English. You can find detailed information on the Internet at **W** www.goethe.de.

A private school teaching German to foreigners that seems to get high marks is the **Europa Sprachenschule** *(Europe Language School;* ☎ 618 88 63, *fax 618 95 57, Taborstrasse 17, Kreuzberg 36; U-Bahn: Schlesisches Tor)* **Map 4**. It offers weekly intensive courses at beginner and advanced levels from €33 (groups up to 15 students) to €90 (groups of five). Other options are available too. For more information, contact the school.

Places to Stay

Berlin attracts a growing number of visitors each year, so at times it can get a little squeezy. It's a good idea to make reservations during the peak months (May to September). The flow thins considerably from November to March when rates may drop and special deals abound. Prices skyrocket again around the holidays (Christmas and New Year), during major events like the Love Parade in July and big trade shows like the International Tourism Fair in early March.

With more than 62,000 beds, Berlin offers the entire gamut of lodging options – hostels to luxury abodes – and, compared to other European capitals remains relatively affordable. New places open up all the time, especially in popular districts like Mitte and Prenzlauer Berg where demand still exceeds availability. Most of these are in the midrange to top-end categories, although there are plenty of independent hostels as well. Now, though, you'll find greater selection and better prices at long-established hotels and pensions in the western districts of Charlottenburg and Wilmersdorf.

Many small hotels and pensions take up one or several floors of historic apartment buildings. Usually you will have to ring the street-level bell to get in. Since many of these family-run places are not staffed around the clock, make a quick call to ensure that someone will be there when you arrive. Upon checking in, you should be given a set of keys (sometimes a deposit is charged) so you can let yourself in at any time.

Some of the older places – especially those converted from large apartments – have rooms with various levels of comfort. While some have private bathrooms (shower or tub and toilet), others may require you to share amenities with other guests. Occasionally, rooms have a private shower but no toilet. This set-up is the reason why there's often such a big range in room rates.

Germany's reputation for cleanliness extends to accommodation; even budget places are usually spotlessly clean. Television and direct-dial phones (or even in-room phones) are not standard services in older hotels, so check ahead if this is important to you. Lifts, on the other hand, are not as rare as you might think and are often of the quaint 'bird-cage' variety.

A wonderful feature of German hotels and pensions is that room rates almost always include breakfast, usually in the form of a lavish buffet with cheeses and cold cuts, jams and honey, various breads and rolls, a choice of cereals and unlimited coffee or tea. Since these are all-you-can-eat affairs, they can easily keep you fed until mid-afternoon. Unless noted, all room rates quoted below include breakfast.

Occasionally you'll find hotels and pensions tucked away in a rear building of a sprawling 19th-century tenement complex. There's usually a bell but no intercom, so you either have to navigate using the layout sketches by the main gate or, better yet, call ahead and ask the proprietor to meet you downstairs.

If you're driving, note that most central hotels don't have a parking lot. Street parking may be elusive, requiring you to leave your car in an expensive public garage (about €13 per night) that may even be located quite a distance from the hotel. Top-end hotels may have their own lots or valet parking, though in either case this will still add around €13 per day to your hotel bill.

Note that this chapter is particularly vulnerable to changes that may occur spontaneously as rooms are renovated, managers switch jobs and independent hotels are bought out by chains. All rates quoted below, therefore, serve merely as guidelines.

CAMPING

Camping facilities in Berlin are neither plentiful nor particularly convenient. All are far from the city centre and complicated to reach unless you're motorised. They fill up quickly, with a lot of space taken up by RVs (recreational vehicles). Call ahead to inquire about vacancy. Office hours at all camping grounds are from 7am to 1pm and from 3pm to 9pm daily. For specifics, contact the Deutscher Campingclub (☎ 218 60 71) at Geisbergstrasse 11 in Schöneberg.

These two camping grounds are relatively convenient to public transport.

Campingplatz Kohlhasenbrück (☎ *805 17 37, Neue Kreisstrasse 36, Zehlendorf*) S-Bahn: No 7 to Griebnitzsee. Person €5, tent €3.50-6.50. Open Mar-Oct. This camping ground is in a peaceful location near a nature preserve overlooking the Griebnitzsee, about 15km south-west of the western centre. From Griebnitzsee station, it's a 10-minute walk. Alternatively, get off at the previous stop, Wannsee, and take bus No 118, which runs directly to the camping ground.

Campingplatz Dreilinden (☎ *805 12 01, Albrechts-Teerofen, Zehlendorf*) Person €5, tent €3.50-6.50. Open Mar-Oct. If Kohlhasenbrück is full, this camping ground is 2km to the east along the Teltow Canal at Albrechts-Teerofen. It's 30 minutes on foot from the Griebnitzsee S-Bahn and 20 minutes to the nearest bus station (No 118), which runs from Wannsee station.

Getting to Berlin's other camping grounds will require at least two changes on public transport.

Campingplatz Kladow (☎ *365 27 97, fax 365 12 45, Krampnitzer Weg 111-117*) Person €5, tent €3.50-6.50. Open year-round. This place is 18km west of the western city centre and caters for both tents and caravans. If you are on the U-Bahn, catch the U7 to Rathaus Spandau. Change from bus No 134 at Alt-Kladow to bus No 234, which goes to the camping ground.

Campingplatz Gatow (☎ *36 54 340, fax 36 80 84 92, Kladower Damm 207-213*) Person €5, tent €3.50-6.50. This alternative, near Campingplatz Kladow, is also served by bus No 134. It's quiet and has well-maintained facilities.

Campingplatz Am Krossinsee (☎ *675 86 87, fax 675 91 50, Wernsdorfer Strasse 45, Köpenick*) Person €5, tent €3.50-6.50.

Open year-round. These grounds are 35km south-east of the city centre. Take the S8 to Grünau, then tram No 68 to Schmückwitz and from here, bus No 755 to Königs Wusterhausen. Once there, you'll be camping on woodsy lakeside grounds with a full roster of amenities, including boat and bike rental.

HOSTELS
DJH Hostels
Berlin's three DJH hostels are open all day year-round but fill up quickly on weekends and throughout summer. In spring and autumn, they're often booked out by noisy school groups.

All require DJH (W www.djh-ris.de) or HI membership cards; see Hostel Cards in the Facts for the Visitor chapter if you don't already have one. None have cooking facilities, but rates include breakfast with lunch and dinner available for an extra fee. To make reservations, contact the hostels directly.

Jugendherberge Berlin International (☎ *261 10 97, fax 265 03 83,* e *jh-berlin@ jugendherberge.de, Kluckstrasse 3, Tiergarten*) **Map 4** U-Bahn: U1/15 to Kurfürstenstrasse. Beds in 4-bed & 5-bed dorms juniors/seniors €18.50/22.50. The most central of the DJH hostels has 350 beds, a small cinema, 24-hour drinks and snack service, and Internet access.

Jugendherberge Ernst Reuter (☎ *404 16 10, fax 404 59 72,* e *jh-ernst-reuter@ jugendherberge.de, Hermsdorfer Damm 48-50, Tegel*) off **Map 1** U-Bahn: Alt-Tegel, then bus No 125 to the door. Beds in 6-bed dorms juniors/seniors €14.30/17.90, curfew 1am. This remote hostel has a TV room, Internet access and various other low-key amusements like table-tennis and board games.

Jugendgästehaus am Wannsee (☎ *803 20 34, fax 803 59 08,* e *jh-wannsee@ jugendherberge.de, Badeweg 1, cnr Kronprinzessinnenweg, Zehlendorf*) S-Bahn: Nikolassee. Beds in 4-bed rooms juniors/seniors €17.90/22. This 264-bed option is in a pleasant if far-flung location on the Grosser Wannsee lake, about 20km southwest of central Berlin. From the S-Bahn station, walk west over the footbridge, turn left at Kronprinzessinnenweg and the hostel will be in sight on the right. This should take no more than 10 minutes. The entire trip from the city centre takes about 45 minutes.

Independent Hostels & Guesthouses

DJH cards are not needed for any of the hostels below. None have curfews and several are run by ex-backpackers who have travelled extensively, know what people want and need, and are extremely savvy and well informed about Berlin.

Charlottenburg *Jugendhotel Berlin (☎ 322 10 11, fax 322 10 12, e info@jugendhotel -berlin.de, Kaiserdamm 3)* **Map 4** Singles/ doubles/triples with bathrooms €24-29 per person, including breakfast, sheets €3.50 for stays under 3 nights. This facility caters primarily to those under 27 but will accept older people on a space-available basis at higher rates ranging from €46 to €90.

Friedrichshain This newly happening district has sprouted several convivial hostels with staff who can make you feel 'plugged in' to Berlin within a day or two.

A&O Backpackers (☎ 29 00 73 65 or 01805-HOSTEL, Boxhagener Strasse 73) **off Map 5** S-Bahn: Ostkreuz. Beds in 4-bed to 10-bed dorms €11.50-13.50, doubles €36, linen €2, breakfast €3. This hostel has a better than average roster of services and facilities, including bike rental, banking, laundry and a beer garden.

Odyssee Globetrotter Hostel (☎/fax 29 00 00 81, e odyssee@hostel-berlin.de, Grün- berger Strasse 23, 2nd backyard, 1st floor) **Map 5** U/S-Bahn: Warschauer Strasse (then a 5-min walk north). Bus: Nos 240 or 147 from Ostbahnhof. Dorm beds €12.50-16.50 per person, singles/doubles with shower €33/49, sheets included, various discounts available. This hostel is run by four young guys who grew up in pre-Wende East Berlin (and can tell a tale or two about those days). Rooms are imaginatively decorated, clean and have lockers. Check-out is at a civilised 1pm and the breakfast buffet costs just €3. The reception area doubles as a lively bar-lounge (both open 24 hours) with pool table

and cheap beers (yes, the parties are legendary). The reviews from readers and travellers have all been positive.

Pegasus Hostel (☎ 29 35 18 10, fax 29 35 11 66, e hostel@pegasushostel.de, Strasse der Pariser Kommune 35) **Map 3** U-Bahn: U5 to Weberwiese, S-Bahn: S3, S5, S7, S9 to Ostbahnhof. Dorm beds €12.50-15, singles/ doubles €26/37, linen €2, breakfast €4. Formerly Frederik's Hostel, this sprawling place in a former Jewish girls' school has sunny, quiet and renovated rooms with sinks, a fully equipped kitchen and Internet access. In summer, the back courtyard is used for barbecue parties.

The Sunflower Hostel (☎ 44 04 42 50, e hostel@sunflower-berlin.de, Helsingforser Strasse 17) **Map 5** U/S-Bahn: Warschauer Strasse. Dorm beds €13-17.50, singles/ doubles €33/40, doubles with shower €48, linen free, breakfast €2.50. This place is also brought to you by the folks of the Odyssee and has the same fun atmosphere and an even better location. There's a bar on the ground floor and nicely painted rooms as well.

Kreuzberg *BaxPax (☎ 69 51 83 22, fax 69 51 83 72, e info@baxpax.de, Skalitzer Strasse 104)* **Map 5** U-Bahn: Görlitzer Bahnhof. Dorm beds €12.50-16, singles/ doubles/triples/quads €28/42/58/72, linen €2. A fairly recent arrival on the hostel scene, this place distinguishes itself with quirky themed rooms (one has GDR paraphernalia, another a bed in an old VW Beetle etc) and a large well-equipped kitchen with terrace. The dorms sleep up to eight people.

Die Fabrik (☎ 611 71 16, fax 618 29 74, e info@diefabrik.com, Schlesische Strasse 18) **Map 5** U-Bahn: Schlesisches Tor. Dorm beds €15.50, singles/doubles/triples/quads from €33/48/61.50/74. Die Fabrik is housed on five floors (no lift) of a former telephone factory. The cheapest beds are in a giant dorm on the ground floor, but smaller rooms are also available for those in need of more privacy. Breakfast (not included) is served at the downstairs cafe called Eisenwaren.

Gästehaus Freiraum (☎ 618 20 08, fax 618 20 06, Wiener Strasse 14, Kreuzberg 36) **Map 5** U-Bahn: U1/12/15 to Görlitzer

Bahnhof. Singles/doubles/triples/quads €22.50/42.50/50/55. This small guesthouse is in a quiet rear courtyard of a renovated turn-of-the-20th-century building and has modern rooms with shared bathrooms and larger apartments with kitchen, TV and private bath. Actual prices depend on the number of people and the length of your stay. Ask about discounts. The guesthouse is attached to a Mitwohnzentrale and is near cafes and nightlife.

Jugendgästehaus Schreberjugend (☎ 615 10 07, fax 61 40 11 50, Franz-Künstler-Strasse 4-10) **Map 5** U-Bahn: U6 or U15 to Hallesches Tor. Beds in 2-bed or 3-bed rooms €20, including breakfast, linen €3 for stays under three nights. This place has 124 rooms and is in a quiet street near the new Jewish Museum.

Hotel Transit (☎ 789 04 70, fax 78 90 47 77, e welcome@hotel-transit.de, Hagelberger Strasse 53-54) **Map 5** Dorm beds €18, singles/doubles/triples/quads with shower €50/57.50/75/100, breakfast included. A school-group favourite, the Transit is also popular with backpackers. Rooms are large, clean and all have a table, safe, stove and sink. It has Internet access and a large communal cafe area with TV.

Mitte *Circus – The Hostel* (☎ 28 39 14 33, fax 28 39 14 84, e info@circus-berlin.de, Rosa-Luxemburg-Strasse 39-41) **Map 3** U-Bahn: U2 to Rosa-Luxemburg-Platz. Beds in 5- or 6-bed room €12.50, singles/doubles/triples/quads €25/20/17.50/15 per person, linen €2. Beg, borrow and/or lie to secure a bed at this hostel. The staff are particularly friendly and helpful, and dorms and public areas are cheerfully painted and clean. Small groups and/or couples might prefer the apartments with private bathroom, kitchen and nice furnishings. Breakfast (not included) is served in the streetside cafe.

Clubhouse Hostel (☎ 28 09 79 79, fax 28 09 79 77, e mailto@clubhouse-berlin.de, Kalkscheunenstrasse 4-5) **Map 3** U/S-Bahn: Friedrichstrasse. Dorm beds €13-15, singles/doubles/triples €25/20/17.50 per person, linen €2, breakfast buffet €3.50. Above the Kalkscheune cultural centre, this place has

quickly developed loyal fans with its friendly staff, central location and large clean rooms.

Mitte's Backpacker Hostel (☎ 28 39 09 65, fax 28 39 09 35, e info@backpacker.de, Chausseestrasse 102) **Map 3** U-Bahn: U6 to Zinnowitzer Strasse. Dorm beds €12-15, doubles/triples/quads €21/19/18 per person. Imaginative and artsy decor make this popular hostel stand out. It attracts a gregarious crowd and a party atmosphere often prevails. Extra services include bike rental (€5 per day), a daily English newspaper, a communal kitchen and Internet access.

Prenzlauer Berg *Lette 'm Sleep* (☎ 44 73 36 23, fax 44 73 36 25, e info@backpackers .de, Lettestrasse 7) **Map 3** U-Bahn: U2 to Eberswalder Strasse. Beds in 3-bed to 6-bed dorms €13-17.50, doubles with kitchenette €45. This friendly, laid-back hostel has a small communal kitchen and TV room and a beer garden in the back. Dorms have sinks and lockers, and Internet access is free. The place has received ringing endorsements from readers who have called it 'spotlessly clean' and 'the most friendly'. It's a five-minute walk from the U-Bahn station and in the midst of a happening nightlife area.

Schöneberg *Studentenhotel Meininger 10* (☎ 78 71 74 14, fax 78 71 74 12, e info@ studentenhotel.de, Meininger Strasse 10) **Map 4** U-Bahn: U4 to Rathaus Schöneberg. Dorm beds €12.50, singles/doubles/triples/quads €30/44/60/80, including breakfast and linen. Despite the name, nonstudents are welcome at this recently revamped place with fee-based Internet, lounge, 24-hour reception and other services.

Jugendgästehaus des CVJM (☎ 264 91 00, fax 261 43 08, e jgh@cvjm-berlin.de, Einemstrasse 10) **Map 4** U-Bahn: U2 or U1/15 to Nollendorfplatz. Beds €20-30. The German YMCA has flat rates for beds in doubles or multi-bed rooms with shared bathrooms.

Tegel The district of Tegel is about 12km north-west of Zoo station.

Backpacker's Paradise (formerly Internationales Jugendcamp Fliesstal; ☎ 433 86 40, *fax 434 50 63, Ziekowstrasse 161)* **off Map 1** U-Bahn: U6 to Alt-Tegel, then bus 222 to Titusweg. Tent space €5, including blankets, foam mattresses and showers; open late June-Aug. If you're on a really tight budget and don't mind 'roughing it', head for the big tent with room for 260. Inexpensive food and self-catering facilities are available, as is Internet access and bike rental. Getting here is quite a haul, though.

Jugendgästehaus Tegel (☎ 433 30 46, fax 434 50 63, Ziekowstrasse 161) **off Map 1** Beds in 3-bed to 8-bed rooms €19, including breakfast and linen. The big Backpacker's Paradise tent is right behind this 220-bed hostel, housed in a stately, redbrick building.

Tiergarten *Haus Wichern (☎ 395 40 72, fax 396 50 92, Waldenser Strasse 31)* **Map 2** U-Bahn: U9 to Turmstrasse. Doubles/quads €23 per person, sheets €3 for stays under 3 nights. Close to the historic Arminius market hall in Tiergarten-Moabit, this contemporary and clean guesthouse is in a neat building with muralled facades depicting various crafts and trades.

Wedding *BDP Gaeste Etage (☎ 493 10 70, fax 494 10 63, Osloer Strasse 12)* **off Map 2** U-Bahn: U8 or U9 to Osloer Strasse. Beds in 2-bed to 9-bed rooms €14, breakfast €1.50-3, linen €4. Run by the Association of German Girl Scouts, this smallish place with 14 rooms has a self-catering kitchen, although you can also order a continental breakfast.

Wilmersdorf *Jugendgästehaus Central (☎ 873 01 88, fax 861 34 85, e jugend.hotel -central@snafu.de, Nikolsburger Strasse 2-4)* **Map 6** U-Bahn: Hohenzollernplatz or Güntzelstrasse. Dorm beds €20 per person, including breakfast, sheets €3.50 for stays under 3 nights. This is an enormous, 450-bed place which goes for the school-group clientele.

Studentenhotel Hubertusallee (☎ 891 97 18, fax 892 86 98, e studentenhotel.hubertus-berlin@t-online.de, Delbrückstrasse 24) **Map 4** Singles/doubles/triples with bathroom

€40/55/65, students €24/35/45, including breakfast. Open Mar-Oct. This hostel is near the Hubertussee lake. From Ku'damm, catch bus No 119 (going west) to the Hasensprung stop or bus No 129 to the Delbrückstrasse stop.

Jugendgästehaus St-Michaels-Heim (☎ 89 68 80, fax 89 68 81 85, Bismarckallee 23) **off Map 4** Beds €17-19 per person. This recent arrival has 35 modern and friendly rooms with shared showers and is located on the Herthasee lake. At the attached hotel, singles/doubles start at €60/75. There's also a self-service restaurant with terrace.

Jugendhotel Vier Jahreszeiten (☎ 873 20 14/17, fax 873 82 23, Bundesallee 31a) **Map 4** U-Bahn: Güntzelstrasse. Beds in 1-bed to 6-bed rooms €20, including breakfast. School groups love this place. During downtime (usually November to February), rates may drop by €4 per person per night.

PRIVATE ROOMS

Berlin's tourist office, the BTM, no longer books private rooms, but several private agencies specialise in this kind of thing. One option is *Bed & Breakfast in Berlin (☎ 44 05 05 82, fax 44 05 05 83, e bedbreakfa@ aol.com, Tietjenstrasse 36)* in Tempelhof. Owner Bernd Rother can find you singles/ doubles/triples from €27.50/43/68, including breakfast and commission but not the 16% VAT.

Other agencies worth trying include *Agentur Wohnwitz (☎ 861 82 22, fax 861 91 92, Holsteinische Strasse 55)* in Wilmersdorf and *Berliner Zimmer (☎ 312 50 03, fax 312 50 13, Goethestrasse 58)* in Charlottenburg.

HOTELS
Bookings

The BTM (☎ 25 00 25, W www.btm.de) handles room reservations for its partner hotels only. Reservations can be made in person at the tourist office branches at the Europa-Center and the Brandenburger Tor (see the Tourist Offices section in the Facts for the Visitor chapter for addresses).

For private booking services you can try Berlin-Direkt-Touristik (toll-free ☎ 0130-21 30 or ☎ 787 77 70, fax 78 77 77 89,

e berlin-direkt@t-online.de) at Feurigstrasse 27 in Schöneberg, which can make free reservations at its 250 member hotels (covering all price categories). Another option is Reservierungsdienst (☎ 822 18 79, fax 821 02 92) at Blissestrasse 62 in Wilmersdorf.

You can also contact hotels or pensions directly (phone, fax and email provided where available) though you may be quoted the most expensive room first. Make it a habit to ask if a cheaper room or rate is available – there often is.

Most of the smaller, independent hotels and pensions don't accept credit-card reservations and may require a down payment by money order or bank draft. There's usually no funny business involved with this kind of thing, but always ask for a written confirmation of your booking and prepayment.

If you're asked to specify your arrival time, be sure to stick to it (or call if you're delayed). Otherwise, if you haven't prepaid anything, you may find that your room has been given to someone else.

Hotels – Budget
Rooms in this category (doubles for €80 or less) have few frills and you'll likely have to share a bathroom, though most usually have an in-room sink. Many places listed here also have larger, more expensive rooms with private bathrooms and more amenities.

Charlottenburg *Hotel Berolina* (☎ 32 70 90 72, fax 32 70 90 73, **e** hotel-pension-berolina@t-online.de, Stuttgarter Platz 17) **Map 6** Singles/doubles/triples/quads €31/41/47/52, breakfast €6 per person. This friendly but old-fashioned pension offers basic accommodation with shared facilities at very acceptable prices. The area is not the most savoury, but the Messe is just a short ride on the S-Bahn.

City Pension Berlin (☎ 327 74 10, fax 324 50 08, **e** city-pension-berlin@t-online.de, Stuttgarter Platz 9) **Map 6** Singles/doubles/triples/quads with shower €32/48/68/75. A few doors down, this family-run place has 20 large, pleasantly furnished rooms with TV and dataport telephones. The helpful owners operate a small private bar

and, if hunger strikes, can also whip up some simple snacks.

Hotel Crystal (☎ 312 90 47, fax 312 64 65, Kantstrasse 144) **Map 6** Singles €35-61, doubles €46-76. Not all rooms are created equal at the Crystal, so inspect before you commit. For a quiet room, ask for one in the back. One reader reported that 'staff are very friendly' and the breakfast 'excellent.'

Pension Fischer (☎ 218 68 08, fax 213 42 25, Nürnberger Strasse 24a) **Map 6** Singles €25.50-36, doubles €36-66. The decor in the 10 rooms may give you '70s flashbacks but who's to complain at these prices? The cheaper rooms share facilities. Breakfast is €5 per person.

Herberge Grosse (☎ 324 81 38, fax 32 76 46 17, **e** berlin@herbergegrosse.de, Kantstrasse 71, 4th floor) **Map 6** U-Bahn: U7 to Wilmerdorfer Strasse. Singles & doubles €55, triples €75 (€12 surcharge for one-night stays), breakfast €8 per person. With three rooms, this place is pretty intimate and feels more like staying at a friend's house. Bathrooms are shared, and guests may use the kitchen and washing machine. Rooms have Scandinavian furniture, direct-dial phones and cable TV; there's free Internet access, bike rentals and a shuttle service to Zoo station, Tegel airport and the ZOB. This one's a winner – if you can snag a room.

Pension Knesebeck (☎ 312 72 55, fax 313 95 07, Knesebeckstrasse 86) **Map 6** Singles/doubles €35/60, with shower €50/75, breakfast €6. Furnishings are eclectic but comfortable at this popular pension run by a friendly proprietor.

Pension München (☎ 85 79 120, fax 85 79 12 22, **e** hotel-pension.muenchen@arcormail.de, Güntzelstrasse 62, 3rd floor) **Map 6** Singles/doubles €33/66, with bath €53/81. This artist-owned pension has lots of character and eight cheerfully decorated rooms with modern amenities. Breakfast is served in a nicely tiled lounge.

Hotel-Pension Majesty (☎ 323 20 61, fax 323 20 63, Mommsenstrasse 55) **Map 6** Singles/doubles €41/51, with shower €56/84. With only four rooms, this place is short on privacy but long on charm. Rooms are tastefully appointed in contemporary style.

Pension Peters (☎ *312 22 78, fax 312 35 19,* e *penspeters@aol.com, Kantstrasse 146)* **Map 6** Singles/doubles €35/51, with bath €56/66. This eight-room pension is nicely furnished with warm lighting, Nordic-style furniture and tasteful artwork.

Pension Viola Nova (☎ *313 14 57, fax 312 33 14,* e *email@violanova.de, Kantstrasse 146)* **Map 6** Singles/doubles €45/60, with shower €55/75, with bath €65/80. Owner Helga Kammertöns tries to match her guests' budget to the room, which is why her snug pension near fashionable Savignyplatz attracts a varied clientele from backpackers to business folk. Rooms are sizeable and have parquet floors and stucco ceilings.

Kreuzberg **Hotel am Anhalter Bahnhof** (☎ *251 03 42, fax 251 48 97,* e *hotel-abb@t-online.de, Stresemannstrasse 36, Kreuzberg 61)* **Map 5** Beds in 5-bed & 6-bed dorms €20.45. Singles/doubles €41/56, with bathroom €61/81. Triples/quads €76/81. Choose from a variety of comfort levels at this friendly pension with an international flair. Rooms sprawl over three floors; pricier ones with private facilities face away from the street. It's fairly close to Potsdamer Platz and the Jewish Museum.

Gasthaus Dietrich Herz (☎ *691 70 43/44, fax 693 11 73, Marheinekeplatz 15)* **Map 5** Singles €45-65, doubles €65-75, breakfast €5. Schnitzel fumes may waft in your window if you're staying at this hotel-restaurant right in the heart of Kreuzberg 61's entertainment district. Some of the 16 homely rooms even have a balcony. Those facing the square are quieter and more expensive.

Pension Kreuzberg (☎ *251 13 62, fax 251 06 38, Grossbeerenstrasse 64)* **Map 5** Dorm beds €21 per person, singles/doubles €40/50. This plain, friendly place caters primarily for backpackers, as is reflected in the low prices.

Mitte **Artist Hotelpension Die Loge** (☎/fax *280 75 13,* e *die-loge@t-online.de, Friedrichstrasse 115)* **Map 3** Singles/doubles €35/56, with bath €51/71, breakfast €6. This pension offers one of the best deals in town, which is why its seven rooms are often booked far in advance. All are equipped with modern amenities and are nicely furnished. The affable young couple who run the place even serve up a romantic candlelit breakfast but only after 11am. Wait for it!

Hotel Honigmond (☎ *284 45 50, fax 28 44 55 11, Tieckstrasse 12)* **Map 3** Singles/doubles €35/50, with bath €50/76, breakfast not included. Upstairs from a traditional restaurant in a 1899 building is this new pension with stucco ceilings, hardwood floors and nicely furnished, clean rooms. In GDR times, the downstairs restaurant, then called Borsig-Eck, was a popular gathering place for dissidents.

Hotel-Pension Merkur (☎ *282 82 97, fax 282 77 65, Torstrasse 156)* **Map 3** Singles/doubles €35/51, with bath €76/85. This family-operated pension is within walking distance of Mitte's most happening nightlife. It's in a ratty-looking building but rooms are adequate.

Pension mitArt (☎ *28 39 04 30, fax 28 39 04 32,* e *mitart@t-online.de, Friedrichstrasse 127)* **Map 3** Singles €49, doubles €66-80. This tiny place has a friendly proprietor and is associated with a contemporary art gallery. More art decorates rooms and public areas, creating a homely feel. Each of the six rooms has hardwood floors and is simply but lovingly furnished.

Prenzlauer Berg **Hotel Transit Loft** (☎ *789 04 70, fax 78 90 47 77,* e *loft@hotel-transit .de, Greifswalder Strasse 219, enter from Immanuelkirchstrasse 14)* **Map 3** Tram: No 2, 3 or 4 to Hufelandstrasse. Dorm beds €19.50, singles/doubles/triples/quads €60/70/90/120. This brand-new hotel has functionally furnished, well-lit rooms with private facilities. It occupies the 3rd and 4th floors of a former warehouse and also has a large dorm for backpackers.

Schöneberg & Tiergarten **Hotel Gunia** (☎ *218 59 40, fax 218 59 44,* e *hotelgunia@ t-online.de, Eisenacher Strasse 10, Schöneberg)* **Map 4** Singles/doubles €40/66, with bath €76/92. This friendly hotel is in a historic building in the heart of the area's gay quarter.

Hotel Les Nations (☎ *392 20 26, fax 392 50 10,* e *les-nations-berlin@t-online.de, Zinzendorfstrasse 6, Tiergarten)* **Map 2** Singles/doubles €45/80, with bath €85/110. This place draws young international travellers with its modern and comfortable rooms. Some are nonsmoking and there's parking on the premises. Rates drop considerably in the off-season.

Wilmersdorf *Pension Curtis* (☎ *883 49 31, fax 885 04 38, Pariser Strasse 39-40, 2nd floor)* **Map 6** Singles/doubles with shower from €38/61. This small and friendly place has discounts for longer stays. If it's fully booked, there are three other pensions offering similar rates in the same building – Austriana, Rügen and Marco Polo.

Hotels – Mid-Range
Hotels in this category (doubles €80 to €140) are comfortable without being formal and usually small enough to offer personal attention. Most rooms more or less meet modern standards, although you may not always find the full range of amenities, especially in older hotels. In-room telephones and TV are likely, and extras like hairdryers and ironing boards are becoming more common as hoteliers are increasingly trying to meet international expectations. Some hotels in this category may still have some cheaper rooms with shared facilities.

Charlottenburg *Hotel-Pension Alexandra* (☎ *885 77 80, fax 88 57 78 18, Wielandstrasse 32)* **Map 6** Singles/doubles €56/76, with bath €79/99. A few steps north of the Ku'damm, this is an attractive pension with nicely refurbished rooms (some in a lavender colour scheme) and a generous breakfast buffet.

Hotel California (☎ *88 01 20, fax 88 01 21 11,* e *info@hotel-california.de, Kurfürstendamm 35)* **Map 6** Singles with bath €99-140, doubles with bath €114-156. Palm trees, movie-theme decor and a rainbow of colours give this place an elegant and cheerful atmosphere. Good shopping, restaurants and theatres are just steps away.

Fitness fans can use the small gym or rent a bicycle (€10 per day).

Hotel-Pension Castell (☎ *882 71 81, fax 881 55 48,* e *messe.castell@t-online.de, Wielandstrasse 24)* **Map 6** Singles €51-84, doubles €56-97. Run with a personal touch, this place offers Art Nouveau style, nicely overhauled and spacious rooms (some with shower only, others with bathroom) and modern amenities at reasonable rates.

Hotel-Pension Funk (☎ *882 71 93, fax 883 33 29, Fasanenstrasse 69)* **Map 6** Singles €34-72, doubles €52-97. Stucco ceilings, Art Nouveau windows, old-fashioned wallpaper and 1920s period furniture are among the nostalgic touches of this charming pension in the former home of silent-movie star Asta Nielsen. It's incredibly good value and very popular, so book early.

Hotel Imperator (☎ *881 41 81, fax 885 19 19, Meinekestrasse 5)* **Map 6** U-Bahn: U1, U9, U15 to Kurfürstendamm. Singles €41-56, doubles €72-92, breakfast €6.50-10. This quirky pension is steps from the Ku'damm and has 11 large rooms that blend antiques with modern furniture. Musicians, actors and other artistic types are among the loyal clients.

Pension am Lietzensee (☎ *325 45 39, fax 322 31 59, Neue Kantstrasse 14)* **Map 4** U-Bahn: U2 to Sophie-Charlotte-Platz, S-Bahn: S4 to Witzleben. Singles €61-72, doubles €87-97. This cute little pension with nine rooms offers most facilities and a lovely location adjacent to Lietzensee lake and its idyllic park. Most rooms have views.

Pension Korfu II (☎ *212 47 90, fax 211 84 32, Rankestrasse 35)* **Map 6** Singles €47-87, doubles €64-104. This place near the Gedächtniskirche offers high quality digs and a lavish breakfast buffet. All 11 rooms have private bath, as well as TV, phone and safe.

Hotel-Pension Nürnberger Eck (☎ *235 17 80, fax 23 51 78 99, Nürnberger Strasse 24a)* **Map 6** Singles/doubles €40/66, with shower €56/92. For 1920s nostalgia, head to this pint-sized pension which has been a hotel since that roaring era of jazz and cabaret. All of the eight rooms feature modern facilities paired with period furniture.

PLACES TO STAY

Original art, some left by former guests, decorates the public areas. Rates are a relative bargain.

Kreuzberg & Friedrichshain

East Side City Hotel (☎ 29 38 33, fax 29 38 35 55, e info@eastsidecityhotel.de, Mühlenstrasse 6, Friedrichshain) **Map 5** Singles €58-95, doubles €69-107. This pleasantly renovated hotel in a 19th-century building is opposite the East Side Gallery, the longest remaining stretch of the Berlin Wall. The Kreuzberg and Friedrichshain entertainment hubs are a short walk away. Rooms are friendly and well-lit.

Juncker's Hotel Garni (☎ 293 35 50, fax 29 33 55 55, e junckers-hotel@t-online.de, Grünberger Strasse 21, Friedrichshain) **Map 5** Singles €48-71, doubles €66-87, breakfast €6. Juncker's offers pretty good value for money and is within walking distance of this district's nightlife scene. The 30 rooms are decked out with contemporary furniture; prices depend on room location and size but all have private facilities.

Hotel Riehmers Hofgarten (☎ 78 09 88 00, fax 78 09 88 08, e info@hotel-riehmers-hofgarten.de, Yorckstrasse 83, Kreuzberg 61) **Map 5** Singles €85-125, doubles €110-140. Deserving of special mention is this artistic 21-room hotel near Viktoriapark. It's integrated into a protected 1891 building complex that wraps around a quiet inner courtyard certain to delight romantics. Rooms are decked out in custom-made classical-modern style furniture; original works by contemporary artists add splashes of colour.

Mitte

Dietrich Bonhoeffer-Haus (☎ 284 671 86, fax 284 67145, e hotel-dbh@t-online.de, Ziegelstrasse 30) **Map 7** Singles €82-102, doubles €122-148. Named for the German theologian and resistance fighter who was killed by the Nazis, this church-affiliated hotel offers a central location, warm atmosphere and pleasantly furnished, modern rooms. In December 1989, the first Round Table meeting that paved the way for free elections in the GDR, and thus reunification, took place here.

Hotel Kastanienhof (☎ 44 30 50, fax 44 30 51 11, e info@hotel-kastanienhof-berlin.de, Kastanienallee 65) **Map 3** Singles €72-82, doubles €92-128. All rooms here have private bathrooms but the more expensive ones are bigger and quieter. There's a nonsmoking breakfast room and the staff are quite savvy. It's halfway between Prenzlauer Berg and Mitte.

Künstlerheim Luise (☎ 28 44 80, fax 28 44 84 48, e info@kuenstlerheim-luise.de, Luisenstrasse 19) **Map 7** Singles/doubles €50-75, doubles €75-120. This place was recently expanded and given a full make-over which saw an international league of artists design each of the 33 rooms.

Hotel Märkischer Hof (☎ 282 71 55, fax 282 43 31, e hotelmh@t-online.de, Linienstrasse 133) **Map 3** Singles €48.50-76, doubles €71.50-102. This place is run with a personal touch and is a good-value base for exploring Mitte's sights and nightlife, even if rooms could use a spruce up.

Schöneberg & Tiergarten

Hotel Delta Berlin (☎ 26 00 20, fax 26 00 21 11, e Delta@cityconact-hotels.de, Pohlstrasse 58, Schöneberg) **Map 4** Singles/doubles €60-105, doubles €68-133. This modern hotel sports creative design and a nice sun terrace. All rooms have private bathrooms and each one looks different; some have circular windows and one even has a circular bathroom. Nonsmoking rooms are available and there's also a bar and room service. Children and dogs are welcome.

Scandotel Castor Berlin (☎ 21 30 30, fax 21 30 31 60, e scandotel@t-online.de, Fuggerstrasse 8, Schöneberg) **Map 4** Singles €94-120, doubles €107-148. This modern behemoth has 78 rooms bathed in a bright colour scheme. There's a bar, a nonsmoking floor and parking in the yard (€6 per night). Children to age 12 stay free in their parents' room (a portable bed is provided).

Hotel Tiergarten (☎ 39 98 96 00, fax 393 86 92, e hotel.tiergarten@t-online.de, Alt-Moabit 89, Tiergarten) **Map 2** Singles €76-107, doubles €92-133. This is a modern establishment catering largely for a business clientele. Amenities include hotel parking and nonsmoking rooms. If you want a quiet room, ask for one at the back.

Wilmersdorf *Hotel Albatros (☎ 89 78 30, fax 89 78 31 00,* e *team@albatros-hotel.de, Rudolstädter Strasse 42)* **Map 4** Singles/doubles €50/61, with bath €74/132. Modern yet quirky, this is a big place with 139 rooms and eight apartments. The decor is fresh, welcoming and colourful and rooms are quite reasonably priced.

Hotel Alexander (☎ 887 16 50, fax 88 71 65 65, Pariser Strasse 37) **Map 6** Singles €92.50-112.50, doubles €107.50-135, extra bed €25. Chrome, marble and floral prints characterise this boutique hotel which counts film makers, artists and business folks among its loyal clientele. Special weekend rates are available on request. Amenities include a small TV (with cable), telephone, minibar and hairdryer.

Hotel Bogota (☎ 881 50 01, fax 883 58 87, e *hotelbogota@t-online.de, Schlüterstrasse 45)* **Map 6** Singles/doubles €44/65, doubles with bath €110. This place gets top marks from several of our readers. Housed in an early 20th-century building, it's inexpensive and quiet, yet close to the Ku'damm action. Furnishings in the 125 rooms are old-fashioned but classy. A bike rental service operates in summer.

Propeller Island Lodge (☎ 891 90 16, fax 892 87 21, w *www.propeller-island.com, Albrecht-Achilles-Strasse 58, Wilmersdorf)* **Map 6** Singles €75-90, doubles €95-110, breakfast €5 per person. If you like the idea of staying in a work of art, hang your hat here, in Berlin's most eccentric hotel. The brainchild of artist/musician Lars Stroschen, it features 30 rooms with furniture and accessories personally designed and handcrafted by him. The result is a series of unique environments perfect for those with imagination and a sense of adventure. There's a room with a circular bed on stilts and another – called the Rubber Cell – that's completely padded in green leather. Or how about the Symbol Room, which is smothered – floor to ceiling – in black & white tiles each sporting a different symbol? Amenities vary slightly. This is not a conventional

hotel, so don't expect a 24-hour reception or room service. Lars takes reservations only by fax and you must arrange your arrival time so someone can be there to let you in.

Hotel Savigny (☎ 881 30 01, fax 882 55 19, e *Hotel.Savigny@t-online.de, Brandenburgische Strasse 21)* **Map 6** Singles/doubles €65/90, extra bed €20. This is a good, well-priced establishment in a traditional building with high ceilings and a 1912 lift. Rooms, 50 in all, are reasonably large and blandly but adequately furnished; all have modern amenities and sparkling private baths. Ask for the newly renovated ones.

Hotel-Pension Wittelsbach (☎ 864 98 40, fax 862 15 32, Wittelsbacherstrasse 22) **Map 6** Singles €66-92, doubles €92-112. This hotel has a special family floor with a veritable fairytale setting featuring a 'Sleeping Beauty' medieval castle and toys galore. Some of it is a bit hokey but kids love it. Quieter accommodation is found on the other floors.

Hotels – Top End

Berlin certainly has no shortage of these gleaming palaces of comfort that supply all the frills and amenities the international jet-setter would expect – cable TV, business desks, minibar, safe, pools, fitness centres, restaurants etc. Naturally such luxury has its price(doubles €140 and over), although prices in Berlin still lag behind those charged in most other European capitals. Note that rates here often don't include breakfast (add about €15 per person), although if you can afford to stay in one of these, this probably doesn't matter much.

Charlottenburg *Hotel Askanischer Hof (☎ 881 80 33, fax 881 72 06, Kurfürstendamm 53)* **Map 6** Singles €100-110, doubles €127-205. For a place with style, try this 1920s hotel that has counted David Bowie and Wim Wenders among its guests. Rooms are large, decked out in Art Nouveau style and have the usual amenities. Nonsmoking rooms and room service are available.

Hotel Bleibtreu (☎ 88 47 40, fax 88 47 44 44, e *info@bleibtreu.com, Bleibtreustrasse 31)* **Map 6** Singles €138-188, doubles

€186-236, breakfast buffet €14.50. If there was such a thing as an 'ecologically correct' hotel, this stylish place would certainly be it. The aesthetic decor is a meditation in understatement, boasting specially designed furniture of untreated oak, 100% virgin-wool carpets underfoot and walls daubed with organic paint. Tucked behind a flower shop, cafe and deli, the Bleibtreu also operates a first-rate restaurant and bar, both popular with locals.

Hecker's Hotel (☎ 889 00, fax 889 02 60, e info@heckers-hotel.com, Grolmannstrasse 35) **Map 6** Singles €116-204, doubles €156-217, breakfast buffet €12.50. This hotel offers cutting-edge cool in its spacious, streamlined public areas, including a glass-fronted lobby. Popular with celebrities in search of privacy, its 72 oversized rooms are decked out with soothing earth-tone furnishings. Some have walk-in wardrobes, king-size beds and marble bathrooms.

Hotel Palace Berlin (☎ 250 20, fax 25 02 11 61, e hotel@palace.de, Budapester Strasse 45) **Map 6** Singles €168-286, doubles €194-311, including breakfast buffet. Some of the 302 rooms at this business-style hotel inside the Europa-Center have views of the Gedächtniskirche. The rooms, recently subjected to a rigorous facelift, are the very definition of luxury (minibar, air-con, TV etc), though it's all done in a rather functional manner. The restaurant First Floor is one of Berlin's best.

Mitte *Adlon Hotel Kempinski (☎ 226 10, fax 22 61 22 22, e adlon@kempinski.com, Unter den Linden 77)* **Map 7** Singles €276-301, doubles €312-337, breakfast buffet €22. The odds of bumping into a celebrity or politician are pretty good at Berlin's premier abode. With front-row vistas of the Brandenburger Tor and offering a sumptuous 'restored-historical' ambience, this full-service hotel leaves no desire unfulfilled. Staff are multilingual, the pool-sauna area makes for some heavenly relaxation, and shopping, nightlife and sights are just a stroll away. Rooms are commensurately lavish.

Hotel Alexander Plaza (☎ 24 00 10, fax 24001777, e info@alexander-plaza.com,

Rosenstrasse 1) **Map 7** Singles €120-186, doubles € 135-201. This historic hotel stands out from among the GDR uglies framing Alexanderplatz. The stylish but functional interior contrasts with the stately restored facade of this 1897 edifice. It's popular with the expense-account crowd, but offers enough personal touches to be a suitable base for leisure visitors as well. Some rooms are nonsmoking and there's a bar and restaurant on the premises.

art'otel berlin mitte (☎ 24 06 20, fax 24 06 22 22, e reservation@artotel.de, Wallstrasse 70-73) **Map 7** Singles €123-173, doubles €148-198. The art of living is celebrated at this glam boutique hotel. It fuses a modernist wing with an 18th-century patrician townhouse via a dramatic atrium. Staying here feels a bit like camping at a museum as public areas and rooms abound with original works by leading contemporary German painter Georg Baselitz. It's expensive, but may well be worth the splurge.

Dorint Am Gendarmenmarkt (☎ 20 37 50, 20 37 51 00, Charlottenstrasse 50-52) **Map 7** Singles €181-278, doubles €202-294. With under 100 rooms, this stylish place has the character of a boutique hotel, yet the amenities of a big 'hotel de luxe'. Noteworthy extras include in-room voice mail and a fitness centre with Roman steam bath and sauna.

Hilton Berlin (☎ 202 30, fax 20 23 42 69, Mohrenstrasse 30, Mitte) **Map 7** Singles €160-240, doubles €179-260, breakfast buffet €18. After a thorough face-lift, the Hilton Berlin sparkles once again in this striking glass palace within walking distance of Gendarmenmarkt. Rooms are furnished in classically elegant style. For a view of the square, book yourself into No 4001, 5001, 5007, 5009, 6013 or 6016.

Prenzlauer Berg *Myer's Hotel Berlin (☎ 440 140, fax 44014104, Metzerstrasse 26)* **Map 3** Tram: No 1 to Metzerstrasse. Singles €85-125, doubles €110-160. A short walk from Kollwitzplatz sits this stylish boutique hotel, a rare high-end entry in Prenzlauer Berg. All 41 rooms are spacious and equipped with all modern amenities.

Tiergarten *Sorat Hotel Spree-Bogen (☎ 39 92 00, fax 39 92 09 99, e spree-bogen@ SORAT-Hotels.com, Alt-Moabit 99)* **Map 2** Singles €127-225, doubles €162-260. This classy hotel occupies a converted dairy and offers a fusion of contemporary chic and early 20th-century-industrial architecture. It's a state-of-the-art affair that sits right on an idyllic stretch of the Spree river, with the government quarter just around the next bend. Minimalist rooms feature designer furniture, and the public areas are friendly and imbued with a creative spirit. The champagne breakfast buffet is sumptuous. Ask about weekend specials.

Grand Hotel Esplanade *(☎ 25 47 80, fax 254 78 82 22, e info@esplanade.de, Lützowufer 15)* **Map 4** Singles €135-273, doubles €135-317, including breakfast buffet. On the opposite – southern – edge of the Tiergarten district is the postmodern Grand Hotel Esplanade. Just look for the mirrored-glass behemoth squatting beside a picturesque stretch of canal. Celebrities, top executives and the merely moneyed relax here with a massage, are chauffeured around in the hotel-owned Rolls Royce or sip a cocktail at the oh-so-fashionable Harry's New York Bar (see the Bars & Pubs section in the Entertainment chapter).

Gay & Lesbian Hotels

By law, no hotel may turn away gay couples, though some may pretend to be full, or frown upon homosexual guests. Fortunately, there's a steadily growing crop of B&Bs, pensions and guesthouses that cater exclusively for gays and lesbians, including these contenders:

enjoy bed & breakfast *(☎ 23 62 36 10, fax 23 62 36 19, w www.ebab.de, Nollendorfplatz 5 – Haus B, Schöneberg)* **Map 4**. Rooms from €20 per person, including breakfast. This private room referral service is an outgrowth of Mann-O-Meter and has an excellent Web site. For both gays and lesbians.

Timmy's Gay B&B *(☎ 81 85 19 88, fax 81 85 19 89, w www.gaybed.de, Perleberger Strasse 7, Tiergarten)* **Map 2** U-Bahn: U9 to Birkenstrasse. Singles/doubles €30/40,

discounts for longer stays. This friendly B&B occupies a nicely renovated late 19th-century building in Alt-Moabit, north of Tiergarten park. It's not close to the major gay districts but hugely popular nonetheless. Reservations are essential.

Frauenhotel Intermezzo *(☎ 22489096, fax 22489097, e frauen@hotelintermezzo .de, An der Kolonnade 14, Mitte)* **Map 7** Beds in 3-bed & 4-bed rooms €30, singles/doubles €40/65, breakfast €5. Run by a trio of young women, this women-only hotel is close to Potsdamer Platz and Unter den Linden. Rooms are largish and have Scandinavian furnishings.

Pension Amsterdam *(☎ 44 00 94 54, fax 448 07 92, e info@pension-amsterdam.de, Gleimstrasse 24, Prenzlauer Berg)* **Map 3** Singles/doubles/triples with bathroom €35/ 70/91, breakfast buffet €6.50. Cheerfully decorated and clean rooms with TV are available at this friendly place on one of the gayest streets in Prenzlauer Berg. Breakfast is served in the attached cafe-restaurant until 3pm and there's free Internet access as well.

Eastside Gayllery *(☎ 43 73 54 84, fax 43 73 54 85, e reservations@eastside-gayllery.de, Schönhauser Strasse 41, Prenzlauer Berg)* **Map 3** Rooms from €35 per person. This guesthouse consists of just a few functional rooms behind a gay shop, but the scene's steps away and host Ulli will quickly fill you in on the local hang-outs. Ask for discounts Monday to Thursday.

ArtHotel Connection *(☎ 210 21 88 00, fax 217 70 30, Fuggerstrasse 33, Schöneberg)* **Map 6** Rooms €56-150, including breakfast. Above the Connection nightclub is this hotel with stylish rooms, most with private facilities. Palm trees add a tropical atmosphere to the breakfast room. Guests are allowed.

Hotel Arco Garni *(☎ 235 14 80, fax 21 47 51 78, e arco-hotel@t-online.de, Geisbergstrasse 30, Schöneberg)* **Map 6** Singles €56-71.50, doubles €71.50-92, including breakfast. Everyone is welcome at this gay-owned hotel in the heart of the gay district. Recently renovated rooms are nicely decked out and offer a full range of amenities. In fine weather, breakfast is served in the garden patio.

Frauenhotel Artemisia (☎ *873 89 05, fax 861 86 53, Brandenburgische Strasse 18,* ⓔ *Frauenhotel-Berlin@t-online.de)* **Map 6** Singles/doubles €55/86, with bath €75/101; ask about special rates. At this stylish and quiet women-only haven each room is bright and individually decorated in soothing salmon and mint and is named after a famous woman. Original art by contemporary women artists decorates the public areas, and there's a nice rooftop terrace for having breakfast or sunbathing in fine weather. There are only 12 rooms, so be sure to book ahead.

LONG-TERM RENTALS

If you're planning to stay in Berlin for a month or longer, you might consider renting a room or an apartment through one of the many *Mitwohnzentrale* (flat-sharing agency) that matches people who are willing to let their digs temporarily with those in need of a temporary home. Accommodation can be diverse: anything from rooms in shared student flats to fully furnished apartments. Rates can vary according to the agency and the type of accommodation required but are always less than what you'd pay in hotels. In Berlin you can expect to pay around €275 per month for a standard room and €400 for a studio apartment. In general, the longer you rent, the less expensive the rate you will have to pay. Even if you're not staying for an entire month, it may still work out cheaper to pay the monthly rent and leave earlier.

Added to the rate will be the agency's commission which comes to around 25% of the rent, plus 16% VAT. In other words, if the month-long rental is €400, your total will be €564 (€100 commission, €64 VAT).

In order to find a place, you first must fill out an application with a Mitwohnzentrale, specifying the desired rental period, the maximum rent you want to pay, the type of accommodation you prefer etc. Next, the agency gives you a list of places that meet your needs. You then need to phone the landlords (you may be able to find someone nice at the agency to do this for you if your German isn't up to it), visit the rooms/apartments that interest you, and pick your favourite. In the case of a successful rental agreement, the entire sum, including commission, is payable to the agency in advance (unless you're staying for several months, in which case you may be able to arrange for monthly payments).

Agencies to try include:

Casa Nostra (☎ 235 51 20, fax 23 55 12 12, Winterfeldtstrasse 46, Schöneberg)
City Mitwohnzentrale (☎ 194 30, fax 216 94 01, ⓔ berlin@city-mitwohnzentrale.com, ⓦ www .city-mitwohnzentrale.com, Hardenbergplatz 14, Charlottenburg)
Erste Mitwohnzentrale (☎ 324 30 31, fax 324 99 77, Sybelstrasse 53, Charlottenburg)
HomeCompany (☎ 194 45, fax 882 66 94, Joachimstaler Strasse 17, Charlottenburg)
Mitwohnagentur am Mehringdamm (☎ 786 20 03, fax 785 06 14, ⓔ info@wohnagentur-berlin.de, Mehringdamm 66, Kreuzberg 61)

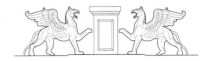

Places to Eat

People from all corners of the world call Berlin home, and it's this United Nations of cuisines that makes eating out in the German capital so exciting. From an unpretentious doner kebab or currywurst to foie gras and Chilean sea bass, from American burgers to Zambian stew, you're sure to find it on a menu somewhere. In fact, finding honest-to-goodness German or Berlin dishes is increasingly becoming a challenge in this most international of European capitals (although this chapter lists a few good candidates). Berlin's not traditionally had a reputation for superb, sophisticated restaurants, but as the boxed text 'Temples of Temptations' shows, a new generation of chefs is proving that haute cuisine is no longer banished.

FOOD
Local Etiquette
Dining out is usually a casual affair and there are few restaurants where dressing up is *de rigeur*. Dinner time starts around 7.30pm to 8pm, so if you're heading for a popular eatery – especially on a Friday or Saturday night – make a reservation. Only in the most formal establishments (and American chains like the Hard Rock Café), or if you've made a reservation, will someone seat you at an assigned table; normally you'll just seat yourself. In student cafes and other casual eateries you may occasionally be asked to share your table with another party. You are expected to consent but you need not socialise with your table mates or even introduce yourself.

Most restaurants figure on only one or two seatings per night, so don't feel that you need to leave quickly after you've finished your meal. You may stay on for another hour or so just nursing a drink, chatting and enjoying the atmosphere. The bill will only be presented to you when you request it.

Service, unfortunately, remains a sore point; you can safely presume it will be bad. Long waits, lukewarm food, inattentiveness and even plain rudeness are rampant. In recognition of this fact, the Berlin Hotel and Restaurant Guild has called upon service personnel to help improve the city's image by adopting a better attitude and being less stingy with smiles. Things seem to be improving, but there's still a long way to go.

Smoking is still widely practised – even in some vegetarian restaurants – and non-smoking sections are rare or ineffective.

Cost
If you don't insist on lavish, sit-down meals, you need not spend a lot of money on food. German Imbiss (snack) stalls are a wonderful way to fill up inexpensively, as are the ubiquitous Turkish takeaway places. At the latter you can get a Turkish *lahmacun* (pizza) for about €2 or a doner kebab (thin meat slices – usually chicken or lamb – served with salad and a garlicky yogurt sauce in a toasted pitta bread) for around €2.50.

Cafes are great places to eat cheaply since they offer not only cakes but also bistro-type dishes like quiche Lorraine, baguette sandwiches, soups etc, usually for under €5. Most are cosy, congenial places where you can also relax over a newspaper or write those postcards.

If you want a more substantial meal, lunch is almost always cheaper than dinner. Chinese and Indian restaurants in particular may offer special three-course bargain lunches for around €5.50. Old-style German restaurants sometimes have a *Stammgericht*, a daily-changing main dish served at lunch time only and also costing around €5.50.

Going out for dinner can also be affordable – even at fancier restaurants – as long as you stick to one main course and a single beverage. If you want alcohol, have beer. If you want wine, order a glass of the house wine and avoid ordering a bottle. Pizzerias are generally great places for cheap meals and also serve pasta and salads; most likely you'll spend €10 or less per person, including one drink.

Smoke Gets in Your Eyes

Berliners are some of the heaviest tobacco smokers in the world. Entering a pub, club or restaurant can be a lung-searing, eye-watering experience that will leave your clothes reeking and your hair in need of an instant wash. Some places do have seating sections for nonsmokers but that makes almost no difference when you're sharing a small room with 50 puffers.

But there are a couple of things you can do to minimise health, hygiene and laundry hazards. As smoke rises, always try to sit on the ground floor of any place you enter. Sitting by a door or window is also a good idea; any draft you have to put up with will be worth it.

When you know you're going to be spending some hours in a packed club or cafe, don't put on the only remaining clean shirt in your suitcase or backpack. If you have long hair, wear it up or pile it up under a hat or a scarf.

Pick places with high ceilings, or modern establishments with efficient ventilation. If you don't mind having an entire restaurant to yourself, have your meal in the afternoon; most kitchens are open all day.

A final point on smoking etiquette. You're in Berlin and the people here smoke. You'll only get incredulous stares if you ask people not to light up. Just pretend you're in an old Bette Davis movie.

A service charge is always included in the bill and German restaurant staff tend to be paid fairly well anyway. However, unless the service was truly abhorrent, most people leave a small tip, sometimes just rounding up the amount of the bill and sometimes leaving about 10%.

DRINKS
Nonalcoholic
Berlin tap water is fine to drink but asking for a glass at a restaurant will raise brows at best and may be refused altogether because they want to sell you an expensive bottle of mineral water (*Mineralwasser*). This almost always has bubbles, although still water is becoming more popular. If you're picky, be sure to specify what you want when ordering. Soft drinks are widely available; of the diet versions, the most common brands available are Coca-Cola and Pepsi Cola. Soft drinks in general taste slightly different from what you're used to (probably sweeter), because they've been reformulated to meet German tastes. A refreshing drink is *Apfelschorle*, which is apple juice mixed with sparkling mineral water.

Coffee is king both in Berlin, in particular, and Germany, in general, and is usually fresh and strong. It comes in cups (*Tasse*) or pots (*Kännchen*) and you should specify which you want when you are ordering. Condensed milk and sugar will usually be served alongside. In trendy cafes you'll often see people nursing huge cups of coffee, called *Milchkaffee* (milk coffee) and containing a large amount of hot milk. Designer coffeehouses in the Starbucks mould have proliferated in the last couple of years. The most common chains are Balzac and Einstein, although they'll soon have competition from the ubiquitous Seattle chain which was planning on opening its first German store in late 2001 – where else but in Berlin?

One warning: the bottomless cup is *not* a concept here, and a single cup can cost as much as €2.50.

If you're ordering tea, and don't want a pot, ask for *ein Glass Tee* (a glass of tea). It'll usually be served in the form of a teabag with sugar and maybe a slice of lemon. If you want milk, ask for *Tee mit Milch*.

Alcoholic

Beer The most common alcoholic beverage is – no surprise – beer, of which the Germans have made a science. All brews adhere to the *Reinheitsgebot* (Purity Law) passed in Bavaria in 1516. There's a confusing number of choices, the most popular being the fairly bitter-tasting *Pils* and the sweeter, foamy *Weizenbier*. *Schwarzbier*, like Köstrizer, is as black as Guinness but not as creamy and heavy-tasting, and is widely available too. Other terms to know are *helles Bier* and *dunkles Bier* which are light and dark beers, respectively. *Berliner Weisse*, or 'Berlin White', is a foaming, low-alcohol wheat beer usually mixed with red (raspberry) or green (woodruff) syrup. *Alsterwasser* is a mix of Pils and lemonade and a popular summer drink.

Wine You'll find wines from around the world in Berlin's restaurants and bars. Those from California and Australia are particularly trendy at the moment and, accordingly, expensive. Chilean wines, on the other hand, offer excellent value. Wines from other European countries, like Spain, Italy and France, are common as well.

Despite what you may have heard – or tasted – back home, German wines are remarkably good. Their reputation as being sweet and headache-inducing is largely undeserved. Germany just doesn't produce a great amount of wine and the Germans drink all the good stuff themselves. It's only the swill that finishes up being exported. In supermarkets, the cheaper wines are almost as cheap as bottled water or soft drinks, and even those are quite good indeed. A delicious bottle of crisp, dry *(trocken)* white wine can easily be found for €2.50.

Riesling, Müller-Thurgau and Silvaner are the three most celebrated German varietals. Unless you order a bottle, wine is usually served in glasses holding 20cl or 25cl. A *Weinschorle* is white wine mixed with sparkling mineral water. Wine is drunk as an aperitif or with meals.

See the Language chapter for a glossary of food and drink terms that might come in useful.

RESTAURANTS

Berliners love going out for dinner and have literally thousands of restaurants and cafes to choose from. Wherever you are in the city, there's no need to travel far since every neighbourhood has its own cluster of eateries running the gamut of cuisines and price categories.

Unless noted otherwise, restaurants mentioned here are open daily for lunch (usually from 11am or noon) and dinner. Those that are dinner-only usually open around 5pm or 6pm. In keeping with Berliners' propensity to go out late and stay out until the early hours of the morning, many restaurants keep their doors open way past dinner time, often until 2am or even 4am on weekends, though food service usually stops around midnight.

American

Juleps (☎ 881 88 23, Giesebrechtstrasse 3, Charlottenburg) **Map 6** Mains €8-16. For more than burgers and ribs, head to Juleps, a warmly lit cocktail bar and restaurant. The menu reflects all shades of the multi-ethnic cauldron that is the USA, though slightly deeper pockets are required to enjoy it all.

Hard Rock Café (☎ 88 46 20, Meinekestrasse 21, Charlottenburg) **Map 6** Mains €7.50-16. A time-worn Trabant adds the local touch to Berlin's branch of the mother of all theme restaurants. It is renowned for its 'pig sandwich' (with smoked pork), though the usual burgers and salads are, of course, available. There's Internet access too.

Pow Wow (☎ 694 56 06, Dieffenbachstrasse 11, Kreuzberg 36) **Map 5** Mains €7.50-12.50. Native American art, a big pool table and juicy burgers (including the vegetarian kind) collaborate to form one of the most fun US-style hang-outs this side of the Statue of Liberty. Steaks and Tex-Mex are also part of the menu, as are a handful of vegetarian items.

Jimmy's Diner (☎ 882 31 41, Pariser Strasse 41, Wilmersdorf) **Map 6** Mains €3-8, burgers €6-7.50. Berlin's oldest diner is perfect for soaking up that *American Graffiti* vibe. Squeeze into one of the crimson faux-leather booths, then sink your teeth into one of them thar juicy burgers.

Fabulous Route 66 50's Diner (☎ *883 16 02, Pariser Strasse 44, Wilmersdorf*) **Map 6** Mains €3-12.50. If Jimmy's is full, try this nearby option. More pricey and a tad over-designed, it's cheerful and serves convincing food. Fun factor: booths with vintage miniature jukeboxes (€0.50 buys two songs).

Australian

Woolloomooloo (☎ *34 70 27 77, Röntgenstrasse 7, Charlottenburg*) **Map 2** Mains €10-18. Dinner only. Craving a bit of 'roo? Kangaroo dinners at Berlin's oldest Australian restaurant go for around €16, though the marinated crocodile steak scores points as well. Wash it all down with pints of foamy Foster's. In summer you can watch the stars sparkle in the placid waters of the Spree.

Chinese

Good Friend (☎ *313 26 59, Kantstrasse 30, Charlottenburg*) **Map 6** Mains €7-17. Open noon-2am daily. For authentic Cantonese head to this bustling place low on ambience but big on delicious food. It's all enjoyed by a hungry clientele that includes lots of Chinese. In case the original dishes prove too challenging, there are others adapted to Western palates.

Bambussprosse (☎ *28 04 76 82, Reinhardtstrasse 11, Mitte*) **Map 7** Lunch specials €3-3.75, mains €3.75-8. Open noon-10pm. This small, largely kitsch-free restaurant has a huge menu that includes duck, pork, chicken and fish but relatively few vegetarian dishes. The lunch special is available 11am-3pm Monday to Friday only. All dishes are available as takeaway, and if your order tallies up to more than €10, delivery is free.

Ostwind (☎ *441 59 51, Husemannstrasse 13, Mitte*) **Map 3** Mains €6.50-13. Open daily for dinner, plus Sun lunch. This is a stylish pastel maze of a restaurant where you can sit at regular tables or in lotus position on pillows in raised booths. The food is creative and above average. The Chinese fondue is a speciality (€12/21 for one/two persons).

French

Cour Careé (☎ *312 52 38, Savignyplatz 5, Charlottenburg*) **Map 6** Mains €8-15. This is a nice brasserie that's especially popular in summer, when you can watch the goings-on in the square from the lovely garden. It's good for snacks like Flammekuche (€6.50) but also well-priced bistro-style mains like lamb cutlets (€10).

Paris Bar (☎ *313 80 52, Kantstrasse 152, Charlottenburg*) **Map 6** Mains €13-25. The staff at this stuffy establishment has seen them all: David Bowie, Jack Nicholson, Madonna, film directors Wim Wenders and Volker Schlöndorff and plenty more celebs. Perhaps that's why they've adopted such a snobby attitude when serving mere mortals with dishes that occasionally overstretch the chef's skills.

Le Cochon Bourgeois (☎ *693 01 01, Fichtestrasse 24, Kreuzberg 36*) **Map 5** Mains €12-20. Dinner only, closed Sun & Mon. It's one thing to make exquisite meals from exquisite ingredients and quite another to do so using ordinary ingredients. At the 'Bourgeois Pig' chef Hannes Behrmann does just that (think pig-snout carpaccio) and usually with great success.

Theodor Tucher (☎ *22 48 94 64, Pariser Platz 6a, Mitte*) **Map 7** Breakfast €5.50-10.50, lunch €10-15, dinner €6-19. The food is creative Mediterranean (fresh fish, pasta, herbs etc) and is served in an environment that's more library than restaurant. Bookshelves blanket the walls, a small bookstore is ensconced on an upstairs landing and author readings and literary salons take place regularly.

Nö (☎ *201 08 71, Glinkastrasse 24, Mitte*) **Map 7** Mains €6-11. Open Mon-Fri for lunch and dinner, dinner only Sat. There's absolutely nothing trendy about this cosily cluttered wine bar and that's why people like it. Come for great wines, perfectly matured cheeses and hearty French fare.

Gugelhof (☎ *442 92 29, Knaackstrasse 37, Prenzlauer Berg*) **Map 3** Breakfast €4-9, mains €8-15. Open from 10am, breakfast until 4pm. Gugelhof blends Swiss, Alsatian and Baden cooking. Reliable standard offerings include raclette (a melted cheese

otsdam's Dutch Quarter consists of orderly red-brick homes.

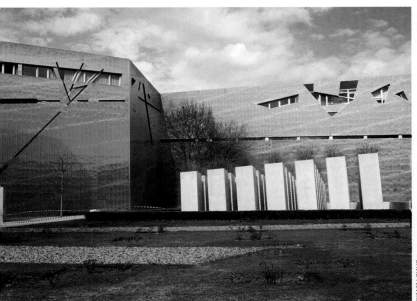

he zinc-clad facade of the Jüdisches Musuem, the largest Jewish museum in Europe.

Serene faces adorn Schloss Glienicke.

Berliner Dom, up close and personal.

Gods, heroes and mythical creatures – reliefs on the Brandenburger Tor.

dish) and choucroute (a sauerkraut-based dish) and, of course, Gugelhupf, a scrumptious dessert enjoyed here by Bill Clinton on his visit to Berlin.

Storch (☎ 784 20 59, *Wartburgstrasse 54, Schöneberg*) **Map 4** Mains €7.50-16. Dinner only. This is a classic neighbourhood-charmer off the tourist circuit. Guests are often greeted by owner Volker Hauptvogel himself. Enjoy exquisite wines while snacking on what may well be the town's best Flammekuche or digging into more substantial mains. Reservations are a good idea.

German

Charlottenburg *Luisen-Bräu* (☎ 341 93 88, *Luisenplatz 1*) **Map 2** Mains €6-15. After a day of sightseeing in and around Schloss Charlottenburg, relax with freshly brewed beer and energy-restoring fare at this microbrewery.

Temples of Temptation

Berlin used to be a culinary wasteland where chefs' imagination stopped at Currywurst and Bouletten (curried sausage and fried beef patties). Times have certainly changed. A new crop of master chefs is cooking up a storm all over town, heralded by critics and celebrated by discerning and deep-pocketed diners. So if you're a serious foodie, want to celebrate a special occasion, or simply want to test the limit of your credit card, make a reservation at any of these culinary temples.

Ana e Bruno (☎ 325 71 10, *Sophie-Charlotten-Strasse 101, Charlottenburg*) **Map 2** Mains €23-30. Dinner only, open Tues-Sat. Bruno Pellegrini has been a food critics' favourite for some time now for his consistently inspired creations from around the Boot. Goat-cheese ravioli with beans and pancetta is a typical offering. Leave room for the spectacular sesame-cracknel parfait with mocha sauce. It's near Schloss Charlottenburg.

E.T.A. Hoffmann (☎ 78 09 88 09, *Yorckstrasse 83, Kreuzberg 61*) **Map 5** Mains €24-30. Dinner only, open Mon-Sat. This culinary temple within the Hotel Riehmers Hofgarten (see Places to Stay) operates under the aegis of Tim Raue, the new shooting star on Berlin's gastronomic scene. He wows diners with innovative takes on haute cuisine using only fresh, seasonal ingredients (chateaubriand with pureed artichokes and truffle sauce was one recent entry). In summer, preferred seating is in the bucolic courtyard.

borchardt (☎ 20 39 71 17, *Französische Strasse 47, Mitte*) **Map 7** Mains €14-23. This is the oldest among the crop of highbrow restaurants sprouting up around Gendarmenmarkt – and still one of the classiest. The ceilings are as tall as the waiter's aprons are long; the food's Franco-German, changes daily but is sometimes served with an unnecessary dollop of attitude.

Margaux (☎ 22 65 26 11, *Unter den Linden 78, Mitte*) **Map 7** Mains €19-36. Open Tues-Sat. It took Michael Hoffmann just one year to become a 'star' chef – a Michelin star, that is. Hoffmann and his team create breathtaking concoctions of classic French cuisine infused with avant-garde touches for a Rolls-Royce crowd. The refined interior – gilded flat ceilings, marble floors – was designed by acclaimed Berlin architect Johanne Nalbach, while former Andy Warhol assistant Ingeborg zu Schleswig-Holstein dreamed up the cheery canvases.

Vau (☎ 202 97 30, *Jägerstrasse 54-55, Mitte*) **Map 7** Mains €30-38. Open Tues-Sat. Also Michelin-starred, Vau, under head chef Kolja Kleeberg, had a similarly stratospheric rise when it opened a few years ago. The ambitious culinary concoctions get a tad too fanciful on occasion, but the presentation is a reliable feast for the eyes. The decor here is cool and minimalist with seating on slim leather banquettes and wicker chairs, and it all gets an elite touch from high-quality canvases.

RT

Kreuzberg *Gasthaus Dietrich Herz (☎ 693 11 73, Marheinekeplatz, Kreuzberg 61)* **Map 5** Mains €3.50-8.50. If you thought a schnitzel was a schnitzel was a schnitzel, go to this time-tested inn to discover that it ain't necessarily so. There are a dozen varieties, some so large they spill off the plate they're served on, and all costing €5.50. Big breakfasts can be had for €3. (Also see the Places to Stay chapter.)

Grossbeerenkeller (☎ 251 30 64, Grossbeerenstrasse 90, Kreuzberg 61) **Map 5** Mains €6.50-12.50. Open 4pm, 6pm Sat. Those nostalgic for the 'old Berlin' should venture down into this rustic cellar. The menu delivers German soul food at its finest, including such delicious artery-cloggers as fried potatoes, roast pork and *Matjes* (pickled herring) in cream sauce.

Weltrestaurant Markthalle (☎ 617 55 02, Pücklerstrasse 34, Kreuzberg 36) **Map 5** Mains €6-15. Attached to the historic Eisenbahn Markthalle (see Market Halls later in this chapter), this eatery also time-warps you back a hundred years. Owned by the same folks as the Tresor nightclub, it attracts an unpretentious clientele of aging Kreuzberg

Berlin Cuisine

Though few locals seem to favour it, there still is such a thing as traditional Berlin cuisine. Overall, it tends to be high-calorie, hearty and heavy on artery-clogging meat dishes. Pork, prepared in umpteen ways, is a staple, including *Kasseler Rippen* (smoked pork chops) and *Eisbein* (pork knuckles). Both usually share the plate with sauerkraut and either mashed or boiled potatoes.

A definite Berlin classic is *Currywurst*, a spicy sausage served with a tangy curried sauce. There's much debate about which Imbiss serves the best concoction.

Ground meat often comes in the form of a Boulette, a cross between a meatball and a hamburger and eaten with a dry roll. Other regulars on Berlin menus are roast chicken, schnitzel, *Sauerbraten* (marinated beef) and *Matjes* (pickled herring).

scenesters and earthy neighbourhood folk who come for the no-nonsense food. The *Königsberger Klopse* (meat dumplings in caper sauce) are a speciality.

Mitte *Historische Weinstuben (☎ 242 41 07, Poststrasse 23)* **Map 7** Mains €6-15. Inside the Nikolaiviertel's Knoblauchhaus, this sedate wine tavern has an outstanding selection of German wines from all regions, including the eastern German growing areas of Saale-Unstrut and Saxony. They go surprisingly well with the hearty Berlin fare served alongside.

Kartoffelkeller (☎ 282 85 48, Albrechtstrasse 14b) **Map 7** Mains €6-10. Potato dishes from seven countries are available in this bourgeois basement restaurant. Expect potato paella with chicken and seafood, feta potato casserole and other such creations.

Kellerrestaurant (☎ 282 38 43, Chausseestrasse 125) **Map 3** Mains €9-14. Lunch & dinner Mon-Fri, dinner-only on Sat & Sun. Brecht devotees can eat just like their idol did at this cellar restaurant in the Brecht-Weigel Memorial House. Many of the Austro-Hungarian dishes served here are based on the recipes of Brecht's wife, Helene Weigel. In summer, dining moves to a placid inner courtyard.

Keyzer Soze (☎ 28 59 94 89, Tucholskystrasse 33) **Map 3** Mains €3-11.50. This is a hip, uncluttered restaurant that takes you on a German culinary journey. *Maultaschen* (ravioli-like noodles) from Swabia, spiced finger-sized sausages from Nuremberg and, of course, the *Berliner Boulette* (hamburger patty) all have their place on the menu. Prices are moderate, and it's often crowded, making service accordingly slow.

Lindenbräu (☎ 25 75 12 80, Bellevuestrasse 3-5) Mains €7.25-15, business lunch €7.50 Mon-Fri. Get your cholesterol fix at this neo-Bavarian beer hall in the Sony Center. There's a large upstairs deck with a view of the central plaza, beer by the metre (€12 for eight 0.2L glasses) and gut-busting portions of traditional southern dishes like *Schweinshaxn* and *Leberkäs*. (See the Potsdamer Platz & Kulturforum map in the Things to See & Do chapter.)

Stäv (☎ *282 39 65, Schiffbauerdamm 8)* **Map 7** Mains €4-12. This place began as an island of Rhenish joie de vivre for homesick Bonn politicians and their entourages, but is now going mostly for the tourist crowd. Both Rhineland and Berlin specialities are served. The strange name, by the way, is an acronym for *Ständige Vertretung*, the euphemism used for the West German embassy in the former GDR.

Zum Nussbaum (☎ *242 30 95, Am Nussbaum 3)* **Map 7** Mains €6-9. The wood-panelled walls of this Berlin classic have hosted the hungry and thirsty since 1571, making it the city's oldest restaurant. Despite steady tourist invasions, the place has remained friendly and affordable.

Prenzlauer Berg *Offenbach Stuben* (☎ *445 85 02, Stubbenkammerstrasse 8)* **Map 3** Mains €8-17. Dinner only. This GDR relic has weathered the Wende in style. It's stuffy but classy and filled with props from a defunct theatre. Carnivores will feel at home since the menu features almost the entire animal world, including duck, lamb, pork and rabbit. Dishes are named after works by the restaurant's namesake, Jacques Offenbach, an operetta composer. Come early as things start to quieten down around 10pm.

Restauration 1900 (☎ *442 24 94, Husemannstrasse 1)* **Map 3** Mains €8-13.50. Right on tourist-heavy Käthe-Kollwitz-Platz is this stylish eatery that serves modern Berlin fare in an Art Deco setting with mirrored walls, dark furniture and crisp white table-linen. Three- and four-course set menus are €20/23.

Spandau *Zitadellenschänke* (☎ *334 21 06, Am Juliusturm)* 7-course meal €40, 5 courses €24, a la carte available too. Dinner only Mon-Fri, lunch and dinner Sat & Sun. Right in the Spandau citadel, the tables groan under the lavish medieval banquets served beneath vaulted ceilings and accompanied by minstrel song. Reservations are recommended since it's the kind of place that draws large office and birthday parties. (See the Spandau map in the Things to See & Do chapter.)

Tiergarten *Alte Meierei* (☎ *39 92 07 20, Alt-Moabit 99)* **Map 2** Mains €14-17. This stylish gem is tucked away in the stables of a former dairy next to the Sorat Hotel Spree-Bogen (see the Places to Stay chapter). It serves updated versions of classic Berlin dishes to a moneyed clientele. If you're a gourmet on a budget, you should go at lunchtime.

Greek

Competition among Greek restaurants is especially fierce in Schöneberg.

Ypsilon (☎ *782 45 39, Hauptstrasse 163)* **Map 4** Mains €7.50-12. Dinner only. This popular neighbourhood eatery has been beautifully spiffed-up and has become a big hang-out for local Greeks and Schöneberg scenesters. Make a meal of the appetisers, best consumed on a balmy summer night in the beer garden. There's live music on weekends.

Nemesis (☎ *781 15 90, Hauptstrasse 154)* **Map 4** Dinner only. Mains €7.50-15. A few doors down is this equally popular restaurant, which is usually packed with communicative folks digging into their souvlaki and hoisting glasses of tart retsina.

Ousies (☎ *216 79 57, Grunewaldstrasse 16)* **Map 4** Mains €5-14. Dinner only. Another place to reminisce about your Greek summer holiday is this bubbly taverna whose exhaustive menu consists mostly of hot and cold appetisers. Order two or three or the excellent sampler (€7.50) and you'll be as happy as Zorba the Greek. A personal favourite that's usually busy, so book ahead.

Ellopia (☎ *446 41 35, Erich-Weinert-Strasse 55, Prenzlauer Berg)* **Map 3** Mains €6-12. Lunch and dinner daily. Minoan-style murals evocative of that ancient civilisation's palace in Knossos form the backdrop at this comfortable eatery. All the staples of Greek cuisine, including 10 meatless platters, are served. If you want the real thing, book a trip at the attached travel agency.

Indian

Charlottenburg *Ashoka Bar* (☎ *313 20 66, Grolmanstrasse 51)* **Map 6** Mains €2.50-6.50. Tease your sinuses with fragrant curries and meat-based dishes that just fly over the counter from the steamy open kitchen of this popular hole-in-the-wall.

Kalkutta (☎ 883 62 93, Bleibtreustrasse 17) **Map 6** Mains €7.50-13. A seductive melange of ginger, coriander and cumin also wafts from this dark and exotically furnished place.

Kreuzberg *Amrit (☎ 612 55 50, Oranienstrasse 203, Kreuzberg 36)* **Map 5**; *(☎ 28 88 48 40, Oranienburger Strasse 45, Mitte)* **Map 3** Mains €6-12.50. With its heavy pine tables and boldly pigmented canvases, Amrit may be furnished like a Swedish living room, but the food is Indian at its finest. Portions are ample, fragrant and steamy. There's even Indian wine.

Chandra Kumari (☎ 694 12 03, Gneisenaustrasse 4, Kreuzberg 61) **Map 5** Mains €4-12. This small, kitsch-free restaurant with saffron-coloured walls serves dishes that blend Sri Lankan and Indian flavours. Vegetarians have plenty of choices, but carnivores might like to know that only free-range meat is used. For a special indulgence, order the *Hochzeitsmenu* (a 'wedding menu', though without the tux and veil), a banquet for two costing €47.50.

Prenzlauer Berg *Himalaya (☎ 441 25 01, Lychener Strasse 3)* **Map 3** Mains €3.50-7. Open noon-midnight. Choose from more than 20 vegetarian plates or try one of their speciality lamb dishes. Chicken, fish and tandoor meals available too. All main courses are served with rice or naan bread and a small salad.

Tandoor (☎ 440 84 93, Rykestrasse 42) **Map 3** Mains €3-4.50. This hole-in-the-wall can't be beaten for price. Dishes are tasty and toothsome but service is slow. The dining area is tiny and Spartan but in summer you can hunker down at wooden sidewalk tables.

Schöneberg *Rani (☎ 215 26 73, Goltzstrasse 32)* **Map 4** Meals €3-6.50. Open 9am-2am. This snug and warmly lit eatery with tasteful decor stands out from the pack of Indian restaurants just south of Winterfeldtplatz. Order at the counter, grab some

cutlery, find a table, then go Pavlovian in anticipation of big plates of basmati rice smothered with meat or vegetable curry. In fine weather, the sidewalk tables are the coolest.

Maharaja (☎ 215 78 25, Goltzstrasse 20) **Map 4** Lunch specials €3.50, mains €3.50-10. Opposite Rani, this place has a bigger menu, friendly table service and a relaxed atmosphere, but it's not nearly as trendy.

International
Charlottenburg *Lubitsch (☎ 882 37 56, Bleibtreustrasse 47)* **Map 6** Mains €6-20. Open from 9.30am, from 6pm Sun. This is a sleek bistro popular with sophisticates chatting and chomping amidst stucco, wood and yellow-hued walls. The menu changes daily.

Marché (☎ 882 75 78, Kurfürstendamm 14-15) **Map 6** Prices €2.15-9. This casual self-service bistro has salad, vegetable, pasta and cake bars as well as various hot dishes prepared to order. Good value too are their special promotions, such as the all-you-can-eat pasta dinner after 6.30pm on Tuesday (€9.50). Children under 1.2 metres-tall eat for free.

Kreuzberg *Bergmann 103 (☎ 694 83 23, Bergmannstrasse 103, Kreuzberg 61)* **Map 5** Snacks €2.50-5, mains €6.50-11.50. Open 9.30am-1am. The menu here suits cosmopolitan culinary tastes. Best bet, perhaps, is the Alsatian Flammekuche, though we hear the Turkish-style dishes are worth trying too. Service, alas, is breathtakingly slow and perfunctory.

Mitte *Ganymed (☎ 28 59 90 46, Schiffbauerdamm 5)* **Map 7** Mains €12.50-21. This revamped GDR leftover sits in the shadow of the Berliner Ensemble theatre (high celebrity quotient). The food is sophisticated German with prices to match. It's all consumed sitting on chocolate-coloured banquettes, surrounded by mirrors, wood and blue Dutch tiles.

Hackescher Hof (☎ 283 52 93, Rosenthaler Strasse 40-41) **Map 7** Mains €6-16. Open 7am-2am, Sat & Sun from 9am. This cafeteria-sized place has sacrificed ts cultured atmosphere to become just another tourist trap. It's almost always full, which keeps staff simmering at potentially explosive stress levels. On the plus side is the sky-high ceiling which helps smoke dissipate more quickly.

Maxwell (☎ *280 71 21, Bergstrasse 22*) **Map 3** Mains €19-25. Dinner only. Beautifully located in a restored courtyard with a large terrace, Maxwell is a good address for those with demanding palates. Using only locally grown products, the chef puts substance before culinary pyrotechnics. The menu changes seasonally and may feature Irish smoked salmon, lobster bisque or duck with black pepper sauce. Deep pockets are required.

Prenzlauer Berg *Weitzmann* (☎ *442 71 25, Husemannstrasse 2*) **Map 3** Breakfast €1.65-12, mains €7.50-11. Outdoor tables at this retro cafe offer front-row views of Käthe-Kollwitz-Platz and the tourist buses prowling through the neighbourhood. The food's German with French touches. Night owls can nurse their hangovers with a 'Schwarzes Frühstück' (black breakfast): black coffee and a cigarette.

Schöneberg *Toronto* (☎ *781 92 30, Crellestrasse 17*) **Map 4** Breakfast €3-8, mains €9-15. Open from 9am Mon-Sat, from 10am Sun. This place is as contemporary and unpretentious as the city after which it's named. The chef's fearlessly blend ethnic cuisines into interesting concoctions, although the biggest crowds come for the excellent breakfasts.

Wilmersdorf *Hamlet* (☎ *882 13 61, Uhlandstrasse 47*) **Map 6** Breakfast €4-9, mains €8-12.50. Open 8am-3am. The menu at this beautiful and stylish brasserie works its way around the Mediterranean. Couscous, grilled chicken breast, scampi and risotti are typical entrees.

Manzini (☎ *885 78 20, Ludwigkirchstrasse 11*) **Map 6** Breakfast €6-10, mains €10-17.50. Open 8am-2am. A few steps away, Manzini is a timelessly trendy tunnel-shaped restaurant where chandeliers dangle

above diners settled into snug green-leather banquettes. The kitchen churns out creative dishes based on seasonal ingredients; the risotti are especially popular.

Italian
Charlottenburg *Ali Baba* (☎ *881 13 50, Bleibtreustrasse 45*) **Map 6** Pizzas €1.50-6.50. Open to 3am. There's no cave and no robbers but the thin-crust pizza is fresh and generously topped. The pasta dishes come in two sizes and are a filling alternative.

XII Apostoli (☎ *312 14 33, Bleibtreustrasse 49*) **Map 6** Breakfast €3.50-10, pizza €8-10, mains from €15. Open 24hrs. Finish up a night on the town with breakfast at this swank eatery with its hilariously over-the-top, church-like decor of Rubenesque cherubs, kitschy frescoes and gaudy chandeliers. At other times, it brims with people with money to burn on pricey pizzas named after the apostles. The business lunch, served Monday to Friday, is good value.

Biscotti (☎ *312 39 37, Pestalozzistrasse 88*) **Map 6** Mains €10-16. Dinner only, open Mon-Sat. This is an upmarket trattoria with wicker, white linen, leafy plants and a refined menu of exquisite pasta, meat and fish dishes.

Pizzeria Piccola Taormina (☎ *881 47 10, Uhlandstrasse 29*) **Map 6** Pizzas €2.75-6.25. You'll be serenaded by Italo pop while munching on generously topped thin-crust pizzas in this bustling, blue-walled labyrinth. The staff are stingy with smiles but who cares when the pizza is generously laden with mushrooms, pepperoni and other goodies? The snack version is just €1. It's self-service.

Kreuzberg *Il Casolare* (☎ *69 50 66 10, Grimmstrasse 30, Kreuzberg 36*) **Map 5** Pizza €5-8, mains €6-12.50. On a scenic stretch of the Landwehrkanal, this no-fuss trattoria is as comfortable as a hug from an old friend. It's run by a North Italian family who serve lots of fresh pasta and daily specials, although it's the thin-crust pizza that keeps the regulars – yuppies to young families – coming back for more.

Sale e Tabacchi (☎ *252 11 55, Kochstrasse 18, Kreuzberg 61*) **Map 7** Mains

€13-24. Open 9am-2am Mon-Fri, 10am-2am Sat & Sun. Integrated into the *taz* newspaper headquarters, this place gets a media crowd, especially at lunch time. The chef likes to spin culinary creations around exquisite ingredients like lobster tails, artichoke hearts and veal cutlets, making eating here a relatively pricey proposition.

Mitte *Cantamaggio* (☎ *283 18 95, Alte Schönhauser Strasse 4)* **Map 3** Mains €10-22. Cantamaggio doled out delicious pasta and more substantial mains long before tourists 'discovered' the Scheunenviertel. Tables here are always crowded – sometimes with actors and directors from the nearby Volksbühne – phone ahead for reservations.

Zucca (☎ *24 72 12 12, Am Zwirngraben, S-Bahn arches 11 and 12)* **Map 7** Breakfast €1.50-8, mains €6-17.50. Zucca is the childhood dream of Klaus Behrendt, a well-known German TV detective. It evokes the elegance of a 1920s coffeehouse, Italian-style: mirrors, chandeliers, antique-y murals, stylish beige and black colours. Food-wise it's a mixed bag of cleverly filled ciabatta sandwiches (from €3) and daily-changing blackboard specials. Good cappuccino too.

Die Zwölf Apostel (☎ *201 02 22, Georgenstrasse, S-Bahn arches 177-180)* **Map 7** Mains €8-16. Open 9am-1am. This place is perfect for capping a day of cultural immersion on Museumsinsel. You'll be unwinding under vaulted S-Bahn arches, watched over by cherubs as you munch on wheelbarrow-sized pizzas delivered straight from the wood-fire oven. Note to the cash-strapped: from noon to 5pm, all pizzas are half-price.

Prenzlauer Berg *Kommandatur Pizzeria* (☎ *44 03 14 68, Knaackstrasse 18)* **Map 3** Mains €5-13. This former smoky anarchist bar has metamorphosed into a chic Italian restaurant popular with tourists and neighbours alike. Sink your teeth into toothsome pizza with creative toppings or go for the tuna carpaccio or any of the fish dishes.

Lappeggi (☎ *442 63 47, Kollwitzstrasse 56)* **Map 3** Mains €8-16. This hip trattoria is often frequented by a mixed clientele of artists, actors, media types and managers.

The fish soup is loaded with finny friends and there's also a bunch of vegetarian dishes. Sneak a peek of the Kollwitzplatz scene from their outdoor tables.

Schöneberg *Lucky Pizzeria* (☎ *781 12 93, Willmanndamm 15)* **Map 4** Mains €3-8. At this popular place the pizza comes in three sizes. It's cosy, cheap and congenial and has been around for more than 30 years – which is saying something in ever-changing Berlin.

Petite Europe (☎ *781 29 64, Langenscheidtstrasse 1)* **Map 4** Mains €10-13. Dinner only. This popular restaurant has a local neighbourhood feel and serves good-value, no-nonsense Italian food in a rustic setting. Show up early if you want a table or, better yet, call for a reservation.

Trattoria á Muntagnola (☎ *211 66 42, Fuggerstrasse 27)* **Map 6** Mains €8-17. Flavour-packed sauces, fresh pasta and substantial meat dishes are the cornerstones of the menu at this neighbourhood Italian. Garlic strands, heavy chandeliers and classic red-white tablecloths do their part in transporting you straight to Sicily.

Japanese
Sachiko Sushi (☎ *313 22 82, Savignypassage, S-Bahn Arch 584, Charlottenburg)* **Map 6** Individual sushi plates €3.50-5.50, lunch special €9.50. Open noon-midnight daily. Sushi servings, sitting on plates coloured to correspond with the price, float by you in a little 'river' built into the oval bar. Your final tab is calculated by adding up the plates. Best buy is the lunch special which gets you three plates plus all the green tea you can drink.

Sushi-Bar (☎ *281 51 88, Friedrichstrasse 115, Mitte)* **Map 3** Sushi plates €8-11. The food is always fresh and excellent at this place located under the Hotelpension die Loge. Nigiri (bars of rice topped with fish slices) cost €2.50-3.50 per two-piece serving and maki-sushi (rice roll with various fillings wrapped in seaweed) tops out at €8.

Tabibito (☎ *624 13 45, Karl-Marx-Strasse 56, Neukölln)* **Map 5** Mains €10-20. Dinner only, open Wed-Mon. Surprise! One of Berlin's best – and most reasonably priced

– sushi bars is not in trendy Mitte but in working-class Neukölln. Authentic and intimate, what's on the menu depends on the season and on what chef Mitsuru finds at the fish market that day. This place is a real find.

Takeaway 'susherias' have also sprouted across Berlin.

Kiraku Sushi (☎ *216 52 02, Motzstrasse 8, Schöneberg)* **Map 4** Maki sushi €2.50-8, nigiri sushi €2.50-3. Open daily. This tiny stand-up eatery and takeaway makes wonderfully fresh sushi and has well-priced lunch specials (€6-7).

Flying Fish Sushi (☎ *782 06 63, Eisenacher Strasse 67)* **Map 4** Maki €2.50-5, nigiri €2.50-3.50 Also recommended in Schöneberg is Flying Fish Sushi.

Sushi Imbiss (☎ *881 27 90, Pariser Strasse 44, Wilmersdorf)* **Map 6**; (☎ *215 49 30, Goltzstrasse 24, Schöneberg)* **Map 4** Nigiri sushi €1.75-2.50, maki sushi €2.50-3. Open daily, from 4pm Sun. These clean holes-in-the-wall serve expertly cut raw fish morsels. You can save by ordering combination platters priced from €5.50-18.

Kosher & Jewish

Thanks to a growing Jewish population – and an increasing interest in Jewish culture – restaurants serving Jewish food have proliferated. Only the first three listed here are strictly kosher.

Arche Noah (☎ *882 61 38, Fasanenstrasse 79, Charlottenburg)* **Map 6** Mains €12-17. Set meals €11-13. Open 11.30am-3.30pm daily & 6.30pm-11pm Sun-Fri. Berlin's oldest kosher restaurant is inside the Jewish Community House. Besides the expansive a la carte menu, multi-course dinners are served daily. For the greatest selection, come on Tuesday night when they bring out a filling all-you-can-eat buffet with 30 items (€17.50). Call ahead for reservations.

Beth Café (☎ *281 31 35, Tucholskystrasse 40, Mitte)* **Map 3** Mains €2-8. Open 11am-10pm Sun-Fri (to 8pm Mon). This is a good-value cafe-bistro with a smoking ban and pretty inner courtyard. Come here for lox on toast, various salads, gefilte fish and other staples of Jewish cuisine. It's affiliated

with the congregation of Adass Jisroel, which also operates *Kolbo*, a small kosher supermarket at Auguststrasse 77–78.

Plaetzl (☎ *217 75 06, Passauer Strasse 4, Schöneberg)* **Map 6** Mains €3.50-7.50. This kosher Imbiss serves salads, vegetarian dishes, gefilte fish and other fare in a relaxed environment. Stock up for home at the integrated supermarket. Another supermarket is *Schalom* (☎ *312 11 31, Wielandstrasse 43, Charlottenburg)* **Map 6**.

A few other restaurants also serve Jewish and Israeli food, but they don't have the Kashrut certificate.

Oren (☎ *282 82 28, Oranienburger Strasse 28, Mitte)* **Map 3** Mains €6-12. Open 10am-1am. Fuse cool moderne design with an eclectic crowd and you get this swank stop in the heart of Mitte's tourist corridor. The Orient-Express platter of mezze (appetisers, €10) is a standout. Noncarnivores have plenty to pick from a menu that's available in Hebrew, English and German.

Rimón (☎ *28 38 40 32, Oranienburger Strasse 26, Mitte)* **Map 3** Mains €7.50-12.50. Housed on the ground floor of the Jewish Cultural Centre, this restaurant is all about Israeli and Eastern European Jewish specialities, from latkes to kreplach to falafel. It's especially packed when the food's served with a side of live klezmer music, about every two weeks.

Am Wasserturm (☎ *442 88 07, Knaackstrasse 22, Prenzlauer Berg)* **Map 3** Mains €10-13. Next to a synagogue, this restaurant has an extensive menu that goes far beyond the usual Jewish food with interesting concoctions, including some vegie choices, for all budgets. The decor features murals and framed explanations of Jewish prayer rituals, but in fine weather, the sunny outdoor terrace is the place to be.

Latin American

Tex-Mex has certainly arrived in Berlin, with 'cantinas' appearing in trendy districts. If you know the real thing, you may be disappointed by the wimpy spicing of many dishes.

Locus (☎ *691 56 37, Marheinekeplatz 4, Kreuzberg 61)* **Map 5** Mains €6-8. Watch kids horsing around on the car-free square from your seat at a rustic outdoor table at this local mainstaywhich serves all the Mexican standards from enchiladas to burritos to fajitas.

Lone Star Taqueria (☎ *692 71 82, Bergmannstrasse 11, Kreuzberg 61*) **Map 5** Mains €4.50-9. This nearby contender serves good-sized and good-looking portions of better than average Mexican food. Don't come if you're starving – it's often crammed and service can be glacial. Happy hour is from 5pm to 8pm.

Frida Kahlo (☎ *445 70 16, Lychener Strasse 37, Prenzlauer Berg*) **Map 3** Breakfast €4-7.50, mains €5.50-11.50. Open from 10am. Surrounded by eclectic objects and pseudo-Aztec wall stencilling, you'll be noshing on gourmet versions of Mexican staples here, from enchiladas to fajitas, in a lively atmosphere. During summer, the action spills out onto the pavement with views of Helmholtz square.

Poco Loco (☎ *881 18 68, Pariser Strasse 18, Wilmersdorf*) **Map 6** Mains €3-8. Open from 3pm. Mixed in among the American diners along here is this kitschy yet fun Mexican cantina where walls are plastered with posters and whimsical dolls and figurines dangle from the ceiling. The food's pretty good and filling.

Middle Eastern & Russian
Pasternak (☎ *441 33 99, Knaackstrasse 22-24, Prenzlauer Berg*) **Map 3** Mains €10-15. Open 10am-2am daily. One of the first restaurants near the historic water tower, Pasternak revives Russian nostalgia with updated versions of traditional favourites (borscht, pelmeni, beef stroganoff). The Farschmacker is a good hangover antidote: vodka plus chopped herring mixed with egg, apple, cucumber and onion on toast. Yum…!

Scarabeo (☎ *885 06 16, Ludwigkirchstrasse 6, Wilmersdorf*) **Map 6** Mains €12-16. Gallery-like and kitsch-free, this classic gourmet Egyptian entry impresses with succulently spiced grilled lamb, chicken or veal. Classic appetisers like baba ghanoush and kibbe (bulgur patties) also tantalise the palate.

Spanish
El Borriquito (☎ *312 99 29, Wielandstrasse 6, Charlottenburg*) **Map 6** Mains €7-13. Open 7pm-5am. El Borriquito offers a rustic Spanish country-inn atmosphere that gets especially lively after midnight when guitar music often erupts spontaneously – let the fiesta begin! Savour the ambience while digging into plates of meaty mains.

Don Quijote (☎ *881 32 08, Bleibtreustrasse 41, Charlottenburg*) **Map 6** Mains €10-15. Dinner daily. This woodsy place with a tiled bar has excellent tapas, fish and paella.

Brazil (☎ *28 59 90 26, Gormannstrasse 22, Mitte*) **Map 3** Mains €10-15. Dinner only. At cavernous, trendy Brazil you'll be dining on fragrant frango estufado (chicken braised in wine), feijoada (hearty stew) and good salads. Wash it all down with tasty caipirinhas.

Bar-Celona (☎ *282 91 53, Hannoversche Strasse 2, Mitte*) **Map 3** Tapas €2-3.50, paella €11-13. This tunnel-shaped establishment has eccentric lamps, yummy paella (a 30-minute wait) and, on some nights, live flamenco music and dancing.

Yosoy (☎ *28 39 12 13, Rosenthaler Strasse 37, Mitte*) **Map 7** Tapas €2.50-4.50, tapas platter €7.50, paella €10 (two-person minimum). This lovely tapas bar transports you straight to the south of Spain with its sunny walls, Moorish tiles and buzzing, down-to-earth atmosphere.

Thai & South-East Asian
Sticks (☎ *312 90 42, Knesebeckstrasse 15, Charlottenburg*) **Map 6** Mains €8-13. Thai-Vietnamese cooking in its infinite variety is on the menu, making it likely that you'll find your favourite among the aromatic noodle and rice dishes as well as duck, tofu and seafood specialities. Vegetarians should ask for the separate menu.

Good Time (☎ *28 04 60 15, Chausseestrasse 1, Mitte*) **Map 3** Mains €6.50-12.50. Ethnic decor, napkins neatly folded into lotus blossoms and a menu that goes beyond the standard Thai repertoire characterise this friendly restaurant. Some dishes have Indonesian inflections.

Kamala (☎ *283 27 97, Oranienburger Strasse 69, Mitte)* **Map 3** Mains €9-14. Another Thai option is this petite basement eatery that's usually packed to the gills. The plain decor contrasts with the colourful dishes, including lip-smacking curries and noodles paired with either meat or vegetables.

Mao Thai (☎ *441 92 61, Wörther Strasse 30, Prenzlauer Berg)* **Map 3** Mains €10-12.50. The owners of Kamala also run this classy spot, where the menu is as intriguing as the carved statuettes and original Asian art. The sublime Thai cuisine has complex flavouring and tends to be on the spicy side. Prices are up there, but for budget gourmets there's a lunch menu for €8 (served until 3pm weekdays). Reservations are advised. There's a nonsmoking section.

Rice Queen (☎ *44 04 58 00, Danziger Strasse 13, Prenzlauer Berg)* **Map 3** Mains €5-9. Cheerfully painted walls and modernist furniture indicate that this is not your usual pan-Asian restaurant. Chef Garry Chan draws upon the ingredients and cooking techniques of Malaysia, China, Thailand and Indonesia to come up with a light and clever crossover cuisine.

Tuk-Tuk (☎ *781 15 88, Grossgörschenstrasse 2, Schöneberg)* **Map 4** Mains €8-16. Dinner only. Stepping into Tuk-Tuk feels like walking into an intimate bamboo den in Jakarta. Soothing gamelan music lets you enjoy your meat- or vegie-based Indonesian dishes in a relaxing ambience.

Angkor Wat (☎ *393 39 22, Paulstrasse 22, Tiergarten)* **Map 2** Mains €10-16. This exotic, cavernous place serves Cambodian fondue, which involves cooking your own meat and vegies in a cauldron right at your table (€30 for two). The other dishes, many of them coconut-milk-based, offer an intriguing cocktail of flavours.

Turkish

There's more to Turkish cuisine than the ubiquitous doner kebab and these restaurants are here to prove it.

Hitit (☎ *322 45 57, Knobelsdorffstrasse 35, Charlottenburg)* **Map 4** Mains €7.50-15. A hit with meat lovers and vegetarians

alike is this cool and elegant eatery with wall reliefs and a marble fountain. The appetiser platter is a winner, though main courses of grilled meat, as well as the meatless casseroles, convince as well. The service is good too.

Bagdad (☎ *612 69 62, Schlesische Strasse 2, Kreuzberg 36)* **Map 5** Mains €7-12. Although named after the Iraqi capital, Bagdad has mostly meaty Turkish mains, as well as salads, which, in summer, are best enjoyed in the relaxing garden. Belly dancers do their thing on Friday and Saturday nights.

Merhaba (☎ *692 17 13, Hasenheide 39, Kreuzberg 36)* **Map 5** Mains €10-13. Quality meats (lamb is a speciality) and vegetables, healthily prepared on the grill are the draw of this top-rated Turkish restaurant. In summer, the big beer garden beckons as well.

Malete (☎ *280 77 59, Chausseestrasse 131, Mitte)* **Map 4** Mains €7.50-12.50. This low-key restaurant gets a mixed clientele of students, office workers and tourists and also serves interesting breakfasts.

Hasir Mitte (☎ *28 04 16 16, Oranienburger Strasse 4, Mitte)* **Map 3** Mains €11-14. The flagship restaurant of this small chain charms with attentive service, exotic decor and deliciously spiced food. The appetiser platter offers a fireworks of flavours and is not to be missed; and neither are the steaming loaves of Fladenbrot.

Miro (☎ *44 73 30 13, Raumerstrasse 29, Prenzlauer Berg)* **Map 3** Breakfast €4-7.50, mains €7-11. Open 10am-midnight. The most coveted tables at this relaxed neighbourhood eatery are the low ones where you sit on fluffy pillows. The food, however, tastes just as good in the main dining room with red-brick walls and wooden floors. All dishes are prepared fresh and many are meatless.

Vegetarian

'Vegetarian' restaurants often serve fish as well. Most restaurants and cafes listed elsewhere in this chapter offer at least one vegetarian dish as well as fresh salads. Indian, Thai, Vietnamese and other Asian eateries also have a good selection of meat-free fare.

PLACES TO EAT

Einhorn (☎ 881 42 41, Mommsenstrasse 2, Charlottenburg) **Map 6**; *(☎ 211 25 04, Wittenbergplatz 5-6, Schöneberg)* **Map 7** Buffet items €1.50 per 100g. Mains €5-7.50. Open 9am-6.30pm Mon-Fri, 10am-4pm Sat. These are simple stand-up places with a buffet of antipasti, salads and daily-changing hot dishes. The Wittenbergplatz branch is great for dropping in after a shopping spree at nearby KaDeWe. The menu makes forays into various cuisines from around the world.

Satyam (☎ 312 90 79, Goethestrasse 5, Charlottenburg) **Map 6** Mains €3-6.50. This easy-going all-vegetarian eatery serves Indian food with flavours from mild to bold.

PI Bar (☎ 0170-527 58 82, Gabriel-Max-Strasse 17, Friedrichshain) **Map 5** Mains €6.50-13.50. At PI, the creativity went as much into the design as into the food, which bears Mediterranean touches. There's a cocktail bar out the back.

Thymian (☎ 69 81 52 06, Gneisenaus-trasse 57, Kreuzberg 61) **Map 5** Mains €8-15. Dinner only, open Tues-Sun. Clever melanges of herbs and spices give the fish and vegetable dishes here that special kick. It's a cosy restaurant with only a few tables, so reservations are advised.

Abendmahl (☎ 612 51 79, Muskauer Strasse 9, Kreuzberg 36) **Map 5** Mains €8-16. Dinner only. This upmarket restaurant has an inventive menu, including fish, and cleverly named dishes like Murder in the Aquarium (fried dorado) or Heavenly Suicide (a dessert). In reference to the restaurant's name 'Last Supper', it's all watched over by a statue of Jesus and religious kitsch. Alas, service is pretty slow, some of the dishes outdistance the chef's skills and portions are model-sized.

Seerose (☎ 69 81 59 27, Mehringdamm 48, Kreuzberg 61) **Map 5** Dishes €2-5. Grains, fresh salads, casseroles and other healthy goodies can be found on the daily-changing buffet at this popular budget eatery. Order at the counter, pay when you leave.

Little Shop of Foods (☎ 44 05 64 44, Kollwitzstrasse 90, Prenzlauer Berg) **Map 3** Meals €3-7. Come here for a journey into the vegetable kingdom. Actually more of a restaurant than a shop, it's a no-nonsense environment enlivened with beautiful floral tiles and wainscoting. The chef turns whatever is fresh and in season into delicious, sometimes eccentric, dishes. 'Yummy', to quote one of our readers.

Hakuin (☎ 218 20 27, Martin-Luther-Strasse 1, Schöneberg) **Map 4** Mains €13-17. Run by a Buddhist organisation, this restaurant makes a celebration out of each meal, using an array interesting ingredients – exotic mushrooms, algae and tofu included. Service can be glacial but the food's delicious.

CAFES

Cafes are an inspired German institution and the number and variety of them in Berlin is astonishing. They're wonderful places to relax over a cup of coffee while reading a newspaper or magazine or chatting away with friends. The afternoon *Kaffee und Kuchen* (coffee and cake) is a German cafe tradition, though these days it's mostly practised by the older generations.

Most cafes are casual eateries attracting people of all ages and walks of life. Most have expanded their culinary repertoire to include hot and cold snacks and some even serve more substantial meals.

Cafes usually make chameleon-like identity changes over the course of a day, starting out as a breakfast place, then offering a small lunch menu and cakes in the afternoon before turning into a restaurant-bar or just a bar at night. In fact, many places listed here would fit just as well into the earlier Restaurant section or the Bars & Pubs section of the Entertainment chapter.

Charlottenburg

Café Hardenberg (☎ 312 26 44, Harden-bergstrasse 10) **Map 6** Breakfast €2.75-5, dishes €2.25-6.50. Students from the art school and Technische Universität across the street treat this sprawling cafe as an extension of the student cafeteria. Alas, the nice stucco ceiling wears a yellow coat of smoke grime and its popularity can have a deleterious effect on the service, so pack some patience.

Café Kranzler (☎ 882 69 11, *Kurfürsten-damm 18-19*) **Map 6** Meals €4-8. Open 8am-midnight. Only a small token cafe, in a rotunda upstairs from the Gerry Weber clothing store, is left of one of the Berlin's oldest coffee houses, in business for some 175 years. Only the name of Helmut Jahn's new business and retail complex into which it is now integrated – the Neue Kranzler Eck – pays homage to more glorious days.

Leysieffer (☎ 882 79 61, *Kurfürstendamm 218*) **Map 6** Breakfast €2.75-14, cakes €3, mains €5-10. Open 9am-8pm Mon-Sat, 10am-6pm Sun. Fans of exquisite chocolates may never make it past the artful displays of the ground-floor store. Those who do venture upstairs will find a courtly cafe-bistro serving refined pastries and savoury morsels beneath tall stucco ceilings and mirrored walls.

Schwarzes Café (☎ 313 80 38, *Kantstrasse 148*) **Map 6** Dishes €4.50-9. Open around the clock, this is a perennial favourite of students and young travellers. It was founded in 1978 by 15 women who charged men DM1 (€0.50) 'admission' with the proceeds benefiting a women's shelter (a practice since abandoned). Breakfast is served any time. It's also famous for its – ahem! – creatively designed toilets.

Café Wintergarten (☎ 882 54 14, *Fasanenstrasse 23*) **Map 6** Breakfast €4.50-14, mains €10-16. Open 9.30am-1am. Intellectuals, artists and shoppers gather at this sophisticated place in the Literaturhaus for conversation, coffee or tasty international fare. In summer, the garden tables are the most coveted.

Friedrichshain
Of the many new places that have sprung up in this district, a few stand out for their congenial atmosphere and cheap prices.

Conmux (☎ 29138 63, *Simon-Dach-Strasse 35*) **Map 5** Mains €4-7.50. In the heart of the main drag, Conmux has industrial decor and builds a menu around vegies, meat and fish prepared in a home-style way.

Truxa (☎ 29 00 30 85, *Wühlischstrasse 30*) **off Map 5** Mains €6-12. Open from around 4pm. Close to Conmux, this friendly

establishment has a Latin-Caribbean theme menu. Capitalising on the salsa craze, free dance lessons are offered every Saturday.

Kreuzberg
Atlantic (☎ 691 92 92, *Bergmannstrasse 100, Kreuzberg 61*) **Map 5** Breakfast €3-10, snacks €3-7. Open 9am-2am. This is one of the most popular cafes for breakfast (served until 4pm) on the strip, although the place never seems to be wanting for customers. A few photos and little else adorn the lemony walls. It's a great spot for absorbing the local scene.

Barcomi's (☎ 694 81 38, *Bergmannstrasse 21, Kreuzberg 61*) **Map 5** Items €1-4.25. Open 9am-midnight Mon-Sat,10am-midnight Sun. This American-style hole-in-the-wall is as busy as Grand Central Station during rush hour. Main attractions are the freshly roasted coffees which go well with the muffins and bagels.

Hannibal (☎ 611 23 88, *Wiener Strasse 69, Kreuzberg 36*) **Map 5** Breakfast €2-8, mains €6-9. Open 8am-3am Mon-Sat, 9am-3am Sun. This is a child-friendly contempo cafe with seats from old S-Bahns and lamps that look like upturned hubcaps. There are lots of low-priced dishes, including burgers and salads, and even an Internet terminal. Breakfast is served until 4pm.

Kichererbse (☎ 694 98 69, *Bergmannstrasse 96, Kreuzbeg 61*) **Map 5** Breakfast €5, mains €3.50-8. Open 10am-1am. For a change in taste, you could try one of the Arabic breakfasts here. Choose from eight varieties; omelette with dates and sweet potato is a typical selection. At other times, sample the couscous dishes or vegetable casseroles.

Café Morena (☎ 611 47 16, *Wiener Strasse 60, Kreuzberg 36*) **Map 5** Dishes €3-8, tapas platters €6.50-9.50. Open 9am-4am. Always busy, this is a classic with a Spanish twist. Best thing: their pancakes, piled high with fruit and drizzled with maple syrup, served until 5pm. At night, the tasty tapas go best with the cocktails or beer.

Morgenland (☎ 611 31 83, *Skalitzer Strasse 35, Kreuzberg 36*) **Map 5** Mains €5-9. An excellent address for breakfast, this cafe fills especially quickly on weekends when hungry acolytes come in waves to feed on the all-you-can-eat buffet for €8. Otherwise the food's pan-European – pasta to lamb to fried fish.

Café Rix (☎ 686 90 20, Karl-Marx-Strasse 141, Neukölln) **Map 5** Breakfast €2-8, mains €3-10. A jewel in downtrodden Neukölln, this cafe integrated within a cultural complex has a lovely Art Deco ambience combined with gold-leaf stucco ceilings. The cross-cultural menu ranges from felafels to tagliatelle to tortilla chips, all of them cheap.

Mitte

Café Adler (☎ 251 89 65, Friedrichstrasse 206) **Map 7** Breakfast €2-6, mains €6-10. Open 9.30am-midnight. This little cafe already stood in its spot when Checkpoint Charlie was still in operation. Now it looks out over the empty intersection but is still a good place for a respite after a visit to the Haus am Checkpoint Charlie museum.

Café Aedes (☎ 285 82 75, Rosenthaler Strasse 40-41) **Map 7** Breakfast €4.50-10, mains €7-10. Open from 10am. Worn-out tourists are nursed back to life with strong cappuccino at this trendy cafe inside the Hackescher Höfe. Locals too are drawn to this artsy place with its cutting-edge interior. The small menu features three meaty and three meatless dishes daily.

Barcomi's (☎ 28 59 83 63, Sophienstrasse 21) **Map 3** Snacks €1.50-5. Open 9am-10pm Mon-Sat, 10am-10pm Sun. Unlike its Kreuzberg cousin, Mitte's Barcomi's is more of a deli than a cafe, though you can still get bagels, muffins and coffee. Other options include marinated cheeses and delicious but expensive build-your-own sandwiches. It's located in the central courtyard of the Sophie-Gips-Höfe.

Café Orange (☎ 282 00 28, Oranienburger Strasse 32) **Map 3** Breakfast €2.50-8, mains €4.50-12. Open 9am-1am. If not invaded by bus-tripping tourists this place next to the New Synagogue is a smart hangout with lofty stucco ceilings and a pleasant atmosphere. Pizza, pasta and salads are very affordable, though more substantial

meat and fish dishes cost around €10. Or you can just come for people-watching and a huge (though pricey) cup of coffee.

Prenzlauer Berg

Anita Wronski (☎ 442 84 83, Knaackstrasse 26-28) **Map 3** Breakfast €3-5, weekend brunch €6.50, mains €4-11. Open 10am-3am. This split-level space was one of the first Prenzlauer Berg cafes. You can observe locals and tourists at play, though the view of the historic water tower through the picture windows is also enjoyable. It's a popular breakfast place on weekends (served until 3pm).

Houdini (☎ 441 25 60, Lychener Strasse 35) **Map 3** Meals €3.50-7. If you've disappeared into the night, you can resurface at this corner cafe where breakfast is served until 5pm. After that, it's on to candlelit dinners of soups, pasta and lavosh wraps.

November (☎ 442 84 25, Husemannstrasse 15) **Map 3** Breakfast €4-9, dishes €7-9. Sparse, uncluttered decor characterises this friendly corner cafe whose huge picture windows gives you that fishbowl feeling. It's perfect for a quiet chat over a strong cuppa (or beer, if you prefer). Breakfast is served until afternoon.

Cafe Xion (☎ 44 03 66 88, Pappelallee 56) **Map 3** Dishes €3-11. The earth-tone colour scheme provides a soothing backdrop for the exhausted night owls landing at this cosy cafe. Breakfast is the busiest time but the mostly meatless mains draw a crowd at other times as well.

Schöneberg

Cafes belong to Schöneberg like froth belongs on cappuccino.

Café Berio (☎ 216 19 46, Maassenstrasse 7) **Map 4** Breakfast €4-25, mains €3-5. Open 8am-1.30am. The two-level Café Berio offers classical music and cakes that are as sweet as the gooiest love letter. It's pretty trendy and especially busy during Saturday's Winterfeldtplatz market. At night, it's swarmed by the gay crowd.

Montevideo (☎ 213 10 20, Victoria-Louise-Platz 6) **Map 6** Breakfast €3.50-9, mains €3.50-12.50. Lose yourself amongst mirrored walls, the cool charm of an American diner and big breakfasts from around the world – Japanese, American, Canadian, Dutch, Italian, Finnish etc.

Phoenix Lounge (☎ 215 75 67, *Kyffhäuser Strasse 14*) **Map 4** Breakfast €3-10, mains €6-9.50. Grab a table, order a large cup of steaming Milchcafe and begin to ponder the vast breakfast menu. Bagels and lox, or maybe the Spanish contender with manchego (cheese) and jamón (smoked ham), or… Take your time – just don't come if you're in a rush.

Sidney (☎ 216 52 53, *Winterfeldtstrasse 40*) **Map 4** Breakfast €3.50-9, dishes €3-8. Open 9am-2pm Sun-Thur, 9am-3am Fri-Sat. This place has a loosely inspired Australian theme that incorporates chrome, wicker and palm trees. It's best on Saturday morning when the picture windows provide first-rate views of the action in Winterfeldtplatz market.

TTT – TeeTeaThé (☎ 21 75 22 40, *Goltzstrasse 2*) **Map 4** Breakfast & mains €4-8. Open 9am-midnight Mon-Sat, from 10am Sun. For a perfectly prepared cup of tea, try TTT, a serene place decorated with East Asian aesthetic restraint. All teas – some 150 varieties – are also available for purchase and there's homemade cakes and snacks as well. Smoking is not permitted.

Tiergarten

Einstein (☎ 261 50 96, *Kurfürstenstrasse 58*) **Map 4**; (☎ 204 36 32, *Unter den Linden 42, Mitte*) **Map 7**. Breakfast €3-12.50, mains €9-19. This Viennese-style coffee house is Berlin's most elegant and stylish cafe distinguished by marble table-tops, big mirrors and comfy red upholstered banquettes. Breakfast, especially on weekends, is the best time to immerse yourself in the ambience. Mains have a distinct Austrian bent.

Café am Neuen See (☎ 254 49 30, *Lichtensteinallee 1*) **Map 6** Breakfast €2.50-12, mains €7-12. In Tiergarten park, this cafe is ideal on balmy summer nights. Beer garden service can be pretty slow, but that just gives you more time for people-watching and looking out over the lake.

The Joy of Breakfast

One of life's little luxuries is a leisurely breakfast, and Berliners have just about perfected the art. Any day of the week, a motley bunch of the city's hungover, idle rich, students and late risers gather at countless cafes to tuck into big plates of eggs, meats, cheeses, breads, butter, jam and a plethora of other foods.

On Sunday, many places lay out truly table-bending brunch buffets that include salads, lox and cream cheese, quiches, pasta, hot meats and whatever else takes the chef's fancy. You can pig out at these all-you-can-eat spreads.

Breakfasts can cost as little as €2.50 for coffee, a croissant and jam, or as much as €12 for a lavish spread with a glass of champagne. At many places, you can order breakfast until 4pm or 5pm. The following spots do more than scramble a few eggs and serve coffee. All are described in greater detail in this chapter.

Charlottenburg
XII Apostoli, Café Hardenberg, Leysieffer, Café Wintergarten, Schwarzes Café

Kreuzberg
Atlantic, Café Adler, Barcomi's, Gasthaus Dietrich Herz, Hannibal, Kichererbse, Melitta Sundström (see Entertainment chapter), Café Morena, Morgenland, Café Rix

Mitte
Aedes East, Barcomi's, Einstein, Gugelhof, Malete, Café Orange, Zucca

Prenzlauer Berg
Frida Kahlo, Houdini, Miro, November, Amsterdam and Schall und Rauch (see Entertainment chapter), Weitzmann, Anita Wronski, Café Xion

Schöneberg
Café Berio, Montevideo, Phoenix Lounge, Sidney, Toronto, TTT

Tiergarten
Café am Neuen See, Einstein

Wilmersdorf
Hamlet, Manzini

PLACES TO EAT

SNACKS & FAST FOOD

Berlin is a paradise for snackers on the go, with Turkish, Greek, Italian, Middle Eastern, Chinese – you name it – specialties available at Imbiss stalls throughout the city.

Soup Kultur (☎ *74 30 82 95, Kurfürstendamm 224, Charlottenburg)* **Map 6**; *(Kantstrasse 56a, Charlottenburg)* **Map 6**; *(Rosa-Luxemburg-Strasse 7, Mitte)* **Map 7** Soups €2.50-4.50. This is a pint-sized stand-up place serving daily 10 different, freshly made soups from around the world – hearty potato to refreshing gazpacho to exotic South African sousboontje.

Gosch (☎ *88 68 28 00, Kurfürstendamm 212, Charlottenburg)* **Map 6**; *(*☎ *25 29 68 20, Alte Potsdamer Strasse 1, Tiergarten)* (see Potsdamer Platz & Kulturforum map in the Things to See & Do chapter) Sandwiches €2-3.50, mains €5.50-11.50. Only the brisk North Sea wind is missing from this stylish fish bistro, a clone of the original branch on the Frisian island of Sylt. Come here for a quick takeaway sandwich or pick your 'poisson' at the counter, then wait while it's being turned into a delicious meal.

Salomon Bagels (☎ *881 81 96, Joachimstaler Strasse 13, Charlottenburg)* **Map 6**; *(*☎ *25 29 76 26, Potsdamer Platz Arkaden, Tiergarten)* (see the Potsdamer Platz & Kulturforum map in the Things to See & Do chapter) Bagel sandwiches €1.25-4.25. The lowly bagel is treated with spiritual reverence here (the back of the menu features 'The history of the bagel as seen from a Solomonic standpoint'). Various stuffings are available, including the classic lox and cream cheese, alongside fresh salads. Bagels alone are €0.75 each.

Bagels & Bialys (☎ *283 65 46, Rosenthaler Strasse 46-48, Mitte)* **Map 7** Dishes €2-5. Bagels, casseroles, salads, soups, shwarma, ciabatta sandwiches – there's something for everyone at this hole-in-the-wall across from the Hackesche Höfe.

Salsabil (☎ *44 04 60 73, Wörther Strasse 16, Prenzlauer Berg)* **Map 3** Dishes €2-5. Eat like a pasha at this clean, friendly oriental Imbiss where you can sink your teeth into plump felafel or shwarma sandwiches while seated at low inlaid wood tables.

Habibi (☎ *61 65 83 46, Oranienstrasse 30, Kreuzberg 36)* **Map 5**; *(Winterfeldtplatz 24, Schöneberg)* **Map 4**; *(*☎ *787 44 28, Akazienstrasse 9, Schöneberg)* **Map 4** Prices €1.75-5. Open to 3am, to 5am Fri & Sat. This chain is the granddaddy of Berlin's felafel and shwarma circuit. Eat a la carte or order the Habibi platter, a generous combination of chickpea balls and meats along with a small salad (€5.50). All branches are great spots to restore balance to the brain after bar-hopping around the neighbourhood.

Hot Dog Laden (☎ *215 69 32, Goltzstrasse 15, Schöneberg)*; *(Motzstrasse 1, Schöneberg)* **both Map 4** Dogs €1.50-2. Dogs go haute at Hot Dog. There's relish and yellow mustard to satisfy the purists, while more adventurous types could sink a fang into a wiener smothered with aromatic chilli. Vegetarian varieties are available too.

Fish & Vegetables (☎ *821 68 16, Goltzstrasse 32, Schöneberg)* **Map 4** Meals €3.75-5.50. 'Cheap, authentic and delicious' describes this Thai kitchen straight from the streets of Bangkok (only cleaner). All dishes pair a sauce – laced with ginger, lemongrass and garlic – with a choice of tofu, tempeh, chicken, pork, fish or shrimp. Order, then take it home or eat here at the stand-up tables.

Shayan (☎ *215 15 47, Goltzstrasse 23, Schöneberg)* **Map 4** Appetisers & salads €3, mains €4-6. 'Kosch Armadid' – Welcome. 'Nusche Yan' – Enjoy your meal. A visit to this little Persian eatery comes complete with a quick language lesson. Seated on banquettes beneath sun-yellow walls, you can munch on such delicacies as chicken with pomegranate and walnut sauce (€6).

Asia Pavillon (☎ *25 29 69 17, Potsdamer Platz Arkaden, Tiergarten)* (see the Potsdamer Platz & Kulturforum map in the Things to See & Do chapter) Meals €2.50-6.25. This self-service eatery on the mall's top floor attracts a stream of famished shoppers with its huge plates of fried noodles.

Nordsee (☎ *213 98 33, Karl-Liebknecht-Strasse 6, Mitte)* **Map 7** Dishes €2-8. Open 10am-9pm Mon-Sat, 11am-9pm Sun. This chain has outlets throughout town serving quick, cheap and fresh-fish sandwiches for takeaway and a selection of hot meals.

FOOD COURTS

KaDeWe (☎ 212 10, 6th floor, Tauentzienstrasse 21, Schöneberg) **Map 6** The food hall here is legendary. Pick from a dozen varieties of caviar, a scrumptious selection of antipasti and a mind-boggling assortment of cheese and sausages (over 1800 varieties of each, we are told). It's all beautifully presented and interspersed with small bars and food counters where the moneyed cap off successful shopping sprees with a glass of Moet & Chandon. Putting together a picnic here would cost you a bundle. If you just want to fill your belly, head up to the cafe on the 7th floor.

Wertheim bei Hertie (☎ 88 00 35 00, Kurfürstendamm 231, Charlottenburg) **Map 6** Prices are lower, the ambience more relaxed, but the assortment is smaller at this food court/cafeteria.

Galeries Lafayette (☎ 20 94 90, Französische Strasse 23, Mitte) **Map 7** This store has a basement food court where gourmets with deep pockets perch at polished counters, sliding oysters down their gullets or digging into plates of calamari rings served on a bed of arugula.

Quartier 205 (Französische Strasse, Quartier 205, Mitte) **Map 7** For more reasonable prices and delicious down-to-earth food, simply wander a couple of buildings south to the small food court in the basement of Quartier 205. The bistro on the right has appetising rice and noodle dishes straight from the pan for around €6, while NK Insel on the left serves filling pasta dishes for €4-5. For dessert you can pick up a scrumptious pastry from the bakery in the centre.

The new **Potsdamer Platz Arkaden** (see the Potsdamer Platz & Kulturforum map in Things to See & Do) also has lots of quick eating choices in the basement, plus a couple of excellent eateries described under Snacks & Fast Food earlier in this chapter.

Turkish Delights

What's the most popular fast food in Berlin? No, not the hamburger and not even the sausage. It's the doughty doner kebab. Everywhere in the city you'll find small take-away restaurants where giant cones of spiced meat rotate on an upright grill, waiting to be shaved into thin slivers which are then stuffed into lightly toasted bread along with fresh salad and a garlicky yoghurt sauce. It's a complete meal usually costing no more than €2.50.

In Turkey, meat has been put through its motions in this fashion for nearly two centuries, but the idea of serving it sandwich-style was born in Berlin. Though nobody can really be sure, credit for the creation is usually given to Mehmed Aygün, an enterprising Turkish emigrant who, at the tender age of 16, opened the first doner stand in Neukölln in 1971. The success of Aygün's savvy sandwich pole-vaulted him to the helm of the small Hasir chain of Turkish restaurants, which includes its flagship at Oranienburger Strasse 4.

The secret to a tasty doner is in the preparation of the huge meat hunk, traditionally consisting of about 90% veal and 10% lamb. Layers of ground meat alternate with thick cut slices which have been marinated in a secret spice mix for up to 24 hours. Relatively new on the scene are the chicken doners whose popularity has increased since the recent hoof-and-mouth and mad cow disease scares. It's estimated that there are now around 1500 doner kebab stands in Berlin selling as many as 100 million portions annually. Not all offer the same standard, but those listed here are all tasty contenders.

Bosporus Grill (☎ 34 20 45 77, Wilmersdorfer Strasse 105, Charlottenburg) **Map 6**

Grill & Schlemmerbuffet Zach (☎ 283 21 53, Brunnenstrasse 197, Mitte) **Map 3** Note: this place is right outside the north-west Rosenthaler Platz U-Bahn exit and not to be confused with the much larger Imbiss nearby on Torstrasse.

Hasir Imbiss (☎ 215 60 60, Maassenstrasse 10, Schöneberg) **Map 4**, (☎ 614 23 73, Adalbertstrasse 10) **Map 5**

Hisar (U-Bahn station Yorckstrasse, Schöneberg) **Map 6**

STUDENT CAFETERIAS

University cafeterias are known within Germany as *Mensas,* which, by the way, comes from the Latin for 'table' and has nothing to do with the intellectual society. Unless noted, mensas are open 11.15am to 2.30pm Monday to Friday. Menus change daily but usually consist of a selection of hot and cold dishes, salads and dessert. You can eat for as little as €3 and will find it hard to spend more than €6. You may be asked to show student ID, or you must pay a little more.

Technische Universität Mensa (☎ 311 22 41, Hardenbergstrasse 34, Charlottenburg) **Map 6** Anyone, student or not, may eat here. Nonstudents pay slightly more, but you can still fill your tray with a three-course lunch for under €5. The *cafe* on the ground floor is open 8am-7.45pm and has drinks, snacks and basic mains for €2.50-3.50. The entrance is across from Steinplatz. On the 2nd floor is a smaller restaurant with higher prices.

Humboldt Universität Mensa (☎ 20 93 27 32, Unter den Linden 6, Mitte) **Map 7** Enter the main portal, take the first door on your left, turn right at the end of the corridor and follow your nose. You must either show student ID (from any university) or pay nonstudent prices.

Mensa der Hochschule für Musik Hanns Eisler (☎ 203 09 23 40, Charlottenstrasse 55, Mitte) **Map 7** Open 8.30am-3pm Mon-Fri. You'll need your student ID to eat at the Mensa of this music academy.

Mensa Freie Universität (☎ 83 00 25 11, Otto-von-Simson-Strasse 23, Zehlendorf) **off Map 1** U-Bahn: U1 to Thielplatz. The Mensa here is nicknamed 'Rostlaube' (Rusty Arbour).

KANTINEN

On weekdays, you can enjoy a hot subsidised meal (€3-5) in a government cafeteria where you clear your own table. Each of Berlin's 12 districts has a town hall and all have Kantinen open to the public, though they only serve lunch.

Central ones include: *Rathaus Charlottenburg (Otto-Suhr-Allee 100)* **Map 2** near Schloss Charlottenburg (in the basement)

and *Rathaus Kreuzberg (Yorckstrasse 4-11)* **Map 5,** on the 10th floor with great views.

Arbeitsämter (employment offices) also have cheap Kantinen. A good one is in *Arbeitsamt IV (5th floor, Charlottenstrasse 90, Kreuzberg 61)* **Map 7** U-Bahn: U6 to Kochstrasse.

SELF-CATERING

To prepare your own food, start your shopping at the discount Aldi, Lidl, Plus or Penny Markt supermarket chains, which have outlets throughout Berlin, as well as the less common Tip. You may have to wait in long checkout queues but you will pay considerably less for basic food items. These are also the cheapest places to buy beer and table wines. More upmarket chains include Kaiser's, Reichelt, Spar and Bolle.

Aldi has a convenient branch on Joachimstaler Strasse **(Map 6)**, on the 1st floor opposite Zoo station, another is at Leibnizstrasse 72 **(Map 6)** near Kantstrasse; both are in Charlottenburg. *Tip* and *Penny Markt* are side by side near the corner of Hohenstaufenstrasse and Martin-Luther-Strasse in Schöneberg. *Kaiser's* locations include those on Nollendorfplatz **(Map 4)** and on Wittenbergplatz in Schöneberg **(Map 6)** and at Bleibtreustrasse 19 in Charlottenburg **(Map 6)**. *Plus* has a branch in the south-eastern corner of Savignyplatz in Charlottenburg **(Map 6)**. *Spar* outlets are everywhere as well.

Lidl has two branches open on Sunday (till 9pm), an absolute rarity; they're in U-Bahn stations Innsbrucker Platz, in Schöneberg, and Ostbahnhof **(Map 5)**, in Friedrichshain.

A few tips on German supermarket etiquette: at the checkout, you must pack your purchases yourself. And you'd better be quick, as you don't want to hold up the queue and draw withering stares from stressed-out hausfraus! Start packing the items away as soon as they've been scanned or punched into the register. Many Germans bring along re-usable plastic or canvas bags to carry their groceries. If you don't have your own, plastic bags are sold for around €0.20.

The best places to buy fresh produce are at farmers' markets (see the Shopping chapter).

Entertainment

Berlin is not just Germany's political capital but also its cultural hub. Nowhere else in the country is the scene as diverse, dynamic and international. This is as true for highbrow pursuits like opera, dance, theatre and classical music as it is for pop and experimental culture in the form of dance clubs, live music venues, cultural centres and cinema.

Berlin has so many places of amusement because Berliners enjoy spending their time and money this way. And since there are no closing times, they do so pretty much all hours.

The city's nightlife takes on different characteristics depending on the district. Charlottenburg (Map 6) has mostly upmarket venues, especially around Savignyplatz and side streets like Bleibtreustrasse and Grolmannstrasse. The western theatre district is on and around the nearby Ku'damm. The area around Gneisenaustrasse, Bergmannstrasse and Marheinekeplatz in Kreuzberg 61 (Map 5) is alternative but with trendy touches, while Kreuzberg 36 (Map 5) along Oranienstrasse and Wiener Strasse has preserved a grungy alternative feel. Around Winterfeldtplatz in Schöneberg (Map 4), you'll find trendy thirty-somethings juggling their alternative lifestyles with the demands of their careers and parenthood. The area around Nollendorfplatz and along Fuggerstrasse and Motzstrasse is one of Berlin's gay meccas.

While the nightlife scenes in the western districts are fairly stable and established, those in the eastern neighbourhoods are still evolving. Mitte, the original post-Wende playground, has become a tourist showcase, especially in the triangle formed by Oranienburger Strasse, Auguststrasse and Hackescher Markt (Map 3). But it's still a fun area for a night out and you shouldn't have any trouble finding a place to your liking. The eastern theatre district is also here along Friedrichstrasse north of Unter den Linden.

Prenzlauer Berg still preserves a bit of an experimental edge, although this is less so around increasingly commercial Käthe-Kollwitz-Platz and its side streets. For more authenticity, head to Knaackstrasse, Lychener Strasse and other streets north of Danziger Strasse.

The most cutting-edge venues are in Friedrichshain, especially along Simon-Dach-Strasse and around Boxhagener Platz, which brims with off-beat bars and restaurants. Drink and food prices are still much lower here than in other, more polished, parts of town. Mühlenstrasse has recently evolved into 'club row'. North of Frankfurter Allee, especially on Rigaer Strasse, a few underground cafes and squatters' clubs are still holding out. These are usually short-lived, not advertised and without a shingle to tip you off to their existence. You'll have to rely on the kindness of strangers to fill you in on what's hot. Guides who conduct the walking tours listed in the Getting Around chapter and people working at the area's hostels are usually good sources.

Listings

Zitty (€2.20) and *Tip* (€2.50) are bi-weekly listings magazines chock-full of insider tips and colourful articles that capture the constantly evolving Berlin Zeitgeist. *Tip* tends to be more mainstream and for a slightly older crowd, while *Zitty* is a tad edgier. Read the free entertainment rag called *030* for one-off parties, club news and trendoid tips. The monthly *Prinz* (€2.50) and *Berlin Programm* (€1.60) are not nearly as up-to-date and plugged-in. Another source is *Ticket* (€0.50), the Thursday supplement to the *Tagesspiegel* daily newspaper.

All publications are written in German, but you should be able to make sense of the listings even with a minimal command of the language.

Tickets

Outlets selling tickets to cultural and sporting events are scattered all over the city. Most agencies accept credit card reservations by phone; a 15% commission charge usually applies. If time permits, tickets will be mailed to you; if not, they'll be waiting for you at the venue's box office.

The ticket hotline operated by the BTM tourist offices (see the Facts for the Visitor chapter) is a good one-stop-shopping source. Other options include Theaterkasse Centrum (☎ 882 76 11, Meineckestrasse 25) **Map 6** and Concert & Theaterkasse City (☎ 313 88 58, Knesebeckstrasse 10) **Map 6**, both in Charlottenburg. In Schöneberg, you'll find Box Office Theaterkasse (☎ 215 54 63, Nollendorfplatz 7) **Map 4**. Another outlet is Showtime (☎ 217 77 54, Tauentzienstrasse 21) **Map 6** in the KaDeWe department store. See the Theatre section for details on Hekticket which offers last-minute half-price theatre tickets.

BARS & PUBS

Bars and pubs are an integral part of Berlin's nightlife. No matter where you are in the city, you're never far from one. A few words on procedure: it's customary to keep a tab instead of paying when you order or when drinks are served.

Charlottenburg

Gainsbourg (☎ 313 74 64, Savignyplatz 5) **Map 6** This American bar speaks to a thirty-something arty crowd. Relax in the warmly lit, clubby atmosphere while sipping one of the award-winning cocktails mixed by master shaker Frido Keiling. There's also a small menu of bistro fare.

Hegel (☎ 312 19 48, Savignyplatz 2) **Map 6** This is the preferred watering hole of academics and cultured expat Russians. It's the place where you can imbibe cleverly named drinks like Zarenblut (Tsar's blood) and Hegel's Todestrunk (Hegel's death drink). Things get downright nostalgic when someone bangs out a few classics on the piano.

Friedrichshain

Boxhagenener Platz and around is entertainment central in this district.

Astro Bar (☎ 29 66 16 15, Simon-Dach-Strasse 40) **Map 5** This bar timewarps you back to the 'spacey' 1960s. Nightly DJ music gets the crowd hopping after 10pm.

Dachkammer (☎ 296 16 73, Simon-Dach-Strasse 39) **Map 5** This place has a split personality: rustic country look, hearty snacks and stacks of magazines downstairs; cool '50s flashback in the cocktail bar upstairs.

Mana Mana (☎ 296 45 89, Niederbarnimstrasse 23) **Map 5** This is a low-key hangout popular with punks (only 'friendly' ones, we're assured). The ever-changing decor is wild and creative, and so are the bands. Cocktails here are dirt-cheap (€3-5).

Supamolly (☎ 292 27 44, Jessnerstrasse 41) **Map 1** This place has morphed from a squatter haunt to a respectable pub with an eclectic program. Usually it's live concerts, but theatre and films pad the schedule.

Die Tagung/Cube Club (☎ 292 87 56, Wühlischstrasse 29) **Map 5** GDR paraphernalia from flags to busts of Lenin and old advertisements let you wallow in pre-Wende nostalgia at the bar. The intimate Cube Club in the basement opens after 11pm Thur-Sat.

For a grittier vibe, visit Rigaer Strasse, where hard-core squatters run some pretty anarchic pubs and cafes. Most open whenever someone feels like it and their existence is constantly threatened by police busts. At the time of writing, a couple of these semi-established hold-outs included **Fischladen** at No 83 and **Schizzotempel** at No 77, both **Map 3**.

Filmriss (☎ 221 96 27, Rigaer Strasse 103) **Map 3** Former squat house gone respectable, this is now a dark and dank cafepub. It also shows old and new cult flicks twice a week (usually Wednesday and Sunday) for free! Get there early, it's small and very popular. Cheap beer, too.

Kreuzberg

Ankerklause (☎ 693 56 49, Kottbusser Damm 104, Kreuzberg 36) **Map 5** Low on aesthetics but high on energy is this Kreuzberg favourite in an old harbour-master's house above the Landwehrkanal. Breakfast on the terrace, sip coffee after shopping at the Turkish Market, drink and talk all night. This place packs 'em in at all hours. Thursday is disco night.

Oranienstrasse is Kreuzberg 36's main entertainment mile.

Bierhimmel (☎ *615 31 22, Oranienstrasse 181*) **Map 5** Bierhimmel is a good place to hang over a paper or a chat. It also draws a sizeable lesbigay contingent, especially on Friday nights. A recent make-over resulted in a mosaic floor, pea-soup-coloured walls and radical seashell chandeliers.

Flammende Herzen (☎ *615 71 02, Oranienstrasse 170*) **Map 5** Walls the colour of a sunset, mirrors and plenty of knick-knacks form the setting of this hip-'n-kitsch watering hole that's also popular with the gay community.

Franken (☎ *614 10 81, Oranienstrasse 19*) **Map 5** Grungy, rough, cool. Come in the wee hours and join the crowd – yuppies to punks – in toasting the rising sun. Then get the hell home to bed.

Schnabelbar (☎ *615 85 34, Oranienstrasse 31*) **Map 5** Schnabelbar has a convivial atmosphere, great music ranging from jazz to house and a minuscule dance floor in the back.

Würgeengel (☎ *615 55 60, Dresdener Strasse 122, Kreuzberg 36*) **Map 5** Open nightly from 7pm. German for 'angel of death', this bar pays homage to the 1962 Luis Buñuel movie by that name. The dramatic blood-red velvet walls, matching big plump sofas and unique tile and stucco ceiling, however, are more reminiscent of a Belle Epoque brothel. They serve killer cocktails, but the place feels like you're in a straitjacket when the post-show crowds from the adjacent Babylon cinema flock in.

Mitte

925 Lounge Bar (☎ *20 18 71 77, Taubenstrasse 19*) **Map 7** If you want to stand out from the deluge of new bars in Mitte, you better think of a clever shtick. At this place it happens to be the must-be-seen-to-be-believed bar wrought from 70kg of real silver (hence the '925' name). Rich-red walls and comfortable club chairs further contribute to the upmarket ambience.

Bar Lounge 808 (☎ *28 04 67 28, Oranienburger Strasse 42/43*) **Map 3** Beautiful scenesters sip potent martinis while socialising in a cool retro ambience at this lounge *du jour* on the tourist mile. A giant

aquarium anchors the place, but full-length drapes curb the fishbowl-effect by keeping out curious stares from passers-by.

Bergwerk (☎ *280 88 76, Bergstrasse 68*) **Map 3** The subdued industrial chic draws a student-ish clientele for beers and snacks. On weekends there's dancing downstairs.

Broker's Bier Börse (☎ *26 47 48 23, Schiffbauerdamm 8*) **Map 7** Open from 8am. In this unique and fun beer hall demand determines the price of drinks. After 5pm, just like in a miniature stock exchange, current prices are posted on a digital board above the bar. If drink orders are up, prices go down – and vice versa. Every once in a while a heavy brass bell is rung and all hell breaks loose because that's when prices go cut-rate. Sure, it's gimmicky and tourists love it, but the fun factor is undeniably real. Food is served as well (mains €5-9).

Jubinal (☎ *28 38 73 77, Tucholskystrasse 34*) **Map 3** This is a similarly happening spot with a nicely calibrated retro look. Music ranges from Klezmer to jazz, and cocktails start at €6.

Kurvenstar (☎ *28 59 97 10, Kleine Präsidentenstrasse 4*) **Map 7** With wacky decor borrowed from the '60s and '70s, this bar-restaurant-club combo mixes it up with music, dancing and food from around the world.

Lore.Berlin (☎ *28 04 51 34, Neue Schönhauser Strasse 20*) **Map 7** Open from 9pm, closed Sun. Sidle up to the 30m-long bar at this ultra-hip joint where discerning drinkers can choose from more than 200 concoctions (€6-10). Check email at a high-speed terminal, then wind down the day enveloped in futuristic and experimental sounds. It's all set in a former coal cellar against the backdrop of ancient heating furnaces. Prepare for plenty of poseurs.

Newton (☎ *20 61 29 90, Charlottenstrasse 57*) **Map 7** Nudes by Newton (Helmut, the photographer, that is) grace the walls at this über-chic place where terminally trendy tourists and locals lounge in clubby red leather armchairs or slurp up the potent cocktails at a bar where the liquor is kept in cages.

Obst und Gemüse (☎ *282 96 47, Oranienburger Strasse 48/49*) **Map 3** This hang-out offers high-energy self-service and takes its name from the fruit and vegetable shop that used to occupy the spot. It's one of the oldest post-Wende bars on the strip and is usually packed to the rafters.

Oscar Wilde (☎ *282 81 66, Friedrichstrasse 112a*) **Map 3** This Irish pub is a patriotic, hard-core drinking establishment with a rough-and-ready crowd, occasional live music and live British soccer league games on TV. Guinness, Kilkenny and Murphy's are on tap and there's pub grub too.

Reingold (☎ *28 38 76 76, Novalisstrasse 11*) **Map 3** A bit removed from tourist-clogged Oranienburger Strasse, this 1930s glamour bar is popular with thirty-something professionals with an intellectual bent: readings by local authors occasionally take place against the backdrop of a huge photograph of Klaus and Erika Mann.

Seven Lounge (☎ *0177-273 24 50, Ackerstrasse 20*) **Map 3** Open from 7pm. Complexion-friendly lighting gives everybody a shot at looking good in this living-room lounge owned by Mo Asumang, erstwhile host of a saucy erotic TV show. Happy-hour (7pm to 8pm) cocktails are €5.

Silberstein (☎ *281 20 95, Oranienburger Strasse 27*) **Map 3** Artsy metal chairs and avant-garde sculptures feature in this gallery-bar where, on some nights, you may have to shoehorn your way inside. Assets include music kept at talking level and a small sushi bar (platters €7.50-14) for those craving a protein burst.

Verkehrsberuhigte Ostzone (☎ *28 39 14 40, Auguststrasse 92*) **Map 3** For a whiff of Ostalgie – new word fusion of Ost (east) and Nostalgie, meaning nostalgia for the GDR – have a drink at this bar creatively furnished with GDR memorabilia and paraphernalia (framed pictures of Honecker and Marx, Trabant parts etc).

Zosch (☎ *280 76 64, Tucholskystrasse 30*) **Map 3** Nearby Zosch is a scene fixture popular with student-age patrons. It has friendly service, vaulted brick ceilings and occasional bands and DJ parties in the basement (often free).

Prenzlauer Berg

Akba Lounge (☎ *441 14 63, Sredzkistrasse 64*) **Map 3** This trendy lounge combines a quiet, tunnel-shaped ground floor cafe with an intimate club upstairs where you'll hear some of the loudest funk played anywhere.

Luna Bar (☎ *447 63 53, Schliemannstrasse 20*) **Map 3** More neighbourhood pub than chic cocktail-lounge, this place is as comfortable as an old shoe. Prices are mercifully low, the clientele a motley melange of colourful locals and young travellers, and the kitchen is always open (snacks €2.50-5.50).

Uluru Resort (☎ *44 04 95 22, Rykestrasse 17*) **Map 3** This friendly Aussie pub often has live music and a boisterous atmosphere.

While the bars around Kollwitzplatz get all the attention, the scene's at least as humming a few blocks away, north of Danziger Strasse. (Take the U2 to Eberswalder Strasse.) Lychener Strasse, for instance, is a happening street.

La Bodeguita del Medio (☎ *442 96 98, Lychener Strasse 6*) **Map 3** This clamorous Cuban bar has a multicultural crowd and a wicked assortment of rum and tequila, plus tapas from €3. It's named after Hemingway's favourite Havana hang-out.

Wohnzimmer (☎ *445 54 58, Lettestrasse 6*) **Map 3** The name translates as 'living room', which aptly describes the comfy and laid-back atmosphere that reigns in this tiny communicative pub-cum-cafe-cum-cocktail bar. Guests at the nearby Lette 'm Sleep hostel get special discounts here.

X-Bar (☎ *443 49 04, Raumerstrasse 17*) **Map 3** You'd need wads of money and lots of stamina to drink yourself through the epic cocktail menu (300 at last count) at this fun bar with walls the colour of a tequila sunrise. Maybe that's why there's not one but two happy hours (6pm to 8pm and midnight to 1am Monday to Saturday, 6pm to 9pm Sunday). There's also a sushi bar in the back.

Schöneberg

You'll find lots of bars and cafes along Maassenstrasse, around Winterfeldtplatz and on Goltzstrasse.

Café M (☎ 216 70 92, *Goltzstrasse 33*) **Map 4** This paradise for poseurs has long had cult status and is still a good place to take in the Schöneberg scene. Despite decor reminiscent of a train station waiting room, it's packed from morn' till morn'.

Mister Hu (☎ 217 21 11, *Goltzstrasse 39*) **Map 4** Despite the Flintstone-esque decor, the two grotto-like rooms somehow manage to be classy, not tacky. Local scenesters sipping inventive cocktails while hunkered over low tables provide another serving of eye-candy.

N.N. Bar (☎ 787 50 33, *Hauptstrasse 159*) **Map 4** This is a chic, tube-shaped lounge with a bar as long as the cocktail menu, soul on the turntable and a staff with attitude. There's dancing on the weekend.

N.N. Train (☎ 78 71 06 17, *Hauptstrasse 162*) **Map 4** The party continues at the nearby N.N. Train, which has taken up shop in a converted S-Bahn carriage. The ambience is more relaxed in the big beer garden, complete with a kiddies playground, in the back.

Slumberland (☎ 216 53 49, *Goltzstrasse 24*) **Map 4** Open from 9.30pm. This beach bar in the heart of urban Berlin has been around forever and still draws in the crowds with plastic palm trees and a sand-covered floor.

Zoulou Bar (☎ 784 68 94, *Hauptstrasse 4*) **Map 4** This tiny establishment seeks to evoke 1930s America and can be more crowded than a Stones concert.

Tiergarten

Tiergarten has a couple of places that are favourites with the expense-account crowd.

Bar am Lützowplatz (☎ 262 68 09, *Lützowplatz 7*) **Map 4** Once named 'Best Bar in Germany', this place features pouting beauties and paunchy gents sipping pricey but perfect cocktails, either at the endless bar or draped over comfortable armchairs. Not suitable for thin wallets, except during happy hour (5pm to 9pm).

Harry's New York Bar ☎ 25 47 88 21, *Grand Hotel Esplanade, Lützowufer 15*) **Map 4** Not to be outdone in the accolade department, Harry's was voted 'Bar of 1996' by *Playboy* magazine. Its refined atmosphere –

enhanced by a black piano and blood-red leather sofas – generally attracts people who are either way too rich or way too thin. Cocktails start at €8.

Berliner Kneipen

Old-fashioned Berlin pubs have their own tradition of hospitality – beer, schnapps, hearty food and a bizarre brand of Berlin humour all served up in rustic, smoke-filled surroundings. Occasionally, you'll come across a *Kneipe* (pub) that natives from the neighbourhood – usually balding working-class stiffs with paunches – have staked out as their private turf. Gruff demeanour and hostile stares greet you as you enter their smoky lair through a heavy wooden door. You, a stranger, have dared to invade their territory (let it be known that there's equal treatment for *all* strangers, German or foreign). Sure, it's local colour, but you'll probably have a better time somewhere else. We've picked out a few places where you can comfortably soak up some atmosphere along with good German beer.

Dicke Wirtin (☎ 312 49 52, *Carmerstrasse 9, Charlottenburg*) **Map 6** Just steps from chic Savignyplatz, this earthy Kneipe often crawls with students from the nearby Technische Universität. The menu features stews and other filling fare for under €5 and six varieties of beer on tap from €2.30.

Zur letzten Instanz (☎ 242 55 28, *Waisenstrasse 14, Mitte*) **Map 7** Stories abound about this historic pub, mysteriously named 'The Final Authority'. As the story goes, about 150 years ago a couple came in from the nearby courthouse to celebrate their just-finalised divorce. By the time they were well oiled and ready to leave, they'd decided to remarry – at which point another guest exclaimed, 'This pub is the court of final authority!' (PS: There's no final word on the couple's fate.)

Zum Nussbaum (☎ 242 30 95, *Am Nussbaum 3, Mitte*) **Map 7** Another historic place, this was once the drinking hole of early-20th-century caricaturist Heinrich Zille and the humourist Otto Nagel. It has recently been re-established as part of the Nikolaiviertel (see the Places to Eat chapter).

ENTERTAINMENT

E&M Leydicke (☎ 216 29 73, *Manstein-strasse 4, Schöneberg*) **Map 4** U-Bahn: U1, U2 or U7 to Yorckstrasse. Open 4pm. Another ancient Berlin pub (founded in 1877), this place bottles its own flavoured schnapps and fruit wines on the premises.

Beer Gardens

As soon as the last winter storms have blown away, pallid Berliners re-acquaint themselves with the sun. Restaurants, bars and cafes start cramming their pavements, gardens or courtyards with tables and chairs to herald beer-garden season. It's convivial and fun, especially in the peak summer months when there's daylight until about 11pm. For sustenance, snacks – sometimes even barbecued ribs, steaks, corn on the cob etc – are usually available.

Golgatha (☎ 785 24 53, *Dudenstrasse 48-64, Kreuzberg 61*) **Map 5** Closed mid-Oct to Mar. This low-key place in Viktoriapark has been around for as long as we can remember and is still great for grilled snacks and cool drinks on a balmy night. A DJ springs into action after 10pm.

Prater (☎ 448 56 88, *Kastanienallee 7-9, Prenzlauer Berg*) **Map 3** Berlin's oldest beer garden is also one of the prettiest and is great for quaffing away beneath a canopy of mature chestnut trees. It's part of a complex that includes a small stage operated by the Volksbühne and an old-fashioned restaurant serving hearty German fare from €5-10.

Loretta am Wannsee (☎ 803 51 56, *Kronprinzessinenweg 260, Zehlendorf*) **off Map 1** S-Bahn: S1, S3 or S7 to Wannsee. This huge garden (over 1000 chairs) is perfect for capping off a hot summer day of swimming in the lake.

Luise (☎ 841 88 80, *Königin-Luise-Strasse 40-44, Zehlendorf*) **off Map 1** U-Bahn: U1 to Dahlem-Dorf. This is a legendary student haunt with space for 700.

Other places with wonderful beer gardens that are covered elsewhere in this book include *Pfefferberg* and *Podewil* (see the Cultural Centres section later in this chapter); and *Café am Neuen See* and *Ypsilon* (see the Places to Eat chapter).

CLUBS

Berlin has a reputation for unbridled and very late nightlife – don't even bother showing up before midnight. Many venues run different parties every night, depending on the DJ and the targeted crowd – techno freaks, *Schlager* (schmaltzy German pop) fans, gays, Latin salsa-lovers – even ballroom dancing is making a comeback! As in other fast-moving Euro capitals, what's flat and what's glossy changes quickly and unexpectedly, which is why serious clubbers should spend some time perusing the listings magazines or look for flyers in cafes and bars.

Getting into clubs is easier in unpretentious Berlin than in other German cities like Munich or Hamburg where the Gucci and Armani crowd rules. Here, imagination usually beats income, so vamp it up with the rest of them. Cover charges (when they apply) range from €2.50 to €10 and sometimes include a drink.

Friedrichshain

By day, tourists from Dublin to Dubuque plow along Mühlenstrasse to marvel at the longest remaining stretch of Berlin Wall, the East Side Gallery. On Friday and Saturday nights, though, the street morphs into 'Club Row' with wild and bizarre parties being staged in around a dozen establishments, including the following.

Maria am Ostbahnhof (☎ 29 00 61 98, W *www.clubmaria.de, Strasse der Pariser Kommune 8-10*) **Map 5** Open 10pm Fri & Sat. Admission €5-10. Maria holds court with drum 'n' bass, house and electronic esoterica at an abandoned postal-distribution centre. At the time of writing, the club's survival in this location was severely threatened so check that it hasn't moved.

Matrix (☎ 29 49 10 47, *Warschauer Platz 18*) **Map 5** Open Tues-Sat. Matrix is an edgy house and techno club popular with ravers barely old enough to vote. It has several dance floors in the red brick arched vaults underneath Warschauer Strasse U-Bahn.

Non Tox (☎ 29 66 72 06, *Mühlenstrasse 12*) **Map 5** Open 11pm Fri-Sat. Admission €4-5. Non Tox has a dark vibe and DJs who 'scratch' a living playing crossover music to an audience that includes mostly regulars.

Ostgut (☎ *29 00 05 97, Mühlenstrasse 26-30*) **Map 5** Open midnight Fri-Sat. Admission €5-10. This is one of *the* places for serious techno-heads to hear tomorrow's sounds today. Hit the dance floor, then chill out in the upstairs Panorama Bar. Also part of the complex is ***lab.oratory***, a hard-core haven for gay men keen on 'sexperimentation' (think parties with names like 'Yellow Facts' and 'Fausthaus' – figure it out). Ostgut is another club whose survival is uncertain as developers are planning on building a large events hall on the grounds. Stay tuned.

Geburtstagsclub (☎ *42 85 13 35, Am Friedrichshain 33*) **Map 3** Open 11pm Thur-Sat. Admission €2.50-5. Away from the Mühlenstrasse strip, right by the Volkspark Friedrichshain, is this feel-good neighbourhood club for the 25 and up crowd. Expect just about the entire musical spectrum, from house to reggae to funk to hip-hop etc.

Kreuzberg

SO36 (☎ *61 40 13 06, Oranienstrasse 190*) **Map 5** Open nightly. This place belongs to Kreuzberg 36 like cream on strawberries. Once the haunt of alternative punks, this trendlessly cool place now has a diversified schedule of live concerts and theme nights – house to hip-hop, ballroom (!) to techno. (Also see the Gay & Lesbian Berlin section later in this chapter.)

Mitte

Adagio (☎ *25 92 95 50, Marlene-Dietrich-Platz 1*) (see the Potsdamer Platz & Kulturforum map in the Things to See & Do chapter) 'Love, Lust and Passion' is the motto of this ballroom-sized hall with fabulous Vegas-style fantasy decor. It's right beneath the musical theatre in DaimlerCity. Thanks to hefty admission and drink prices, the crowd consists mostly of yuppies, middle-aged Berlin tourists and suits with expense accounts. Pity.

Delicious Doughnuts (☎ *28 09 93 74, Rosenthaler Strasse 9*) **Map 3** Open 11pm. Owners Axel and Peter have created a happening lounge-club with homely, romantic

Techno Town

Lay down a bass track that sounds like direct thermonuclear hits on an oil drum, toss in some eerie electronic wailing and gasping snatches of melody, run it through some Star Wars technology and deliver it all through speakers the size of God's summer home. Then add a curiously mellow crowd of twenty-something ravers with pierced anatomy, plastic miniskirts, tight T-shirts and – more often than not – loaded up on Ecstasy or an assortment of other synthetic-fun enhancers.

Somewhere post a DJ who manipulates the sound and the crowd like a postmodern fakir charming his snake. Pour it all into a venue with decor from the sexual dream of a robot, with bodies writhing rhythmically from midnight until way past dawn. And there you have it: Techno 101. A sound, a mantra and a way of life that Berlin has somehow made its own.

Rave. Gabber. Jungle. Trance. The variations seem endless. Techno was inspired by the machine-music first spun by the Düsseldorf band Kraftwerk – which, in turn, was influenced by Detroit-grown House – in the 1970s.

Then, in 1989, a small group of Berlin techno-heads started what would become a worldwide phenomenon: the Love Parade. From 150 ravers in the first year, attendance grew steadily, peaking in 1999 when 1.5 million people danced through Tiergarten park. Since then, the numbers have declined; only about 600,000 joined the party in 2001. Maybe it's because there's now so many 'Love Parades'. Vienna has one, so does Moscow, Paris, even Tel Aviv and Cape Town. Or maybe it's because techno has just gone irrevocably commercial: thumpa thumpa at the supermarket, in elevators, in TV commercials. Or perhaps the first generation of techno pioneers has simply grown up and discovered that pseudo-political slogans like 'Friede, Freude, Eierkuchen' (Peace, Happiness, Pancakes) just don't sound as profound anymore – if they ever did.

touches in the heart of Mitte. There's a different beat nightly – house to electrojazz to '60s to soul.

Knaack Club (☎ 44 27 06 01, Greifswalder Strasse 224) **Map 7** This is a comfortable dance club that began as a youth club in the 1950s. Admission is often free or cheap. Low intimidation factor.

Mudd Club (☎ 27 59 49 99, Grosse Hamburger Strasse 17) **Map 7** Berlin's Mudd Club pays homage to the legendary Soho original, the hub of the New York underground in the '70s and '80s. The cellar venue is a bit hard to find as it's set back from the street and down a steep staircase.

Der Grüne Salon (Green Salon; ☎ 28 59 89 36, Rosa-Luxemburg-Platz, inside the Volksbühne theatre) **Map 3** An atmosphere of smoky sophistication and nostalgia reigns at this intimate venue, which is a throwback to the wicked '20s. Its salsa, tango and swing nights are legendary (check about dance lessons), and evenings featuring chansons, comedy shows or readings draw a full house as well. High celeb quotient.

Der Rote Salon (Red Salon; ☎ 24 06 58 06, Rosa-Luxemburg-Platz) **Map 3** Open 9pm. The retro red armchairs and chandeliers form a glam backdrop for readings, concerts and dance parties at this place, also within the Volksbühne theatre. Post-premiere parties are especially well attended.

Oxymoron (☎ 28 39 18 86, Rosenthaler Strasse 40-41) **Map 7** Admission €3-13. This place inside the Hackesche Höfe changes stripes with the movement of the sun. By day, the opulent baroque salon in front – complete with plump velvet sofas, gold-leaf mirrors and chandeliers – caters for the cafe crowd. After dark, it morphs into an eats-and-lounge act before turning into a chic club after 11pm when jazz and rock seamlessly blend with drum 'n' bass and soft hiphop. The door policy is liberal, but sneakers (tennis shoes) are better left at your hotel.

Sage Club (☎ 278 98 30, Köpenicker Strasse 76) **Map 7** U-Bahn: Heinrich-Heine-Strasse. Open Thur-Sun. Admission €5. Goons at the door decide who's rich or flamboyant enough to enter this phantasmagoric dance emporium where a 'fire'-spewing

dragon hovers above the dance floor. Crowds spread out over two dance floors, three bars (72 cocktails), a lounge for chilling and a garden. Sound-wise it's funk, soul, rock, house and trance.

Sophienklub (☎ 282 45 52, Sophienstrasse 6) **Map 3** No one will accuse this club of trendsetting, but that's just fine with regulars. Those who find much of Berlin's club life a tad too twisted will feel comfortable here. There are two floors with diverse sounds – soul, funk, R&B or Brit pop.

Tresor/Globus (☎ 609 37 02, Leipziger Strasse 128a) **Map 7** Open 11pm Wed, Fri & Sat. Admission €2.50-10. Global house sounds envelop you as you enter Globus, the ground-floor club in this legendary two-for-one haunt. Stairs lead down to Tresor, inside the money vault of a former department store and one of the birthplaces of the Berlin techno revolution in the early 1990s. Alas, its days may be numbered as construction on nearby Leipziger Platz is getting closer. Check the local listings before heading out.

WMF (☎ 28 38 88 50, Ziegelstrasse 23) **Map 7** This is a Berlin classic that's been forced to move more than once and is likely to be displaced again soon (check the listings magazines for updates). Sunday is 'GayMF' (see Clubs under Gay & Lesbian Berlin later in this chapter).

Prenzlauer Berg

Duncker (☎ 445 95 09, Dunckerstrasse 64, Prenzlauer Berg) **Map 3** S-Bahn: S8 or S10 to Prenzlauer Allee. This former GDR youth club looks foreboding, but behind the shabby brick facade awaits a lively club with good cocktails, friendly folk and a pleasant garden.

Schöneberg, Tiergarten & Wilmersdorf

90 Grad (☎ 23 00 59 54, Dennewitzstrasse 37, Schöneberg) **Map 4** Open 9pm Wed, 11pm Fri-Sat. Admission €7.50-10. This is still a swank spot after many years in the party business, but the elite door policy is a major turn-off. DJs spin a wild mix of everything, except techno, while perched in a giant chancel in the middle of the dance floor. Thursday is gay night.

El Barrio (☎ 262 18 53, W *www.el -barrio.de, Potsdamer Strasse 84, Tiergarten)* **Map 4** Open 10pm Tues-Sun. For fiery salsa nights, head to this cellar where couples writhe to sultry Latin rhythms. There's occasional live music, and dance classes in salsa and merengue are offered regularly. Call for a schedule or check the Web site.

Far Out (☎ 32 00 07 17, *Kurfürstendamm 156, Wilmersdorf)* **Map 6** Open Tues-Sun. Admission free-€5. One of oldest party venues in the CityWest, Far Out is anything but and definitely lacks the edge of eastern clubs. It is, however, a comfortable place to swing a leg. If you're over 30, entry is free during Wednesday's 'Forever Young' parties.

GAY & LESBIAN BERLIN

Nicknamed 'Homopolis', Berlin has the biggest and most happening gay and lesbian scene in Germany. It's estimated that up to 500,000 gays and lesbians call Berlin home today. The tradition goes back to 1897 when sexual behaviourist Magnus Hirschfeld laid the groundwork for the gay and lesbian rights movement in this city. British writer Christopher Isherwood lived in Schöneberg in the 1920s. In 2001, with the election of Klaus Wowereit as governing mayor after Diepgen's resignation (see History in the Facts about Berlin chapter), Berlin became only the second European city (after Paris) to be led by an openly gay politician.

Anything goes in today's gay Berlin – and we mean *anything*. The wildest parties take place only once or twice a month and change venues often. Before clubbing you can eat at a gay-owned and/or operated restaurant and nurse a drink at one of the many gay cafes and bars. Darkrooms are very common and basically *de rigeur* at new pubs or bars.

Berlin Clubs Under Fire

Berlin's club scene is legendary. Smaller, underground venues especially have sparked impulses that have resonated around the world, the best example being the popularity explosion of techno. It all started after the Wende, when pioneers of the genre moved into abandoned and often semi-ruined GDR era buildings. Tresor found a home in the vault of a former department store. E-Werk opened in a converted power station. Maria am Ostbahnhof took over a postal distribution centre. All it took was a wild idea, lots of creativity and a little money. Sure, some clubs teetered on the edge of legality but even they were ultimately tolerated by the authorities who, in the aftermath of reunification, had bigger fish to fry.

But as with so much in Berlin, times are a-changin'. Some of the most popular establishments are being forced to close or move to other locations, kicked out by developers with visions of office buildings, apartment complexes and events facilities. This, of course, is nothing new. Clubs have had to move before. The difference now is that Berlin is running out of suitable locations, as gentrified Mitte and increasingly commercial Prenzlauer Berg have become too expensive for many of these shoe-string operations.

So is Berlin's club scene dying?

Not if the newly founded Club Commission can help it. The goal of this increasingly vocal cooperative of club owners is to keep alive the creative underground scene where new and unconventional sounds and movements can thrive. They lobby against increasing commercialisation and the unfettered growth of regulations in the hope that city representatives, investors and developers will allow clubs to continue using empty buildings. The group points to 'the scene' as an economic as well as an image factor. Said spokesperson Marc Wahlberg in an interview with the news weekly *Der Spiegel*, 'Businesses who've relocated to Berlin in recent years have come because this is an attractive place for younger people to live. And they value the city not because we've got three opera houses and highly subsidized musical theatres, but because of the experimental, trend-setting venues that have sprung up here in the last 10 years.' Ten years hence, will techno have gone tango?

The scene concentrates in four districts: around Nollendorfplatz in Schöneberg **Map 4**; Oranienstrasse in Kreuzberg 36 **Map 5**; along Mühlenstrasse in Friedrichshain **Map 5**; and in Prenzlauer Berg, particularly on Gleimstrasse **Map 3**.

The freebie *Siegessäule* is the Berlin bible for all things gay and lesbian, while *Sergej* is strictly for men. *Zitty* and *O30* also have listings. Gay guidebooks include the bilingual *Berlin von Hinten* (Berlin from Behind) by Robin Rauch, *Homopolis* by Micha Schulze, and *Lesbisches Berlin* by Traude Bührmann, all available at lesbigay and some mainstream bookstores.

Cinemas

Kino International (☎ 247 56 00, *Karl-Marx-Allee 33, Mitte*) **Map 3** With its dangling Bohemian glass chandeliers, wainscotting, glitter curtain and parquet floor, the Kino is a show in itself. On Monday nights, it goes 'MonGay' with homo-themed classics, imports and previews of upcoming features. The glam lobby-bar opens at 9pm, showtime is 10.30pm.

Xenon (☎ 782 88 50, *Kolonnenstrasse 5-6, Schöneberg*) **Map 4** The city's second-oldest movie theatre shows predominantly lesbigay flicks with lots of imports. Watch out for Dykescreen, its occasional lesbian film series.

Cafes & Bars

Roses (☎ 615 75 70, *Oranienstrasse 187, Kreuzberg 36*) **Map 5** Roses has over-the-top queeny decor (coloured lights, carpeted walls and Madonna sculptures), strong drinks and a chatty party vibe.

Melitta Sundström (☎ 692 44 14, *Mehringdamm 61, Kreuzberg 61*) **Map 5** Start your day with latte and omelettes at this relaxed cafe with an intellectual air and walls smothered in brightly pigmented art.

Schall und Rauch (☎ 448 07 70, *Gleimstrasse 23, Prenzlauer Berg*) **Map 3** A bistro by day (mains €5-10), this trendy place turns into a chic cocktail bar when the moon gets high. It has an award-winning design and designer prices willingly paid by a young and buff crowd. There's a daily breakfast buffet (€5) but it's the Sunday brunch (€7) that has cult status.

Cafe Amsterdam (☎ 448 07 92, *Gleimstrasse 24, Prenzlauer Berg*) **Map 3** Next door, meet and mingle at this popular place, which usually throbs with house and techno beats. In the daytime, people come for the breakfast buffet (€5) or the cake buffet.

Café PositHIV (☎ 216 86 54, *Alvenslebenstrasse 26, Schöneberg*) **Map 4** Open Tues-Sun. This volunteer-run cafe provides a fun and relaxed environment for those infected with HIV, their friends and anyone else for that matter.

Clubs *Die Busche* (☎ 589 15 85, *Mühlenstrasse 11-12, Friedrichshain*) **Map 5** Open 9.30pm Wed, Fri & Sat. Admission varies. The ghosts of communism have long been exorcised from what used to be the only gay disco in GDR-era Berlin, but the place is still alive and kicking. Loud music, mirrored rooms and a young, mixed (read: bi-lesbigay-straight) clientele make up the ingredients for its raunchy dance parties.

SO36 (☎ 61 40 13 06, *Oranienstrasse 190, Kreuzberg 36*) **Map 5** A long-time cult club, the 'Esso' has several theme nights for lesbigays, such as Electric Ballroom (techno) on Monday, Hungry Hearts (House) on Wednesday and Cafe Fatal (German pop and ballroom dancing) on Sunday. Gayhane, a multicultural party, is a real hoot – think Turkish and German pop, transvestites, belly dancing etc. It takes place on the fourth Saturday of the month. On the third Friday of the month, lesbian women and drag queens get down during the glamorous 'Jane Bond Night'.

SchwuZ Basement (693 70 25, *Mehringdamm 61, Kreuzberg 61*) **Map 5** On Saturday, Melitta Sundström (see Cafes earlier in this section) turns into the warm-up bar for this mainstream dance club in the SchwuZ gay centre behind the cafe. Come here to check out the most outrageous drag queens and to get sweaty on the two dance floors.

WMF (☎ 28 38 88 50, *Ziegelstrasse 23, Mitte*) **Map 7** On Sunday, WMF goes 'GayMF' and becomes *the* place to wind up the weekend during their 'Gay T-Dance'.

Some patrons like to fortify themselves during the Cake Club at the Bar Lounge 808 before heading here (see Bars & Pubs later in this section).

Other venues with occasional gay-lesbian events include: *Tränenpalast*, *Tresor*, *Sage Club*, *Oxymoron*, *Kalkscheune* and *90 Grad*. For addresses, check under the Clubs and Cultural Centres sections earlier in this chapter.

Special Events

For specific information on gay events, contact *Mann-O-Meter* (☎ 216 80 08) **Map 4**. February sees the award ceremony of the Teddy – the Gay and Lesbian film prize – as part of the Berlin International Film Festival. The Leather Meet takes place around Easter, while the Gay & Lesbian Run is in May. June wouldn't be complete without the Christopher Street Parade. The Lesbian Film Festival is held in October, followed in November by the Verzaubert (Enchanted) International Queer Film Festival.

Men Only

Bars Schöneberg, which used to be the epicentre of Berlin's bar scene, now has serious competition from boomtown Prenzlauer Berg.

Greifbar (☎ 444 08 28, *Wichertstrasse 10, Prenzlauer Berg*) **Map 3** This is a simple cruising den with a busy darkroom where you can retreat to Portacabins for some privacy. It draws a slightly older clientele of active gays aged around 30.

Pick Ab (☎ 445 85 23, *Greifenhagener Strasse 16, Prenzlauer Berg*) **Map 3** As the name suggests, this place has a very cruisy atmosphere fuelled by eye-candy decor and clientele. Age-wise, it's a mixed bag.

Stiller Don (☎ 445 59 57, *Erich-Weinert-Strasse 67, Prenzlauer Berg*) **Map 3** Another leftover from the GDR era, this place is busiest on Monday nights when a low-key crowd comes for beer and free peanuts.

Andreas Kneipe (☎ 218 32 57, *Ansbacher Strasse 29, Schöneberg*) **Map 6** This old-timey pub has a convivial ambience and is a good place to meet locals, even in the daytime.

Hafen (☎ 214 11 18, *Motzstrasse 19, Schöneberg*) **Map 4** Hafen is full of gay yuppies fortifying themselves before they move on to (some say sneak into) Tom's Bar (see later in this section).

Lenz (☎ 217 78 20, *Eisenacher Strasse 3, Schöneberg*) **Map 4** The deal in this beautiful cocktail bar is 150 different drinks served by handsome bartenders to buff boyz.

Prinzknecht (☎ 218 14 31, *Fuggerstrasse 33, Schöneberg*) **Map 6** Next to Connection (see the Clubs section later in this section) is this chic American-style bar with bare brick walls, chrome lamps and posters of Georgia O'Keefe's floral paintings.

Tom's Bar (☎ 213 45 70, *Motzstrasse 19, Schöneberg*) **Map 4** Open from 10pm. Tom's, next door to Hafen, is often the next stop on the party circuit. Its dark, cavernous bar is a serious pick-up place and there's also an active cellar. If you're OFB ('out for business') don't arrive here before midnight.

Clubs *Metropol* (☎ 21 73 68 41, *Nollendorfplatz 5, Schöneberg*) **Map 4** This old theatre, its facade festooned with seductive nude sculptures, has seen many incarnations but is currently home to high-intensity gay nights, including Cocker Party, and Cilli Bom with an oriental theme.

Connection (☎ 218 14 32, *Fuggerstrasse 33, Schöneberg*) **Map 6** On Friday and Saturday nights, this is one of the oldest and most popular gay discos in town. The warren of underground darkrooms is legendary. Upstairs there are three floors of cruising action, a mirrored dance floor and blaring techno music.

Saunas *Apollo Sauna* (☎ 213 24 24, *Kurfürstenstrasse 101, Charlottenburg*) **Map 6** Open 1pm-7am Mon-Fri, 24 hrs Sat & Sun. This traditional gay sauna has steam rooms, cruising hallways and cabins. It's famous for its Slivovitz sauna infusions.

Gate Sauna (☎ 229 94 30, *Wilhelmstrasse 81, Mitte*) **Map 7** Open 11am-7am Mon-Fri, 24 hrs Sat & Sun. One of the biggest and most active saunas is south-east of the Brandenburger Tor. Apart from two floors of modern and clean saunas and steam rooms, it has a bar, TV and video room.

Treibhaus Sauna *(☎ 448 45 03, Schönhauser Allee 132, Prenzlauer Berg)* **Map 3** Open 3pm-7am Mon-Fri, 24 hrs Sat & Sun. This is one of the nicest saunas in town.

Lockers at any of these places cost €10-15 (cabins are an extra €5-6). Weekday specials and student discounts are sometimes available.

Cruising Check with Mann-O-Meter for the latest on the cruising scene. In the meantime, the following are some 'classic' haunts: Löwenbrücke bridge in the Tiergarten near the Siegessäule; the Märchenbrunnen in Volkspark Friedrichshain **Map 3**, and the area around the parking lot on Pappelplatz in Grunewald. Nude swimming days (Tuesday, Wednesday and Friday) at the Alte Halle in the Stadtbad Charlottenburg **Map 2** are also popular.

Women Only

Berlin's lesbian scene used to have its headquarters in Schöneberg, but Kreuzberg has lately caught on as well. In addition to the all-women venues listed here, there are also one-off and monthly women-only parties at such places as SchwuZ, Kalkscheune and Tränenpalast. One major organiser is ***MegaDykes*** *(☎ 78 70 30 94)*; look for their flyer or check the listings magazines.

Die 2 *(☎ 302 52 60, Spandauer Damm 168, Charlottenburg)* **Map 1** Lesbians of all ages and styles gather at this down-homey bar which runs a disco on Wednesday, Friday and Saturday nights.

Schoko Café *(☎ 615 15 61, Mariannenstrasse 6, Kreuzberg 36)* **Map 5** Above an all-women Turkish hamam (bathhouse), this is a multicultural meeting point, including a sizeable English-speaking contingent. There's a popular disco on the second Saturday of the month.

Café Seidenfaden *(☎ 283 27 83, Dircksenstrasse 47, Mitte)* **Map 7** Open 1pm-7pm Sun-Fri. Men, alcohol and smoking are banished from this simple, communicative cafe that's especially geared to women recovering from alcohol or drug addiction.

pe *(☎ 218 75 33, Kalckreuthstrasse 10, Schöneberg)* **Map 4** The city's oldest lesbian bar (formerly known as Pour Elle, since 1973) has come under new ownership and is now more mixed, with only Saturday reserved for 'Women Only'.

Begine *(☎ 215 43 25, Potsdamer Strasse 139, Schöneberg)* **Map 4** Things have calmed down considerably since the days when this historic building was occupied by female squatters. Now it's a cafe and cultural centre for women, primarily lesbians, with an intellectual bent. There are concerts, readings and films as well as the Begine Disco on the fourth Saturday of the month.

CULTURAL CENTRES

Cultural centres are an important part of Berlin's entertainment scene. These multiuse venues are generally housed in unusual spaces, such as former warehouses, department stores, breweries and other large buildings. Various forms of entertainment are offered, including all or a mix of the following: cinema, dance, live music, theatre, bars, cafes, restaurants, exhibits and even circus acts. Events range from mainstream to 'out there', usually with a good dose of multiculturalism thrown in.

Tempodrom *(☎ 263 99 80, Anhalter Bahnhof, off Möckernstrasse, Kreuzberg 61)* **Map 5** This beloved Berlin institution, sorely missed since 1998, was scheduled to reopen in late 2001. Forced to move from its previous Tiergarten location because of the construction of the New Federal Chancellery, the private venue will resume its eclectic performance schedule in brand-new permanent tent-like digs on the grounds of the former Anhalter Bahnhof.

Kalkscheune *(☎ 28 39 00 65, Johannisstrasse 2, Mitte)* **Map 3** This place holds forth with an eclectic program that ranges from the sophisticated (tango, jazz, chansons) to the wildly popular *Schöne Party* (Fun Party) for the over-25 set.

Podewil *(☎ 24 74 96, Klosterstrasse 68-70, Mitte)* **Map 7** U-Bahn: U2 to Klosterstrasse. This place offers a mixed bag of film, dance, theatre and live music as well as a cafe, all in a palais dating from 1704.

The beer garden is open to 9.30pm in fine weather.

Tacheles *(☎ 282 61 85, Oranienburger Strasse 54-56, Mitte)* **Map 3** This dilapidated, graffiti-covered building is like an adventure playground for adults. Its post-atomic look belies an active cultural program that includes dance, jazz concerts, the ***Café Camera***, cabaret, readings, workshops, bizarre art galleries and studios, a cinema, theatre and more. The beer garden out the back is great in summer, and there's also the ***Zapata*** nightclub. (Also see Things to See & Do – Mitte.)

Tränenpalast *(Palace of Tears, ☎ 206 10 00, Reichstagsufer 17, Mitte)* **Map 7** In a retired border-crossing facility, this 'palace' offers a wide roster of multicultural entertainment, from smooth jazz to sultry flamenco, wacky cabaret to heady readings.

Kulturbrauerei *(☎ 441 92 69, Knaackstrasse 97, Prenzlauer Berg)* **Map 3** The original red-brick buildings of this 19th-century brewery have been turned into a happening nightlife mega-complex with a motley mix of cinema, theatre, dance club, restaurant and cafe.

Pfefferberg *(☎ 449 65 34, Schönhauser Allee 176, Prenzlauer Berg)* **Map 3** Also converted from a brewery, the more alternative Pfefferberg promotes cross-cultural projects. There's live music in the concert hall, dancing in the Subground dance club, food and drink in the happening rooftop beer garden and art in the gallery.

UFA-Fabrik *(☎ 75 50 30, Viktoriastrasse 10-18, Tempelhof)* **Map 1** U-Bahn: U6 to Ullsteinstrasse. Another multimedia culture club is housed in the former UFA film studios. There's music, theatre, dance, cabaret and circus shows year-round. From June to September performances are on an outdoor stage.

Akademie der Künste *(☎ 39 07 60, Hanseatenweg 10, Tiergarten)* **Map 2** Berlin's Academy of Arts is an international cooperative of artists and their supporters that traces its roots to the Prussian Academy of Arts, founded in 1696 by King Friedrich I. It puts on changing art exhibits alongside a lively schedule of readings, film, dance and theatre performances, discussions,

workshops etc. A new building is taking shape at Pariser Platz 4 in its original pre-war space.

Haus der Kulturen der Welt *(☎ 39 78 71 75, John-Foster-Dulles-Allee 10, Tiergarten)* **Map 2** The House of World Cultures brings contemporary artists, especially those from Africa, Latin America and Asia, to Berlin. Performances in dance, music, theatre, art, film and literature are supplemented by festivals and highbrow symposia and conferences. It's housed in a fascinating building, described in more detail in the Architecture special section.

Die Insel *(☎ 53 60 80 20, Alt-Treptow 6, Treptow)* **off Map 1** S-Bahn: S6, S8, S9 or S10 to Plänterwald. Insel is a former GDR youth club housed in a mock medieval castle on a Spree island, reached via a romantic bridge. There's something for everybody, from workshops for youths to live rock concerts, open-air cinema (June to September), dance parties of all musical stripes. There's even a family cafe (on weekends) where parents can relax while the tots are being entertained with crafts projects or puppet theatre.

LIVE MUSIC
Classical
Classical music fans have plenty to pick from just about any night of the week, except during the summer hiatus. A concert at the Philharmonie or the Konzerthaus is a special treat. Aficionados under 27 who are planning a longer Berlin stay or are making repeated visits to the city should look into the Classic Card deal (see boxed text 'Making an Art of Discounts' in the Facts for the Visitor chapter).

Konzerthaus Berlin *(☎ 20 30 90, Gendarmenmarkt 2, Mitte)* **Map 7** Standing tickets €6, seats €6-40, more during special concerts. The lavish Schinkel-designed Konzerthaus is one of Berlin's top classical venues. The 'house band' is the renowned Berliner Symphonie Orchester helmed by Eliahu Inbal. There are two auditoriums as well as the music club for literary and children's events. Organ concerts (€7) also take place here.

Hochschule für Musik Hanns Eisler (☎ *203 09 24 11, Charlottenstrasse 55, Mitte*) **Map 7** This top-rated music academy maintains several orchestras, a choir and even a big band, which collectively stage as many as 400 performances annually, including concerts, musicals and operas. Many events are free or low-cost.

Berliner Philharmonie (☎ *25 48 80, Herbert-von-Karajan-Strasse 1, Tiergarten*) (see the Potsdamer Platz & Kulturforum map in the Things to See & Do chapter) Standing tickets €7, seats €15-51, more during special events. The Philharmonie – the name of both the building and the orchestra that plays here – is arguably the finest place in Berlin to hear classical music thanks to its supreme acoustics. Sir Simon Rattle will take over from Claudio Abbado as musical director in the summer of 2002. The adjacent ***Kammermusiksaal*** is a smaller chamber-music venue. There isn't a bad seat in either house.

Deutsches Symphonie-Orchester (☎ *20 29 87 11 for tickets, Charlottenstrasse 56, Mitte*) Tickets €9-55. This orchestra, led by Kent Nagano, is an outgrowth of the RIAS Symphonie Orchester founded in 1946 and financed by the USA until 1953. Without its own permanent venue, it performs at the Philharmonie, the Konzerthaus and in the Otto-Braun-Saal at the National Library at Potsdamer Strasse 33.

Hochschule der Künste (*University of the Arts;* ☎ *31 85 22 04, Hardenbergstrasse 33, Charlottenburg*) **Map 6** The concert hall here is also busy in season.

Jazz
Jazz junkies will have no problem getting their fill in Berlin, which has lately grown an increasingly respectable scene fuelled by local performers as well as national and international talent.

A-Trane (☎ *313 25 50, Bleibtreustrasse 1, Charlottenburg*) **Map 6** Open nightly. Admission €5-20, Mon & Tues usually free. The audience can be a bit precious, but the talent – both emerging and established – is the main reason to come. Styles run the gamut from modern jazz and bebop to avant-garde, mainstream and vocal jazz. It's an intimate place with round cocktail tables and there's not a bad seat in the house.

Quasimodo (☎ *312 80 86, Kantstrasse 12a, Charlottenburg*) **Map 6** Open 9pm daily, shows start around 10pm. Admission €7.50-12.50, Tues & Wed €2.50, including a drink. Quasimodo attracts high-calibre national and international acts. Its petite size puts you close to the stage, but the low ceiling, black walls and smoky air may make you feel just a tad claustrophobic. The spacious upstairs cafe is a good place for respite from the crowd or a pre-show drink.

Junction Bar (☎ *694 66 02, Gneisenaustrasse 18, Kreuzberg 61*) **Map 5** Open 8pm. Admission €3.50-6. Check your lungs at the door when descending into this cellar establishment where you'll be showered by everything from traditional jazz to jazz-rap. The upstairs bar serves snacks.

b-flat (☎ *280 63 49, Rosenthaler Strasse 13, Mitte*) **Map 3** Open 8pm. Admission €2.50-7.50. Jazz is still the main event at this popular place, but lately Latin nights (mostly salsa and tango) have spiced things up a bit.

Jazzbar Pfandleihe (☎ *28 09 71 59, Linienstrasse 98, Mitte*) **Map 3** There's live jazz here from 9pm or 10pm daily, plus a Sunday jazz brunch and a Monday jam session. Happy hour is from 6pm to 9pm. Enter through the courtyard between Torstrasse 164 and Linienstrasse 98.

Take the A-Trane to Jazzville

Schlot (☎ *448 21 60, Chausseestrasse 18, Mitte)* **Map 3** Open from 7.30pm. Admission €4-7.50. Schlot, which translates as 'chimney', is an unpretentious venue that kicked off immediately after Germany's reunification and quickly garnered a reputation for its fine jazz and cabaret. Managed by a pair of marathon runners, it has an interesting and eclectic mix of acts and styles presented in a spacious setting of iron, red-brick and wood.

Flöz (☎ *861 10 00, Nassauische Strasse 37, Wilmersdorf)* **Map 4** U-Bahn: U7 or U9 to Berliner Strasse. Open daily, concerts from 9pm. Modern jazz, folk and rock are on the musical menu at this old-timey cellar haunt, which is popular with an older and wiser clientele.

Big Venues

Megastars like Janet Jackson, U2, the Three Tenors and touring productions – á la *Lord of the Dance* – usually appear at one of these big venues.

Olympia Stadion (☎ *30 06, 33, Olympischer Platz 3, Charlottenburg)* **Map 1** Undergoing gradual renovation until late 2004, this historic stadium can hold up to 70,000 spectators.

Waldbühne (☎ *23 08 82 30, Am Glockenturm, Charlottenburg)* **Map 1** U-Bahn: U2 to Olympia-Stadion Ost, then free shuttle or bus No 18. This open-air amphitheatre is in operation from May to September. There's oodles of space for more than 20,000 people to file in and enjoy rock, pop and classical concerts. Popular, too, are the movie nights with films projected onto a giant screen.

Max-Schmeling-Halle (☎ *44 30 45, Am Falkplatz, cnr Gaudystrasse & Prenzlauer Berg)* **Map 3** This 8100-seat hall, completed in 1997, is home to Berlin's professional basketball team, Alba, and also hosts concerts, theatre and conferences.

Velodrom (☎ *44 30 45, Paul-Heyse-Strasse 26, cnr Fritz-Riedel-Strasse & Prenzlauer Berg)* **Map 3** Major bicycling races and other top sporting and music events, as well as conferences, are held at this 11,000-seat hall.

OPERA & MUSICALS

Deutsche Oper Berlin (☎ *343 84 01, Bismarckstrasse 35, Charlottenburg)* **Map 6** Opera tickets €9-72, ballet tickets €9-36. Weekday performances are rarely sold out. Berlin's largest opera house is a 1961 glass-and-steel behemoth that may lack in visual grandeur but not in performance quality. After the death of long-time artistic director Götz Friedrich, it is now guided by Udo Zimmermann, himself a composer. He promises a motley mix, from romantic operas to lesser-known works such as Luigi Nono's *Intoleranza*. All operas are performed in the original language.

Staatsoper Unter den Linden (☎ *208 28 61 for schedule,* ☎ *20 35 40 box office,* ☎ *204 47 62 ticket availability, Unter den Linden 5-7, Mitte)* **Map 7** Tickets €8-60. The National Opera, under the leadership of Daniel Barenboim, hosts lavish productions with international talent in a neoclassical music temple. Felix Mendelssohn-Bartholdy once served here as music director. Barenboim places much emphasis on baroque operas and German romantic warhorses as well as on works by later composers, such as Wagner. In 2001, film director Doris Dörrie produced Mozart's *Cosi fan tutte*. All operas are performed in the original language.

Komische Oper (☎ *47 99 74 00, Behrenstrasse 55-57, Mitte)* **Map 7** Tickets €8-55, box office at Unter den Linden 41. Musical theatre, light opera, operetta and dance theatre are the mainstays at this opera house founded in 1947. There's less of an elite touch here, where the repertory is more light-hearted and often performed in a theatrical way. All productions are sung in German.

Neuköllner Oper (☎ *68 89 07 77, Karl-Marx-Strasse 131-133)* **Map 5** U-Bahn: U7 to Karl-Marx-Strasse. Tickets €7.50-20. This place, in working-class Neukölln, is much more avant-garde than its name might suggest. The repertory includes rare operas by Mozart and Schubert, but also children's and experimental shows. It's all staged with little money and much creativity in a refurbished pre-war ballroom and attracts an unpretentious, young audience.

Musical Theater Berlin (☎ 01805-44 44, Marlene-Dietrich-Platz 1) (see the Potsdamer Platz & Kulturforum map in the Things to See & Do chapter) Tickets €42-110. This state-of-the-art musical theatre in DaimlerCity opened in June 1999 with the world premiere of *Der Glöckner von Notre Dame* (The Hunchback of Notre Dame), based on the novel by Victor Hugo. All performances are in German.

Theater des Westens (☎ 882 28 88 or 01805-99 89 99, Kantstrasse 12, Charlottenburg) **Map 6** Tickets €17-60. Near Zoo station, this is Berlin's traditional venue for musicals, both touring and home-grown productions. These are usually performed in German and quality varies widely. Note that it's hard to see much from the cheapest seats.

CABARET

A number of venues are trying to revive the lively and lavish variety shows in vogue during the Golden Twenties. Programs include dancers, singers, jugglers, acrobats and other entertainers who each perform a short number.

Chamäleon Varieté (☎ 282 71 18, Rosenthaler Strasse 40-41, Mitte) **Map 7** Admission €15-20 Mon-Thur, €25 Fri-Sat, midnight show €14. Shows Mon-Sat at 8.30pm, Sun at 7pm, midnight shows Fri and Sat. This is an intimate venue in a former ballroom in the Hackesche Höfe. Slapstick to jugglers, burlesque to trapeze artists – enjoy the show from your seat at a little coffeehouse table with candle-light.

Friedrichstadtpalast (☎ 23 26 24 74, Friedrichstrasse 107, Mitte) **Map 7** Tickets €12.50-40. Shows are often sold out at the 2000-seat Friedrichstadtpalast, the largest musical-revue theatre in Europe. Ritzy Las Vegas-style productions, featuring an 80-head ballet of leggy dancers and excellent in-house orchestra and singers, ensure an entertaining evening.

Scheinbar Varieté (☎ 784 55 39, Monumentenstrasse 9, Schöneberg) **Map 4** U-Bahn: U7 to Kleistpark. Tickets (available before the show) €6-10. Shows 8.30pm Wed-Sat. To say Scheinbar is tiny is an understatement. Yet the intimacy of the venue

makes for good views of the stage and gives you a chance to chat with the performers after the show.

Pantomimes, jugglers and clowns are part of the mix and many get their start here before moving on to bigger venues like the glamorous Wintergarten (see following).

Wintergarten-Das Varieté (☎ 25 00 88 88, Potsdamer Strasse 96, Tiergarten) **Map 4** Tickets €18-50. Tickets are hot at the cool Wintergarten which revives the tradition of vaudeville. Every night, top magicians, clowns, acrobats and artistes from around the world appear beneath the theatre's starry sky ceiling. It's a classy venue, with lots of polished brass, velvet and young women selling candy from trays. The line-up changes every few months and quality can vary, but it's definitely worth checking out. The original Wintergarten (1887–1944) was in the Hotel Central on Friedrichstrasse.

Bar jeder Vernunft (☎ 883 15 82, Schaperstrasse 24, Wilmersdorf) **Map 6** Tickets €15-30. Entertainers appearing at this wonderful venue have a veritable cult following and shows – often with a camp or bizarre bent – are often sold out in advance. Part of the draw is certainly the exquisite setting: a historic Art Nouveau-style tent decked out with dazzling mirrors and booths bathed in red-velvet and candlelight. After the show, the place turns into a relaxed piano bar open to anyone; in summer there's a nice beer garden as well.

'Cabaret, by the way, is not to be confused with 'Kabarett', which is political satire featuring a team of *Kabarettisten* in a series of stand-up monologues or skits. They can be hilarious – if your German is up to it! The main troupes are:

Die Stachelschweine (The Porcupines; ☎ 261 47 95, Europa-Center, Charlottenburg) **Map 6** Tickets €10-20. Shows Tues-Sat.

Die Wühlmäuse (The Voles; ☎ 30 67 30 11, Pommernallee 2-4, Charlottenburg) **Map 1** Tickets €12.50-40. Shows Tues-Sat.

BKA-Berliner Kabarett Anstalt (☎ 251 01 12, Mehringdamm 32-34, Kreuzberg) **Map 5** Shows daily €11-18.

Die Distel (The Thistle; ☎ 204 47 04, Friedrichstrasse 101, Mitte) **Map 7** Tickets €13-40. Shows Tues-Sat.

Gaze at the stars at the Carl Zeiss Planetarium.

Golden Gallery, Schloss Charlottenburg.

The Metropol Theater features erotic friezes.

Schloss Cecilienhof, Potsdam, where Stalin, Churchill and Truman met in 1945.

Statues of Martin Luther and Philipp Melanchthon grace the Markt in Lutherstadt-Wittenberg.

Cabaret in Berlin: Let the Good Times Roll – Again!

For all intents and purposes, Berlin *is* cabaret. No other form of entertainment is so intensely linked with the German capital – and not just since Bob Fosse gave us the classic movie, *Cabaret*, starring Liza Minelli. Cabaret came of age in the free-wheeling Golden Twenties. Night after night, dozens of theatres dazzled crowds with a varied program of singers, showgirls, jugglers, magicians and other artists, many of whom had run away from the circus.

Cabaret's spirit was nurtured by the political and societal circumstances of the 1920s. The collapse of the monarchy had brought an end to centuries of censorship, and artists were quick to capitalise on their new-found freedom. Political satire flourished, with inherently corrupt Weimar Republic politicians providing plenty of fodder for biting routines. At the same time, the crippling hyperinflation of 1923 imbued people with a sense of fatalism, driving them to party as though there was no tomorrow. The arrival of new music – especially jazz (or *Yatz*, as it was called here) – further loosened libidos. Berlin became Europe's party town – the capital of cocaine and decadence. It was a world of lurid delights and amoral dalliances so cleverly chronicled by Christopher Isherwood in *Goodbye to Berlin*, which formed the basis for *Cabaret*.

Hitler's rise to power put an instant cork into this brief period of unbridled laissez-fare; war and division followed. Since reunification, though, cabaret has undergone a renaissance, albeit in a much tamer form. You're more likely to encounter parodies of the *Pirates of Penzance* than an opium-besotted androgyne. Even drag queens have become respectable. In places such as the Wintergarten and the Friedrichsstadtpalast you'll find carefully choreographed spectacles, but even smaller venues such as the Bar jeder Vernunft and Chamäleon Varieté provide a glimpse of the wild days of the Golden Twenties.

CASINO

Spielbank Berlin (☎ *85 59 90, Marlene-Dietrich-Platz; slot machine admission €1, to tables €2.50)* Open 10.30-3am, over 21 only. This is part of the entertainment complex within the Potsdamer Platz development (see the Potsdamer Platz & Kulturforum map in the Things to See & Do chapter). It claims to be Germany's largest casino with tables and slot machines spread over three floors and divided into the Casino Leger (no dress code) and Casino Royal (formal dress).

THEATRE

Theatre has flourished in Berlin for more than a century. With more than 100 theatres – from big, highbrow venues to smaller experimental outfits – there really is something to suit everybody. In the eastern city centre, they cluster around Friedrichstrasse; in the CityWest they line up along Ku'damm. Many theatres are closed Monday and from mid-July to late August.

Good seats are usually available on the evening of a performance, as unclaimed tickets are sold 30 minutes before curtain time. You'll often see other theatre-goers trying to sell an extra ticket; it's perfectly fine to buy from these people but make sure the ticket is legit and watch out for scalpers. Some theatres offer discounts of up to 50% to students and seniors.

Half-price theatre tickets are also available to everyone from Hekticket on the day of the performance. Branches are on the ground floor in the Zoo-Palast cinema, ***Hekticket*** (☎ *24 31 24 31, Hardenbergstrasse 29a, Charlottenburg)* **Map 6** and *(☎ 230 99 30, Liebknechtstrasse 12, Near Alexanderplatz)* **Map 7**. Obviously, choices are limited to what's officially left unsold that day. Sales commence at 2pm daily and tickets must be bought and paid for in person at the Hek-ticket office but will actually be waiting for you at the venue.

Listed here is a small selection of the-atres, nearly all of them in Mitte. Check the listings magazines for smaller, experimental theatres. Berlin's not stuffy, so you can come dressed as you please.

Major Stages

Renaissance-Theater Berlin (☎ *312 42 02, Hardenbergstrasse 6, Charlottenburg)* **Map 6** Tickets €11-29. The productions here are a little more on the lightweight, entertaining side but also include premieres of contem-porary German playwrights.

Deutsches Theater (☎ *28 44 12 25, Schumannstrasse 13a, Mitte)* **Map 7** Tickets €5-30. This theatre has a rich tradition and counts Max Reinhardt among its former directors (1905–33). Since reunification, though, it hasn't really been able to connect with its audiences, but that may change now that Bernd Willms, previously of the Maxim-Gorki-Theater, is at the helm. He's brought with him a young, energetic ensem-ble cast, which also plays at the smaller *Kammerspiele* (studio theatre) next door.

Berliner Ensemble (☎ *28 40 81 55, Bertolt-Brecht-Platz 1, Mitte)* **Map 7** Tick-ets €6-30. Bertolt Brecht's old theatre (*The Threepenny Opera* premiered here) was taken over by acclaimed director Claus Pey-mann in 1999. Look for lots of Austrian writers as well as German classics and Shakespeare. The theatre building itself is gorgeous and cheap tickets are usually available.

Volksbühne am Rosa-Luxemburg-Platz (☎ *240 67 72, Linienstrasse 227, Mitte)* **Map 3** Tickets €10 or €15. Sex, blood, screams and pain: the graphic performances here are not for tender souls. Nonconformist and rad-ical, cutting-edge and provocative are the maxims of its eccentric leader Frank Castorf and his league of guest directors. This style resonates especially with younger folk: about one in three theatre-goers at Volksbühne is aged between 15 and 35. Even more off-beat performances take place at the *Berliner*

Prater (*Kastanienallee 7-9, Prenzlauer Berg)* **Map 4** on a smaller stage.

Maxim Gorki Theater (☎ *20 22 11 29, Am Festungsgraben 2, Mitte)* **Map 7** Tick-ets €11-23, discount for advance bookings. Volker Hesse, the new director, is a fan of contemporary plays and collaborations with other innovative groups. Quality here is uniformly high, and productions often pro-voke debate.

Schaubühne am Lehniner Platz (☎ *89 00 23, Kurfürstendamm 153, Wilmersdorf)* **Map 6** Tickets €8-28, students (advance bookings only) for all seats €7. In a convert-ed 1920s cinema, this place is run by inter-nationally acclaimed dance theatre chore ographer Sasha Waltz and director Thomas Ostermeier whose productions run the gamut from *Shopping & Fucking* to classics such as *Danton's Death*.

English-Language Theatre

Friends of Italian Opera (☎ *691 12 11, Fidicinstrasse 40, Kreuzberg 61)* **Map 5** Maximum ticket €15, students €10. De-spite its name, this troupe has nothing to do with fat ladies in frills (actually its name is code for 'Mafia'). It is, in fact, Berlin's old-est English-language theatre. Both resident Berlin troupes and visiting ensembles per-form almost nightly at the 60-seat venue.

STUEKkE (☎ *42 02 81 48, Palisaden-strasse 48, Friedrichshain)* **Map 3** This is a small fringe theatre that specialises in contemporary plays by British or American writers, although performances are not al-ways in English.

Children's & Youth Theatre

Berlin has several youth-oriented theatres, all of which perform in German.

Grips Theater (☎ *391 40 04, Altonaer Strasse 22, Tiergarten)* **Map 2** U-Bahn: U9 to Hansaplatz. Tickets €5-13. The best, and best-known, is Grips Theater which does high-quality, topical and critical plays for children and teenagers.

People of any age and language back-ground can enjoy puppet theatre. Established troupes include *Berliner Figurentheater* (☎ *786 98 15, Yorckstrasse 59, Kreuzberg)*

Map 5, *Puppentheater Firlefanz (☎ 283 35 60, Sophienstrasse 10, Mitte)* **Map 3** and *Schaubude Puppentheater Berlin (☎ 423 43 14, Greifswalder Strasse 81-84, Prenzlauer Berg)* **Map 3**.

Cabuwazi (☎ 533 72 44) The mysterious name stands for 'Chaotisch-Bunter Wander Zirkus' (Chaotic and Colourful Travelling Circus), a nonprofit program that trains kids aged 10 to 17 as circus artistes who then perform at venues around town. Call or check the listings magazines for upcoming shows.

DANCE

Classical ballet is performed at the Staatsoper Unter den Linden and the Deutsche Oper (see the Opera section earlier in this chapter), while scantily-clad showgirls strut their stuff at the Friedrichstadtpalast (see the Cabaret section earlier in this chapter).

Berlin's independent dance scene has also announced that it wants to be taken seriously and several venues and companies are doing their best to ensure that the city has a place among Europe's centres of dance. Along with Sasha Waltz' Schaubühne am Lehniner Platz (see Theatre earlier in this chapter), the following venues all feature high-calibre modern and experimental dance. Check the listings magazines for upcoming shows.

Hebbel Theater (☎ 25 90 04 27, Stresemannstrasse 29, Kreuzberg) **Map 5**
Sophiensaele (☎ 283 52 66, Sophienstrasse 18, Mitte) **Map 3**
Tanzfabrik Berlin (☎ 786 58 61, Möckernstrasse 68, Kreuzberg) **Map 5**
Tanzwerkstatt Berlin im Kunsthaus Podewil (☎ 24 74 96, Klosterstrasse 68-70, Mitte) **Map 7**

CINEMAS

Films are pretty pricey, with Saturday night tickets at fancy multiplex cinemas costing as much as €9. Seeing a show on *Kinotag* (film day, usually Tuesday or Wednesday) or before 5pm saves about €2.50. The big cinemas show mostly mainstream Hollywood movies dubbed into German.

Smaller independent neighbourhood theatres are usually a bit cheaper and may offer student discounts. Many show movies in their original language (no subtitles) which is denoted by the acronym 'OF' (Originalfassung); those shown *with* subtitles are denoted 'OmU' (Original mit Untertiteln).

Discovery Channel IMAX Theater Berlin (☎ 44 31 61 31, Marlene-Dietrich-Platz 4) (see the Potsdamer Platz & Kulturforum map in the Things to See & Do chapter) This big cinema screens the usual IMAX documentaries about travel, space and wildlife.
Cinestar IMAX im Sony Center (☎ 26 06 62 60, Potsdamer Strasse 4) (see the Potsdamer Platz & Kulturforum map in the Things to See & Do chapter) This is yet another IMAX with 2D *and* 3D shows.
Cinemaxx (☎ 44 31 63 16, Potsdamer Platz 5, Mitte) (see the Potsdamer Platz & Kulturforum map in the Things to See & Do chapter) This state-of-the-art mega-complex is the main venue of the International Film Festival. Up to 20 movies are on the program at any given time.
Cinemas that have frequent showings of OmU or OF films include:
Die Kurbel (☎ 883 53 25, Giesebrechtstrasse 4, Charlottenburg) **Map 6** This place shows recent-release Hollywood movies in the original English.
Babylon (☎ 61 60 96 93, Dresdner Strasse 126, Kreuzberg 36) **Map 5** U-Bahn: U1, U8, or U15 to Kottbusser Tor. Babylon also shows mostly recently released mainstream fare.
Eiszeit (☎ 611 60 16, Zeughofstrasse 20, Kreuzberg 36) **Map 5** U-Bahn: U1 to Görlitzer Bahnhof. There's a daily changing program of more obscure, alternative film fare here.
Acud (☎ 44 35 94 98, Veteranenstrasse 21, Mitte) **Map 7** Lesser-known movies from around the world are shown in the original version here, usually at 8pm.
Central (☎ 28 59 99 73, Rosenthaler Strasse 39, Mitte) **Map 7** This arty cinema next to the Hackescher Höfe shows films with an intellectual bent.
Hackesche Höfe (☎ 283 46 03, Rosenthaler Strasse 40/41, Mitte) **Map 7** New and old movies – mostly from Anglo countries – are shown at this small cinema.
Odeon (☎ 78 70 40 19, Hauptstrasse 116, Schöneberg) **Map 4** U-Bahn: U4 to Innsbrucker Platz or S1, S45 or S46 to Schöneberg. Come here for English-language recent releases.
Arsenal (☎ 26 95 51 00, Potsdamer Strasse 21, Sony Center, Tiergarten) (see the Potsdamer Platz & Kulturforum map in the Things to See & Do chapter) A potpourri of nonmainstream movies from around the world – usually dubbed into English – can be seen at this brand-new theatre.

ENTERTAINMENT

SPECTATOR SPORTS
Athletics
The ISTAF, an international track and field meet, is held in early September at the Olympic Stadium. Call ☎ 30 38 44 44 to book tickets. Later the same month, you have the opportunity to watch or participate in the Berlin Marathon. The route starts at Charlottenburger Tor on Strasse des 17 Juni and finishes at the Gedächtniskirche. Call ☎ 302 53 70 for information.

Basketball
Berlin's European-class basketball team, ALBA, won the German championship in the 1997–98 season. Games take place at the *Max-Schmeling-Halle (☎ 44 30 45 information, 44 30 44 30 tickets, Am Falkplatz, cnr Gaudystrasse)* **Map 3** Tickets start at €6 for national league games, €12 for European league games. Home games usually take place at 3pm Saturday. The stadium seats about 8000.

Horse Racing
Berlin has three racecourses.

Galopprennbahn Hoppegarten (☎ 03342-389 30, Goetheallee 1, Dahlwitz-Hoppegarten) S-Bahn: S5 to Hoppegarten. Standing room €4, seats €5-10. Races usually 1pm Sun Apr-Oct; call to confirm. Built in 1867 north-east of the city, this is one of the fanciest European racetracks and is 2350m long.

Trabrennbahn Karlshorst (☎ 50 01 70 or ☎ 25 09 92 92 for recorded information, Treskowallee 129, Lichtenberg) S-Bahn: S3 to Karlshorst. Tram: No 26, 27 to Treskowallee/Ehrlichstrasse. Admission €1/0.50. Meetings 2pm Sat, sometimes 6pm Tues (free entry). This track dates back to 1862 but was completely destroyed in WWII. After the war, it was the only trotting course in the GDR.

Trabrennbahn Mariendorf (☎ 740 11 21, Mariendorfer Damm 222, Tempelhof) U-Bahn: U6 to Alt-Mariendorf. Bus: No 176 or 179 to Trabrennbahn. Races 6.30pm Wed free, 1.30pm Sun €2.50/1.50 year-round. Founded in 1913, this is the trotting course of choice for hobnobbing politicos and businessfolk.

Ice Hockey
Ice hockey is hugely popular in Berlin, which has two teams in the national league. The Berlin Capitals play at the *Deutschlandhalle (☎ 885 60 00, Messedamm 26, Charlottenburg)* S-Bahn: S5, S75 to Eichkamp. Standing room tickets adult/concession/children under 11 €11/8/5, seats €20-40/15-25/7.50-20. Tickets are available at the box office, at the head office at Kurfürstendamm 214 and at general ticket outlets.

The other Berlin team, EHC Eisbären, plays at the *Sportforum Hohenschönhausen (☎ 97 18 40 40 for tickets, Steffenstrasse, Hohenschönhausen)* S-Bahn: S75 to Hohenschönhausen, then tram No 15 to Simon-Bolivar-Strasse. Standing-room tickets €12.50, seats €20-33. They're sold at the box office, ticket outlets or via the ticket hotline.

Soccer
Berlin's Bundesliga (National League) club Hertha BSC enjoys a loyal fan-base that regularly flocks into the Olympic Stadium for home games. Kick-off is usually at 3.30pm Saturday. The playing season lasts from early September until around May/June with a winter break from December to January.

Tickets (hotline ☎ 01805-43 78 42) cost €5 to €50. The stadium is packed if a famous team like Bayern München or Borussia Dortmund is visiting; otherwise, you should be able to get tickets without any trouble on game day at the stadium box office which opens two hours before kick-off. Advance tickets are available at ticket offices, online (Ⓦ www.herthabsc.de) or by calling the hotline.

Two national-championship finals take place every year in Berlin. In January there is the annual indoor soccer championship, hosted by the DFB (the German National Soccer Association) and played in the *Max-Schmeling-Halle (☎ 44 30 44 30 for information)* **Map 3**. Hugely popular is the DFB Pokalendspiel, the German National Soccer Association cup final. It's played at the Olympic Stadium but tickets are hard to come by and should be ordered months in advance by writing to Berliner Fussball-bund, Humboldtstrasse 8a, 14193 Berlin; or call ☎ 896 99 40 for details.

Tennis

The German Open women's tournament takes place every May at the Rot-Weiss Tennis Club in the Grunewald forest near the Hundekehlesee lake. It usually attracts high-ranking players and is a very popular event. Martina Hingis, Conchita Martinez and Amelie Mauresmo were the winners in 1999, 2000 and 2001, respectively. Tickets, especially for the later rounds, are tough to get; try the BTM hotline on ☎ 25 00 25, major ticket outlets or the tennis club directly on ☎ 89 57 55 20/21.

Shopping

Penny pinchers to power shoppers – anyone can buy just about anything under the sun in Berlin. Unlike, say, London with Oxford Street or New York with Fifth Avenue, shopping in the German capital is not concentrated in a single artery. Each neighbourhood offers its own take on shopping with a special mix of stores. Charlottenburg specialises in mainstream clothing; Friedrichstrasse has haute couture; multi-ethnic Kreuzberg is lined with second-hand and junk stores; Mitte brims with art galleries, hip local designer fashions and bizarre knick-knack boutiques. Also give the flea markets a try; they're often treasure troves of things unique to Berlin.

WHAT TO BUY
Antiques & Collectibles
Antique and collectible stores cluster along Goltzstrasse in Schöneberg (furniture, household goods, lamps), around Savignyplatz in Charlottenburg (jewellery, upmarket classic furniture and Berlin collectibles), on Bergmannstrasse in Kreuzberg 61 (funky clothing, accessories, and decorative arts) and along Husemannstrasse in Prenzlauer Berg (GDR memorabilia, furniture, and books).

In Kupfergraben, just off the northern tip of Museumsinsel, is the Berliner Kunst & Nostalgiemarkt, not really a market but a series of shops housed in the S-Bahn arches between Planckstrasse and Geschwister-Scholl-Strasse. Shops specialise in periods like Art Nouveau or the 1950s, or in collectibles such as lamps, military regalia or porcelain. Cheap it ain't, though with some luck you might still find some bargains.

Books
General Interest Pursue your German literary interests at the following stores.

Hugendubel (☎ 21 40 60, Tauentzienstrasse 13, Charlottenburg) **Map 6**; *(☎ 253 91 70, Potsdamer Platz Arkaden, Tiergarten)* (see the Potsdamer Platz & Kulturforum map in the Things to See & Do chapter) This

excellent chain has a superb selection, including novels in English and Lonely Planet books. Browsing is encouraged and comfortable sofas invite reading. You may even bring books to the in-store cafe.

Kiepert (☎ 31 18 80, Hardenbergstrasse 4-5, Charlottenburg) **Map 6**; *(☎ 201 71 30, Friedrichstrasse 63, Mitte)* **Map 7** These shops have a similar assortment of books as Hugendubel.

Berlin Story (☎ 20 45 38 42, Unter den Linden 10, Mitte) **Map 7** This central store offers one-stop-shopping for Berlin-related maps, videos, magazines and books of all kinds (guides, cookbooks, history, etc), many in English.

For international papers and magazines in a range of languages, try the *Presse Zentrum (☎ 313 98 49, main hall, Zoo station)* or the *Europa Presse Center (ground floor, Europa-Center)*, both in Charlottenburg **(Map 6)**.

English Cosmopolitan Berlin has a number of bookstores which specialise in English-language publications.

Books in Berlin (☎ 313 12 33, Goethestrasse 69, Charlottenburg) **Map 6** Roll up for new and used English-language books.

Marga Schoeller Bücherstube (☎ 881 11 12, Knesebeckstrasse 33-34, Charlottenburg) **Map 6** Visit this well-established shop for its sophisticated assortment of art and theatre literature as well as feminist works and nonfiction.

Fair Exchange (☎ 694 46 75, Dieffenbacherstrasse 58, Kreuzberg 61) **Map 5** For used books this place is worth a try.

British Bookshop (☎ 238 46 80, Mauerstrasse 83-84, Mitte) **Map 7** This friendly store has books on the history of Berlin and of Germany in general, an excellent selection of the latest British and US novels, and general reference books on subjects like German cuisine, the arts and travel, including Lonely Planet books. Staff are multilingual and very knowledgeable.

Travel Most bookshops have a travel section, but some stores specialise in guidebooks and maps.

Outdoor (☎ 693 40 80, Bergmannstrasse 108, Kreuzberg 61) **Map 5** This shop has many books and maps at discounted prices and caters especially for budget travellers.

Reisebuch (☎ 28 38 61 07, Auguststrasse 89, Mitte) **Map 3** Get in the mood for China, Italy or whatever country takes your fancy when browsing this neat store run by a couple of enterprising young women.

Schropp Landkarten (☎ 23 55 73 20, Potsdamer Strasse 129, Schöneberg) **Map 4** With the right map from this place, you'll have no excuse for getting lost. Choose from topographical, hiking, biking and driving maps from around the world, plus an assortment of travel books.

Another source is *Globetrotter Ausrüstungen* (see the Camping, Outdoor & Sports Gear section later in this chapter).

Speciality For those hard-to-find speciality tomes, browse through any of these stores.

Bücherbogen (☎ 318 69 50, inside S-Bahn arch No 593, Savignyplatz, Charlottenburg) **Map 6** This bookstore is part of a small chain specialised in architecture and art, with many titles in English. Check the Yellow Pages for additional branches.

Hammet (☎ 691 58 34, Friesenstrasse 27, Kreuzberg 61) **Map 5** For detective and crime stories, including many in English, come to this store, named after Dashiell Hammet.

Richard Schikowski (☎ 218 54 95, Motzstrasse 30, Schöneberg) **Map 4** This shop has a unique offering of books on the occult.

Gay & Lesbian Most mainstream bookstores have lesbigay sections, but for selection and knowledgeable staff these places are hard to beat.

Prinz Eisenherz (☎ 313 99 36, Bleibtreustrasse 52, Charlottenburg) **Map 6** This

---

Weird, Whacky, Useful – Uniquely Berlin

There's no final frontier to your shopping experience in Berlin. In this city where creativity is king lots of unusual stores have opened up in recent years. We introduce you to a small selection of some of the more bizarre boutiques in town.

Berliner Zinnfiguren *(☎ 315 70 00, Knesebeckstrasse 88, Charlottenburg)* **Map 6** Open 10am-6pm Mon-Fri, 10am-3pm Sat. Build up your own Prussian army – en miniature – at this traditional tin figurine store, in business since 1934. The more pacifist-minded can choose from a collection of historical characters. Many items are hand-painted.

Mondos Arts *(☎ 42 01 07 78, Schreinerstrasse 6, Friedrichshain)* **Map 3** Open 10am-7pm Mon-Fri, 11am-4pm Sat. The best of GDR culture is kept alive at this funky store named for the brand of condoms once sold behind the Iron Curtain. The store's founders were also the initiators of the (ultimately successful) campaign to save the *Ampelmännchen*, the little man on the lights at pedestrian crossings in the GDR. He now graces everything from t-shirts to mousepads and makes for a whimsical souvenir.

Laden der Blindenanstalt von Berlin *(☎ 25 88 66 12, Oranienstrasse 26, Kreuzberg 36)* **Map 5** Open 9am-4.45pm Mon-Thur, to 3.45pm Fri. Intricate baskets and fashionable brushes in all shapes and forms are sold at this store. What's unique about it? It's all made by the handy folks of Berlin's Institute for the Blind. Pretty cool stuff.

Berliner Bonbonmacherei *(☎ 44 05 52 43, Oranienburger Strasse 32, Mitte)* **Map 3** Open noon-8pm Wed-Sat. Sneak a peek into the basement kitchen of this cute candy shop in the Heckmann-Höfe to see traditional caramels and sweets being made by hand.

Bärliner *(☎ 41 71 75 07, Rykestrasse 26, Mitte)* **Map 3** Open 2pm-8pm Tues-Fri, 11am-2pm Sat. Berlin's trusty symbol, the bear, takes centre stage at this store. Choose from an entire stuffed zoo full of cuddly companions, from the handmade collector's version for hundreds of euros to the cute little one that'll fit into any backpack.

is one of the best shops for literature and books for gay men, with a smaller selection for lesbians.

Chronika Buchhandlung (☎ *693 42 69, Bergmannstrasse 26, Kreuzberg 61*) **Map 5** Come here for a big selection of literature by women and for women – straight or lesbian.

Adam (☎ *448 07 67, Gleimstrasse 23, Prenzlauer Berg*) **Map 3** Though more geared towards gay men, Adam also has some stuff for lesbians and even stocks condoms and dildos.

Bruno's (☎ *21 47 32 93, Nürnberger Strasse 53, Wilmersdorf*) **Map 6** Here gay men browse for international magazines, novels, coffee-table books and travel guides. There are also videos for sale and rent.

Fashion

Mainstream The obvious places to look for mainstream clothing are the malls (see the *Where to Shop* section later in this chapter), which have chain and individual boutiques and larger stores. Other good strips are on Wilmersdorfer Strasse, Kurfürstendamm and Tauentzienstrasse in Charlottenburg.

Gap (☎ *219 00 90, Tauentzienstrasse 13, Charlottenburg*) **Map 6** This American chain sells well-made, classic casual wear for men and women.

Diesel Jeans Store (☎ *88 55 14 53, Kurfürstendamm 17, Charlottenburg*) **Map 6** West of Gap, this store has the entire collection of the fashionably overpriced Diesel label.

Peek & Cloppenburg (☎ *24 90 51, Tauentzienstrasse 19, Charlottenburg*) **Map 6** Solid, quality clothing for men and women at decent prices is sold at this multi-storey store, just west of the KaDeWe.

Hennes & Mauritz (*H&M;* ☎ *882 62 99, Tauentzienstrasse 13a, Charlottenburg*) **Map 6** (☎ *201 20 10, Friedrichstrasse 79, Mitte*) **Map 7**. Young fashions at low prices is the name of the game at the ubiquitous H&M, a Swedish chain, with branches around town.

East & West (☎ *55 48 91 96, Frankfurter Allee 111, Friedrichshain*) **Map 1** A good selection of casual wear, including Diesel, Levi's and Big Star, is on sale at this funky store decked out like an American ranch.

Berlin Designers The following places are worth checking for up-to-the-minute creations from local designers.

Groopie de Luxe (☎ *217 20 38, Goltzstrasse 39, Schöneberg*) **Map 4** This place has one-off outfits from hip local designers, including its own label Groopie Couture, and accessories of superior quality. You'll look good anywhere from a trance party to a 1930s swing night. Mid- to upper-priced.

Claudia Skoda (☎ *885 10 09, Kurfürstendamm 50, Charlottenburg*) **Map 6** (☎ *280 72 11, Linienstrasse 156, Mitte*) **Map 3** Claudia Skoda's understated women's clothes have been a major presence on Berlin's design scene for a long time. The cucumber-cool aluminium-clad store in Charlottenburg is where you go for custom-tailored couture, while the Mitte branch has her ready-to-wear line.

Eisdieler (☎ *285 73 51, Kastanienallee 12, Mitte*) **Map 3** Not just flavour of the month – the urban streetwear designed by this five-person cooperative and sold in a former ice cream parlor has established itself firmly in the Berlin design world. Stock up on t-shirts, pants and sweaters, then sprinkle it all with jewellery, shoes, bags and other accessories.

Nix (☎ *281 80 44, Auguststrasse 86, Mitte*) **Map 3** The name stands for New Individual X-tras, a line of unusual – and quite affordable – fashions for hip women, men and children designed by the team of Barbara Gebhardt and Angela Herb.

Tagebau (☎ *28 39 08 90, Rosenthaler Strasse 19, Mitte*) **Map 3** This warehouse-sized space is another cooperative of six young designers. Browse for whimsical hats by Angela Klöck, jewellery made from unusual materials (bone, fur) by Eva Sörensen and Michaela Binder, striking costumes by Gizella Koppany, formal fashions by Karsten Fischer and furniture by Diemo Alfóns.

Ultramarin (☎ *441 87 94, Wörther Strasse 33, Prenzlauer Berg*) **Map 3** Variety is the name of the game here: garish colour for urban trendoids, romantic fabrics, classic business outfits, even theatrical wedding dresses. It's all custom-tailored.

Vintage Used clothing stores can be found along Bergmannstrasse and Mehringdamm in Kreuzberg 61, Oranienstrasse in Kreuzberg 36, Rosenthaler Strasse in Mitte and Maassenstrasse and Goltzstrasse in Schöneberg.

Humana (Joachimstaler Strasse 43, Charlottenburg) **Map 6**; *(☎ 422 20 18, Frankfurter Tor 3, Friedrichshain)* **Map 3**; *(☎ 21 75 21 04, Nollendorfplatz 6, Schöneberg)* **Map 4** Humana is a chain of thrift stores with many branches – some of them almost department-store sized – throughout town.

Checkpoint (☎ 694 43 44, Mehringdamm 57, Kreuzberg 61) **Map 5** The recent fad for anything '70s may have peaked, but you wouldn't know it when browsing through this store's collection of bell-bottoms and psychedelic nylon shirts.

Colours (☎ 694 33 48, 1st floor, rear Bergmannstrasse 102, Kreuzberg 61) **Map 5** This huge loft is crammed with vintage goodies suitable for the office or your next period costume party. In the mix are party dresses, jeans, jackets, shirts and other garments from various decades. Most items are in good condition.

Sterling Gold (☎ 28 09 65 00, Heckmann-Höfe, off Oranienburger Strasse 32, Mitte) **Map 3** Discover your inner Grace Kelly when slipping into one of the superb gowns and cocktail dresses from the '50s to the '80s sold here. It's not cheap, but everything's classy and in good shape.

Monroe (☎ 440 84 48, Kollwitzstrasse 102, Prenzlauer Berg) **Map 3** This place is affiliated with Checkpoint in Kreuzberg and has a similar assortment of new and used clothes and shoes at cut-rate prices.

Maassen 10 (☎ 215 54 56, Maassenstrasse 10, Schöneberg) **Map 4** This hole-in-the-wall, near the Hasir Imbiss eatery, specialises in cheap used or slightly flawed Levi's jeans and other casual mainstream clothing.

Garage (☎ 211 27 60 Ahornstrasse 2, Schöneberg) **Map 4** This basement warehouse is Nirvana for the cash-strapped treasure hunter. Everything's priced by weight (1kg for €13), but you really have to pick your way through the countless racks as items are often tattered or soiled.

Made in Berlin (☎ 262 24 31, Potsdamer Strasse 106, Schöneberg) **Map 4** Cash-poor but style-savvy Berliners poke through the racks of this popular store, which has better quality gear than its sister store Garage.

Eccentric & Clubwear There are several places where you can get kitted-out for a night of clubbing.

Kaufhaus Schrill (☎ 882 40 48, Bleibtreustrasse 46, Charlottenburg) **Map 6** This place has clothing and eccentric accoutrements to put together electric fantasy outfits that'll add a spark to any party.

Planet (☎ 885 27 17, Schlüterstrasse 35, Charlottenburg) **Map 6** This store is the 'headquarters' of this musician-owned clothing label. The serious – and well-heeled – techno crowd comes here to put together eye-catching outfits.

Waahnsinn Berlin (☎ 282 00 29, Rosenthaler Strasse 17, Mitte) **Map 3** Open noon-8pm Mon-Sat. You'll need a whacky sense of aesthetics coupled with a good dose of humour to find a new favourite among the outrageous outfits, accessories and home furnishings at this shop. But you're guaranteed to make a splash on the club circuit.

Lingerie & Erotica If you are planning after-hours activities you may want to visit these stores for suitable attire.

Hautnah (☎ 882 34 34, Uhlandstrasse 170, Charlottenburg) **Map 6** Hautnah has three floors stocked with everything girls and boys with imagination might need for a naughty night.

Fishbelly (☎ 28 04 51 80, Sophienstrasse 7a, Hackesche Höfe, Mitte) **Map 7** Get your nocturnal niceties at Jutta Teschner's sleek lingerie shop whose motto is 'sexy wear for sexy women'. From briefs to bustiers to babydolls – you'll find big names and her own designs.

Schwarze Mode (☎ 784 59 22, Grunewaldstrasse 91, Schöneberg) **Map 4** This shop does fetish fashions of the weirdest variety. Browse the erotic bookstore next door for ideas, then stock up here on latex, leather and rubber.

Les Dessous (☎ 883 36 32, *Fasanenstrasse 42, Wilmersdorf*) **Map 6** For the finest in bodywear, head to Les Dessous where the money you part with may outweigh that silken negligee you get in return.

Shoes Put the final touches on your fashion make-over at the following footgear emporia.

Riccardo Cartillone (☎ 313 29 57, *Savignyplatz 4, Charlottenburg*) **Map 6**; (☎ 28 09 96 94, *Neue Schönhauser Strasse 7, Mitte*) **Map 7** Footwear from around the 'Boot' (as in Italy) for fashion-conscious women is what you'll find here.

Calypso (☎ 28 54 54 15, *Rosenthaler Strasse 23, Mitte*) **Map 3** This store is crammed with historic footwear for women. Step up to browse through a vast assortment of lace-up boots from the '20s, stiletto heels from the '60s, platform shoes from the '70s and other must-have retro styles.

Orlando (☎ 28 04 78 58, *Rosenthaler Strasse 48, Mitte*) **Map 7** The store's design is for purists: wooden floor, wooden shelves. Fortunately, more imagination has gone into the design of the stylish boots sold here mostly at reasonable prices.

Schuhtick Last Minute (☎ 214 09 80, *Maasenstrasse 5, Schöneberg*) **Map 4** Schuhtick has some of the coolest trotters in town – office to nightclub – but usually with stratospheric price tags. Relief is in sight at this outlet branch where many styles ring in for well under €50.

Galleries

Berlin has about 300 private galleries holding forth in stately patrician villas, converted warehouses or factories and spacious, elegant storefronts. There are two main areas: in Charlottenburg along Fasanenstrasse, Knesebeckstrasse, Mommsenstrasse, Pestalozzistrasse and other Ku' damm side streets; and in Mitte along Auguststrasse, Sophienstrasse, Gipsstrasse, Torstrasse and other streets in and around the Hackesche Höfe. Predictably, the former scene is more established, highbrow

and mainstream, while the latter has a more experimental, avant-garde edge.

The best up-to-date source is the bi-monthly German-English *Berlin Artery – Der Kunstführer* (€1.80), available at newsstands, bookstores and galleries. For new off-beat galleries, check for flyers in bars and clubs.

Jewellery

Jewellery designers producing unique handmade pieces abound in Berlin. Most have combination studio-stores and can customise their creations to suit your personal tastes. As you'd imagine, none of this comes cheap... Here's a small selection:

Treykorn (☎ 31 80 23 54, *Savignyplatz 13, Savignypassage, Charlottenburg*) **Map 6** Sabine and Andreas Treykorn's rings, necklaces and bracelets have avant-garde flair and are made and displayed at their edgy jewellery gallery cum studio.

Fritz & Fillmann (☎ 615 17 00, *Dresdener Strasse 20, Kreuzberg 36*) **Map 5** Manuel Fritz and Manuela Fillmann have a way with precious metals. Their innovative and very wearable designs are museum quality and are for sale along with works by other jewellery artists from around Germany.

Schmucklabor (☎ 28 38 46 82, *Oranienburger Strasse 32, Heckmann-Höfe, Mitte*) **Map 3** Here in the Heckmann-Höfe, gold, silver and platinum are wrought into eccentric one-of-a-kind designs with an industrial edge. Very Berlin.

Doris Imhoff Schmuck & Perlen (☎ 78 71 67 00, *Akazienstrasse 26, Schöneberg*) **Map 4** Stock up on pearls and make your own costume jewellery or choose from among the store owner's own inventive creations.

Music

Zweitausendeins (☎ 312 50 17, *Kantstrasse 41, Charlottenburg*) **Map 6** Much of world music, classical and pop is sold at steep discounts here.

L&P Classics (☎ 88 03 30 43, *Knesebeckstrasse 33, Charlottenburg*) **Map 6** This place has an excellent assortment of classical music, including hard to find works by famous and lesser-known composers.

Canzone (☎ *312 40 27, S-Bahn Arch 583, Savignyplatz, Charlottenburg*) **Map 6** Good service and great selection in world music – rare to mainstream – are the hallmarks of this established store.

Space Hall (☎ *694 76 64, Zossener Strasse 33, Kreuzberg 61*) **Map 5** This space is cutting-edge space and has 'out-of-this-world' selection of mostly techno and house; it's a frequent stop for DJs.

Saturn (☎ *24 75 16, Alexanderplatz 8, Mitte*) **Map 7** (☎ *25 92 40, Alte Potsdamer Strasse 7, Tiergarten*) (see Postdamer Platz map in the Things to See & Do chapter) This huge electronics store has some of the best prices on mainstream CDs as well as lots of discount offers. There are even listening stations, so you can try before you buy – still a rarity in Germany.

DNS Recordstore (☎ *247 98 93, Alte Schönhauser Strasse 39-40, Mitte*) **Map 3** Vinyl purists can combine nostalgia with a craving for millennial sounds (drum 'n bass, techno, trip-hop, acid, etc). A handful of turntables are available for a test-listen.

Flashpoint (☎ *44 65 09 59, Schivelbeiner Strasse 47, Prenzlauer Berg*) **Map 3** For the latest club sounds – drum 'n bass, trance, goa, classic techno and more – go to Flashpoint.

Mr Dead & Mrs Free (☎ *215 14 49, Bülowstrasse 5, Schöneberg*) **Map 4** In a similar vein is this store which specialises in UK and US imports and independent labels, including vinyl.

Outdoor, Camping & Sports Gear

Der Aussteiger (☎ *441 04 14, Schliemannstrasse 46, Prenzlauer Berg*) **Map 3** For outdoor, expedition and camping gear, have a look at the range here.

Globetrotter Ausrüstungen (☎ *850 89 20, Bundesallee 88, Steglitz*) **Map 1** U-Bahn: Walter-Schreiber-Strasse. Although this is one of the best-known and largest stores, it's a bit out of the way.

Bannat (☎ *882 76 01, Lietzenburger 65, Wilmersdorf*) **Map 6** This is among the biggest outdoor gear emporia in the west of the city.

Mont K (☎ *448 25 90, Kastanienallee 83, Prenzlauer Berg*) **Map 3** Dedicated hikers, climbers and outdoor fans will find all the karabiners and water-tight boots they'll need for the next adventure. The young sales team also has an arsenal of tips to offer.

Step by Step (☎ *784 84 60, Kaiser-Wilhelm-Platz 4, Schöneberg*) **Map 4** This place has an excellent selection of hiking boots and other outdoor equipment.

Niketown (☎ *250 70, Tauentzienstrasse 7b, Charlottenburg*) **Map 6** Try the Berlin branch of Niketown for general sports equipment.

Karstadt Sport (☎ *88 02 40, Joachimstaler Strasse 5-6*) **Map 6** This multi-storey department store near Zoo station has equipment and outfits for any sport – tennis to caving.

Porcelain & Gifts

Meissener Porzellan (☎ *204 35 81, Unter den Linden 39, Mitte*) **Map 7** This shop sells the famous porcelain manufactured in that Saxon city. It is lovely to look at but, with prices starting at about €50 for an unpainted piece, it's a gaspingly expensive purchase. Even a painted ashtray measuring 7cm by 10cm will set you back around €150.

KPM (*Königliche Porzellan Manufaktur,* ☎ *881 18 02, Kurfürstendamm 26a, Charlottenburg*) **Map 6** This royal porcelain manufacturer has its own line of beautiful pieces in a similar price bracket as Meissener.

Rosenthal Studio (☎ *881 70 51, Kurfürstendamm 216, Charlottenburg*) **Map 6**. This is a branch of the nationwide chain selling tableware, vases and cutlery. Quality is extremely high and designs range from traditional to contemporary.

O-Ton Keramik (☎ *615 38 66, Oranienstrasse 165a, Kreuzberg 36*) **Map 5** You can watch all the stock being made in the back of the shop. Pottery includes expensive but very idiosyncratic handmade vases, bowls, pots, cups etc.

WHERE TO SHOP

Kurfürstendamm/Tauentzien-strasse – Charlottenburg (Map 6)

The Ku'damm, the premier shopping mile in the CityWest, stretches west of the Gedächtniskirche for about 3km, while Tauentzienstrasse wends its way south-east of Breitscheidplatz to Wittenbergplatz. The focus is on chain boutiques flogging affordable young fashions. The more exclusive shops – haute couture, porcelain etc – are mostly in the side streets such as Fasanenstrasse and Bleibtreustrasse. Thrown into the mix are electronics stores, pharmacies, perfume stores, home furnishings, and department stores.

Indoor malls include the Ku'damm Karree just west of Uhlandstrasse U-Bahn station, which is anchored by the four-storey electronics store ProMarkt, and the Europa-Center on Breitscheidplatz has a supermarket, newsstands, boutiques and restaurants.

Tauentzienstrasse is dominated by the KaDeWe department store (see the Department Stores section later in this chapter).

Wilmersdorfer Strasse – Charlottenburg (Map 6)

Berlin's first pedestrian zone stretches from Kantstrasse to Bismarckplatz. Along here you'll find chains like H&M, department stores like Hertie and Karstadt and large clothing stores like C&A. It is here that locals buy affordable mainstream wares for daily use. Get off at the Wilmersdorfer Strasse stop of the U7.

Bergmannstrasse – Kreuzberg 61 & Oranienstrasse – Kreuzberg 36 (Map 5)

There are lots of trendy second-hand clothing stores, book stores and boutiques selling ethnic accessories amongst the cafes and restaurants along here.

Hackesche Höfe & Around – Mitte (Maps 3 & 7)

Edgy galleries, boutiques with off-the-wall home accessories, music stores, jewellery studios and many one-of-a-kind places have proliferated here in recent years. Spend an afternoon browsing in Berlin's hippest shopping area.

Friedrichstadtpassagen – Mitte (Map 7)

Berlin's most sophisticated shopping takes place in this stylish trio of indoor malls along Friedrichstrasse (U-Bahn: U6 to Französische Strasse) in Mitte. It is anchored by the Galeries Lafayette, a branch of the famous Parisian department store (see Department Stores later in this section) and connected by an underground tunnel to Quartier 205 and Quartier 206. The latter houses Departmentstore, a rather mundane name for an exclusive emporium of fashions, furniture, houseware, perfume and other goodies from around the world, catering for those with discerning tastes and wallets to match.

Alexanderplatz – Mitte (Map 7)

The shopping here is centred around the vast Galeria Kaufhof department store, with a good assortment of mainstream items. Saturn is a megastore for electronics with good prices but poor service. Smaller boutiques round out the offerings. Take any U/S-Bahn train that stops at Alexanderplatz.

Potsdamer Platz Arkaden – Tiergarten

This stylish three-storey shopping mall is an excellent place to shop. There's an interesting range of boutiques, speciality stores, a Hugendubel bookstore and chains selling everything from funky eyewear to cigars to books to tuxedos. In the basement are several supermarkets and a food court. More restaurants and a popular ice cream parlour are on the top floor. There's also a post office on the ground floor. (See the Potsdamer Platz & Kulturforum map in the Things to See and Do chapter.)

Pariser Strasse/Olivaer Platz – Wilmersdorf (Map 6)

Mid-range to upmarket boutiques selling fashionable and sometimes one-of-a-kind clothing and accessories are gathered along Pariser Strasse. It gets more exclusive the closer you get to Olivaer Platz, where expensive designer boutiques cluster. From Ku'damm, take bus No 109, 119, 129 or 219 west and get off at the Olivaer Platz stop.

Altstadt Spandau – Spandau

Spandau's old town is entirely pedestrianised which makes for some relaxed shopping. There's nothing trendy about it, but if you just want to browse for conventional clothes, toiletries, household goods, stationery and such, you should be able to find what you need along Breite Strasse and Carl-Schurz-Strasse. Take the U7 and get off either at Altstadt Spandau or Rathaus Spandau.

DEPARTMENT STORES

KaDeWe (☎ 212 10, *Tauentzienstrasse 21, Schöneberg*) **Map 6** 'If we don't have it, it probably doesn't exist' is the motto of this renowned consumer temple. Short for Kaufhaus des Westens (Department Store of the West), it is truly one of Europe's grand stores, with about 30 million shopping fetishists leaving the registers ringing with about a quarter billion euros each year. In general, prices are competitive, if not low. The food hall on the 6th floor is legendary (see the Places to Eat chapter).

Wertheim bei Hertie (☎ 88 00 30, *Kurfürstendamm 231, Charlottenburg*) **Map 6** Berlin's second-largest department store is a nice complement to the KaDeWe. This one's less upmarket, slightly cheaper and has almost as good a selection.

Galeries Lafayette (☎ 20 94 80, *Französische Strasse 23, Friedrichstadtpassagen, Mitte*) **Map 7** This transplant of the French department store is more interesting for its architecture than its exclusive designer offerings. Built like a circular atrium, its centrepiece is a funnel-shaped translucent glass core where the light bounces around in an impressive display. The French designer clothing, accessories and cosmetics are pretty average and expensive. There's a food court in the basement (see the Places to Eat chapter).

Dussmann – Das Kulturkaufhaus (☎ 20 25 24 40, *Friedrichstrasse 90, Mitte*) **Map 7** Open 10am-10pm. Dussman is a hip place to stock up on books (three floors), CDs (two floors) and GDR-era books and memorabilia. Unique services include free reading glasses if you left yours at home, gift wrapping, and portable chairs to rest weary legs. It's all rounded out by a cultural program that includes cabaret nights, live TV talkshows and readings. Another bonus: it's open till 10pm.

Stilwerk (☎ 31 51 50, *Kantstrasse 17, Charlottenburg*) **Map 6** An emporium of good taste is this galleria where you'll find everything for house and home – from egg cups to chrome cooking utensils to full professional kitchens – at 57 international design stores. While here, also pop into ***Rahaus*** (☎ 313 21 00, *Kantstrasse 151*) **Map 6**, on the opposite corner, for knickknacks, home accessories and furniture with whimsical, modernist designs.

MARKETS
Farmers' Markets

Türkenmarkt (*Turkish Market, Maybachufer, Kreuzberg 36*) **Map 5** Open noon-6.30pm Tues & Fri. Heaps of regular and exotic fruit and vegetables, mountains of delicious bread loaves, buckets spilling over with olives, delicious arrays of feta cheeses – this mouthwatering culinary bonanza is what you'll find at this bazaar-like slice of Istanbul. Prices are as low as you'll find anywhere in town and the people are friendly and helpful. Good picnic items include spiced feta spread, best eaten with a freshly baked *simit*, a ring-shaped sesame loaf.

Winterfeldtmarkt (*Winterfeldtplatz, Schöneberg*) **Map 4** Open 8am-2pm Wed & Sat. Considered the best of Berlin's neighbourhood produce markets, its fruit and vegetables are among the freshest and the selection is good too, though prices tend to be quite high. Stalls selling dairy products, meats and sausages are here as well. To get a sense of the Schöneberg scene, you should come on Saturday around noon. After browsing, jostle for a table at one of the many cafes flanking the square and indulge in a late breakfast.

Flea & Antique Markets

Berlin's many flea markets are great for unearthing unique souvenirs, often for pennies. Look for typical Berlin curiosities, bric-a-brac, antiques, eccentric clothing and simply cheap used stuff. Bargaining is definitely encouraged and, depending on your skills, you should be able to get vendors to knock 10% to 50% off the asking price. Following is a list of regular markets.

Strasse des 17 Juni – Charlottenburg, **(Map 6)** Open 10am-5pm Sat & Sun. On Strasse des 17 Juni just west of the S-Bahn stop Tiergarten, this market is a tourist favourite and has good Berlin memorabilia. It's expensive but fun to browse.

Boxhagener Platz – Friedrichshain, **(Map 5)** U-Bahn: U5 to Frankfurter Tor. Open 11am-6pm Sun. This is a great street market with no professionals and dirt-cheap stuff. Anything goes – GDR memorabilia, plain old junk and plenty of funky stuff.

Flohmarkt am Moritzplatz – Kreuzberg 36, **(Map 5)** U-Bahn: U8 to Moritzplatz. Open 8am-4pm Sat & Sun. This one's pretty junky, but if you ferret around long enough you'll probably find decent treasure amongst the trash.

Berliner Kunst & Nostalgiemarkt – Mitte, **(Map 7)** Open 11am-5pm Sat & Sun. This tourist-oriented market is along Am Kupfergraben off the north-western tip of Museumsinsel. You'll find collectibles, books, ethnic crafts and GDR memorabilia (not always authentic) but expect to pay a pretty penny. Take bus No 100 to Lustgarten, then walk north for a few minutes, or get off at U/S-Bahn station Friedrichstrasse, then walk east along Georgenstrasse for 10 minutes.

Flohmarkt am Arkonaplatz – Mitte, **(Map 3)** U-Bahn: U8 to Bernauer Strasse. Open 10am-4pm Sun. This is a fun market with lots of locals selling stuff at reasonable prices. With luck you'll unearth fine treasure from the post-WWII collectibles (mostly '50s to '70s), bric-a-brac, furniture and more.

Flohmarkt Rathaus Schöneberg – Schöneberg, **(Map 4)** U-Bahn: U4 to Rathaus Schöneberg. Open 9am-4pm Sat & Sun. Pros and nonpros mix it up at this neighbourhood market, which often has good deals on used clothing and books.

Flohmarkt Spandau – Spandau, U-Bahn: U7 to Rathaus Spandau, then bus No 131, 331 or 231 north to Hohenzollernring. Open 8am-4pm Sat & Sun. On Streitstrasse, corner of Hohenzollernring, this flea market has lots of private vendors, which makes for an interesting selection and reasonable prices.

Market Halls

Berlin has some of the few surviving market halls in Germany. These are wonderful places for chowing down on earthy snacks while stocking up on cheeses, breads, hams and produce. The halls were erected by the city late in the 19th century in order to move street markets indoors. The first such hall opened in 1886 and by 1900 there were 14 of them. Some didn't survive the wars, others were closed for lack of profitability. The remaining three are high-ceilinged, fairly ornate structures that time-warp you back to a different age. All are open from 8am to 6pm on weekdays and to 1pm on Saturday.

Arminius Markthalle (Arminiusstrasse 2, Tiergarten-Moabit) **Map 2** U-Bahn: U9 to Turmstrasse. This market has been housed in a red and yellow brick building since 1891. A few years ago, the Lange's Imbiss (immediately on your left as you enter from Arminiusstrasse) gained fame as the main set for a well-known German TV series. Black and white photographs featuring the stars posing with the staff are proudly displayed in the stand-up eating section across the aisle.

Marheineke Markthalle (Marheinekeplatz, Kreuzberg 61) **Map 5** U-Bahn: U7 to Gneisenaustrasse. Unfortunately this market has more stalls selling cheap toys and clothes than produce, dairy goods or meats – though there is some of that as well.

Eisenbahn Markthalle (Eisenbahnstrasse 43-44, Kreuzberg 36) **Map 5** U-Bahn: U1 or U15 to Görlitzer Bahnhof. This market is quite downtrodden, but the cool Weltrestaurant on its western flank provides a welcome contrast (see the Places to Eat chapter).

Excursions

Almost everything worth seeing around Berlin is in the surrounding state of Brandenburg, including Potsdam, Brandenburg (the town), the former Sachsenhausen concentration camp at Oranienburg, the Spreewald, Cottbus, Rheinsberg, Chorin and Niederfinow. All these destinations are adequately served by train from Berlin.

Efficient rail links also mean that cities farther afield, such as Lutherstadt-Wittenberg in the state of Saxony-Anhalt and the Saxon cities of Dresden and Leipzig, are within easy reach and make for good excursions from the German capital.

Brandenburg

Encircling Berlin, the state of Brandenburg seems to have a hard act to follow, but it has more than its share of attractions. It is a region of lakes, marshes, rivers and canals connecting the Oder and Elbe rivers via the Havel and the Spree, thus making it prime boating, fishing, hiking and cycling territory.

Brandenburg was originally settled by the Wends – the ancestors of the Sorbs – but they were overpowered in 1157 by Albrecht der Bär (Albert the Bear), who became the *Markgraf* (margrave) of Brandenburg. Friedrich I of the Hohenzollern dynasty arrived in the early 15th century, and by 1618 the electors of Brandenburg had acquired the eastern Baltic duchy of Prussia, eventually merging the two states into a powerful union called the Kingdom of Prussia. By 1871, this kingdom brought all the German states under its control, leading to the establishment of the German Empire.

Organised Tours

Berolina (☎ 88 56 80 30), Severin + Kühn (☎ 880 41 90) and BVB (☎ 88 68 37 11), who provide guided bus tours of Berlin, also offer four-hour tours to Potsdam and Sanssouci (with commentary in English and German) for €33. Reservations are necessary. For the same price, they all also run seven-hour tours of the Spreewald from May to early October. The Spreewald tour includes a punt-ride on the canals. (See the Organised Tours section in the Getting Around chapter.)

POTSDAM
☎ 0331 • pop 142,000

Potsdam, on the Havel River some 24km south-east of central Berlin, is the capital of Brandenburg state and the most popular day trip from Berlin. The city rose to prominence in the mid-17th century when Elector Friedrich Wilhelm (ruled 1640–88) made it his second residence after Berlin. Later, with the creation of the Prussian kingdom, Potsdam became a royal seat and garrison town, and in the mid-18th century Friedrich II (Frederick the Great, ruled 1740–86) built many of the marvellous palaces in Sanssouci Park to which visitors flock today.

In April 1945, RAF bombers devastated the historic centre of Potsdam, including the Stadtschloss (City Palace) on Alter Markt, but fortunately most of the palaces in the park escaped undamaged. The Allies chose Schloss Cecilienhof for the Potsdam Conference of August 1945, which finalised the division of Berlin and Germany into occupation zones.

The Potsdam suburb of Babelsberg is the site of a historic – and now once again working – film studio as well as German-film theme park. In 2001, Potsdam hosted the *Bundesgartenschau* (National Garden Show) in parks and gardens throughout town, for which this already lovely city was further spruced up.

The Potsdam tourist office (☎ 27 55 80, fax 275 58 29, ℮ information@potsdam.de) is at Friedrich-Ebert-Strasse 5, beside the Alter Markt. From April to October, hours are 9am to 7pm Monday to Friday and 10am to 4pm weekends. From November to March, it's open 10am to 6pm weekdays and till 2pm on weekends. Staff here also sell the

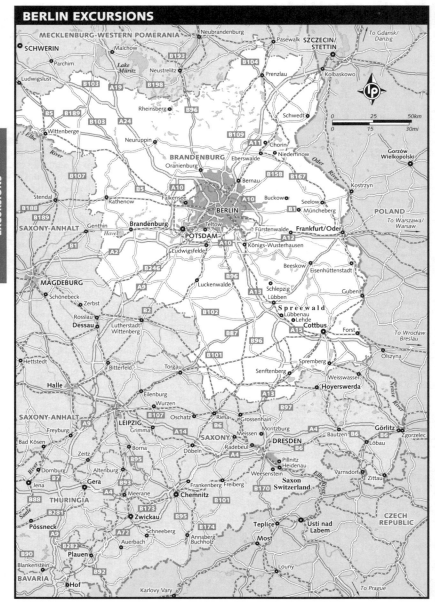

EXCURSIONS

Berlin WelcomeCard (see Tourist Offices in the Facts for the Visitor chapter), which also entitles you to some discounts in Potsdam.

The Sanssouci tourist office (☎ 969 42 00), with information on the park palaces, is near the old windmill opposite Schloss Sanssouci. It's open 8.30am to 5pm daily from April to October and 9am to 4pm the rest of the year.

Sanssouci Park

Sprawling Sanssouci Park *(admission free; open dawn to dusk)* is located west of the Potsdam city centre. The palaces and out-buildings, which are on Unesco's World Heritage List, all have different hours and admission prices. A day ticket (adult/concession €15.50/10.25) allows entry to all palaces and other sights in the park, but you have to work pretty fast to make it pay off.

Sanssouci Park is inexcusably poorly signposted; do yourself a favour and pick up a free map at the tourist office for better orientation. The palaces are spaced fairly far apart – for example it's about 2km between the Neues Palais and Schloss Sanssouci and about 15km to complete the entire circuit. Sadly, cycling in the park is strictly *verboten*.

Schloss Sanssouci

The highlight of Sanssouci Park is the Knobelsdorff-designed Schloss Sanssouci *(tours adult/concession €8/5; open 9am-5pm Tues-Sun Apr-Oct, 9am-4pm Nov-Apr)*. Built in 1747, it is a celebrated rococo palace with glorious interiors. As it can only be seen on a guided tour, arrive early and avoid weekends and holidays, or you may not get a ticket at all. Only 2000 visitors a day are allowed entry (Unesco's rule) so tickets are usually sold out by 2.30pm – even in the shoulder seasons. Entry is guaranteed if you're in Potsdam on an escorted tour (see Organised Tours later in this chapter) or if you join one operated by the Potsdam tourist office *(☎ 275 58 50; adult/concession €20/10 Apr-Oct)*.

Inside the palace, our favourite rooms include the frilly rococo **Konzertsaal** (Concert Hall) and the bed chambers of the **Damen-flügel** (Ladies' Wing), including a 'Voltaire slept here' one. From the palace's northern terrace you can see **Ruinenberg** (1754), a group of classical 'ruins' – a folly built by Friedrich II.

Around Schloss Sanssouci

Just opposite the palace is the **Historische Mühle** *(Historical Windmill; ☎ 969 42 02; adult/concession €1.50/0.50; open 10am-6pm daily Apr-Oct, Sat-Sun only Nov-Mar)*, which was designed to give the palace grounds a rustic appeal.

The palace is flanked by the twin **Neue Kammern** *(New Chambers; tours adult/concession €3/2.50; open 10am-5pm Tues-Sun mid-May–mid-Oct, 10am-5pm Sat-Sun Apr–mid-May)*, which served as a guesthouse and orangery. It includes the large Ovidsaal, with its gilded reliefs and green-and-white marble floor, and Meissen porcelain figurines in the last room to the west.

Nearby, the **Bildergalerie** *(Picture Gallery; ☎ 969 42 02; tours adult/concession €3/2.50; open 10am-5pm Tues-Sun mid-May–mid-Oct)* was completed in 1764 as Germany's first purpose-built art museum. It contains a rich collection of 17th-century paintings by Rubens, Van Dyck, Caravaggio and others.

Just west of the Neue Kammern is the **Sizilianischer Garten** (Sicilian Garden) of subtropical plants, which was laid out in the mid-19th century.

Orangerieschloss & Around

The Renaissance-style Orangery Palace *(☎ 969 42 02; tours adult/concession €3/2.50; open 10am-5pm Tues-Sun mid-May–mid-Oct)* was built in 1864 as a guesthouse for foreign royalty. It contains six sumptuous rooms, including the **Raphaelsaal** with copies of the Italian Renaissance painter's work done by 19th-century German artists. The **tower** *(admission €1)* on the western side can be climbed for great views over the Neues Palais and the park. Part of the Orangerieschloss' west wing is still used to keep some of the more sensitive plants alive in the cold German winter.

Two interesting buildings west of the Orangerieschloss – and within easy walking

EXCURSIONS

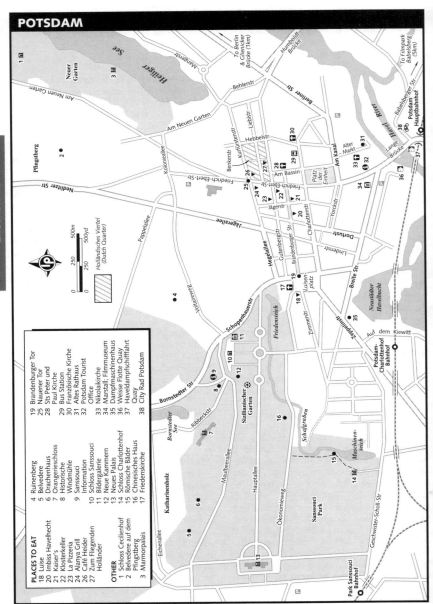

POTSDAM

PLACES TO EAT
18 Luise
20 Imbiss Havelhecht
21 Kaiser's
22 Klosterkeller
23 La Pizzeria
24 Alanya Grill
26 Café Heider
27 Zum Fliegenden Holländer

OTHER
1 Schloss Cecilienhof
2 Belvedere auf dem Pfingstberg
3 Marmorpalais
4 Ruinenberg
5 Belvedere
6 Drachenhaus
7 Orangerieschloss
8 Historische Windmühle
9 Sanssouci Information
10 Schloss Sanssouci
11 Bildergalerie
12 Neue Kammern
13 Neues Palais
14 Schloss Charlottenhof
15 Römische Bäder
16 Chinesisches Haus
17 Friedenskirche
19 Brandenburger Tor
25 Nauener Tor
28 Sts Peter und Paul Kirche
30 Französische Kirche
31 Altes Rathaus
32 Potsdam Tourist Office
33 Nikolaikirche
34 Marstall; Filmmuseum
35 Dampfmaschinenhaus
36 Weisse Flotte Quay
37 Haveldampfschifffahrt Quay
38 City Rad Potsdam

distance – are the pagoda-like **Drachenhaus** (Dragon House), built in 1770, housing a cafe-restaurant (closed Mon), and the rococo **Belvedere**, the only building in the park to suffer serious damage during WWII but which was fully restored in 1999.

Neues Palais

At the far west of Sanssouci Park, the late-baroque Neues Palais *(☎ 969 42 02; tours adult/concession €6/5 Apr-Oct & €5/4 Nov-Mar; open 9am-5pm Sat-Thur Apr-Oct, 9am-4pm Sat-Thur Nov-Mar)* was built in 1769 as the summer residence of the royal family. It is one of the biggest, most imposing buildings in the park and the one to see – aside from Schloss Sanssouci itself – if your time is limited. The tour takes in about a dozen of the palace's 200 rooms, including the **Grottensaal** (Grotto Hall), a rococophile's delight of shells, fossils and baubles set into the walls and ceilings; the **Marmorsaal**, a large banquet hall of white Carrara marble with a wonderful ceiling fresco; the **Jagdkammer** (Hunting Chamber) with lots of dead furry things and fine gold tracery on the walls; and several chambers fitted out from floor to ceiling in rich-red damask. Note the *Fahrstuhl* (1899), an electric 'stair lift' that transported aging royals from the ground to the 1st floor.

The **Schlosstheater** in the south wing has classical music concerts on weekends.

Schloss Charlottenhof & Around

At the southern edge of the park is Karl Friedrich Schinkel's main contribution, the 1826 Schloss Charlottenhof *(☎ 969 42 02; tours adult/concession €4/3; open 10am-5pm Tues-Sun mid-May–mid-Oct)*. It must be visited on a 30-minute German-language tour – but don't wait around too long if the queues are lengthy. In truth, the exterior (modelled after a Roman villa) is more interesting than the interior, especially the Doric portico and the bronze fountain to the east.

A short distance to the north-east, on the edge of the little Maschinenteich (Machine Pond), are the **Römische Bäder** *(Roman Baths; ☎ 969 42 02; tours adult/concession €3/2.50; open 10am-5pm Tues-Sun mid-*

May–mid-Oct), built in 1836 by a pupil of Schinkel and never used. The floor mosaics and caryatids inspired by the baths at Herculaneum are impressive, but we also liked the flounder spitting into a clamshell near the entrance.

Follow the path north along the west bank of the Schafgraben to Ökonomieweg, then head west to arrive at what many consider to be the pearl of the park: the **Chinesisches Haus** *(Chinese Teahouse; admission €1; open 10am-5pm Tues-Sun mid-May–mid-Oct)*, dating from 1757. It's a wonderful circular pavilion of gilded columns, palm trees and figures of Chinese musicians and animals (one of the monkeys is said to have the features of Voltaire).

Altstadt

The baroque **Brandenburger Tor** (Brandenburg Gate), on Luisenplatz at the western end of the old town, pales in comparison to its namesake in Berlin but is actually older (1770). From this square, pedestrianised Brandenburger Strasse runs east to the **Sts Peter und Paul Kirche** (Church of Saints Peter and Paul), completed in 1868. The **Französische Kirche** (French Church), to the south-east on Charlottenstrasse and once the seat of the town's Huguenots, was built in 1753.

North-west of here, on Friedrich-Ebert-Strasse is another monumental arch, the **Nauener Tor** (Nauen Gate), completed in 1755. It's on the edge of the **Holländisches Viertel** (Dutch Quarter), bounded by Friedrich-Ebert-Strasse, Hebbelstrasse, Kurfürstenstrasse and Gutenbergstrasse, which has 134 gabled red-brick houses built for Dutch workers who came to Potsdam in the 1730s at the invitation of Friedrich Wilhelm I. The homes have been prettily restored and now house galleries, cafes and restaurants.

South of here, past the monumental Platz der Einheit, looms the great neoclassical dome of Schinkel's **Nikolaikirche** (1850). It stands on Alter Markt the eastern side of which is anchored by the **Altes Rathaus** *(admission free; open Tues-Sun)*, which now contains several art galleries upstairs.

EXCURSIONS

West of the Alter Markt on Breite Strasse and housed in the **Marstall**, the former royal stables designed by Knobelsdorff in 1746, is the **Filmmuseum** (☎ 271 81 12, Schloss-strasse 1; adult/concession €6/2; open 10am-6pm daily). Documenting the history of film making at the studios in nearby Babelsberg, it's a real delicacy for film buffs. You can see a bioscope, the prototype projector invented by Max Skladanowsky in 1895 (see the Film section in the Facts about Berlin chapter), as well as dressing rooms of UFA's leading ladies, including Marlene Dietrich. You can also watch excerpts from classics like *Metropolis* and *The Blue Angel* and learn all about Hans Albers, one of Germany's main movie stars. The complex also contains a cinema (tickets €3-4.50) and a cafe.

The tiled facade and spindly minaret east of here, along Breite Strasse, does not belong to a mosque but to the **Dampfmaschinen-haus** (Steam Pump House; tours adult/concession €2/1.50; open 10am-5pm Sat-Sun mid-May–mid-Oct), built in 1842 to bring water to the fountains in Park Sanssouci.

Due north of this Moorish pump house, on the south-eastern edge of Sanssouci Park, is the **Friedenskirche** (Church of Peace; admission free; open 9am-6pm daily May-Oct, noon-3pm daily Nov-Apr). A pile, completed in 1854 in neo-Romanesque style, it contains the mausoleum of Friedrich Wilhelm IV (ruled 1840–61).

Neuer Garten

This winding lakeside park, on the west bank of the Heiliger See and north-east of the city centre, is a fine place to relax after all the baroque-rococo and high art of Sanssouci Park. It was built in 1786 under Friedrich Wilhelm II and bears the genius of landscape architect Peter Joseph Lenné.

Within the park, the freshly restored **Marmorpalais** (Marble Palace; ☎ 969 42 02; tours adult/concession €3/2.50 Apr-Oct, €2/1.50 Nov-Mar; open 10am-5pm Tues-Sun Apr-Oct, 10am-4pm Sat-Sun Nov-Mar) sits right on the lake and was designed by Carl Gotthard Langhans in 1792. Note the gilded angels dancing around the cupola.

Farther north is **Schloss Cecilienhof** (☎ 969 42 02; tours adult/concession €5/4 Apr-Oct, €4/3 Nov-Mar; open 9am-5pm Apr-Oct, 9am-4pm Nov-Mar, closed Mon), an English-style country manor best known as the site of the 1945 Potsdam Conference. Large photographs of the participants – Stalin, Truman and Churchill – are displayed inside.

For some of the best views over Potsdam, head west of the park to lovely **Belvedere** (☎ 969 42 02; adult/concession €3.50/2.50; open 10am-6pm Fri-Sun Apr-May & Aug-Sep, 10am-8pm Fri-Sun June-July, 10am-4pm Fri-Sun Oct, 11am-4pm Sat-Sun Nov only), a recently reopened structure atop the Pfingstberg.

Filmpark Babelsberg

Filmpark Babelsberg (☎ 01805-34 56 72, August-Bebel-Strasse 26-53, Enter from Grossbeerenstrasse; adult/concession €14.50/ 13; open 10am-6pm mid-Apr–Oct, 10am-8pm July-Aug), Germany's one-time response to Hollywood, is located east of the city centre. Filming has resumed (see the 'Hollywood on the Havel' boxed text), though the main reason for coming here is the theme park that's sprung up – Universal Studios-style – on the grounds. New attractions are added yearly, but current favourites include a stunt show inside a giant fake volcano; a simulated 'last' dive aboard a Russian submarine (perhaps not too appropriate given the Kursk disaster in 2000); and the 30-minute studio tour aboard a tram around the backlot to new and former film sets. You can also watch animals being trained as actors and tour the warped **Caligari Hall** the expressionistic facade of which is definitely a neat piece of film architecture. There's also a **guided tram ride** (in German) around the backlot for a peek at the sound stages and production studios, as well as the props and costumes room.

To get to the park, take the S7 to Babelsberg and then bus No 690 or 698 to Ahornstrasse. Alternatively, get off the S-Bahn at Griebnitzsee and take bus No 696 to the Drewitz stop.

Hollywood on the Havel

Before there was Paramount (1914) and Warner Brothers (1918), the reels were already spinning in the Babelsberg dream factory, half a world away from Hollywood. Production on the first movie, *Der Totentanz* (Dance of Death), starring Asta Nielsen, began in 1912. By the '20s, the talent of celebrated directors such as Fritz Lang, FW Murnau, Ernst Lubitsch and Josef von Sternberg fuelled the Babelsberg myth.

Under the UFA banner, the studio churned out movie after movie, many of them now cherished classics, such as Lang's *Metropolis*. One of the world's first mega-productions, it required the building of a gigantic production stage (still the largest in Europe) and 36,000 extras. By 1945, some 1300 films had come out of Babelsberg, including the first German talkie *The Blue Angel*, starring Marlene Dietrich, and countless Nazi propaganda flicks.

After WWII, from the ashes of UFA rose DEFA, the top production company in the GDR which primarily made antifascist and internationally successful children's fare. After the Wende, the French Vivendi group bought what is now called Studio Babelsberg and put film director Volker Schlöndorff (*Tin Drum*) at the helm. Several post-production facilities, computer-animation firms and TV and radio production companies also set up shop here. Filming (which stopped around 1990) has resumed and Babelsberg is slowly reclaiming its role on the world stage of movie making.

Weisse Flotte (☎ 275 92 20; *boat tours 9am-3.45pm daily Apr-early Oct*) operates boats on the Havel and the lakes around Potsdam, departing from the dock below the Hotel Mercure near Lange Brücke. Tours include trips to Wannsee (€7.75 return), Werder (€8.25) and Spandau (€11).

Haveldampfschifffahrt (☎ 270 62 29; *tours adult/concession €9/5; tours daily except Mon & Fri mid-Apr–late Sept*) has steamboat tours of the same areas leaving from the southern end of Lange Brücke, opposite the Weisse Flotte quay.

Places to Eat
Klosterkeller (☎ 29 12 18, *Friedrich-Ebert-Strasse 94*) Mains €9.45-12.75. This rustic place serves traditional regional dishes and also has a wine bar, beer garden and cocktail bar.

Café Heider (☎ 275 42 11, *Friedrich-Ebert-Strasse 29*) Specials €4.25-11.25. Across the road, right by the Nauen Gate, this was a prime meeting spot for GDR-era intellectuals.

Zum Fliegenden Holländer (☎ 27 50 30, *Benkerstrasse 5*) Mains €5-17, 2-course set lunch €8. You'll find friendly service, nice new woodwork and fine German cuisine at this airy pub-restaurant in the Dutch quarter.

Luise (☎ 90 36 63, *Luisenplatz 6*) Mains €5.25-14.50. Imaginative Californian-Italian cuisine makes this modern place with park views popular – make reservations.

La Pizzeria (☎ 280 04 29, *Gutenbergstrasse 90*) Meals €4.75-15.75. Recently redone, La Pizzeria is popular with locals for its well-priced pizzas and pastas.

For quick bites, the colourful **Alanya Grill** at Friedrich-Ebert-Strasse 86 has doners and other Turkish specialities, and **Imbiss Havelhecht** is a fish market/snack bar at Brandenburger Strasse 25. Self-cater at **Kaiser's** supermarket, Brandenburger Strasse 30.

Getting There & Away
Getting to Potsdam is easy and convenient. The S7 links central Berlin with Potsdam Hauptbahnhof, south-east of the town centre, about every 10 minutes. The trip takes about 33 minutes. Regional DB trains are faster but operate on a more limited schedule. You need a transit pass covering zones A, B and C (€2.40).

Getting Around
Potsdam has its own local trams and buses that are integrated with Berlin's public transport network. To get to the Altstadt from Potsdam Hauptbahnhof, take bus No 609 or 638 or tram No 92, or walk (about 1km to Brandenburger Strasse). Tram No 92 continues north to the Neuer Garten with Schloss Cecilienhof. Bus No 695 goes to Schloss Sanssouci, the Orangerieschloss

EXCURSIONS

and the Neues Palais. For Schloss Charlottenhof, take tram No 98 to the end.

City Rad Potsdam (☎ 61 90 52, winter ☎ 280 05 95) rents bikes near the Hauptbahnhof, although the facility may move. Rental fees (plus up to €75 deposit) are €10 per day for touring/trekking bikes (students get a 30% discount). It also offers a four-hour guided bike tour on Saturday at 10am for an additional €10 per person.

BRANDENBURG
☎ 03381 • pop 82,600

Brandenburg, about 60km south-west of Berlin, is the oldest town in the March of Brandenburg, with a history going back to at least the 6th century when Slavs settled near the site of today's cathedral. Although badly damaged in WWII, the town is being restored, and its baroque churches and waterside setting make it a worthwhile day trip.

The Havel River, the Beetzsee and their canals split Brandenburg into three sections: the Neustadt on an island in the centre, Dominsel to the north, and the Altstadt to the west. The sections are connected by six bridges. The train station is 1.5km south of the central Neustädtischer Markt.

A small tourist office (☎ 194 33, fax 22 37 43), at Hauptstrasse 51, is open 10am to 6pm Monday to Friday, and to 5pm Saturday (2pm November to March).

Walking Tour
Begin a stroll through Brandenburg at the Romanesque **Dom St Peter und Paul** (☎ 20 03 25, Domlinden 25; admission free; open 10am-4pm Mon-Fri, 10am-5pm Sat, 11am-5pm Sun), on the northern edge of Dominsel. Begun in 1165 by Premonstratensian monks and completed in 1240, it contains the wonderfully decorated Bunte Kapelle (Coloured Chapel), with its vaulted and painted ceiling; the carved 14th-century Böhmischer Altar (Bohemian Altar); a fantastic baroque organ (1723); and the **Dommuseum** (☎ 20 03 25, Domlinden 25; adult/concession €2.50/1.50; open 10am-4pm Mon-Fri, 10am-5pm Sat, 11am-5pm Sun), full of liturgical treasures upstairs. Much of the cathedral is being

renovated, so some items may have been moved around or out.

From the cathedral walk south on St Petri to Mühlendamm. Just before you cross the Havel to the Neustadt, look left at the **Hauptpegel** which measures the river's water level. On the other side is the **Mühlentorturm** (Mill Gate Tower) that once marked the border between the separate towns of Dominsel and Neustadt.

Molkenmarkt, the continuation of Mühlendamm, runs parallel to Neustädtischer Markt, leading to the **Pfarrkirche St Katharinen**, a 14th-century Gothic-hall church that originally consisted of two separate chapels; note the 'Meadow of Heaven' painted ceiling. South-west of here, at the end of Steinstrasse, is the **Steintorturm**, the second of the four remaining city towers.

To reach the Altstadt, walk back up Steinstrasse to pedestrianised Hauptstrasse and then west over the Havel to the **Museum im Frey-Haus** (☎ 52 20 48, Ritterstrasse 96; adult/concession €2/1; open 9am-5pm Tues-Fri, 10am-5pm Sat-Sun). It's a local history museum with much emphasis on the EP Lehmann factory, which produced cute mechanical toys and pottery.

A short distance north-east is the redbrick Gothic **Altstädtische Rathaus**, a gem-box with a **statue of Roland** (1474) in front symbolising the town's judicial independence.

Places to Eat
Blaudruck Café (☎ 22 57 34, Steinstrasse 21) Mains €4.50-13. The menu's limited during the day, but at night you can dine on regional fare in the wine cellar, sans electric lighting.

Dom Café (☎ 52 43 27, Burghof 11) Mains €3-11.25. Open 11am-6pm. Here's a great place for salads, fresh fish and homemade cakes, adjacent to the cathedral.

Bismarck Terrassen (☎ 30 09 39, Bergstrasse 20) Mains €6-14. See if you don't feel Prussian while dining on elegant French-German food with a view of a park. Inside's a festival of Bismarck memorabilia.

Cheap bites include **Pizzeria No 31** (Steinstrasse 31), **Orient Grill** (Steinstrasse 43) with doners from €2, and an *Asia-Imbiss* (*Steinstrasse 65*).

Getting There & Around

Frequent regional trains link Brandenburg with Zoo station (€8.50, 35 minutes).

Tram Nos 6 and 9 run from Brandenburg Hauptbahnhof to Hauptstrasse via Steinstrasse and Neustädtischer Markt. A single ride is €1.05 and a day ticket is €2.30. Velo (☎ 31 74 72), Gerostrasse 15 in the Altstadt, rents bikes per day/weekend for €6/12.50.

SPREEWALD

The Spreewald, the watery 'Spree Forest' (287 sq km) of rivers, canals and streams 90km south-east of Berlin, is the closest thing the capital has to a playground. Day trippers and weekend warriors come here in droves to punt on more than 400km of waterways, hike the countless nature trails and fish in this region designated a Unesco Biosphere Reserve in 1990. The focal points of most of this activity are the twin towns of Lübben and Lübbenau. The Spreewald is also home to most of Germany's Sorbian minority (see boxed text 'The Sorbs') who call the region the Blota. Its unofficial capital is Cottbus.

Lübben & Lübbenau

There's an ongoing debate among Berliners over Lübben (Lubin in Sorbian, population 15,000) and Lübbenau (Lubnjow, population 21,450), which lie 13km apart. Which is the more historical/touristy/picturesque 'Spreewald capital'?

Lübben, a tidy and attractive town and the centre of the drier Unterspreewald (Lower Spreewald), has a history predating that of Lübbenau by at least two centuries, boasts more interesting architecture and feels like a 'real' town.

Lübbenau, in the Oberspreewald (Upper Spreewald), is equally picturesque but positively crammed year-round with tourists trying to get out onto the canals on *Kähne* (punt boats) – once the only way to travel in these parts. A visit to both towns has its merits.

Lübben's Hauptbahnhof is on Bahnhofstrasse, south-west of the central Markt. To reach the centre of town walk north-east

EXCURSIONS

The Sorbs

The ancestors of the Sorbs, Germany's only indigenous minority (population 60,000), were the Slavic Wends, who settled between the Elbe and Oder rivers in the 5th century in an area called Lusatia (Luzia in Sorbian, from *luz* or 'meadow').

Lusatia was conquered by the Germans in the 10th century, subjected to brutal assimilation throughout the Middle Ages and partitioned in 1815. Lower Sorbia, centred around the Spreewald and Cottbus (Chosébuz), went to Prussia while Upper Sorbia around Bautzen (Budessin), 53km north-east of Dresden, went to Saxony. Upper Sorbian, closely related to the Czech language, enjoyed certain prestige in Saxony while the Kingdom of Prussia attempted to suppress Lower Sorbian, which is similar to Polish. The Nazis tried to eradicate both.

Though the Sorbs were protected under the GDR, their proud folk traditions and costumes didn't suit the bland 'proletarian' regime. Since German unification, however, interest in their culture has been revived through radio and TV broadcasts and theatre performed in their language. The more colourful Sorbian festivals include the **Vogelhochzeit** or Birds' Wedding on January 25, a horseback **Easter procession,** and a symbolic 'witch-burning' on April 30, a local variant of the **Walpurgisnacht.**

For further details, contact the Sorbian Institute (☎ 03591-497 20), at Bahnhofstrasse 6, 02625 Bautzen or the Institute of Sorbian Studies (☎ 0341-973 76 50), at Augustusplatz 9, 04109 Leipzig.

– Jeremy Gray

along Friedensstrasse and then through the Hain, a large park. The tourist office is in Schloss Lübben (☎ 03546-30 90, fax 25 43), Ernst-von-Houwald-Damm 15, and is open 10am to 6pm Monday to Friday, to 4pm Saturday, and to 3pm Sunday, with shorter hours in winter.

Lübbenau's Hauptbahnhof and bus station are on Poststrasse, about 600m south of the tourist office (☎ 03542-36 68, fax 467 70) at Ehm-Welk-Strasse 15. From April to October, it's open 9am to 6pm Monday to Friday, and to 4pm weekends. The rest of the year hours are 9am to 4pm weekdays only. Also in Lübbenau is the Haus für Mensch und Natur (☎ 03542-89 21 11, fax 89 21 40), Schulstrasse 9, where you can learn more about the Spreewald Biosphere Reserve. Its hours are 10am to 5pm daily April to October and 10am to 4pm weekdays only November to March.

Hiking The Spreewald has hiking and walking trails to suit everyone. If you plan on doing some serious hiking, pick up a map at either tourist office.

From Lübben an easy trail follows the Spree south to Lübbenau (13.2km) and north to Schlepzig (12.3km). From Lübbenau you can follow a **nature trail** (30 minutes) west to Lehde, the 'Venice of the Spreewald', with its wonderful **Freilandmuseum** (☎ 03542-24 72; adult/student/child aged 2-12 €3/2/1; open 10am-6pm Apr-mid-Sept, 10am-5pm mid-Sept–Oct) of traditional Sorbian thatched houses and farm buildings. The Leiper Weg, which starts near the Grosser Hafen on Dammstrasse in Lübbenau, is part of the **E10 European Walking Trail** from the Baltic to the Adriatic and leads south-west to Leipe, accessible by boat only since 1936 (you can also take a punt back). Another popular walk is from the Topfmarkt in Lübbenau north-east to the Wotschofska restaurant (3km), crossing 14 small bridges.

Boating The Kahnfährhafen in Lübben, the little harbour where you can board **punts** (per person per hour €2.50-3.50), is along the Spree south-west of the tourist office.

Bootsverleih Gebauer (☎ 03546-71 94) has one/two-person kayaks for €3.50/4 for the first hour and €2/2.50 for each additional hour. Day rates are €15/17.50 weekdays and €17.50/21 weekends. Canoes for the first hour/subsequent hour cost €5/3.50 and per weekday/weekend €25/28.

In Lübbenau there's the Kleiner Hafen on Spreestrasse, about 100m north-east of the tourist office, and the Grosser Hafen, 300m south-east on Dammstrasse. Boats can be rented per hour for approximately €2.50 – a tour of the canals takes about two hours. The area around the Grosser Hafen has any number of boat companies vying for business; a good option is **Manfred Francke** (☎ 27 22, Dammstrasse 72).

Places to Eat – Lübben *Goldener Löwe* (☎ 03546-73 09, Hauptstrasse 15) Mains €7-11. This is a somewhat touristy but decent place, with a lovely beer garden and freshwater fish dishes.

Café Ambiente (☎ 03546-18 33 07, Cnr Renatestrasse & Gerichtsstrasse) Meals €4-7. Open 8am-6pm. This cafe does breakfast, light meals and afternoon coffee.

There are several *Imbisse* on and around Hauptstrasse.

Places to Eat – Lübbenau *Lübbenauer Hof* (☎ 03542-831 62, Ehm-Welk-Strasse 20) Mains €9-12. Cosy but expanding, this is one of the more upmarket options in town.

Pension Spreewald-Idyll (☎ 03542-22 51, Spreestrasse 13) Mains €7-12. This restaurant/beer garden attached to a pension serves local fish, plus some game dishes.

Strubel's (☎ 03542-27 98, Dammstrasse 3, Enter from Apothekengasse) Mains €6-12.50. Try Strubel's if you want eel, pike or perch pulled from the Spree.

Cottbus

Cottbus (Chosebuz in Sorbian, population 115,000), about 115km south-east of Berlin, is a pretty town with some wonderful architecture and a decent number of cultural offerings. The tourist office (☎ 0355-242 54, fax 79 19 31) is at Karl-Marx-Strasse 68 in the Spree Galerie shopping centre and is open 9am to 6pm weekdays, to 1pm or 2pm Saturday.

The **Sorbische Kulturinformation Lodka** (☎ 0355-79 11 10; Wendisches Haus, August-Bebel-Strasse 82) provides information about the Sorbs – and serves authentic Sorbian specialities at its cafe.

Those interested in Sorbian culture should check out the **Wendisches Museum/Serbski muzej** (☎ 79 49 30, Mühlenstrasse 12; adult/child €2/1; open 8.30am-5pm Mon-Fri, 2pm-6pm Sat-Sun). This museum thoroughly examines this Slavic people's history, language and culture.

Other places worth inspecting are the 15th-century **Oberkirche** on Oberkirchplatz, west of the central Altmarkt; the Art Nouveau **Staatstheater** on Schillerplatz to the south-west; **Branitzer Park** to the south-east with its lovely 18th-century baroque Schloss and the Seepyramide, a curious 'floating' grass-covered pyramid in a little lake.

Getting There & Around

Regional trains departing hourly from Berlin Ostbahnhof serve Lübben (€11.50, 50 minutes), Lübbenau (€13, one hour) and Cottbus (€16.50, 1½ hours).

The Lübben tourist office rents bicycles for €5 per day, as does Karl-Heinz Oswald (☎ 03546-40 63), An der Spreewaldbahn 6, north-west of the centre. In Lübbenau, you can try Kretschmann (☎ 03542-433) at Poststrasse 16.

SACHSENHAUSEN MEMORIAL & MUSEUM

In 1936 the Nazis opened a 'model' **Konzentrationslager** (Concentration camp; ☎ 03301-20 02 00; admission free; open 8.30am-6pm Tues-Sun Apr-Sept & 8.30am-4.30pm Tues-Sun Oct-Mar) for men in a disused brewery in Sachsenhausen, near the town of Oranienburg (population 26,000), about 35km north-west of Berlin.

Inmates (political undesirables, gays, Jews, Gypsies – the usual Nazi targets) were forced to make bricks, hand grenades and weapons, counterfeit dollar and pound banknotes (to flood Allied countries and wreak economic havoc) and even to test-out boot leather for days on end on a special track. By 1945 about 220,000 men from 22 countries had passed through the gates of Sachsenhausen KZ. About 100,000 died.

After the war, the Soviets and GDR leaders set up *Spezillager No 7* (Special Camp No 7) for political prisoners, ex-Nazis, monarchists or whoever didn't happen to fit into *their* mould. An estimated 60,000 people were interned at the camp between 1945 and 1950, and up to 12,000 are believed to have died here. There's a mass grave of victims at the camp and another one 1.5km to the north.

The walled camp (31 hectares) is an easy, signposted 20-minute walk north-east of Oranienburg train station. You can also catch bus No 804 or 805 as far as the corner of Bernauer Strasse and Strasse der Einheit.

Maps, brochures and books are for sale at the camp information office.

Getting There & Away

The fastest way to travel to Oranienburg is by RB train from Berlin-Lichtenberg, which makes the trip in 30 minutes. Alternatively, take the S1 to its northern terminus, which offers more frequent departures but takes about twice as long. Either way, tickets cost €2.40.

RHEINSBERG
☎ 033931 • pop 5300

Rheinsberg, some 90km north of Berlin, has much to offer visitors: a charming Renaissance palace, walks in the lovely Schlosspark, boating on the lake and Rhin River and some top-notch restaurants.

The town hugs the south-eastern shore of Grienericksee, a large lake. The central Markt lies about 1km north-west of the train station. In the Markt's Kavalierhaus, you'll find the friendly tourist office (☎ 20 59, fax 347 04) open 9.30am to 5pm Monday to Saturday and 10am to 2pm Sunday. Buses stop on Mühlenstrasse just south of Schlossstrasse.

Schloss Rheinsberg

A moated castle stood on Grienericksee from the early Middle Ages to protect the March of Brandenburg's northern border from the marauders of Mecklenburg. But Schloss

Rheinsberg (☎ 726 11; tours adult/concession €5/4 Apr-Oct, €4/3 Nov-Mar, including Tucholsky exhibit; admission free to park; open 9.30am-5pm Tues-Sun Apr-Oct & 10am-4pm Nov-Mar) as we see it today only began to take shape in 1566, when its owner, Achim von Bredow, had it rebuilt in the Renaissance style. Friedrich Wilhelm I bought and expanded it in 1734 for his 22-year-old son, Crown Prince Friedrich (the future Friedrich II). He also cleaned up the town – paving roads, plastering house facades and tiling roofs.

Friedrich, who spent four years here studying and preparing for the throne (1734–40), later said this period was the happiest of his life. He oversaw much of the remodelling of the palace by Johann Gottfried Kemmeter and Knobelsdorff; some say this was his 'test-run', on a minor scale, for the much grander Schloss Sanssouci (1747) in Potsdam.

During WWII art treasures from Potsdam were stored at Schloss Rheinsberg. Alas, the palace was looted in 1945 and used as a sanatorium by the communists from 1953. Today, it is a mere shadow of its former self, but it is being renovated.

A tour of the palace takes in about two dozen, mostly empty, rooms on the 1st floor, including the oldest ones: the **Hall of Mirrors**, where young Friedrich held flute contests; the **Tower Chamber**, where the future king studied and which he re-created in the Berliner Schloss in 1745; and the **Bacchus Room** with a ceiling fresco of a worn looking Ganymede. Among our favourites, though, are the **Lacquer Room**, with its chinoiserie; **Prince Heinrich's bedchamber**, with an exquisite trompe l'oeil ceiling; and the rococo **Shell Room**.

The ground floor of the north wing contains the **Kurt Tucholsky Gedenkstätte**, a museum dedicated to the life and work of the writer (1890–1935). He wrote a popular novel called *Rheinsberg – ein Tagebuch für Verliebte* (Rheinsberg – A Lovers' Diary) in which the young swain Wolfgang traipses through the Schloss with his beloved Claire in tow, putting the palace and the town of Rheinsberg firmly on the literary map.

Places to Eat
Zum Alten Fritz (☎ 20 86, Schlossstrasse 11) Mains €4.75-12.25. This is an excellent place for north-German specialities like *Krustenbraten* (ham with beans and parsley potatoes) and fish dishes.

Seehof (☎ 383 03, Seestrasse 19c) Mains €7.25-14.25. This is a 1st-class restaurant with a lovely back courtyard. The owners are knowledgeable about the local performing arts scene.

Schloss Rheinsberg (☎ 27 77, Seestrasse 13) Mains €7-13.75. Inside the Deutsches Haus Hotel, the town's silver-service restaurant has regional German cooking with prices to match.

The Rhin Passage shopping centre at the southern end of town has reasonable lunch places, including **Al Castello** (☎ 380 84) with pizzas and pastas from €3.50/4.25, and **Garden** Chinese restaurant (☎ 378 11) with weekday lunches from €6.50.

Getting There & Away
RE trains from Charlottenburg to Rheinsberg leave every two hours (€12.80, 2¼ hours). The train station in Rheinsberg is 1km southeast of the Markt on Berliner Strasse.

CHORIN
Kloster Chorin (Chorin Monastery; ☎ 03 33 66-703 77, Am Chorin 11a; adult/child €2.50/1.50, parking €2.50; open 9am-6pm Apr-Oct & 9am-4pm Nov-Mar), in the little town by the same name some 60km northeast of Berlin, is considered to be one of the finest red-brick Gothic structures in northern Germany. Every summer it hosts the Choriner Musiksommer, a world-class music festival.

There is no tourist office, but the reception desk at the Hotel Haus Chorin (☎ 03 33 66-500), Neue Klosterallee 10, acts as a sort of de facto information centre.

Kloster Chorin was founded by Cistercian monks in 1273, and 500 of them laboured over six decades to erect their monastery and church of red brick on a granite base. The monastery was secularised in 1542 following Elector Joachim II's conversion to Protestantism and, after the Thirty Years' War, it fell into disrepair. Renovation of the structure, which was instigated by Schinkel, has gone on in a somewhat haphazard fashion since the early 19th century.

The entrance to the monastery is through the bright-red and ornate western facade, leading to the central cloister and ambulatory, where the music festival is held. To the north is the early-Gothic **Klosterkirche** with its carved portals and long lancet windows in the apse. Have a look along the walls at floor level to see the layer of granite supporting the porous handmade bricks. The celebrated **Choriner Musiksommer** takes place at 3pm on most weekends from June to August – expect to hear some top talent. For more information contact the organisers at ☎ 03334-65 73 10, Schickelstrasse 5, in Eberswalde Finow. Tickets are also available from ticket agencies in Berlin. Chamber music concerts are also held in the church, said to have near-perfect acoustics, at 4pm sometimes on Sunday from late May to August.

Getting There & Away
Take a regional train from Lichtenberg to Eberswalde or from Ostbahnhof to Britz, then bus No 912 from either town straight to the monastery (€8.70, one hour). Alternatively, travel directly to Chorin train station from Ostbahnhof (€8.70, 50 minutes), then walk about 3km along a marked trail.

NIEDERFINOW
The **Schiffshebewerk** *(ship's lift; ☎ 03 33 69-461, Hebewerkstrasse; adult/child €1/ 0.50; open 9am-6pm May-Sept & 9am-4pm Oct-Apr)* at Niederfinow (population 700), about 10km south-east of Chorin and 50km north-east of Berlin, is one of the most remarkable feats of engineering from the early 20th century (1934).

It's also fun, especially for kids. Ships sail into a sort of giant bathtub which is then raised or lowered, water and all, 36m between the Oder River and the Oder-Havel Canal. This being Germany, technical data about the structure is posted everywhere ('60m high, 27m wide, 94m long' etc), but it's still an amazing sight watching 1200-tonne barges laden with coal on the hoist.

WASSER- UND SCHIFFFAHRTSAMT EBERSWALDE

The Schiffshebewerk in action above the water

The lift can be viewed from Hebewerkstrasse for free, but it's much more fun to climb the steps to the upper platform to view the 10-minute operation from above.

Getting There & Away
Niederfinow is directly served hourly by a regional train from Berlin-Lichtenberg (€8.70, 55 minutes). The Schiffshebewerk is about 2km to the north of the station, and the way is signposted.

Beyond Brandenburg

LUTHERSTADT-WITTENBERG
☎ 03491 • pop 53,000

Lutherstadt-Wittenberg is about 100km south-west of Berlin in the state of Saxony-Anhalt. It is best known as the place where Martin Luther launched the Reformation in 1517, an act of the greatest cultural importance to all of Europe and indeed the world. Wittenberg was also famous for its university where Luther was a full theology professor, and for being the seat of the elector of Saxony until 1547. Renaissance painter Lucas Cranach the Elder also lived here at that time.

EXCURSIONS

Martin Luther was the central figure in the Reformation.

From Wittenberg's main train station the city centre is a 15-minute walk down Collegienstrasse, the main thoroughfare. All of the city's chief sights are within the Altstadt ring. The main street, Collegienstrasse, runs east-west through the Markt and becomes Schlossstrasse at its western end.

Wittenberg-Information (☎ 49 86 10, fax 48 86 11) at Schlossplatz 2, opposite the Schlosskirche, is open 9am to 6pm weekdays, 10am to 3pm Saturday and 11am to 4pm Sunday. For a self-guided tour of the town, pick up an audioguide (€5) or *The Historic Mile* (€2.50), a good English-language guidebook to the city.

Lutherhalle Wittenberg

The Lutherhalle (☎ 420 30, Collegienstrasse 54; adult/concession €3.50/2; open 9am-6pm Tues-Sun Apr-Sept & 10am-5pm Tues-Sun Oct-Mar) is among the world's most exhaustive museums dedicated to the Reformation. It's housed in a former Augustinian monastery that served as Luther's home and workplace for more than four decades. Here, he penned his most important works and lectured his students in the building's auditorium. You can still see the original rooms today but, alas, not until at least late 2002 while the museum is being renovated. In 1996, the Lutherhalle, along with other Luther sites in Wittenberg and

other towns in Saxony-Anhalt, was designated as a Unesco World Cultural Heritage Site.

The **Luthereiche**, the site where Luther burned a copy of the papal bull threatening his excommunication, is on the corner of Lutherstrasse and Am Bahnhof.

Melanchthon Haus

The house where humanist Philipp Melanchthon (1497–1560) lived for 24 years has been preserved in close to its original state and is now a museum (☎ 40 26 71, Collegienstrasse 60; adult/concession €2.50/1.50; open 9am-6pm Tues-Sun Apr-Sept & 9am-5pm Oct-Mar). Melanchthon was a disciple and close friend of Luther and helped Luther translate the Bible into German. He eventually became a reformer himself. He came to town in 1518 as a university lecturer and stayed until his death. Melanchthon's reformist ideas went far beyond religious matters – his primary goal was to overhaul the German education system, which at that time taught entirely in Latin.

Stadtkirche

On Kirchplatz, a few steps east of the Markt, the Stadtkirche is chock-full with art treasures. The large altarpiece here was designed jointly by Lucas Cranach the Elder and his son and completed in 1547. It shows Luther, Melanchthon and other Reformation figures, as well as Cranach the Elder himself, in biblical contexts. In 1525 Luther married the ex-nun Katharina von Bora in this church, where he also preached. Take note of the octagonal bronze baptismal font and the many fine paintings, especially Cranach the Younger's *The Lord's Vineyard* behind the altar in the south-east corner of the church.

Markt

On the northern side of the Markt is the **Rathaus** (1523–40), a banner example of an affluent central-German Renaissance town hall. In front of the Rathaus are two large **statues**. The one in the centre of the square is of Luther (1821), and on his right side is Melanchthon (1865).

Cranachhaus

Just off Markt is the home where Lucas Cranach the Elder lived during his time in Wittenberg. The home is accessible from a picturesque courtyard. Inside is the superbly renovated **Galerie im Cranachhaus** (☎ 420 19 17, Markt 4; admission €2, open 10am-5pm Tues, Wed & Fri, 10am-6pm Thur, 1pm-5pm Sat-Sun), which has rotating art exhibitions as well as a groovy audio-visual presentation.

Out the back, pick up some black-and-white sketches of Martin Luther in the **Historische Druckerstube** (open 9am-5pm Mon-Fri), which still sets type and prints by hand.

Schloss Wittenberg

At the western end of town is Wittenberg Palace (1499) with its huge, rebuilt **Schlosskirche** (Schlossstrasse; admission free, tours in German €1; open 2pm-5pm Mon, 10am-5pm Tues-Sat, 11.30am-5pm Sun May-Oct; open to 4pm Nov-Apr). A replica of the door, onto which Luther is said to have nailed his 95 Theses on 31 October 1517, is here. The original door was destroyed by fire in 1760 and has been replaced by a bronze memorial (1858) inscribed with the theses in Latin. Luther's tombstone lies below the pulpit, and Melanchthon's is opposite.

Hundertwasser Schule

North-east of the centre is the Martin-Luther-Gymnasium, a school whimsically remodelled by Viennese architect Friedensreich Hundertwasser in his signature fairytale style. It's a spectacular sight, with its mosque-like cupolas, bright kooky facade and rooftop vegetation. It's a 20-minute walk from the centre: go up Berliner Strasse, turn right into Schillerstrasse and it's the fourth corner on the left (at Strasse der Völkerfreundschaft.)

Places to Eat

Much of the town's food scene is along Collegienstrasse. Try Speckkuchen, a pizza-like dough topped with bacon and eggs scrambled with cream and onions. Lutherbrot is a crumptious gingerbread-like concoction with chocolate and sugar icing.

Stadtkantine (☎ 41 13 89, Coswigerstrasse 19) Dishes €3-4. This is the best bet for a quick, cheap hot meal – try the stuffed pork roulade.

Creperie Lorette (☎ 40 40 45, Collegienstrasse 70) Meals €3-8. This is a charming little place with OK crepes with various filling (both sweet and savoury), great salads and friendly service.

Zum Schwarzen Baer (☎ 41 12 00, Schlossstrasse 2) Snacks €2.50-3.50, mains to €10. This is a great place for potato-based snacks and even pizza and full meals built around Germany's favourite tuber. There's a cool pub in the back.

Zur Schlossfreiheit (☎ 40 29 80, Coswigerstrasse 24) Mains €6-10. Come here for historical theme dishes, such as Lutherschmaus (duck in a peppery sultana sauce).

Getting There & Away

Wittenberg is directly served by fast ICE trains every two hours from Ostbahnhof (€23, one hour); regional trains require a change in Jüterbog and take 1¾ hours but cost only €16.

DRESDEN

☎ 0351 • pop 485,000

About 200km south of Berlin, Dresden, capital of the state of Saxony, was famous throughout Europe as 'the Florence of the north' in the 18th century. During the reigns of August der Starke (August the Strong, ruled 1694–1733) and his son August III (ruled 1733–63), Italian artists, musicians, actors and master craftsmen, particularly from Venice, flocked to the court at Dresden.

The Italian painter Canaletto depicted the rich architecture of the time in many paintings that now hang in Dresden's Alte Meister Gallery in the Zwinger; also here are countless masterpieces purchased for August III with income from Saxon silver mines.

In February 1945 much of Dresden was devastated during Anglo-American fire-bombing raids, killing around 35,000 people at a time when the city was jammed with refugees and the war was almost over. It is generally recognised that the bombing of

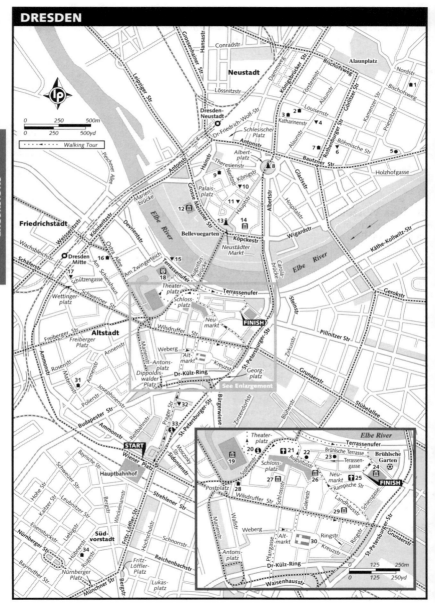

DRESDEN

PLACES TO STAY		10	El Español	19	Zwinger;
1	Pension Edith	11	Kügelgenhaus		Zwinger Museums
2	Jugendhotel Die Boofe	15	Opernrestaurant	20	Dresden-Information
3	Hostel Mondpalast	17	brennNessel	21	Katholische Hofkirche
7	Rothenburger Hof	32	CaféBörse	22	Fürstenzug
9	Hotel Martha Hospiz			23	Kasematten
16	art'otel Dresden	**OTHER**		24	Albertinum;
28	Hotel Kempinski Taschenberg	5	Pfunds Molkerei		Albertinum Museums
	Palais; Sophienkeller	8	Schiller Monument	25	Frauenkirche
31	Jugendgästehaus Dresden	12	Japanisches Palais;	26	Verkehrsmuseum
34	Jugendherberge Rudi Arndt		Ladesmuseum für	27	Residenzschloss;
			Vorgeschichte		Hausmannsturm
PLACES TO EAT		13	Goldener Reiter	29	Stadtmuseum
4	Scheunecafé	14	Museum für Volkskunst	30	Kreuzkirche
6	Raskolnikoff	18	Semperoper	33	Dresden-Information

Dresden was inspired more by vengeance than strategic necessity. Much of the city's baroque splendour has been restored and even the famous Frauenkirche is scheduled to reopen by 2006.

Dresden's centre is conveniently compact. The Elbe River splits the town in a rough V-shape, with the Neustadt, the bohemian pub quarter to the north and the Altstadt to the south. Most of Dresden's priceless art treasures are south of the Elbe in two large buildings, the Albertinum and the Zwinger, at opposite sides of the Altstadt. The Brühlsche Terrasse, a lovely riverside walkway, connects the two.

From the Hauptbahnhof, the pedestrianised Prager Strasse leads north into this old centre. Most trains also stop at the Neustadt train station. To get to the main sights from here, walk east on Antonstrasse to Albertplatz, then south on pedestrianised Hauptstrasse to Augustusbrücke which connects Neustadt and Altstadt.

Dresden-Information can help you find suitable accommodation. It's just north of the Hauptbahnhof, at Prager Strasse 21 (☎ 49 19 20, fax 49 19 21 16 ⓔ info@dresden-tourist .de, Ⓦ www.dresden-tourist.de). It's open 9am to 7pm Monday to Friday and until 4pm Saturday. A second office is in Schinkelwache at Theaterplatz 2 near the Zwinger. It's open 10am to 6pm Monday to Friday and to 4pm Saturday.

Both offices sell the 48-hour Dresden Card (€15) which gives admission to 11 museums, minor discounts on city tours and river boats and unlimited public transportation. If you're in town just for the day, it may not be such a good deal, as 24-hour transport tickets for singles/families cost €4/6, and museum day passes, good for admission to most major museums (including the 'must-sees' at the Zwinger and the Albertinum) go for €6/3.50. Note that children under 16 enter free at these museums if accompanied by their parents.

Altstadt

A 10-minute walk north along Prager Strasse from the Hauptbahnhof brings you to the Altmarkt area, the historic hub of Dresden. On the right you'll see the rebuilt **Kreuzkirche** (1792), Dresden's main Protestant church. It's famous for its 150-strong boys' choir, whose singing can usually be enjoyed for free during church services at 6pm on Saturday and 9.30am on Sunday. There are fine views from the church tower (€1/0.50).

Cross the wide Wilsdruffer Strasse to the baroque **Landhaus**, now home of the **Stadtmuseum** (*City Historical Museum;* ☎ *49 86 60, adult/concession €2/1; open 10am-6pm Tues-Sun*) which chronicles the city's history until 1989.

Neumarkt

North-west up Landhausstrasse is Neumarkt, lorded over by the **Frauenkirche**, still wrapped in scaffolding. Until 1945 it was Germany's greatest Protestant church, its enormous dome known as the 'stone bell'. The bombing raids of 13 February 1945 flattened it, and the GDR decided to leave the rubble as a war memorial.

After reunification, the movement to rebuild the church gained momentum and a huge archaeological dig and reconstruction project began, incorporating the more than 10,000 remaining original pieces. Reassembly of this huge puzzle is scheduled for completion in 2006 (Dresden's 800th anniversary), but – get this – funding has been so generous that it appears likely to finish early. To view the progress, take a one-hour guided tour (several daily, free, donations welcomed, German only).

On the western side of Neumarkt is the 16th-century Johanneum, formerly the royal stables and now the interesting **Verkehrsmuseum** *(Museum of Transport; ☎ 864 40, Augustusstrasse 1; adult/child €2/12; open 10am-5pm Tues-Sun)* with its fascinating collection of penny-farthings, trams, dirigibles, carriages and other historic vehicles.

The back (northern side) of the building, fronting Augustusstrasse, is smothered with the 102m-long **Fürstenzug** (Princes' Procession), an eye-popping mural made of 24,000 Meissen tiles depicting all Saxon rulers from 1123 to 1904.

Schlossplatz

Augustusstrasse leads directly to Schlossplatz and the baroque **Katholische Hofkirche** (1755), the former court church and now Dresden's cathedral, whose crypt contains the heart of August der Starke. Just south of the church is the multi-turreted **Residenzschloss** (Royal Palace), a confection in neo-Renaissance style. Under reconstruction until at least 2006, it will reopen as a major museum centre. Meanwhile, changing exhibits take place in the palace tower, the **Hausmannsturm** *(☎ 491 46 22; adult/child €2.50/1.50, but this may vary; open 10am-5pm Tues-Sun Apr-Oct)*. From its viewing platform you can also catch a glimpse of the palace's beautiful sgraffito-clad inner courtyard and enjoy bird's-eye views of the city's major landmarks.

Semperoper

On its western side, Hofkirche flanks another of Dresden's great squares, the Theaterplatz, clearly dominated by the glorious Semperoper *(☎ 491 17 05, for tours ☎ 491 14 96, Theaterplatz 2; tours adult/concession €4.50/3 daily)* which has had a tumultuous history. The original, designed by Gottfried Semper, was opened in 1841 but burned down in 1869 and was rebuilt by his son Manfred from 1871–78. Again destroyed in 1945, it reopened in 1985 after the communists invested millions in its restoration. The Dresden opera has a tradition going back 350 years, and saw the premieres of works by Richard Strauss, Carl Maria von Weber and Richard Wagner.

Tickets for the Semperoper start at €15, but they're usually booked out as much as a year in advance.

Zwinger

Dresden's most famous building complex is the vast late-baroque Zwinger (1728). Its lovely, fountain-studded courtyard is framed by an open-air gallery and several charming portals (one is reachable via a long footbridge over a moat).

The Zwinger houses five museums of which the **Gemäldegalerie Alte Meister** *(Old Masters Gallery; ☎ 491 46 22, Theaterplatz 1; adult/concession €3.50/2; open 10am-6pm Tues-Sun)* is the one to see if you're pressed for time. All the heavy-hitters of the art world are represented, including Italian Renaissance artists Raffael and Titian and Dutch and Flemish masters like Rubens, Rembrandt and Vermeer. The museum is housed in the Semperbau facing Theaterplatz. Admission also gives entry to the **Rüstkammer** *(armoury; ☎ 491 46 26, Theaterplatz 1; armoury only adult/concession €1.50/1; open 10am-6pm Tues-Sun)*, with its superb collection of ceremonial weapons.

On the opposite side of the courtyard is the **Mathematics and Physics Salon** *(☎ 491 46 60, Zwinger; adult/concession €1.50/1; open 10am-6pm Fri-Wed)* with old instruments, globes and timepieces. The dazzling **Porcelain Collection** *(☎ 491 46 22, Glockenspielpavillon)*, one of the world's most

Potsdam's Brandenburger Tor.

A grand staircase leads to Dresden's Zwinger.

Home of opera in Dresden, the Semperoper has had a tumultuous history.

ANDREA SCHULTE-PEEVERS

Brühlsche Terrasse – riverside in Dresden.

ANDREA SCHULTE-PEEVERS

Baroque sculptures adorn the Zwinger complex.

JOHN BORTHWICK

Karl Marx and comrades watch over Augustusplatz in Leipzig.

famous, is closed for renovation until at least late 2002. Also here is the **Museum für Tierkunde** *(Zoological Museum; ☎ 495 25 03, Zwinger/Unterm Kronentor; adult/concession €1/0.50; open 10am-6pm Wed-Mon)*, which has natural history exhibits.

Brühlsche Terrasse

This spectacular riverside promenade begins just east of Augustusbrücke. Known as the 'Balcony of Europe', it is an elevated footpath above the southern embankment of the Elbe. In summer it's a must for strolling, with great views of the river, the paddle-steamers and, across the Elbe, the Goldener Reiter statue and Neustadt.

Beneath the promenade is the Renaissance brick bastion commonly known as the **Kasematten**. The museum inside *(☎ 491 47 86; adult/child €3/2; open 10am-5pm Apr-Oct daily, 10am-4pm Nov-Mar)* has audio-guides in English and other languages.

Albertinum

The Albertinum *(☎ 491 47 14, Brühlsche Terrasse; adult/concession €3.50/2; open 10am-6pm Fri-Wed)* is just off the eastern end of the promenade. Like the Zwinger, it houses several museums packed with glorious art treasures. Here you'll find the **Galerie Neue Meister** (Gallery of New Masters), with renowned 19th and 20th century paintings, including many impressionists. Not to be missed is the **Grünes Gewölbe** (Green Vault), one of the world's finest collections of jewel-studded precious objects. Eventually the Grünes Gewölbe will be relocated to its original site in the Royal Palace. Treasures include the world's biggest green diamond – all 41 carats' worth – tiny sculptures fashioned from odd-shaped pearls, and a stunning group of 137 gem-studded figures. Also in the Albertinum is the **Skulpturensammlung**, which includes classical and Egyptian works, and the **Münzkabinett**, which traces the history of coins from the 7th century to 1871.

Neustadt

Despite the name, Neustadt is an old part of Dresden largely untouched by the wartime bombings. After reunification it became the centre of the city's alternative scene, but with encroaching gentrification it's gradually losing its hard-core bohemian edge. Königsstrasse, which runs parallel to and to the west of Hauptstrasse, is developing into a swish shopping district.

A major sight is the **Goldener Reiter** (1736), an equestrian statue of August der Starke at the northern end of Augustusbrücke. From here, Hauptstrasse, a pleasant pedestrian mall, leads to Albertplatz, where you'll find a nice marble **Schiller Monument**.

Neustadt museums include the **Museum für Volkskunst** *(Museum of Folk Art; ☎ 803 08 17, Köpckestrasse 1; adult/child €1.50/1, open 10am-6pm Tues-Sun)* with three floors documenting the common people's lives in Saxony through the ages. On display are painted armoires, baskets, pottery, toys, Christmas decorations, Saxon and Sorbian folkloric costumes and lots more. On nearby Palaisplatz is the **Japanisches Palais** (1737), containing the famous **Landesmuseum für Vorgeschichte** *(State Archeaology Museum; ☎ 892 66 03, Palaisplatz 11; adult/child €4.50/3, open 10am-6pm Tues-Sun)*.

Pfunds Molkerei

It's billed as 'the world's most beautiful dairy shop', and for good reason: from top to bottom, the interior of Pfunds Molkerei *(☎ 816 20, Bautzner Strasse 79)* is a gorgeous riot of hand-painted tiles and enamelled sculptures. Founded by the Pfund brothers in 1880, the dairy claims to have invented condensed milk. The shop sells lovely wines, cheeses and milk. Upstairs there's also a cafe-restaurant upstairs with a strong milk-products theme.

Organised Tours

Hamburger Hummelbahn *(☎ 494 04 04)* offers city tours taking in all major sights aboard double-decker buses and cutesy 'choo-choo' trains. Tours (in German) leave from Postplatz several times daily, last 90 minutes and for adult/concession cost from €13/12.

Stadtrundfahrt Dresden *(☎ 899 56 50)* operates year-round sightseeing tours on the get-on, get-off as often as you wish principle for adult/child aged 14-17 costs €15/8. Buses, which depart at regular intervals from Theaterplatz/Augustusbrücke, make 19 stops and are equipped with headphones for non-German speakers.

Places to Stay
Room rates are pretty stratospheric, although a few budget places have emerged in recent years. The tourist office operates a room-reservation service at ☎ 49 19 22 22 per person for a fee of €2.50.

Jugendgästehaus Dresden (☎ 49 26 20, fax 492 62 99, e jghdresden@djh-sachsen .de, Maternistrasse 22) Singles €24, 2- or 3-bed rooms juniors/seniors €16.50/20, add €2.50 for private shower and toilet. This is a fantastic place in an old communist party training centre.

Hostel Mondpalast (☎/fax 804 60 61, e mondpalast@t-online.de, Katharinenstrasse 11-13) Dorm beds €12.50, singles/doubles €20/32. This is a leading Neustadt budget option with theme-decorated rooms and a great pub next door.

Jugendhotel Die Boofe (☎ 801 33 61, fax 801 33 62, e boofe@t-online.de, Louisenstrasse 20) Singles/doubles €28/41.50. Rooms are nicer than your average hostel, but it can get a bit noisy – there's a pub downstairs and a fire station next door.

Jugendherberge Rudi Arndt (☎ 471 06 67, fax 472 89 59, Hübnerstrasse 11) Dorm beds juniors/seniors €15.50/18. This non-DJH hostel is in a historic residential neighbourhood, 20 minutes' walk south of the Hauptbahnhof.

Pension Edith (☎/fax 802 83 42, Priesnitzstrasse 63) Singles/doubles with shower €39/51.50. This pension, in a quiet spot, has basic rooms. It's small, so book well ahead.

Hotel Martha Hospiz (☎ 817 60, fax 817 62 22, e marthahospiz.dresden@t-online .de, Nieritzstrasse 11) Singles/doubles with bath €70/100. Peace and quiet reign in this ample yet lovely inn with cheerful country furnishings.

Rothenburger Hof (☎ 812 60, fax 812 62 22, e kontakt@dresden-hotel.de, Rothenburger Strasse 15-17) Singles/doubles €52.50/82.50. In the middle of Neustadt,

this hotel has clean rooms, a bright atmosphere, and even a steam room and sauna.

art'otel dresden (☎ 492 20, fax 492 27 77, e dresden@artotel.de, Ostra-Allee 33) Singles/doubles €215/255. There's a gallery next door, a slick restaurant and fanciful rooms.

Hotel Kempinski Taschenberg Palais (☎ 491 20, fax 491 28 12, e reservation@ kempinski-dresden.de, Taschenberg 3) Singles/doubles €205/230. Luxury drips from the walls of this restored 18th-century mansion just opposite the Zwinger. 'Specials' may sometimes be available.

Places to Eat
Café Börse (☎ 490 64 11, Prager Strasse 8a) Mains €4.45-8.75. Drinks and crepes are the thing in this contemporary place. So is the people-watching from the deck above busy Prager Strasse.

The Altstadt has a handful of places worth checking out.

brennNessel (☎ 494 33 19, Schützengasse 18) Mains €5-9.25. This country-style place has vegetarian specialities like wholemeal noodles and feta in bell-pepper sauce, and leek, potato and sunflower-seed casserole.

Sophienkeller (☎ 49 72 60, Taschenberg 3) Set dinners €12.50-20, mains €8-14. Decorated like a fair in 1730 and serving good local specialities and wines, Sophienkeller also offers performances by singers in 18th-century garb.

Opernrestaurant (☎ 491 15 21, Theaterplatz 2) Mains €6-15. Opposite the Semperoper, this facility offers stylish surroundings and varied cuisine from Italian to German, at equally stylish prices. A nice spot for drinks after a performance.

More restaurants can be found in the Neustadt, including the following.

Raskolnikoff (☎ 804 57 06, Böhmische Strasse 34) Mains €3.50-12. This bohemian place has cheap Russian dishes like *borscht* (beetroot soup) and *wareniki* (dough baked with potatoes and mushrooms). It's located underneath the Galerie Erhardt sign.

Scheunecafé (☎ 803 66 19, Alaunstrasse 36) Banquet for two €17.50. This is good-value Indian food in a rock-n-roll atmosphere – the set-menu is five delicious courses.

Kügelgenhaus (☎ 527 91, Hauptstrasse 13) Mains €6.50-11. For something special, dine here, below the Museum of Early Dresden Romanticism. It has a good range of local Saxon dishes, and there's a basement beer cellar.

El Español (☎ 804 86 70, An der Dreikönigskirche 7) Dishes €3.75-12.75. Readers have written to recommend this cosy Spanish place in a ritzy neighbourhood.

Getting There & Away

Despite the distance from Berlin, Dresden is only a two-hour EC train ride away (€30 each way) with departures every two hours from Ostbahnhof. If you're driving, take the A113 to the A13 south. With an early departure from Berlin, it's possible to 'do' the Dresden highlights in a day, although this fabulous city is certainly worth an overnight stay.

Getting Around

Dresden's transport network, for a one-zone single ticket charges €1.50 and for four-ride strip tickets €5, while 24-hour passes are €4 (single) or €6 (family).

LEIPZIG

☎ 0341 • 480,000

Leipzig is an important business and transport centre in eastern Germany with a strong tradition in the arts. During the Wende, Leipzig became the 'Stadt der Helden', or City of Heroes, for its leading role in the 1989 democratic revolution. Its residents organised protests against the communist regime in May of that year; by October, they were taking to the streets by the hundreds of thousands, placing candles on the steps of Stasi headquarters and attending peace services at St Nicholas Church. Their actions resonated: on November 9, the Wall collapsed.

Since the discovery of rich silver mines in the nearby Erzgebirge (Ore Mountains) in the 16th century, Leipzig has enjoyed almost continual prosperity. It has hosted trade fairs since medieval times, and during the communist era these provided a key east-west interface. After reunification, the city spent huge sums on an ultra-modern fairground with the aim of re-establishing its position as one of Europe's great fair cities.

Leipzig has some of the finest classical music and opera in the country, and its art and literary scenes are flourishing. It was home to Bach, Wagner and Mendelssohn, and to Goethe, who set a key scene of *Faust* in the cellar of his favourite watering hole. And Leipzig's university attracts students from all over the world.

Leipzig's city centre lies within a ring road that outlines the town's medieval fortifications. From the newly renovated Hauptbahnhof (which houses a huge shopping mall), cross Willy-Brandt-Platz and continue south along Nikolaistrasse for five minutes; the central Markt is just a couple of blocks south-west. Leipzig's dazzling fairgrounds (or Neue Messe) are 5km north of the Hauptbahnhof (take tram No 16).

The excellent Leipzig Tourist Service (☎ 710 42 60/65, fax 710 42 71, e lipsia@ aol.com) is at Richard-Wagner-Strasse 1, near the Hauptbahnhof. It's open 9am to 7pm Monday to Friday, to 4pm Saturday and to 2pm Sunday. Staff sell the one- or three-day Leipzig Cards (€5/10.50), which grants free or discounted admission to museums and the zoo, plus unlimited public transport.

Historic Centre Walking Tour

This 4km circuit commences at the Markt and moves clockwise to Augustusplatz before exploring the attractive area south of the old quarter. It's a 1½-hour walk, but will take the best part of a day with all the stops.

On the Markt, the Renaissance **Altes Rathaus** (1556), one of Germany's most stunning town halls, houses the **Stadtgeschichtliches Museum** (*City History Museum; ☎ 96 51 30; adults/child €2.50/1.25; open 10am-6pm Tues-Sun*). Move south across the street and you'll enter the sunset-coloured baroque **Apelshaus** (1607) with lovely bay windows. Now a shopping mall known as the Königshaus Passage, in its

EXCURSIONS

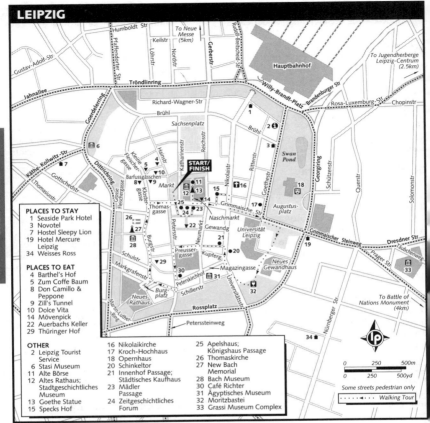

LEIPZIG

PLACES TO STAY
1 Seaside Park Hotel
3 Novotel
7 Hostel Sleepy Lion
19 Hotel Mercure Leipzig
34 Weisses Ross

PLACES TO EAT
4 Barthel's Hof
5 Zum Coffe Baum
8 Don Camillo & Peppone
9 Zill's Tunnel
10 Dolce Vita
14 Mövenpick
22 Auerbachs Keller
29 Thüringer Hof

OTHER
2 Leipzig Tourist Service
6 Stasi Museum
11 Alte Börse
12 Altes Rathaus; Stadtgeschichtliches Museum
13 Goethe Statue
15 Specks Hof
16 Nikolaikirche
17 Kroch-Hochhaus
18 Opernhaus
20 Schinkeltor
21 Innenhof Passage; Städtisches Kaufhaus
23 Mädler Passage
24 Zeitgeschichtliches Forum
25 Apelshaus; Königshaus Passage
26 Thomaskirche
27 New Bach Memorial
28 Bach Museum
30 Café Richter
31 Ägyptisches Museum
32 Moritzbastei
33 Grassi Museum Complex

heyday its impressive list of overnight guests included Peter the Great and Napoleon.

The Königshaus Passage leads directly into the **Mädler Passage**, surely one of the world's most beautiful shopping arcades. A mix of neo-Renaissance and Art Nouveau, it opened as a trade hall in 1914 and was renovated at great expense in the early 1990s. Today it's home to chi-chi shops, restaurants, cafes and most notably, **Auerbachs Keller** (see Places to Eat later in this section).

The north exit of Mädler Passage leads to Naschmarkt – so named for the edible goodies once peddled here – which is dominated

by the **Alte Börse** (1687), the ornate former trading house. In front is a **statue of Goethe** (1903), who studied law at Leipzig University. Today the Alte Börse is a cultural centre, with year-round concerts, plays and readings.

From the Naschmarkt, continue east along Grimmaische Strasse and turn left down a corridor toward **Specks Hof**, another shopping arcade. At the eastern portal of Specks Hof you'll see the **Nikolaikirche** (St Nicholas Church), built in 1165. This unusual edifice blends Romanesque and late-Gothic architecture with an amazing neoclassical interior. More recently, the church was the chief meeting point for peaceful demonstrators from May 1989. A pamphlet tells the story of how 600 loyal party members who were sent into the church to break up the services ended up listening to the sermon and joining the protesters.

Head south-east on Nikolaistrasse, then continue east on Grimmaische Strasse to reach Augustusplatz, where you can get a crash course in 20th-century monumental architecture. The square is strewn with glass structures that glow at night, lending the concrete slabs some much-needed warmth.

To the north is the functional **Opernhaus** (opera house) built in 1960, while the mini-shadow on your left is cast by the 11-storey **Kroch-Hochhaus** (1928), Leipzig's first 'skyscraper', now part of the university. Note the Art Deco lobby.

At the square's other end is the unforgiveably boxy **Neues Gewandhaus** (1981), which hosts classical and jazz concerts. Occupying much of the square's western flank is the giant GDR-era **Universität Leipzig** (1975), with its skyscraper nicknamed 'Uniriese' (University Giant) or 'Weisheitszahn' (Wisdom Tooth) by locals. It's supposed to look like an open book.

Moving south past the Gewandhaus, you'll arrive at the **Moritzbastei**, once part of the city fortifications and now a huge student club. Swinging around north on Universitätsstrasse you'll come across the **Schinkeltor** on the western side of the university building. This mid-19th-century gate is the only surviving bit of the original university to survive WWII and the GDR.

Just west of the Schinkeltor is the **Innenhof Passage**, in the spectacularly renovated Städtisches Kaufhaus. Exit on the west side, cross the street and continue west on Preussergasse to Petersstrasse, one of the city's main shopping boulevards. Turn left on Peterstrasse, and soon you'll see **Café Richter** (☎ 960 52 35, Peterstrasse 43), the oldest coffee retailer in town (since 1879). This fabulous eclectic building, with its golden iron spiral staircase, is worth a gander; the luscious beans (around 500g for €4) are wonderful too.

Take a few more steps south, then turn west into Markgrafenstrasse to Burgplatz, dominated by the baroque **Neues Rathaus** (New Town Hall). Recently renovated, the interior makes it one of the finest municipal buildings in Germany, with a grand staircase straight out of a Donald Trump dream. In the lobby are rotating art exhibitions, mostly on historical themes.

Continue north on Burgstrasse to get to the **Thomaskirche** (1212), with the tomb of composer Johann Sebastian Bach in front of the altar. The church was extended and converted to the Gothic style in 1496, and was the site of the baptisms of Richard Wagner, Karl Liebknecht and all of Bach's children.

Bach worked here as a cantor from 1723 until his death in 1750. Outside the church is the **New Bach Memorial** (1908) showing the composer standing against an organ, with his left-hand jacket pocket turned inside-out (he always claimed to be broke – not surprising with 20 children from two marriages). Concerts by the famous *Thomanerchor*, the boys' choir once led by Bach, are held regularly.

North of here Burgstrasse joins up with Thomasgasse; turn right and you'll find yourself back at the Markt in a minute or two.

Museums

Opposite Thomaskirche is the **Bach Museum** (☎ 96 41 10, Thomaskirchhof 16; adult/concession €3/2; open 10am-5pm). It has portraits, manuscripts and other memorabilia focusing on the composer's life in Leipzig. Bach wrote some of his greatest works – including *Johannes Passion, Matthäus Passion, Weinachtsoratorium and h-Moll Messe* – in this city.

In the Runde Ecke (Round Corner) building is the former local headquarters of the GDR Ministry for State Security (Stasi), now the **Stasi Museum** (☎ 961 24 43, Dittrichring 24; admission free; open 2pm-6pm Wed-Sun). It contains exhibits on propaganda, preposterous disguises, surveillance photographs and, in the back, mounds and mounds of papier-mache the Stasi created when they shredded and then soaked secret documents before the fall of the GDR. Printed explanations in English are available.

Opened in 1999, the **Zeitgeschichtliches Forum Leipzig** (*Leipzig Forum of Contemporary History;* ☎ *222 20; Grimmaische Strasse 6; admission free; open 9am-6pm Tues-Fri, 10am-6pm Sat-Sun*) is a haunting and uplifting museum on the history of the GDR from division to dictatorship to resistance. You can see legendarily harsh GDR cleaning products and video clips of families stifling tears as the Berlin Wall was being built between them. An English-language pamphlet translates the main captions.

The **Ägyptisches Museum** (*Egyptian Museum;* ☎ *973 70 10, Leipzig University, Schillerstrasse 6; adult/child €1.50/0.75; open 1pm-5pm Tues-Sat, 10am-1pm Sun*) has a 9000-piece collection of Egyptian antiquities and ranks among the most important of such collections in Europe. Displays include stone vessels from the 3rd millennium BC, Nubian decorative arts, and sarcophagi.

The **Grassi Museum Complex** at Universität Leipzig, at Täubchenweg 2 and 2c, contains three museums.

The **Museum für Völkerkunde** (*Ethnological Museum;* ☎ *214 20; Täubchenweg 2 & 2c; adult/concession €2.50/1; open 10am-5.30pm Tues-Fri, 10am-5pm Sat-Sun*) has a huge collection of cultural exhibits from around the world. The **Musikinstrumenten-Museum** (*☎ 214 21 20, Täubchenweg 2 & 2c; adult/concession €2.50/1; open 10am-5pm Tues-Sat, 10am-1pm Sun*) boasts a collection of almost 1000 musical instruments. The **Museum für Kunsthandwerk** (*☎ 214 21 75, Täubchenweg 2 & 2c; adult/concession €2.50/1; open 10am-6pm Tues-Sun, to 8pm Wed*) displays local arts and crafts. Note that the complex was closed for renovations at the time of writing, with exhibits moved elsewhere around town, but it should have reopened by the time you read this.

Völkerschlachtdenkmal

South-east of the centre is Leipzig's monolithic Völkerschlachtdenkmal (*Battle of Nations Monument; adult/concession €2.50/ 1.25; open 10am-5pm May-Oct*), a 91m-high monument built in 1913 commemorating the decisive victory by the combined Prussian, Austrian and Russian forces over

Napoleon's army 100 years earlier. Climb the tower for a good view of the city and surrounding area.

Organised Tours

Leipzig Tourist Service (*☎ 710 42 60/65, fax 710 42 71; Richard-Wagner-Strasse 1*) runs a two-hour guided walk from Monday to Saturday at 4pm, starting from its office for €5. From April to December there are also daily bus tours. A two-hour tour leaves at 10.30am for adult/concession costing €10/8 or one for 2½ hours leaves at 1.30pm for adult/concession and costs €14/10.

Places to Stay

Keep in mind that Leipzig's hotels raise their prices and fill up quickly during large trade shows, so check ahead if you plan to spend the night. Leipzig Tourist Service runs a free room-finding service (*☎ 710 42 55*), with singles/doubles from around €22.50/40.

Jugendherberge Leipzig-Centrum (*☎ 245 70 11, fax 245 70 12, Volksgartenstrasse 24*) Juniors/seniors €12/14.50. Tram: No 17, 27, 37 or 57 to Löbauer Strasse. This DJH-hostel is in the eastern suburb of Schönefeld, in an office-type block.

Hostel Sleepy Lion (*☎ 993 94 80, fax 993 94 82,* e *info@hostel-leipzig.de, Käthe-Kollwitz-Strasse 3*) 4-bed to 8-bed dorms €14-15, singles/doubles €23/36, linen €2, breakfast €2.50. Opened in 2000, this playful independent hostel is the best deal in the centre of town. Large rooms all have lockers and their own en suite bath and toilet. Internet access is €2.50 per hour, and bikes can be rented per day for €5.

Weisses Ross (*☎ 960 59 51, Rossstrasse 20*) Singles/doubles €30/47.50, with shower €35/55. The Weisses Ross is newly renovated, although the neighbourhood is nothing special.

Hotel Mercure Leipzig (*☎ 214 60, fax 960 49 16,* e *Mercure_Leipzig@t-online.de, Augustusplatz 5-6*) Singles/doubles €49.50/ 69.50. Despite its joyless facade, the location is tiptop, rooms are comfortable and the breakfast is good.

Novotel (*☎ 995 80, fax 995 82 00,* e *h1784 @ accorhotels.com, Goethestrasse*

11) Rooms from €82.50. Opposite the train station, this is one of the few air-conditioned hotels in the city.

Seaside Park Hotel *(☎ 985 20, fax 98 57 50,* **e** *seaside-hotels@regionett.de, Richard-Wagner-Strasse 7)* Singles/doubles from €97.50/116.50. The Seaside occupies a nice Art Nouveau house in the town centre. The hotel also boasts a commendable restaurant.

Places to Eat

Zum Coffe Baum *(☎ 961 00 60, Kleine Fleischergasse 4)* Mains €7.95-12.95. Leipzig's oldest coffeehouse also has a restaurant and cafe as well as a free coffee museum on the top floor. Composer Robert Schumann met friends here, and you can sit at his regular table.

Mövenpick *(☎ 211 77 22, Am Naschmarkt 1-3)* Buffet €9.75. This restaurant offers outstanding value, with a nightly buffet where you can help yourself to imaginative salads, casseroles and desserts.

Thüringer Hof *(☎ 994 49 99, Burgstrasse 19)* Mains €8.50-13. Said to have been Martin Luther's favourite pub, this place has been entirely restored. There's a traditional vaulted-ceiling restaurant in front and an atrium in the back.

Barthel's Hof *(☎ 141 31 13, Hainstrasse 1)* Buffet lunch €7.50, mains €10-17.50. This is a sprawling, historic place with a fantastic lunch buffet and some quirky Saxon dishes (eg, *Heubraten* – marinated lamb roasted on hay).

Barfussgässchen, one block west of the Markt, is an alleyway chock-a-block with outdoor tables in fine weather.

Dolce Vita *(☎ 960 67 28, Barfussgässchen 2-8)* Dishes €3.75-14.50. This is a rustic, popular Italian place. Sit downstairs if you are bothered by smoke.

Don Camillo & Peppone *(☎ 960 39 10, Barfussgässchen 11)* Dishes €4.50-16. This is Dolce Vita's more upmarket cousin, across the street.

Zill's Tunnel *(☎ 960 20 78, Barfussgässchen 9)* Mains €6.45-13.25. This place offers wonderful Saxon specialities – the roast venison in red wine is particularly good.

Auerbachs Keller *(☎ 21 61 00, Mädler Passage)* Mains €6.75-12.25. Founded in 1525, this is one of Germany's classic restaurants. Goethe's *Faust – Part I* includes a scene here, in which Mephistopheles and Faust carouse with students before they ride off on a barrel. The historic section of the restaurant includes the Goethe room (where the writer constantly drank – excuse us, gleaned inspiration), the Weinfass and, beneath that, the genuinely spooky Hexenküche. Note the carved tree-trunk hanging in the Weinfass, featuring witches, Faust astride the barrel and a hooved Mephisto in hot pursuit.

Getting There & Away

Located about 160km south of Berlin, Leipzig is quickly reached by ICE train leaving every other hour from Ostbahnhof (€33, 1½ hours). Although it is possible to get a good overview of Leipzig's main sights on a long day trip, for a more thorough investigation you might consider spending the night.

Getting Around

Trams are the main form of public transport in Leipzig, with the most important lines converging on Willy-Brandt-Platz outside the Hauptbahnhof. Fares are zone *and* time-based. Short journeys are €0.95 and must be completed within 15 minutes. Tickets for travel throughout Leipzig are €1.30 and good for 60 minutes; four trip strip-tickets are €4.75.

Language

High German is the official and proper form of German throughout the country, though most people also speak a local or regional dialect. The same is true of Berlin, though only a small number of native Berliners speak pure Berlinisch.

The good news is that both High and Low German are distant relatives of English and many words survive in the current vocabulary, which makes things easier for English speakers.

The bad news is that, unlike English, German has retained clear formal distinctions in gender and case. Though not as difficult as Russian, which has more cases, German does have its tricky moments. Fortunately Germans are used to hearing foreigners make a hash of their grammar, and any attempt to speak the language is well received.

All German school children learn a foreign language – usually English – which means most can speak it to a certain degree. You might have problems finding English speakers in eastern Germany, however, where Russian was the main foreign language taught in schools before the *Wende* (change) in 1989.

Berlin is Germany's most multicultural city (with people from 185 nations), so it's not surprising that a multitude of languages are spoken here. In 1999, 30% of immigrants were of Turkish descent, while people from the former states of Yugoslavia accounted for 15% of the city's population. Other large groups are Poles (6.5%) and immigrants from the former Soviet republics (5.6%). There are also about 13,000 Italians and 11,000 Greeks.

The words and phrases in this language guide should help you through the most common travel situations. Those with the desire to delve further into the language should get a copy of Lonely Planet's *German phrasebook*, which contains a useful two-way dictionary.

Pronunciation

English speakers sometimes hold onto their vowels too long when speaking German, which causes comprehension problems. Nevertheless, there are long vowels, like *pope*, and short ones, like *pop*. Another common mistake is a tendency to pronounce all vowels as if they have umlauts (**ä**, **ö** and **ü**). It's worth practising the difference, as they often change the tense and meaning of a word. In most other respects German pronunciation is fairly straightforward. There are no silent letters, and many foreign words (eg, *Band*, for 'rock band') are pronounced roughly the same as in English.

Vowels

a	short, as the 'u' in 'cut', or long, as in 'father'
au	as the 'ow' in 'vow'
ä	short, as in 'hat', or long, as in 'hare'
äu	as the 'oy' in 'boy'
e	short, as in 'bet', or long, as in 'obey'
ei	as the 'ai' in 'aisle'
eu	as the 'oy' in 'boy'
i	short, as in 'inn', or long, as in 'marine'
ie	as in 'siege'
o	short, as in 'pot', or long, as in 'note'
ö	as the 'er' in 'fern'
u	as in 'pull'
ü	similar to the 'u' in 'pull' but with lips stretched back

Consonants

Most consonants and their combinations are roughly similar to English ones, with a few exceptions. At the end of a word, consonants **b**, **d** and **g** sound a little more like 'p', 't' and 'k' respectively. There are no silent consonants.

ch	throaty, as in Scottish *loch*
j	as the 'y' in 'yet'
ng	always one sound, as in 'strong'
qu	as 'kv'
r	trilled or guttural

s	as in 'see' or as the 'z' in 'zoo'
sch	as the 'sh' in 'shore'
st	usually pronounced 'sht'
sp	usually pronounced 'shp'
v	more like an English 'f'
w	as an English 'v'
z	as the 'ts' in 'tsar'

Grammar

German grammar can be a nightmare for English speakers. Nouns come in three genders: masculine, feminine and neutral – the corresponding forms of the definite article ('the' in English) are *der*, *die* and *das*, with the basic plural form, *die*. Nouns and articles will alter according to the case (nominative, accusative, dative and genitive). Note that German nouns always begin with a capital.

You should be aware that German uses polite and informal forms for 'you' (*Sie* and *Du* respectively). When addressing people you don't know well you should always use the polite form (though younger people will be less inclined to expect them). In this language guide we use the polite form unless indicated by 'inf' (for 'informal') in brackets.

Greetings & Civilities

Hello.	*Hallo.*
Good morning.	*Guten Morgen.*
Good day.	*Guten Tag.*
Good evening.	*Guten Abend.*
Goodbye.	*Auf Wiedersehen.*
Bye.	*Tschüss.*
Yes.	*Ja.*
No.	*Nein.*
Where?	*Wo?*
Why?	*Warum?*
How?	*Wie?*
Maybe.	*Vielleicht.*
Please.	*Bitte.*
Thank you (very much).	*Danke (schön).*
You're welcome.	*Bitte or Bitte sehr.*
Excuse me.	*Entschuldigung.*
I'm sorry/Forgive me.	*Entschuldigen Sie, bitte.*
I'm sorry. (to express sympathy)	*Das tut mir leid.*

Language Difficulties

I understand.	*Ich verstehe.*
I don't understand.	*Ich verstehe nicht.*
Do you speak English?	*Sprechen Sie Englisch?/Sprichst du Englisch?* (inf)
Does anyone here speak English?	*Spricht hier jemand Englisch?*
What does ... mean?	*Was bedeutet ...?*
Please write it down.	*Bitte schreiben Sie es auf.*

Paperwork

first name	*Vorname*
surname	*Familienname*
nationality	*Staatsangehörigkeit*
date of birth	*Geburtsdatum*
place of birth	*Geburtsort*
sex (gender)	*Geschlecht*
passport	*Reisepass*
identification	*Ausweis*
visa	*Visum*

Small Talk

What's your name?	*Wie heissen Sie?/Wie heisst du?* (inf)
My name is ...	*Ich heisse ...*
How are you?	*Wie geht es Ihnen?/Wie geht's dir?* (inf)
I'm fine, thanks.	*Es geht mir gut, danke.*
Where are you from?	*Woher (kommen Sie/ kommst du)?* (inf)
I'm from ...	*Ich komme aus ...*

Getting Around

What time does the ... leave/arrive?	*Um wieviel Uhr fährt ... ab/kommt ... an?*
boat	*das Boot*
bus	*der Bus*
train	*der Zug*
tram	*die Strassenbahn*

Where is the ...?	*Wo ist ...?*
bus stop	*die Bushaltestelle*
metro station	*die U-Bahnstation*
train station	*der Bahnhof*
main train station	*der Hauptbahnhof*
airport	*der Flughafen*
tram stop	*die Strassenbahn- haltestelle*

I want to go to ...	*Ich möchte nach ... fahren.*

Signs

Eingang/Einfahrt	**Entrance**
Ausgang/ Ausfahrt	**Exit**
Notausgang	**Emergency Exit**
Auf/Offen/ Geöffnet	**Open**
Zu/Geschlossen	**Closed**
Rauchen Verboten	**No Smoking**
Polizei	**Police**
WC/Toiletten	**Toilets**
Herren	**Men**
Damen	**Women**

the next	*der/die/das nächste*
the last	*der/die/das letzte*
ticket office	*Fahrkartenschalter*
one-way ticket	*einfache Fahrkarte*
return ticket	*Rückfahrkarte*
1st/2nd class	*erste/zweite Klasse*
timetable	*Fahrplan*
platform number	*Gleisnummer*
luggage locker	*Gepäckschliessfach*

I'd like to hire ...	*Ich möchte ... mieten.*
a bicycle	*ein Fahrrad*
a motorcycle	*ein Motorrad*
a car	*ein Auto*

Directions

Where is ...?	*Wo ist ...?*
How do I get to ...?	*Wie erreicht man ...?*
Is it far from here?	*Ist es weit von hier?*
Can you show me (on the map)?	*Könnten Sie mir (auf der Karte) zeigen?*

street	*die Strasse*
suburb	*der Vorort*
town	*die Stadt*
behind	*hinter*
in front of	*vor*
opposite	*gegenüber*
straight ahead	*geradeaus*
(to the) left	*(nach) links*
(to the) right	*(nach) rechts*
at the traffic lights	*an der Ampel*
at the next corner	*an der nächsten Ecke*
north	*Nord*
south	*Süd*
east	*Ost*
west	*West*

Around Town

I'm looking for ...	*Ich suche ...*
a bank	*eine Bank/ Sparkasse*
the church	*die Kirche*
the city centre	*das Stadtzentrum*
the ... embassy	*die ... Botschaft*
my hotel	*mein Hotel*
the market	*den Markt*
the museum	*das Museum*
the post office	*das Postamt*
a public toilet	*eine öffentliche Toilette*
a hospital	*ein Krankenhaus*
the police	*die Polizei*
the tourist office	*das Fremden- verkehrsbüro*

I want to change some money/ travellers cheques.	*Ich möchte Geld/ Reiseschecks wechseln.*
What time does ... open/close?	*Um wieviel Uhr macht ... auf/zu?*
I'd like to make a phone call.	*Ich möchte telefonieren.*

beach	*der Strand*
bridge	*die Brücke*
castle/palace	*die Burg/das Schloss*
cathedral	*der Dom*
forest	*der Wald*
island	*die Insel*
lake	*der See*
market	*der Markt*
monastery/convent	*das Klostere*
mountain	*der Berg*
river	*der Fluss*
sea	*das Meer/die See*
tower	*der Turm*

Accommodation

I'm looking for ...	*Ich suche...*
a hotel	*ein Hotel*
a guesthouse	*eine Pension*
a youth hostel	*eine Jugendherberge*
a camping ground	*einen Campingplatz*

Where is a cheap hotel?	*Wo findet man ein preiswertes Hotel?*

Please write the address?	*Könnten Sie bitte die Adresse aufschreiben?*
Do you have a room available?	*Haben Sie ein Zimmer frei?*
How much is it per night/person?	*Wieviel kostet es pro Nacht/Person?*
May I see it?	*Darf ich es sehen?*
Where is the bathroom?	*Wo ist das Badezimmer?*
It's very noisy/ dirty/expensive.	*Es ist sehr laut/ dreckig/teuer.*

I'd like to book a ...	*Ich möchte ... reservieren.*
bed	*ein Bett*
cheap room	*ein preiswertes Zimmer*
single room	*ein Einzelzimmer*
double room	*ein Doppelzimmer*
room with two beds	*ein Zimmer mit zwei Betten*
room with shower and toilet	*ein Zimmer mit Dusche und WC*
dormitory bed	*ein Bett im Schlafsaal*

for one night	*für eine Nacht*
for two nights	*für zwei Nächte*
I'm/We're leaving now.	*Ich reise/Wir reisen jetzt ab.*

Shopping

I'd like to buy ...	*Ich möchte ... kaufen*
How much is that?	*Wieviel kostet das?*
Do you accept credit cards?	*Nehmen Sie Kreditkarten?*
bookshop	*Buchladen*
chemist/pharmacy	*Apotheke* (medicine) *Drogerie* (toiletries)
department store	*Kaufhaus*
laundry	*Wäscherei*
more/less	*mehr/weniger*
bigger/smaller	*grösser/kleiner*

Health

I need a doctor.	*Ich brauche einen Arzt.*
Where is a hospital?	*Wo ist ein Krankenhaus?*
I'm ill.	*Ich bin krank.*

Emergencies

Help!	*Hilfe!*
Call a doctor!	*Rufen Sie einen Arzt!*
Call the police!	*Rufen Sie die Polizei!*
Leave me alone.	*Lassen Sie mich in Ruhe.*
Get lost!	*Hau ab!* (inf)
I'm lost.	*Ich habe mich verirrt.*
Thief!	*Dieb!*
I've been raped/ robbed!	*Ich bin vergewaltigt/ bestohlen worden!*

It hurts here.	*Es tut hier weh.*
I'm pregnant.	*Ich bin schwanger.*

I'm ...	*Ich bin ...*
diabetic	*Diabetiker*
epileptic	*Epileptiker*
asthmatic	*Asthmatiker*

I'm allergic to antibiotics/ penicillin.	*Ich bin allergisch auf Antibiotika/ Penizillin.*

antiseptic	*Antiseptikum*
aspirin	*Aspirin*
condoms	*Kondome*
diarrhoea	*Durchfall*
medicine	*Medikament*
the pill	*die Pille*
sunblock cream	*Sonnencreme*
tampons	*Tampons*

Times & Dates

What time is it?	*Wie spät ist es?*
It's (10) o'clock.	*Es ist (zehn) Uhr.*
It's half past nine.	*Es ist halb zehn.*
in the morning	*morgens/vormittags*
in the afternoon	*nachmittags*
in the evening	*abends*
When?	*wann?*
today	*heute*
yesterday	*gestern*

Monday	*Montag*
Tuesday	*Dienstag*
Wednesday	*Mittwoch*
Thursday	*Donnerstag*

Friday	*Freitag*
Saturday	*Samstag/Sonnabend*
Sunday	*Sonntag*
January	*Januar*
February	*Februar*
March	*März*
April	*April*
May	*Mai*
June	*Juni*
July	*Juli*
August	*August*
September	*September*
October	*Oktober*
November	*November*
December	*Dezember*

Numbers

1	*eins*
2	*zwei /zwo*
3	*drei*
4	*vier*
5	*fünf*
6	*sechs*
7	*sieben*
8	*acht*
9	*neun*
10	*zehn*
11	*elf*
12	*zwölf*
13	*dreizehn*
14	*vierzehn*
15	*fünfzehn*
16	*sechzehn*
17	*siebzehn*
18	*achtzehn*
19	*neunzehn*
20	*zwanzig*
21	*einundzwanzig*
22	*zweiundzwanzig*
30	*dreissig*
40	*vierzig*
50	*fünfzig*
60	*sechzig*
70	*siebzig*
80	*achtzig*
90	*neunzig*
100	*einhundert*
1000	*eintausend*
10,000	*zehntausend*

| one million | *eine Million* |

FOOD & DRINK

breakfast	*Frühstück*
lunch	*Mittagessen*
dinner	*Abendessen*
menu	*Speisekarte*
restaurant	*Gaststätte/Restaurant*
pub/bar	*Kneipe*
supermarket	*Supermarkt*
snack bar	*Imbiss*

I'm a vegetarian.	*Ich bin Vegetarier(in).*
I'd like something to drink, please.	*Ich möchte etwas zu trinken, bitte.*
It was very tasty.	*Es hat mir sehr geschmeckt.*
The bill, please?	*Die Rechnung, bitte.*
Please keep the change.	*Das stimmt so.* (lit: 'that's OK as is')

Menu Decoder

Eating at a restaurant in a foreign country can easily be bewildering. Fortunately, throughout Germany, you'll usually find menus posted outside the entrance, giving you all the time you need to decide whether something speaks to your tastes. We've put together a short list of useful vocabulary terms to help you steer what you hunger for onto your plate.

Soups (*Suppen*)

Brühe – bouillon
Erbsensuppe – pea soup
Frühlingssuppe or *Gemüsesuppe* – vegetable soup
Hühnersuppe – chicken soup
Linsensuppe – lentil soup
Tomatensuppe – tomato soup

Meat (*Fleisch*)

Boulette – a cross between a meatball and a hamburger, eaten with a dry roll
Brathuhn – roast chicken
Bratwurst – fried pork sausage
Currywurst – a spicy sausage served with a tangy curried sauce
Eisbein – pickled pork knuckles
Ente – duck
Fasan – pheasant
Frikadelle – flat meatball
Hackbraten – meatloaf

Hackfleisch – chopped or minced meat
Hirsch – male deer
Huhn or Hähnchen – chicken
Kalbfleisch – veal
Kaninchen or Hase – rabbit
Kasseler Rippen – smoked pork chops
Lammfleisch – lamb
Putenbrust – turkey breast
Reh – venison
Rindfleisch – beef
Rippenspeer – spare ribs
Sauerbraten – marinated and roasted beef
Schinken – ham
Schnitzel – pounded meat, usually pork,
  breaded and fried
Schweinefleisch – pork
Truthahn – turkey
Wild – game
Wildschwein – wild boar

Seafood *(Meeresfrüchte)*
Aal – eel
Austern – oysters
Barsch – perch
Dorsch – cod
Fisch – fish
Forelle – trout
Hummer – lobster
Karpfen – carp
Krabben – shrimp
Lachs – salmon
Matjes – pickled herring
Miesmuscheln or Muscheln – mussels
Scholle – plaice
Seezunge – sole
Thunfisch – tuna

Vegetables *(Gemüse)*
Blumenkohl – cauliflower
Bohnen – beans
Brokkoli – broccoli
Erbsen – peas
Gurke – cucumber
Kartoffel – potato
Kohl – cabbage; can be *rot* (red), *weiss*
  (white) or *grün* (green)
Möhre – carrot
Paprika – bell/sweet pepper
Pilze – mushrooms
Rosenkohl – brussels sprouts

Spargel – asparagus
Tomate – tomato
Zwiebel – onion

Fruit *(Obst)*
Ananas – pineapple
Apfel – apple
Apfelsine or Orange – orange
Aprikose – apricot
Banane – banana
Birne – pear
Erdbeere – strawberry
Kirschen – cherries
Pampelmuse – grapefruit
Pfirsich – peach
Pflaume – plum
Weintrauben – grapes
Zitrone – lemon

Some Common Dishes
Auflauf – casserole
Eier, Rühreier – eggs, scrambled eggs
Eintopf – stew
Königsberger Klopse – meatballs in caper
  sauce
Kohlroulade – cabbage leaves stuffed with
  minced meat
Rollmops – pickled herring
Salat – salad

Cooking Methods
Frittiert – deep-fried
Gebacken – baked
Gebraten – pan-fried
Gefüllt – stuffed
Gegrillt – grilled
Gekocht – boiled
Geräuchert – smoked
Geschmort – braised
Paniert – breaded

Drinks *(Getränke)*
Bier – bier
Kaffee – coffee
Milch – milk
Mineralwasser – fizzy bottled mineral water
Saft – juice
Tee – tea
Wein – wine

Glossary

You may encounter the following terms and abbreviations while in Berlin. For other terms, see the Language chapter.

(pl) indicates plural

Abfahrt – departure (trains & buses)
ADAC – Allgemeiner Deutscher Automobil Club (German Automobile Association)
Allee – avenue
Altstadt – old town
Ankunft – arrival (trains & buses)
Apotheke – pharmacy
Arbeitsamt – employment office
Arbeitserlaubnis – work permit
Ärztlicher Notdienst – emergency medical service
Aufenthaltserlaubnis – residency permit
Auflauf, Aufläufe (pl) – casserole
Ausgang, Ausfahrt – exit
Ausländerbehörde – Foreigners' Office
Autobahn – motorway
Autonom – left-wing anarchist
AvD – Automobilclub von Deutschland (Automobile Club of Germany)

Bahnhof – train station
Bahnpolizei – train station police
Bahnsteig – train station platform
Bau – building
Bedienung – service, service charge
Behinderte – (pl) disabled persons
Berg – mountain
Bezirk – district
Bibliothek – library
Bierkeller – cellar pub
Bratkartoffeln – fried or roasted potatoes
BRD – Bundesrepublik Deutschland or, in English, FRG (Federal Republic of Germany). The official name for Germany today; orginally applied to the former West Germany.
Brücke – bridge
Brunnen – fountain or well
Bundesland – federal state
Bundesrat – upper house of the German Parliament

Bundestag – lower house of the German Parliament
Busbahnhof – large bus station

CDU – Christliche Demokratische Union (Christian Democratic Union), center-right party

DB – Deutsche Bahn (German national railway)
DDR – Deutsche Demokratische Republik or, in English, GDR (German Democratic Republic). The name for the former East Germany. *See also* BRD.
Denkmal – memorial
Deutsche Reich – German Empire. Refers to the period 1871-1918.
DJH – Deutsches Jugendherbergswerk (German youth hostel association)
Dom – cathedral
DZT – Deutsche Zentrale für Tourismus (German National Tourist Office)

Eingang – entrance
Eintritt – admission
EU-Aufenthaltserlaubnis – EU residency permit

Fahrplan – timetable
Fahrrad – bicycle
FDP – Freie Demokratische Partei (Free Democratic Party), center party
Fest – festival
Feuerwehr – fire brigade
Flohmarkt – flea market
Flughafen – airport
Franks – Germanic people influential in Europe between the 3rd and 8th centuries
Freikorps – WWI volunteers
Fremdenverkehrsamt – tourist office
Fremdenzimmer – tourist room
FRG – Federal Republic of Germany; *see also* BRD
Frühstück – breakfast

Garten – garden
Gasse – lane or alley

Gastarbeiter – literally 'guest worker'; labourer arriving from Turkey, Yugoslavia, Italy or Greece in the 1960s to help rebuild Germany
Gästehaus, Gasthaus – guesthouse
Gaststätte – informal restaurant
GDR – German Democratic Republic (the former East Germany); *see also* BRD, DDR
Gedenkstätte – memorial site
Gepäckaufbewahrung – left-luggage office
Gespräch – reverse charge telephone call
Gestapo – Nazi secret police
Glockenspiel – literally 'bell play'; carillon sounded by mechanised figures often in the form of religious or historical characters
Gründerzeit – literally 'foundation time'; the period of industrial expansion in Germany following the founding of the German Empire in 1871

Hafen – harbour, port
halbtrocken – semi-dry (wine)
Hauptbahnhof – main train station
Hauptpostlagernd – poste restante
Heilige Römische Reich – the Holy Roman Empire, which lasted from the 8th century to 1806. The German lands comprised the bulk of the Empire's territory.
Herzog – duke
Hitlerjugend – Hitler Youth, organisation for boys
Hochdeutsch – literally 'High German'; standard spoken and written German developed from a regional Saxon dialect
Hof, Höfe (pl) – courtyard
Hotel Garni – a hotel without a restaurant where you are only served breakfast

Imbiss – snack bar, takeaway stand; *see* Schnellimbiss
Insel – island

Jugendgästehaus – youth guesthouse, usually of a higher standard than a youth hostel
Jugendherberge – youth hostel
Jugendstil – Art Nouveau

Kabarett – cabaret
Kaffee und Kuchen – literally 'coffee and cake'; traditional afternoon coffee break
Kaiser – emperor; derived from 'Caesar'
Kanal – canal
Kantine, Kantinen (pl) – government subsidised cafeterias in public buildings like town halls
Kapelle – chapel
Karte – ticket
Kartenvorverkauf – ticket booking office
Kino – cinema
Kirche – church
Kloster – monastery, convent
Kneipe – bar or pub
Kommunales Kino – alternative or studio cinema
Konditorei – cake shop
König – king
Konsulat – consulate
Konzentrationslager (KZ) – concentration camp
korrekt – correct, proper
Kristallnacht – literally 'night of broken glass'. The attack on Jewish synagogues, cemeteries and businesses by Nazis and their supporters on the night of 9 November 1938 that marked the beginning of full-scale persecution of Jews in Germany. Also known as Reichspogromnacht.
Kunst – art
Kurfürst – prince elector

Land, Länder (pl) – state
Landtag – state parliament
Lesbe, Lesben (pl) – lesbian
lesbisch – lesbian (adj)
lieblich – sweet (wine)
Lied – song

Markgraf – margrave; German nobleman ranking above a count
Markt – market
Marktplatz (often abbreviated to Markt) – marketplace or central square
Mehrwertsteuer (MWST) – value-added tax
Mensa – university cafeteria
Mietskaserne, Mietkasernen (pl) – tenement built around successive courtyards
Milchcafé – milk coffee, *café au lait*
Mitfahrzentrale – ride-sharing service

Mitwohnzentrale – an accommodation-finding service (usually long-term)
Münzwäscherei – coin-operated laundrette

Nord – north
Notdienst – emergency service

Ossis – literally 'Easties'; nickname for East Germans
Ost – east
Ostalgie – word fusion of Ost and Nostalgie, meaning nostalgia for GDR days
Ostpolitik – former West German chancellor Willy Brandt's foreign policy of 'peaceful coexistence' with the GDR

Palast – palace
Pannenhilfe – roadside breakdown assistance
Parkhaus – car park
Parkschein – parking voucher
Parkscheinautomat – vending machine selling parking vouchers
Passage – shopping arcade
Pfand – deposit for bottles and sometimes glasses (in beer gardens and stores)
Pfund – pound (500 grams)
Plattenbauten – prefab housing developments
Platz – square
Post or Postamt – post office

Rathaus – town hall
Reich – empire
Reichspogromnacht – *see* Kristallnacht
Reisezentrum – travel centre in train or bus stations
Rezept – prescription
Rezeptfrei – over-the-counter medications

Saal, Säle (pl) – hall, large room
Sammlung – collection
Säule – column, pillar
Schatzkammer – treasury
Schiff – ship
Schiffahrt – literally 'boat way'; shipping, navigation
Schloss – palace, castle
Schnaps – schnapps
Schnellimbiss – stand-up food stall

Schwul, Schwule (pl) – gay
See – lake
Sekt – sparkling wine
Selbstbedienung (SB) – self-service (restaurants, laundrettes etc)
Sozialistische Einheitspartei Deutschland – Socialist Unity Party of Germany, or SED
SPD – Sozialdemokratische Partei Deutschlands (Social Democrat Party of Germany), centre-left party
SS – Schutzstaffel; organisation within the Nazi party that supplied Hitler's bodyguards, as well as the concentration-camp guards and the Waffen-SS troops in WWII
Stadt – city or town
Stadtbad, Stadtbäder (pl) – public bath
Stadtwald – city or town forest
Stasi – GDR secret police (from Ministerium für Staatssicherheit, or Ministry of State Security)
Stau – traffic jam
Stehcafé – stand-up café
Strasse (often abbreviated to Str) – street
Süd – south
Szene – scene (ie where the action is)

Tageskarte – daily menu or day ticket on public transport
Tal – valley
Teich – pond
Thirty Years' War – pivotal war in Central Europe (1618-48) that began as a German conflict between Catholics and Protestants
Tor – gate
Trabant – GDR-era car, boasting a 2-stroke engine
Trampen – hitchhiking
Treuhandanstalt – trust established to sell off GDR assets after the Wende
trocken – dry (wine)
Trödel – junk, bric-a-brac
Trümmerberg – artificial hill built from wartime rubble
Trümmerfrau – 'rubble women', ie women who cleaned up bricks and rebuilt houses after WWII
Turm – tower

Übergang – transit point
Ufer – bank

verboten – forbidden
Verkehr – traffic
Viertel – quarter, district

Wald – forest
Waldfrüchte – wild berries
Wäscherei – dry cleaner, laundrette
Wechselstube – currency exchange office
Weg – way, path
Weihnachtsmarkt – Christmas market
Wende – 'change' or 'turning point' of 1989, ie the fall of communism that led to the collapse of the GDR and ultimately to German reunification
Wessis – literally 'Westies'; nickname for West Germans

West – west
Wurst – sausage

Zahnarzt – dentist
Zeitung – newspaper
Zeitgeist – the spirit or outlook of a specific time or period
Zimmer Frei – room available (accommodation)
Zimmervermittlung – room-finding service; *see also* Mitwohnzentrale
ZOB – Zentraler Omnibusbahnhof (central bus station)
Zuckerbäckerstil – wedding-cake style of architecture which was typical of the Stalin era

Lonely Planet Guides by Region

Lonely Planet is known worldwide for publishing practical, reliable and no-nonsense travel information in our guides and on our Web site. The Lonely Planet list covers just about every accessible part of the world. Currently there are 16 series: Travel guides, Shoestring guides, Condensed guides, Phrasebooks, Read This First, Healthy Travel, Walking guides, Cycling guides, Watching Wildlife guides, Pisces Diving & Snorkeling guides, City Maps, Road Atlases, Out to Eat, World Food, Journeys travel literature and Pictorials.

AFRICA Africa on a shoestring • Botswana • Cairo • Cairo City Map • Cape Town • Cape Town City Map • East Africa • Egypt • Egyptian Arabic phrasebook • Ethiopia, Eritrea & Djibouti • Ethiopian Amharic phrasebook • The Gambia & Senegal • Healthy Travel Africa • Kenya • Malawi • Morocco • Moroccan Arabic phrasebook • Mozambique • Namibia • Read This First: Africa • South Africa, Lesotho & Swaziland • Southern Africa • Southern Africa Road Atlas • Swahili phrasebook • Tanzania, Zanzibar & Pemba • Trekking in East Africa • Tunisia • Watching Wildlife East Africa • Watching Wildlife Southern Africa • West Africa • World Food Morocco • Zambia • Zimbabwe, Botswana & Namibia
Travel Literature: Mali Blues: Traveling to an African Beat • The Rainbird: A Central African Journey • Songs to an African Sunset: A Zimbabwean Story

AUSTRALIA & THE PACIFIC Aboriginal Australia & the Torres Strait Islands •Auckland • Australia • Australian phrasebook • Australia Road Atlas • Cycling Australia • Cycling New Zealand • Fiji • Fijian phrasebook • Healthy Travel Australia, NZ & the Pacific • Islands of Australia's Great Barrier Reef • Melbourne • Melbourne City Map • Micronesia • New Caledonia • New South Wales • New Zealand • Northern Territory • Outback Australia • Out to Eat – Melbourne • Out to Eat – Sydney • Papua New Guinea • Pidgin phrasebook • Queensland • Rarotonga & the Cook Islands • Samoa • Solomon Islands • South Australia • South Pacific • South Pacific phrasebook • Sydney • Sydney City Map • Sydney Condensed • Tahiti & French Polynesia • Tasmania • Tonga • Tramping in New Zealand • Vanuatu • Victoria • Walking in Australia • Watching Wildlife Australia • Western Australia
Travel Literature: Islands in the Clouds: Travels in the Highlands of New Guinea • Kiwi Tracks: A New Zealand Journey • Sean & David's Long Drive

CENTRAL AMERICA & THE CARIBBEAN Bahamas, Turks & Caicos • Baja California • Belize, Guatemala & Yucatán • Bermuda • Central America on a shoestring • Costa Rica • Costa Rica Spanish phrasebook • Cuba • Cycling Cuba • Dominican Republic & Haiti • Eastern Caribbean • Guatemala • Havana • Healthy Travel Central & South America • Jamaica • Mexico • Mexico City • Panama • Puerto Rico • Read This First: Central & South America • Virgin Islands • World Food Caribbean • World Food Mexico • Yucatán
Travel Literature: Green Dreams: Travels in Central America

EUROPE Amsterdam • Amsterdam City Map • Amsterdam Condensed • Andalucía • Athens • Austria • Baltic States phrasebook • Barcelona • Barcelona City Map • Belgium & Luxembourg • Berlin • Berlin City Map • Britain • British phrasebook • Brussels, Bruges & Antwerp • Brussels City Map • Budapest • Budapest City Map • Canary Islands • Catalunya & the Costa Brava • Central Europe • Central Europe phrasebook • Copenhagen • Corfu & the Ionians • Corsica • Crete • Crete Condensed • Croatia • Cycling Britain • Cycling France • Cyprus • Czech & Slovak Republics • Czech phrasebook • Denmark • Dublin • Dublin City Map • Dublin Condensed • Eastern Europe • Eastern Europe phrasebook • Edinburgh • Edinburgh City Map • England • Estonia, Latvia & Lithuania • Europe on a shoestring • Europe phrasebook • Finland • Florence • Florence City Map • France • Frankfurt City Map • Frankfurt Condensed • French phrasebook • Georgia, Armenia & Azerbaijan • Germany • German phrasebook • Greece • Greek Islands • Greek phrasebook • Hungary • Iceland, Greenland & the Faroe Islands • Ireland • Italian phrasebook • Italy • Kraków • Lisbon • The Loire • London • London City Map • London Condensed • Madrid • Madrid City Map • Malta • Mediterranean Europe • Milan, Turin & Genoa • Moscow • Munich • Netherlands • Normandy • Norway • Out to Eat – London • Out to Eat – Paris • Paris • Paris City Map • Paris Condensed • Poland • Polish phrasebook • Portugal • Portuguese phrasebook • Prague • Prague City Map • Provence & the Côte d'Azur • Read This First: Europe • Rhodes & the Dodecanese • Romania & Moldova • Rome • Rome City Map • Rome Condensed • Russia, Ukraine & Belarus • Russian phrasebook • Scandinavian & Baltic Europe • Scandinavian phrasebook • Scotland • Sicily • Slovenia • South-West France • Spain • Spanish phrasebook • Stockholm • St Petersburg • St Petersburg City Map • Sweden • Switzerland • Tuscany • Ukrainian phrasebook • Venice • Vienna • Wales • Walking in Britain • Walking in France • Walking in Ireland • Walking in Italy • Walking in Scotland • Walking in Spain • Walking in Switzerland • Western Europe • World Food France • World Food Greece • World Food Ireland • World Food Italy • World Food Spain **Travel Literature:** After Yugoslavia • Love and War in the Apennines • The Olive Grove: Travels in Greece • On the Shores of the Mediterranean • Round Ireland in Low Gear • A Small Place in Italy

Lonely Planet Mail Order

Lonely Planet products are distributed worldwide. They are also available by mail order from Lonely Planet, so if you have difficulty finding a title please write to us. North and South American residents should write to 150 Linden St, Oakland, CA 94607, USA; European and African residents should write to 10a Spring Place, London NW5 3BH, UK; and residents of other countries to Locked Bag 1, Footscray, Victoria 3011, Australia.

INDIAN SUBCONTINENT & THE INDIAN OCEAN Bangladesh • Bengali phrasebook • Bhutan • Delhi • Goa • Healthy Travel Asia & India • Hindi & Urdu phrasebook • India • India & Bangladesh City Map • Indian Himalaya • Karakoram Highway • Kathmandu City Map • Kerala • Madagascar • Maldives • Mauritius, Réunion & Seychelles • Mumbai (Bombay) • Nepal • Nepali phrasebook • North India • Pakistan • Rajasthan • Read This First: Asia & India • South India • Sri Lanka • Sri Lanka phrasebook • Tibet • Tibetan phrasebook • Trekking in the Indian Himalaya • Trekking in the Karakoram & Hindukush • Trekking in the Nepal Himalaya • World Food India **Travel Literature:** The Age of Kali: Indian Travels and Encounters • Hello Goodnight: A Life of Goa • In Rajasthan • Maverick in Madagascar • A Season in Heaven: True Tales from the Road to Kathmandu • Shopping for Buddhas • A Short Walk in the Hindu Kush • Slowly Down the Ganges

MIDDLE EAST & CENTRAL ASIA Bahrain, Kuwait & Qatar • Central Asia • Central Asia phrasebook • Dubai • Farsi (Persian) phrasebook • Hebrew phrasebook • Iran • Israel & the Palestinian Territories • Istanbul • Istanbul City Map • Istanbul to Cairo • Istanbul to Kathmandu • Jerusalem • Jerusalem City Map • Jordan • Lebanon • Middle East • Oman & the United Arab Emirates • Syria • Turkey • Turkish phrasebook • World Food Turkey • Yemen **Travel Literature:** Black on Black: Iran Revisited • Breaking Ranks: Turbulent Travels in the Promised Land • The Gates of Damascus • Kingdom of the Film Stars: Journey into Jordan

NORTH AMERICA Alaska • Boston • Boston City Map • Boston Condensed • British Columbia • California & Nevada • California Condensed • Canada • Chicago • Chicago City Map • Chicago Condensed • Florida • Georgia & the Carolinas • Great Lakes • Hawaii • Hiking in Alaska • Hiking in the USA • Honolulu & Oahu City Map • Las Vegas • Los Angeles • Los Angeles City Map • Louisiana & the Deep South • Miami • Miami City Map • Montreal • New England • New Orleans • New Orleans City Map • New York City • New York City City Map • New York City Condensed • New York, New Jersey & Pennsylvania • Oahu • Out to Eat – San Francisco • Pacific Northwest • Rocky Mountains • San Diego & Tijuana • San Francisco • San Francisco City Map • Seattle • Seattle City Map • Southwest • Texas • Toronto • USA • USA phrasebook • Vancouver • Vancouver City Map • Virginia & the Capital Region • Washington, DC • Washington, DC City Map • World Food New Orleans **Travel Literature:** Caught Inside: A Surfer's Year on the California Coast • Drive Thru America

NORTH-EAST ASIA Beijing • Beijing City Map • Cantonese phrasebook • China • Hiking in Japan • Hong Kong & Macau • Hong Kong City Map • Hong Kong Condensed • Japan • Japanese phrasebook • Korea • Korean phrasebook • Kyoto • Mandarin phrasebook • Mongolia • Mongolian phrasebook • Seoul • Shanghai • South-West China • Taiwan • Tokyo • Tokyo Condensed • World Food Hong Kong • World Food Japan **Travel Literature:** In Xanadu: A Quest • Lost Japan

SOUTH AMERICA Argentina, Uruguay & Paraguay • Bolivia • Brazil • Brazilian phrasebook • Buenos Aires • Buenos Aires City Map • Chile & Easter Island • Colombia • Ecuador & the Galapagos Islands • Healthy Travel Central & South America • Latin American Spanish phrasebook • Peru • Quechua phrasebook • Read This First: Central & South America • Rio de Janeiro • Rio de Janeiro City Map • Santiago de Chile • South America on a shoestring • Trekking in the Patagonian Andes • Venezuela **Travel Literature:** Full Circle: A South American Journey

SOUTH-EAST ASIA Bali & Lombok • Bangkok • Bangkok City Map • Burmese phrasebook • Cambodia • Cycling Vietnam, Laos & Cambodia • East Timor phrasebook • Hanoi • Healthy Travel Asia & India • Hill Tribes phrasebook • Ho Chi Minh City (Saigon) • Indonesia • Indonesian phrasebook • Indonesia's Eastern Islands • Java • Lao phrasebook • Laos • Malay phrasebook • Malaysia, Singapore & Brunei • Myanmar (Burma) • Philippines • Pilipino (Tagalog) phrasebook • Read This First: Asia & India • Singapore • Singapore City Map • South-East Asia on a shoestring • South-East Asia phrasebook • Thailand • Thailand's Islands & Beaches • Thailand, Vietnam, Laos & Cambodia Road Atlas • Thai phrasebook • Vietnam • Vietnamese phrasebook • World Food Indonesia • World Food Thailand • World Food Vietnam

ALSO AVAILABLE: Antarctica • The Arctic • The Blue Man: Tales of Travel, Love and Coffee • Brief Encounters: Stories of Love, Sex & Travel • Buddhist Stupas in Asia: The Shape of Perfection • Chasing Rickshaws • The Last Grain Race • Lonely Planet ... On the Edge: Adventurous Escapades from Around the World • Lonely Planet Unpacked • Lonely Planet Unpacked Again • Not the Only Planet: Science Fiction Travel Stories • Ports of Call: A Journey by Sea • Sacred India • Travel Photography: A Guide to Taking Better Pictures • Travel with Children • Tuvalu: Portrait of an Island Nation

LONELY PLANET

You already know that Lonely Planet produces more than this one guidebook, but you might not be aware of the other products we have on this region. Here is a selection of titles that you may want to check out as well:

Munich
ISBN 1 86450 055 7
US$14.95 • UK£8.99

Germany
ISBN 1 74059 078 3
US$24.99 • UK£14.99

German phrasebook
ISBN 0 86442 451 5
US$5.95 • UK£3.99

Bavaria
ISBN 1 74059 013 9
US$17.99 • UK£11.99

Central Europe
ISBN 1 86450 204 5
US$24.99 • UK£14.99

Central Europe phrasebook
ISBN 1 86450 226 6
US$7.99 • UK£4.50

Europe on a shoestring
ISBN 1 86450 150 2
US$24.99 • UK£14.99

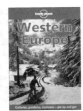

Western Europe
ISBN 1 86450 163 4
US$27.99 • UK£15.99

Europe phrasebook
ISBN 1 86450 224 X
US$8.99 • UK£4.99

Berlin City Map
ISBN 1 86450 005 0
US$5.95 • UK£3.99

Frankfurt City Map
ISBN 1 74059 016 3
US$5.99 • UK£3.99

Frankfurt Condensed
ISBN 1 86450 223 1
US$11.99 • UK£6.99

Available wherever books are sold

Index

Text

Bold indicates maps.

Bold indicates maps.

Places to Stay

Places to Eat

Boxed Text

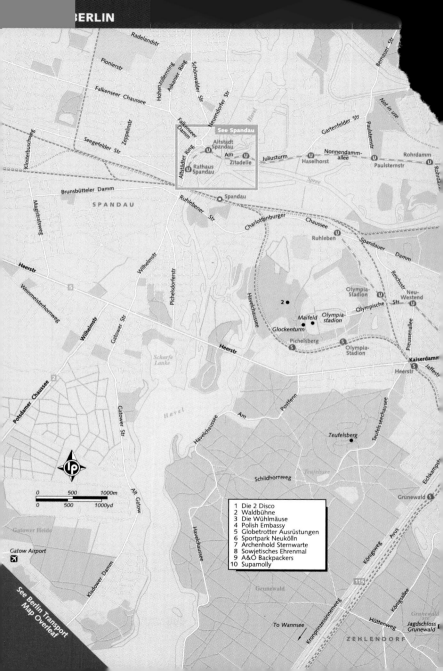

See Spandau

Radelandstr
Pionierstr
Falkenseer Chaussee
Hohenzollernring
Askanier Ring
Schönwalder Str
Meyerndorfer Str
Falkenseer Damm
Zeppelinstr
Seegefelder Str
Klosterbuschweg
Not in use
Bernauer Str
Gartenfelder Str
Paulsternstr
Rohrdamm
Altstadt Spandau
Juliusturm
Nonnendamm- allee
Am Zitadelle
Haselhorst
Paulsternstr
Rathaus Spandau
Altstädter Ring
Falkenseer Damm
Brunsbütteler Damm
Magistratsweg
SPANDAU
Spandau
Ruhlebener Str
Charlottenburger Chaussee
Spree
Ruhleben
Spandauer Damm
Heerstr
Weinmeisterhornweg
Wilhelmstr
Pichelsdorferstr
Havelchaussee
Gatower Str
Olympia- Stadion
Neu- Westend
Olympische Str
Reichsstr
Preussenallee
2
Maifeld
Glockenturm
Olympia- stadion
Olympische
Scharfe Lanke
Heerstr
Pichelsberg
Olympia- Stadion
Kaiserdamm
Heerstr
Jaffestr
Havel
Postfenn
Am
Havelchaussee
Teufelsberg
Teufelssechaussee
Eichkampstr
Schildhornweg
Teufelssee
Grünewald
Potsdamer Chaussee
Alt Gatow
Gatower Str

0   500   1000m
0   500   1000yd

Gatower Heide

Gatow Airport

Grunewald
Grunewald
115
Kronprinzessinnenweg
Königsweg
Avus
Königsallee
Jagdschloss Grunewald

Kladower Damm
Havelchaussee

To Wannsee
Hüttenweg
ZEHLENDORF

See Berlin Transport Map Overleaf

1 Die 2 Disco
2 Waldbühne
3 Die Wühlmäuse
4 Polish Embassy
5 Globetrotter Ausrüstungen
6 Sportpark Neukölln
7 Archenhold Sternwarte
8 Sowjetisches Ehrenmal
9 A&O Backpackers
10 Supamolly

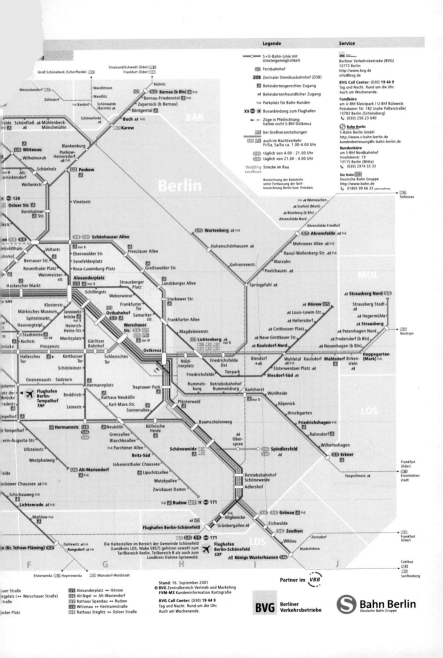

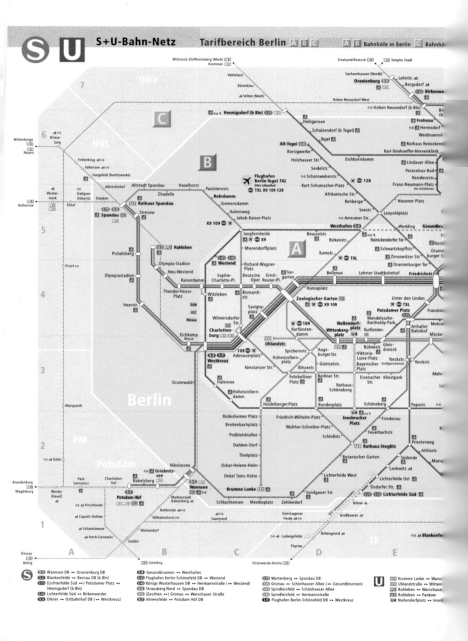

MAP 2 - WESTERN CHARLOTTENBURG & NORTHERN TIERGARTEN

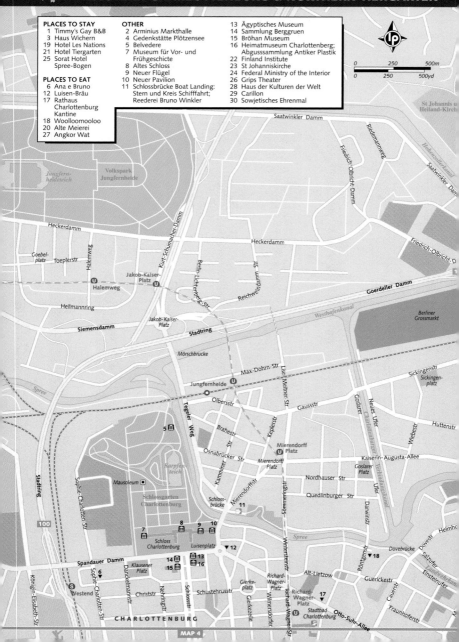

PLACES TO STAY
1 Timmy's Gay B&B
3 Haus Wichern
19 Hotel Les Nations
21 Hotel Tiergarten
25 Sorat Hotel Spree-Bogen

PLACES TO EAT
6 Ana e Bruno
12 Luisen-Bräu
17 Rathaus Charlottenburg Kantine
18 Woolloomooloo
20 Alte Meierei
27 Angkor Wat

OTHER
2 Arminius Markthalle
4 Gedenkstätte Plötzensee
5 Belvedere
7 Museum für Vor- und Frühgeschicte
8 Altes Schloss
9 Neuer Flügel
10 Neuer Pavilion
11 Schlossbrücke Boat Landing: Stern und Kreis Schifffahrt; Reederei Bruno Winkler

13 Ägyptisches Museum
14 Sammlung Berggruen
15 Bröhan Museum
16 Heimatmuseum Charlottenberg; Abgusssammlung Antiker Plastik
22 Finland Institute
23 St Johanniskirche
24 Federal Ministry of the Interior
26 Grips Theater
28 Haus der Kulturen der Welt
29 Carillon
30 Sowjetisches Ehrenmal

MAP 4

PLACES TO STAY
- 7 Pension Amsterdam
- 17 Lette'm Sleep
- 28 Eastside Gayllery
- 60 Myer's Hotel Berlin
- 61 Hotel Transit Loft
- 64 Hotel Kastanienhof
- 68 Hotel-Pension Merkur
- 73 Mitte's Backpacker Hostel
- 78 Hotel Honigmond
- 83 Artist Hotelpension Die Loge; Sushi-Bar
- 84 Hotel Märkischer Hof
- 98 Pension mitArt
- 123 Circus - The Hostel
- 131 Pegasus Hostel

PLACES TO EAT
- 2 Ellopia
- 11 Café Xion
- 18 Frida Kahlo
- 21 Houdini
- 24 Himalaya
- 30 Rice Queen
- 32 Salsabil
- 34 Offenbach Stuben
- 35 Miro
- 40 Little Shop of Foods
- 43 Tandoor
- 44 Mao Thai
- 46 Weitzmann
- 47 Restauration 1900
- 48 Ostwind
- 49 November
- 51 Gugelhof
- 52 Lappeggi
- 53 Anita Wronski
- 55 Am Wasserturm
- 56 Pasternak
- 57 Kommandatur Pizzeria
- 70 Maxwell
- 76 Bar-Celona
- 81 Good Time
- 82 Malete
- 86 Amrit
- 90 Kolbo
- 91 Beth Café
- 94 Keyzer Soze
- 100 Kamala
- 104 Oren
- 106 Rimón
- 108 Grill & Schlemmerbuffet Zach
- 112 Brazil
- 118 Barcomi's
- 122 Cantamaggio

BARS & CLUBS
- 3 Stiller Don
- 4 Greifbar
- 6 Schall und Rauch
- 10 Pick Ab
- 12 Duncker
- 15 Luna Bar
- 23 La Bodeguita del Medio
- 26 Volksbühne am Berliner Prater; Prater Beer Garden
- 33 X-Bar
- 41 Akba Lounge
- 42 Uluru Resort
- 62 Knaack Club
- 63 Pfefferberg
- 67 Seven Lounge
- 69 Jazzbar Pfandleihe
- 71 Bergwerk
- 77 Schlot
- 79 Reingold
- 85 Obst und Gemüse
- 87 Verkehrsberuhigte Ostzone
- 93 Jubinal
- 95 Bar Lounge 808
- 97 Oscar Wilde Irish Pub
- 99 Kalkscheune; Clubhouse Hostel
- 101 Zosch
- 105 Silberstein
- 113 Delicious Doughnuts
- 114 b-flat
- 127 Geburtstagsclub
- 134 Filmriss
- 136 Fischladen
- 138 Schizzotempel

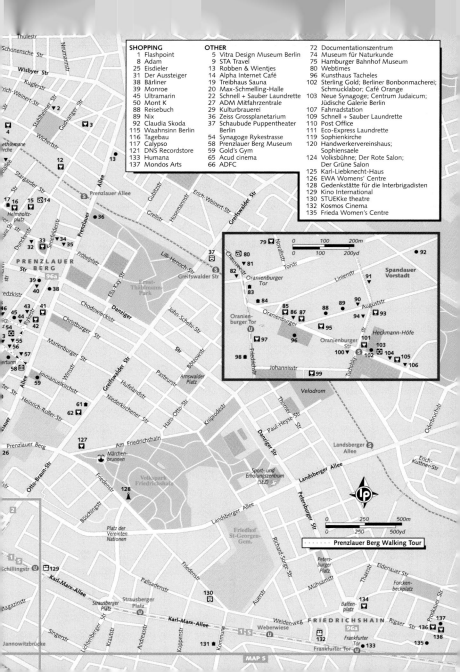

SHOPPING
1 Flashpoint
2 Adam
25 Eisdieler
31 Der Aussteiger
38 Bärliner
39 Monroe
45 Ultramarin
50 Mont K
88 Reisebuch
89 Nix
92 Claudia Skoda
115 Waahnsinn Berlin
116 Tagebau
117 Calypso
121 DNS Recordstore
133 Humana
137 Mondos Arts

OTHER
5 Vitra Design Museum Berlin
9 STA Travel
13 Robben & Wientjes
14 Alpha Internet Café
19 Treibhaus Sauna
20 Max-Schmelling-Halle
22 Schnell + Sauber Laundrette
27 ADM Mitfahrzentrale
29 Kulturbrauerei
36 Zeiss Grossplanetarium
37 Schaubude Puppentheater Berlin
54 Synagoge Rykestrasse
58 Prenzlauer Berg Museum
59 Gold's Gym
65 Acud cinema
66 ADFC

72 Documentationszentrum
74 Museum für Naturkunde
75 Hamburger Bahnhof Museum
80 Webtimes
96 Kunsthaus Tacheles
102 Sterling Gold; Berliner Bonbonmacherei; Schmucklabor; Café Orange
103 Neue Synagoge; Centrum Judaicum; Jüdische Galerie Berlin
107 Fahrradstation
109 Schnell + Sauber Laundrette
110 Post Office
111 Eco-Express Laundrette
119 Sophienkirche
120 Handwerkervereinshaus; Sophiensaele
124 Volksbühne; Der Rote Salon; Der Grüne Salon
125 Karl-Liebknecht-Haus
126 EWA Womens' Centre
128 Gedenkstätte für die Interbrigadisten
129 Kino International
130 STUEKke theatre
132 Kosmos Cinema
135 Frieda Women's Centre

Prenzlauer Berg Walking Tour

MAP 5

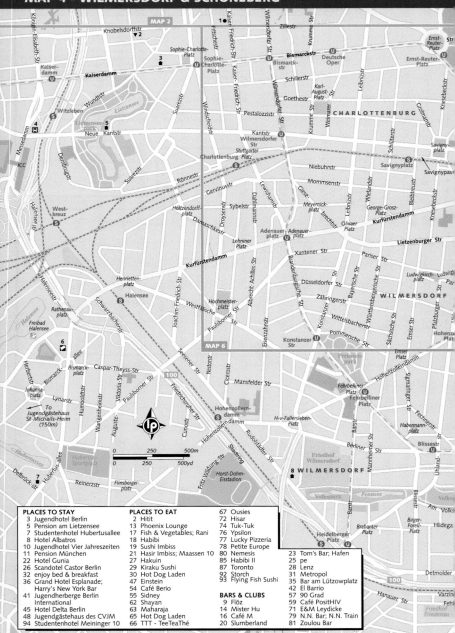

MAP 4 - WILMERSDORF & SCHÖNEBERG

PLACES TO STAY
3 Jugendhotel Berlin
5 Pension am Lietzensee
7 Studentenhotel Hubertusallee
8 Hotel Albatros
10 Jugendhotel Vier Jahreszeiten
11 Pension München
22 Hotel Gunia
26 Scandotel Castor Berlin
32 enjoy bed & breakfast
36 Grand Hotel Esplanade;
   Harry's New York Bar
41 Jugendherberge Berlin
   International
45 Hotel Delta Berlin
48 Jugendgästehaus des CVJM
94 Studentenhotel Meininger 10

PLACES TO EAT
2 Hitit
13 Phoenix Lounge
17 Fish & Vegetables; Rani
18 Habibi
19 Sushi Imbiss
21 Hasir Imbiss; Maassen 10
27 Hakuin
29 Kiraku Sushi
30 Hot Dog Laden
47 Einstein
54 Café Berio
55 Sidney
62 Shayan
63 Maharaja
65 Hot Dog Laden
66 TTT - TeeTeaThé

67 Ousies
72 Hisar
74 Tuk-Tuk
76 Ypsilon
77 Lucky Pizzeria
78 Petite Europe
80 Nemesis
85 Habibi II
87 Toronto
92 Storch
93 Flying Fish Sushi

BARS & CLUBS
9 Flöz
14 Mister Hu
16 Café M
20 Slumberland

23 Tom's Bar; Hafen
25 pe
28 Lenz
31 Metropol
35 Bar am Lützowplatz
42 El Barrio
57 90 Grad
59 Café PositHIV
71 E&M Leydicke
79 N.N. Bar; N.N. Train
81 Zoulou Bar

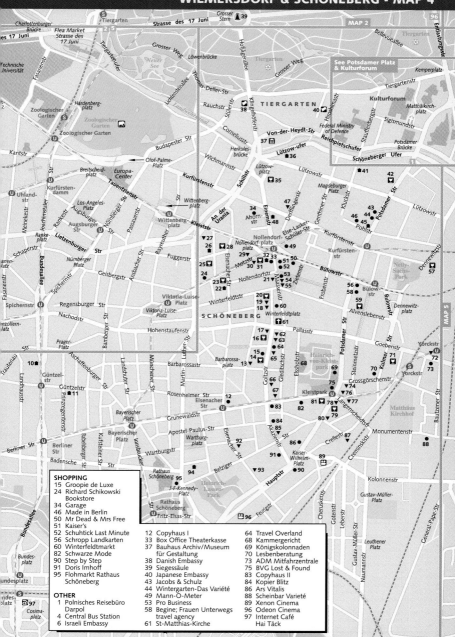

SHOPPING
15 Groopie de Luxe
24 Richard Schikowski Bookstore
34 Garage
46 Made in Berlin
50 Mr Dead & Mrs Free
51 Kaiser's
52 Schuhtick Last Minute
56 Schropp Landkarten
60 Winterfeldtmarkt
82 Schwarze Mode
90 Step by Step
91 Doris Imhoff
95 Flohmarkt Rathaus Schöneberg

OTHER
1 Polnisches Reisebüro Darpol
4 Central Bus Station
6 Israeli Embassy
11 Güntzelstr
12 Copyhaus I
33 Box Office Theaterkasse
37 Bauhaus Archiv/Museum für Gestaltung
38 Danish Embassy
39 Siegessäule
40 Japanese Embassy
43 Jacobs & Schulz
44 Wintergarten-Das Varieté
53 Mann-O-Meter
53 Pro Business
58 Begine; Frauen Unterwegs travel agency
61 St-Matthias-Kirche
64 Travel Overland
68 Kammergericht
69 Königskolonnaden
70 Lesbenberatung
73 ADM Mitfahrzentrale
84 BVG Lost & Found
83 Copyhaus II
84 Kopier Blitz
86 Ars Vitalis
88 Scheinbar Varieté
89 Xenon Cinema
96 Odeon Cinema
97 Internet Café Hai Täck

MAP 5 - KREUZBERG 36 & 61

PLACES TO STAY
2 Odyssee Globetrotter Hostel;
  Juncker's Hotel-Garni
8 The Sunflower Hostel
13 East Side City Hotel
39 Gästehaus Freiraum
41 Bax Pax
45 Die Fabrik Hostel; Eisenwaren
51 Jugendgästehaus Schreberjugend
54 Hotel am Anhalter Bahnhof
61 Pension Kreuzberg
63 Hotel Transit
66 Hotel Riehmers Hofgarten;
  E.T.A. Hoffmann Restaurant
86 Gasthaus Dietrich Herz

PLACES TO EAT
4 PI Bar
6 Truxa
7 Conmux
16 Abendmahl
17 Weltrestaurant Markthalle
22 Habibi
32 Hasir Imbiss
37 Amrit
38 Morgenland
40 Hannibal
42 Café Morena
44 Bagdad
50 Il Casolare
58 Grossbeerenkeller
67 Rathaus Kreuzberg Kantine
69 Chandra Kumari
71 Seerose
76 Bergmann 103
78 Atlantic
79 Kichererbse
83 Locus
87 Barcomi's
88 Lone Star Taqueria
99 Thymian
100 Pow Wow

103 Le Cochon Bourgeois
104 Merhaba
107 Tabibito
110 Café Rix

BARS & CLUBS
1 Mana Mana
3 Dachkammer;
  Astro Bar
5 Tagung/Cube Club
9 Maria am Ostbahnhof
10 Ostgut; lab.oratory
11 Non Tox
12 Die Busche
14 Matrix
21 Franken
23 Schnabelb...
26 Würgeeng...
31 Flammend...
  Herzen
33 Bierhimme...
34 Roses
36 SO 36
49 Ankerklau...
80 Junction B...
95 Golgatha

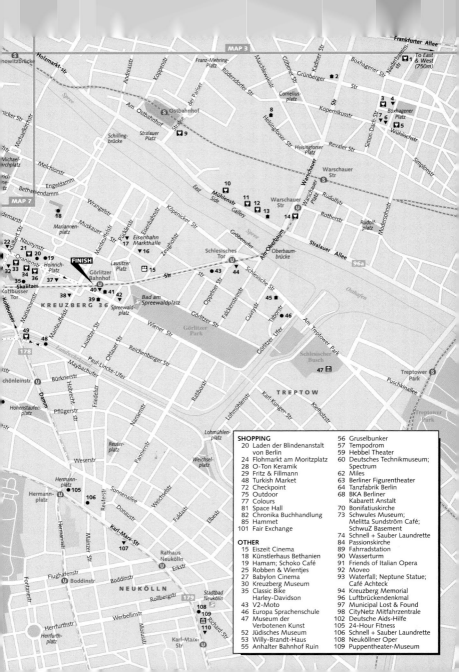

MAP 3

FINISH

SHOPPING
20 Laden der Blindenanstalt von Berlin
24 Flohmarkt am Moritzplatz
28 O-Ton Keramik
29 Fritz & Fillmann
48 Turkish Market
72 Checkpoint
77 Colours
81 Space Hall
82 Chronika Buchhandlung
85 Hammet
101 Fair Exchange

OTHER
15 Eiszeit Cinema
18 Künstlerhaus Bethanien
19 Hamam; Schoko Café
25 Robben & Wientjes
27 Babylon Cinema
30 Kreuzberg Museum
35 Classic Bike Harley-Davidson
43 V2-Moto
46 Europa Sprachschule
47 Museum der Verbotenen Kunst
52 Jüdisches Museum
53 Willy-Brandt-Haus
55 Anhalter Bahnhof Ruin
56 Gruselbunker
57 Tempodrom
59 Hebbel Theater
60 Deutsches Technikmuseum; Spectrum
62 Miles
63 Berliner Figurentheater
64 Tanzfabrik Berlin
68 BKA Berliner Kabarett Anstalt
70 Bonifatiuskirche
73 Schwules Museum; Melitta Sundström Café; SchwuZ Basement
74 Schnell + Sauber Laundrette
84 Passionskirche
89 Fahrradstation
90 Wasserturm
91 Friends of Italian Opera
92 Moveo
93 Waterfall; Neptune Statue; Café Achteck
94 Kreuzberg Memorial
96 Luftbrückendenkmal
97 Municipal Lost & Found
98 CityNetz Mitfahrzentrale
102 Deutsche Aids-Hilfe
105 24-Hour Fitness
106 Schnell + Sauber Laundrette
108 Neuköllner Oper
109 Puppentheater-Museum

MAP 6 - CHARLOTTENBURG

Citywest Walking Tour

CHARLOTTENBURG

WILMERSDORF

START/FINISH

Deutsche Oper

Ernst-Reuter-Platz

Technische Universität

Zoo Station

Zoologischer Garten

Europa Center

Neues Kranzler Eck

Bundesallee

Streets:
Strasse des 17 Juni
Grosser Weg
Neuer See
Tiergarten
Landwehrkanal
Charlottenburger Brücke
Fasanenstr
Hardenbergstr
Steinplatz
Goethestr
Knesebeckstr
Grolmanstr
Uhlandstr
Savignyplatz
Kantstr
Schlüterstr
Leibnizstr
Schillerstr
Wilmersdorfer Str
Bismarckstr
Krumme Str
Weimarer Str
Karl-August-Platz
Niebuhrstr
Mommsenstr
Pestalozzistr
Stuttgarter Platz
Kaiser-Friedrich-Str
Fritschestr
Lewishamstr
Dahlmannstr
Sybelstr
Droysenstr
Damaschkestr
Lehniner Platz
Albrecht-Achilles-Str
Westfälische Str
Paulsborner Str
Hochmeisterplatz
Nestorstr
Brandenburgische Str
Konstanzer Str
Düsseldorfer Str
Xantener Str
Adenauerplatz
Olivaer Platz
Leibnizstr
Wielandstr
George-Grosz-Platz
Bleibtreustr
Knesebeckstr
Savignypassage
Kurfürstendamm
Budapester Str
Tauentzienstr
Nürnberger Str
Kurfürstenstr
Wittenbergplatz
Bayreuther Str
Martin-Lutherstr
Fuggerstr
Hohenstaufenstr
Viktoria-Luise-Platz
Ansbacher Str
Passauer Str
Geisbergstr
Regensburger Str
Augsburger Str
Los-Angeles-Platz
Rankestr
Joachimstaler Str
Lietzenburger Str
Nürnberger Platz
Spichernstr
Nachodstr
Pariser Str
Emser Str
Fasanenstr
Meinekestr
Schaperstr
Ludwigkirchplatz
Ludwigkirchstr
Pfalzburger Str
Hohenzollerndamm
Hohenzollernplatz
Salzburger Str
Bayerische Str
Württembergische Str
Zähringerstr
Wittelsbacherstr
Pommersche Str
Meyerinckplatz
Gieselerstr
Adenauerplatz
Wilmersdorfer Str
Lichtensteinallee
Tiergartenufer
Hardenbergplatz
Breitscheidplatz
Olof-Palme-Platz
Wittenbergplatz

Flea Market Strasse des 17 Juni

Schaubühne am Lehniner Platz

0 250 500m
0 250 500yd

MAP 6 - CHARLOTTENBURG

PLACES TO STAY
31 Pension Knesebeck
45 Herberge Grosse
46 Hotel Berolina
47 City Pension Berlin
54 Hotel Crystal
55 Pension Peters
56 Pension Viola Nova
71 Hotel Palace Berlin
87 Pension Fischer;
   Hotel-Pension Nürnberger Eck
90 Pension Korfu II
96 Hecker's Hotel
97 Hotel California
109 Hotel Askanischer Hof
110 Hotel-Pension Alexandra
111 Hotel-Pension Majesty
117 Hotel-Pension Castell
118 Hotel Bogota
119 Hotel Bleibtreu
125 Hotel-Pension Funk
134 Hotel Imperator
146 Pension Curtis
147 Hotel Alexander
149 Propeller Island Lodge
150 Hotel Savigny
151 Hotel-Pension Wittelsbach
152 Frauenhotel Artemisia
159 Jugendgästehaus Central
160 Hotel Arco Garni
161 ArtHotel Connection;
   Connection Nightclub

PLACES TO EAT
4 Satyam
8 Café Hardenberg
9 Technical University Mensa
11 Café am Neuen See
27 Cour Careé
30 Sticks
32 Ashoka Bar
35 Good Friend
37 Schalom
43 Biscotti
44 Soup Kultur
49 El Borriquito
50 XII Apostoli
57 Schwarzes Café
59 Sachiko Sushi
62 Paris Bar
67 Marché
79 Einhorn - Schöneberg
84 Plaetzl
93 Café Kranzler; BVG Top Tour
100 Einhorn - Charlottenburg
101 Don Quijote
102 Ali Baba
104 Lubitsch
105 Kalkutta
113 Bosporus-Grill
114 Juleps
122 Pizzeria Piccola Taormina

126 Café Wintergarten;
   Literaturhaus
127 Gosch
129 Leysieffer
131 Soup Kultur; easyEverything
133 Salomon Bagels
138 Hard Rock Café
141 Scarabeo
142 Poco Loco
143 Sushi Imbiss
144 Fabulous Route 66 50's Diner
145 Jimmy's Diner
155 Hamlet
156 Manzini
163 Trattoria á Muntagnola
164 Montevideo
165 Tip
166 Penny Markt

BARS & CLUBS
25 Dicke Wirtin
28 Gainsbourg
34 A-Trane
53 Hegel
82 Andreas Kneipe
148 Far Out
162 Prinzknecht

SHOPPING
2 Kiepert
15 Humana
16 Aldi Supermarket;
   AGW Exchange
24 Stilwerk
26 Riccardo Cartillone
29 Berliner Zinnfiguren
33 Prinz Eisenherz
39 Books in Berlin
41 Aldi Supermarket
42 Zweitausendeins
51 Treykorn
52 Bücherbogen
58 Plus Supermarket
60 Canzone
61 Rahaus
64 Karstadt Sport; Cyberb@r
66 Diesel Jeans Store
78 Niketown
80 Kaiser's Supermarket
83 KaDeWe; Showtime;
   BTM Tourist Office Info Point
85 Peek & Cloppenburg
86 Bruno's
88 Hennes & Mauritz
89 Hugendubel; Gap;
   Jopp Frauen Fitness Studio
91 Wertheim bei Hertie
94 KPM
98 L&P Classics
99 Marga Schoeller Bücherstube
103 Kaufhaus Schrill
106 Kaiser's Supermarket

107 Planet
108 Claudia Skoda
120 Ku'damm Karree;
   Story of Berlin
123 Hautnah
140 Bannat
158 Les Dessous

OTHER
1 Deutsche Oper Berlin
3 Concert & Theaterkasse City
5 Post Office
6 Renaissance-Theater Berlin
7 STA Travel
10 Hochschule der Künste
12 Aquarium
13 Zoo Elephant Gate
14 Zoo-Palast Cinema; Hekticket
17 BVG Information Kiosk
18 Reisebank
19 Amerika Haus
20 Erotik-Museum
21 Theater des Westens
22 Quasimodo
23 Fit Fun
36 Das Verborgene Museum
38 STA Travel
40 Schnell + Sauber Laundrette
48 Rainbow Tours
63 Lufthansa City Centre
65 Main Post Office
68 Kaiser-Wilhelm Gedächtniskirche
69 Euro-Change
70 BTM Main Tourist Office
72 SixtBudget
73 Hertz; Avis
74 Apollo Sauna
75 Europcar
76 Thermen am Europa-Center
77 Die Stachelschweine
81 American Express
92 Tempelhofer Sightseeing Tours
95 Jüdisches Gemeindehaus,
   Arche Noah
112 Schwulenberatung
   (Gay Advisory Service)
115 Kurbel Cinema
116 Alternativ Tours
121 Institut Français;
   French Consulate
124 Käthe-Kollwitz-Museum
128 Severin + Kühn
   Sightseeing Tours
130 Berolina Bus Tours
132 BVB Bus Tours
135 Theaterkasse Centrum
136 City-Wache Police Station
137 CityNetz
139 Berliner AIDS-Hilfe
153 Tennis & Squash City
154 Schnell + Sauber Laundrette
157 Bar jeder Vernunft

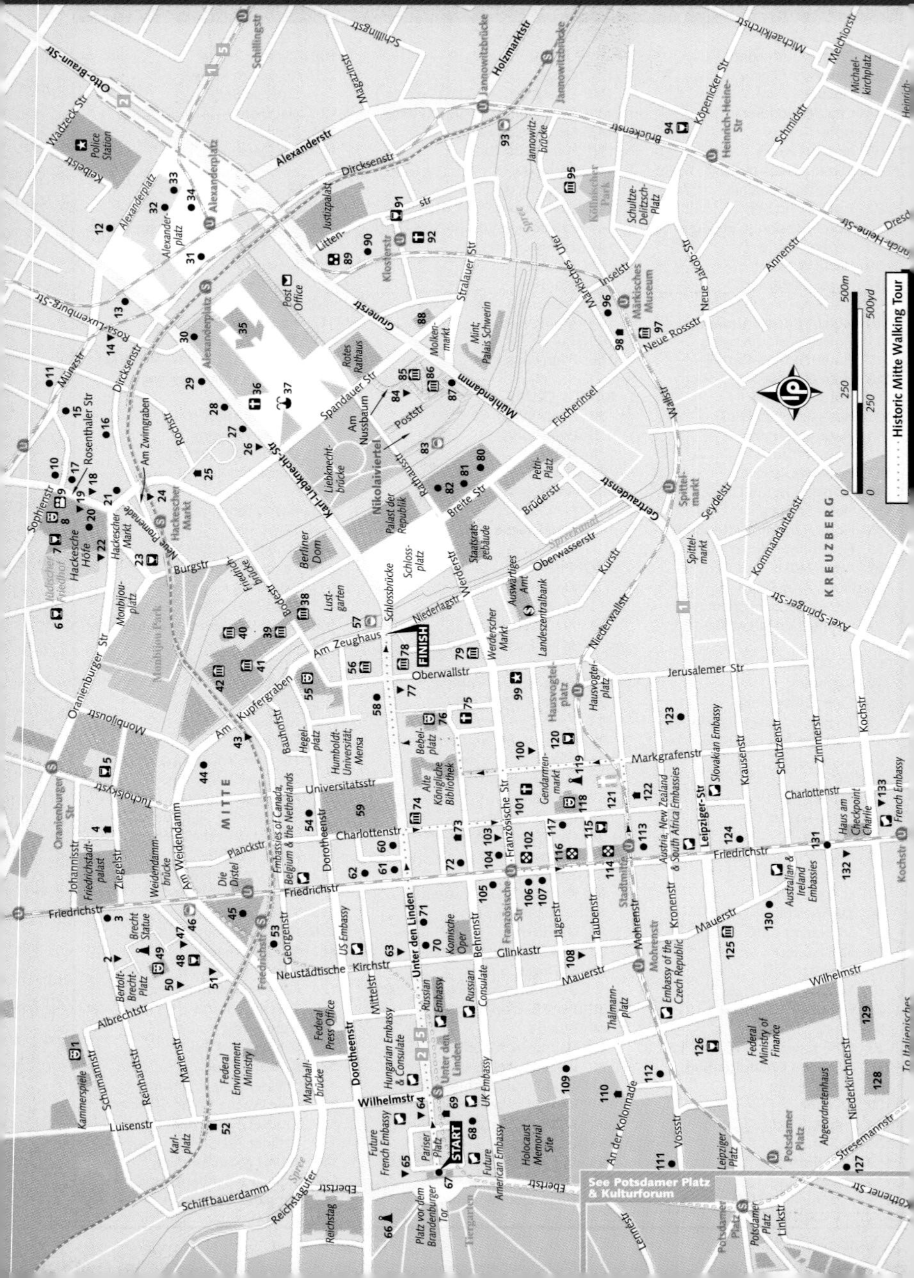

MAP 7 - MITTE

Otto-Braun-Str

Schillingstr

Wadzeckstr

Police Station

Keibelstr

Alexanderplatz

Dircksenstr

Alexanderstr

Holzmarktstr

Janowitzbrücke

Michaelkirchstr

Mehlerstr

Michaelkirchstr

Köpenicker Str

Heinrich-Heine-Str

Schulze-Delitzsch-Platz

Annenstr

Dresden

Neue Jacob-Str

Heinrich-Heine-Str

Historic Mitte Walking Tour

KREUZBERG

Rosaluxemburg-Str

Münzstr

Rosenthaler Str

Sophienstr

Am Zwinger

Hackescher Markt

Karl-Liebknecht-Str

An Neuen Promenade

Hackesche Höfe

Hackescher Markt

Burgstr

Monbijouplatz

Oranienburger Str

Spandauer Str

Am Nußbaum

Liebknecht-brücke

Berliner Dom

Nikolaiviertel

Palast der Republik

Breite Str

Petri-Platz

Spittel-markt

Seydelstr

Mühlendamm

Fischerinsel

Am Zwinger

Post Office

Rotes Rathaus

Stralauer Str

Klosterstr

Littenstr

Justizplatz

Dircksenstr

Alexanderstr

Sprée

Märkisches Museum

Mint: Palais Schwein

Neue Rossstr

Inselstr

Wallstr

Mühlendamm

Am Kupfergraben

Monbijoupark

Oranienstr

Tucholskystr

Friedrichstr

Weidendamm-brücke

Am Weidendamm

Planckstr

MITTE

Am Kupfergraben

Bauhofstr

Hegel-platz

Humboldt Universität; Mensa

Universitätsstr

Dorotheenstr

Charlottenstr

Friedrichstr

Lust-garten

Schloss-brücke

Schloss-platz

Staatsrats-gebäude

Niederlagstr

Werderscher Markt

Oberwasserstr

Auswärtiges Amt

Landeszentralbank

Am Zeughaus

FINISH

Oberwallstr

Werderstr

Hausvogtei-platz

Hausvogteiplatz

Jerusalemer Str

Am Kupfergraben

Die Distel

US Embassy

Georgenstr

Neustädtische Kirchstr

Friedrichstr

Bertolt Brecht Platz

Brecht Statue

Ziegelstr

Embassies of Canada Belgium & the Netherlands

Bebel platz

Alte Königliche Bibliothek

Gendarmen-markt

Markgrafenstr

Charlottenstr

Slovakian Embassy

Kochstr

Schützenstr

Zimmerstr

Haus am Checkpoint Charlie

Unter den Linden

Französische Str

Französische Str

Jägerstr

Taubenstr

Mohrenstr

Stadtmitte

Austria, New Zealand & South Africa Embassies

Friedrichstr

Australian & Ireland Embassies

Charlottenstr

Kronenstr

Mauerstr

Wilhelmstr

Embassy of the Czech Republic

Federal Ministry of Finance

Niederkirchnerstr

Stresemann Str

To Italienisches

Russian Embassy

Russian Consulate

Komische Oper

Glinkastr

Behrenstr

Mohrenstr

Thälmann-platz

Mauerstr

Kronenstr

Leipziger Str

Leipziger Platz

Potsdamer Platz

Potsdamer Platz

An der Kolonnade

Vossstr

Voßstr

Hungarian Embassy & Consulate

Federal Press Office

Dorotheenstr

Mittelstr

Unter den Linden

UK Embassy

Wilhelmstr

Future French Embassy

Pariser Platz

START

Holocaust Memorial Site

Future American Embassy

Platz vor dem Brandenburger Tor

Ebertstr

Reichstag

Schiffbauerdamm

Marschall-brücke

Federal Environment Ministry

Albrechtstr

Reinhardtstr

Marienstr

Luisenstr

Karl-platz

Kammerspiele

Schumannstr

Johannisstr

Friedrichs-palast

Friedrichstr

Oranienburger Str

Schiffbauerdamm

See Potsdamer Platz & Kulturforum

Linienstr

250 0 500m
250 0 500yd

MAP 7 - MITTE

PLACES TO STAY
4 Dietrich-Bonhoeffer-Haus
25 Hotel Alexander Plaza
52 Künstlerheim Luise
69 Adlon Hotel Kempinski
73 Dorint Am Gendarmenmarkt
98 art'otel berlin mitte
110 Frauenhotel Intermezzo
122 Hilton Berlin

PLACES TO EAT
2 Bambussprosse
14 Soup Kultur
18 Bagels & Bialys
19 Yosoy
22 Hasir Mitte
24 Zucca
26 Nordsee
43 Die Zwölf Apostel
47 Ganymed
50 Kartoffelkeller
51 Stäv
63 Einstein
64 Margaux
65 Theodor Tucher
77 Opernpalais
84 Zum Nussbaum
100 Vau
103 borchardt
108 Nö
132 Café Adler
133 Sale e Tabacchi
134 Arbeitsamt IV Kantine

BARS & CLUBS
5 WMF
6 Mudd Club
7 Sophienklub
23 Kurvenstar
48 Broker's Bier Börse
91 Zur letzten Instanz
94 Sage Club
115 Newton Bar
120 925 Lounge Bar
126 Tresor/Globus

SHOPPING
10 Orlando
17 Riccardo Cartillone
32 Saturn
44 Berliner Kunst &
   Nostalgiemarkt
62 Dussmann – Das
   Kulturkaufhaus
71 Meissener Porzellan
102 Galeries Lafayette
104 Hennes & Mauritz
113 Kiepert
114 Quartier 205
116 Quartier 206,Departmentstore
130 British Bookshop

THEATRE & MUSIC
1 Deutsches Theater
8 Puppentheater Firlefanz
49 Berliner Ensemble
55 Maxim Gorki Theater
76 Staatsoper Unter
   den Linden
90 Podewil; Café Podewil;
   Tanzwerkstatt Berlin
117 Hochschule für Musik
   Hanns Eisler;
   Mensa
118 Konzerthaus

OTHER
3 Fahrradservice
9 Central Cinema;
   Blindenwerkstatt Otto
   Weidt
11 Atlas Reisewelt
12 PPS
13 Europcar
15 Goethe Institute;
   Lore.Berlin
16 Café Seidenfaden
20 Café Aedes;
   Chamäleon Variété;
   Fahrradstation; Oxymoron;
   Hackesches Hof-Theater;
   Cinema; Fishbelly Lingerie
21 British Council
27 Polnisches Kultur-Institut
28 Haus Ungarn;
   Ungarn Tours
29 Jopp Frauen Fitness
   Studio
30 Hekticket
31 World Time Clock
33 Atlas Reisewelt
34 ADM Mitfahrzentrale
35 TV Tower; Telecafé;
   BTM Info-Cafe
36 Marienkirche
37 Neptune Fountain
38 Altes Museum
39 Neues Museum
   (under reconstruction)
40 Alte Nationalgalerie
41 Pergamon Museum
42 Bodemuseum
45 Tränenpalast
46 Reederei Bruno Winkler
53 Fahrradstation –
   Friedrichstrasse
54 STA Travel
56 Zeughaus
57 Berliner Wassertaxi
   Service
58 Neue Wache
59 Alte Staatsbibliothek
60 Berlin Story

61 Tempelhofer Sightseeing
   Tours
66 Wall Victims' Memorial
67 Brandenburg Tor;
   BTM Tourist Office
68 Future Academy of Arts
70 Komische Oper
   Box Office
72 Healthland
74 Guggenheim Museum
75 St Hedwigs Kathedrale
78 Kronprinzenpalais;
   Deutsches Historisches
   Museum (temporary)
79 Friedrichwerdersche Kirche;
   Schinkelmuseum
80 Berliner Stadtbibliothek
81 Ribbeckhaus;
   Zentrum für Berlin-Studien
82 Neuer Marstall
83 Stern und Kreis Boat
   Landing – Nikolaiviertel
85 Museum Nikolaikirche
86 Museum Knoblauchhaus;
   Historische Weinstuben
87 Ephraim-Palais
88 Altes Stadthaus
89 Franziskaner Klosterkirche
92 Parochialkirche
93 Stern und Kreis Boat
   Landing – Jannowitzbrücke
95 Märkisches Museum;
   Wusterhausensche Bär
96 Otto-Nagel-Haus
97 Museum Kindeit & Jugend
99 Police Station
101 Französischer Dom;
   Hugenottenmuseum
105 Euro-change
106 Sputnik Travel
107 American Express
109 Gate Sauna
111 Former Site of
   Hitler's Bunker
112 Former Site of
   Hitler's New Chancellery
119 Schiller Statue
121 Deutscher Dom;
   German History Exhibit
123 Czech Centre;
   Cedok Travel
124 Thomas Cook
125 Museum für
   Kommunikation
127 Zahnklinik Medeco
128 Martin-Gropius-Bau
129 Topography of Terror;
   Former Gestapo
   Headquarters; Wall
131 Former Checkpoint
   Charlie

MAP LEGEND

CITY ROUTES

Freeway	Freeway		Unsealed Road
Highway	Primary Road		One Way Street
Road	Secondary Road		Pedestrian Street
Street	Street		Stepped Street
Lane	Lane		Tunnel
	On/Off Ramp		Footbridge

REGIONAL ROUTES

	Tollway, Freeway
	Primary Road
	Secondary Road
	Minor Road

BOUNDARIES

	International
	State
	Disputed
	Fortified Wall

HYDROGRAPHY

	River, Creek		Dry Lake; Salt Lake
	Canal		Spring; Rapids
	Lake		Waterfalls

TRANSPORT ROUTES & STATIONS

	Train		Cable Car, Funicular
	S-Bahn		Ferry
	U-Bahn		Walking Trail
	Underground Train		Walking Tour
	Tramway		Path

AREA FEATURES

	Building		Market		Beach		Campus
	Park, Gardens		Sports Ground		Cemetery		Plaza

POPULATION SYMBOLS

○ **CAPITAL**	National Capital	● **CITY**	City	● Village	Village
◉ **CAPITAL**	State Capital	● Town	Town		Urban Area

MAP SYMBOLS

■ Place to Stay	▼ Place to Eat		● Point of Interest

✈	Airport		Cinema	⚓	Monument		Stately Home
⊖	Bank	☍	Cycling		Museum		Swimming Pool
	Bus Stop		Embassy, Consulate		Parking		Synagogue
	Bus Terminal	☏	Fountain		Police Station		Theatre
▲	Camping	✛	Hospital		Post Office		Tomb
	Castle, Chateau		Internet Cafe		Pub or Bar	❶	Tourist Information
	Cathedral, Church	※	Lookout		Shopping Centre		Zoo

Note: not all symbols displayed above appear in this book

LONELY PLANET OFFICES

Australia
Locked Bag 1, Footscray, Victoria 3011
☎ 03 8379 8000 fax 03 8379 8111
email: talk2us@lonelyplanet.com.au

USA
150 Linden St, Oakland, CA 94607
☎ 510 893 8555 TOLL FREE: 800 275 8555
fax 510 893 8572
email: info@lonelyplanet.com

UK
10a Spring Place, London NW5 3BH
☎ 020 7428 4800 fax 020 7428 4828
email: go@lonelyplanet.co.uk

France
1 rue du Dahomey, 75011 Paris
☎ 01 55 25 33 00 fax 01 55 25 33 01
email: bip@lonelyplanet.fr
www.lonelyplanet.fr

**World Wide Web: www.lonelyplanet.com *or* AOL keyword: lp
Lonely Planet Images: lpi@lonelyplanet.com.au**